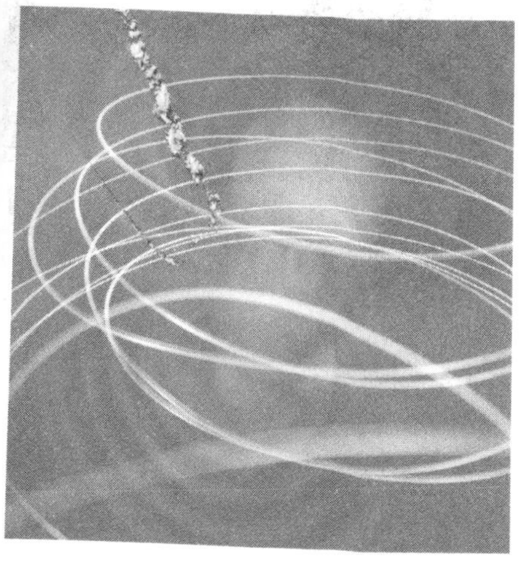

Cisco Certification: Bridges, Routers, and Switches for CCIEs

Andrew Bruce Caslow, CCIE # 3139

Valeriy Pavlichenko, CCIE # 3765

Prentice Hall PTR, Upper Saddle River, NJ 07458

http://www.phptr.com

Library of Congress Cataloging-in-Publication Data

Caslow, Andrew Bruce.
Cisco certification: bridges, routers, and switches for CCIEs /
Andrew Bruce Caslow.
p. cm.
ISBN 0-13-082537-9 (alk. paper)
1. Electronic data processing personnel--Certification.
2. Internetworking (Telecommunication)--Examinations--Study guides.
I. Title.
QA76.3.C377 1998
004.6'076--dc21 98-31189
CIP

Editorial/production supervision: *Maria Molinari*
Acquisitions editor: *Mary Franz*
Editorial assistant: *Noreen Regina*
Cover design director: *Jerry Votta*
Cover designer: *Amy Rosen / Scott Weiss*
Manufacturing manager: *Alexis Heydt*
Marketing manager: *Lisa Konzelmann*
Technical editor: *Valeriy Pavlichenko*

Prentice-Hall, Inc.
A Simon & Schuster Company
Upper Saddle River, NJ 07458

Prentice Hall books are widely used by corporations and government agencies for training, marketing, and resale.
The publisher offers discounts on this book when ordered in bulk quantities.
For more information, contact Corporate Sales Dept.; Phone 800-382-3419; FAX: 201-236-7141
E-mail (Internet): corpsales@prenhall.com
Or write: Prentice Hall PTR, Corp. Sales Department, One Lake Street,Upper Saddle River, NJ 07458

Printed in the United States of America

10 9 8 7 6 5 4 3 2 1

ISBN 0-13-082537-9

Prentice-Hall International (UK) Limited, *London*
Prentice-Hall of Australia Pty. Limited, *Sydney*
Prentice-Hall Canada Inc., *Toronto*
Prentice-Hall Hispanoamericana, S.A., *Mexico*
Prentice-Hall of India Private Limited, *New Delhi*
Prentice-Hall of Japan, Inc., *Tokyo*
Simon & Schuster Asia Pte. Ltd., *Singapore*
Editora Prentice-Hall do Brasil, Ltda., *Rio de Janeiro*

When we think about the future of the world, we always have in mind its being at the place where it would be if it continued to move as we see it moving now. We do not realize that it moves not in a straight line, but in a curve, and that its direction is changing constantly.

Ludwig Wittgenstein

Contents

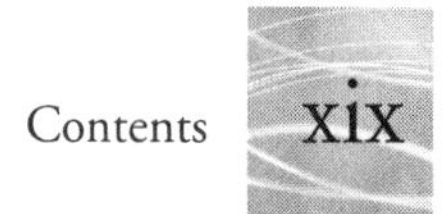

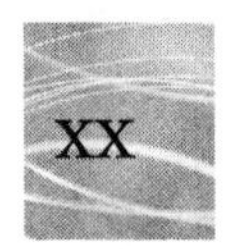

Chapter 16 IPX Configuration 495

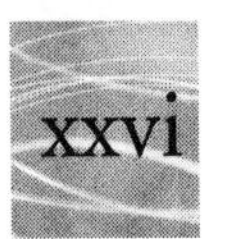

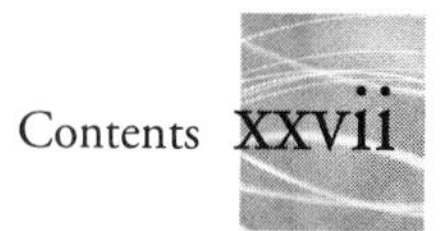

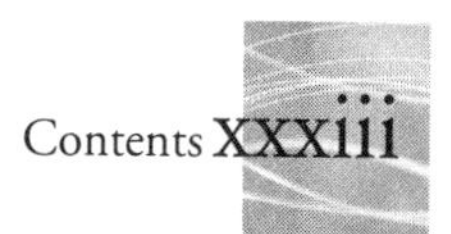

Preface

For the next ten years, the opportunities for internetwork professionals will be immense. However, the challenge of possessing the proper knowledge base and skill set will be faced by every internetworking professional. The challenge is two-fold: (1) how does one develop his internetworking knowledge base and skill sets to the highest possible level and (2) how does one stay current in this rapidly changing field! Cisco Systems offers a solution: the Cisco IOS (Internetworking Operating System). By mastering the Cisco IOS, an internetworking professional can supply virtually any internetworking solution. The IOS has its origins in the routing world but has expanded to LAN switching, ATM switching, mulitlayer switching, voice-data integration and security.

From an internetwork education perspective, the IOS configuration set, show commands and debugging tools provide a technician with a valuable insight into how internetworking technologies operate. For example, having access to IOS debugging tools and a network protocol analyzer such as a Network Associates Sniffer in a testbed environment allows a technician to develop a strong technical understanding of how internetwork protocols operate at a high level of technical detail. IOS debugging tools should be used with extreme caution in a production internetwork. However, in an educational environment, IOS debugging tools should be used to enhance the internetwork education process. One of the goals of this book is to demonstrate how debug output can be used to enhance the internetwork education process.

A broader goal of this book is to demonstrate the power of the Cisco IOS from both a production and education perspective. An internetwork professional that learns the IOS well enough to attain CCIE certification has developed an internetworking knowledge base and skill set that will allow him to accelerate his learning of other internetworking technologies. Therefore, mastering the Cisco IOS and the related internetworking technologies to the point of attaining CCIE certification should be viewed as a foundational beginning rather than an end. Once you have attained your CCIE, you must look ahead to what new internetworking topics you will master. However, as you learn new topics, you will apply the precious internetworking analysis skills you developed while you prepared for CCIE certification.

In sum, I hope this book assists in developing the reader's internetwork analysis skills. By developing methodologies to think like a quality internetworking professional, you will be able to rapidly adapt to the constant changes occurring in this industry. By developing methodologies to think like a quality internetworking professional, you will be better prepared to attain your CCIE. Therefore, a clear road to optimizing your internetworking analysis skills is mastering the Cisco IOS. Once you learn how to speak IOS and think IOS to the highest level of technical detail, improved internetworking analysis skills come along with the territory. Good luck on your journey to CCIE certification!

Acknowledgments

Writing this book was a tremendous challenge. The potential topics of CCIE certification are vast, ever expanding and ever changing. In order to cover the wide range of topics covered in this book, assistance from several associates in the Cisco community was required. In particular, I would like to thank Valeriy Pavlichenko (CCIE) for providing technical editing services. Valeriy is one of the most disiplined and systematic internetworking engineers in the business. Without his feedback, much of the work of this book would not have been done. Secondly, special thanks must be given to Brent Baccala, the editor of the Internet Encyclopedia at **www.freesoft.org**. Brent provided key contributions to Chapters Nine, Eleven and Fourteen. Brent Baccala is blessed with a tremendous combination of brilliant technical insight and strong writing skills. Brent's ability to explain highly technical topics clearly has been tremendous inspiration to me. Finally, special thanks must be given to fellow Cisco Certified Instructor and CCIE Rajah Chowbay. Rajah assisted in drafting Chapter Seven of this book as well as provided tremendous influence in the structure in each and every chapter of this book.

Thanks must also be given to Mr. Albert Spaulding and his company ARS, Ltd. (Alexandria, Virginia) for providing the time and resources to write this book. Thank you Mr Spaulding and ARS!

Specific contributions to the book came from the following associates:

Paul Bourghese (CCIE and Certified Cisco Instructor) for developing Chapter Twenty-Four.

James Park (CCIE and Certified Cisco Instructor) for editing Chapters Sixteen, Seventeen and Twenty-Five.

Fred Ingham (CCIE and Certified Cisco Instructor) for editing Chapters Twenty-One as well as Chapters Twenty-Three through Twenty-Nine.

Summantra Roy (CCIE) for reviewing Chapter Twenty-One.

Guillermo "The Marine!!" Rastelli for providing graphics and logistics support.

Lourdes Pol for proofreading the book.

All ARS Bridges, Routers and Switches for CCIEs students. They are the best and brightest in the internetworking industry! Remember my students, "Can you spot the issue?"

Writing this book also required extensive support of friends and family. Special thanks goes out to my mother, my brothers and sisters, my dear friends Spottie, the Constable of France and the Schwarz Graf. Finally, I must thank my wife Lania and two daughters Andreina and Gabriela for their love and support during the long lonely months of writing this book.

For more information about topics in this book see **www.cciecert.com.**

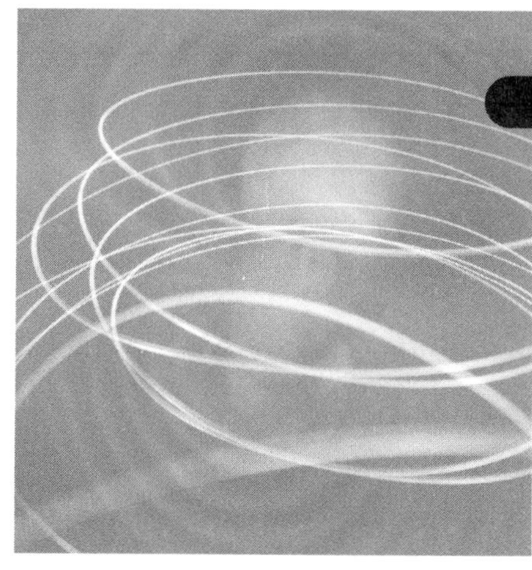

ONE

Introduction to CCIE Certification

Topics Covered in This Chapter

- The Influence of the OSI Model
- The Influence of Graduate School Examination Testing Formats
- What This Book Does Not Cover
- CCIE Test Nondisclosure Policy
- The Cisco Web Site
- The Origins of This Book
- CCIE Defined
- Roadmap of This Book
- Warm Up "Issue Spotting" Scenario
- Six Key Ingredients for CCIE Certification Success

The purpose of this book is to provide Certified Cisco Internetworking Expert (CCIE) candidates a structured roadmap to prepare for CCIE certification. Potential topics involved in CCIE certification testing are vast and ever expanding. Originally, CCIE certification focused primarily on routing and bridging. Today, it still covers these topics, but has expanded to ATM and LAN switching. As the scope of internetworking expands, so will the topics encountered in CCIE certification.

Even though CCIE certification topics are expanding and changing, all topics fall under the technological classification of "internetworking." Internetworking topics can be categorized and ordered. By categorizing and ordering internetworking topics, CCIE candidates can formulate a structured and systematic approach to certification preparation. This book provides such an approach.

This book is not an end but a beginning. It provides a suggested template for CCIE preparation. You, the CCIE candidate, must fill out the template. You must expand the template with additional research and extensive hands-on experience with potential CCIE topics.

At the end of your CCIE certification effort, you should have accumulated stacks of configuration scripts and debug traces as well as downloaded white papers, sample configurations, and configuration guidebooks from Cisco's web site. If you are a serious CCIE candidate, you will have created a detailed outline of the topics you have covered. The outline will reference configuration scripts you have created, debug traces you have generated, and the reference materials you have accumulated. You will also create a number of different checklists for each topic studied. The checklists will help you structure and refine your internetworking analysis methods. This book provides a framework for the outline you need to create. It also provides several sample checklists to help you to begin building your own.

This book contains multiple extracts from configuration scripts, show commands, and debug traces; it also contains several thought-provoking scenarios to test your internetworking analysis skills. If you are going to be successful in your pursuit of CCIE certification, you must use the analysis techniques presented in this book as mere suggestions. As such, you must expand and modify them to meet your needs and formulate your own scenarios. Ideally, your scenarios will be actual cases on production internetworks.

This book is structured in six levels; each level defines a discrete categorization of internetworking technology. The names of the six levels are:

Level One:	Physical and Data-Link Layer Technologies
Level Two:	IP Addressing, IP IGP Routing, and Route Redistribution
Level Three:	IP Exterior Gateway Protocol Routing
Level Four:	Non-IP Routing Protocols (IPX, AppleTalk, and DECNET)
Level Five:	Nonroutable Protocols
Level Six:	Managing Internetwork Traffic

A detailed description of what is covered in each level is provided later in this chapter. Each level builds upon the previous one. Within each level is a progression of topics. Topics within each level build upon each other. Upon completion of each chapter, there is a checklist. If you complete all of the items on the checklist, you are ready to go to the next chapter. At the end of every level (defined in this book by a collection of chapters), there is an aggregated checklist of all chapters within a level.

The structure of this book is influenced by two primary sources: the OSI Model and commonly used graduate school examination testing formats.

The Influence of the OSI Model

The structure of this book is like the structure of the OSI Model — both are layered. The subject matter of this book focuses primarily on the first three

layers of the OSI Model: the physical, data-link, and network layers. In fact, this book interprets and divides the network layer into three sublayers:

- Sublayer One: Network Layer Addressing or Routed Protocol Addressing (IP, IPX, AppleTalkDDP)
- Sublayer Two: Network Layer Internal Gateway Routing Protocols (RIP, OSPF, NLSP)
- Sublayer Three: (IP only) Network Layer External Gateway Routing Protocols (BGP4)

In classic internetwork troubleshooting, if a process defined at a lower layer of the OSI Model is malfunctioning, all of the higher layers will be adversely affected. The same layered approach applies to internetwork configuration—i.e., if the configuration of a lower level process is performed incorrectly, the configuration of all higher level processes will be adversely affected. Therefore, it is important that CCIE candidates master lower level topics in the six level model presented in this book before addressing higher level topics. Remember, the potential subject matter of CCIE certification is vast. You must maintain a structured preparation strategy.

In the last fifteen years, the changes that have occurred in the field of internetworking have been staggering; however, one thing has not changed: the most common method of discussing internetworking technologies involves referencing the OSI Model. Just about every class and every book written in the field of internetworking refers to the OSI Model. Many will argue that the layers of the OSI Model do not accurately correspond to newer technologies such as ATM. However, such critics propose to develop a new layered model for ATM. Therefore, it is safe to say that one thing all internetwork engineers find useful is to view internetworking issues (design, configuration, and troubleshooting) from the perspective of a layered model.

This book will apply the concept of a layered internetwork model to a layered approach to learning. The method of how we learn internetworking will ultimately affect how we design, configure, monitor, and troubleshoot in internetworking. Therefore, not only will this book provide a layered approach to learning about internetwork technology, it will also foster a layered approach to internetwork analysis. This will be a case of how we learn about something will ultimately affect how we interact with something.

The Influence of Graduate School Examination Testing Formats

A common format of a graduate school exam is the "issue spotting and analysis" format. This format involves a generally worded question presented to the test taker that involves a scenario or "fact pattern." Once the scenario is presented, the test taker is asked to "spot the issues" and analyze potential problems within the scenario and offer solutions.

Typically, the issues to be spotted and analyzed are hidden from the test taker. The test taker must proactively analyze the scenario to determine the precise issue or set of issues to be analyzed. Many times graduate students in medicine, engineering, and law receive real-world case-study scenarios as their "issue spotting and analysis" exams.

This book will approach CCIE certification preparation in a similar manner. In scenarios contained within this book, you will be presented with a group of routers and/or switches. You will be asked to configure the routers and switches in a specific way. The scenarios will be worded or the configurations set up so that special problems can arise if you are not intimately familiar with the subject matter. You will not be explicitly told about the potential problems. You must "spot the issues."

For example, you may be asked to configure an OSPF domain with variable-length subnets for the address space of 10.0.0.0. Some of the OSPF subnets for 10.0.0.0 will be twenty-four bits. Other subnet masks will be 26 bits. You will also be asked to configure a RIP domain with twenty-four bit subnets for network 10.0.0.0. Once both OSPF and RIP are configured, you will be asked to exchange routing table information between OSPF and RIP via the process of route redistribution. Finally, you will be asked to be able to ping all of the interfaces in both the RIP and OSPF domains from anywhere in the internetwork.

To the trained internetwork engineer, the issue that emerges immediately is the conflict of the subnetting rules of RIP versus the subnetting rules of OSPF. RIP supports a fixed-length subnet mask. If subnetting is applied to RIP, all subnets in a RIP domain must use the same size mask and they must be contiguous. OSPF supports variable-length subnet masking and discontiguous subnets. In the scenario above, when redistribution is performed, OSPF could recognize all RIP routes but RIP could not recognize all OSPF routes. As a result, routers in the RIP domain cannot ping all of the interfaces in the OSPF domain.

Two possible solutions for this issue are route summarization within OSPF or use of IP classless with the RIP domain.

If the reader has ever been involved with migrating an internetwork from RIP to OSPF, the scenario described above may sound familiar. Many organizations migrate to OSPF because of its ability to support variable-length subnet masking. However, organizations (especially large ones) cannot perform a routing protocol migration over night. While gradually migrating from RIP to OSPF and applying variable-length subnet masking to the new OSPF domain, a common problem or "issue" is the inability of the legacy protocol RIP to recognize the different length subnets of OSPF. You must honestly ask yourself: if you were on an internetworking job site, would you have been

able to spot the issue of a subnet mask mismatch problem between RIP and OPSF?

With the scenario described above, the poorly prepared engineer would not have even spotted the issue. If an internetworking engineer did not know how the rules of subnetting applied to RIP and OSPF and how these rules can create a potential conflict when redistribution occurs between these two protocols, he or she would be completely lost in a scenario with the facts described above. To the well prepared, the issue sticks out like a sore thumb. Good CCIE certification preparation involves working through scenarios that are loaded with such hidden issues. The well-prepared CCIE candidate will proactively search for such issues when any configuration scenario is presented. Ideally, the scenarios the CCIE candidate is working on are real-world scenarios encountered on the job.

Issue spotting scenarios are good preparation for real-world activities. In many instances, an internetwork engineer will receive a customer trouble ticket that states a general problem with no specific information regarding why the problem developed. For example, you may receive the following trouble ticket: "Customer cannot access mail server." You must attack the problem in a systematic, incremental, and sequential manner. As you apply your test and evaluation methods, you will spend a lot of time and effort determining what is "not" the problem. Eventually, you will come upon a specific issue (or issues) that is the source of the problem. It is at this point that you have "spotted the issue." If you are an experienced internetworking engineer, you have been using "issue spotting" techniques for a long time. The scenarios in this book will force you to articulate "issue spotting skills" and become intimately aware of them.

To help develop and improve your "issue spotting" skills, many chapters end with exercises titled "Can You Spot the Issues?" As a warm up, an extensive "issue spotting" scenario will be presented at the end of this chapter.

What This Book Does Not Cover

This book focuses on configuring, monitoring, and troubleshooting Cisco routers and switches with the Cisco Internetwork Operating System (IOS). It is not a book about designing internetworks or configuring other critical non-Cisco internetworking components such as CSU/DSUs and firewalls. Many of the scenarios presented in this book are extracted from real-world scenarios encountered by the author—yes, names are changed to protect the innocent! Other scenarios are extracted from controlled testbed environments. Therefore, in order for this book to be useful in a real-world setting, it must be supplemented by other texts on critical topics beyond Cisco router and switch configuration. However, the author of this book feels confident to say that this book is a complete and comprehensive reference for building a complex

Cisco router and switch testbed. By building a complex testbed and using some of the Cisco analysis tools such as the "debug" utility, an internetwork engineer can apply some of the scenarios presented in this book to his or her own testbed to view IOS analysis tools first hand. The debug traces generated on a router in a test-bed should be similar to those presented in this book. Even though an internetworking engineer will not use certain Cisco debug tools on a production network, viewing the debug traces in a test-bed network for specific internetworking technologies will strengthen one's understanding of how certain protocols and processes operate. This understanding will sharpen internetworking analysis skills that will ultimately be applied to real-world production environments.

CCIE Test Nondisclosure Policy

Cisco is adamant about maintaining the value of the CCIE by maintaining a strict nondisclosure policy on the CCIE examinations. This book adheres to the nondisclosure provision. Any references to the CCIE examinations themselves contained in this book are directly referenced from the Cisco public web site. To stay current on Cisco test taking policies, requirements, and Cisco recommended test preparation measures, reference the Cisco web site at www.cisco.com.

The Cisco Web Site

Even though Cisco maintains a strict nondisclosure policy with CCIE examination, it provides a substantial amount of information on CCIE certification topics on its web site.

The Cisco web site also contains a wealth of information to help CCIE candidates prepare for certification. The Cisco web site contains white papers, design guides, frequently asked questions (FAQs), forums, and sample configurations. All of these resources are useful in strengthening your knowledge of internetworking technologies and Cisco solutions. Cisco is a highly dynamic company. It is mandatory to frequently check its web site for any changes in the CCIE program or any updates to its products.

The Origins of This Book

This book was written by CCIEs and Certified Cisco Instructors employed at the Certified Cisco Training Partner, Automation Research Systems (ARS) Limited in Alexandria, Virginia. During certified Cisco courses, students constantly

ask, "Is what we are covering relevant for CCIE certification?" The answer often is "yes and no." Yes, the material covered in Cisco certified courses is the subject matter of CCIE certification. However, the material covered in almost all of the Cisco certified courses is introductory in nature. It does not go to the level of technical detail that CCIE certification preparation demands. Certified Cisco courses provide an excellent starting point for CCIE preparation; however, they only get you to a 60–65 percent level of preparation.

Information on the Cisco web site supports this. The Cisco web site lists three key elements for successful CCIE certification preparation: formal training, real-world hands-on experience, and a structured self-study program. The Cisco web site lists a number of Cisco Certified courses to take for CCIE preparation, but it also lists the requirement of two years of field experience. While gaining as much field experience as possible is absolutely valuable, it does not assure that a CCIE candidate will touch on all of the topics that could be encountered in the CCIE certification process.

A required supplement to the field experience component is a structured self-study program. A structured self-study program must involve the systematic coverage and review of the eight volume Cisco IOS Configuration Guide and Command Reference as well as Cisco published documents on LAN switching and ATM solutions. To close the gap where the Cisco Certified courses leave off, a CCIE candidate must review the material of all eight volumes of the IOS configuration guides and similar guides for LAN switching and ATM. The Configuration Guides are available in hard copy, CD-ROM, or via the Cisco public web site. In conjunction with reviewing the Configuration Guides, CCIE candidates are recommended to read other papers that Cisco makes freely available on its web site. Paper titles include:

- OSPF Design Guide
- BGP Design Guide
- BGP Five Lesson Tutorial
- DLSW+ Design Guide
- Internetworking Design Guide
- Internetworking Case Studies

Like other Cisco training partners and some universities (Witchita State University), ARS launched a specialized CCIE certification course titled Bridges, Routers, and Switches (BRS) for CCIEs. It is an intensive course that systematically reviews the core elements of Cisco router and switch configuration. The structure of the course is the six level approach used by this book. The course is heavily hands-on and is designed for students possessing a high degree of experience. A frequent comment among students of the BRS class is, "It is the most hands-on Cisco class I have ever taken. After the first day, I was humbled to learn how little I really knew." The class is not a normal nine-to-five class. It is more like a nine in the morning to ten at night class, with a three router to one student ratio or one two student team working on racks of six routers and one catalyst switch.

It is impossible to cover all of the material in this book in a single course. To remedy this, ARS introduced two post-classroom support services to assist CCIE candidates to prepare in a manner that is modular and self-paced: CCIE preparation lab time and CCIE preparation weekend study groups. CCIE lab time allows candidates to focus on individual topics in a hands-on environment. Attendees of the weekend CCIE study group sessions held in the Washington, D.C. area have access to equipment and work on problems in a team environment. Students from Richmond to New York City would drive in to participate in the study sessions.

As popularity of the CCIE practice lab and the follow up study groups increased, ARS developed a virtual CCIE preparation lab, where students from around the world can dial into a rack of routers and prepare.

This book is the product of the BRS course and study groups. It is a tested and proven method for CCIE certification preparation. By purchasing this book, you are getting the primary text of the ARS Bridges, Routers and Switches for CCIEs course. With current BRS students, as soon as they sign up for the course, this book plus supplements are shipped to them.

Listed below is a suggested approach to preparing for the CCIE certification:

1. Read this book.
2. Construct your personal outline of topics to study for CCIE certification. Structure the outline on the six levels described in this book. Also, structure your outline along the lines of the topics covered in the IOS Configuration Guides. IOS Configuration Guides are available on the Cisco web site.
3. Within the outline, list what topics you have experience with and which you do not.
4. Continue to strengthen the topics you have hands-on experience with by gaining more hands-on experience on these topics. Attempt to gain hands-on experience on the topics you have little or no hands-on experience with.
5. Take recommended certified Cisco courses from Cisco training partners that are recommended at the end of some of the chapters in this book (ACRC, CIT, etc.).
6. Take the ARS course Bridges, Routers, and Switches for CCIEs (BRS) or equivalent.
7. Use the ARS CCIE lab and/or virtual ARS CCIE lab or equivalent. If you can, build your own CCIE practice lab.
8. Form and attend CCIE study groups.
9. Keep a progress chart of your strengths and weaknesses. Use the checklists in this book as a detailed supplement to your progress chart.
10. Perform as many practice tests and scenarios as possible.

11. Again, obtain as much hands-on experience as possible!
12. Take the official test.

CCIE Defined

Introduced in 1993, Cisco introduced CCIE program. CCIE certification is a two part certification that involves passing two tests: one written and one hands-on. A CCIE candidate must pass the written test before taking the hands-on examination.

Originally, a single CCIE certification existed. Today, the CCIE certification may be attained under three disciplines, as detailed in the next three sections.

Routing and Switching

The Routing and Switching CCIE certification focuses on design, configuration, and troubleshooting issues involving IP routing, non-IP desktop protocols (IPX, AppleTalk, DECNET), nonroutable technologies (transparent bridging, source-route bridging and DLSw+), LAN switching (VLANs and catalyst configuration), and underlying (WAN) technologies (Frame-Relay, ATM, ISDN).

ISP/Dial

The ISP Dial CCIE certification focuses on designing configuring and troubleshooting IP routing, dialup issues, security, remote access, and WAN technologies.

WAN Switching

The WAN Switching CCIE certification focuses on the former Stratacom product line. Stratacom is a carrier class WAN switch manufacturer acquired by Cisco in 1996. Topics include designing, configuring and troubleshooting the interconnection of Stratacom products (IGX-IGX, BPX-BPX, IGX to BPX), the configuration voice services, managing traffic, and configuring ATM as well as Frame-Relay.

Once CCIE certification is attained, you are required to maintain the certification by adhering to recertification requirements. Access the Cisco web site for more details on each of these certifications.

The Cisco web site supplies general parameters defining what topics are addressed in each certification and what Cisco equipment is involved with each certification.

The CCIE Written Exam

The written exam is a 100-question, two-hour long computer-based test administered by Sylvan Prometric. It covers a wide range of internetworking issues, ranging from cabling to source route bridging to ATM. You are graded and given your score immediately after you have completed the test. You must call Sylvan Prometric to register for the written test and find out which Sylvan location offers the test. The passing score for the written test is 65% for non-Cisco employees and 70% for Cisco employees.

See the Cisco web site for a current list of topics covered on the CCIE written test and a recommended reading list.

The CCIE Hands-On Lab

The hands-on exam is two days in length. You are assigned a collection of various types of Cisco internetworking equipment relevant to your specific CCIE certification (Routing and Switching, ISP Dial, or WAN Switching). According to the CCIE page on the Cisco web site, "you are instructed to build, configure, and test complex internetworks to provided specifications." Once you have configured and tested the equipment as specified, "faults" will be placed in your configuration and you must find the faults and fix them.

You cannot bring in any materials with you to the CCIE lab. You are limited to accessing printed copies of the IOS document set (the eight volume Configuration Guide and Command Reference) and the official Cisco CD-ROM documentation set.

The CCIE candidate must receive no less than an 80% grade to pass the CCIE lab exam.

Currently, the CCIE lab is administered at the following sites:

- San Jose, California
- Research Triangle Park, North Carolina
- Halifax, Canada
- Brussels, Belgium
- Sydney, Australia
- Peking, China
- Tokyo, Japan

The CCIE certification process is an ever-evolving state. Reference the Cisco web page for any updates.

Six Key Ingredients for CCIE Certification Success

1. Knowledge Base of Internetworking Technology.
2. Knowledge Base of the Cisco IOS: Knowledge base of how to use the Cisco IOS to configure, maintain, monitor, and troubleshoot the above-mentioned technology.
3. Be Able to Spot Issues and Potential Problems: Be able to rapidly and proactively spot issues and potential problems in configuring and troubleshooting.
4. Strong Internetwork Analysis Skills: You must be able apply your internetwork and Cisco IOS knowledge base in a systematic and incremental manner in a live internetwork environment.
5. Hands-on Experience: It is absolutely essential that all four of the ingredients listed above were developed in a hands-on environment.
6. Test Taking Time and Task Management Skills: CCIE certification is based upon tests. It is recommended to have a test taking strategy for all CCIE examinations. Like most tests, time is one of your most vital resources. Have a proactive time management strategy when taking any of the CCIE certification tests.

Roadmap of This Book

As mentioned earlier, the core of this book is divided into six levels:

- Level One: Physical and Data-Link Layer Configuration Tasks (Chapters 3—8)
- Level Two: Configuring IP Addressing, IP IGP Routing Protocols, and Redistribution (Chapters 9—13)
- Level Three: Configuring IP Exterior Gateway Protocols (Chapter 14)
- Level Four: Configuring non-IP Routing Protocols (Chapters 15—19)
- Level Five: Configuring non-Routable Protocols (Chapters 20—22)
- Level Six: Managing Internetwork Traffic (Chapters 23—29)

Chapters Two and Three are basic chapters and will be a review for many. However, they give all readers a common reference point with which to begin the book with. Chapter Thirty is a troubleshooting chapter providing a summary of troubleshooting techniques for all six levels. Chapter Thirty-One provides listings of CCIE certification preparation checklists and general test-taking techniques. Chapter Thirty-Two provides a final set of internetwork configuration scenarios.

The core of this book is the subject matter of the six levels. Displayed below is a more detailed description of what is covered in each of the six levels.

Level One: Physical and Data-link Layer Configuration Tasks

Level One lays the physical and data-link layer foundation of the entire internetwork. If you can't complete Level One tasks, you go no farther. You will encounter different technologies at Level One, but the technologies can be grouped and categorized. General categories include: LAN interface configuration, WAN interface configuration, Non-Broadcast Multiple Access Configuration (Frame-Relay, X.25 and ATM) and switched configuration (ISDN and Asynchronous).

Level One Topics Include:

- Interface Configuration Basics
- Overview of all Available Physical Interfaces for Cisco Routers and Switches
- Overview of all Logical Interfaces for Cisco Routers and Switches
- General Troubleshooting Tools and Techniques for all Interface Types
- Configuring Troubleshooting Frame-Relay
- Configuring and Troubleshooting ISDN/DDR
- Configuring and Troubleshooting the Catalyst 5000
- Configuring and Troubleshooting ATM

Once you have mastered the topics above, you have laid a solid foundation for Level Two.

Level Two: Configuring IP Addressing, IP IGP Routing Protocols, and Redistribution

Level Two lays the network layer foundation of the entire internetwork. Level Two will challenge you with IP address planning issues. You must know the relationship between IP addressing, subnetting, and route summarization. Furthermore, you must know how to apply these topics to different routing protocols. You must know the mechanics of routing protocol configuration for: RIP, IGRP, OSPF, and EIGRP. You must know how to configure these protocols over complex Level One technologies such as Frame-Relay, ATM, and ISDN. Finally, you must know how to redistribute routing information from one routing protocol to another. To practice Level Two configuration issues, take five to ten routers or Catalysts with Route Switch Modules and configure at least three different routing protocols among them. After you have completed all Level Two tasks, you should be able to ping every interface in your internetwork.

If you can't complete Level Two Tasks, you cannot complete Level Three Tasks, or any type of Level Four Tasks that rely on tunneling traffic through an IP network, or Level Five tasks like DLSW+ that require IP to be working properly.

Level Two Topics Include:

- IP Address Planning
- IP Addressing and its Relationship to Interior Gateway Routing Protocols (RIP, IGRP, EIGRP, OSPF)
- Variable-Length Subnetting
- Route Summarization
- IP Classless
- Using Static and Default Routes
- Configuring RIP
- Configuring IGRP
- Configuring OSPF
- Configuring EIGRP for IP
- Configuring IP Routing Protocols over Frame-Relay
- Configuring IP Routing Protocols over ISDN
- All topics of Route Redistribution
- Using Distribute-Lists to Control Routing Table Propagation
- Configuring NAT

The first two levels are absolutely critical for going onto layers three through six. Everything is based-lined with IP.

Once you have mastery of Level One and Level Two topics, you have turned the corner in CCIE certification preparation. Everything builds upon this foundation.

Level Three: Configuring IP Exterior Gateway Protocols

Level Three topics build directly upon Level Two topics. Level Two topics dealt with routing IP within one autonomous system. Level Two focused exclusively on interior gateway routing protocols. Level Three addresses routing IP between autonomous systems. Level Three focuses on BGP4. An external BGP4 speaker will never announce a network that is not within its own IGP routing table. Therefore, if Level Two IGP routing issues are not operating properly, Level Three topics will not operate properly. Internal BGP4 speakers must have a routable path to other internal BGP speakers. Again, this path is dependent upon the performance of Level Two IGP routing protocols.

Level Three is the end of the line for IP routing configuration. If you have mastered Levels One, Two, and Three, you are able to design, implement, maintain, and troubleshoot large-scale IP internetworks.

Level Three Topics Include:

- Establishing EBGP neighbor relationships
- Establishing IBGP neighbor relationships
- Announcing networks to BGP neighbors
- Using the no synchronization command
- Using the next-hop-self command
- Load balancing between BGP neighbors
- Aggregating BGP routes
- Filtering BGP announcements

Level Four: Configuring non-IP Routing Protocols

We perform a significant change of course with Level Four topics. We move away from exclusively IP routing configuration issues and begin to examine configuring non-IP routing protocols such as IPX, AppleTalk, and DECNET. Even though we move away from exclusively IP routing issues, we draw upon our understanding of IP routing to accelerate our learning of IPX, AppleTalk, and DECNET. When IPX routing is examined, we address similar issues that we encountered with IP interior routing at Level Two. Topics such as configuring distance vector routing protocols (IP RIP can be compared to IPX RIP), link state routing protocols (OSPF can be compared to NLSP), and hybrid routing protocols (IP EIGRP can be compared to IPX EIGRP). AppleTalk and DECNET also have similar parallels to IP routing configuration.

Finally, a popular configuration for all Layer Four protocols is to tunnel them through an IP network. If Layers One, Two, and Three are not operational, tunneling Layer Four protocols through an IP network will not work.

Level Four Topics Include:

- Configuring IPX to run concurrently with IP
- Tunneling IPX through an IP network
- Configuring EIGRP for IPX
- Configuring NLSP
- Performing IPX redistribution
- Configuring IPX over Frame-Relay
- Configuring IPX over ISDN DDR
- Creating Static SAP entries
- Adjusting IPX timers
- Configuring AppleTalk to run concurrently with IP
- Tunneling AppleTalk through an IP network
- Configuring EIGRP for AppleTalk
- Configuring AppleTalk over Frame-Relay

- Configuring AppleTalk over ISDN/DDR
- Complex AppleTalk ZONE configuration
- Configuring DECNET to run concurrently with IP
- Tunneling DECNET through an IP network
- Configuring a multiple area DECNET network
- Manually configuring the designated router in a DECNET area

Level Five: Configuring Nonroutable Protocols

Whenever a packet enters a router, the router must either route the packet or bridge it. So far, we have focused our attention on routing. At Level Five, we take an in-depth look at Cisco's non-routing configurations, i.e., transparent bridging, concurrent routing and bridging, integrated routing and bridging, source-route bridging, and DLSW+.

Level Five Topics Include:

- Configuring Transparent Bridging on Routers and Catalyst Switches
- Configuring the Spanning Tree Protocol on Routers and Catalyst Switches
- Configuring Concurrent Routing and Bridging
- Configuring Integrated Routing and Bridging
- Configuring Source-Route Bridging
- Configuring Source-Route Transparent Bridging
- Configuring Source-Route Translational Bridging
- Configuring Concurrent Routing and Bridging
- Configuring Integrated Routing and Bridging
- Configuring LAT
- Configuring DLSW+ for SNA
- Configuring DLSW+ for NETBIOS
- Overview of STUN and BSTUN

Level Six: Managing Internetwork Traffic

With Level Six, we put the finishing touch on five preceding levels. Once traffic of any and all of the protocols configured in levels two through five are operating properly, we begin to control and filter the traffic with access-lists, access-expressions, queue-lists, dialer-lists, and route-maps. We will only consider working with Level Six topics until all preceding levels are stable. If we begin working on Level Six topics before the preceding level's tasks are complete, we can never be sure that our Level Six configurations are working properly.

Level Six topics can be grouped and categorized in the following manner. From a structural perspective, all Level Six topics include at least two components: some type of list defined in global configuration mode (access-list, dialer-list, queue-list, route-map, etc.) and some type of command that applies the list (access-group, dialer-group, IP policy, DLSW remote peer statement, etc.).

From a subject matter standpoint, layer six topics can be categorized by data-link layer operation and network layer operation.

Level Six Topics Include:

- Access-List Overview
- Comparing Data-Link Access-Lists and Access-Expressions to Network-Layer Access-Lists
- Configuring IP Standard and Extended Access-Lists
- Configuring IPX Access-Lists
- Configuring AppleTalk Access-Lists
- Configuring DECNET Access-Lists
- Configuring LSAP Access-Lists
- Configuring MAC Address Access-Lists
- Creating Access-Expressions
- Configuring NETBIOS Name Filters
- Configuring Queuing
- Configuring Policy Routing and Route Maps
- Using Access-Lists with DDR Dialer-Lists

Working Through the Six Levels and Working With the IOS

The Cisco IOS is a "mode oriented" operating system developed exclusively for routers and switches. The three primary modes of the Cisco IOS are:

- User
- Privileged
- Configuration

User Mode

User Mode is the first mode accessed when accessing the router command line interface. User mode is a highly restrictive environment. A limited set of commands can be performed in user mode. In user mode, commands include a limited set of show commands. The running and startup configuration cannot be viewed in user mode. Debug commands cannot be run in user mode. Configuration mode cannot be accessed in user mode.

Privileged Mode

All commands from user mode can be executed in privileged mode in addition to other show commands, debug commands, and clear commands. Configuration mode can be accessed in privileged mode only.

Configuration Mode

Configuration mode contains many modes within it. The most commonly used configuration modes are:

- Global configuration mode
- Interface configuration mode
- Routing protocol configuration mode
- Line configuration mode

When progressing through each of the six levels presented in this book, a listing of relevant IOS commands will be supplied. The IOS commands will be categorized in the following manner:

- Configuration Commands
    1. Global Configuration Commands
    2. Interface Configuration Commands
    3. Routing Protocol Configuration Commands
    4. Other Configuration Commands
- Show Commands
- Debug Commands
- Clear/shut/reload Commands
- Other Commands

As much as possible, this book will attempt to associate relevant show and debug commands with each specific configuration command used. CCIE candidates must train themselves to remember that whenever any configuration command is entered into the IOS some type of immediate result will occur. To determine whether a given result is the one desired, show commands and debug tools can be used to verify that the proper outcome has been achieved. A good practice to perform while learning new IOS commands is:

1. Enter a single configuration command. (Remember virtually every configuration command takes effect immediately).
2. Exit the configuration mode to privileged mode.
3. Perform relevant show and debug commands related to the configuration command entered in Step One.
4. View the output of the show and debug commands. Do the show and debug commands reflect a change in the router's operation due to the configuration command entered in Step One?

5. Enter configuration mode again.
6. Enter another single command.
7. Repeat Steps Two through Four.

By stressing this, CCIE candidates will learn how to think incrementally.

Also, IOS commands will be presented in a manner that introduces the most basic and essential configuration commands first. Once the basic and essential commands are introduced, commands that build upon these commands will be introduced and examined. For a quick refresher of basic IOS commands and IOS modes, see Appendix A.

A Warm Up "Issue Spotting" Scenario

You get a call from a customer who tells you that their accounting department cannot access a set of database servers in another city. They have been down for twenty minutes and the company is losing thousands of dollars a minute. You have no time to lecture the customer on faults in their network's design, you must solve the problem. A required element of performing internetwork troubleshooting is possessing strong "issue spotting skills." Is the problem a Frame-Relay issue? Is it an IP addressing overlap issue? Is it a routing protocol issue? Once you have spotted the issue, you can begin working on a solution to a given internetworking problem. If you can't spot the issue, you will never know where to begin to provide a solution to the problem. The following exercise involves a complex sample configuration scenario. It is a warm-up exercise to set the pace for the rest of the book. Throughout the book, you will encounter more scenarios that will test your issue spotting skills as well as your IOS configuration and IOS troubleshooting skills. When reading the scenario, make note that each paragraph after the introduction, includes at least one issue you must spot and/or configuration steps you must perform. Some paragraphs contain multiple issues. The scenario is a complex one. It is an amalgamation of real-world scenarios encountered by the author. The names have been changed to protect the innocent.

Read the scenario as if it were an examination. Take a sheet of paper and write down the issues you spot in each paragraph. Also, write down what technologies you must possess knowledge of to perform the configuration tasks described in each paragraph. After the scenario introduction, each paragraph is numbered to help you keep track of your comments. An answer key is provided in Appendix B. Good Luck!

Scenario Introduction

You are the internetwork engineer hired to configure, test, and validate the scenario described below for the Wolzac Media Corporation. The Wolzac Media Corporation (WMC) is a mass-media conglomerate that owns newspapers, television stations, and Web-based information services. It has grown rapidly over the last five years through acquiring other media companies.

As you read the scenario and view the diagram, you may question many design points; however, you cannot alter the design at this time. The equipment has been purchased, shipped, and delivered. Before the customer wants to place the equipment into production, it wants to create a testbed. You must build the testbed to the customer's specifications. If you want to show the customer why the design is flawed, you must first build the customer's configuration precisely to customer specifications and then point out design flaws. No whining, no side-stepping: just do it! Remember, build the configuration exactly to customer specifications.

The testbed needs to be configured according to the layout displayed in Figure 1–1. You need to go to the customer's site, unbox the six Catalyst 5000 switches, four LightStream 1010's, five Cisco 4700 routers, six Cisco 25xx routers (a combination of Model 2501, 2503, and 2513 routers), and four 2509 routers. You are going to take with you a Cisco 2522 router to configure as a

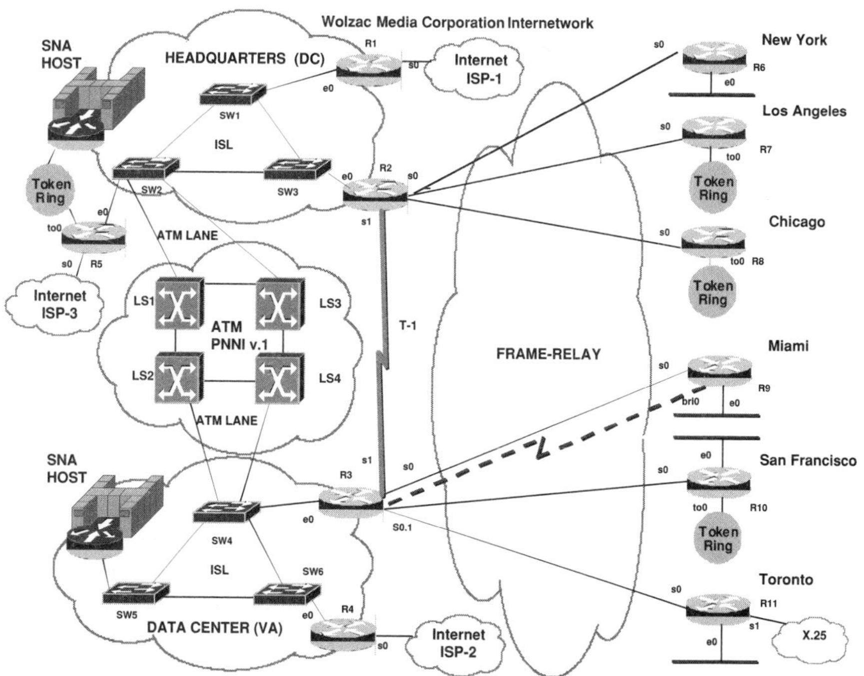

FIGURE 1–1 A Warm Up "Issue Spotting" Scenario

Frame-Relay switch and an ISDN simulator. The customer has an extensive inventory of synchronous serial cables (both DCE and DTE) so that you can connect routers back-to-back to simulate the internetwork. It has a surplus of MAUs and Ethernet hubs to simulate equipment used at the regional offices as well as legacy equipment that must be supported at the Headquarters and Data Center sites. Finally, it has an extra inventory of Cisco 2500 routers and one old 7000 router that can be used to simulate routers used by ISPs and other organizations.

Headquartered in Washington D.C., WMC's facility is a ten story building with 1000 employees. Approximately 20 miles away, it has a second data center with 700 employees in a Washington D.C. suburb, Reston, Virginia. It has six regional offices throughout the United States and Canada.

WMC is upgrading its internetworking infrastructure with a complete Cisco solution. Currently, it has two Cisco routers for WAN connectivity between its Headquarters and Data Center (a single T-1 circuit) and a collection of Cabletron MMAC and SynOptics 3000 hubs at each site. WMC plans to phase out the Cabletron and SynOptics equipment and install Catalyst multilayer switches. The initial phase of the upgrade will involve installing six Catalyst switches—three at the headquarters site and three at the suburban data center. The Catalyst switches will be configured with Ethernet 10/100 modules to connect legacy equipment as well as fast-ethernet modules for ISL trunking. The groups of Catalyst switches at both the headquarters and data center will be configured with ATM LANE modules that will connect into a mesh of four Cisco LightStream ATM switches. Two of the LightStream switches will reside at its Headquarters and the other two at the Data Center. The existing T-1 connection between the two sites will remain.

SPOTTING ISSUES AND LISTING CONFIGURATION STEPS

PARAGRAPH 1 • All of the Catalysts in the Headquarters site will be interconnected via Fast-EtherChannel. Switch-2 (Sw2) will be interconnected to Switch-4 (Sw4) in Reston via ATM LANE. All of the Catalysts in the Reston, Virginia Data Center will also be interconnected via FastEtherChannel. Fast-EtherChanel configuration will be performed on the two ports of each Catalyst Supervisor Module. You have been told that there has been a mix up in the equipment shipped to WMC. Six Supervisor One Modules have been shipped to the WMC Headquarters and six supervisor two modules have been shipped to the Data Center. You are going to build your testbed at the Washington D.C. office. Can you perform Fast-EtherChannel configuration on the Supervisor One Modules? Do you need to have someone from the Data-Center bring the Supervisor Two Modules?

PARAGRAPH 2 • WMC management knows very little about Fast-EtherChannel and LANE. Management went to a seminar and heard about LECS, LEC, BUS, and LES, but it does not know how to configure it. A contract consultant mentioned that planning the spanning tree election is going to be important among the switches. WMC management is skeptical of this. spanning tree was used for bridges and not switches. Is spanning tree important in the configuration of Catalyst switches? What does this mean and how can a spanning tree election be influenced? You must explain and provide a LANE configuration. If spanning tree is important, make Sw1 the root of the spanning tree and Sw2 the backup root of the spanning tree.

PARAGRAPH 3 • Six VLANs will be configured within the switched network. VLAN membership will be static; however, dynamic VLAN membership is a future consideration. You must configure a static VLAN configuration and explain and demonstrate what configuration steps are involved with dynamic VLAN memberships. Ports associated with all six VLANs will be dispersed throughout all of the Catalyst switches. For some reason, WMC management wants the management connection of each Catalyst to be in the VLAN number associated with its switch number. For example, the management connection of Sw1 will be in VLAN 1; the management connection of Sw2 will be in VLAN 2; the management connection of Sw3 will be in VLAN 3, etc. WMC management admits that the LAN switched environment is completely new to them. They do not know what the name of the management connection is on the Catalyst switches or how to configure it. They just know that they do not want to access each Catalyst switch through the console port only. They want to TELNET to each Catalyst from anywhere on the WMC internetwork.

PARAGRAPH 4 • Switch-6 contains a Route-Switch Module. Router R3 has a Fast-Ethernet interface. A solution must be formulated to allow devices on different VLANs to communicate with each other except for devices on VLAN 3. VLAN 3 MUST BE EXCLUDED FROM THE INTER-VLAN ROUTING SOLUTION. VLAN 4 contains mission critical UNIX-based billing systems that all of the remote sites must access via TCP/IP. Management wants to know if there is a way to provide redundant paths and transparent redundant default gateways to the UNIX-based billing systems.

PARAGRAPH 5 • VLANs 1—5 will be subnets of the 172.16.0.0 prefix. A 24-bit subnet mask will be used for VLANs 1—5. VLAN 6 will use the 172.16.0.0 prefix; however, it must use a 26-bit subnet mask. You must select a specific subnet number to meet these requirements. Routers R1—R5 have a single ethernet or fast-ethernet interface (R1 and R5 have an ethernet interface; routers R2, R3, and R4 have fast-ethernet interfaces). WMC management was told that inter-VLAN routing can be performed with a single ethernet interface on a router. It was referred to as "one-armed routing" or "routing on a stick." Is this true? Must the interface be a fast-ethernet interface?

PARAGRAPH 6 • Router R1's Ethernet interface must be in VLAN 1; routers R2 and R4 ethernet interfaces must be in VLAN 2; router R3's Fast-ethernet interface must be in VLANs 1, 3, 4, and 6; router R5's ethernet interface must be in VLAN 3. Routers R1—R4 and the RSM in Sw6 will be part of OSPF area 0. All of R5's interfaces will be in a RIP version 1 domain. Any other interfaces in VLAN 3 must also be in the RIP domain.

Paragraph 7 • A strong possibility exists that router R5 will be connected to another router from a new WMC subsidiary. If interconnected, the subsidiary router will advertise a total of five additional 172.16.0.0 subnets to R5. Management wants you to simulate the subsidiary interconnection by creating five virtual interfaces and assigning an additional five 172.16.0.0 subnetworks to advertise via RIP on R5 to all other WMC routers How can you create virtual subnetworks and interfaces on Cisco routers? Someone mentioned the use of loopback interfaces. Are they involved in any way? Management wants to know if different length subnet masks can be used with RIP version 1? If they can't be, can they be used with other routing protocols such as RIP version 2, IGRP, EIGRP, and OSPF?

Paragraph 8 • Once all of this is performed, all routers should be able to ping all other router interfaces and switch management interfaces and vice-versa. For some reason, R5 cannot ping any interfaces in VLAN 6. VLAN 6 interfaces are assigned a 172.16.0.0 prefix with a 26-bit subnet mask. Why can't R5 ping any of the interfaces on VLAN 6? What is a solution?

Paragraph 9 • OSPF area 0 needs to be extended over the Frame-Relay cloud from router R2 to routers R6 and R7. Routers R6 and R7 must be able to ping each other as well as R2. No frame-relay map statements can be used on any of the routers. The New York router (R6) will be advertising three additional networks to corporate headquarters. The network subnet addresses are 172.16.100.16, 172.16.100.32, and 172.16.100.48. All of the subnets are in OSPF area 10 and all of them have a 26-bit subnet mask assigned to them. Assign one of these addresses to the ethernet 0 interface of router R6 and the other two to virtual interfaces. Summarize them into one advertisement so that all other routers can access the networks (including router R5).

Paragraph 10 • The Los Angeles router (R7) will be advertising four additional networks to WMC corporate headquarters. Assign the Token-Ring interface a 172.16.0.0 prefix with a 21-bit subnet mask. Create three virtual interfaces with a 140.10.0.0 prefix and a 30-bit subnet mask. Summarize the three 140.10.0.0 subnets with a 26-bit subnet mask. Assign all Los Angeles interfaces (except Serial0) to OSPF area 22.

Paragraph 11 • The Chicago router is running IGRP only. It will be advertising three 172.16.0.0 prefixes with 24-bit subnet masks to headquarters. Make sure that all other WMC OSPF routers view the Chicago subnets as a single entry with a 22-bit mask.

Paragraph 12 • An unforeseen problem has arisen that you must solve. Router R2 needs to maintain two OSPF connections with routers R6 and R7 over a single Frame-Relay interface (Serial0) using no Frame-Relay map statements. Router R2 must also maintain an IGRP connection over the same Frame-Relay interface (Serial0). How can this be performed? WMC management read something about subinterfaces used with Frame-Relay and ATM connections. If subinterfaces can be used to solve this problem, you can use one and only one subinterface on R2 to solve the OSPF/IGRP over the same physical Frame-Relay interface problem. Do not use any subinterfaces on R7. Do not let any IGRP advertisements out on any other interfaces on router R2 other than the single interface connecting R2 to R7.

PARAGRAPH 13 • After you have successfully configured IGRP between R2 and R7, strange things begin happening to R2's routing table. Many of the networks that it learned from OSPF are being listed as being learned from IGRP and router R7. As a result, packets are not getting to the proper destination. The network is broken! Why? What is a remedy?

PARAGRAPH 14 • Once you have solved the above problem, R7 cannot ping many of the other interfaces in the WMC corporate internetwork. Why? What is a solution?

PARAGRAPH 15 • Router R3 is running EIGRP over all of its Frame-Relay connections. The Miami office focuses on media services for the Caribbean and South America. Maintaining a reliable connection to corporate headquarters is critical. An ISDN backup solution has been specified so that if the Frame-Relay PVC goes down an ISDN back up connection will be established. When the Frame-Relay PVC is active again, the ISDN connection must go back to "stand-by" mode.

PARAGRAPH 16 • Horse-racing is very popular in Florida. WMC wants to provide up to date horse-race results from Florida thoroughbred race horse tracks. All Florida racetracks have ISDN services to transfer race results to WMC in Miami. However, the Miami router has only one BRI0 interface and it is used to back up the Frame-Relay PVC to corporate headquarters. Is there any way to use the single BRI0 interface for both hot back services and brief switched connections to Florida racetracks? Security is important to WMC. Configure all ISDN connections with CHAP authentication. Make sure that the ISDN calls do not stay up forever or that calls are not constantly being made. WMC does not want a $1,500.00 ISDN bill for a single BRI interface!

PARAGRAPH 17 • The San Francisco office has three 172.16.0.0 subnetworks, each with a 26-bit subnet mask. Assign two of these subnets to the physical LAN interfaces on R10 and one to a logical interface. Summarize all of the subnets as a single 172.16.0.0/24 subnet. Also, create a single 24-bit subnet for the 10.100.1.0 prefix and assign it to another logical interface. Do not use a "network" statement to assign this network to the EIGRP process running on router R10. However, make sure that this address appears in all other WMC routers' routing tables.

PARAGRAPH 18 • The Toronto office is a recent acquisition to WMC. Its three networks also use the 10.0.0.0 address space. In fact, one of its subnetworks is identical to the 10.100.1.0/24 subnet advertised by R10 in San Francisco. Aside from reassigning another unique address to the 10.100.1.0/24 subnet in Toronto, is there a solution that will let these subnets co-exist? You have a friend named Nat who possibly can help you with this problem. Assign the 10.100.1.0 subnetwork to a logical interface on router R11. Assign a 10.32.0.0/11 subnetwork to interface ethernet 0 and 10.1.1.0/24 subnet address to the Serial-1 interface.

Paragraph 19 • Prior to acquiring the Toronto office, WMC maintained an X.25 connection to a news service in Paris. WMC wants to retain this X.25 connection. Take an extra router out of WMC inventory and connect it back to back to the R11 Serial-1 interface. Configure X.25 over this connection. Make R11 the X.25 DTE device.

Paragraph 20 • Router R3 is connected to routers R10 and R11 through a multipoint subinterface. No other subinterfaces are configured on routers R3, R10, and R11. For some reason, routers R10 and R11 can ping R3, but they cannot ping each other. For some reason, R10 cannot see any routes R11 is advertising and vice versa. Why is this the case and how do we remedy the problem?

Paragraph 21 • Videoconferencing is a very hot item at WMC. Corporate executives saw one of WMC's competitors using it extensively with Microsoft NetMeeting. WMC needs a videoconferencing solution that does not wastefully consume bandwidth. A scenario WMC wants to avoid is opening a separate TCP connection (and ultimately a separate video datastream) for every NetMeeting viewer. Do you have any suggestions? If so, configure your solution between all of the routers and test it with the ping command.

Paragraph 22 • The regional manager of the Chicago office has an "intranet" web server in his office. He only wants Chicago office employees to access it. He wants his employees to access Internet e-mail and Internet web sites only. Only Chicago technical staff needs more access than Internet mail and web services. He believes that nontechnical staff do not need TELNET, FTP, or any other services. He feels that "if they want to TELNET, FTP, and play DOOM, let them go home and do that on their private Internet accounts." He does not want any non-Chicago employees to access any of his office's resources. How do you let people go out but not come in? What is the result of restricting inbound traffic to just mail and web traffic? What happens to DNS requests? What happens to routing updates?

Paragraph 23 • The Internet is changing WMC's business. A mass-media company without an Internet strategy is a dinosaur. NBC, ABC, CBS, and CNN all have robust Web-based Internet services. WMC must have the same. WMC has mirrored Web server farms in its headquarters facility and its Reston data center. WMC is currently connected to the Internet through a single ISP (ISP-

1) through router R1. However, as the diagram reflects, WMC has immediate plans to become multihomed to three different ISPs. It has registered for an autonomous system number and it has been assigned the number 100.

PARAGRAPH 24 • Each of the three ISPs supplied WMC with IP addresses to use to form EBGP neighbor relationships as well as autonomous system numbers. Each of the three ISPs warned WMC that is was using unregistered IP addresses within its internal network. None of the ISPs will advertise the WMC 172.16.0.0 and 10.0.0.0 networks to the Internet. WMC has been supplied with a block of Class C addresses from each of the three ISPs. WMC must find a way to convert its unregistered private addresses to registered Internet addresses. Any type of conversion scheme used must allow single registered IP addresses to be used by many internal WMC users since WMC internal addresses exceed the amount of registered addresses assigned to the company. Finally, the IP address conversion solution must be able to set aside statically configured exceptions for Web, mail, and DNS servers. Once again, you have a friend named Nat who can help you with these issues.

PARAGRAPH 25 • WMC management is completely lost on the topic of BGP configuration. You must determine which routers are going to be EBGP speakers and which are going to be IBGP speakers. You must determine whether WMC must redistribute the entire BGP routing table into its internal internetwork or whether it is possible to announce default networks from each of the WMC BGP speakers to the rest of the internal WMC routers?

You must determine whether synchronization must be enabled or disabled on the WMC BGP routers.

You must determine how to address the next-hop reachability issue with each WMC BGP speaker.

You must determine how WMC will announce its networks to other BGP speakers.

You must determine how to filter BGP updates on an autonomous system basis or on a network prefix basis.

You must determine whether a full mesh needs to be maintained between all WMC IBGP connections.

You must determine what BGP attribute manipulation (if any) you want to apply.

PARAGRAPH 26 • Take three spare routers out of WMC inventory and connect them back to back to the Serial interface identified as the Internet connection on routers R1, R4, and R5 in Diagram-1. Make sure that the spare routers are also connected to each other. This will assure multiple paths in your testbed. Multiple BGP paths to announced networks gives a greater range of scenarios to test and validate with. All of the spare routers out of WMC inventory have passwords on them and nobody knows what the passwords are. You need to break into the routers and find or change the password. One of the spare routers is an old Cisco 7000. Also, one of the spare routers has no IOS; it keeps booting up with the ROM-based IOS. You must make another router with the IOS a TFTP server and copy the IOS to the router without one.

Paragraph 27 • Like many corporations, WMC was an intensive NetWare 3.x shop. In 1996, it had over fifty NetWare 3.x file servers and 100 HP printers with JetDirect cards advertising themselves as NetWare print servers. In addition to this, WMC has other server processes running such as backup/archive servers and SAA gateways for SNA traffic. With all of these servers, SAP traffic is heavy on the WMC network.

Paragraph 28 • Since 1996, some experimentation was performed with NetWare 4.x and IntraNetWare but a complete upgrade to either of these platforms has occurred. Now, a full-scale operating system religious war is raging between upgrading to IntraNetWare or NT. NT is making many inroads at WMC. Fifteen NT servers are already installed and there is a strong possibility that all NetWare servers will be upgraded to NT servers. Windows 95 has clearly become the client OS of choice at WMC. End users are accessing NetWare servers via Windows 95 IPX connections. Many departments also want to use the Windows 95 networking features. Many departments have been having difficulty with running NETBIOS over IPX.

Paragraph 29 • NetWare and IPX are used throughout WMC. Enable IPX on every VLAN, LAN, and WAN link. Use IPX/RIP on the LAN links and EIGRP on the WAN links. Make sure that all IPX interfaces on all routers can be pinged.

Paragraph 30 • WMC management does not want to waste bandwidth on excessive IPX routing and SAP broadcasts. How can deploying IPX for EIGRP help solve the problem? Also, WMC management wants only IP traffic to travel over its WAN links. Is there a way to tunnel IPX traffic through an IP network? If there is, configure it using EIGRP over the Frame-Cloud using routers R2, R6, and R7. As a comparison, configure IPX with EIGRP directly on the WAN interfaces of the multipoint interface of router R3 and the physical serial interfaces of routers R10 and R11. Are there any issues here? Compare the issues to the problems we had with running IP over the same interfaces on routers R3, R10, and R11.

Paragraph 31 • You are in a testbed environment and you do not have multiple servers. Is there any way you can generate SAP traffic on Cisco routers? If so, how? Once you have discovered a method of generating SAP traffic, create some type of filter that allows only fileservers with the internal IPX numbers of 1234 and ABCD into the SAP table of router R6. Use the correct node address with the IPX internal network number.

Paragraph 32 • Many Novell clients timeout when trying to attach to a server through a Catalyst switch. Are there any remedies to consider?

PARAGRAPH 33 • The Miami office has multiple NetWare devices. Make sure that the ISDN link will never become active due to a RIP, SAP, or Serialization advertisement but let NCP traffic initiate a call. If RIP and SAP traffic is blocked, will static route and server advertisement statements be required in Miami?

PARAGRAPH 34 • On Windows 95 workstations, many IPX services are not being seen in the Network Neighborhood. It seems as if only IPX services on a local segment are being seen. What do you need to do to see all IPX services in Network Neighborhood from remote networks?

PARAGRAPH 35 • A bizarre IPX configuration requirement has been requested for review. Software developers want to write NETBIOS over IPX applications. For some unexplainable reason, they need to bridge IPX packets on the ethernet interfaces of routers R10 and R11 and the Serial0.1 subinterface of router R3. Can this bridged traffic somehow be routed out other interfaces on the same routers participating in IPX routing? Can the exact same scenario be performed for IP traffic on the same routers with the same interfaces? Do not configure this scenario, but be prepared to give a detailed explanation of whether it can or cannot be performed. If requested, be prepared to configure your solution for both IPX and IP on the above listed routers and interfaces.

PARAGRAPH 36 • As with many mass-media companies, Apple workstations are plentiful. Apple workstations are still the favorite of many desktop publishing and graphics professionals. Since WMC has grown through acquisition and since its business relies so heavily on graphics and desktop publishing, AppleTalk traffic runs throughout the WMC internetwork.

Enable AppleTalk on every VLAN, LAN, and WAN link. Use unique zone names for each link. For the Ethernet interfaces on the regional office routers, configure the zone WMC-WORLD in addition to a unique zone name. Make WMC-WORLD the default zone for each Ethernet interface. Use RTMP on the LAN links and EIGRP on the WAN links. Make sure that all AppleTalk interfaces on all routers can be pinged. Like IPX, tunnel AppleTalk over IP on routers R2, R6, and R7. As a comparison, configure AppleTalk with EIGRP directly on the WAN interfaces of the multipoint interface of router R3 and the physical serial interfaces of routers R10 and R11. Are there any issues here? Compare the issues to the problems we had with running IP and IPX over the same interfaces on routers R3, R10, and R11. How are the issues solved?

PARAGRAPH 37 • End systems on the Ethernet segments of New York, Miami, and Toronto use a legacy advertisement billing service residing on a DEC host attached to VLAN 2. The service is accessible only by the nonroutable protocol LAT developed by the Digital Equipment Corporation (DEC). Come up with a solution to allow LAT traffic from the regional offices to access the DEC host on VLAN 2. The solution will "translate" into a real success for WMC.

Paragraph 38 • WMC has two IBM 3090 mainframes. One is located at corporate headquarters and the second is in the Reston Data Center. WMC has replaced the mainframe Front End Processors with Cisco routers with channel interface processors ("CIP" cards). You do not need to manage the CIP interface; however, everything beyond the CIP interface is your responsibility. WMC has been using RSRB for several years and it wants to migrate to DLSW+. What are the differences between RSRB and DLSW+?

Paragraph 39 • When working with DLSW+, how much do you need to know about source-route bridging, transparent bridging, source-route transparent bridging, and source-route translational bridging? Explain in detail.

Paragraph 40 • Each of the satellite offices must access the mainframes via SNA. The Los Angeles, Chicago, and San Francisco regional offices also have SNA applications residing on AS-400's that all offices must access. What are the minimum commands required for DLSW+ configuration? When can FST or TCP encapsulation mode be used? How does making my local peer statement "promiscuous" assist in making DLSW+ more scalable? Precisely, how do you configure a partial mesh of DLSW+ connections to provide reachability from all peers to all peers throughout the WMC network. Apply this configuration to routers connected to the Frame-Relay cloud only.

Paragraph 41 • For some reason, DLSW+ peer connections will not be established with the Chicago office. The grouchy Chicago regional manager is enraged. Remember, he was the person that wanted to filter as much traffic as possible on his connection to corporate. He wanted to restrict his WAN traffic to only Internet mail and Web services. By the way, did you place an access-list on the Chicago WAN interface?

Paragraph 42 • What is the difference between a DLSW+ keepalive and an LLC2 timer?

Paragraph 43 • You must allow bridged traffic to pass between the Ethernet and Token-Ring local interfaces on router R10 in San Francisco. Can you do this with DLSW+? Is this a source-route translational bridging problem?

Paragraph 44 • DLSW+ traffic is mission critical. The bandwidth requirements are minimal since it is primarily terminal traffic. However, the small amount of bandwidth it requires had better be there when it needs it. If WAN links should ever get congested, make sure that DLSW+ traffic receives 50% of the available bandwidth. Make sure that NetWare traffic receives 25% of the remaining available bandwidth and all other traffic shares the remainder.

Paragraph 45 • Your testbed involves several pieces of Cisco equipment. You have been given four Cisco 2509 routers with octopus cables. You are told to make them terminal servers. By configuring them as terminal servers and plugging the RJ-45 connectors of the octopus cables into the console ports of each router and switch, you have control over that device just as you would if you are directly connected to the device's console port. Large Cisco installations use terminal server to remotely manage many Cisco devices. You need to configure four terminal servers for WMC and you need to show WMC how to use them.

Summary

Let's begin to follow the roadmap laid out by this book. We will constantly refer back to the WMC scenario presented in this chapter. We will encounter additional scenarios as well. For the experienced Cisco internetwork engineer, the next two chapters will be a review. For the readers that fit into this category, just skim the next two chapters and go to Chapter Four. For those new to Cisco, the next two chapters provide a basic starting point for learning about the Cisco technological strategy of providing an end-to-end internetworking solution and how Cisco solutions are categorized into a hierarchical three-level model of "core, distribution and access." From a hands-on perspective, Chapter Two covers the steps involved with the initial configuration and inspection of a new Cisco router and switch. Chapter Three provides an overview of different interface types available for Cisco routers and switches. It also covers interface configuration, monitoring, and troubleshooting basics. The contents of Chapters Two and Three contain introductory Cisco information that apply to all chapters following them.

Getting Started

Topics Covered in This Chapter:

- Tools and Techniques Used to Perform Initial Inspection of Routers and Switches
- Overview of Router and Switch Boot Up Process
- Remotely Accessing Routers and Switches
- General Router and Switch Configuration Guidelines
- IOS Command Line Shortcuts

A rack of routers and switches is your Tabula Rasa....

When performing an internetwork installation, many components are usually involved. For example, if a company with a headquarters office and four regional offices wants to interconnect its offices together via Frame-Relay, a minimum of five routers (one for each office) will be involved. Most systems integrators will ship all of the equipment to one site (normally the systems integrator's office) and configure and test the equipment in an experimental testbed environment. Once the equipment has been successfully configured and tested, it is shipped to its final destination. In this chapter, we will start from the beginning of Cisco router and switch configuration, the moment when the equipment arrives at the office. We will go through the procedures involved with powering on a router and switch for the first time, inspecting its hardware components, and the Internetwork Operating System (IOS) shipped on the router. Before we begin with actual configuration issues, let's review the Cisco technological vision and how Cisco categorizes and orders its vast and sometimes incomprehensible router and switch product line.

The Cisco End-to-End Solution

Cisco prides itself as being the only internetworking company with a robust end-to-end internetworking solution. Cisco provides routing, (LAN) switching, (ATM) switching, and voice-data integration as well as other internetworking solutions. The Cisco end-to-end solution is not merely a hardware solution. It is a software and customer support solution as well. Cisco has received international acclaim for the feature rich multiplatform IOS. From a technical support perspective, Cisco's Technical Assistance Centers (TAC) provide twenty-four hour, seven day a week technical support and documentation is readily available on Cisco web sites and freely accessible CD-ROMs.

The benefits of an organization implementing a single vendor end-to-end internetworking solution can be characterized by the scenario below:

An organization's internetworking infrastructure is made up of one vendor's routers, a different vendor's LAN switches, and yet a third vendor's ATM switches. Most of the organization's data flows through all three of these components. If there is a major network failure, the source of the problem could reside with any of these components. In many cases, the router vendor will blame the LAN switch vendor or ATM switch vendor and the LAN switch vendor will blame the router vendor or the ATM switch vendor, etc. A linear increase in the number of different vendors used to build an internetwork infrastructure can create an exponential increase in finger pointing when the network has problems. While the organization's network is down, the different vendor's are wasting time blaming each other. While the vendor's are blaming each other, the organization with the broken internetwork suffers. This is clearly a lose–lose proposition. As internetworks scale in size, the organization becomes more vulnerable to these inter-vendor squabbles.

By having as few as possible vendors to supply internetwork components, the scenario described above can be avoided; however, a new set of problems can arise: a single vendor solution may lock an organization into a proprietary solution; a single vendor may not be able to provide the "best in breed" solutions for each internetwork product category.

Regarding the proprietary solution issue, Cisco makes its products highly modular from a hardware and software perspective. From a hardware perspective, many of Cisco's products (all of Cisco's high-performance platforms) are highly modular. You first purchase a router or switch chassis, then you select which route switch processor or supervisor module, and finally you select the type of interface modules you want to populate the chassis with. From a software perspective, the Cisco IOS is the most robust, most broadly deployed, and most modular in the industry. It possesses both Cisco proprietary features and open systems features. Cisco prides itself on being a "technologically agnostic" company. The IOS usually offer at least two solutions (many times even more) to solve a given internetworking requirement.

Regarding the issue of finding a single internetwork vendor to provide the best of breed in every internetwork product category, this is a more difficult question to answer. Cisco has many competitors in different categories of internetworking. Many of them make excellent products. From a hardware perspective, some competitor's products out perform Cisco products. However, from a software perspective, very few competitor's products out perform the Cisco IOS. Cisco views itself more as a software company than a hardware company.

Many internetworking companies are trying to supply an end-to-end solution, but none can match the depth and breadth of the Cisco product line. Recent mergers between Wellfleet and SynOptics formed Bay Networks; Bay Networks in turn merged with Northern Telecom. Cisco itself continues to expand and enrich its end-to-end solutions through acquisitions as well. When Cisco acquires a company, many times the acquisition compromises commitment to providing a single IOS for its entire product line. This was the case with the acquisition of Crescendo, the original maker of the Catalyst product line. The Catalyst OS is markedly different from the router IOS. However, as products like the Catalyst become digested into the Cisco product line, they become more IOS like. For example, the Catalyst 5000 now possesses many of the commands the IOS has. The full IOS runs on a number of the Catalyst modules such as the route switch module, LANE module, and the ATM Switch Processor module. Finally, the Catalyst 2916 and the Catalyst 8500 layer three switch both possess a complete IOS command line interface.

From a technician's perspective, having a single IOS available on multiple platforms makes configuring, maintaining, and troubleshooting different platforms easier. If a technician masters the router IOS, he will encounter the same IOS on the LightStream product line, on the Catalyst 8500 layer three switch, on the Catalyst 2916 layer two switch, and on many of the Catalyst 5000 modules. It is Cisco's goal to provide range of hardware options that are as modular as possible that all support a single IOS.

Core, Distribution, and Access

The Cisco Hierarchical Internetworking Model

A common Cisco architectural model used to categorize Cisco's range of product offerings is a three tier hierarchical internetwork model made up of a core-level, distribution level, and access level. The hierarchical internetwork model is not an idea conceived by Cisco. The American PSTN telephone network has been based upon a hierarchy of Central Offices for decades (Regional Central Offices, Sectional Central Offices, Primary Central Offices, Toll Central Offices, and End Central Offices).

Originally, the Cisco three tier internetworking hierarchy categorized different types of routers only. Now the three tier hierarchy can be used to categorize a mixed environment of routers and switches. A plausible representation of an integrated hierarchical internetwork is displayed below:

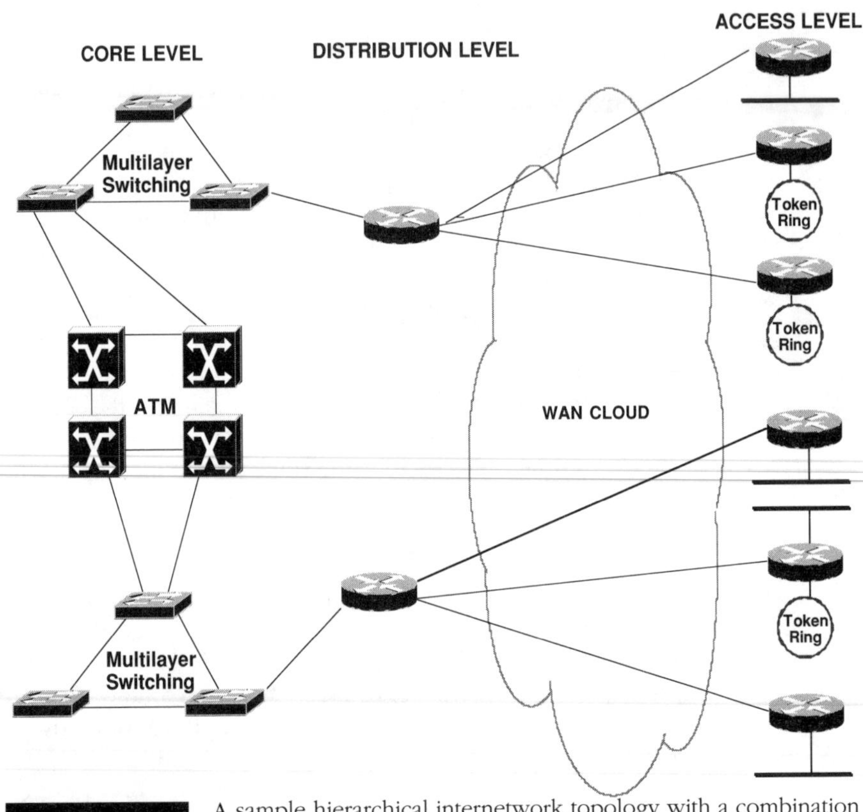

FIGURE 2–1 A sample hierarchical internetwork topology with a combination of routers and switches.

This model will be referred to several times throughout this book. A brief description of each of the three levels is provided below. Brief references will be made to specific router and switch models. A slightly more detailed description of different Cisco router and switch models will be provided in Chapters Three and Six. For comprehensive descriptions of Cisco products, access the Cisco web site.

The Core-Level

Just as "all roads lead to Rome" all internetwork segments lead to the Core. The Core is the top level aggregation point for the entire internetwork. The Core-level is focused on switching packets, frames, and cells as fast as possible. The core should be designed with routers and switches that can forward packets as fast as possible and with connections that possess ample bandwidth. Core routers should not be performing tasks such as access-list filtering, network address translation, encryption, or compression. These tasks should be performed as far out on the edge of the internetwork as possible: at the distribution or access levels.

Three resources you never want any routers or switches to exhaust are:

1. CPU Cycles
2. Memory
3. Bandwidth

Since core-level routers and switches are the aggregation point of an organization's entire internetwork, it is especially important that core routers and switches do not run out of the resources listed above. Therefore, Cisco core routers and switches are configured with high-speed switching architectures, high-performance microprocessors (multiple high-performance processors), a large amount of memory, and high bandwidth connections.

Traditionally, the core-level was composed of high speed routers with high speed connections. In the late 1980's and early 1990's, Cisco made its mark with the AGS+ router. It was during this time that Cisco captured the Internet routing market with routers like the AGS+. The AGS+ became the core router used in the infrastructure of virtually every ISP in the early 1990's. In 1993, Cisco introduced the Model 7000 router. The Model 7000 router is the direct descendant of the AGS+ and the direct predecessor of the current model 7500 core router. Today, model 7500 routers can be loaded with high performance route switch processors and high performance interface processors such as the versatile interface processor (VIP) for optimized routing. Even with the optimized features of the 7500 series routers, many internetwork designers were searching for alternative core routing technologies such as ATM switching or packet over SONET switching.

Cisco is innovating in new core-level switching technologies with products like the gigaswitch router (GSR) Model 12000 router, the Catalyst 8500 layer three switch, the Catalyst 5000 with a supervisor III module and a NetFlow feature card, and with the LightStream and Stratacom family of ATM switches.

The Model 12000 router (GSR) contains both optimized hardware and software features. From a hardware perspective, the GSR is designed with an optimized crossbar switching fabric and can be configured with OC-3, OC-12, and OC-48 interface processors. From a software perspective, the GSR supports Cisco Express forwarding that optimizes layer three WAN switching.

Core-level campus area networks can deploy the Catalyst 8500 layer three switch for wire speed forwarding of IP and IPX traffic over ethernet, fast-ethernet, and gigabit ethernet. From a hardware perspective, the Catalyst 8500, performs layer three forwarding of IP and IPX packets at the hardware level. From a software perspective, the Catalyst 8500 uses the same Cisco Express Forwarding technology of the Model 12000 router.

Optimized core-level routing can also be performed with Catalyst 5000 switches with Supervisor III Modules and NetFlow Feature cards. If an ATM core is desired, the LightStream and Stratacomm ATM switches can be deployed for core-level ATM switching.

The Distribution Level

The distribution level is the intermediary between the core and the access levels. The distribution level terminates all of the access level connections and aggregates them to the core. Many times over subscription is performed at the distribution level. For every T-1 connection to the core, a distribution-level router may have five T-1 connections from the access-level. Common distribution class routers are the 4000 family and 3600 family of routers. It is not uncommon to see 7200 and 7500 routers also deployed at the distribution level of large-scale internetworks.

Access-list filtering, compression and encryption can be performed at the distribution level of a hierarchical routed internetwork; however, it is optimal for the access-level routers to perform these tasks.In a campus-area network, routers at the distribution level must perform access-list filtering, compression, and encryption. In these networks, access-level equipment do not consist of routers but rather of hubs or LAN switches. Common campus-level distribution routers are Model 4000, 7200, or even 7500 routers with a fast-ethernet interface or a Route Switch Module residing in a Catalyst 5000.

The Access-Level

The access-level is a local network's driveway into the internetwork. In a WAN environment, it is the terminating point for a local user segment connected either directly to the core or to a distribution-level router. For example, it is the branch office of a bank that has a single ethernet connection that connects to headquarters over a 128 Kbps fractional T-1 line. Common access-level routers are the Model 1600, 2500, and 2600 routers. In a WAN environment, access-level routers should perform access-list filtering, compression, network address translation, and encryption.

In a campus-area network, the access-level is a shared hub or a switched LAN. Neither of these devices have the intelligence to perform access-list filtering, compression, network address translation, and encryption.

Therefore, these activities must be performed by the campus LAN distribution-level device: a router.

Designing an internetwork hierarchically facilitates a design that scales well, facilitates redundancy, facilitates traffic control, and limits the scope of internetwork failure. A brief explanation of some of the benefits of a hierarchical internetwork design is provided below.

Scalability

If an internetwork is built according to this model, new access points can be interconnected to distribution points in a modular "building block" approach. If too many access points connect to a single distribution point, a second distribution point can be created. and access points can be divided between them.

Redundancy

Providing complete redundancy within a large internetwork can be financially impossible. Instead of attempting to provide redundancy for the whole network, provide redundancy between distribution routers and core routers and another level of redundancy between all core routers. This will assure that only a part of the network is down at any time and not the whole network.

Limit the Scope of Failure

This benefit is closely related to redundancy. A hierarchical network model can provide "circuit breaker" functionality to an internetwork. By compartmentalizing internetwork design within a hierarchy, we can better assure that one network failure at the access or distribution level does not bring down the entire enterprise.

Facilitates Traffic Control

Certain types of traffic such as routing table updates and IPX SAP updates should not be aggregated and broadcast all over the internetwork. Placing access-lists on access- or distribution-level routers can prevent this type of traffic from wastefully consuming core-level bandwidth. A hierarchical design can provide well-defined blocking points for undesirable traffic.

In the warm-up scenario in Chapter One, you were assigned the task of creating a massive testbed involving different model routers, LightStream ATM switches, and Catalyst switches. The equipment in that scenario can be categorized in the hierarchical model displayed above.

It is useful to be aware of this design principle when installing and configuring internetworking equipment.

When creating a testbed that involves many pieces of equipment, it is useful to organize the equipment on a rack-by-rack basis where each rack reflects the equipment's position in the internetworking hierarchy.

Now that we have a better understanding of Cisco's ambitious strategic focus of being the premier end-to-end internetworking company and how Cisco categorizes its products into a three-level hierarchical architecture of core, distribution, and access, let's address the hands-on topic of inspecting, testing, and configuring a brand new router or switch.

Initial Inspection of Routers and Switches

When unpacking routers and switches for the first time, visually locate and record the model of each router and switch. Record the number and type of interfaces. Some routers are fixed configuration routers with interfaces built into them. Others are modular routers that come shipped with no interfaces. For modular routers, you normally receive the interfaces separately. Once the hardware is removed from the packaging and all hardware components are assembled, power up the router and make sure it performs the boot-up process properly. You can view the router boot-up process by plugging one end of the console cable supplied with the router into the console port of the router and the other end into a serial port of a PC (for example, COM1) running Windows 95 and HyperTerminal (or equivalent). The default console terminal settings should be set at a speed of 9600 bps, 8-bits, no parity, and 1 stop bit. All routers are configured with a console port and an auxiliary port. A Catalyst switch also comes configured with a console port. The console port is used for connecting directly to the router or switch. The auxiliary port is used for remote access to the router through an asynchronous modem. A brief discussion of auxiliary port access will be provided later in this Chapter.

Unfortunately, different Cisco routers and switches have different console port interfaces. The two most common console interfaces are DB-25 and RJ-45. Check the router and/or switch you have received to see what type of console interface it possesses. The router will come shipped with the appropriate console cables and connectors.

Once you have located the console connection on your router or switch, plugged in the appropriate cable with the appropriate connector, and have activated a terminal access program like Windows 95 HyperTerminal, you are ready to watch your router or switch boot up for the first time. Make note that the console output displayed during the boot-up process is different for different Cisco platforms. The following Cisco router and switch platforms generate the same type of console messages during the boot-up process:

```
Cisco routers 1600, 2500, 2600, 3600,3810,4000, 7200, 7500,12000
Catalyst 8500
LightStream 1010
```

The Catalyst 5000 family generates a different set of messages during its boot-up process. In this Chapter, we are going to focus on the boot-up process of Cisco 2500, 2600, 3600, 4000, and 7500 routers as well as Light Stream 1010 ATM switches and Catalyst 5000 switches.

Cisco Router and LightStream 1010 Boot-Up Process

When powering-on a router for the first time, it is absolutely important that you are able to successfully access the console port. Within seconds of applying power to the router, you should see the following three lines while plugged into the router's console port:

The first three lines seen during the boot-up process of a Cisco 2500 router:

```
System Bootstrap, Version 5.2(8a), RELEASE SOFTWARE
Copyright (c) 1986–1995 by Cisco Systems
2500 processor with 6144 Kbytes of main memory
```

The first three lines seen during the boot-up process of a Cisco 4000 router:

```
System Bootstrap, Version 5.3(10) [tamb 10], RELEASE SOFTWARE
(fc1)
Copyright (c) 1994 by Cisco Systems, Inc.
C4500 processor with 16384 Kbytes of main memory
```

The first three lines seen during the boot up of a Cisco 7500 router:

```
System Bootstrap, Version 5.3.2(3.2) [kmac 3.2], RELEASE SOFTWARE
Copyright (c) 1994 by Cisco Systems, Inc.
RSP processor with 32768 Kbytes of main memory
```

The first three lines seen during the boot up of the LightStream 1010 ATM Switch:

```
System Bootstrap, Version 201(1025), SOFTWARE
Copyright (c) 1986–1996 by Cisco Systems
ASP processor with 16384 Kbytes of main memory
```

Notice that line three displays the router processor and the amount of memory in each router and ATM switch. Check to make sure that the amount of memory displayed matches how much you physically installed in the router or ATM switch. If you do not see something similar to the three lines displayed above during the first few seconds of the router or LightStream switch boot-up process, check that you have a good console cable. Also, check that your terminal session is configured properly in your workstation (for example, HyperTerminal on Windows 95).

If both of these prove to be working properly, you need to perform hardware troubleshooting on your Cisco router. If you do not see the lines displayed above within seconds of powering on your router, more than likely you have a memory problem. See Chapter 30 for more information on router troubleshooting.

If the router has no configuration, it will end the boot-up process at "setup" mode. You are about to access "setup" mode when you are prompted with the following message:

```
Notice: NVRAM invalid, possibly due to write erase.
     --- System Configuration Dialog ---

At any point you may enter a question mark '?' for help.
Use ctrl-c to abort configuration dialog at any prompt.
Default settings are in square brackets '[]'.
Would you like to enter the initial configuration dialog? [yes]:
```

If you decline to enter the initial configuration dialog, you will end up at the following prompt:

```
Router>
```

From this point, you can begin configuring your router. If you encounter the following three prompts, your router is not fully operational:

```
>
rommon 1 >
Router(boot)>
```

The first two prompts, ">" and "rommon1>" indicate that your router has booted, but has not loaded an IOS. You are in the "ROM Monitor" mode. By pressing the question mark key, a list of microprocessor specific commands will be listed to assist you in getting your router properly booted. When you are in this mode, think of your router as being in a coma—it is alive but in a vegetative state.

If you boot your router and you end up with the "Router(boot)>" prompt, your router is still not operational. You have loaded an emergency backup copy of the IOS that allows you to perform IOS commands but does not allow the router to route. For example, if you go into configuration mode and you type the command "router ?," you should receive a listing of the routing protocols you can enable; however, when a router is in (boot) mode, no routing process can be enabled:

```
r4(boot)#configuration terminal
Enter configuration commands, one per line. End with CNTL/Z.
r4(boot)(config)#router ?
% Unrecognized command
```

See Chapter Thirty for details on how to recover from situations where routers do not boot up properly.

Catalyst 5000 Boot-Up Process

The Catalyst 5000 multilayer switch boot-up process takes much longer than a router boot-up process. Common prompts seen during the initial phase of a Catalyst 5000 switch (with a Supervisor I module) boot-up process are:

```
ROM Power Up Diagnostics of Mar 26 1997
Init NVRAM Log
LED Test .................. done
ROM Checksum .............. passed
Dual Port RAM r/w Test ..... passed
ID PROM ................... passed
System DRAM Size(mb) ....... 20
DRAM Data Bus Test ......... passed
DRAM Address Test .......... passed
DRAM Byte/Word Access Test .. passed
EARL Test ................. passed

BOOTROM Version 2.2(2), Dated Mar 26 1997 16:29:34
BOOT date: 06/23/98 BOOT time: 22:56:43
SIMM RAM address test
SIMM Ram r/w 55aa
SIMM Ram r/w aa55
Uncompressing NMP image. This will take a minute...
```

After approximately four to five minutes of testing the different modules and loading the Catalyst IOS, a successful Catalyst boot-up process will terminate with the following console prompt and messages:

Cisco Systems Console

```
Enter password:
7/4/1998,20:27:00:SYS-5:Module 1 is online

Console>
7/4/1998,20:27:22:SYS-5:Module 3 is online
7/4/1998,20:27:25:SYS-5:Module 2 is online
7/4/1998,20:27:33:SYS-5:Module 4 is online
```

For each module that is installed in a Catalyst 5000, a console message should be displayed that the specific module is now "online." Also, under healthy operational conditions, the system status (LED) for all modules on a Catalyst should be green.

It is important to be aware of the different stages of the Catalyst 5000 boot-up process. When watching the Catalyst boot-up process, you will notice different LEDs changing colors (green, orange, and red). You will also notice the console generating different messages at different times. If you watch the Catalyst 5000 boot-up process closely, you will notice that the LED color changes occur in synchronization with the display of many of the console messages. A general chronology of the Catalyst 5000 of the console messages displayed and the associated LED color changes is provided below:

Upon boot up all module status LED's are red.
Within seconds of boot up, the supervisor module status LED turns orange.
All other modules status LEDs are red.
During testing of the EARL, the supervisor status LED turns back to red.
All other modules status LEDs are red.
Once the Catalyst 5000 boot ROM is loaded, the supervisor status LED turns green.
All other modules status LEDs are red.

During a RAM test, the supervisor module status LED turns RED again.
All other modules status LEDs are red.

As the NMP image is uncompressed, the supervisor LED turns orange.
All other modules status LEDs are red.

Once the NMP image is loaded, the supervisor status LED turns green.
All other modules status LED turns orange.

Supervisor ports go through a self-test. They will flash between the combinations of orange and green. Finally, all active LEDs in the supervisor module turn green.

Finally, a console message similar to the one listed below appears for the supervisor module:

7/4/1998,20:27:00:SYS-5:Module 1 is online

All ports on other modules go through a self-test. After several seconds of self-testing, the status LEDs of the nonsupervisor modules turn green and a console message is displayed that they are now "on-line."

Displayed below is a sample display of the Catalyst 5000 boot-up process. To the right of each line is a description of the Supervisor module LED status light color and the approximate time elapsed from the moment the boot-up process began to reach the specified stage:

ROM Power Up Diagnostics of Mar 26 1997
Init NVRAM Log

LED Test .... done (red/one second)
ROM Checksum .... passed (orange/less than five seconds)
Dual Port RAM r/w Test ..... passed (orange/less than five seconds)
ID PROM .... passed (orange/less than five seconds)
System DRAM Size (mb) .... 20 (orange/less than five seconds)
DRAM Data Bus Test .... passed (orange/less than five seconds)
DRAM Address Test .... passed (orange/less than five seconds)
DRAM Byte/Word Access Test .. passed (orange/less than five seconds)
EARL Test .... passed (red/six seconds)

BOOTROM Version 2.2(2), Dated Mar 26 1997 16:29:34 (green/twenty-six seconds)
BOOT date: 06/23/98 BOOT time: 22:56:43
SIMM RAM address test (red/ begin at fifty-five seconds)
SIMM Ram r/w 55aa (red)
SIMM Ram r/w aa55 (red)
Uncompressing NMP image. This will take a minute... (orange)

Perform A Show Version on A Router

Once you have visually inspected and recorded the model of the router and the number and type of interfaces of each device, perform a show version on each router, Catalyst Switch, and LightStream ATM Switch. (If you need a refresher on basic IOS commands and modes, see Appendix A.) Make sure that the number and type of interfaces recorded during the visual inspection matches the number and type of interfaces listed at the bottom of the show version display. If they do not, one of the router's interfaces or controllers could be malfunctioning.

For example, if you see a total of two ethernet interfaces in a router, the show version should list two ethernet interfaces. In the show version listing displayed below, a total of two Ethernet, two token-ring, and four serial interfaces are listed.

```
r2#show version
Cisco Internetwork Operating System Software
IOS (tm) 4500 Software (C4500-JS-M), Version 11.2(11), RELEASE
SOFTWARE (fc1)
Copyright (c) 1986-1997 by cisco Systems, Inc.
Compiled Mon 29-Dec-97 20:50 by ckralik
Image text-base: 0x600088A0, data-base: 0x607F2000

ROM: System Bootstrap, Version 5.2(7) [rchiao 7], RELEASE
SOFTWARE (fc1)
BOOTFLASH: 4500 Bootstrap Software (C4500-BOOT-M), Version
10.3(10), RELEASE SOFTWARE (fc1)

r2 uptime is 1 day, 2 hours, 52 minutes
```

```
System restarted by power-on at 19:10:12 UTC Wed Jan 10 1996
System image file is " flash:c4500-js-mz_112-11.bin ", booted via
flash

cisco 4700 (R4K) processor (revision B) with 16384K/4096K bytes
of memory.
Processor board ID 02596706
R4600 processor, Implementation 32, Revision 2.0 (Level 2 Cache)
G.703/E1 software, Version 1.0.
Bridging software.
SuperLAT software copyright 1990 by Meridian Technology Corp).
X.25 software, Version 2.0, NET2, BFE and GOSIP compliant.
TN3270 Emulation software.
2 Ethernet/IEEE 802.3 interface(s)
2 Token Ring/IEEE 802.5 interface(s)
4 Serial network interface(s)
128K bytes of non-volatile configuration memory.
8192K bytes of processor board System flash (Read/Write)
4096K bytes of processor board Boot flash (Read/Write)

Configuration register is 0x102
```

From a hardware perspective, the show version also lists the amount of memory and flash contained in the router or switch.

Be alert for any type of hardware anomalies on the routers. For example, look at the power light to the immediate right of the AUX port on a 2500 router. If it is flickering, you have a hardware problem with that router. Contact your Cisco product supplier immediately.

Record the IOS Loaded on the Router

Once you have performed an inspection on the physical components of the routers and switches, locate and record the IOS version being used by the router or switch. This is also performed with the show version command:

```
r2#show version
Cisco Internetwork Operating System Software
IOS (tm) 4500 Software (C4500-JS-M), Version 11.2(11), RELEASE
SOFTWARE fc1)
Copyright (c) 1986-1997 by cisco Systems, Inc.
Compiled Mon 29-Dec-97 20:50 by ckralik
Image text-base: 0x600088A0, data-base: 0x607F2000

ROM: System Bootstrap, Version 5.2(7) [rchiao 7], RELEASE
SOFTWARE (fc1)
BOOTFLASH: 4500 Bootstrap Software (C4500-BOOT-M), Version
10.3(10), RELEASE SOFTWARE (fc1)

r2 uptime is 1 day, 2 hours, 52 minutes
```

```
System restarted by power-on at 19:10:12 UTC Wed Jan 10 1996
System image file is "flash:c4500-js-mz_112-11.bin", booted via
flash

cisco 4700 (R4K) processor (revision B) with 16384K/4096K bytes
of memory.
Processor board ID 02596706
R4600 processor, Implementation 32, Revision 2.0 (Level 2 Cache)
G.703/E1 software, Version 1.0.
Bridging software.
SuperLAT software copyright 1990 by Meridian Technology Corp).
X.25 software, Version 2.0, NET2, BFE and GOSIP compliant.
TN3270 Emulation software.
2 Ethernet/IEEE 802.3 interface(s)
2 Token Ring/IEEE 802.5 interface(s)
4 Serial network interface(s)
128K bytes of non-volatile configuration memory.
8192K bytes of processor board System flash (Read/Write)
4096K bytes of processor board Boot flash (Read/Write)

Configuration register is 0x102
```

In the show version display listed above, the second line lists the following IOS running on a 4000 router:

4500 Software (C4500-JS-M), Version 11.2(11)

The IOS was developed for a model 4500 router. It is major release 11.2 with maintenance release (11) and the IOS runs from RAM (-M). This is reconfirmed in the middle of the show version display with the following line:

```
System image file is "flash:c4500-js-mz_112-11.bin", booted via
flash
```

This line lists the precise file name as it appears in the router's flash memory.

Knowing how to determine what release and what type of IOS is running on a router or switch is critical for proper router configuration and administration. Different IOS images possess different features and capabilities. For example, if the IOS is pre-11.2 release, you cannot configure integrated routing and bridging or network address translation on that router. Selecting the correct IOS feature set and the right version is essential to maintaining optimal router and switch performance.

When selecting an IOS to download for a given router or switch, three key elements to be aware of when are:

1. Router or switch platform
2. Release
3. Software Feature Set

If you have the proper Cisco maintenance agreement, you can download multiple IOS images directly from Cisco's web site. Cisco has many tools that help select the correct IOS type for your needs. Cisco has an "IOS Planner" that guides you through the IOS selection process under Software Center on the Cisco web site.

If you use the Cisco IOS planner, the first parameter to be selected is router or switch platform. Once a platform has been selected, then a major release must be selected. Recent router IOS major releases are:

10.3
11.0
11.1
11.2
11.3

A number in parenthesis following a major release number is a maintenance release number. For example, if you see the following on the second line of a show version display:

```
2500 Software (C2500-DS40-L), Version 11.2(11)
```

The IOS running on the specific router is version 11.2 with maintenance release (11).

Finally, a feature set must be selected. The traditional classification of IOS image software feature sets have been based upon the following three categories:

IP FEATURE SET • An IP IOS image supports the IP based processes and protocols only. If you want to enable IPX or AppleTalk routing on an IP IOS image, you will be unsuccessful.

DESKTOP FEATURE SET • ·A desktop image is one that possesses support for not only IP but IPX, AppleTalk, DECNET and other desktop protocols.

ENTERPRISE FEATURE SET • Enterprise is the most feature rich software feature set supplied.

More feature sets exist other than the three listed above. Also, there are many variations of the IP, Desktop, and Enterprise feature sets. A sampling of the variations are listed below:

DESKTOP
DESKTOP PLUS
DESKTOP/COMMSERVER
DESKTOP/IBM
ENTERPRISE
ENTERPRISE 40

ENTERPRISE PLUS
ENTERPRISE/APPN PLUS
IP ONLY
IP PLUS 40 (1605)
IP/IBM/APPN

IOS images are several megabytes in size. If you are going to download an IOS image or copy an IOS image to a router or switch, make sure you do this on a high bandwidth link. Also, make sure that the target router has enough flash to store the image locally.

Performing a Show Version on a Catalyst Switch

The Catalyst also has a show version command that provides a summary of the current hardware, firmware, and operating system configurations residing on the switch:

```
Cat1> show version
WS-C5000 Software, Version McpSW: 3.1(2) NmpSW: 3.1(2a)
Copyright (c) 1995-1998 by Cisco Systems

NMP S/W compiled on Feb 20 1998, 18:56:57
MCP S/W compiled on Feb 20 1998, 19:09:39

System Bootstrap Version: 2.2(2)

Hardware Version: 2.3 Model: WS-C5000 Serial #: 005595422

Module Ports Model    Serial # Hw   Fw   Fw1   Sw

------ ----- ---------- --------- ------ ------- ------- --------------------
1  2  WS-X5009  17ABCDE22 2.3  2.2(2) 2.2(1) 3.1(2a)
2  2  WS-X5156  17ABCDE22 2.0  1.3   1.3   3.2(6)
3  12 WS-X5213A 17ABCDE22 2.1  3.1(1)      3.1(2)
g
   DRAM          FLASH          NVRAM
Module Total  Used  Free  Total  Used  Free  Total Used Free
------ ------- ------- ------- ------- ------- ------- ----- ----- -----
1    20480K  8195K 12285K  4096K  3584K  512K 256K 106K 150K

Uptime is 0 day, 0 hour, 11 minutes
```

You can also use the show module command to obtain a listing of the different modules residing in a Catalyst. The show modules command provides a more detailed description of the modules residing in the Catalyst. In the listing below, an ATM OC-3 LANE module resides in module two. This line card has the model number WS-X5156. If you compare the line card listing displayed in the show version command with the listing in the show module command, you see that both listings reference a WS-X5156 residing in module two. However, the show module command gives you a more detailed description of the module. From a basic hardware troubleshooting perspective, the show module command gives you a summary status of the module in the far right column of the module listing. Notice in the show module displayed below, all modules possess an "OK" status. Possible listings for the status column are: ok, disable, faulty, other, standby, error.

```
Cat1> show module
Mod Module-Name      Ports Module-Type      Model  Serial-Num Status
--- ------------------- ----- --------------------- --------- --------- -------
1           2   100BaseTX Supervisor WS-X5009 17ABCDE22 ok
2           2   UTP OC-3 Dual-Phy ATM WS-X5156 17AEFGH22 ok
3           12  10/100BaseTX Ethernet WS-X5213A 17AEFGH22 ok

Mod MAC-Address(es)             Hw   Fw   Sw
--- -------------------------------------- ------ ------- ----------------
1  00-10-11-3b-70-00 thru 00-10-11-3b-73-ff 2.3  2.2(2) 3.1(2a)
2  00-e0-1e-e4-fe-3e            2.0  1.3   3.2(6)
3  00-e0-1e-e7-97-18 thru 00-e0-1e-e7-97-23 2.1  3.1(1) 3.1(2)
```

Tracking IOS versions for the Catalyst 5000 product line is tricky. Different Catalyst IOS versions are available for different Catalyst Supervisor modules. Also, different IOS versions are available for different Catalyst line cards. You can determine which software version is being used by a Catalyst supervisor module and each line card by referencing the column on the far right in the module's listing; it is in the middle of the show version display.

The primary Catalyst 5000 IOS image is the network management processor (NMP) image. You can determine which NMP image you are running in either the show version or show module display. The NMP image version number is listed on the second line of the show version display and on the far right-hand (Sw) column of the Module MAC Address(es) listing in the bottom half of the show module display. Major releases of Catalyst 5000 NMP images are:

2.1
2.2
2.3
2.4
3.1
3.2
4.1

Remotely Connecting To a Router or Switch

Normally, initial inspection of a router is through a terminal session with the terminal directly connected to the console port. Direct connection to the console port is the most simple and direct way to connect to a router or switch; however, it is extremely inconvenient. If the only way to access a router or switch is through a direct connection to the console port, an internetwork engineer must always walk to the physical location of a given router or switch and plug into the specific device's console port. This is an extremely unscalable solution when a technician must administer several Cisco devices.

Fortunately, there are a number of different methods of remotely accessing a router or switch. Remote access to a router or switch can be performed through four different methods:

1. via a TELNET session
2. via the router auxiliary port through an asynchronous modem or to a Catalyst switch via the SL0: interface
3. via the router or switch console port through a terminal server
4. via an SNMP management station like CiscoWorks or CiscoWorks for Switched Internetworks

Accessing a Router or Switch Via a TELNET Session

The most common method of remotely accessing a router or switch is through a TELNET session. On a router, TELNET access requires that at least one interface has a reachable connection through a given internetwork. Configuration requirements for TELNET access to a router is:

1. an ip address must be assigned to a routable interface
2. a routing table or default route must be established to direct return path TELNET traffic
3. line configuration of a vty password must be performed. A configuration example follows:

   ```
   r1(config)#line vty 0 4
   r1(config-line)#login
   r1(config-line)#password cisco
   ```

4. an enable password must be supplied

Remember Cisco passwords are case sensitive. By default, if you do not supply a line vty password, you cannot access a router via TELNET. If you do not supply an enable password to a router, you cannot access the privileged mode of the router via TELNET.

WHEN ACCESSING A ROUTER THROUGH A TELNET SESSION, CONSOLE SESSION MESSAGES AND DEBUG OUTPUT ARE NOT SEEN BY

DEFAULT. YOU MUST ENABLE "TERMINAL MONITOR" ON THE ROUTER THAT IS HOSTING THE TELNET SESSION FOR CONSOLE SESSION MESSAGES AND DEBUG TRACES TO BE VIEWED VIA A GIVEN TELNET SESSION. THIS IS EXTREMELY IMPORTANT TO REMEMBER!

Configuring TELNET access to a Catalyst 5000 switch is covered in detail in Chapter Six. It involves assigning an IP address to the logical SC0: interface on a Catalyst 5000 and providing a default route for the SC0: interface. See Chapter Six for more details.

Accessing a Router or Switch Via an Asynchronous Modem Connection

If you are unable to access the router or switch via a TELNET session over an internetwork, a router or switch can be configured so that dialup access via an asynchronous modem can be performed using a router's auxiliary port or a Catalyst switch's SL0: port. This method requires that the same configuration steps performed in configuring TELNET access on the router or switch. The only difference is that an IP address will be supplied to the asynchronous interface mapped to the auxiliary port on a router or an IP address will be supplied to the SL0: interface of a Catalyst switch. In addition to this, appropriate asynchronous modem configuration commands must be entered on both the router and switch. Once the appropriate asynchronous modem configuration commands are entered on the router or switch, a technician can dial-in and access the device via TELNET. This method is normally used during emergency situations only.

Accessing a Router or Switch Via a Network Management Station

SNMP-based network management systems provide a proactive method of monitoring and managing a multicomponent complex internetwork through a graphical user interface (GUI). Popular network management programs such as HP OpenView have been used for years to manage servers, end systems, and internetworking components on large-scale internetworks. CiscoWorks and CiscoWorks for Switched Internetworks are specialized network management programs designed to manage Cisco equipment on UNIX, Windows NT, and Windows 98 platforms. When the SNMP agent is enabled on a Cisco router or switch, all monitoring and management can be performed from the GUI of a network management console.

In order to allow a Cisco router to be managed by a remote network management system like CiscoWorks, enter the following global configuration command:

```
Router2-2(config)#snmp-server community <authentication-string> ?
```

```
<1-99> Std IP accesslist allowing access with this community string
ro   Read-only access with this community string
rw   Read-write access with this community string
view  Restrict this community to a named MIB view
<cr>
```

From global-configuration mode, enter the SNMP-server community command followed by a user specified authentication string. If this is all you enter, you will be limited to READ-ONLY access to the router. If you want READ-WRITE access, you must specify the "rw" parameter after the authentication-string.

In order to allow a Catalyst switch to be managed by a network management system like CiscoWorks for Switched Internetworks, enter the following Catalyst SET command:

```
Cat1 (enable) >set snmp community ?
Usage: set snmp community <access_type> [community_string]
  (access_type = read-only|read-write|read-write-all)
```

Cisco is aggressively innovating in the area of network management. It is constantly introducing windows-based and Web-based network management tools such as the Cisco Resource Manager. Check the Cisco web site for the latest Cisco network management solutions.

Accessing a Router or Switch Via a Terminal Server

If your internetworking environment involves many pieces of Cisco equipment and you need to be accessing the console port of each device, a terminal server is an extremely useful tool. Without the terminal server, console port access can be attained only by physically connecting your terminal directly into the console port of each and every specific device. For example, if you have three routers and one Catalyst switch in a rack and you need to access the console port of each device, you will need to physically move your connection from the console port of one device to another. This is an immensely exasperating activity!

Terminal servers provide an alternative to having to physically move your console connection from device to device. Terminal servers are used to remotely administer and troubleshoot groups of routers. For example, you can TELNET to a terminal server and the terminal server with its asynchronous connections provides direct console connections to multiple Cisco devices. Terminal servers are also used by router programmers to perform remote "step level" debugging on router software. Terminal servers allow you to reboot your router without completely losing your connection to the router.

Terminal servers are usually a 2509 router that have traditionally been configured with an eight port asynchronous octopus cable. Each RJ-45 connection of the octopus cable is placed inside the console connection of each router to be accessed by the terminal server. By doing this with a model 2509 router, you can maintain eight console connections to eight different routers and switches by performing a reverse TELNET to each console port.

To configure a terminal server, three basic steps must be performed in corresponding configuration modes:

1. Line command configuration
2. Configuring one IP address in interface configuration mode
3. Configuring an ip host table on global configuration mode

Line Command Configuration

From global configuration mode of a model 2509 router, type the following two commands:

```
Term_Srvr(config)#line 1 8
Term_Srvr(config-line)#transport input all
```

These two commands allow all eight of a 2509 router's asynchronous interfaces to support reverse TELNET sessions. Next, a single IP address must be created on the terminal server.

IP Address Configuration

Configure an IP address on a physical interface or a loopback interface. Typically, the terminal server will be connected to some other network. At the very least a single ethernet or serial interface will be configured with an IP address. If more than one path to the terminal server exists, consider using a loopback interface. A loopback interface is an internal logical interface that can be created within a router. It will never go down unless the entire router goes down.

Configuring IP Host Table

Once an IP address is assigned to an interface, an IP host table must be created referencing this IP single address for each entry and a unique reverse TELNET port. Three elements of information will be included on each line of the IP host table:

1. IP host name
2. IP address
3. Reverse TELNET port address.

The reverse TELNET port addresses used will range from 2001 to 2008 on the 2509 router. Whichever router will have octopus cable connection number one placed into its console port should have the reverse TELNET port 2001 on the line of the router's name. Whichever router will have octopus cable connection number two placed into its console port should have the reverse TELNET port 2002 on the line of the router's name.

The IP host table is created in global configuration mode. Listed below are two sample entries of an IP host table:

```
ip host r1 2001 1.1.1.1
ip host r2 2002 1.1.1.1
```

Notice how the numbers in the router names correspond to the last digit of the reverse TELNET port. Also, notice how the same IP address is used for each entry.

Listed below is a complete configuration script of a terminal server. Note how the IP address is assigned to a loopback address. All entries in the IP host table reference this IP address. Note how a single entry is placed under "line 1 8": "transport input all."

```
Term_Srvr#sh run
Building configuration...

Current configuration:
!
version 11.2
service udp-small-servers
service tcp-small-servers
!
hostname Term_Srvr
!
enable password cisco
!
no ip domain-lookup
!
interface Loopback0
    ip address 1.1.1.1 255.0.0.0
!
interface Ethernet0
no ip address
!
interface Serial0
no ip address
    shutdown
!
interface Serial0.1
!
interface Serial1
```

```
     no ip address
     shutdown
!
ip host r1 2001 1.1.1.1
ip host r2 2002 1.1.1.1
ip host r3 2003 1.1.1.1
ip host r4 2004 1.1.1.1
ip host r5 2005 1.1.1.1
ip host fr 2006 1.1.1.1
!
line con 0
line 1 8
     transport input all
line aux 0
line vty 0 4
     password cisco
     login
!
end
```

Once the terminal server is configured and the RJ-45 connectors of the 2509's octopus cable are placed in the correct console ports of your rack of routers and switches, you can test the operation of your terminal server.

Simply type in the name of a router listed in your IP host table at either the user or privileged mode prompt of the Terminal Server and press ENTER. You will then be at the command line prompt of the specified router. A sample of what you will see is displayed below:

```
Term_Srvr>r5
Trying r5 (1.1.1.1, 2005)... Open
Router>
```

Once you have successfully gained access to another router through the Terminal Server, press the following key sequence to return to the Terminal Server: CONTROL+SHIFT+6, x..

If you attempt to access another router through the Terminal Server and you encounter a message like the one displayed below:

```
Term_Srvr>r2
Trying r2 (1.1.1.1, 2002)...
% Connection refused by remote host
```

Check the status of the lines of the Terminal Server with the "show line" command:

```
Term_Srvr>sh line
```

Tty Typ	Tx/Rx	A Modem	Roty	AccO	AccI	UsesNoiseOverruns
* 0 CTY			14	0	0/0	

* 1	TTY	9600/9600	host	7	0	102/311
* 2	TTY	9600/9600	host	9	7	104/315
* 3	TTY	9600/9600	host	10	0	100/300
* 4	TTY	9600/9600	host	5	1	101/302
* 5	TTY	9600/9600	host	9	0	0/0
6	TTY	9600/9600	host	2	0	0/0
7	TTY	9600/9600	host	0	0	0/0
8	TTY	9600/9600	host	0	0	0/0
9	AUX	9600/9600		0	0/0	
10	VTY		2	0	0/0	
11	VTY		14	0	0/0	
12	VTY		2	0	0/0	
13	VTY		0	0	0/0	
14	VTY		0	0	0/0	

An Asterisk on the left side of a line denotes the particular line is in use. To check if you are already using the line, type the "show sessions" command:

```
Term_Srvr>show sessions
```

Conn Host	Address	Byte	Idle	Conn Name
1 r1	1.1.1.1	0	0 r1	
2 r2	1.1.1.1	0	0 r2	
3 r3	1.1.1.1	0	0 r3	
4 r4	1.1.1.1	0	0 r4	
* 5 r5	1.1.1.1	0	0 r5	

Sessions are opened and retained when you first initiate a reverse TELNET session to a router connected to the Terminal Server. Each session has a connection number. This connection number is displayed on the first column of the show sessions display. Instead of typing the router's name to access the router again, simply type in the session connection number. To many, setting up sessions with remote routers connected to the Terminal Server is the most efficient means of using the Terminal Server. In the show sessions listing above, notice how the numbers of the session connections match the numbers in the names of the routers. By doing this, the Terminal Server user only needs to type a single number to access the specific router. This is a great time saver.

Troubleshooting the Terminal Server

If you try to access a router from a Terminal Server and you get a "connection refused" message, type "show line" to view the status of the line. If the line has an asterisk next to it, type the following command sequence using the number of the specific line:

```
Term_Srvr#clear line 1
[confirm]
[OK]
```

If many lines are being shown as being used and you want to clear them all, simply type "exit." This will terminate your entire console session. Press ENTER again and you will begin a new console session. Listed below is an example of what you see when you terminate a console session:

```
Term_Srvr>exit
(You have open connections) [confirm]
Closing: r1 !
Closing: r2 !
Closing: r3 !
Closing: r4 !
Closing: r5 !
```

If you want to terminate only one specific session, use the "disconnect" command:

```
TERM-SERVER#disconnect 2
Closing connection to r5 [confirm]
```

With many versions of the IOS, Terminal Server configurations may result in lines listed as being used when they never have been used. A remedy to this problem is adding the "Modem host" command in line configuration mode in addition to the "transport input all" command.

Make Sure the Routers and Switches Have the Default Configurations Only

If the routers are configured with the default configuration script only, they will boot up into SETUP mode.

```
Notice: NVRAM invalid, possibly due to write erase.
    --- System Configuration Dialog ---
At any point you may enter a question mark '?' for help.
Use ctrl-c to abort configuration dialog at any prompt.
Default settings are in square brackets '[]'.
Would you like to enter the initial configuration dialog? [yes]:
You can exit and terminate SETUP mode by typing CONTROL+C.
```

If your routers do not have a default configuration and you want to configure them from scratch, perform a write erase on each router and reload them. With a Catalyst switch, perform a CLEAR CONFIG ALL and reload the switch.

Assign Your Routers and Switches a Name

Once you have checked and verified the physical components of your routers and switch, recorded the IOS running on each router and switch, configured and tested the terminal server (if one is supplied) or configured the routers and switches for SNMP read–write access (if an SNMP network management system is supplied), and assured that the routers and switches have default configurations running, it is time to supply your routers and switches a name. If you use a terminal server, it is suggested to assign your routers and switches the same name used in the Terminal Server IP host table. Once each of your routers and switches has been configured with a name, conduct a final test on your terminal server or SNMP management station.

If No DNS Server is Supplied, Disable DNS Lookups on the Routers

If no DNS server is supplied on your internetwork, disable DNS lookups on the routers with the following global configuration command:

```
No ip domain-lookup
```

If you do not do this, every time you accidentally mistype something at the user or enable prompt, the IOS will try to resolve the mistyped string with an IP address. The IOS interprets your mistyped string as a DNS name and will by default try to resolve it. An example of the console messages you will see when this happens are displayed below:

```
Router#xyxyxyx
Translating "xyxyxyx"...domain server (255.255.255.255)
% Unknown command or computer name, or unable to find computer
address
```

The IOS attempted to resolve the string "xyxyxyx" to an IP address. If no DNS server is supplied, disable DNS lookups with "no ip domain-lookup."

Cisco IOS Shortcuts

Listed below are router IOS shortcuts that can help save time when using the Cisco IOS command line interface:

- CONTROL+R (Repaints a line)

Many times when you are typing, you will be rudely interrupted by an IOS message. Instead of re-typing an entire line, use CONTROL+R to repaint a line of text. An example of using CONTROL+R is displayed below:

```
London#show
%LANCE-5-LOSTCARR: Unit 0, lost carrier. Transceiver problem?ip
London#show ip interface
```

Two other time-saving commands are CONTROL+A and CONTROL+E:

- CONTROL+A (Go to the beginning of the line)
- CONTROL+E (Go to the end of the line)

To cancel a command such as a PING or TRACE, type:

- CONTROL+SHIFT+6

The following three commands can save keystrokes:

- Wr t (Write terminal; Display current running configuration)
- Wr (Write; Save current running configuration to NVRAM)
- U al (undebug all)

"U al" is especially useful. When debug massages are being generated so rapidly that you can't get to the command line, type "u al" and look for the "All debugging has been disabled" message."

For a quick reference of navigating through the Cisco IOS, refer to Appendix A.

Summary

After reading this chapter, you are able to perform an initial inspection of recently shipped routers and switches; you are able to verify the key hardware components of a router or switch; you are able to initiate a direct console session and determine whether the router or switch is booting up properly; you are able to determine what IOS version the router or switch is running; you are able to configure the router or switch for remote access via a TELNET session, Terminal Server session or make the device available for SNMP network management. Finally, you have learned some IOS command line shortcuts, to make navigating the IOS easier.

If you are assembling a collection of routers and switches in a testbed environment, the state of your testbed configuration should include the following:

- All of your routers now have names.
- You know what version of the IOS each one is running and you know what type of interfaces each has.
- Each router has a clean startup configuration and a default running configuration.
- If no domain name server is supplied, you have disabled automatic DNS lookups with "no ip domain-lookup."
- If a terminal server has been supplied, you have successfully configured it.

Now, it is time to undertake Level One: Physical and Data-Link Layer Interface Configuration. Now you are ready to begin connecting cables to router interfaces as well as switch ports and getting all specified interfaces in an up/up state.

Professional Development Checklist

Upon completion of this chapter, you should be able to:

- Initiate a direct console session with a router or switch
- Configure a router for remote TELNET access
- Allow an SNMP management station to access a router or switch with read-write privileges
- Allow an SNMP management station to access a router or switch with read-only privileges
- Configure a terminal server
- Disable DNS look-ups on the router
- Review IOS command line short cuts

For Further Study

- Cisco Certified Course: Introduction to Cisco Router
- Configuration, Cisco Systems, Inc.
- Cisco IOS Configuration Guide, Volume I, Cisco Systems, Inc., 1989–1998.

URLs

- **www.cciecert.com**
- **www.mentorlabs.com**
- **www.cisco.com**

Can You Spot The Issues?

1. The terminal server is configured with the script displayed below. For some reason, the terminal server cannot access any of the routers it is connected to. Why?

```
Term_Srvr#sh run
Building configuration...

Current configuration:
!
version 11.2
service udp-small-servers
service tcp-small-servers
!
hostname Term_Srvr
!
enable password cisco
!
no ip domain-lookup
!
interface Loopback0
     ip address 1.1.1.1 255.0.0.0
!
interface Ethernet0
no ip address
!
interface Serial0
no ip address
     shutdown
```

```
!
interface Serial0.1
!
interface Serial1
     no ip address
     shutdown
!
ip host r1 2001 11.11.1.1
ip host r2 2002 11.11.1.1
ip host r3 2003 11.11.1.1
ip host r5 2005 11.11.1.1
ip host r4 2004 11.11.1.1
ip host fr 2006 11.11.1.1
!
line con 0
line 1 8
     line aux 0
line vty 0 4
     password cisco
     login
!
end
```

2. Whenever the command "conf t" is mistyped at the console ("conft") and the ENTER key is pressed, the following message appears:

```
Router#conft
Translating "conft"...domain server (255.255.255.255)
```

After several seconds have passed, the following message is displayed:

```
% Unknown command or computer name, or unable to find computer
address
```

You find this to be annoying. How can you prevent this from happening whenever you accidentally mistype a command?

3. You are asked to supply list and description of all of the options for accessing a Cisco router or switch. The client has heard about SNMP, dialing into routers and switches, something called a terminal server and TELNET access. The client is confused. You need to explain to the client the difference between all of these access methods. Which one is the most reliable and why? Which one is the most accessible and why?

General Guidelines for Cisco Router Interface and Catalyst Port Configuration

Topics Covered In This Chapter

- Overview of Physical Interfaces Used in Cisco Routers
- Overview of Logical Interfaces Used in Cisco Routers
- Overview of ARP, Inverse ARP, and MAP Statements Used on Router Interfaces
- Examine the tools used to verify the operational status of an interface
- Examine the tools used to verify the operational status of Catalyst switch ports

Chapter Two introduced methods of validating that Cisco routers and switches were booting up properly with the correct hardware and operating system components. Methods of remotely accessing routers and switches as well as Internetwork Operating System (IOS) shortcuts were also introduced. Chapter Three introduces router and switch interfaces and ports.

All routers have interfaces and all local-area network (LAN) switches have ports. Some of the interfaces and ports a router or switch possesses are physical and some are logical. From the Cisco Model 1600 router and up, all routers possess a limit on the number of interfaces each may possess. This limit is defined by an IOS value known as the interface descriptor block (IDB). A common interface descriptor block value for many IOS images is 300 (many versions of the IOS support more). You may be wondering how any single router could have three hundred or more interfaces. The answer is that many of the interfaces will be logical. These interfaces will be created within the IOS itself.

This chapter introduces different types of interfaces available in Cisco routers and switches. It will cover both physical and logical interfaces. The first part of this chapter will provide a general overview of general guidelines for router interface configuration, monitoring, and troubleshooting. At the end of the chapter, general guidelines for Catalyst port and interface configuration will be examined and a comparison to router interface configuration will be supplied.

Introduction to Router Interfaces

The importance of router interfaces cannot be overemphasized. A router without interfaces (either physical or logical) is like a car with no tires. A router with one of its configured interfaces operationally disabled is like a car with a flat tire. From a configuration perspective, the vast majority of configuration commands are performed in global configuration mode or interface configuration mode. Many monitoring and troubleshooting techniques involve show commands monitoring the status of an interface or statistics of traffic flowing through an interface.

The Taxonomy of Cisco Router Interfaces

Router interfaces can be categorized in the following three groups:

1. LAN interfaces
2. Wide-area network (WAN) interfaces
3. Logical interfaces

Combinations of these interfaces can be found on the following partial list of Cisco router platforms:

Model 700 router family
Model 1000 router
Model 1600 router
Model 2500 router family
Model 2600 router family
Model 3600 router family
Model 3810 Multiaccess Concetrator
Model 4000 router family
Model 5x00 router family (Universal Access Servers)
Model 7200 router family
Model 7500 router family
Model 12000 router family

Catalyst Route Switch Model
Catalyst 8500 layer three switch family

As you can see, the range of Cisco router products is extensive. Even though the listing above displays the most popular Cisco router products, the list is incomplete and it is ever changing. For a complete and current listing of Cisco router models, access the Cisco web site.

You may be overwhelmed by the number of choices of different Cisco routers; however, keep this one point in mind: all of these routers (with the exception of the some small office/home office routers such as the Model 700 series) use the same IOS. From a perspective of configuration monitoring and troubleshooting, all of these platforms are the same. For example, all of these routers begin interface configuration with the following sequence of commands:

```
r1# configure terminal
r1(config)#interface serial 0 (serial = interface-type; 0 = interface number)
r1(config-if)#
```

Different routers possess different interface types. The interface type on a given router is dependent upon what interfaces the router is physically configured with. In the example above, the interface type defined is a serial interface. The number following the interface type is the interface number. This number can be preceded by a slot number or a slot number and a port adapter module number. Interface slot numbers and ports adapter numbers are found on the modular configuration routers such as the Model 7500, 7200, and 3600. Displayed below is an example of accessing interfaces on a Model 7500 router. Notice that the slot number of the interface must be specified:

```
core-7513-dc# configure terminal
core-7513-dc(config)#interface serial 3/0
core-7513-dc(config-if)#
```

To obtain a better understanding of the different types of interfaces available for different types of Cisco router platforms, lets revisit the hierarchical categorization of the Cisco router product line. Cisco groups its router product-line in the hierarchical internetwork model presented at the beginning of Chapter Two:

Core
Distribution
Access

The following sections provide a brief overview of which interface types are used with which Cisco router:

Core-Level Routers

Popular core routers are:

Cisco 7500 router family
Cisco 12000 router family
Cisco 7200 router family
Cisco Catalyst 5000 RSM
Cisco Catalyst 8500 Layer Three Switch family

These routers possess architectures for high-speed layer three switching. All of these core class routers have high-performance backplanes and processors, as well as the capacity to be configured with significant memory. From an interface perspective, many of the core router interfaces also possess optimized hardware features. All of the core routers are modular. A base unit core router comes configured with no interfaces. They must be populated with interface modules and interface processors.

Provided below are brief thumbnail summaries of the primary distinguishing characteristics of Cisco's core router family. For more information on these routing platforms, access www.cisco.com. Cisco provides a staggering amount of information on all of its products on its web site.

The Cisco 7500 Router Family

The 7500 family is the direct descendant of the Cisco AGS/AGS+/Model 7000 line. It can be configured with a broad range of high-performance, hot swappable interface processors with the following types of connections:

Ethernet
Fast-Ethernet
Token-Ring
FDDI
Channelized T-1
Channelized T-3
Asynchronous Transfer Mode (ATM)
Channel Interface Processor
HSSI
Synchronous Serial
ISDN PRI

The 7500 family routers can accept interface processors from older 7000 model routers. The 7500 provides a high level of port density and applies distributed processing technologies with products such as the versatile interface processor (VIP) cards. From a redundancy standpoint, all Model 7500 routers support hot swappable interface processors. The Model 7507 and 7513 routers support dual power supplies and dual route switch processors. Since it can accommodate so many different interface types and protocols and since it possesses a high level of redundancy, the Model 7500 is Cisco's multipurpose core router solution. The 7500 router cannot forward layer three packets as rapidly as the 12000 gigabit switch router or Catalyst 8500 layer three switch. They are more specialized core router platforms. For example, both the Model 12000 and the Catalyst 8500 are limited to the number of interface types supported and the number of protocols they can route.

The Cisco 7200 Router Family

The 7200 router family has a smaller physical footprint than the 7500. It cannot interchange interface modules with the 7500. It does not possess as many interface slots as the larger 7500 routers (7507 and 7513). Currently, the maximum number of interface module slots for a Model 7200 router is six. The maximum number of interface slots for a Model 7500 router is eleven. Like the 7500, the Model 7200 also supports a broad range of interface types including:

Ethernet
Fast-Ethernet
Token Ring
FDDI
ATM
ATM CES
Packet Over DS3/E3
Serial
ISDN PRI
Channelized Serial
ISDN BRI
HSSI
Channelized Port Adaptor

A key design feature of the 7200 router is its support of circuit emulation for voice-data integration solutions. In summary, the Model 7200 is multipurpose router that is less expensive and possesses fewer features than the Model 7500.

The Cisco 12000 Router Family

The Model 12000 router provides carrier-class IP forwarding. At the heart of the Model 12000 router is a multigigabit crossbar switch fabric. This architecture switches IP packets to and from high-performance line cards with SONET interfaces ranging from OC-3 (155 Mbps), OC-12 (622 Mbps), and OC-48 (2.4 Gbps). The 12000 IOS possesses the same user interface and tools as the standard IOS; however, it possesses optimized IP switching features such as Cisco

Express Forwarding to optimize the IP routing process. The Model 12000 router supports both IP over SONET and ATM.

Cisco Catalyst 5000 Route Switch Module

At the heart of the Cisco 7500 core router is the Route Switch Processor. It is the high-performance switching engine of the Model 7500 router. The Catalyst Route Switch Module (RSM) takes the 7500 Route Switch Processor technology and inserts it into a Catalyst 5000 multilayer switch. The RSM provides core router layer three switching capabilities between VLANs within a Catalyst 5000. The standard RSM configuration is without any physical interfaces. It creates logical VLAN interfaces. It is used solely for routing between VLANs. However, the RSM can be configured with a VIP. When configured with a VIP, the Catalyst can also possess external routing interfaces that are currently available on the Model 7500 routers. Therefore, a Catalyst 5000 with both a RSM and a VIP is a multipurpose layer two switch and multipurpose layer three switch in one box!

Cisco Catalyst 8500 Layer Three Switch Router

For years, Cisco has been promoting an architecture known as "CiscoFusion." CiscoFusion is the merging of layer three routing, LAN switching, and ATM switching into a single architecture. The Catalyst 8500 is the embodiment of CiscoFusion. The Catalyst 8500 is a layer three switch (what Cisco calls a "switch router") that forwards IP and IPX packets at wire speed. Like all other core router solutions described, it runs the Cisco IOS. Currently, two types of Catalyst 8500 switch routers are offered:

Catalyst 8500 Campus Switch Router (CSR)
Catalyst 8500 Multiservice Switch Router (MSR)

The Catalyst 8500 CSR performs wire speed Fast-Ethernet, Gigabit Ethernet switching as well as maintains ATM OC-3, OC-12, and Packet over SONET uplinks. The Catalyst 8500 MSR provides all the features of the Catalyst 8500 CSR in addition to ATM switching across T-1 and OC-48 connections. The Catalyst 8500 MSR supports ATM Forum defined internetworking services such as MPOA. The Catalyst 8500 is an ideal core-level platform for integrating voice, video, and data traffic.

Distribution-Level Routers

Distribution class routers are:

Cisco 4000 router family
Cisco 3600 router family

The 4000 and 3600 are the mid-range Cisco router platforms. The 4000 and 3600 do not have the processing speed, memory capacity, or port density of the core-level routers; however, they do support a broad range of interface types including:

Ethernet
Fast-Ethernet
Token-Ring
ISDN BRI
Channelized T-1/ISDN PRI
FDDI
ATM
Synchronous Serial
High-Speed Serial

Even though they do not possess the same performance features as the core-level routers, Model 4000 and 3600 routers possess high-performance processors and a capacity for a significant amount of memory. Like the core routers, distribution class routers are modular. A base unit distribution class router comes configured with no interfaces. They must be populated with interface modules. Unlike core routers, distribution routers possess limited redundancy features. They do not have redundant power supplies and main processors. They do not support hot swappable interface cards.

For larger organizations, the Model 7200, the RSM and even the Model 7500 router are used as distribution class routers. Distribution class routers are often used to terminate WAN traffic from branch offices or the Internet into a private campus network.

The Model 4000 and 3600 cannot interchange interface cards. The newer Model 3600 is able to interchange interface cards with the Model 2600 and Model 1600 Access Level routers. For voice/data integration requirements, the Model 3600 router supports the following voice/fax interfaces:

FXS voice/fax interface card
FXO voice/fax interface card
E&M voice/fax interface card

Access-Level Routers

Access-class routers are:

Cisco 700 family
Cisco 1000
Cisco 1600 family
Cisco 2500 family
Cisco 2600 family

The most common access-class router sold by Cisco is the 2500 model router. Over one million model 2500 routers have been sold. Most 2500 routers are sold as fixed configuration routers.

The new model 1600 and 2600 access-class routers possess a modular design. Certain interface modules from the 1600, 2600, and 3600 routers can be interchanged. Like the Model 3600, the Model 2600 router possesses voice/data integration support.

Access-Class Routers are commonly configured with the following interface types:

Synchronous serial
Synchronous/Asynchronous serial
Ethernet
Token-Ring
ISDN BRI

Like the Model 3600 router, the Model 2600 router supports the following voice/fax interfaces:

E&M voice/fax interface card
FXS voice/fax interface card
FXO voice/fax interface card

For higher performance interfaces such as Fast-Ethernet, FDDI, ISDN PRI, and ATM, you need to purchase a distribution-level router. However, attempting to stay current on all Cisco product announcements is like painting a moving train. Access the Cisco web site to stay current for any new interface announcements for Cisco Access-Level routers.

Specialized Routers

The following routers deserve special attention beyond the classification of being either core-, distribution- or access-level routers.

Remote-Access Routers

AS-5x00 Family of Universal Access Servers

THE VOICE/DATA INTEGRATION ROUTERS

Model 3600, 2600, and MC-3810 routers

Even though these routers can be placed in either the distribution- or access-levels of the Cisco internetworking hierarchy, they provide unique features that require a more detailed description.

The Remote-Access Routers, AS-5200 and AS-5300, provide highly scalable remote access solutions for both Asynchronous Modem access and ISDN access. The AS-5200 can support multiple asynchronous dial-in connections over Channelized T-1/ISDN PRI connections. Therefore, with an AS-5200, a single channelized T-1/ISDN PRI connection can support multiple dial-in asynchronous Modem connections. You do not need to manage exterior Modem banks with the AS-5200. The AS-5300 applies the AS-5200 model to a higher performance architecture. The AS-5200 uses the same base router architecture as a Model 2500 router. The AS-5300 uses the same base router architecture as a Model 4700 router. Both the AS-5200 and AS-5300 apply robust IOS features for deploying Virtual Private Dialup Network (VPDN) technologies such as Layer 2 Forwarding (L2F). Cisco rounds out its AS-5x00 product line with the high capacity carrier class AS-5800.

The model 3600, 2600, and 3810 routers provide voice/data integration solutions. The 3600 and 2600 routers provide a voice over IP solution. The MC-3810 router provides a voice over HDLC, Frame-Relay, and ATM solution. By installing an MC-3810, 3600, or 2600 router in a branch office, a company can send both its voice and data traffic over the same connection! With the 3600 and 3810 routers, you can literally plug a standard telephone into a voice port residing on the router, get a dial tone, and make a telephone call! Or you can plug individual telephones and your PBX into your router and make telephone calls! All this can be done on a MC-Cisco 3810 or 3600 router using the IOS! INCREDIBLE!!!Voice/Data integration is one of the hottest areas in internetworking. It can be assured that many more Cisco voice/data integration solution will be offered on more Cisco platforms. Access Cisco's web site for the latest voice/data integration offerings.

Interface Overview Summary

From plugging a $10.00 Radio Shack telephone in a Cisco router to plugging a carrier class 2.6 Gbps OC-48 connection into a Cisco router, a Cisco router can make the connection. Not only can it make the connection, all of these different types of connections can be configured, monitored, and troubleshooted with the same IOS! This is why Cisco states that it has the most robust end-to-end internetworking solution. The following section introduces the basic commands used to perform basic interface monitoring and interface activation.

Basic IOS Tools Used to Monitor Status

On virtually every Cisco router model, you can discover what interfaces a router possesses with the following four IOS commands:

- Show version

  Show version was used in Chapter Two to verify that the IOS recognized all of the installed hardware components in a router or switch (memory, flash, and interfaces). For example, if a router is installed with two Ethernet interfaces and two serial interfaces, show version will list two Ethernet and two serial interface in its display under normal conditions. Show version does not specify which slots the interfaces are in. It merely acknowledges that the IOS is aware of specific interfaces installed in a given router. If an installed interface does not appear in the summary interface listing at the bottom of the show version display, more than likely there is a hardware problem with the unlisted interface.

- Show interfaces

  Show interface provides a wide range of information for a specific interface. The following is a sample show interface display:

```
r1#show interfaces serial 0
Serial0 is up, line protocol is up
 Hardware is HD64570
 MTU 1500 bytes, BW 1544 Kbit, DLY 20000 usec, rely 255/255, load 1
 255
 Encapsulation HDLC, loopback not set, keepalive set (10 sec)
 Last input 00:00:07, output 00:00:03, output hang never
 Last clearing of "show interface" counters never
 Input queue: 0/75/0 (size/max/drops); Total output drops: 0
 Queuing strategy: weighted fair
 Output queue: 0/1000/64/0 (size/max total/threshold/drops)
   Conversations 0/1/256 (active/max active/max total)
   Reserved Conversations 0/0 (allocated/max allocated)
 5 minute input rate 0 bits/sec, 0 packets/sec
 5 minute output rate 0 bits/sec, 0 packets/sec
   5446 packets input, 121310 bytes, 0 no buffer
   Received 5446 broadcasts, 0 runts, 0 giants, 0 throttles
   0 input errors, 0 CRC, 0 frame, 0 overrun, 0 ignored, 0 abort
   8176 packets output, 107862 bytes, 0 underruns
   0 output errors, 0 collisions, 1812 interface resets
   0 output buffer failures, 0 output buffers swapped out
   3627 carrier transitions
   DCD=up DSR=up DTR=up RTS=up CTS=up
```

Notice that the show interface command displayed above is followed by a specific interface type and port number. If you only type "show interface," the IOS will provide a listing similar to the display above for every interface defined in the router. It is recommended to specify a particular interface when using the show interface command.

Not only does the show interface command supply information on the operational status of a given interface, it also supplies information on the amount and type of traffic that has been sent and received on an interface. Information displayed in the show interface command will change depending upon how the interface is configured. For example, if you configure a nondefault encapsulation type or the queuing method on an interface, show interface will display additional information to reflect the configuration change.

Statistics displayed in the show interface display are cumulative. If you want to reset the counters and monitor statistics for a fixed period of time, use the clear counters command in the IOS privileged mode:

```
r1#clear counters serial 0
Clear "show interface" counters on this interface [confirm]
%CLEAR-5-COUNTERS: Clear counter on interface serial0 by console
```

The show interface command will be used throughout this book. Network layer equivalents (show ip interface, show ip ospf interface, show ipx interface, show appletalk interface, show decnet interface) will also be used extensively.

The most commonly referenced listing in the show interface command is the first line of the display "interface-x/port-y is up, line protocol is up." Common combinations listed in this first line of the show interface display will be examined in the next section.

- Show controllers

  From a hardware perspective, all interfaces are managed by a controller. To view controller statistics or to verify that a cable has been attached to a given interface, use the show controllers command. The show controllers command is discussed later in this chapter.

- Ship interface brief

  To obtain a brief summary of the status of all interfaces in a router, type "show ip interface brief." Use this command even if you don't have IP addresses assigned to interfaces. As seen below, it provides a clean summary of all interfaces status:

```
Interface      IP-Address   OK?  Method  Status           Protocol
Ethernet0      unassigned   YES  unset   up               up
Serial0        unassigned   YES  unset   down             down
Serial1        unassigned   YES  unset   administratively down down
TokenRing0     unassigned   YES  unset   up               up
```

Default Router Interface Configuration

In order for an interface to transmit and receive traffic, the first line must list:

interface-x/port-y is up, line protocol is up

If an interface does not have an "UP/UP" state, it will not forward traffic The default configuration for router interfaces is:

1. All interfaces are administratively shutdown.
2. All interfaces have no network layer address assigned to them.

Overview of Router Interface States

The "show interface" commands displays range of statistics for a given interface. The first line of a show interface statement provides a useful summary of the status of the interface. Notice that two listings are displayed on the first line. Displayed below are some combinations of first line listings of the show interface command:

- Interface X is down, line protocol is down
- Interface X is up, line protocol is down
- Interface X is up, line protocol is up
- Interface X is administratively down, line protocol is down

The first listing refers to the physical layer status of the interface. If it is down, a useful IOS command to troubleshoot a physical layer issue is the show controller command. The second listing (line protocol) reflects the data-link layer status of the interface. This listing maintains an "up" state by successfully sending and receiving keepalives. Use "show run" to determine whether the keepalive setting has been changed. If the keepalive is set to the default of ten seconds, it does not appear in the configuration script. Failure to send and receive keepalives can be caused by the following configuration errors:

1. No clock rate set on the DCE serial interface
2. Encapsulation type mismatch on a point-to-point serial interface
3. LMI mismatch on a pre-IOS 11.2 frame-relay interface
4. Keepalive timer mismatch on interfaces sharing the same link

If interfaces are misconfigured, the keepalives cannot be exchanged. If keepalives cannot be exchanged, the IOS reports the interface is in a data-link layer "down" state. As mentioned earlier, to obtain a brief summary of the status of all interfaces in a router, use the "show ip interface brief" command. This command provides a neatly condensed summary of the operational status of all interfaces.

In order to remove an interface from its default operational state—administratively shutdown—enter the no shutdown command in interface configuration mode:

```
r1#conf t
Enter configuration commands, one per line. End with CNTL/Z.
r1(config)#interface serial 0
r1(config-if)#no shutdown
%LINK-3-UPDOWN: Interface Serial0, changed state to up
%LINEPROTO-5-UPDOWN: Line protocol on Interface Serial0, changed
state to up
```

When the no shutdown interface configuration command is entered, console messages appear listing that the interface is now in an "Up" state from a physical layer perspective and in an "Up" state from a data-link layer perspective.

Special Characteristics of Cisco Router LAN Interfaces
Ethernet

Many Cisco routers come configured with 15-pin AUI Ethernet interfaces that require an external transceiver. Some models, especially the 4000 family have interface modules that have both 10BASE-T and AUI interfaces that default to the AUI interface. For these routers, you must configure the 10BASE-T interface with the "media-type 10BASET" interface configuration command.

The AUI interface is standard with Cisco 2500 routers. Some 2500 series routers have both AUI and 10BASET Ethernet interfaces.

When an unattached Ethernet interface is administratively enabled, it attains a physical layer UP state and a data-link layer DOWN state (UP/DOWN). This is unlike most other physical interfaces. With a Token-Ring or a synchronous serial interface, if the interface is completely disconnected, the interface is in a (DOWN/DOWN) state. Therefore, if an Ethernet interface's state is "UP/DOWN," check the physical connection first.You can spoof an unattached Ethernet interface into an UP/UP state by disabling keepalive messages on the interface. This is useful in a lab environment when you want to use an unattached Ethernet interface for simulation purposes.

Useful tools for troubleshooting Ethernet connection problems are:

- Show controllers e # (# = interface number)
- Debug Ethernet interface

Sample messages of debug Ethernet interface are displayed below for an interface with no connection:

```
%LANCE-5-LOSTCARR: Unit 0, lost carrier. Transceiver problem?
%LANCE-5-LOSTCARR: Unit 0, lost carrier. Transceiver problem?
```

To connect a router Ethernet 10BASET interface to a 10BASET hub or LAN switch, use a straight through cable. To connect one router Ethernet interface to another router Ethernet interface cable, use a crossover cable. To directly connect a PC with an Ethernet interface directly to a router Ethernet interface, use a crossover cable. Directly connecting a PC with an Ethernet interface directly to a router Ethernet interface is useful when upgrading the IOS image on a router.

Fast-Ethernet

Fast-Ethernet takes CSMA/CD technology to a 100 Mbps speed. Cisco routers provide a range of Fast-Ethernet interface offerings. Common Fast-Ethernet interfaces on Cisco routers are RJ-45 and the 40-pin, DB-40 Media-Independent Interface (MII). The MII interface is oftentimes used for fiber based Fast-Ethernet connections

Fast-Ethernet interfaces can be used as ISL trunking interfaces for Catalyst 5000 connectivity. By performing trunking between a router and a switch, the router can provide inter-VLAN routing.

Providing inter-VLAN routing with a Fast-Ethernet interface also involves creating subinterfaces. More information will be supplied on Fast-Ethernet subinterfaces later in the chapter.

Fast-Ethernet can be configured to perform in either half-duplex or full-duplex mode.

Token-Ring

Token-Ring interfaces require a number of configuration parameters. By default, no ring-speed is defined on a Cisco token-ring interface. Therefore, it is required that you manually set the ring-speed on a Token-Ring interface. When you change set the ring-speed on a Token-Ring interface, it re-initializes the interface. During this re-initialization process, the entire router console is frozen for a few seconds.

If you administratively enable a Token-Ring interface without it being connected to a MAU or comparable device, the interface will maintain the following status:

```
TokenRing0 is initializing, line protocol is down.
```

Also, the following error message will appear:

```
%TR-3-OPENFAIL: Unit 0, open failed: Lobe Test, failed
%LINK-3-UPDOWN: Interface TokenRing0, changed state to down
%LINK-5-CHANGED: Interface TokenRing0, changed state to initializing
```

Therefore, when you enable a Token-Ring interface make sure that it is physically connected into a MAU or comparable device. Unlike an unattached Ethernet interface, that maintains an UP/DOWN state, the unattached Token-Ring interface will maintain an initializing/down state. If "debug Token events" is enabled, the following messages will be generated by the unattached Token-Ring interface:

```
%TR-3-OPENFAIL: Unit 0, open failed: Lobe Test, failed
%TR-3-BADSTART: Unit 0, Start completion and wrong idb state - state= 0
TR0: reset from 30534BA
TR0: txtmr: 0x0, msclk: 0xDEDE4, qt: 0 (0ms) starting.
%TR-3-INITFAIL: Unit 0, init failed. result code=0x3, error code=0x22
-Traceback= 30539AE 305681C 3053CD6 30534C2
%TR-3-OPENFAIL: Unit 0, open failed: Lobe Test, failed
%TR-3-BADSTART: Unit 0, Start completion and wrong idb state - state= 0
TR0: reset from 30534BA
TR0: txtmr: 0x0, msclk: 0xE22C8, qt: 0 (0ms)
```

Also, remember that when you change the ring speed or bridge parameters (source-route bridging, source route transparent bridging, or source-route translational bridging), the Token-Ring interface will be immediately set to a down state and begin reinitializing. After a few seconds, it will be back to an up state.

Useful Token-Ring troubleshooting tools are:

```
Show controllers token # (# = interface number)
Debug token ring (Debugs significant Token Ring events.)
Debug token events (Debugs Token Ring input and output.)
Show Inm status
```

WAN Interfaces

SYNCHRONOUS SERIAL INTERFACES

Cisco synchronous serial interfaces are extremely versatile. By setting the appropriate encapsulation type on a serial interface, the following WAN protocols can be supported:

```
Router(config-if)#encapsulation ?
 atm-dxi         ATM-DXI encapsulation
 bstun           Block Serial tunneling (BSTUN)
 frame-relay     Frame Relay networks
 hdlc            Serial HDLC synchronous
 lapb            LAPB (X.25 Level 2)
 ppp             Point-to-Point protocol
 sdlc            SDLC
 sdlc-primary    SDLC (primary)
 sdlc-secondary  SDLC (secondary)
 smds            Switched Megabit Data Service (SMDS)
 stun            Serial tunneling (STUN)
 x25             X.25
```

When you change the encapsulation on an interface, make sure both sides of the connections match. If they do not, the interface will maintain an "up/down" state.

DETERMINING DTE AND DCE INTERFACES

In most configurations, a router's serial interface acts as the DTE. However, in some cases such as in configuring a Cisco router to provide SDLC tunneling with STUN, the router interface can be configured as a DCE device. If the router interface is a DCE interface, it must supply clock. An interface is configured to supply clock with the "clock rate" interface configuration command. (See Appendix A for Configuration Basics.)

Whether the interface is acting as a DTE or DCE, it has nothing to do with the characteristics of the interface itself. DTE and DCE status is determined by the configuration of the cables attached to the interface. You can determine which end is DTE and which is DCE with the "show controllers" command. When you type the "show controllers" command, make sure you include a space between the word serial or letter "s" and the interface number. If no space is included, you will get an error message.

Again, if an interface is acting as a DCE, it must supply clock. If you want to simulate a WAN connection and you want to connect router serial interfaces back to back, one router interface must supply clock. Use the "show controllers" command to determine which interface is DCE and which is DTE. On the interface that is DCE, enter the "clock rate" interface configuration command. When entering in a value for "clock rate," make note that different cable types support different maximum speeds. For example, a V.35 cable supports a maximum clock rate of 4 Mbps. Other cable types such as RS-232 only support different maximum clock rates.

In the show controllers listing below, notice that a V.35 cable is attached to interface serial 0 on router R2. Also, make note that the V.35 connection is the DTE end of the cable. This is displayed on line three of the show controllers display:

```
R2r#show controllers s 0
HD unit 0, idb = 0xDB2D4, driver structure at 0xE0050
buffer size 1524 HD unit 0, V.35 DTE cable
cpb = 0x41, eda = 0x4940, cda = 0x4800
RX ring with 16 entries at 0x414800
00 bd_ptr=0x4800 pak=0x0E0D5C ds=0x41EC68 status=80 pak_size=0
01 bd_ptr=0x4814 pak=0x0E0B8C ds=0x41E5B0 status=80 pak_size=0
```

In the show controllers listing below, notice that a V.35 cable is attached to interface serial 0 on router R1. Also, make note that the V.35 connection is the DCE end of the cable with a defined clock rate of 56Kbps. This is displayed on line three of the show controllers display:

```
r1#sh controllers s 0
HD unit 0, idb = 0xF2DF4, driver structure at 0xF7B70
buffer size 1524 HD unit 0, V.35 DCE cable, clockrate 56000
cpb = 0x62, eda = 0x4000, cda = 0x4014
RX ring with 16 entries at 0x624000
00 bd_ptr=0x4000 pak=0x0FA1DC ds=0x62C988 status=80 pak_size=273
01 bd_ptr=0x4014 pak=0x0FA74C ds=0x62DDB0 status=80 pak_size=0
```

In the show controllers listing below, no cable is attached to interface serial 1. This is displayed on line three of the show controllers display:

```
Router#show controllers s 1
HD unit 1, idb = 0xE3CC4, driver structure at 0xE8A40
buffer size 1524 HD unit 0, No cable
cpb = 0x42, eda = 0x3140, cda = 0x3000
RX ring with 16 entries at 0x423000
00 bd_ptr=0x3000 pak=0x0EB61C ds=0x42CDB0 status=80 pak_size=0
01 bd_ptr=0x3014 pak=0x0EB44C ds=0x42C6F8 status=80 pak_size=0
```

Configure the clock rate on the interface that has the DCE connection of the synchronous cable attached. The clock rate command is an interface configuration command. An example of how to use the command is displayed below:

```
Router(config)#interface serial 0
Router(config-if)#clock rate 56000
```

Other WAN Interfaces

ATM INTERFACES

Cisco supports ATM router interfaces that operate at OC-3 speeds and higher. They can be configured back-to-back or configured to communicate directly to an ATM switch. Configuring PVCs for an ATM interface is similar to configuring PVCs for Frame-Relay. Coverage of ATM will be supplied in Chapter Seven.

ISDN INTERFACES

Cisco supports two different interface types for ISDN: the BRI interface and the PRI interface. Both interfaces must establish communications with the ISDN switch before passing data.

The ISDN PRI interface is found on the channelized T-1 card for Cisco 4000 and 7500 series routers.

Extensive coverage of ISDN configuration is provided in Chapter Five.

Asynchronous Interfaces

Asynchronous interfaces support dial-up modems. Like ISDN PPP, and Dial on Demand Routing (DDR) DDR are used to configure asynchronous interfaces. Unlike ISDN, asynchronous interfaces use in-band signaling and require chat scripts. The auxiliary port on a Cisco router can be configured as an asynchronous interface.

Virtual Interfaces

A distinguishing feature of the Cisco IOS is its use of virtual interfaces. The IOS supports several virtual interfaces. The most commonly used virtual interfaces are listed below:

- Subinterfaces
- VLAN interfaces
- Channelized interfaces
- Loopback interfaces
- Dialer interfaces
- Tunnel interfaces
- Bridge virtual interfaces
- Null interfaces

A brief description of each is provided below.

Subinterfaces

Subinterfaces are used in situations where multiple logical connections are set up and maintained over a single physical interface. Situations where subinterfaces are used are:

1. Frame-Relay
2. ATM
3. Fast-Ethernet/ISL

Two types of subinterfaces exist: point-to-point and multipoint.

Subinterfaces and Frame-Relay

Subinterfaces play a key role in Frame-Relay configuration. They simplify large-scale hub and spoke configurations They provide a solution to split-horizon issues when distance vector routing protocols are used in a Frame-Relay hub and spoke environment. Using subinterfaces with Frame-Relay is covered in the next chapter.

Subinterfaces and ATM

Configuring subinterfaces in an ATM environment is similar to Frame-Relay. Subinterfaces will allow partial mesh topologies to circumvent the split horizon issue for distance vector routing protocols. Subinterfaces also play a key role in router configuration in ATM LANE. Multipoint subinterfaces are used to configure ATMLEC and LES BUS services. Using subinterfaces with ATM is covered in Chapter Seven.

Subinterfaces and Fast Ethernet/ISL

Using subinterfaces with Fast Ethernet ISL allows a single physical interface to route between multiple VLANs. Each subinterface will be used to provide connectivity to a specific VLAN. Use of ISL subinterfaces will be provided in the Configuring Catalyst 5000 chapter (Chapter Six).

Changing Existing Subinterfaces

When an attempt is made to change an existing subinterface to a different type (for example from point-to-point to multipoint), the following prompt is encountered:

```
r3#conf t
Enter configuration commands, one per line. End with CNTL/Z.
r3(config)#inte s0.1 p
r3(config)#inte s0.1 point-to-point
% Warning: cannot change link type
r3(config-subif)#
```

In order to perform the change, remove the unwanted subinterface and reboot the router.

In the scenario below, a subinterface is removed in the following manner:

```
r3(config-if)#no inte s0.1
r3(config)#
r3(config)#^Z
```

Notice there is no error. However, when sh ip interface is typed we see a "deleted" prompt next to the deleted subinterface.

Completely screwed up routing table: See original manuscript.

```
r3#sh ip interface brief
Interface     IP-Address    OK?  Method   Status              Protocol
Ethernet0     169.20.1.1    YES  manual   up                  up
Serial0       172.16.1.3    YES  manual   administratively    down down
Serial0.1     172.16.3.3    YES  manual   deleted             down*****
Serial1       unassigned    YES  not set  administratively    down down
```

In order to remedy this situation, reboot the router.

Channelized T-1 and T-3 Interfaces

Channelized T-1 and T-3 interfaces allow a single physical T-1 or T-3 to be divided into separate logical interfaces. Channelized T-1 and T-3 services are available on the Channelized T-1 or Channelized T-3 interface processor card. This card is available on 4000 and 7500 model routers. The benefit of Channelized T-1 and T-3 cards is the ability to maintain multiple WAN connections over a single physical interface. Instead of buying multi-port fast serial processor interface cards, a single Channelized T-1 card can support up to twenty-four DS-0 connections. For example, one channelized interface could use a Frame-Relay encapsulation. A second could be configured with an X.25 encapsulation. A third could be configured with an HDLC encapsulation. Channelized interfaces sometimes get confused with subinterfaces. Unlike a channelized interface, subinterfaces do not use an encapsulation type different from the primary interface they are defined under. Listed below are the core configuration commands for a Channelized T-1 card. In the configuration below, two channelized serial interfaces are created with the channel-group statement under the controller T1 heading. The first channel-group command creates logical interface serial 0:0. It is using the T-1 timeslots 1–5. The second channel-group command creates logical interface serial 0:1. It is using T-1 timeslots 6–8. As soon as the channel-group command is entered, the logical interfaces are created and the following console messages appear:

```
%LINEPROTO-5-UPDOWN: Line protocol on Interface Serial0:0,
changed state to up
%LINEPROTO-5-UPDOWN: Line protocol on Interface Serial0:1,
changed state to up
```

Here is the core configuration of a basic channelized T-1 interface:

```
controller T1 0
framing esf
clock source line primary
linecode b8zs
channel-group 0 timeslots 1–5
channel-group 1 timeslots 6–8
!
!
interface serial 0:0
ip address 172.16.40.1 255.255.255.0
encapsulation x25
x25 address 111122223333444
 x25 map ip 172.16.40.2 12341234123455 broadcast
!
```

```
interface serial 0:1
 ip address 10.1.1.1 255.255.255.0
 encapsulation frame-relay
```

Notice that the interfaces created from the channelized T-1 interface are using completely different encapsulation types. They are operating as if they are two physically separate interfaces. In the show interface commands below, examine the last line of the display for both serial 0:0 and serial 0:1. At the end of both displays is a listed of the channels used by both.

```
r4#show interfaces s0:0
Serial0:0 is up, line protocol is up
 Hardware is DSX1
 Internet address is 172.16.40.1/24
 MTU 1500 bytes, BW 280 Kbit, DLY 20000 usec, rely 255/255, load 1/255
 Encapsulation X25, loopback not set
 LAPB DTE, modulo 8, k 7, N1 12056, N2 20
   T1 3000, interface outage (partial T3) 0, T4 0
   State DISCONNECT, VS 0, VR 0, Remote VR 0, Retransmissions 0
   Queues: U/S frames 0, I frames 0, unack. 0, reTx 0
   IFRAMEs 0/0 RNRs 0/0 REJs 0/0 SABM/Es 0/0 FRMRs 0/0 DISCs 0/0
 X25 DTE, address 111122223333444, state R1, modulo 8, timer 0
   Defaults: cisco encapsulation, idle 0, nvc 1
    input/output window sizes 2/2, packet sizes 128/128
   Timers: T20 180, T21 200, T22 180, T23 180, TH 0
   Channels: Incoming-only none, Two-way 1-1024, Outgoing-only none
   RESTARTs 0/0 CALLs 0+0/0+0/0+0 DIAGs 0/0
 Last input never, output never, output hang never
 Last clearing of "show interface" counters never
 Queueing strategy: fifo
 Output queue 0/40, 0 drops; input queue 0/75, 0 drops
 5 minute input rate 0 bits/sec, 0 packets/sec
 5 minute output rate 0 bits/sec, 0 packets/sec
   0 packets input, 0 bytes, 0 no buffer
   Received 0 broadcasts, 0 runts, 0 giants, 0 throttles
   0 input errors, 0 CRC, 0 frame, 0 overrun, 0 ignored, 0 abort
   0 packets output, 0 bytes, 0 underruns
   0 output errors, 0 collisions, 26 interface resets
   0 output buffer failures, 0 output buffers swapped out
   0 carrier transitions
 Timeslot(s) Used:1-5, Transmitter delay is 0 flags

Serial0:1 is up, line protocol is up
 Hardware is DSX1
```

```
Internet address is 10.1.1.1/24
MTU 1500 bytes, BW 168 Kbit, DLY 20000 usec, rely 255/255, load 1/255
Encapsulation FRAME-RELAY, loopback not set, keepalive set (10 sec)
LMI enq sent 0, LMI stat recvd 0, LMI upd recvd 0, DTE LMI down
LMI enq recvd 0, LMI stat sent 0, LMI upd sent 0
LMI DLCI 1023 LMI type is CISCO frame relay DTE
FR SVC disabled, LAPF state down
Broadcast queue 0/64, broadcasts sent/dropped 0/0, interface broadcasts 0
Last input never, output never, output hang never
Last clearing of "show interface" counters never
Input queue: 0/75/0 (size/max/drops); Total output drops: 0
Queueing strategy: weighted fair
Output queue: 0/1000/0 (size/max total/drops)
  Conversations 0/0/64 (active/max active/threshold)
  Reserved Conversations 0/0 (allocated/max allocated)
5 minute input rate 0 bits/sec, 0 packets/sec
5 minute output rate 0 bits/sec, 0 packets/sec
  0 packets input, 0 bytes, 0 no buffer
  Received 0 broadcasts, 0 runts, 0 giants, 0 throttles
  0 input errors, 0 CRC, 0 frame, 0 overrun, 0 ignored, 0 abort
  0 packets output, 0 bytes, 0 underruns
  0 output errors, 0 collisions, 23 interface resets
  0 output buffer failures, 0 output buffers swapped out
  0 carrier transitions
 Timeslot(s) Used:6-8, Transmitter delay is 0 flags
```

Loopback Interfaces

Loopback interfaces are internal interfaces that reside on the router. The benefit of a loopback interface is that it will only go down if the entire router goes down. For this reason, loopback interfaces are used by OSPF, BGP, and DLSw+. When loopback interfaces are used on routers running OSPF, the highest number IP address on a loopback interface is used as the OSPF RID. It is important for OSPF to have stable RID assignments. If the RID was extracted from an IP address on a physical interface and the physical interfaces failed, the OSPF process could experience a RID change. If the router rebooted and the interface that was used for the RID assignment was still inactive, the OSPF process would use another RID. Since the router had a new RID, all other OSPF routers would treat it as a new and different router. The result would be that all OSPF routers affected would have inaccurate information in their topological databases.

For BGP and DLSw+, loopback interfaces can be used to establish more fault-tolerant BGP neighbor and DLSw+ peering sessions. If a physical address was used by BGP and DLSw+ to establish these connections, and the interface went down, the entire connection will be lost. By using a loopback interface, this situation can be avoided. If a loopback interface is used by BGP and DLSW+ it must be reachable by the remote peer.

Loopback interfaces are also useful for generating router traffic in a lab environment. AppleTalk cannot be configured on a loopback interface. NLSP cannot be configured on a loopback interface.

Dialer Interfaces

Dialer interfaces are logical interfaces used by DDR with dialer rotary groups and dialer profiles configurations. Use of dialer interfaces will be covered in detail in the ISDN/DDR chapter (Chapter Five).

Tunnel Interfaces

Tunnel interfaces allow the IOS to take IPX, AppleTalk, and DECNET traffic and encapsulate it in IP packets. By doing this the non-IP traffic can be transported over an IP network. Non-IP protocol tunneling will be covered in the Configuring IPX, AppleTalk, and DECNET chapters.

Bridge Virtual Interface

The Bridge Virtual Interface (BVI) is a critical component in integrated routing and bridging (IRB), a Level Five topic. The BVI acts as the routed interface for a collection of interfaces in a single bridge group. Prior to IRB and its component BVI, network layer protocols could be bridged over specified interfaces and routed over others on the same router but the bridged traffic could never be forwarded to the routed traffic. By enabling IRB and creating a BVI, network layer traffic that is bridged can be forwarded to the BVI and from the BVI routed out an interface participating in routing. IRB is useful when migrating from a bridged environment to a routed environment. It is also an important tool to use on the Catalyst 8500 layer three switch. If you wanted to directly connect three servers to the Catalyst 8500 and have them reside on the same network layer segment, you would place them all in the same bridge-group, enable IRB, create a BVI, and through the BVI route to the rest of the internetwork.

It is extremely important to understand the importance of IRB and the BVI. This is a brief summary of the subject. Coverage of IRB and the Bridge Virtual Interface will be provided in Chapter Twenty.

Null Interfaces

Null interfaces are useful for route summarization. For example, if a collection of subnets reside in a BGP speaker's routing table that need to be summarized, a static route with the summary address can be configured. The unique characteristic of the static route created will be that it points to a null interface. BGP will advertise the static route pointing to the null interface. Downstream BGP speakers will not be impacted by the null interface. They will forward the traffic destined to the summary address to the BGP speaker that sourced the routing advertisement. (In this case, the BGP speaker with the static route using the null interface.) When packets destined to valid subnets arrive at the sourcing BGP speaker, the IP longest match rule will apply and packets will be successfully forwarded. Packets destined for subnets not listed in the BGP speakers routing table will match the summarized static route entry using the null interface. These packets will be dropped. More details on IP routing and the longest match rule are provided in Chapter Nine.

EIGRP automatically inserts a entry into its routing table pointing to a null interface when its manual route summarization command is used.

USING THE CISCO DISCOVERY PROTOCOL

The Cisco Discovery Protocol (CDP) is a Cisco proprietary data-link layer protocol that provides a degree of reachability information of directly connected neighbors. It is an extremely useful tool to determine operational status of an interface's physical and data-link layer.

Displayed below is a sample CDP listing:

```
r4#show cdp neighbor
Capability Codes: R - Router, T - Trans Bridge, B - Source Route Bridge
          S - Switch, H - Host, I - IGMP
Device ID     Local      Intrfce     Holdtme     Capability      Platform Port ID
r2            Ser 0      170         R           2500            Ser 0.2
r1            Ser 0      127         R           2500            Ser 0.2
```

The first interface listing, "Local Interface" is the local interface that the listed neighbor is seen on. In the example above, "sh cdp neighbor" was typed on router "r4." Router r4 sees neighbor r2 through its serial 0 interface. The second interface listing "Port ID" at the far right of each cdp listing is the interface on the remote neighboring router that is being used to transfer the cdp information. To summarize the example above:

```
R4 sees r2 through r4's serial 0 interface. R2 sees r4 through its serial 0.2
interface.
R4 sees r1 through r4's serial 0 interface. R1 sees r4 through its serial 0.2
interface.
```

With the show cdp neighbor detail command, you can obtain more information about directly connected devices such as the neighbor's device type (router, bridge or switch), a neighbor's network layer address and a neighbor's IOS version. Displayed below is CDP information obtained from a neighboring Catalyst 5000 switch:

```
r1#sh cdp neighbors detail
-------------------------

Device ID: 005595422

Entry address(es): IP address: 172.16.10.5

Platform: WS-C5000, Capabilities: Trans-Bridge Switch

Interface: Ethernet1, Port ID (outgoing port): 3/8

Holdtime : 119 sec

Version : WS-C5000 Software, Version McpSW: 3.1(2) NmpSW: 3.1(2a)

Copyright (c) 1995-1998 by Cisco Systems
```

Displayed below is the output of a show cdp neighbor command executed on a Catalyst 5000 switch:

```
Cat1 (enable) sh cdp neighbor detail

Device-ID: r1

Device Addresses: IP address: 172.16.10.6

Holdtime: 176 sec

Capabilities: ROUTER

Version: Cisco Internetwork Operating System Software

IOS (tm) 4500 Software (C4500-JS-M), Version 11.2(11), RELEASE SOFTWARE (fc1)

 Copyright (c) 1986-1997 by cisco Systems, Inc.

Platform: cisco 4700

Port-ID (Port on Device): Ethernet1

Port (Our Port): 3/8
```

CDP is also used by network management programs like CiscoWorks for Switched Internetworks for network discovery purposes.

MAPPING NETWORK LAYER ADDRESSES TO DATA-LINK ADDRESSES

Routers' interfaces and their associated data-link and physical layer protocols ultimately provide transport to network layer protocols such as IP, IPX, AppleTalk, and DECNET. Protocols and IOS configuration commands have been developed to map network layer addresses to data-link layer addresses.

One such protocol is ARP in the TCP/IP protocol suite. It maps a remote IP address with a remote MAC address on a multi-access network such as a LAN or VLAN. On WAN interfaces, different data-link to network layer mapping tools are used. Some are standards based others are Cisco specific.

When examining the four basic types of WAN interfaces, we can see how data-link layer to network layer mapping occurs on a Cisco router. The basic types of interfaces are:

1. Dedicated point-to-point connections (DS-0, DS-1, etc.)
2. Switched connections (ISDN BRI, ISDN PRI, ASYCHRONOUS)
3. PVC-Based Nonbroadcast Multi-Access (NBMA) Networks (Frame-Relay, ATM, X.25)
4. SVC-Based NBMA Networks (Frame-Relay, ATM, X.25)

For the first type of connection, dedicated point-to-point connections, Cisco routers need no mapping procedures. The router will operate on the premise that there is a single connection on each end of a point-to-point interface. Whatever the network layer address is on the local point-to-point interface, the remote network layer address must match.

For switched connections, ISDN and asynchronous connections, the router still forwards network layer packets based upon the address assigned to local switched interfaces. However, since the very essence of a switched connection is that the link becomes active only when data needs to be sent and that connections can be dynamically set up with multiple remote sites, the router must be supplied with some type address (for example, a dial string) to initiate a call. If the router is configured to call multiple remote sites, manually created dialer map statements or dialer profiles must be used to match the correct remote network layer address with the correct dial string.

For PVC-based NBMA networks, the router cannot assume that there is a single destination for any physical port. The distinguishing characteristic of an NBMA interface is that multiple PVCs can be assigned to a single physical interface. Cisco routers provide multiple solutions to map the correct local NBMA address (Frame-Relay DLCI or ATM VPI VCI) to the correct remote network layer address. These solutions include inverse ARP, map statements, and subinterfaces.

SVC-based NBMA networks such as ATM, Frame-Relay, and X.25, provide a mapping challenge that combines the mapping issues of switched technologies such as ISDN with the mapping issues of PVC-based NBMA networks. Just as a single physical interface can support multiple PVCs, a single physical port can support multiple SVCs in an NBMA network. Manual mapping statements are a common solution to map multiple remote network layer sites to remote X.121, NSAP, or E.164 addresses. For ATM, dynamic mapping of SVCs to network layer protocols is provided by Classical IP (RFC 1577) and ATM LANE.

When discussing the process of mapping network layer addresses to other addresses, the Cisco point-to-point subinterface (a virtual interface) needs to be mentioned. Point-to-point subinterfaces remove the need for manual mapping statements for NBMA PVC connections. This virtual interface makes a single Frame-Relay DLCI or ATM VPI/VCI appear as a traditional dedicated physical point-to-point interface to the Cisco router. Recall how Cisco routers treat dedicated physical point-to-point interface. Such interfaces have no need for any mapping statements because they are up all of the time and there is only one destination at the end of the link. Point-to-point subinterfaces allow the Cisco router to treat a single Frame-Relay DLCI or ATM VPI/VCI pair as if it is a traditional point-to-point link. Subinterfaces will be covered in detail in Chapters Four and Seven.

Clearly, mapping statements and mapping issues will emerge when configuring many WAN protocols. A summary listing of the most common manual map statements and dynamic mapping protocols is provided below.

Manual Map Statements

Dialer Map

Dialer maps are used by switched PSTN connections such as ISDN and asynchronous interfaces. Dialer map statements map a remote network layer address to a dial-string via a remote ASYNC or ISDN interface. Example:

Dialer map ip 172.16.1.1 5551111

The syntax above can be interpreted in plain English as:

"To get to the ip address 172.16.1.1 call 5551111"

Dialer map statements can be viewed in a summary format with the "show dialer map" statement. A mutually exclusive alternative to dialer map statements is dialer profiles. See Chapter Five for more details on dialer map statements and dialer profiles.

Frame-Relay Map

Frame-relay maps are used for PVC-based Frame-Relay connections. Frame-Relay map statements map a remote network layer address to a local DLCI. Example:

Frame-relay map ip 172.16.1.1 101

The syntax above can be interpreted in plain English as:

"To get to the ip address 172.16.1.1 use local DLCI 101"

Frame-relay map statements can be viewed in summary format with the "show frame map" statement. Alternatives to frame-relay map statements are inverse arp and point-to-point subinterfaces. See Chapter Four for more details on frame-relay map statements and its alternatives.

Map-Lists

Map-lists are used to map ATM PVC, ATM SVC, and SMDS SVCs addresses to a network layer address. Map-Lists are defined in the "map-list" configuration mode. Once the map-list is defined, it is applied to an interface with the map-group command.

```
r4(config-map-list)#ip 172.16.1.1 ?
 atm-nsap   ATM NSAP
 atm-vc     ATM VC
 class      Frame Relay static map class name
 smds       ATM SMDS E.164
```

Dynamic Mapping Protocols

Manual mapping statements create a number of configuration and scalability challenges. A number of WAN-based protocols have been developed to automate the remote network address to either remote or local data-link layer address mapping process. The most commonly used dynamic mapping protocols are:

Inverse ARP for Frame-Relay and ATM PVCs
ATM Classical ARP for ATM SVCs
ATM LANE for ATM SVCs

When there is a problem with this mapping process, it can usually be detected with a debug ip packet "encap failed" message. USE EXTREME CAUTION WHEN USING DEBUG IP PACKET. ON ROUTER FORWARDING EVEN A MINIMAL AMOUNT OF IP TRAFFIC, DEBUG IP PACKET CAN SEVERELY IMPACT ROUTER PERFORMANCE BY CONSUMING CPU CYCLES. DEBUG IP PACKET IS USEFUL TO USE IN A LEARNING ENVIRONMENT.

Mapping issues will be key topics in Chapter Four "Configuring Frame-Relays, Chapter Five "Configuring ISDN/DDR," and Chapter Seven "Configuring ATM."

Ports and Interfaces on a Catalyst 5000

So far, we have been reviewing router interfaces. Now, let's review Catalyst 5000 ports and interfaces. Like the Cisco core router product line, the Catalyst 5000 family of switches is modular in design. At the very least, a modular supervisor module must be included within every Catalyst configuration.

Different Supervisor modules exist: (Supervisor I, II, and III.) Supervisor modules usually come configured with a console port and two ethernet interfaces; however, only specific Supervisor modules (Supervisor II and higher) support features such as Fast-EtherChannel.

The port types supported on a Catalyst 5000 are vast, varied and ever expanding. Listed below is a brief summarization of different types of ports that can be installed inside of a Catalyst 5000:

The full range of 10BASE/100BASE Ethernet ports (both copper and fiber)
Gigabit Ethernet ports
Token-Ring ports
FDDI/CDDI ports
ATM LAN Emulation OC-3 Single-Mode and Multi-Mode Fiber
ATM OC-12 ports
T1/E1 ATM Trunk
T1/E1 Circuit Emulation
25 Mbps ATM

On a Catalyst switch, the words ports and interfaces are not interchangeable. On Catalyst switches, layer-two switched connections are called "ports." Ports on a Catalyst are not administratively shutdown by default. As soon as a device is plugged into a Catalyst switch, the port autosenses characteristics of the connection speed and the port become active. The default settings of all Catalyst ports are:

all ports are enabled
all Ethernet 10/100 ports are set to "autosense"
all Token-Ring 4/16 ports are set to "autosense"
all ports belong to VLAN 1

Four useful commands for monitoring and troubleshooting individual Catalyst 5000 ports are:

show modules
show port status
show port module/port
show mac module/port

Show module gives you a quick view on the status of all the modules in a Catalyst 5000 switch. Make note of the "status" column on the far right of the first listing (the module listing) in the show module display. Under normal circumstances, the status of all modules is "ok."

```
Console> (enable) show module
Mod   Module-Name   Ports        Module-Type     Model      Serial-Num  Status
----- ------------- ------------ --------------- ---------- ----------- -------
1     2             100BaseTX    Supervisor      WS-X5009   005595422   ok
2     2             UTP OC-3     Dual-Phy ATM    WS-X5156   007509575   ok
3     12            10/100BaseTX Ethernet        WS-X5213A  007420511   ok

Mod   MAC-Address(es)                            Hw     Fw      Sw
----- ------------------------------------------ ------ ------- ----------
1     00-10-11-3b-70-00 thru 00-10-11-3b-73-ff   2.3    2.2(2)  3.1(2a)
2     00-e0-1e-e4-fe-3e                          2.0    1.3     3.2(6)
3     00-e0-1e-e7-97-18 thru 00-e0-1e-e7-97-23   2.1    3.1(1)  3.1(2)
```

Show port status is the equivalent of show ip interface brief on a router. Show port status provides a single line general summary of the status of all ports. Show port status can be entered with a parameter specifying an individual module or port.

```
Console> (enable) show port status
Port Name   Status            Vlan     Level    Duplex   Speed Type
----------- ----------------- -------- -------- -------- ------------
1/1         notconnect 1      normal   half     100      100BaseTX
1/2         notconnect 1      normal   half     100      100BaseTX
2/1         notconnect trunk  normal   full     155      OC3 UTP ATM
2/2         notconnect trunk  normal   full     155      OC3 UTP ATM
3/1         connected 1       normal   a-half   a-10     10/100BaseTX
3/2         notconnect 1      normal   auto     auto     10/100BaseTX
3/3         notconnect 10     normal   auto     auto     10/100BaseTX
3/4         notconnect 10     normal   auto     auto     10/100BaseTX
3/5         notconnect 2      normal   auto     auto     10/100BaseTX
3/6         inactive  22      normal   auto     auto     10/100BaseTX
3/7         inactive  22      normal   auto     auto     10/100BaseTX
3/8         notconnect 1      normal   auto     auto     10/100BaseTX
3/9         notconnect 1      normal   auto     auto     10/100BaseTX
3/10        notconnect 1      normal   auto     auto     10/100BaseTX
3/11        notconnect 12     normal   auto     auto     10/100BaseTX
3/12        notconnect 12     normal   auto     auto     10/100BaseTX
```

Show port and show mac provide a greater level of detail on individual port statistics. If you type in these commands without specifying an individual port or module, you will be flooded with information from all of the ports on the switch. It is best to use these commands with a specific reference to a specific port. Examples of show port and show mac are displayed below:

```
Console> (enable) sh port 3/1
Port Name   Status              Vlan      Level     Duplex    Speed Type
----------  ----------          ----------  --------  ----------  ----------------
3/1         connected 1          normal    a-half    a-10      10/100BaseTX

Port   Security   Secure-Src-Addr   Last-Src-Addr   Shutdown Trap
------ ----------- ---------------------- ------------------- ---------------------
3/1    disabled                      No              disabled

Port   Broadcast-Limit   Broadcast-Drop
-----  --------------------  ---------------------
3/1     -                  0

Port   Align-Err   FCS-Err   Xmit-Err   Rcv-Err   UnderSize
------ ----------- ----------- ----------- ----------- --------------
3/1    0           0         5           0         0

Port   Single-Col   Multi-Coll   Late-Coll   Excess-Col   Carri-Sen   Runts   Giants
-----  -------------  ---------------  ------------  --------------  -------------  ---------  ----------
3/1    9384         1046         0           0            0           0       0

Last-Time-Cleared
--------------------------
Sun Jul 5 1998, 12:39:45
```

As reflected in the show port display above, show port lists general port configuration parameters as well as port errors and collisions. Show mac (displayed below) provides summary information on what has been sent and received on a given port. By using show mac, you can determine whether a given port is transmitting or receiving frames. Both show port and show mac display cumulative totals of port statistics. Just as with a router interface, you can use the "clear counters" command to reset the show port and show mac counters.

An example of using the clear counters command can be related to the show port 3/1 displayed above. Notice at the bottom of the display. It lists that collisions have occurred on this port. When did these collisions occur? Are these aggregate numbers accumulated over several months? Or did 99% of the collisions occur over the last hour? You cannot tell this with the show port command alone. You must clear the show port counters and monitor the statistics closely.

```
Console> (enable) show mac 3/1
MAC    Rcv-Frms   Xmit-Frms   Rcv-Multi   Xmit-Multi   Rcv-Broad   Xmit-Broad
------- ------------- --------------- ------------- -------------- -------------- ----------------
3/1    28         241         3           227          11          0
```

```
MAC   Dely-Exced  MTU-Exced  In-Discard  Lrn-Discrd  In-Lost  Out-Lost
----- ----------- ---------- ----------- ----------- -------- ---------
3/1   0           0          0           0           0        0

Port  Rcv-Unicast  Rcv-Multicast  Rcv-Broadcast
----- ------------ -------------- --------------
3/1   14           3              11

Port  Xmit-Unicast  Xmit-Multicast  Xmit-Broadcast
----- ------------- --------------- ---------------
3/1   14            228             0

Port  Rcv-Octet  Xmit-Octet
----- ---------- -----------
3/1   3185       16780

Last-Time-Cleared
--------------------------
Sun Jul 5 1998, 12:39:45
```

If you want to view comparative listings of traffic sent and received over a range of ports, use the show mac command with the module option:

```
Console> (enable) sh mac 3
MAC   Rcv-Frms   Xmit-Frms  Rcv-Multi  Xmit-Multi  Rcv-Broad  Xmit-Broad
----- ---------- ---------- ---------- ----------- ---------- -----------
3/1   109865     2211536    40         1637086     90         574426
3/2   0          0          0          0           0          0
3/3   0          0          0          0           0          0
3/4   278707147  124        260589510  235         18117564   0
3/5   0          0          0          0           0          0
3/6   0          0          0          0           0          0
3/7   0          0          0          0           0          0
3/8   318952     184196580  193134     177254876   39         6941775
3/9   402980     95594574   314450     84275628    45468      11319009
3/10  1278       247413269  1278       237201166   0          10212103
3/11  247413269  1278       237201166  1278        10212103   0
3/12  0          0          0          0           0          0

MAC   Dely-Exced  MTU-Exced  In-Discard  Lrn-Discrd  In-Lost  Out-Lost
----- ----------- ---------- ----------- ----------- -------- ---------
3/1   0           0          1           0           0        38
3/2   0           0          0           0           0        0
3/3   0           0          0           0           0        0
```

3/4	0	0	9537836	0	0	0
3/5	0	0	0	0	0	0
3/6	0	0	0	0	0	0
3/7	0	0	0	0	0	0
3/8	0	0	0	0	0	0
3/9	0	0	0	0	0	0
3/10	0	0	0	0	0	0
3/11	0	0	11023904	0	5100	0
3/12	0	0	0	0	0	0

Port	Rcv-Unicast	Rcv-Multicast	Rcv-Broadcast
3/1	109735	40	90
3/2	0	0	0
3/3	0	0	0
3/4	0	260589511	18117564
3/5	0	0	0
3/6	0	0	0
3/7	0	0	0
3/8	125719	193134	39
3/9	43040	314450	45468
3/10	0	1279	0
3/11	0	237201166	10212103
3/12	0	0	0

Port	Xmit-Unicast	Xmit-Multicast	Xmit-Broadcast
3/1	25	1637086	574426
3/2	0	0	0
3/3	0	0	0
3/4	0	238	0
3/5	0	0	0
3/6	0	0	0
3/7	0	0	0
3/8	0	177254878	6941775
3/9	0	84275628	11319009
3/10	0	237201166	10212103
3/11	0	1279	0
3/12	0	0	0

Port	Rcv-Octet	Xmit-Octet
3/1	7042537	168612273
3/2	0	0

```
3/30   0
3/4    9786571738   9761
3/50   0
3/60   0
3/70   0
3/8    20730676     7549716736
3/9    26393888     2314387717
3/10   84344        7508995553
3/11   7508995472   84344
3/12   0            0

Last-Time-Cleared
--------------------------------
Sun Jul 5 1998, 12:39:45

Console> (enable)
```

From the show mac module display, you can obtain a comparison of traffic flowing through each port on a given module.

The word "interface" is reserved for logical connections that are used to remotely administer the switch. They are called the SC0 and the SL0 interfaces. However, when referencing RSM connections (both logical and physical), the term interface is used. To view the status of the logical interfaces in a Catalyst switch, type show interface:

```
Console> (enable) show interface
sl0: flags=51<UP,POINTOPOINT,RUNNING>
 slip 0.0.0.0 dest 0.0.0.0
sc0: flags=63<UP,BROADCAST,RUNNING>
   vlan 10 inet 172.16.200.1 netmask 255.255.255.0 broadcast
172.16.200.255
```

When determining whether to use the word "port" or "interface" to reference a router or switch connection, keep these general rules in mind:

Refer to Data-Link Layer based connections as "ports."
Refer to Network Layer based connections as "interfaces."

Remember that a Catalyst is not just a data-link layer switch. It is a multilayer switch. An RSM can be inserted into a Catalyst 5000. The RSM is a fully functioning router module. When the RSM is accessed for configuration purposes, the administrator encounters the standard router IOS. Standard RSMs come with no physical interfaces. The primary interface for an RSM is a logical VLAN interface that is used to route traffic between VLANs. An RSM can be coupled with a VIP card. The VIP card can be configured with the same port adapter modules used with the VIP on a model 7500 router. When a Catalyst is installed with a VIP configured with physical interfaces, the interfaces are configured and managed from the RSM just as they would be in a standalone router. Remember the RSM and its associated VIP card is a standalone entity inside of the Catalyst 5000. The RSM shares the same power supply as the other Catalyst modules; however, it runs its own IOS.

Additional coverage of Catalyst 5000 ports and interfaces will be provided in Chapter Six.

Summary

Given the material covered in this chapter, you now possess a general overview of the different types of interfaces found in different types of routers. Router interfaces can be categorized in several ways:

Physical and logical
LAN and WAN
Data Communications and Voice Communications
Core, distribution, and access

Cisco continues to expand the type and sophistication of the interfaces it offers. For example, Cisco routers now can be equipped with FXO and FXS ports that allow a standard telephone or PBX to be attached to a router. With the FXO/FXS ports, a router can now transport voice calls from directly connected POTS telephones! From the perspective of sophistication, the Cisco Catalyst 8500 layer three switch performs IP and IPX switching services at wire speed.

Regardless of the type or classification of the router interface, the Cisco IOS provides a uniform method of configuring, monitoring, and troubleshooting interfaces.

You know what IOS commands can be used on all routers to verify what types of interfaces a given router possesses. You also know what show commands to use to obtain the operational status of router interfaces.

Listed below is a summary of the key interface show commands:

```
Show version
Show ip interface brief
Show interface
Show controllers
Show running-config
Show cdp neighbor
```

Know what the utility of each command is for any interface you are configuring and monitoring.

Let's return to the scenario presented in Chapter One: the WMC Corp. scenario. In this scenario, ten routers, one RSM, six Catalyst 5000 switches, and four LightStream switches are included in the configuration. The routers had a combination of Ethernet, Fast-Ethernet, Token-Ring, Synchronous serial and ISDN BRI interfaces. If all cabling is performed on this scenario and all router interfaces were connected to the correct devices (ISDN NT-1, CSU-DSU, Catalyst switch, etc.), you should be able to verify the interface type in each router and switch, administratively enable the interfaces and ports and observe their operational status. You can do this if you are physically present in the testbed or remotely connected to the testbed via a TELNET session. (What Cisco tool will allow access to all Cisco devices remotely from the console port? The answer is not a set of very long console cables! The answer is a terminal server.)

If your interfaces are not in an "up/up" state, your higher layer configuration statements will not work. It is imperative that you feel comfortable with this very basic process. It is mandatory you practice cabling up a testbed of routers and switches, administratively enabling specified interfaces, creating virtual interfaces when requested and monitoring all interfaces.

Performing the IOS commands to administratively enable an interface, setting the clock rate for the synchronous serial DCE interface, creating virtual interfaces and monitoring all interfaces is a basic but an essential set of skills to possess. This chapter has completely skipped the critical technical issues of cabling and DCE configuration. For example, in a real-world production environment, you rarely connect the synchronous serial interface of one router into the back of another. In a real-world production environment you plug a router's synchronous serial port into a CSU/DSU. The CSU/DSU has its own set of configuration and cabling issues. These issues are not within the scope of this book. See the books listed at the end of this chapter for some good references on this topic.

On the Catalyst 5000, your primary interface monitoring and troubleshooting tools are:

Show module
Show port status

Show port module/port
Show mac module/port
Show mac module
Show cdp neighbor

In the next four chapters, coverage will include configuring Frame-Relay, ISDN with Dial On-Demand Routing, Catalyst 5000 with multiple VLANs, and ATM configuration. Each of these topics poses several configuration challenges.

Professional Development Checklist

Upon completion of this chapter, you should know how to:

- Determine what types of interfaces are inside of a router
- Check the status of all interfaces in a router
- Administratively enable interfaces
- For back to-back serial connections, determine which end is DTE and which is DCE
- Configure back-to back serial connections
- List and describe the use of Cisco virtual interfaces
- List and describe the use of WAN map statements and dynamic mapping protocols
- Describe the difference between Catalyst ports and Catalyst interfaces
- Use all of the show commands listed in the command summary to access interface status

For Further Study

- Introduction to Cisco Router Configuration, Cisco Systems, Inc., 1989–1998.

Interfaces in general are covered in Volume I of the IOS Configuration Guide and Command Reference. Additional information on WAN interfaces is supplied in Volume IV of the IOS Configuration Guide and Command Reference.

URLs

- **www.cciecert.com**
- **www.mentorlabs.com**
- **www.cisco.com**

Can You Spot the Issues?

1. Routers R1 and R2 are connected through a back-to-back serial interface.

   Both routers R1 and R2 have administratively enabled their interface.
   The interfaces are in an Up/Down state.
   How can you get the interfaces in an Up/Up state? What do you need to check?

2. Routers R1 and R2 are connected back-to-back through a synchronous serial interface zero on reach router. Show controllers shows R2 as the DCE. The interface configurations are supplied below. Will this configuration work? If not, what is the problem?

R1 Serial 0 Interface Configuration

interface serial 0
ip address 172.16.40.1 255.255.255.0

R2 Serial 0 Interface Configuration

interface serial 0
ip address 172.16.40.1 255.255.255.0
encapsulation ppp

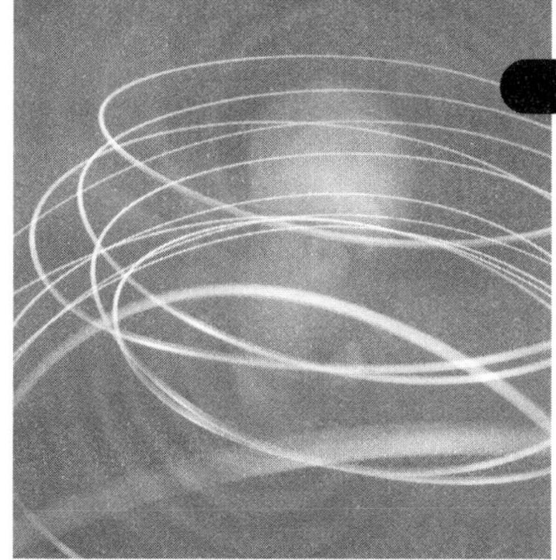

FOUR

Configuring Frame-Relay: "To Map or Not to Map? That is the Question...."

Topics Covered In This Chapter

- Frame-Relay Configuration Between Two Sites
- Frame-Relay Configuration Between Multiple Sites
- Frame-Relay Partial Mesh Configuration
- Using Subinterfaces with Frame-Relay
- Configuring Routing Protocols Over Frame-Relay
- Frame-Relay Switch Configuration
- Troubleshooting Frame-Relay

Nonbroadcast multi-access (NBMA) networks are widely popular today. Starting with X.25 in the 1970s and joined by Frame-Relay, SMDS, and (ATM) in the 1990s, NBMA networks allow a router to set up and maintain several logical connections over a single physical port. NBMA networks can be configured with either permanent virtual circuits (PVCs) or switched virtual circuits (SVCs).

Out of the NBMA technologies mentioned above, Frame-Relay is currently the most preferred for new installations. Once a mastery of Frame-Relay design and configuration is achieved, it is much easier to acquire a strong understanding of X.25, ATM, and SMDS. Therefore, the remainder of this chapter will be focused solely on Frame-Relay design and configuration issues.

Frame-Relay networks propose several design and configuration challenges. At the network layer address level, every connection within a given Frame-Relay network appears as if all are on the same network. For PVC-based configurations, every remote network layer address, such as IP or IPX, will need to be mapped to a local DLCI in Frame-Relay.

For example, consider a Frame-Relay network consisting of four connections. Each Frame-Relay connection will require a mapping for each remote network layer address to a local DLCI.

Remedies have been developed for the above mentioned scenario. One such remedy is inverse ARP (RFC 1263). Inverse ARP dynamically maps remote network layer addresses to local DLCIs on a Frame-Relay DTE. Inverse ARP can only map addresses from remote Frame-Relay devices that maintain a directly connected PVC to the device performing the inverse ARP. Inverse ARP can provide a complete set of mappings in a full-mesh Frame-Relay topology. In a partial mesh topology, inverse ARP cannot provide a complete set of remote network address to DLCI mappings.

Cisco provides two primary solutions to the limitations of inverse ARP-Frame-Relay map statements and subinterfaces. Frame-Relay map statements statically map remote network layer addresses to a local DLCI. Frame-Relay map statements perform in a static manner what inverse ARP does dynamically. However, Frame-Relay map statements possess more functionality than inverse ARP. They allow a network address of a remote Frame-Relay connection that is *not* directly connected to a local Frame-Relay device to be mapped to a local DLCI. This feature is of particular benefit in a partial-mesh Frame-Relay topology.

Subinterfaces subdivide DLCIs and associate them with one or more logical interfaces. Two types of subinterfaces are available, point-to-point and multipoint. A point-to-point subinterface can only accommodate a single DLCI at any given time. Point-to-point subinterfaces are treated by the Cisco Internetwork Operating System (IOS) like a physical point-to-point interface and do not need either inverse ARP or Frame-Relay map statements. Multipoint interfaces can accommodate one or more DLCIs at any given time. Multipoint DLCIs rely on either inverse ARP or Frame-Relay map statements for proper operation.

From the perspective of network layer routing, nonbroadcast networks create issues with distance vector routing protocols such as RIP and IGRP. Since a single physical port can support multiple logical connections, Frame-Relay can be configured so that data received on one connection will be forwarded out another connection on the same physical port. While Frame-Relay supports data forwarding of this type at the data-link level between logical connections, the network layer protocols, primarily distance vector routing protocols, are not aware of the different logical connections. In order to prevent routing loops, virtually every distance vector routing protocol supports the rule of split horizon. The rule of split horizon is as follows: if routes are learned from an interface on a router, those routes can never be advertised back out of the interface they were learned on.

This creates acute routing issues and problems when distance vector routing protocols are configured over Frame-Relay. Distance vector routing protocol issues, such as split-horizon, and issues created by link state routing protocols, such as OSPF, will be covered in this chapter.

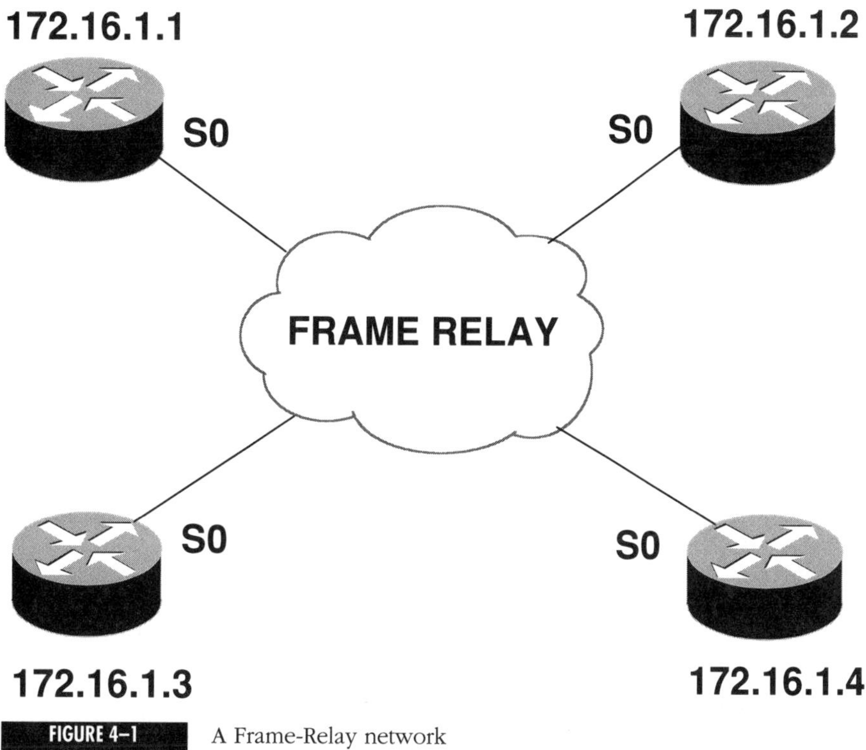

FIGURE 4–1 A Frame-Relay network

It is imperative that internetworking engineers understand multiple combinations of Frame-Relay configuration. This chapter will start with the most basic Frame-Relay configuration and build to the complex. By the end of this chapter, you will need to know the following:

- Configuring a Frame-Relay full mesh network with physical interfaces only
- Configuring a Frame-Relay full mesh network with logical interfaces only
- Configuring a Frame-Relay full mesh network with a combination of logical and physical interfaces
- Configuring a Frame-Relay partial mesh network (hub and spoke) with physical interfaces only
- Configuring a Frame-Relay partial mesh network (hub and spoke) with logical interfaces only
- Configuring a Frame-Relay partial mesh network (hub and spoke) wtih a combination of logical and physical interfaces
- When to use inverse ARP
- When to use Frame-Relay map statements
- When to use point-to-point subinterfaces
- When to use multipoint subinterfaces

- How to configure distance vector routing protocols for Frame-Relay
- How to configure EIGRP for Frame-Relay
- How to configure OSPF for Frame-Relay
- How to configure a Cisco router as a Frame-Relay switch

Key tools to use to verify Frame-Relay configurations are:

- Show Frame-Relay pvc
- Show Frame-Relay map
- Debug ip packet
- Debug frame packet
- Clear frame-relay-inarp
- Shutdown/no shutdown
- Write/reload

Remember these general Frame-Relay troubleshooting principles:

- Troubleshoot both sides of the Frame-Relay connection
- Be incremental with your analysis of Frame-Relay

Configuring Frame-Relay on a Cisco Router

The Minimum Frame-Relay Configuration: Encapsulation Frame-Relay and Inverse ARP

The minimum Frame-Relay configuration on a Cisco router consists of a single command:

```
Router(config)#interface serial 0
Router(config-if)#encapsulation frame-relay
Router(config-if)#no shutdown
```

With this single command, a Cisco router is ready to act as a Frame-Relay DTE device. Once this command is typed and the interface is administratively enabled, the following process will occur on a Cisco router:

1. The interface is administratively enabled.
2. The Frame-Relay switch announces the configured DLCIs to the router.
3. Once the DLCIs have attained an active state, inverse ARP is performed to map remote network layer addresses to local DLCIs.

After these three steps have occurred, a router with a Frame-Relay interface can ping a remote router's network layer address on the same Frame-Relay cloud. This three-step progression is reflected and verified by the following router console prompts and show commands.

Immediately after a Frame-Relay interface is administratively enabled, the following console prompt appears:

```
%LINEPROTO-5-UPDOWN: Line protocol on Interface Serial0, changed
state to up
%LINK-3-UPDOWN: Interface Serial0, changed state to up
%FR-5-DLCICHANGE: Interface Serial0 - DLCI 101 state changed to
ACTIVE
```

If a Frame-Relay DLCI attains a state other than ACTIVE—other possibilities include INACTIVE and DELETED—check the Frame-Relay switch configuration to make sure its configuration matches the configuration of the router acting as the Frame-Relay DTE device.

Once these messages appear, the following show command can be entered to verify that the Frame-Relay PVC(s) are active and operational:

```
Router#show frame-relay pvc
PVC Statistics for interface Serial0 (Frame Relay DTE)
DLCI = 102, DLCI USAGE = LOCAL, PVC STATUS = ACTIVE, INTERFACE =
Serial0
input pkts 2        output pkts 2        in bytes 76
out bytes 76        dropped pkts 0       in FECN pkts 0
in BECN pkts 0      out FECN pkts 0      out BECN pkts 0
in DE pkts 0        out DE pkts 0
pvc create time 00:24:02, last time pvc status changed 00:24:02
```

Once Frame-Relay PVCs are active, enter the following command to verify that inverse ARP has successfully mapped remote network layer addresses to the appropriate DLCI:

```
Router#sh frame-relay map
Serial0 (up): ipx AAA1234.00e0.1eb9.2a0f dlci 102(0x66,0x1860), dynamic,
     broadcast,, status defined, active
Serial0 (up): ip 172.16.1.2 dlci 102(0x66,0x1860), dynamic,
     broadcast,, status defined, active
```

Notice that the router dynamically learned the remote IP and IPX addresses of the remote Frame-Relay devices through inverse ARP. Note that inverse ARP operated for both IP and IPX. Inverse ARP will support the following protocols:

- IP
- IPX
- AppleTalk
- DECNET
- VINES
- XNS
- ISO CLNS

A Word of Caution About Inverse ARP

Inverse ARP will resolve a remote network layer address with a local DLCI even if the remote IP address does not belong to the local subnet. For example, assume ROUTER-1 has a local Frame-Relay interface with an IP address of 172.16.34.1/24. Assume that Router-1 maintains a PVC to a remote Frame-Relay peer (ROUTER-2) that has an ip address of 10.1.1.1/24. When the PVC is activated, inverse ARP is performed and it resolves the remote IP address of 10.1.1.1 to the local DLCI of ROUTER-1. We now have an IP address mismatch. This can be detected by performing a show frame map.

Once the problem is detected and the remote side Frame-Relay router configures the correct address, inverse ARP will be performed again. Now the incorrect address and the correct address will appear in the inverse arp map table. You must manually clear inverse ARP with a clear frame-inarp command to remove any undesired inverse-arp entries.

A Frame-Relay Configuration Supporting Multiple Sites

The simple configuration described above is adequate for a Frame-Relay configuration between only two sites. However, Frame-Relay configurations become more complex when many sites are involved. For example, consider the following scenario.

One headquarters site needs to maintain connectivity between two satellite offices. The configuration must allow all sites to be able to communicate with each other. Therefore, both satellite offices must communicate with headquarters as well as with each other. The headquarters site is configured with two PVCs, one connected to each of the satellite sites. The configuration is called a partial mesh or hub and spoke topology.

If the minimal configuration described in the previous section is used (configuring the routers with the encapsulation Frame-Relay statement only), the following results would occur.

HEADQUARTERS

```
headquarters#show frame-relay map
Serial0 (up): ip 172.16.1.3 dlci 112(0x70,0x1C00), dynamic,
     broadcast,, status defined, active
Serial0 (up): ipx AAA1234.0000.0c92.c1f9 dlci 101(0x65,0x1850), dynamic,
     broadcast,, status defined, active
Serial0 (up): ipx AAA1234.00e0.1eb9.2a05 dlci 112(0x70,0x1C00), dynamic,
     broadcast,, status defined, active
Serial0 (up): ip 172.16.1.1 dlci 101(0x65,0x1850), dynamic,
     broadcast,, status defined, active
```

SATELLITE OFFICE ONE

```
Satellite-1#show frame-relay map
```

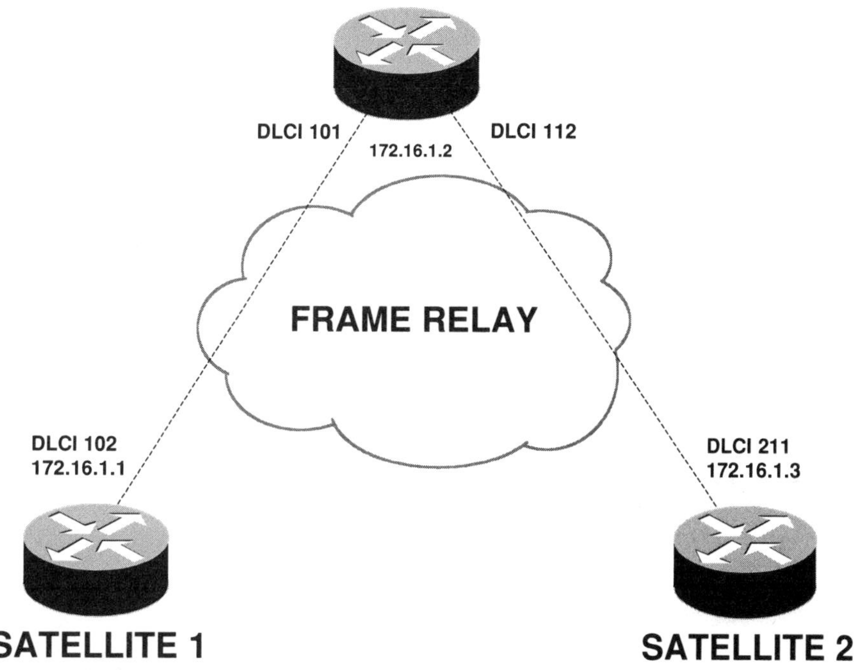

FIGURE 4–2 A partially meshed Frame-Relay topology.

```
Serial0 (up): ipx AAA1234.00e0.1eb9.2a0f dlci 102(0x66,0x1860), dynamic,
     broadcast,, status defined, active
Serial0 (up): ip 172.16.1.2 dlci 102(0x66,0x1860), dynamic,
     broadcast,, status defined, active
```

SATELLITE OFFICE TWO

```
Satellite-2#sh frame-relay map
Serial0 (up): ipx AAA1234.00e0.1eb9.2a0f dlci 211(0xD3,0x3430), dynamic,
     broadcast,, status defined, active
Serial0 (up): ip 172.16.1.2 dlci 211(0xD3,0x3430), dynamic,
     broadcast,, status defined, active
```

Notice that inverse ARP resolved all of the addresses for the headquarters router from both spokes. Both spokes resolved only the addresses from the headquarters router. As a result, the headquarters router can reach both satellite routers and vice-versa but the spokes cannot reach each other.

When Satellite-2 attempted to ping Satellite-1, the following output was generated from debug ip packet:

```
Satellite-2#ping 172.16.1.1
```

Type escape sequence to abort.
Sending 5, 100-byte ICMP Echos to 172.16.1.1, timeout is 2 seconds:

```
IP: s=172.16.1.3 (local), d=172.16.1.1 (Serial0), len 100, sending
IP: s=172.16.1.3 (local), d=172.16.1.1 (Serial0), len 100, encapsulation
failed.
IP: s=172.16.1.3 (local), d=172.16.1.1 (Serial0), len 100, sending
IP: s=172.16.1.3 (local), d=172.16.1.1 (Serial0), len 100, encapsulation
failed.
```

"Encapsulation failed" reflects a problem with the underlying data-link layer operation. To examine general Frame-Relay operations, enable debug frame packet:

```
Satellite-2#debug frame packet
Frame Relay packet debugging is on
Satellite-2#ping 172.16.1.1
```

Type escape sequence to abort.
Sending 5, 100-byte ICMP Echos to 172.16.1.1, timeout is 2 seconds:

```
Serial0:Encaps failed--no map entry link 7(IP).
Serial0:Encaps failed--no map entry link 7(IP).
Serial0:Encaps failed--no map entry link 7(IP).
Serial0:Encaps failed--no map entry link 7(IP).
Serial0:Encaps failed--no map entry link 7(IP).
Success rate is 0 percent (0/5)
```

The router correctly sent the packet out of the Frame-Relay interface. The destination IP address is part of the same subnet of the IP address configured on the Frame-Relay interface. Since no DLCI-to-IP address mapping exists in the Satellite-2 router's Frame-Relay map table, the packet gets dropped at the interface.

THE LIMITATIONS OF INVERSE ARP

Inverse ARP only resolves network addresses of remote Frame-Relay connections that are directly connected. Inverse ARP alone cannot resolve the unreachability problems between two spokes in a partial mesh topology.

SOLUTIONS TO THE LIMITATIONS OF INVERSE ARP

The limitations of inverse ARP can be remedied with three configuration alternatives:

1. Add an additional PVC between the Satellite-1 and Satellite-2
2. Configure Frame-Relay Map Statements

3. Configure Point-to-Point Subinterfaces

ADDING A PVC BETWEEN THE TWO SPOKES: THE FULL-MESH SOLUTION

When a PVC is added between the two spokes, a full-mesh topology is created. All Frame-Relay connections have a direct link to each other. As a result, all Frame-Relay interfaces can maintain a complete inverse ARP map table of all remote network addresses.

```
Satellite-2#show frame-relay pvc
PVC Statistics for interface Serial0 (Frame Relay DTE)
DLCI = 211, DLCI USAGE = LOCAL, PVC STATUS = ACTIVE, INTERFACE = Serial0
input pkts 114          output pkts 125          in bytes 10868
out bytes 11410         dropped pkts 0           in FECN pkts 0
in BECN pkts 0          out FECN pkts 0          out BECN pkts 0
in DE pkts 0            out DE pkts 0
out bcast pkts 114                               out bcast bytes 10314
pvc create time 00:50:45, last time pvc status changed 00:47:06

DLCI = 302, DLCI USAGE = LOCAL, PVC STATUS = ACTIVE, INTERFACE = Serial0
input pkts 8            output pkts 7            in bytes 536
out bytes 556           dropped pkts 2           in FECN pkts 0
in BECN pkts 0          out FECN pkts 0          out BECN pkts 0
in DE pkts 0            out DE pkts 0
out bcast pkts 7        out bcast bytes 556
pvc create time 00:02:08, last time pvc status changed 00:01:58

Satellite-2#show frame-relay map
Serial0 (up): ipx AAA1234.0000.0c92.c1f9 dlci 302(0x12E,0x48E0), dynamic,
     broadcast,, status defined, active
Serial0 (up): ipx AAA1234.00e0.1eb9.2a0f dlci 211(0xD3,0x3430), dynamic,
     broadcast,, status defined, active
Serial0 (up): ip 172.16.1.1 dlci 302(0x12E,0x48E0), dynamic,
     broadcast,, status defined, active
Serial0 (up): ip 172.16.1.2 dlci 211(0xD3,0x3430), dynamic,
     broadcast,, status defined, active
```

Although adding an additional PVC remedied the problem, it is not a scalable solution. As more Frame-Relay connections are added, more PVCs will need to be added to maintain a full mesh topology. The following formula can be used to calculate the number of PVCs needed to maintain a full-mesh:

$$(n*(n-1))/2$$

where n denotes the Frame-Relay peers.

This formula is applied in the following table. Notice how a linear increase of Frame-Relay connections causes an exponential increase of Frame-Relay PVCs:

TABLE 4.1

Number of Connections	Number of PVCs
2	1
3	3
4	6
5	10
6	15
7	21
8	28
9	36
10	45

As the numbers in the table above reflect, maintaining a full-mesh frame-relay network does not scale well.

Using Frame-Relay Map Statements

Instead of adding additional PVCs to maintain a full-mesh topology and using inverse ARP to maintain a complete mapping of all remote local network addresses, Frame-Relay map statements can be used to statically map local DLCI, to unknown remote network layer addresses. Frame-Relay map statements can be used for the following protocols:

```
Satellite-1(config-if)#frame-relay map ?
apollo          Apollo Domain
appletalk       AppleTalk
bridge          Bridging
clns            ISO CLNS
decnet          DECnet
dlsw            Data Link Switching
ip              IP
ipx             Novell IPX
llc2            llc2
qllc            qllc protocol
rsrb            Remote Source-Route Bridging
stun            Serial Tunnel
```

vines	Banyan VINES
xns	Xerox Network Services

The complete syntax of the Frame-Relay map statement is:

Satellite-1(config-if)#frame-relay map ip x.x.x.x nnnn

active	Always compress TCP/IP headers
broadcast	Broadcasts should be forwarded to this address
cisco	Use CISCO Encapsulation
ietf	Use RFC1490 Encapsulation
nocompress	Do not compress TCP/IP headers
payload-compression	Use payload compression
tcp	TCP header compression parameters
<cr>	

x.x.x.x = ip address

nnnn = DLCI number 16-1007

The broadcast parameter is required for protocols such as OSPF. In this scenario, a single Frame-Relay map statement would be required on each of the Satellite routers. This will provide reachability from all Frame-Relay connections to all Frame-Relay connections.

The configuration for each of the satellite routers will include the following.

SATELLITE ONE CONFIGURATION

```
interface Serial0
ip address 172.16.1.1 255.255.255.0
encapsulation frame-relay
frame-relay map ip 172.16.1.3 102

Satellite-1#show frame-relay map
Serial0 (up): ip 172.16.1.3 dlci 102(0x66,0x1860), static,
       CISCO, status defined, active
Serial0 (up): ip 172.16.1.2 dlci 102(0x66,0x1860), dynamic,
        broadcast,, status defined, active
```

SATELLITE TWO CONFIGURATION

```
interface Serial0
ip address 172.16.1.3 255.255.255.0
encapsulation frame-relay
frame-relay map ip 172.16.1.1 211

Satellite-2#show frame-relay map
Serial0 (up): ip 172.16.1.1 dlci 211(0xD3,0x3430), static,
       CISCO, status defined, active
Serial0 (up): ip 172.16.1.2 dlci 211(0xD3,0x3430), dynamic,
       broadcast,, status defined, active
```

This configuration option alleviates the need to maintain a Frame-Relay full-mesh topology. When a spoke router wants to send a packet to another spoke router, the Frame-Relay map statement directs the packet out of the spoke's PVC. When the packet arrives at the hub router, the hub router is able to redirect the packet out the correct PVC since it has a complete DLCI to remote network address mapping of all spokes.

Even though Frame-Relay map statements remove the need to maintain a full-mesh topology, Frame-Relay map statements also present scalability issues. For every additional spoke added, n-1 Frame-Relay map statements need to be added to each spoke (where n = number of spokes in a Frame-Relay hub and spoke topology). An additional frame-relay map statement will need to be included if the conditions described in the next section are met. IT IS CRITICAL THAT YOU ARE AWARE OF HOW FRAME-RELAY MAP STATEMENTS DISABLE INVERSE ARP. Read the next section, "A Word of Caution When Using Frame-Relay Map Statements" for further information.

Subinterfaces further simplify Frame-Relay configurations on Cisco routers. Two types of subinterfaces are available in the Cisco IOS, point-to-point, and multipoint. We will first examine using point-to-point subinterfaces. Coverage of multipoint subinterfaces will be provided later in the chapter.

A Word of Caution When Using Frame-Relay Map Statements

Consider the configuration displayed above. Each spoke has one inverse-arp entry to the hub and one frame-relay map statement to the other spoke. This is an operational configuration; however, if the router is reloaded, inverse-arp will be disabled for any DLCI that is used with a frame-relay map statement. A rule to remember when using frame-relay map statements is: when you configure a frame-relay map statement for a particular protocol (IP, IPX, DECNET, etc.), inverse-arp will be disabled for that specific protocol only for the DLCI referenced in the frame-relay map statement.

In the example above, inverse-arp had already occurred when the frame-relay map statement was entered. If the frame-relay map statement is saved to the startup configuration, inverse arp will not be performed for the protocol on the specific DLCI referenced in the frame-relay map statement. Inverse-arp will work for other protocols on the DLCI referenced in the frame-relay map statement. It will also work for the protocol referenced in the frame-relay map statement but on a different DLCI.

Therefore, as a rule: when configuring frame-relay map statements, make note of the protocol and the DLCI specified. If there are any inverse-arp mappings for that same protocol referencing the same DLCI, replace the inverse-arp entries with frame-relay map statements.

Configuring Frame-Relay Point-to-Point Subinterfaces

By using point-to-point subinterfaces, the Cisco router can treat each PVC as if it were a separate point-to-point interface on the router. By doing so, the NBMA characteristics of Frame-Relay can be circumvented. Conventional point-to-point interfaces cannot be subdivided into multiple logical interfaces. Standard point-to-point interfaces have no concept of DLCI number, inverse ARP, or local DLCI address to remote network address mappings. This gives us the best of both worlds: the Frame-Relay service is supplying multiple PVCs over a single physical interface and the point-to-point subinterface is subdividing each PVC as if it were a physical point-to-point interface. **By providing this functionality, point-to-point subinterfaces completely by pass the DLCI to network address mapping issue.** A further discussion of point-to-point subinterfaces is supplied after the next example.

The configuration of a point-to-point subinterface is displayed below. It involves a minimum of two commands:

```
Interface Serial0.1 point-to-point
Frame-relay interface-dlci dlci-number
```

Rules to remember when configuring point-to-point subinterfaces are:

- No Frame-Relay map statements can be used with point-to-point subinterfaces
- One and only one DLCI can be associated with a single point-to-point subinterface

Let's take a look at the configuration files and show frame map statements.

SATELLITE ONE

```
interface Serial0
no ip address
encapsulation frame-relay
!
interface Serial0.1 point-to-point
ip address 172.16.1.1 255.255.255.0
frame-relay interface-dlci 102
Satellite-1#show frame-relay map
Serial0.1 (up): point-to-point dlci, dlci 102(0x66,0x1860),
        broadcast status defined, active
```

SATELLITE TWO

```
interface Serial0
no ip address
encapsulation frame-relay
!
interface Serial0.1 point-to-point
ip address 172.16.1.3 255.255.255.0
```

```
frame-relay interface-dlci 211
!
Satellite-2#sh frame-relay map
Serial0.1 (up): point-to-point dlci, dlci 211(0xD3,0x3430),
       broadcast status defined, active
```

The Frame-Relay mapping process is remedied by using point-to-point subinterfaces. Note how the Frame-Relay map statement is different for a point-to-point subinterface. Note that it does not contain the same information that an inverse ARP entry or Frame-Relay map contains. With inverse ARP and the frame-relay map statement, there is an entry of the remote network address with its associated DLCI for each and every listing generated by the show frame-relay map statement. With point-to-point subinterfaces, no reference to a remote network address is displayed. Where there is a remote network address for a Frame-Relay map statement and inverse ARP, there is the entry "point-to-point dlci" for point-to-point subinterface listings generated by the show Frame-Relay map command.

Notice from the following show commands how the subinterface configured above on the satellite-2 router is treated as a separate interface. Other IOS commands such as show ip route, show ip interface brief, and show frame pvc represent the subinterface along with other interfaces in the router.

```
Satellite-2#show ip route
Codes: C - connected, S - static, I - IGRP, R - RIP, M - mobile, B - BGP
D - EIGRP, EX - EIGRP external, O - OSPF, IA - OSPF inter area
N1 - OSPF NSSA external type 1, N2 - OSPF NSSA external type 2
E1 - OSPF external type 1, E2 - OSPF external type 2, E - EGP
i - IS-IS, L1 - IS-IS level-1, L2 - IS-IS level-2, * - candidate default
U - per-user static route, o - ODR
Gateway of last resort is not set
172.16.0.0/24 is subnetted, 3 subnets
C    172.16.1.0 is directly connected, Serial0.1
R    172.16.2.0 [120/2] via 172.16.1.2, 00:00:20, Serial0.1
R    172.16.3.0 [120/2] via 172.16.1.2, 00:00:20, Serial0.1

Satellite-2#show ip interface brief
Interface    IP-Address    OK? Method Status    Protocol
Ethernet0    unassigned    YES unset            administratively down down
Serial0      unassigned    YES unset up         up
Serial0.1    172.16.1.3    YES NVRAM up         up
Serial1      unassigned    YES unset            administratively down down

Satellite-2#sh frame pvc
PVC Statistics for interface Serial0 (Frame Relay DTE)
DLCI = 211, DLCI USAGE = LOCAL, PVC STATUS = ACTIVE, INTERFACE =
Serial0.1
```

```
input pkts 7          output pkts 6          in bytes 720
out bytes 834         dropped pkts 0         in FECN pkts 0
in BECN pkts 0        out FECN pkts 0        out BECN pkts 0
in DE pkts 0          out DE pkts 0
out bcast pkts 6      out bcast bytes 834
pvc create time 00:01:28, last time pvc status changed 00:01:28
```

GENERAL RULES OF FRAME-RELAY SUBINTERFACES

Subinterfaces divide a single interface into multiple logical interfaces. There are two types of subinterfaces: point-to-point and multipoint.

POINT-TO-POINT SUBINTERFACES

A point-to-point Frame-Relay subinterface can have one and only one DLCI associated with it. A point-to-point subinterface does not use Frame-Relay map statements. If multiple point-to-point subinterfaces are configured for a single router and each subinterface has an IP address assigned to it, each IP address must be assigned from a different network or subnetwork address space.

An exciting aspect of point-to-point subinterfaces is that the router treats them as point-to-point interfaces. The following error messages will never appear on a packet exiting a point-to-point subinterface:

```
Serial0:Encaps failed--no map entry link 7(IP).
```

Since this is the case, the entire issue of remote network address to local DLCI mapping can be avoided.

MULTIPOINT SUBINTERFACES

A multipoint subinterface can have multiple DLCIs assigned to it. Multipoint subinterfaces share many of the characteristics of a physical Frame-Relay interface. Frame-relay map statements can be used with multipoint subinterfaces. Inverse ARP can be used with multipoint subinterfaces.

THE "FRAME-RELAY INTERFACE DLCI" STATEMENT

The Frame-Relay interface DLCI command is used to assign specific DLCIs to specific subinterfaces (both point-to-point and multipoint). Without the Frame-Relay interface DLCI command, all DLCIs are assigned to the physical interface. If 10 DLCIs are announced to a Cisco router from a Frame-Relay switch and only seven of the DLCIs are explicitly assigned to existing subinterfaces on the switch, the remaining DLCIs will be assigned to the physical interface.

ROUTING OVER FRAME-RELAY

DISTANCE VECTOR ROUTING PROTOCOLS AND SPLIT-HORIZON

Frame-Relay creates configuration challenges for routing protocols. For distance vector routing protocols such as IP RIP, IGRP, IPX RIP, RTMP as well as hybrid routing protocols with distance vector characteristics such as IP EIGRP, IPX EIGRP, and AppleTalk EIGRP, the rule of split horizon can cause routing table update problems on a hub and spoke Frame-Relay topology.

The rule of split-horizon states that when a particular network is learned from a specific interface, that same network can never by advertised out of that same interface. For example, if ROUTER-1 learned about the 10.0.0.0 network on Serial0, split-horizon will prevent ROUTER-1 from ever advertising 10.0.0.0 out its Serial0 interface. The rule of Split-Horizon is applied at the network layer with distance vector routing protocols. Distance vector routing protocols have no awareness of the multiconnection, multi-PVC nature of Frame-Relay that operates at the data-link layer. Therefore, a network layer process (the rule of split-horizon) prevents a data-link layer process (the forwarding of packets from one Frame-Relay PVC to another) from occurring.

Distance vector routing protocols do not know that routing information may arrive on one PVC on a physical interface and need to go out other PVCs on the same physical interface. Distance vector routing protocols are completely unaware of the existence of different PVCs. They still see routing traffic coming in one physical port only. This is a case where a process on one layer of the OSI Model is unaware of what a lower layer is doing.

How split-horizon can cause problems in a Frame-Relay network can be manifested in examing the network topology of the Headquarters and two satellite companies. Satellite-1 can send routing updates to headquarters but headquarters cannot send these updates out to Satellite-2 due to split-horizon.

This problem does not occur on a full-mesh Frame-Relay network because every router has a direct connection to every other router. All routing updates are sent directly to all other routers. Split-horizon only blocks routing updates in a hub and spoke topology. A Cisco IOS remedy to this split horizon problem is to disable split-horizon on the hub router in a Frame-Relay network. This can be performed at the interface configuration mode.

```
headquarters(config-if)#no ip split-horizon ?
eigrp Enhanced Interior Gateway Routing Protocol (EIGRP) <cr>
headquarters(config-if)#no ipx split-horizon ?
eigrp Enhanced Interior Gateway Routing Protocol (EIGRP)
headquarters(config-if)#no appletalk eigrp-splithorizon ?
<cr>
headquarters(config-if)#no decnet split-horizon ?    <cr>
```

Notice that split-horizon is used by many protocol suites including IP, IPX, AppleTalk, and DECNET. Split-horizon cannot be disabled for IPX/RIP. Split-horizon can be disabled for IPX EIGRP and AppleTalk EIGRP and AppleTalk RTMP. In order for Cisco to conform to the IPX RIP protocol specification, split-horizon cannot be disabled for this routing protocol.

Split-horizon can be disabled for all IP distance vector routing protocols. In fact, when encapsulation Frame-Relay is activated on a physical interface, the IOS automatically disables split-horizon. For both point-to-point and multipoint subinterfaces, split-horizon is enabled.

Reference the bulleted list below for the default settings of IP split-horizon for the interface types listed:

- Split-horizon is disabled on Frame-Relay physical IP interfaces
- Split-horizon is enabled on Frame-Relay point-to-point IP subinterfaces
- Split-horizon is enabled on Frame-Relay mulitpoint IP subinterfaces

If the remedy to overcoming split-horizon issues in a hub and spoke Frame-Relay topology is to disable it, does this solution expose the network to problems that split-horizon was designed to prevent? When split-horizon is disabled, is the network now vulnerable to routing loops? The answer to this question is: *absolutely*. But there is a remedy to this vulnerability—distribute-lists. Distribute-lists allow a network administrator to control what routes a router will advertise out of an interface or to another neighbor or accept on a specified interface. Skillful use of distribute-lists is an absolute must for any internetworking engineer. It will be covered extensively in the IP redistribution chapter (Chapter 11). Once distribute-lists are mastered in an IP environment, it is easy to learn how they work in IPX, AppleTalk, and DECNET.

Configuring IP, IPX, AppleTalk, and DECNET routing protocols is revisited in Chapters 14—19. These Chapters are dedicated configuring non-IP routing protocol suites. Please note for now that you must be aware of addressing split-horizon issues in hub and spoke Frame-Relay topologies.

OSPF AND NETWORK TYPE MISMATCHES

OSPF is not affected by the rule of split-horizon since it does not apply it. However, OSPF has its own set of Frame-Relay configuration issues. When an OSPF interface is enabled, it identifies itself as being an interface of a certain network type: BROADCAST if the OSPF interface is connected to an Ethernet, Token-Ring, or FDDI network; POINT_TO_POINT if the interface is connected to a conventional point-to-point wide-area network (WAN) connection such as a T-1; or NON_BROADCAST if it is connected to an NBMA network such as Frame-Relay or ATM. An example of how this network type is identified in a Cisco environment is displayed below.

For an OSPF connection on an Ethernet network the network type is "BROADCAST":

```
Satellite-2#show ip ospf interface e0
Ethernet0 is up, line protocol is up
Internet Address 172.16.33.17/24, Area 0
Process ID 100, Router ID 172.16.1.3, Network Type BROADCAST,
Cost: 10
Transmit Delay is 1 sec, State WAITING, Priority 1
No designated router on this network
No backup designated router on this network
Timer intervals configured, Hello 10, Dead 40, Wait 40,
Retransmit 5
Hello due in 00:00:02
Wait time before Designated router selection 00:00:22
Neighbor Count is 0, Adjacent neighbor count is 0
Suppress hello for 0 neighbor(s)
```

For an OSPF connection with a conventional Frame-Relay interface (conventional meaning that it is not using subinterfaces), the network type is "NON_BROADCAST"

```
headquarters#show ip ospf interface Serial 0
Serial0 is up, line protocol is up
Internet Address 172.16.1.2/24, Area 0
Process ID 100, Router ID 172.16.1.2, Network Type NON_BROADCAST,
Cost: 64
Transmit Delay is 1 sec, State WAITING, Priority 1
No designated router on this network
No backup designated router on this network
Timer intervals configured, Hello 30, Dead 120, Wait 120,
Retransmit 5
Hello due in 00:00:06
Wait time before Designated router selection 00:01:36
Neighbor Count is 0, Adjacent neighbor count is 0
Suppress hello for 0 neighbor(s)
```

For an OSPF connection with a point-to-point subinterface on a Frame-Relay network, the network type is POINT_TO_POINT:

```
Serial0.1 is up, line protocol is up
Internet Address 172.16.1.1/24, Area 0
Process ID 100, Router ID 172.16.3.1, Network Type
POINT_TO_POINT, Cost: 64
Transmit Delay is 1 sec, State POINT_TO_POINT,
Timer intervals configured, Hello 10, Dead 40, Wait 40,
Retransmit 5
Hello due in 00:00:08
Neighbor Count is 0, Adjacent neighbor count is 0
Suppress hello for 0 neighbor(s)
```

When Frame-Relay is configured on the physical interface Serial 0, it has an OSPF network type of NON_BROADCAST. When Frame-Relay is configured on the point-to-point subinterface Serial 0.1, it is assigned the network type of POINT_TO_POINT. This causes an acute problem with OSPF. For OSPF to exchange routing information with a neighbor on the same network (in order for OSPF neighbors to form an adjacency), the two neighbors must possess the same "hello parameters." When Frame-Relay is configured with a combination of physical interfaces and logical interfaces, OSPF network type mismatches are likely to occur. The following debug messages were generated between one Frame-Relay peer with OSPF configured on a physical interface and a second Frame-Relay peer configured on a point-to-point subinterface:

```
OSPF: Mismatched hello parameters from 172.16.1.1
Dead R 40 C 120, Hello R 10 C 30 Mask R 255.255.255.0 C 255.255.255.0
OSPF: Mismatched hello parameters from 172.16.1.1
Dead R 40 C 120, Hello R 10 C 30 Mask R 255.255.255.0 C 255.255.255.0
OSPF: Mismatched hello parameters from 172.16.1.1
Dead R 40 C 120, Hello R 10 C 30 Mask R 255.255.255.0 C 255.255.255.0
```

OSPF configured on a physical Frame-Relay interface assumes the default OSPF interface type of nonbroadcast. An OSPF nonbroadcast interface has settings of 30 seconds for HELLO intervals and 120 seconds for DEAD intervals. A point-to-point subinterface is defined by OSPF as a point-to-point interface type. An OSPF point-to-point interface has settings of 10 seconds for HELLO intervals and 40 seconds for DEAD intervals. In situations where OSPF is configured on one Frame-Relay physical interface and OSPF is also configured on another Frame-Relay peer's point-to-point subinterface interface, default OSPF configurations will create an "hello mismatches," the OSPF adjacencies will not form and OSPF will not work.

A remedy to the problem is using the Cisco IOS interface configuration command "IP OSPF NETWORK" to make sure that OSPF interface types match between OSPF speakers on a Frame-Relay network. The options of this command are listed below:

```
Satellite-1(config-if)#ip ospf network ?
broadcast                  Specify OSPF Type of Network
nonbroadcast               Specify OSPF Type of Network
point-to-multipoint        Specify OSPF Type of Network
```

By using this command with one of the three options listed above, we can assure that OSPF neighbors on the same Frame-Relay network will have the same network type. A popular selection for OSPF networks is the point-to-multipoint option. By adding this interface configuration statement to every OSPF interface on the Frame-Relay network, the problem of OSPF network type mismatches will be avoided. More information on OSPF over NBMA networks such as Frame-Relay will be presented in the Configuring OSPF chapter.

SURVEY THE PRIMARY COMBINATIONS

We've got all the pieces now. Let's examine the following combinations and determine when to use inverse ARP, when to use Frame-Relay map statements, and when to use the Frame-Relay interface DLCI command in a hub and spoke Frame-Relay topology.

- All physical interfaces: Physical interface at the hub and physical interfaces at the spokes
- All subinterfaces: Multipoint subinterface at the hub and point-to-point subinterfaces at the spokes
- Physical interface at the hub: logical point-to-point subinterface at the spokes, and
- Logical multipoint subinterface at the hub: physical interfaces at the spokes

For many internetworking engineers, there is a lot of confusion about when to use Frame-Relay map statements, when to use Frame-Relay interface-DLCI statements, and when to rely on inverse ARP. The next set of examples will help clarify when to use each of these configuration techniques.

We will use the following tools to verify and debug our Frame-Relay configurations:

```
Sh frame map
ping
Debug ip packet
Debug frame packet
Debug ip icmp
```

Initially, we will deliberately provide an incomplete configuration of a Frame-Relay hub and spoke topology. Since the configuration is incomplete, the debug tools listed above will allow us to determine what needs to be done to complete the configuration.

The objective of this exercise is twofold. One, to provide a detailed and incremental view of how Frame-Relay configurations operate and two, to introduce a method of troubleshooting Frame-Relay problems with Cisco IOS show and debug commands.

All Physical Interfaces

CONFIGURING A HUB AND SPOKE FRAME-RELAY CONFIGURATION WITH FRAME-RELAY MAP STATEMENTS AND NO FRAME-RELAY SUBINTERFACES *REVISITED*

Three routers are configured in a frame relay hub and spoke topology.

At first, there are no map statements on any of the routers. The spoke routers learned the hub's remote IP address through inverse ARP. The spokes can successfully ping the hub.

When SPOKE-1 (the "pinging" side) without configuration statements trys to ping SPOKE-2 (the "pinged" side), the following debug IP packet messages are generated:

```
IP: s=172.16.3.1 (local), d=172.16.3.2 (Serial0), len 100,
sending
IP: s=172.16.3.1 (local), d=172.16.3.2 (Serial0), len 100,
encapsulation failed
IP: s=172.16.3.1 (local), d=255.255.255.255 (Serial0), len 31,
sending broad/multicast.
```

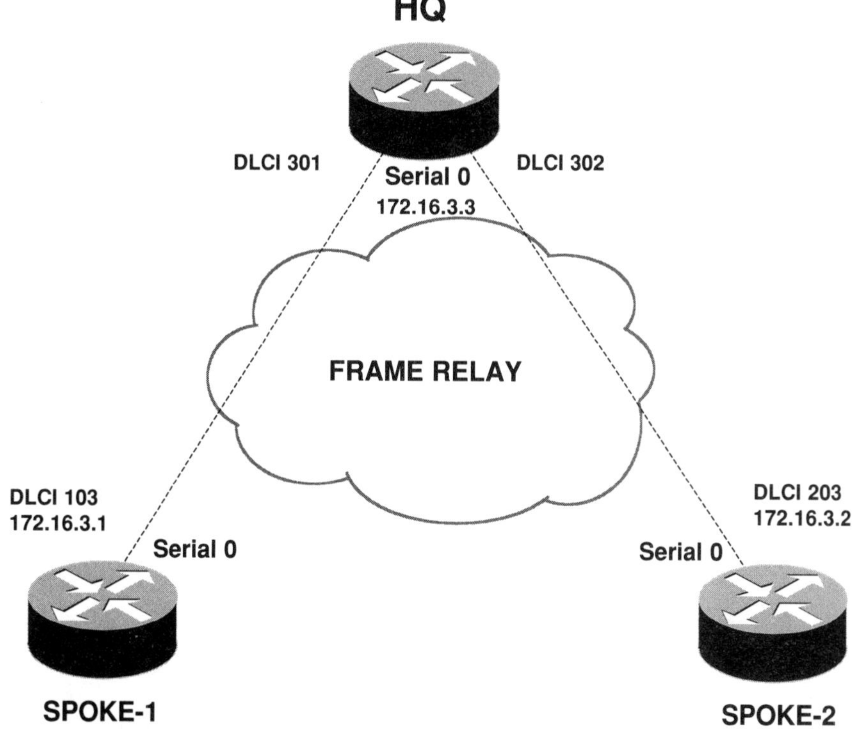

FIGURE 4–3 An all physical interfaces Frame-Relay configuration


```
IP: s=172.16.3.1 (local), d=172.16.3.2 (Serial0), len 100,
sending
IP: s=172.16.3.1 (local), d=172.16.3.2 (Serial0), len 100,
encapsulation failed
IP: s=172.16.3.1 (local), d=255.255.255.255 (Serial0), len 31,
sending broad/multicast.
```

When you enable debug IP packet and you see the packets going out of the correct interface but they are displaying an "encapsulation failed" message, immediately examine what is happening at the data-link layer (in this case, examine what is happening with Frame-Relay). This message can be translated as saying, "Everything is alright with the IP packet forwarding process, but something is wrong with lower level processes that IP depends on." Debug IP packet does not know how to specifically identify what the lower level problem is. It merely represents it with an "encapsulation failed" message. We must turn on a data-link debugging tool, in this case debug frame packet, to examine what is happening at this level.

From debug frame packet, we see:

```
Serial0:Encaps failed--no map entry link 7(IP)
Serial0:Encaps failed--no map entry link 7(IP).
Serial0:Encaps failed--no map entry link 7(IP).
```

Debug frame packet displays that the ping is unsuccessful because the destination IP address does not have a Frame-Relay map entry. Remember, this is a spoke-to-spoke ping. Inverse ARP cannot supply spoke-to-spoke remote network layer to DLCI mappings. As a remedy, we will add a Frame-Relay map statement to SPOKE-1. When the Frame-Relay map statement is added, we get the following message:

```
IP: s=172.16.3.1 (local), d=172.16.3.2 (Serial0), len 100,
sending.
IP: s=172.16.3.1 (local), d=172.16.3.2 (Serial0), len 100,
sending.
IP: s=172.16.3.1 (local), d=172.16.3.2 (Serial0), len 100,
sending.
IP: s=172.16.3.1 (local), d=172.16.3.2 (Serial0), len 100,
sending.
```

Notice how "encap failed" messages from "debug ip packet" have disappeared. However, notice that all of the messages state that SPOKE-1 is sending only. It is not receiving any packets back from SPOKE-2. When we examine debugging messages from the "pinged side," SPOKE-2, we see the following:

```
IP: s=172.16.3.1 (Serial0), d=172.16.3.2 (Serial0), len 104, rcvd
3
ICMP: echo reply sent, src 172.16.3.2, dst 172.16.3.1
IP: s=172.16.3.2 (local), d=172.16.3.1 (Serial0), len 104,
sending
Serial0:Encaps failed--no map entry link 7(IP)
IP: s=172.16.3.2 (local), d=172.16.3.1 (Serial0), len 100,
encapsulation failed
Serial0(i): dlci 203(0x30B1), pkt type 0x800, datagramsize 104
```

```
IP: s=172.16.3.1 (Serial0), d=172.16.3.2 (Serial0), len 104, rcvd
3
ICMP: echo reply sent, src 172.16.3.2, dst 172.16.3.1
IP: s=172.16.3.2 (local), d=172.16.3.1 (Serial0), len 104,
sending
Serial0:Encaps failed--no map entry link 7(IP)
```

SPOKE-2 is receiving the ICMP packets from SPOKE-1. This means that SPOKE-1 (with its single Frame-Relay map statement) sent its ICMP echo request destined for SPOKE-2 down its PVC terminated at the hub router, HQ. HQ took the packet and forwarded out of its DLCI connected to SPOKE-2 because the HUB has both a mapping and a DLCI for both SPOKE-1 and SPOKE-2. **(EMPHASIS: NO MANUAL CONFIGURATION STATEMENTS FOR THE HUB!!) SPOKE-2 has received SPOKE-1's packet. It must send an ICMP reply, but when it trys, it gets an "encap failed."**

The remedy is supplied by a configuring single Frame-Relay map statement on SPOKE-2 point to the remote IP address of SPOKE-1. Everything should work fine once this single statement is entered. Proper operation is reflected by the debug messages generated by SPOKE-2 below:

```
IP: s=172.16.3.1 (Serial0), d=172.16.3.2 (Serial0), len 104, rcvd
3
ICMP: echo reply sent, src 172.16.3.2, dst 172.16.3.1
IP: s=172.16.3.2 (local), d=172.16.3.1 (Serial0), len 104,
sending
Serial0(o): dlci 203(0x30B1), pkt type 0x800(IP), datagramsize
104
IP: s=172.16.3.1 (Serial0), d=172.16.3.2 (Serial0), len 104, rcvd
3
ICMP: echo reply sent, src 172.16.3.2, dst 172.16.3.1
IP: s=172.16.3.2 (local), d=172.16.3.1 (Serial0), len 104,
sending
Serial0(o): dlci 203(0x30B1), pkt type 0x800(IP), datagramsize
104
```

Notice no "encap failed" messages are being displayed. Notice that SPOKE-2 is now both sending and receiving packets. *Everything is working fine with two single static map statements at the spokes and nothing done at the hub.*

The following is a sample of the inbound and outbound traffic at the hub router HQ from debug frame packet:

```
Serial0(i): dlci 301(0x48D1), pkt type 0x800, datagramsize 176
Serial0(i): dlci 301(0x48D1), pkt type 0x800, datagramsize 176
Serial0(i): dlci 302(0x48E1), pkt type 0x800, datagramsize 104
Serial0(o): dlci 302(0x48E1), pkt type 0x800(IP), datagramsize 60
Serial0(o): dlci 301(0x48D1), pkt type 0x800(IP), datagramsize
104
```

Notice that HQ is both sending and receiving packets out of both of its DLCIs.

Listed below are the configurations and Frame-Relay map listings from SPOKE-1, SPOKE-2, and HQ.

SPOKE-1

```
interface Serial0
ip address 172.16.3.1 255.255.255.0
encapsulation frame-relay
frame-relay map ip 172.16.3.2 103 broadcast

r1#SH FRAM MAP
Serial0 (up): ip 172.16.3.2 dlci 103(0x67,0x1870), static,
      broadcast,
        CISCO, status defined, active
Serial0 (up): ip 172.16.3.3 dlci 103(0x67,0x1870), dynamic,
      broadcast,, status defined, active
```

SPOKE-2

```
interface Serial0
ip address 172.16.3.2 255.255.255.0
encapsulation frame-relay
frame-relay map ip 172.16.3.1 203 broadcast

r2#SH FRAM MAP
Serial0 (up): ip 172.16.3.1 dlci 203(0xCB,0x30B0), static,
      broadcast,
        CISCO, status defined, active
Serial0 (up): ip 172.16.3.3 dlci 203(0xCB,0x30B0), dynamic,
      broadcast,, status defined, active
```

HQ

```
interface Serial0
ip address 172.16.3.3 255.255.255.0
encapsulation frame-relay

r3#sh fram map
Serial0 (up): ip 172.16.3.1 dlci 301(0x12D,0x48D0), dynamic,
      broadcast,, status defined, active
Serial0 (up): ip 172.16.3.2 dlci 302(0x12E,0x48E0), dynamic,
      broadcast,, status defined, active
```

SUMMARY

When using only physical interfaces in a hub and spoke topology, you need to add a Frame-Relay map statement on the spoke routers to assure spoke-to-spoke reachability. *Nothing needs to be done to the hub router.*

Frame-Relay interface-DLCI statements are useless in a physical interface only configuration because the whole purpose of the Frame-Relay interface-DLCI command is to *associate a particular DLCI to a particular subinterface.* When subinterfaces are not used, the DLCIs are automatically associated with the physical interface.

Please note the previous "word of caution about frame-relay map statements." When a Frame-Relay map statement is used, inverse-arp is disabled for the protocol referenced in the Frame-Relay map statement on the DLCI referenced in the Frame-Relay map statement. Since the spokes in this example are using the same protocol (IP) and the same DLCI in the frame-relay map statement as is being used in the pre-existing inverse-arp statements between each spoke and the hub, the inverse-arp statements should be replaced with frame-relay map statements. Everything is working fine with a combination for inverse-arp and Frame-Relay map statements when inverse-arp is performed before the Frame-Relay map statement is entered. However, if the router should be reloaded for any reason or if the interface should be shut down for any reason, inverse-arp will be disabled and the spokes will not have a mapping to the hub.

Note how the troubleshooting was performed:

- It was incremental.
- It was sequential.
- It was layered: for data-link layer troubleshooting debug frame packet was used; for network layer troubleshooting, debug ip packet and debug ip icmp were used.
- It was performed from both sides of the connection: spoke to hub, spoke-1 to hq, and spoke-2 to hq, spoke to spoke, and spoke-1 to spoke-2.

ALL SUBINTERFACES USING FRAME-RELAY INTERFACE DLCI STATEMENTS ONLY

With the same hub and spoke topology used in the all physical interfaces configuration used in the previous section, the routers are now configured using exclusively subinterfaces. SPOKE-1 and SPOKE-2 are configured with point-to-point subinterfaces and HQ is configured with a multipoint subinterface. With the following configurations, all routers could ping each other.

SPOKE-1

```
interface Serial0.2 point-to-point
ip address 172.16.3.1 255.255.255.0
frame-relay interface-dlci 103

SPOKE-1#SH FRAME MAP
Serial0.1 (up): point-to-point dlci, dlci 103(0x67,0x1870),
       broadcast status defined, active
```

SPOKE-2

```
interface Serial0.2 point-to-point
ip address 172.16.3.2 255.255.255.0
frame-relay interface-dlci 203

SPOKE-2#SH FRAME MAP
Serial0.1 (up): point-to-point dlci, dlci 203(0xCB,0x30B0),
       broadcast status defined, active
```

HQ

```
interface Serial0.1 multipoint
ip address 172.16.3.3 255.255.255.0
frame-relay interface-dlci 301
frame-relay interface-dlci 302

HQ#SH FRAME MAP
Serial0 (up): ip 172.16.3.1 dlci 301(0x12D,0x48D0), dynamic,
       broadcast,, status defined, active
Serial0 (up): ip 172.16.3.2 dlci 302(0x12E,0x48E0), dynamic,
       broadcast,, status defined, active
```

Notice how the entries in the sh frame map statement differ between point-to-point subinterfaces and multipoint subinterfaces. The entries under SPOKE-1 and SPOKE-2 are listed as "point-to-point DLCI." The entries under HQ list an inverse ARP entry with a remote network address (in this case IP) with a local DLCI. Additional spoke routers could be added using this all subinterface configuration model and no additional Frame-Relay map statements would be needed. This makes this configuration a highly scalable one.

This configuration presents a set of different issues. All Frame-Relay connections are able to ping each other; however, if we are running a distance vector routing protocol with this configuration, we now have a problem with distance vector routing protocols such as RIP and IGRP. The following routing table was generated by SPOKE-1.

SPOKE-1#SH IP ROUTE
Codes: C — connected, S — static, I — IGRP, R — RIP, M — mobile, B — BGP
D — EIGRP, EX — EIGRP external, O — OSPF, IA — OSPF inter area
N1 — OSPF NSSA external type 1, N2 — OSPF NSSA external type 2
E1 — OSPF external type 1, E2 — OSPF external type 2, E — EGP
i — IS-IS, L1 — IS–IS level-1, L2 — IS–IS level-2, * — candidate default
U — per-user static route, o — ODR

Gateway of last resort is not set

```
R  156.10.0.0/16 is possibly down, routing via 172.16.3.3,
Serial0.1
R  169.11.0.0/16 [120/1] via 172.16.3.3, 00:00:00, Serial0.1
R  169.10.0.0/16 [120/1] via 172.16.3.3, 00:00:00, Serial0.1
R  174.10.0.0/16 is possibly down, routing via 172.16.3.3,
Serial0.1
R  169.12.0.0/16 [120/6] via 172.16.3.3, 00:00:00, Serial0.1
R  174.11.0.0/16 is possibly down, routing via 172.16.3.3,
Serial0.1
R  172.20.0.0/16 [120/1] via 172.16.3.3, 00:00:00, Serial0.1
C   172.16.3.0 is directly connected, Serial0.1
```

Notice the "possibly down" networks. These networks were being advertised successfully when the hub was configured on a physical interface because split-horizon is disabled by default. On a multipoint subinterface, split-horizon is enabled by default. Routes from the spoke routers will not get advertised out to other spokes because of split-horizon. If split-horizon is disabled on the multipoint subinterface, all of the routes will be propagated and the possibly down statements will disappear. If OSPF were enabled with the configurations displayed above, network type mismatches would occur.

PHYSICAL INTERFACE AT THE HUB AND POINT-TO-POINT SUBINTERFACES AT THE SPOKE

Everything works with the following configurations. Note how the show frame map statements differ.

SPOKE-1

```
interface Serial0
no ip address
encapsulation frame-relay
!
interface Serial0.1 point-to-point
ip address 172.16.3.1 255.255.255.0
frame-relay interface-dlci 103
SPOKE-1#SH FRAME MAP
Serial0.1 (up): point-to-point dlci, dlci 103(0x67,0x1870),
       broadcast status defined, active
```

SPOKE-2

```
interface Serial0
no ip address
encapsulation frame-relay
!
interface Serial0.1 point-to-point
ip address 172.16.3.2 255.255.255.0
frame-relay interface-dlci 203
SPOKE-2#SH FRAM MAP
```

```
Serial0.1 (up): point-to-point dlci, dlci 203(0xCB,0x30B0),
       broadcast status defined, active
```

HQ

```
interface Serial0
ip address 172.16.3.3 255.255.255.0
encapsulation frame-relay

r3#SH FRAM MAP
Serial0 (up): ip 172.16.3.1 dlci 301(0x12D,0x48D0), dynamic,
       broadcast,, status defined, active
Serial0 (up): ip 172.16.3.2 dlci 302(0x12E,0x48E0), dynamic,
       broadcast,, status defined, active
```

MULTIPOINT SUBINTERFACE AT THE HUB AND PHYSICAL INTERFACES AT THE SPOKES

With our last combination, we have come full circle. We are now back to configuring Frame-Relay map statements on the following:

SPOKE-1

```
interface Serial0
ip address 172.16.3.1 255.255.255.0
encapsulation frame-relay
frame-relay map ip 172.16.3.2 103 broadcast
!
SPOKE-1#sh fram map
Serial0 (up): ip 172.16.3.2 dlci 103(0x67,0x1870), static,
       broadcast,
         CISCO, status defined, active
Serial0 (up): ip 172.16.3.3 dlci 103(0x67,0x1870), dynamic,
       broadcast,, status defined, active
```

SPOKE-2

```
interface Serial0
ip address 172.16.3.2 255.255.255.0
encapsulation frame-relay
frame-relay map ip 172.16.3.1 203 broadcast
SPOKE-2#sh fram map
Serial0 (up): ip 172.16.3.1 dlci 203(0xCB,0x30B0), static,
       broadcast,
         CISCO, status defined, active
Serial0 (up): ip 172.16.3.3 dlci 203(0xCB,0x30B0), dynamic,
       broadcast,, status defined, active
```

HQ

```
interface Serial0
```

```
no ip address
encapsulation frame-relay
!
interface Serial0.1 multipoint
ip address 172.16.3.3 255.255.255.0
frame-relay interface-dlci 301
frame-relay interface-dlci 302
HQ#sh fram map
Serial0.1 (up): ip 172.16.3.1 dlci 301(0x12D,0x48D0), dynamic,
       broadcast,, status defined, active
Serial0.1 (up): ip 172.16.3.2 dlci 302(0x12E,0x48E0), dynamic,
       broadcast,, status defined, active
```

For the hub, notice how everything is minimally configured. Notice how all of the map statements in "sh frame map" are dynamic. They could have been replaced with static map statements but it's not necessary.

With multipoint subinterfaces, you can use either Frame-Relay interface-DLCI statements or Frame-Relay map statements. One will perform dynamic configuration with inverse ARP. The other will statically configure the mappings. *Both do not need to be used concurrently.*

POINT-TO-POINT SUBINTERFACES AT THE HUB

Configuring point-to-point subinterfaces at the hub overcomes the problem of split-horizon without having to disable it. Each PVC will be assigned its own subinterface and the router will treat it as a regular physical point-to-point interface. However, when this configuration is used, each subinterface must be configured as a separate subnet.

If the hub was configured with exclusively point-to-point subinterfaces and the hub was configured with PVCs connecting it to 10 different spokes, 10 different IP subnetworks would need to be configured for each subinterface.

FRAME-RELAY INTERFACE DLCI VS FRAME-RELAY MAP

A common point of confusion with Frame-Relay configuration is when to use Frame-Relay map statements and when to use Frame-Relay interface-DLCI statements. Sometimes attempts are made to use both statements on the same interface or multipoint subinterface. When this is done, surprising results may occur.

If you have a number of Frame-Relay map statements on a physical interface or on a multipoint subinterface and you type a Frame-Relay interface-DLCI statement referencing the *same* DLCI that the map statements were referencing, all of the map statements *will be erased*.

If you have a number of Frame-Relay map statements on a physical interface and you type a Frame-Relay interface-DLCI statement referencing *a different* DLCI that the map statements were referencing, all of the map statements *will remain*.

However, once a Frame-Relay interface-DLCI statement is entered, many map statements can be entered and the interface-DLCI statement will not be removed.

```
interface Serial0
encapsulation frame-relay
frame-relay map ip 172.16.3.4 103 broadcast
frame-relay map ip 172.16.3.5 103 broadcast
frame-relay map ip 172.16.3.6 103 broadcast
frame-relay interface-dlci 103
```

When an attempt is made to remove the interface-DLCI statement with Frame-Relay map statements existing referencing the same DLCI, the following message is generated:

```
interface Serial0
r1(config-if)#no frame-relay interface-dlci 103
%Cannot remove PVC as being referenced by map statement
```

Configuring a Router as a Frame-Relay Switch

With minimal configuration, a Cisco router with multiple serial interfaces can be converted into a Frame-Relay switch. It is essential that internetworking engineers know how to perform this configuration. The commands for configuring a router as a Frame-Relay switch are as follows:

- At global configuration mode type: frame-switch(config)#frame-relay switching
- At the interface mode of interface Serial1, type:

```
frame-switch(config-if)#encapsulation frame-relay
frame-switch(config-if)#frame-relay intf-type dce
frame-switch(config-if)#frame-relay route 102 interface s2 201
```

- At the interface mode of interface Serial2, type:

```
frame-switch(config-if)#encapsulation frame-relay
frame-switch(config-if)#frame-relay intf-type dce
frame-switch(config-if)#frame-relay route 201 interface s1 102
```

The values 102 and 201 in the last statement, "frame-relay route" for both steps two and three are merely examples. Use whatever values you choose between the range of 16 and 1007.

It is extremely important that you know how to interpret the Frame-Relay route configuration command. The first value entered (in the example above: 102 in step two) is the DLCI number that will be announced out of the interface under which this command was typed. If the Frame-Relay route statement was entered under the Serial1 interface on the Frame-Relay switch, DLCI 102 will be announced to whatever router is attached to interface one on the Frame-Relay switch.

The second half of the Frame-Relay route statement in the example above configures the end-point of the other end of the PVC created. All traffic sourced from DLCI 102 on the Serial1 interface of the Frame-Relay switch is destined for DLCI 201 on interface Serial2 of the Frame-Relay switch.

A common-sense method of interpreting the Frame-Relay route statement is:

> All data from DLCI xxx on interface Sx will be destined to DLCI yyy on interface Sx.

Translating the Frame-Relay route statement from STEP TWO in the example above with this statement would yield:

> All data from DLCI 102 on interface S1 will be destined for DLCI 201 on interface S2.

Finally, STEP THREE displays how a mirrored Frame-Relay route statement must be entered on interface Serial2 to complement the Frame-Relay route statement on Serial1.

Two samples of Frame-Relay switch configurations are supplied below. The first is of a full-mesh topology. The second is of a hub and spoke topology.

FULL-MESH FRAME-RELAY SWITCH CONFIGURATION SCRIPT

Note how each interface has two Frame-Relay route statements associated with it. Each Frame-Relay route statement has a complement under another interface.

```
frame-switch#sh run
Building configuration...
Current configuration:
!
version 11.2
no service udp-small-servers
no service tcp-small-servers
!
hostname frame-switch
!
!
frame-relay switching
!
interface Ethernet0
no ip address
shutdown
!
```

```
interface Serial0
no ip address
shutdown
!
interface Serial1
no ip address
encapsulation frame-relay
clockrate 56000
frame-relay intf-type dce
frame-relay route 101 interface Serial2 102
frame-relay route 112 interface Serial3 211
!
interface Serial2
no ip address
encapsulation frame-relay
clockrate 56000
frame-relay intf-type dce
frame-relay route 102 interface Serial1 101
frame-relay route 203 interface Serial3 302
!
interface Serial3
no ip address
encapsulation frame-relay
clockrate 56000
frame-relay intf-type dce
frame-relay route 211 interface Serial1 112
frame-relay route 302 interface Serial2 203
!
!
!
no ip classless
!
!
line con 0
line aux 0
line vty 0 4
login
!
end
```

HUB AND SPOKE FRAME-RELAY SWITCH CONFIGURATION SCRIPT

Notice how Serial1 is configured to serve the hub router. It has two Frame-Relay route statements while Serial2 and Serial3 only have one. Note how the two Frame-Relay route statements under Serial1 are complemented by the Frame-Relay route statements under Serial2 and Serial3.

```
frame-switch#sh run
Building configuration...
Current configuration:
```

```
!
version 11.2
no service udp-small-servers
no service tcp-small-servers
!
hostname frame-switch
!
!
frame-relay switching
!
interface Ethernet0
no ip address
shutdown
!
interface Serial0
no ip address
shutdown
!
interface Serial1
no ip address
encapsulation frame-relay
clockrate 56000
frame-relay intf-type dce
frame-relay route 101 interface Serial2 102
frame-relay route 112 interface Serial3 211
!
interface Serial2
no ip address
encapsulation frame-relay
clockrate 56000
frame-relay intf-type dce
frame-relay route 102 interface Serial1 101
!
interface Serial3
no ip address
encapsulation frame-relay
clockrate 56000
frame-relay intf-type dce
frame-relay route 211 interface Serial1 112
!
!
!
no ip classless
!
!
line con 0
line aux 0
line vty 0 4
```

```
login
!
end
```

CHECKING STATUS OF DLCIS ON A FRAME-RELAY SWITCH

On the Frame-Relay switch "show frame route" can be typed to get a listing of the status of all the PVCs.

frame-switch#show frame route

Input Intf	Input Dlci	Output Intf	Output Dlci	Status
Serial1	101	Serial2	102	active
Serial1	112	Serial3	211	active
Serial2	102	Serial1	101	active
Serial3	211	Serial1	112	active

Under normal conditions, all PVCs should have an "active" status. If any are inactive check the following:

1. The interface configuration of both interfaces related to the "inactive" status listing on the Frame-Relay switch
2. Closely examine the Frame-Relay route statements related to the "inactive" status listing on the Frame-Relay switch
3. The configurations of the routers acting as Frame-Relay DTE devices

LMI

Local Management Interface (LMI) is a set of enhancements to the primary Frame-Relay specification. LMI provides a number of functions including defining keep-alive and status messages sent between the Frame-Relay switch and the Frame-Relay DTE.

With LMI, the Frame-Relay switch and DTE device exchange keep-alive messages every 10 seconds. Every 60 seconds, a full status inquiry is generated listing all DLCIs active for a given Frame-Relay interface. When LMI keep-alive messages get out of sequence, all Frame-Relay connectivity can be lost.

LMI traffic can be viewed with debug frame LMI. Listed below are samples of healthy and unhealthy LMI messages generated by debug frame LMI.

Healthy LMI Debug Messages — Notice that DTE is in the UP state. DTE (myseq) is incrementing by one and SWITCH (yourseq) is incrementing by one. Every 60 seconds, a full status inquiry will be received announcing all of the DLCIs source by the switch.

```
Serial0(in): Status, clock 6799604, myseq 27
RT IE 1, length 1, type 0
KA IE 3, length 2, yourseq 7 , myseq 27
PVC IE 0x7 , length 0x6 , dlci 301, status 0x2 , bw 0
PVC IE 0x7 , length 0x6 , dlci 302, status 0x2 , bw 0
```

```
PVC IE 0x7 , length 0x6 , dlci 304, status 0x2 , bw 0
Serial0(out): StEnq, clock 6809584, myseq 28, yourseen 7, DTE up
datagramstart = 0x400078, datagramsize = 13
FR encap = 0xFCF10309
00 75 01 01 01 03 02 1C 07
Serial0(in): Status, clock 6809600, myseq 28
RT IE 1, length 1, type 1
KA IE 3, length 2, yourseq 8 , myseq 28
Serial0(out): StEnq, clock 6819584, myseq 29, yourseen 8, DTE up
datagramstart = 0x400078, datagramsize = 13
FR encap = 0xFCF10309
00 75 01 01 01 03 02 1D 08
```

Unhealthy LMI Debug Messages — Notice in the LMI messages displayed below, the DTE is in a down state. Notice that all the messages are outbound. The DTE sequence numbers are incrementing by one and the switch sequence numbers are remaining constant.

```
Serial0(out): StEnq, clock 6699584, myseq 17, yourseen 139, DTE
down
datagramstart = 0x400078, datagramsize = 13
FR encap = 0xFCF10309
00 75 01 01 00 03 02 11 8B
Serial0(out): StEnq, clock 6709584, myseq 18, yourseen 139, DTE
down
datagramstart = 0x400078, datagramsize = 13
FR encap = 0xFCF10309
00 75 01 01 00 03 02 12 8B
Serial0(out): StEnq, clock 6719584, myseq 19, yourseen 139, DTE
down
datagramstart = 0x400078, datagramsize = 13
FR encap = 0xFCF10309
00 75 01 01 00 03 02 13 8B
```

If this condition persists, the Frame-Relay device will drop all PVCs. This is reflected by the router console messages displayed below.

```
%FR-5-DLCICHANGE: Interface Serial0 - DLCI 301 state changed to
INACTIVE
%FR-5-DLCICHANGE: Interface Serial0 - DLCI 302 state changed to
INACTIVE
%FR-5-DLCICHANGE: Interface Serial0 - DLCI 304 state changed to
INACTIVE
%FR-5-DLCICHANGE: Interface Serial0 - DLCI 301 state changed to
DELETED
%FR-5-DLCICHANGE: Interface Serial0 - DLCI 302 state changed to
DELETED
%FR-5-DLCICHANGE: Interface Serial0 - DLCI 304 state changed to
DELETED
```

SHOW FRAME-RELAY LMI

To obtain an estimate of the stability of your Frame-Relay connections, use the show frame lmi command. The second to last line of this command reflects the number of LMI status messages sent and received. Under ideal conditions, these values should be equal. Finally, take note of the last entry "Num Status Timeouts." Under ideal conditions, this entry should have a value of zero. If there are any anomolies to the values in sh frame lmi, perform a debug frame lmi and watch the lmi packets enter and exit the router.

```
show frame lmi
LMI Statistics for interface Serial0 (Frame Relay DTE) LMI TYPE =
CISCO
```

Invalid Unnumbered info 0	Invalid Prot Disc 0
Invalid dummy Call Ref 0	Invalid Msg Type 0
Invalid Status Message 0	Invalid Lock Shift 0
Invalid Information ID 0	Invalid Report IE Len 0
Invalid Report Request 0	Invalid Keep IE Len 0
Num Status Enq. Sent 653	Num Status msgs Rcvd 649
Num Update Status Rcvd 0	Num Status Timeouts 3

CISCO IOS VS 11.2 LMI AUTO-SENSING

Cisco supports the following three types of LMI: Cisco, ANSI, Q933a. Prior to IOS version 11.2, the LMI type configured on the Frame-Relay switch must match the LMI-type manually configured on the Cisco router acting as a Frame-Relay DTE. With IOS version 11.2, Cisco routers have LMI auto-sensing. Even when the LMI has been changed on the router while the frame connections are active, the link will temporarily go down due to LMI mismatch but will eventually come back up and LMI auto-sense to adapt to the change. This is an 11.2 feature only.

SUGGESTED CONFIGURATION STRATEGIES FOR FRAME-RELAY

If you encounter a Frame-Relay configuration scenario on a job site, a suggested approach for getting started is listed below.

1. Read the customer requirement carefully.
2. Be able to spot the issues. Common issues can be spotted by asking the following questions:
   - Is it a full-mesh topology or is it a hub and spoke topology?
   - If hub and spoke, should physical or logical interfaces be configured at the hub?
   - If hub and spoke, should physical or logical interfaces be configured at the spokes?
   - What routing protocol is the customer using?

3. If the topology is a partial mesh/hub and spoke topology, be aware of the spoke to spoke reachability issues. Debug frame packet will be useful in verifying spoke-to-spoke reachability.
4. If the configuration involves a combination of logical and physical interfaces, remember which interfaces will need the Frame-Relay interface DLCI statement, which will need the Frame-Relay map statement and which interfaces can rely sole on inverse ARP.
5. If the configuration involves the following three components:
   - a partial mesh/hub and spoke topology,
   - distance-vector routing protocols are being configured over the Frame-Relay network, or
   - a physical or multipoint subinterface is being used at the hub, remember to disable split-horizon at the hub.
6. If the configuration involves the following two components:
   - a combination of logical and physical interfaces used on Frame-Relay connections, and
   - OSPF running over the Frame-Relay network, remember to check for network type mismatches for OSPF.
7. If you change a network layer address on a Frame-Relay interface, clear the Frame-Relay ARP cache on all remote Frame-Relay connections.
8. Remember the progression of using your show/verification tools:
   - Once the interface has been configured with the Frame-Relay encapsulation and is administratively enabled, you should see the DLCIs be announced to appropriate router and attain an "ACTIVE" state.
   - Type show frame pvc to make sure all of the DLCIs are present and active. If subinterfaces have been configured, make sure the right DLCIs are assigned to the correct subinterface.
   - Type show frame map to examine all of the Frame-Relay mappings.

Summary

This chapter began with a brief description of NBMA networks in general and Frame-Relay in particular. This Chapter investigated and demonstrated some of the NBMA characteristics of Frame-Relay. In order for a network layer packet to be forwarded out a physical Frame-Relay interface, a mapping between the remote network layer address and a local DLCI needs to exist. This mapping can be supplied dynamically via inverse-arp or statically via a Frame-Relay map statement. If a mapping was not supplied, debug frame packet will generate the following messages:

```
Serial0:Encaps failed--no map entry link 7(IP).
```

The NBMA characteristics can be circumvented by using point-to-point subinterfaces. When assigning individual DLCIs to a point-to-point subinterface, the IOS treats each DLCI as a conventional point-to-point link.

The NBMA characteristics of Frame-Relay pose several routing protocol configuration challenges. For distance vector routing protocols, the issue involved the rule of split-horizon. For link-state protocols, the rule involved interface type mismatches.

This Chapter provided an introduction to the foundational topics of basic Frame-Relay configuration. If you do not master the topics covered in this Chapter, you will not be able to continue on with more advanced Frame-Relay topics such as traffic shaping and Frame-Relay SVCs. A good measurement of your Frame-Relay knowledge base can be obtained by comparing what has been covered in this Chapter with what is covered in the IOS Configuration Guide Frame-Relay chapter. You can access this chapter through Cisco's on-line documentation at the following URL: **http://www.cisco.com/univercd/home/home.htm.**

Under this URL, access the following hot-links:

Cisco Product Documentation
Cisco IOS Software
Cisco IOS Release
Cisco IOS XX.XX (XX.XX = the version of the IOS)
Configuration Guides, Command References
Wide Area Networking Configuration Guide
Configuring Frame-Relay

This chapter has emphasized configuring IP over Frame-Relay. In upcoming chapters, configuring IPX, AppleTalk, and DECNET will be covered. It is essential to baseline all data-link layer configurations with IP first. If you can't get IP working over your data-link protocols like Frame-Relay, more than likely you will not be able to get IPX or Appletalk to work as well. Remember, baseline everything with IP!

Other Frame-Relay Topics to Review

Once the topics of this chapter have been mastered, spend some time examining the topics below:

- Configuring Frame-Relay Switched Virtual Circuits
- Configuring Frame-Relay Traffic Shaping
- Configuring Compression over Frame-Relay, and
- Configuring Frame-Relay Discard Eligibility.

These topics should be relatively easy to grasp once you have attained a strong understanding of the material covered in this chapter. It cannot be over estimated how important it is to master the material covered in this chapter. If you want to consider yourself minimally competent in Frame-Relay configuration, the issues presented in this chapter should be second nature to you.

Finally, the topics covered in this chapter lay an excellent foundation for you to learn about ATM PVC configuration and configuring routing protocols over an ATM PVC-based network. Both Frame-Relay and ATM are NBMA networks. Many of the same issues you examined in this Chapter will be seen again in Chapter Seven, the Configuring ATM Chapter.

Professional Development Checklist

To consider yourself to be minimally competent in basic Frame-Relay configuration, you should be able to perform the following tasks with a Cisco router:

- Configure a Frame-Relay switch to supply a full-mesh topology
- Configure routers with Frame-Relay interfaces with the encapsulation frame-relay command only
- Configure a Frame-Relay switch to supply a partial-mesh/hub and spoke topology
- Address the spoke-to-spoke reachability issue with Frame-Relay map statements or subinterfaces
- Possess an awareness of routing issues in a Frame-Relay environment

If you don't feel comfortable with these topics, do not go to the next chapter. It is essential that a strong understanding of Frame-Relay be attained before you get into ISDN and Level Two IP topics. *It cannot be stressed enough how important it is to have a strong understanding of Frame-Relay.*

For Further Study

- Cisco IOS Wide-Area Networking Configuration Guide, Cisco Systems, Inc., 1989–1998.
- Cisco IOS Wide-Area Networking Command Reference, Cisco Systems, Inc., 1989–1998.

These two resources are available in hard copy, CD-ROM, and on the Cisco web site at **www.cisco.com**. Extensively search the Cisco web site for sample Frame-Relay configuration scripts and white papers.

URLs

- **www.cciecert.com**
- **www.mentorlabs.com**
- **www.cisco.com**

Can You Spot the Issues?

1. WMC wants to install a Frame-Relay network between its headquarters site and three satellite offices. Each satellite office must be able to communicate with both headquarters and each other. WMC wants to configure the entire Frame-Relay network using inverse-arp but they do not want to pay for a full mesh Frame-Relay topology. Do you see any problems with this scenario?
2. The Wolzac management has a second recommendation. They want a single DLCI announced to each spoke and they want a Frame-Relay map statement on each spoke router providing reachability to the other spoke routers. Since there are three satellite offices, WMC management estimates that only two Frame-Relay map statements will be needed for each spoke. They believe that inverse-arp will provide an adequate dynamic mapping between each spoke and each hub. Something troubles you about this configuration. It somehow relates to having only a single DLCI being announced to each spoke router and the danger of mixing Frame-Relay map statements with the inverse-arp process. What is wrong here? Can you spot the issue?

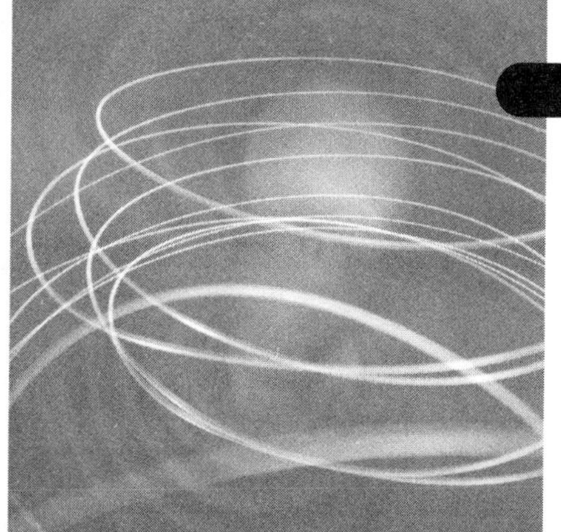

F I V E

Configuring ISDN and Dial-on-Demand Routing

Topics Covered In This Chapter

- ISDN Technical Overview
- DDR Technical Overview
- Configuring ISDN interfaces on Cisco Routers
- Configuring DDR with the Dialer String Statement
- Configuring DDR with Dialer Map Statements
- Configuring DDR with PPP and PPP CHAP
- Configuring DDR with Dialer Profiles
- Configuring Routing Protocols over ISDN/DDR
- Configuring Dial Back-Up over ISDN/DDR
- Troubleshooting ISDN/DDR

The two topics of this chapter work closely together. Integrated Services Digital Network (ISDN) was developed by an international standards organization (formerly known as the CCITT; now known as the ITU-T) to usher in end-to-end digital telephone service for the public switched telephone network (PSTN). ISDN is designed to provide services for both voice and non-voice traffic over an all digital PSTN. Dial-on-demand routing (DDR) is a technology developed by Cisco to harness ISDN services by routers. Although DDR provides routing services over all switched PSTN connections [both plain old telephone service (POTS) and ISDN], its greatest performance is attained over ISDN connections. By applying DDR to ISDN connections, Cisco routers provide an attractive alternative wide-area network (WAN) connectivity solution for sites that generate low volume traffic.

ISDN Overview

Since its inception, the PSTN has been built for analog voice services. Up until the 1960s, the architecture of the PSTN was circuit switched connections carrying analog signals. In the 1960s, dedicated digital connections were introduced to carry voice traffic between PSTN central offices. These digital connections were based upon the "digital signal level zero" or "DS-0." A DS-0 is a single digital voice channel operating at 64,000 bits/sec.

DS-0s were aggregated into groups of 24 channels to form DS-1s. DS-1s comprise what is commonly known as T-1 circuits. Eventually, DS-1 services were offered to end users. However, these connections were dedicated. Since the connections were dedicated, they were expensive and did not scale well.

The CCITT (now the ITU-T) developed ISDN as an architecture to provide switched digital services to transport both voice and nonvoice services over the existing PSTN infrastructure. With ISDN, PSTN subscribers (end users) can send voice, data, and video on the same switched connection. By doing so, ISDN provided a switched, "on-demand" fully digital alternative to dedicated circuits. In November 1992, all major American PSTN carriers participated in National ISDN, a promotion to demonstrate the national deployment of ISDN services throughout the United States. Many carriers have aggressively deployed ISDN in their regions; however, end-user adoption to ISDN has not been as successful as forecasted.

In the mid-1990s, ISDN became a popular method of Internet access for small offices and residences. In the commercial environment, ISDN is popular for accessing remote offices with light traffic requirements and as a hot backup technology for other types of WAN connections such as Frame-Relay.

ISDN services are provisioned to subscribers with three different types of channels:

B Channel	64 Kbps
D Channel	16 Kbps or 64 Kbps
H Channel	384 Kbps (H0) and others

These channel types are combined to offer the following two ISDN interface types:

```
ISDN Basic Rate Interface (BRI)       1 D Channel + 2 B Channels
ISDN Primary Rate Interface (PRI)     1 D Channel + 23 B Channels
                                      1 D Channel + 30 B Channels
```

The D Channel is primarily used for signaling to setup and tear down B and H Channels. The D Channel can also be used for packet switching. A unique factor of the D Channel is that it transports "common-channel" signaling. Common-channel signaling transports signaling messages for multiple data-channels thereby freeing data-channels of over head traffic. B Channels are used for transferring all types of end user traffic: voice, video, and data.

Since the D Channel carries signaling information for B Channels, end users receive a full 64 Kbps "clear channel" for each B Channel. B Channels are used both by ISDN basic rate interface (BRI) and primary rate interface (PRI) interfaces.

H Channels are used by ISDN PRI interfaces only. The H0 channel is equivalent to six B Channels. H Channels are typically used for high-bandwidth services such as videoconferencing.

Another development worth noting is the development of Broadband ISDN. Broadband ISDN is based upon a virtual circuit unchannelized architecture. The core technology of Broadband ISDN is asynchronous transfer mode (ATM). ATM will be covered in Chapter Seven. For the remainder of the chapter, references to ISDN will be for Narrowband ISDN. The core technologies of Narrowband ISDN are the BRI and PRI interfaces mentioned above.

ISDN Components

ISDN hardware, wiring, and physical layer signaling specifications are categorized and outlined in the ISDN "functional groupings" and "reference points." "Functional groupings" define characteristics and interaction between different ISDN physical components. "Reference points" define logical points to separate "functional groups." The goal of defining the "functional groups" and "reference points" is to promote and facilitate standardization of ISDN components.

Examples of ISDN components defined within the category of "functional groupings" are:

NT1 (Network Termination 1) is the boundary between the carrier's ISDN network and the customer premise equipment.
NT2 (Network Termination 2) is a device that manages switching functions and is oftentimes part of a private branch exchange (PBX).
TE1 (Terminal Equipment Type 1) Devices that use the standard ISDN interface. Examples of TE1 devices are digital ISDN telephones and Cisco 2503 routers with a BRI interface.
TE2 (Terminal Equipment Type 2) Devices that do not use the standard ISDN interface. TE2 devices require a terminal adapter (TA).
TA (Terminal Adapter) A Terminal Adapter is used by a TE2 to interconnect into a standard ISDN interface.

Examples of ISDN "reference points" are defined in ITU-T Recommendation I.411:

Reference Point R is the connection between a TE2 and a TA.
Reference Point S is the connection between the end user CPE and the NT1.
Reference Point T is the connection between the NT2 and the NT1.

If no NT2 device is being used (which is the case for virtually all BRI users), the end user customer premises equipment (CPE) to carrier interface is called the S/T interface.

Reference Point U is the exterior terminating point for the carrier PSTN network. The U reference point is comprised of a single pair of wire.

ISDN Layers

Protocols used on the ISDN D Channel are ordered and categorized in a layered format. Two protocols worth mentioning are Q.921 and Q.931. Q.921 is a derivative of high-level data-link control (HDLC). Like HDLC, it is a data-link layer protocol. Q.921 provides constant communication between the ISDN end device and the switch. Q.931 is a network layer protocol. It provides a series of messages for ISDN call set up and tear down. Q.931 uses Q.921 as a transport. Debugging Q.921 and Q.931 output is useful in troubleshooting ISDN connectivity problems. It will be covered later in this chapter.

Dial-on-Demand Routing Overview

DDR is software bundled in the Cisco IOS to provide internetworking services over switched connections such as ISDN or POTS connections. Optimal performance from DDR is attained when it is used over ISDN connections. Combined with the rapid call setup and bandwidth of ISDN, DDR is used for exchanging data between different sites on an "as needed" or "on demand" basis.

A primary benefit of DDR is that it allows a network administrator to specify what types of traffic will initiate an ISDN call. For example, if a network administrator only wants Web traffic to initiate an ISDN connection, DDR will be configured to conform to this policy. Cisco labels traffic that has been specified by DDR to initiate a call as "interesting traffic."

Once "interesting traffic" has initiated a call, all other traffic by default may traverse the ISDN connection. However, only "interesting traffic" will keep the connection active. For example, if what has been specified as "interesting traffic" does not pass over a DDR connection for a period less than the "DDR idle timer," the connection will be terminated.

Working with DDR requires expertise in creating access control lists called "dialer-lists" to define "interesting traffic." If a DDR dialer-list is configured so broadly that it allows undesirable traffic to initiate and maintain an ISDN connection, the result can be that a client receives a $1,000.00 telephone bill for a single ISDN line. If a DDR dialer-list is configured to restrictively, the result can be that critical traffic does not get through.

Two types of DDR implementations currently are available in the Cisco IOS: legacy DDR and Dialer profiles. Legacy DDR applies commands directly

to the physical ISDN interface and relies heavily on dialer-map statements. Dialer profiles apply minimal commands to the ISDN physical interface. Most Dialer profile commands are applied to a virtual interface: the dialer interface. Finally, dialer profiles do not use any dialer map statements.

The main focus of this chapter will be on the configuration of DDR in an (IP) environment. DDR configuration for other protocols such as (IPX), AppleTalk, and DECENT will be covered in Level Four (Chapters 16–18). Keep in mind a sound understanding of DDR with IP will make for a smooth transition into the other protocols.

Configuring ISDN on Cisco Routers

When configuring and implementing routing over ISDN, you are dealing with two protocol stacks running in parallel: one running over the D Channel and another running over the B Channels:

	D Channel	**B Channel**
Data-Link Layer	Q.921	PPP, HDLC
Network Layer	Q.931	IP, IPX, AppleTalk

The ISDN order of operation is as follows:

1. Q.921 signaling between the router ISDN interface and ISDN switch over the D Channel.
2. Q.931 call set up messages are exchanged between calling and called parties over the D Channel. Once the call is set up, virtually all of the D Channel operations are complete. From this point forward, virtually all of the traffic is B Channel traffic.
3. B Channel Data-Link Layer negotiation and establishment (PPP, HDLC, etc.)
4. Network Layer protocols applied over the B Channel (IP, IPX, etc.)

It is essential that you understand the dual stack nature of ISDN configuration. When troubleshooting ISDN configurations, you must know what protocols use the D Channel and what protocols use the B Channels.

ISDN Syntax Overview

When reviewing ISDN configuration commands, it must be stressed that ISDN commands configured on the router must have a complementary configuration on the ISDN switch. For example, if a switch does not have service profile identifier (SPID) numbers configured, you don't need to configure a SPID number on the router. If your is switch is not configured to support caller-id, you cannot configure ISDN caller-id on the interface on your router.

Selecting the ISDN Switch-Type

ISDN configuration on Cisco routers begins with selecting the ISDN switch-type that the router is connected to. This is performed by entering the following global-configuration statement for routers with ISDN BRI interfaces:

```
R3(config)#isdn switch-type ?
   basic-1tr6          1TR6 switch type for Germany
   basic-5ess          AT&T 5ESS switch type for the U.S.
   basic-dms100        Northern DMS-100 switch type
   basic-net3          NET3 switch type for UK and Europe
   basic-ni1           National ISDN-1 switch type
   basic-nwnet3        NET3 switch type for Norway
   basic-nznet3        NET3 switch type for New Zealand
   basic-ts013         TS013 switch type for Australia
   ntt                 NTT switch type for Japan
   vn2                 VN2 switch type for France
   vn3                 VN3 and VN4 switch types for France
```

Once a switch-type is selected and the BRI interface is administratively enabled with the "no shutdown" command, you can immediately determine whether your interface is properly communicating with the ISDN switch by typing `show isdn status` and `debug isdn q921`.

If the router is properly communicating to the ISDN switch, the information listed in `show isdn status` should be similar to what is displayed below:

```
R3#sh isdn stat
The current ISDN Switchtype = basic-ni1
ISDN BRI0 interface
   Layer 1 Status:
      ACTIVE
   Layer 2 Status:
      TEI = 64, SAPI = 0, State = MULTIPLE_FRAME_ESTABLISHED
   Layer 3 Status:
      0 Active Layer 3 Call(s)
   Activated dsl 0 CCBs = 0
   Total Allocated ISDN CCBs = 0
```

Note that layer 1 status is active and layer 2 has attained a state of MULTIPLE_FRAME_ESTABLISHED. Compare these parameters with those listed below.

The following `show isdn status` command lists information of a router that is not communicating with the ISDN switch. Note that the layer 1 status is deactivated and the layer 2 state is TEI_ASSIGNED.

```
R3#sh isdn stat
The current ISDN Switchtype = basic-ni1
ISDN BRI0 interface
   Layer 1 Status:
      DEACTIVATED
```

```
Layer 2 Status:
   TEI = 64, SAPI = 0, State = TEI_ASSIGNED
Layer 3 Status:
   0 Active Layer 3 Call(s)
Activated dsl 0 CCBs = 0
```

If you cannot communicate with the ISDN switch, you can go no farther with your configuration. This is the absolute starting point of ISDN operation.

ISDN PRI Interface Configuration

With ISDN PRI interfaces on Cisco routers such as the model 3600, 4000, and 7500, a PRI switch-type must be defined and PRI controller commands must be entered. Examples of the configuration commands for the controller are displayed below.

```
hostname r4
!
!
isdn switch-type primary-5ess
!
controller T1 0
framing esf
linecode b8zs
pri-group timeslots 1-24
!
interface Serial0:23
n
o ip address
no ip mroute-cache
no cdp enable
!
```

From global configuration mode you will enter controller configuration mode and configure parameters for encoding and frame format. You will also need to build a PRI group and assign time slots to it.

```
controller T1 0
framing esf
linecode b8zs
clock source line
pri-group timeslots 1-24
```

Like an ISDN BRI interface configuration, a PRI switch type must be specified in global configuration mode:

```
r4(config)#isdn switch-type ?
primary-4ess  AT&T 4ESS switch type for the U.S.
primary-5ess  AT&T 5ESS switch type for the U.S.
primary-dms100 Northern Telecom switch type for the U.S.
primary-net5  European switch type for NET5
primary-ntt   Japan switch type
primary-ts014  Australia switch type
```

Once these commands are entered, the Internetwork operating system (IOS) will create 24 interfaces—all identified as serial interfaces numbered zero through twenty-three. Interface S0:23 is the D-Channel. You can check whether your ISDN PRI interface is properly communicating with the ISDN switch with the same commands used for ISDN BRI interfaces: `show isdn status` and `debug isdn q921`:

```
r4#sh isdn status
The current ISDN Switchtype = primary-5ess
ISDN Serial0:23 interface
Layer 1 Status:
 ACTIVE
Layer 2 Status:
 TEI = 0, State = MULTIPLE_FRAME_ESTABLISHED
Layer 3 Status:
 0 Active Layer 3 Call(s)
Activated dsl 0 CCBs = 0
Total Allocated ISDN CCBs = 0
```

You can obtain a summary of the status of each ISDN channel with the `show isdn` services command:

```
r4#sh isdn service
PRI Channel Statistics:
ISDN Se0:23, Channel (1-31)
Activated dsl 0
State (0=Idle 1=Propose 2=Busy 3=Reserved 4=Restart 5=Maint)
0 0 0 0 0 0 0 0 0 0 0 0 0 0 0 0 0 0 0 0 0 0 0 0 3 3 3 3 3 3 3 3
Channel (1-31) Service (0=Inservice 1=Maint 2=Outofservice)
0 0 0 0 0 0 0 0 0 0 0 0 0 0 0 0 0 0 0 0 0 0 0 0 0 0 0 0 0 0 0 0
```

Notice that only the first twenty-three are idle and the remaining eight are reserved. In North America, a PRI is comprised of twenty-three 64 Kbps B Channels and 1 64 Kbps D Channel. In Europe and other parts of the world, an ISDN PRI is comprised of thirty 64 Kbps B Channels and one 64 Kbps channel.

ISDN Interface Configuration Commands

The Cisco IOS provides many interface configuration options for ISDN:

```
R3(config-if)#isdn ?
  all-incoming-calls-v120  Answer all incoming calls as V.120
  answer1                  Specify Called Party number and subaddress
  answer2                  Specify Called Party number and subaddress
  caller                   Specify incoming telephone number to be verified
  calling-number           Specify Calling Number included for outgoing calls
  fast-rollover-delay      Delay between fastrollover dials
  incoming-voice           Specify options for incoming calls.
  not-end-to-end           Specify speed when calls received are not isdn
                           end to end
  sending-complete         Specify if Sending Complete included in
                           outgoing SETUP message
  spid1                    Specify Service Profile IDentifier
  spid2                    Specify Service Profile IDentifier
  static-tei               Specify a Static TEI for ISDN BRI
  twait-disable            Delay National ISDN BRI switchtype from
                           activating interface on powerup
  x25                      Configure x25 over the D channel
```

The above listed commands can only be used if the ISDN switch is configured to support these features. The most commonly configured ISDN interface configuration commands are "`isdn spid1`" and "`isdn spid2`." Service profile identifiers (SPIDs) are used to announce the ISDN device to the switch. If SPIDs are required, your ISDN configuration will not work unless the SPIDs are properly configured. For most installations in the United States, SPIDs are required. However, in many testbed and lab environments, SPIDs are not required. For practical purposes, you should be intimately familiar with ISDN configurations where SPIDS are required and configurations where they are not required.

ISDN SHOW Commands

The IOS provides the following show commands to monitor ISDN usage:

```
Sh isdn stat
Sh isdn hist

Sh isdn active
Sh inte bri0 (shows the status of the D Channel)
Sh inte bri0 1 and sh inte bri 2 (shows the status of both the B
Channels)
```

ISDN Debug Commands

Cisco provides excellent debugging tools for ISDN. These tools allow you to see what is happening on the D Channel with both the calling and the called party.

```
Debug isdn q921
Debug isdn q931
```

`Debug isdn q921` provides data-link layer debugging of q.921 messages. Much of the `debug isdn q.921` messages display S-Frame events of the LAPD protocol.

`Debug isdn q931` provides network-layer debugging of q.931 messages. Performing debug at this level is extremely useful to assure that the ISDN call is being set up, maintained and terminated properly.

Listed below are sample Q.931 traces of ISDN calls being set up:

Call Setup

CALLING PARTY

In the debug trace below, take note of the direction of the messages (TX and RX) and the types of the messages:

```
ISDN BR0: TX -> SETUP pd = 8 callref = 0x04
      Bearer Capability i = 0x8890
      Channel ID i = 0x83
      Keypad Facility i = '2001'
ISDN BR0: RX <- CALL_PROC pd = 8 callref = 0x84
      Channel ID i = 0x89
ISDN BR0: RX <- CONNECT pd = 8 callref = 0x84
ISDN BR0: TX -> CONNECT_ACK pd = 8 callref = 0x04
```

Four message types are exchanged between the calling party and the switch:

```
SETUP
CALL_PROC
CONNECT
CONNECT_ACK
```

CALLED PARTY

As with the calling party, take note of the direction of the messages (TX and RX) and the types of the messages in the debug trace below:

```
ISDN BR0: RX <- SETUP pd = 8 callref = 0x0C
      Bearer Capability i = 0x8890
      Channel ID i = 0x89
      Signal i = 0x40 - Alerting on - pattern 0
```

```
      Calling Party Number i = 'A', 0x80, '2019992002'
      Called Party Number i = 0xC1, '2019992001'
      Locking Shift to Codeset 6
      Codeset 6 IE 0x3C i = 0x1103, '2019992002'
ISDN BR0: TX -> CONNECT pd = 8 callref = 0x8C
      Channel ID i = 0x89
ISDN BR0: RX <- CONNECT_ACK pd = 8 callref = 0x0C
      Signal i = 0x4F - Alerting off
```

Three message types are exchanged between the called party and the switch:

```
SETUP
CONNECT
CONNECT_ACK
```

Notice that only the calling party received a CALL_PROC. The called party neither transmitted nor received a CALL_PROC.

CALL TEARDOWN

The next series of debug traces displays a sample trace of Q.931 messages during call teardown.

CALLING PARTY DISCONNECTING

```
ISDN BR0: TX -> DISCONNECT pd = 8 callref = 0x03
      Cause i = 0x8090 - Normal call clearing
ISDN BR0: RX <- RELEASE pd = 8 callref = 0x83
ISDN BR0: TX -> RELEASE_COMP pd = 8 callref = 0x03
```

CALLED PARTY DISCONNECTING

```
ISDN BR0: RX <- DISCONNECT pd = 8 callref = 0x0B
      Cause i = 0x8090 - Normal call clearing
ISDN BR0: TX -> RELEASE pd = 8 callref = 0x8B
ISDN BR0: RX <- RELEASE_COMP pd = 8 callref = 0x0B
```

LINE IS BUSY

The following debug trace displays the Q.931 messages generated when a line is busy.

```
ISDN BR0: TX -> SETUP pd = 8 callref = 0x01
      Bearer Capability i = 0x8890
      Channel ID i = 0x83
      Keypad Facility i = '2001'
ISDN BR0: RX <- CALL_PROC pd = 8 callref = 0x81
      Channel ID i = 0x89
ISDN BR0: RX <- DISCONNECT pd = 8 callref = 0x81
```

```
      Cause i = 0x8191 - User busy
ISDN BR0: TX -> RELEASE pd = 8 callref = 0x01
ISDN BR0: RX <- RELEASE_COMP pd = 8 callref = 0x81.
```

NO CHANNELS ARE AVAILABLE

No local channels are available to make the call. In a few seconds, we see local release of channels and you can make the call. Sometimes this error is seen when clear interface bri0 is used.

```
ISDN BR0: TX -> SETUP pd = 8 callref = 0x02
      Bearer Capability i = 0x8890
      Channel ID i = 0x83
      Keypad Facility i = '2002'
ISDN BR0: RX <- RELEASE_COMP pd = 8 callref = 0x82
      Cause i = 0x81A2 - No channel available
ISDN BR0: Setup was rejected, cause = 22.
```

ISDN CONFIGURATION SUMMARY

At a minimum, only two commands are required for ISDN configuration on a Cisco router.

```
ISDN switch-type (global configuration command)
No shut (interface command)
```

Once these two commands are entered, type `show isdn status` to make sure the router is properly communicating with the ISDN switch.

All other ISDN commands are optional. You can configure them on the router only if the ISDN switch is configured to support them.

With just two minimum commands, ISDN is ready for service on a Cisco router. (Many times SPID numbers are also required. Your carrier will inform you if SPIDs are required.) Now DDR must be configured. DDR is the Cisco service that determines what type of traffic will initiate an ISDN call and specifically what number must be called.

Configuring DDR

KNOWING FRAME-RELAY HELPS YOU LEARN DDR

To best learn DDR, review the configuration options of Frame-Relay:

The first configuration option of Frame-Relay was a minimal configuration that involved a single command: "encapsulation frame-relay."

This configuration was adequate for simple configurations, but it was not adequate for more complex configurations. Frame-Relay map statements were used for more complex configurations.

Finally, subinterfaces were introduced to make Frame-Relay configurations easier, more flexible and more scalable.

We will follow the same progression with DDR:

First we will configure and examine a simple minimal configuration focusing on using the dialer string command. We will push this configuration to its limits.

Second, we will look at the DDR equivalent to frame-relay map statements, dialer map statements. In many ways, dialer map statement syntax is very similar to frame-relay map statements.

Finally, just as point-to-point Frame-Relay subinterfaces did away with frame-relay map statements, we will do away with dialer map statements with Dialer Profiles.

DDR Overview

Listed below are the basic operational steps that occur when traffic passes over a DDR link.

1. "Interesting traffic" is defined by the network administrator.
2. Interesting traffic initiates a call using a dialer map or dialer string in a dialer profile.
3. The call is set up using the ISDN Q.931 signaling protocol.
4. Data is transferred over the ISDN link.
5. The DDR connection is maintained as long as "interesting traffic" is transferred over the connection before the "dial idle timer" expires.
6. Once the dial idle timer expires, Q.931 tears the connection down.

Once again, recall Frame-Relay map statements from the previous chapter. Dialer maps are the functional equivalent to Frame-Relay maps. A difference is that dialer maps are used for switched connections. Frame-Relay map statements are used with permanent (PVC) connections. DDR Dialer map statements map a remote network layer address with a remote telephone number or "dial string." Frame-Relay maps mapped a remote network layer address with a local DLCI number.

An alternative to the Frame-Relay map statement is the point-to-point subinterfaces. Point-to-point subinterfaces make a single PVC appear as physical point to point connection. With point-to-point subinterfaces, Frame-Relay map statements are not needed.

A parallel can be drawn between the relationship of Frame-Relay map statements and point-to-point subinterfaces with the relationship of dialer map statements with dialer profiles. Just as point-to-point subinterfaces do not use Frame-Relay map statements, Dialer Profiles do not use dialer map statements. Just as a point-to-point subinterface appears to the IOS as another physical interface, Dialer Profile interfaces also appear to the IOS as another physical interface.

DDR SYNTAX OVERVIEW

USING DIALER-LIST AND DIALER-GROUP

There is a single global configuration DDR command: dialer-list. Dialer-list is a required DDR command. It defines what type of traffic will be defined as "interesting." Again, "interesting" traffic is traffic that will initiate a DDR call. Dialer-lists can define interesting traffic in a very broad manner or in a very granular manner. To configure dialer-lists to be granular, configure them with access-lists. Access-lists are a Level Six topic and they will be covered in Chapters twenty-four and twenty-five.

Displayed below is a listing of all the protocol types that can be defined as "interesting."

```
r1-2522(config)#dialer-list 1 protocol ?
   appletalk               AppleTalk
   bridge                  Bridging
   clns                    OSI Connectionless Network Service
   clns_es                 CLNS End System
   clns_is                 CLNS Intermediate System
   decnet                  DECnet
   decnet_node             DECnet node
   decnet_router-L1        DECnet router L1
   decnet_router-L2        DECnet router L2
   ip                      IP
   ipx                     Novell IPX
   llc2                    LLC2
   vines                   Banyan Vines
   xns                     XNS
```

Dialer-List commands only define what is interesting. Configuring a dialer-list alone is completely ineffective. To apply a dialer-list, we need to enter the interface configuration command: dialer-group.

If the dialer-group statement is not applied to the desired interface, no calls will be initiated. The `debug ip packet` and `debug dialer packet` command allows us to see what happens when the dialer-group statement is omitted.

```
IP: s=172.16.1.1 (local), d=172.16.1.2 (BRI0), len 100, sending
BRI0: ip (s=172.16.1.3, d=172.16.1.2), 100 bytes, uninteresting
(no dialer-group defined)
IP: s=172.16.1.1 (local), d=172.16.1.2 (BRI0), len 100,
encapsulation failed.
IP: s=172.16.1.1 (local), d=172.16.1.2 (BRI0), len 100, sending
BRI0: ip (s=172.16.1.1, d=172.16.1.2), 100 bytes, uninteresting
(no dialer-group defined)
IP: s=172.16.1.1 (local), d=172.16.1.2 (BRI0), len 100,
encapsulation failed.
```

Router-1 has the IP address 172.16.1.1 configured on its ISDN BRI0 interface. It is trying to ping ROUTER-2 with the IP address of 172.16.1.2. ROUTER-1 is correctly forwarding the ICMP packets to BRI0. However, since there is no dialer-group applied to the interface, we get the message "uninteresting" (no dialer-group defined). Finally, we see a message that we saw in Configuring Frame-Relay "encapsulation failed."

When a dialer-list is configured and the dialer-group is applied to inte bri0, we see the following debug messages from debug ip packet and debug dialer packet:

```
R3#ping 172.16.1.1
Type escape sequence to abort.
Sending 5, 100-byte ICMP Echos to 172.16.1.1, timeout is 2
seconds:
!!!!!
Success rate is 100 percent (5/5), round-trip min/avg/max = 40/
41/44 ms
R3#
IP: s=172.16.1.2 (local), d=172.16.1.1 (BRI0), len 100, sending
BRI0: ip (s=172.16.1.2, d=172.16.1.1), 100 bytes, interesting (ip
PERMIT)
IP: s=172.16.1.1 (BRI0), d=172.16.1.2 (BRI0), len 100, rcvd 3
IP: s=172.16.1.2 (local), d=172.16.1.1 (BRI0), len 100, sending
BRI0: ip (s=172.16.1.2, d=172.16.1.1), 100 bytes, interesting (ip
PERMIT)
IP: s=172.16.1.1 (BRI0), d=172.16.1.2 (BRI0), len 100, rcvd 3
```

Notice that the IP addresses are being sent to the proper interface. Debug dialer is identifying the IP packets as "interesting" and marking them with "ip PERMIT" and finally the interface is receiving ping response from the remote ISDN interface.

It is recommended that you start out with the basic dialer-list configuration statement:

```
Dialer-list 1 protocol ip permit
```

Apply this dialer-list to the desired interface with the interface configuration command: dialer-group.

This statement permits all IP traffic. Once you have determined that DDR is working with this very basic dialer-list statement make your dialer-list more granular. As mentioned earlier, you can make dialer-lists more granular by applying access-lists with dialer-lists. Access-lists are covered on Chapters Twenty-four and Twenty-five.

REMEMBER: BASLINE EVERYTHING WITH A BASIC IP CONFIGURATION.

The Minimum ISDN/DDR Configuration

In the configurations listed below, both routers maintain the minimum configuration statements.

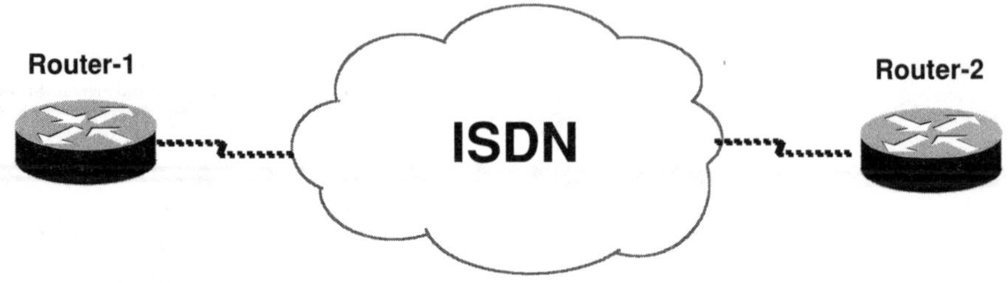

FIGURE 5–1 A minimal ISDN configuration

ROUTER-1#SHOW RUN

```
version 11.3
no service password-encryption
!
hostname ROUTER-1
!
!
isdn switch-type basic-ni1
!
interface Ethernet0
 no ip address
 shutdown
!
interface Serial0
 no ip address
 no ip mroute-cache
 shutdown
 no fair-queue
!
interface Serial1
 no ip address
 shutdown
!
interface BRI0
 ip address 172.16.1.1 255.255.255.0
 dialer string 2002
 dialer-group 1
!
ip classless
dialer-list 1 protocol ip permit
!
!
line con 0
```

```
line aux 0
line vty 0 4
 login
!
end
```

ROUTER-2#SHOW RUN

```
!
hostname ROUTER-2
!
!
isdn switch-type basic-ni1
!
interface Ethernet0
      no ip address
      shutdown
!
interface Serial0
      no ip address
      shutdown
!
interface Serial1
      no ip address
      shutdown
!
interface BRI0
      ip address 172.16.1.2 255.255.255.0
      dialer string 2001
      dialer-group 1
!
no ip classless
!
dialer-list 1 protocol ip permit
!
line con 0
line aux 0
line vty 0 4
      login
!
end
```

As the configurations of both ROUTER-1 and ROUTER-2 reflect, a minimum ISDN/DDR configuration for IP traffic includes five configuration commands (two global and three interface).

Global Configuration Commands

```
Isdn switch-type basic-nil
Dialer-list 1 protocol ip permit
```

Interface Configuration Commands

```
Dialer-group 1
Dialer string 2001
Ip address 172.16.1.1 255.255.255.0
```

The dialer string statement defines the telephone number to call to set up the ISDN connection. If the dialer string is omitted, the following debug messages are generated by debug dialer packet and debug dialer events:

```
BRI0: ip (s=172.16.1.1, d=172.16.1.2), 100 bytes, interesting (ip
PERMIT)
BRI0: Dialing cause ip (s=172.16.1.1, d=172.16.1.2)
BRI0: No dialer string, dialing cannot occur.
BRI0: ip (s=172.16.1.1, d=172.16.1.2), 100 bytes, interesting (ip
PERMIT)
BRI0: Dialing cause ip (s=172.16.1.1, d=172.16.1.2)
BRI0: No dialer string, dialing cannot occur.
```

Notice the message "No dialer string, dialing cannot occur."

When the dialer string is included, the following messages are displayed on the router console:

```
%LINK-3-UPDOWN: Interface BRI0:1, changed state to up
%LINEPROTO-5-UPDOWN: Line protocol on Interface BRI0:1, changed
state to up
%LINK-3-UPDOWN: Interface BRI0:2, changed state to up
%LINEPROTO-5-UPDOWN: Line protocol on Interface BRI0:2, changed
state to up
%ISDN-6-CONNECT: Interface BRI0:1 is now connected to 2002
%ISDN-6-CONNECT: Interface BRI0:2 is now connected to 2019992002
```

Notice that BRI0:1 and BRI0:2 (both B channels) have been activated. This can be further verified by the show dialer command:

```
ROUTER-1#sh dialer
BRI0 - dialer type = ISDN
Dial String Successes  Failures  Last called Last status
2002          3          0         00:00:14    successful   Default
0 incoming call(s) have been screened.
0 incoming call(s) rejected for callback.
BRI0:1 - dialer type = ISDN
Idle timer (120 secs), Fast idle timer (20 secs)
Wait for carrier (30 secs), Re-enable (15 secs)
Dialer state is data link layer up
Dial reason: ip (s=172.16.1.1, d=172.16.1.2)
Time until disconnect 114 secs
Current call connected 00:00:14
Connected to 2002
BRI0:2 - dialer type = ISDN
```

```
Idle timer (120 secs), Fast idle timer (20 secs)
Wait for carrier (30 secs), Re-enable (15 secs)
Dialer state is data link layer up
Time until disconnect 107 secs
Connected to 2019992002
```

Show dialer is a very useful command. It lists the remote telephone number (dial string) this interface is configured to call. It lists the status of both B Channels. It lists the settings for certain timers, most importantly the "dial idle timer." The dial idle timer listed as "idle timer" in show dialer is used to disconnect the call if no interesting traffic travels over the DDR connection during the length of time specified by the idle timer. For example, the dialer idle timer in the listing above is 120 seconds. After 120 seconds, the connection is torn down and the following messages are displayed:

```
%ISDN-6-DISCONNECT: Interface BRI0:1 disconnected from 2002 ,
call lasted 120 seconds
%LINK-3-UPDOWN: Interface BRI0:1, changed state to down
%LINEPROTO-5-UPDOWN: Line protocol on Interface BRI0:1, changed
state to down
%ISDN-6-DISCONNECT: Interface BRI0:2 disconnected from 2019992002
, call lasted 120 seconds
%LINK-3-UPDOWN: Interface BRI0:2, changed state to down
%LINEPROTO-5-UPDOWN: Line protocol on Interface BRI0:2, changed
state to down
```

Note that the call "lasted 120 seconds," the length of time of the idle timer.

THE LIMITATIONS OF USING THE DIAL STRING COMMAND

Although this configuration is simple, it is very limited and nonscalable. In this configuration, HDLC encapsulation is being used. The preferred encapsulation type is PPP. PPP is supported by virtually all end system platforms. With PPP, PAP, and CHAP authentication can be used as well as compression techniques.

The minimal configuration is undesirable due to the following three limitations:

INEFFICIENT USE OF THE B CHANNELS • The B Channels usage is inefficient because both B Channels are set up to support two unidirectional traffic flows. When possible, it is more efficient to use only one B Channel for bidirectional traffic flow. Use the second B Channel only when bandwidth requirements necessitate. In up coming configurations, configuring DDR with PPP encapsulation and dialer maps will allow connections to be establishing using a single B Channel with traffic flowing bidirectionally.

BOTH SIDES OF THE CONNECTION REQUIRE A DIAL STRING • In many configurations, it is desirable to exclude a dialer string from one side of the connection. This prevents a specific connection from ever initiating a call. The connection may receive calls, but it can never initiate a call. With PPP encapsulation and dialer map statements, you can configure DDR so that only one side of a connection possesses a dialer string. With the dialer string statement, it is impossible to distinguish multiple network-layer next-hop addresses with multiple dialer strings. With dialer map statements, network-layer next-hop addresses can be mapped to different dialer strings.

USING A DIALER STRING CONFIGURATION FOR CONNECTING TO MULTIPLE SITES

A dialer string configuration becomes impractical when multiple connections are involved. Assume a scenario where one headquarters router needs to connect to two different satellite offices. If you enter two dialer string statements

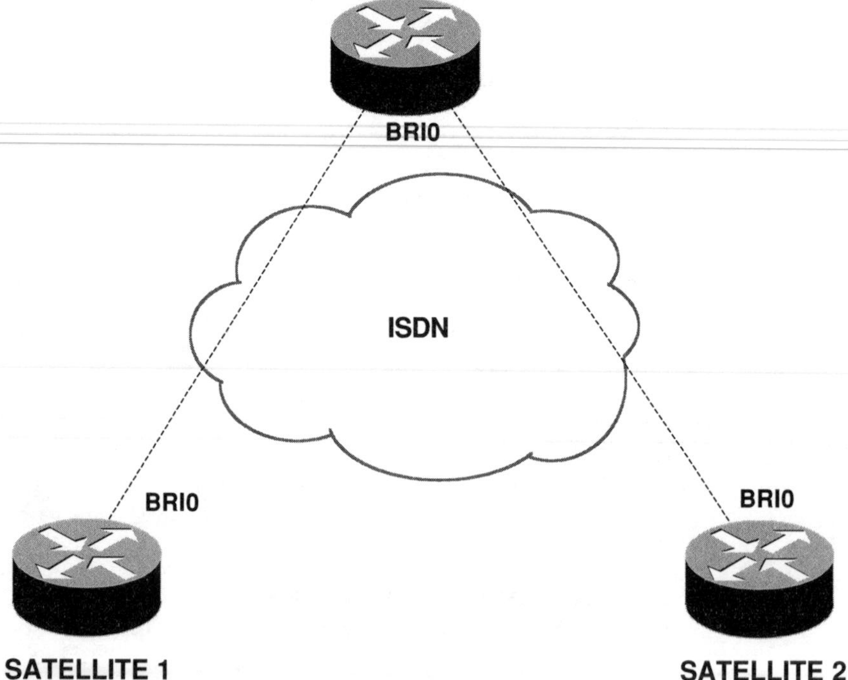

FIGURE 5–2 A multi-site ISDN configuration

with the telephone numbers of each satellite site, you end up with the following configuration for the HEADQUARTERS router:

```
interface BRI0
      ip address 172.16.1.1 255.255.255.0
      dialer string 2002
```

```
dialer string 2003
dialer-group 1
```

Notice that there are now two dial strings associated with BRI0. The router has no way of determining which dial string to use to connect to a specific IP address. For example, SATELLITE-1 has the IP address of 172.16.1.2 and a telephone number of 2002. SATELLITE-2 has the IP address of 172.16.1.3 and a telephone number of 2003. If HEADQUARTERS attempts to ping 172.16.1.2, it will call the first number (2002) and try to ping 172.16.1.2. In this case, this will work. If HEADQUARTERS attempts to ping 172.16.1.3, it will still call the first number on its list (2002) but it will not find 172.16.1.3. The ping will be unsuccessful. This is verified by the following `debug isdn q931` traces.

When we attempt to ping 172.16.1.2 with `debug isdn q931` enabled, the following debug messages are generated:

```
ISDN BRO: TX -> SETUP pd = 8 callref = 0x01
      Bearer Capability i = 0x8890
      Channel ID i = 0x83
      Keypad Facility i = '2002'
```

Notice the dial string used is 2002.

When an attempt to ping 172.16.1.3 with `debug isdn q931` enabled, the following debug messages are generated:

```
ISDN BRO: TX -> SETUP pd = 8 callref = 0x01
      Bearer Capability i = 0x8890
      Channel ID i = 0x83
      Keypad Facility i = '2002'
```

Notice the dial string used is still 2002 because it is the first dial string listed in the configuration script.

To further demonstrate this point, three invalid dial strings are added (2004, 2005, 2006) in the configuration script in the following order:

```
interface BRI0
      ip address 172.16.1.1 255.255.255.0
      dialer string 2004
      dialer string 2005
      dialer string 2006
      dialer string 2002
      dialer string 2003
      dialer-group 1
```

With this configuration, the following debug isdn q931 messages are generated when interesting traffic (in this case IP ping traffic) initiates a call:

```
ISDN BRO: TX -> SETUP pd = 8 callref = 0x02
```

```
        Bearer Capability i = 0x8890
        Channel ID i = 0x83
        Keypad Facility i = '2004'
ISDN BR0: RX <- CALL_PROC pd = 8 callref = 0x82
        Channel ID i = 0x89
ISDN BR0: RX <- DISCONNECT pd = 8 callref = 0x82
        Cause i = 0x819B - Destination out of order
ISDN BR0: TX -> RELEASE pd = 8 callref = 0x02
ISDN BR0: RX <- RELEASE_COMP pd = 8 callref = 0x82.
ISDN BR0: TX -> SETUP pd = 8 callref = 0x03
        Bearer Capability i = 0x8890
        Channel ID i = 0x83
        Keypad Facility i = '2005'
ISDN BR0: RX <- CALL_PROC pd = 8 callref = 0x83
        Channel ID i = 0x89
ISDN BR0: RX <- DISCONNECT pd = 8 callref = 0x83
        Cause i = 0x819B - Destination out of order
ISDN BR0: TX -> RELEASE pd = 8 callref = 0x03
ISDN BR0: RX <- RELEASE_COMP pd = 8 callref = 0x83.
ISDN BR0: TX -> SETUP pd = 8 callref = 0x04
        Bearer Capability i = 0x8890
        Channel ID i = 0x83
        Keypad Facility i = '2006'
ISDN BR0: RX <- CALL_PROC pd = 8 callref = 0x84
        Channel ID i = 0x89
ISDN BR0: RX <- DISCONNECT pd = 8 callref = 0x84
        Cause i = 0x819B - Destination out of order
ISDN BR0: TX -> RELEASE pd = 8 callref = 0x04
ISDN BR0: RX <- RELEASE_COMP pd = 8 callref = 0x84.
ISDN BR0: TX -> SETUP pd = 8 callref = 0x05
        Bearer Capability i = 0x8890
        Channel ID i = 0x83
        Keypad Facility i = '2002'
ISDN BR0: RX <- CALL_PROC pd = 8 callref = 0x8A
        Channel ID i = 0x89
ISDN BR0: RX <- CONNECT pd = 8 callref = 0x8A
```

Notice that ISDN q931 attempted to call every number in the list until it found a number that worked. In this case, the number is 2002. To allow dial strings to be associated with the correct remote network address, other dialer maps or dialer profiles must be used. Dialer profiles will be discussed later in this chapter.

USING DIALER MAP STATEMENTS WITH PPP

Dialer map statements can be used in place of dialer string commands. The commands are mutually exclusive. If you try to type in a dialer map when a dial string currently exists on the interface, the following error message is generated:

```
Router(config-if)#dialer map ip 172.16.1.3 2003
%Cannot change dialer map when dialer string present.
```

To use dialer map statements, you must remove all dial string statements from the interface.

If we add the following two dialer map statements to the HEADQUARTERS router, the router will always use the correct dial string to call the appropriate remote network address.

HEADQUARTERS CONFIGURATION (THE CALLING PARTY)

```
interface BRI0
      ip address 172.16.1.1 255.255.255.0
      encapsulation ppp
      dialer map ip 172.16.1.1 2001
      dialer map ip 172.16.1.2 2002
      dialer-group 1
```

With Frame-Relay, we have a "show frame-relay map" statement to view all next-hop network layer address to local DLCI mappings. With DDR, we have a show dialer map statement to view all next-hop network layer address to remote dialer string mappings. With Frame-Relay, we had both static and dynamic map entries. With DDR, we also have static and dynamic entries. Headquarters has two static map statements listed. Satellite-1 has one dynamic map statement listed. Compare this to the Frame-Relay hub-and spoke configuration in Chapter Four.

```
HEADQUARTERS#sh dialer map
Static dialer map ip 172.16.1.3  (2003) on BRI0
Static dialer map ip 172.16.1.2  (2002) on BRI0
```

Take note of the absence of both a dialer string statement and a dialer map statement from SATELLITE-1.

By using PPP encapsulation and the dynamic dialer mapping feature of the Cisco IOS, only one DDR command needs to be provided to configure SATELLITE-1: the dialer-group command. Since SATELLITE-1 has no dialer map or dialer string, it cannot initiate a call to any other remote site. It can receive calls only.

SATELLITE-1 CONFIGURATION (THE CALLED PARTY)

```
interface BRI0
      ip address 172.16.1.2 255.255.255.0
      encapsulation ppp
      dialer-group 1
SATELLITE-1#sh dialer map
Dynamic dialer map ip 172.16.1.1 name 2019992001 () on BRI0
```

When SATELLITE-1 attempts to initiate a call, it generates the following debug dialer messages:

```
BRI0: ip (s=172.16.1.2, d=172.16.1.1), 100 bytes, interesting (ip
PERMIT)
BRI0: Dialing cause ip (s=172.16.1.2, d=172.16.1.1)
BRI0: No dialer string, dialing cannot occur.
BRI0: ip (s=172.16.1.2, d=172.16.1.1), 100 bytes, interesting (ip
PERMIT)
BRI0: Dialing cause ip (s=172.16.1.2, d=172.16.1.1)
BRI0: No dialer string, dialing cannot occur.
```

By examining the show dialer listing below, notice that only one B Channel is being used to maintain a given connection. In the first configuration using dial strings and HDLC encapsulation, both channels were used to establish one call. Using two B Channels to establish a call is inefficient. Using dialer map statements with PPP encapsulation, two calls can be placed at the same time over the same BRI interface.

```
HEADQUARTERS#sh dialer
BRI0 - dialer type = ISDN
Dial String  Successes  Failures  Last called  Last status
2002         10         250       00:00:05     successful
2003         5          3         00:00:10     successful
0 incoming call(s) have been screened.
BRI0:1 - dialer type = ISDN
Idle timer (120 secs), Fast idle timer (20 secs)
Wait for carrier (30 secs), Re-enable (15 secs)
Dialer state is data link layer up
Dial reason: ip (s=172.16.1.1, d=172.16.1.3)
Time until disconnect 110 secs
Current call connected 00:00:11
Connected to 2003
BRI0:2 - dialer type = ISDN
Idle timer (120 secs), Fast idle timer (20 secs)
Wait for carrier (30 secs), Re-enable (15 secs)
Dialer state is data link layer up
Dial reason: ip (s=172.16.1.1, d=172.16.1.2)
Time until disconnect 114 secs
Current call connected 00:00:07
Connected to 2002
```

The next section examines the PPP connection negotiation process. It is this process that allows the router to perform connection establishment over a single BRI channel.

USING PPP

PPP specifications are outlined in RFC 1548. RFC 1548 describes PPP in the following manner.

The PPP provides a standard method for transporting multi-protocol datagrams over point-to-point links. PPP is comprised of three main components:

1. A method for encapsulating multiprotocol datagrams.
2. A link control protocol LCP for establishing, configuring, and testing the data-link connection.
3. A family of network control protocols (NCPs) for establishing and configuring different network-layer protocols.

The following NCPs are supported by Cisco's implementation of PPP: LEX, DECCP, OSICP, VINESCP, XNSCP, IPCP, CCP, CDP, BRIDGECP, LLC2

ATALKCP, IPXCP, and NBFCP. PPP runs over ISDN B Channels only. The Q.921/Q.931 protocols run over the D Channel only.

Sh interface bri0 lists statistics on the D Channel
Sh interface bri0 1 on sh interface bri0 2 lists statistics on the B Channel. Compare show interface bri0

```
HEADQUARTERS#sh interfaces bri0
BRI0 is up, line protocol is up (spoofing)
   Hardware is BRI
   Internet address is 172.16.1.1/24
   MTU 1500 bytes, BW 64 Kbit, DLY 20000 usec, rely 255/255, load
   1/255
   Encapsulation PPP, loopback not set
   Last input 00:00:00, output 00:00:00, output hang never
   Last clearing of "show interface" counters never
   Input queue: 0/75/0 (size/max/drops); Total output drops: 0
   Queuing strategy: weighted fair
   Output queue: 0/64/0 (size/threshold/drops)
      Conversations 0/1 (active/max active)
      Reserved Conversations 0/0 (allocated/max allocated)
   5 minute input rate 0 bits/sec, 0 packets/sec
   5 minute output rate 0 bits/sec, 0 packets/sec
      10482 packets input, 59828 bytes, 0 no buffer
      Received 0 broadcasts, 0 runts, 0 giants
      0 input errors, 0 CRC, 0 frame, 0 overrun, 0 ignored, 0 abort
      10449 packets output, 60010 bytes, 0 underruns
      0 output errors, 0 collisions, 21 interface resets
      0 output buffer failures, 0 output buffers swapped out
      19 carrier transitions
```

With sh interface bri0, there is no reference to LCPs or NCPs. With show interface bri0 1 and bri0 2, there is a listing for LCP and NCP status. In the show interface bri0 1 below, note the listing of "LCP Open" and "Open: IPCP, CDP."

```
HEADQUARTERS#sh interfaces bri0 1
BRI0:1 is up, line protocol is up
   Hardware is BRI
   MTU 1500 bytes, BW 64 Kbit, DLY 20000 usec, rely 255/255, load
   1/255
   Encapsulation PPP, loopback not set, keepalive set (10 sec)
   LCP Open
   Open: IPCP, CDP
   Last input 00:00:00, output 00:00:01, output hang never
   Last clearing of "show interface" counters never
   Input queue: 0/75/0 (size/max/drops); Total output drops: 0
   Queuing strategy: weighted fair
   Output queue: 0/64/0 (size/threshold/drops)
      Conversations 0/1 (active/max active)
      Reserved Conversations 0/0 (allocated/max allocated)
   5 minute input rate 0 bits/sec, 0 packets/sec
   5 minute output rate 0 bits/sec, 0 packets/sec
      1747 packets input, 144598 bytes, 0 no buffer
      Received 40 broadcasts, 0 runts, 0 giants
      4 input errors, 0 CRC, 0 frame, 0 overrun, 0 ignored, 4 abort
      1775 packets output, 139488 bytes, 0 underruns
      0 output errors, 0 collisions, 21 interface resets
      0 output buffer failures, 0 output buffers swapped out
      300 carrier transitions
```

PPP operation begins with a negotiation process. The states and phases the PPP negotiation process uses can be followed by enabling debug ppp negotiation. A sample PPP negotiation process is displayed below:

```
BR0:1 PPP: Treating connection as a callin
BR0:1 PPP: Phase is ESTABLISHING, Passive Open
BR0:1 LCP: State is Listen
BR0:1 PPP: I pkt type 0xC021, datagramsize 14
BR0:1 LCP: I CONFREQ [Listen] id 3 len 10
BR0:1 LCP:     MagicNumber 0xE06515C8 (0x0506E06515C8)
BR0:1 LCP: O CONFREQ [Listen] id 3 len 10
BR0:1 LCP:     MagicNumber 0xE0FB5C2D (0x0506E0FB5C2D)
BR0:1 LCP: O CONFACK [Listen] id 3 len 10
BR0:1 LCP:     MagicNumber 0xE06515C8 (0x0506E06515C8)
BR0:1 PPP: I pkt type 0xC021, datagramsize 14
BR0:1 PPP: I pkt type 0x8021, datagramsize 14
BR0:1 PPP: I pkt type 0x8207, datagramsize 8
BR0:1 LCP: I CONFACK [ACKsent] id 3 len 10
BR0:1 LCP:     MagicNumber 0xE0FB5C2D (0x0506E0FB5C2D)
BR0:1 LCP: State is Open
BR0:1 PPP: Phase is UP
BR0:1 IPCP: O CONFREQ [Closed] id 3 len 10
BR0:1 IPCP:    Address 172.16.1.2 (0x0306AC100102)
```

```
BR0:1 CDPCP: O CONFREQ [Closed] id 3 len 4
BR0:1 IPCP: I CONFREQ [REQsent] id 3 len 10
BR0:1 IPCP:    Address 172.16.1.1 (0x0306AC100101)
BR0:1 IPCP: O CONFACK [REQsent] id 3 len 10
BR0:1 PPP: I pkt type 0x8021, datagramsize 14
BR0:1 PPP: I pkt type 0x8207, datagramsize 8
BR0:1 IPCP:    Address 172.16.1.1 (0x0306AC100101)
BR0:1 CDPCP: I CONFREQ [REQsent] id 3 len 4
BR0:1 CDPCP: O CONFACK [REQsent] id 3 len 4
BR0:1 IPCP: I CONFACK [ACKsent] id 3 len 10
BR0:1 IPCP:    Address 172.16.1.2 (0x0306AC100102)
BR0:1 IPCP: State is Open
BR0:1 CDPCP: I CONFACK [ACKsent] id 3 len 4
BR0:1 CDPCP: State is Open
BR0 IPCP: Install route to 172.16.1.1
See RFC 1548 for a listing of different PPP states and phases.
```

PPP ADVANCED CONFIGURATION PARAMETERS

Cisco's PPP implementation offers many options. Listed below are all of the PPP interface configuration parameters:

```
r1-2522(config-if)#ppp ?
  max-bad-auth
  authentication        Set PPP link Authentication method
  bridge                Enable ppp bridge translation
  callback              Set PPP link callback option
  chap                  Set CHAP authentication parameters
  compression           Enable PPP Compression control negotiation
  multilink             Make interface multilink capable
  negotiation-timeout   Negotiation timeout period
  pap                   Set PAP authentication parameters
  reliable-link         Use LAPB with PPP to provide a reliable link
  use-tacacs            Use TACACS to verify PPP Authentications
```

PPP AUTHENTICATION

One of the biggest benefits of using PPP is its authentication features. Two authentication techniques are available with PPP: PAP and CHAP. PAP involves a two-step process where the password is actually transferred over the network in clear text. CHAP (RFC 1994) involves a three-step process where the password itself is never passed over the network. The focus of this section is on PPP CHAP authentication.

In order to configure PPP authentication on a Cisco router, a user/password database must be created in global configuration mode. If you don't want to create a local database, you can use a RADIUS or TACACS+ server to manage a user/password combination. We will discuss only configuring a local database on a router.

When creating the local database, enter in the router host name of the remote PPP peer router and the same password for each peer. For example, if you wanted to configure basic PPP authentication between a router with a host name of HEADQUARTERS and a router with a hostname of SATELLITE-1, you will enter the following configuration statements on each router.

CONFIGURATION FOR ROUTER HEADQUARTERS

```
Username SATELLITE-1 password abc123
```

CONFIGURATION FOR ROUTER SATELLITE-1

```
Username HEADQUARTERS password abc123
```

Make sure that the name entered in the user database is identical to the remote peer's router host name. Also, make sure that both sides of the PPP peering connections are using identical passwords. Both username entries and passwords are case-sensitive.

If you want the PPP process to use a name other than a router's host name for the authentication process, enter the following interface configuration command:

```
HEADQUARTERS(config-if)#ppp chap hostname XXX
XXX is the alternate CHAP hostname.
```

If you change your local PPP chap hostname, make sure that this name is entered in the remote PPP peer's local database.

Once the database has been created, you must enter the following three interface configuration commands:

1. Encapsulation ppp
2. PPP authentication chap
3. Dialer map protocol next-hop-address name remote PPP authentication name

These three interface configuration commands are applied to the sample configurations below.

HEADQUARTERS INTERFACE CONFIGURATION

```
HEADQUARTERS(config)#inte bri0
HEADQUARTERS(config-if)#encapsulation ppp
HEADQUARTERS(config-if)#ppp authentication chap
HEADQUARTERS(config-if)#dialer map ip 172.16.1.2 name SATELLITE-1
2002
HEADQUARTERS(config-if)#dialer map ip 172.16.1.3 name SATELLITE-2
2003
```

SATELLITE-1 INTERFACE CONFIGURATION

```
SATELLITE-1(config)#inte bri0
SATELLITE-1(config-if)#encapsulation ppp
SATELLITE-1(config-if)#ppp authentication chap
SATELLITE-1(config-if)#dialer map ip 172.16.1.1 name HEADQUARTERS
```

Notice how the dialer map statement of HEADQUARTERS has a dial string and the SATELLITE-1 dialer map does not. This means that only HEADQUARTERS can make a call to SATELLITE-1. SATELLITE-1 cannot call HEADQUARTERS. If you wanted both sides to call each other, supply a dial string on both sides.

When you see the following error message repeatedly displayed, you have a PPP authentication problem:

```
%LINK-3-UPDOWN: Interface BRI0:1, changed state to up
%LINK-3-UPDOWN: Interface BRI0:1, changed state to down
%LINK-3-UPDOWN: Interface BRI0:1, changed state to up
%LINK-3-UPDOWN: Interface BRI0:1, changed state to down
%LINK-3-UPDOWN: Interface BRI0:1, changed state to up
%LINK-3-UPDOWN: Interface BRI0:1, changed state to down
```

If you see this error message, check your configuration first. Check your database entries as well as the required interface configuration commands. To pinpoint the authentication problem, use the following debug tools:

```
Debug ppp negotiation
Debug ppp authentication
```

With debug ppp authentication enabled, the following messages were generated when a CHAP authentication session was initiated and a PPP peer did not have the name SATELLITE-1 in its database:

```
PPP BRI0:1: O CHAP CHALLENGE(1) id 30 len 28
PPP BRI0:1: Send CHAP challenge id=30 to remote
PPP BRI0:1(i): pkt type 0xC223, datagramsize 32
PPP BRI0:1: I CHAP CHALLENGE(1) id 21 len 28
PPP BRI0:1: CHAP challenge from SATELLITE-1
PPP BRI0:1: USERNAME SATELLITE-1 not found.
PPP BRI0:1: Unable to authenticate for peer.
```

When the name of the challenging peer is not in the database of the receiving peer, the authentication process never goes beyond the challenge phase. Compare this debug trace with the following successful CHAP authentication process.

The following debug ppp authentication trace displays a successful CHAP authentication process:

```
PPP BRI0:1: O CHAP CHALLENGE(1) id 46 len 28
PPP BRI0:1: Send CHAP challenge id=46 to remote
```

```
PPP BRI0:1: I CHAP CHALLENGE(1) id 37 len 28
PPP BRI0:1: CHAP challenge from SATELLITE-1
PPP BRI0:1: O CHAP RESPONSE(2) id 37 len 28
PPP BRI0:1(i): pkt type 0xC223, datagramsize 8
PPP BRI0:1: I CHAP SUCCESS(3) id 37 len 4
PPP BRI0:1: Passed CHAP authentication with remote.
PPP BRI0:1(i): pkt type 0xC223, datagramsize 32
PPP BRI0:1: I CHAP RESPONSE(2) id 46 len 28
PPP BRI0:1: CHAP response received from SATELLITE-1
PPP BRI0:1: CHAP response id=46 received from SATELLITE-1
PPP BRI0:1: O CHAP SUCCESS(3) id 46 len 4
PPP BRI0:1: Send CHAP success id=46 to remote
PPP BRI0:1: remote passed CHAP authentication.
```

In the successful authentication process, three fundamental phases are executed:

- CHALLENGE
- RESPONSE
- SUCCESS

Notice that all three phases are present in the debug trace above. Also, note O and I letters preceding the word CHAP. These letters reflect that the message was generated by an input (I) or output (O) packet. If you don't see combination of input and output packets, check to see if all the packets are inbound or outbound. In troubleshooting, this can be useful to determine the source of the problem.

When the username of the far-side router is misspelled on the calling router, the following debug message is received:

```
PPP BRI0:2: Send CHAP challenge id=2 to remote
PPP BRI0:2: CHAP challenge from satellite-1
PPP BRI0:2: USERNAME satellite-1 not found.
PPP BRI0:2: Unable to authenticate for peer.
```

When the username of the far-side router is spelled correctly, but the password is misspelled on the calling router, the following debug message is received:

```
PPP BRI0:1: Send CHAP challenge id=51 to remote
PPP BRI0:1: CHAP challenge from r2-2503
PPP BRI0:1: Failed CHAP authentication with remote.
Remote message is: MD compare failed
```

DDR PHYSICAL INTERFACE COMMANDS

So far, we have seen the following interface configuration commands related to DDR:

```
Dialer-group
Dialer string
```

```
Dialer map
Encapsulation ppp
PPP authentication chap
```

Out of the interface configuration commands listed above, the dialer map command is the most feature rich and the most commonly misconfigured.

The Dialer map can be configured for the following types of traffic:

```
appletalk            AppleTalk
bridge               Bridging
clns                 ISO CLNS
decnet               DECnet
ip                   IP
ipx                  Novell IPX
llc2                 LLC2
snapshot             Snapshot routing support
vines                Banyan VINES
xns                  Xerox Network Services
```

So far, we have only worked with IP configurations. Later in this chapter, we will review the "snapshot" traffic type. In later chapters, configuration of IPX, AppleTalk, and DECNET over DDR will be covered.

Once the traffic type is connected, the dialer map statement supports the following parameters:

```
WORD                 Dialer string
   broadcast         Broadcasts should be forwarded to this address
   class             dialer map class
   modem-script      Specify regular expression to select modem
                     dialing script
   name              Map to a host
   spc               Semi Permanent Connections
   speed             Set dialer speed
   system-script     Specify regular expression to select system
                     dialing script
```

So far, we have seen the following parameters used in dialer map statements: dial string and name.

INCREMENTALLY ADDING COMPLEXITY TO THE DIALER MAP STATEMENT: ADDING THE BROADCAST PARAMETER

The broadcast parameter allows broadcast traffic to be forwarded and broadcasts will reset the idle timer.

Just as with Frame-Relay map statements, the dialer map broadcast parameter is required for proper OSPF operation over a DDR link. When the broadcast parameter is added, you will see broadcasts initiate and sustain DDR connections. The following show dialer statement displays this:

```
HEADQUARTERS#sh dialer
BRI0 - dialer type = ISDN
Dial String  Successes  Failures  Last called  Last status
2002         6          0         00:00:13     successful
0 incoming call(s) have been screened.
BRI0:1 - dialer type = ISDN
Idle timer (120 secs), Fast idle timer (20 secs)
Wait for carrier (30 secs), Re-enable (15 secs)
Dialer state is data link layer up
Dial reason: ip (s=172.16.1.1, d=255.255.255.255)
Time until disconnect 105 secs
Current call connected 00:00:14
Connected to 2002
BRI0:2 - dialer type = ISDN
Idle timer (120 secs), Fast idle timer (20 secs)
Wait for carrier (30 secs), Re-enable (15 secs)
Dialer state is idle
```

Please note that when the broadcast parameter is added, the DDR link can stay up indefinitely due to constant broadcast traffic. To remedy this situation, granular dialer-lists must be configured.

OTHER COMMONLY USED DIALER INTERFACE CONFIGURATION COMMANDS

- Idle-timeout
- Fast-idle
- Load-threshold

Once these commands are entered, they impact all connections established through the interface.

With IOS version 11.2, Cisco introduced a more modular method of DDR configuration that allows the parameters to be applied to logical dialer interfaces and disposes of using dialer map statements: Dialer Profiles. Dialer Profiles is the next generation implementation of DDR. When you obtain a solid understanding of Dialer Profiles, it is more than likely they will be your preferred method of DDR configuration.

DIALER PROFILES

Dialer Profiles separate many of the configuration parameters used in legacy DDR configurations from the physical interface. Instead of configuring the physical interface, a logical dialer interface is configured. When a call needs to be made using the logical dialer interface, it is bound to a physical interface within a "dialer pool."

THE BENEFITS OF DIALER PROFILES

With Legacy DDR configurations, parameters such as BRI connection speed and dialer idle timers are configured directly on a physical interface. All connections established using that interface will have these parameters applied. With Dialer Profiles, these parameters are configured on the logical dialer interface and are applied only when a connection uses that logical dialer interface. At the time of connection set up, these parameters are bound and applied to a physical interface. With Dialer Profiles, physical interfaces maintain a minimal configuration. The complexity of configuration is shifted to the logical dialer interface.

In an upcoming section, we will review using the IOS dial backup feature. With this feature, a primary interface can be identified and a backup interface can be designated to be used if the primary fails. ISDN/DDR is ideal for acting as the backup interface. When applying dial backup to a legacy ISDN/DDR configuration, the physical interface is placed in "standby" mode. When an interface is in "standby" mode no other traffic can pass over it. This is a tremendous limitation of using dial backup with legacy ISDN/DDR. With dialer profiles, the logical dialer interface is in standby mode and the physical interfaces are free to be used for other services.

DIALER PROFILE CONFIGURATION REQUIREMENTS

Configuration of a Physical Interface
Configuration of a Logical Dialer Interface
Optional MAP-CLASS Configuration

You cannot have legacy dialer configuration statements on the physical interface when you are trying to configure dialer profiles. If you try to type a Dialer Profile statement on an interface configured for legacy DDR, you get an error message:

```
r4(config-if)#dialer pool-member 1
%Remove Legacy DDR Configuration first
```

If you try to add legacy DDR commands to an interface configured for dialer profiles, you get the following results:

```
r4(config-if)#dialer-group 1
%Remove Dialer Profile Configuration first
```

CONFIGURATION OF THE PHYSICAL BRI/ASYNC INTERFACE:

First, remove all legacy DDR commands from the physical interface. This includes:

```
Dialer map statements
Dialer group statements
Network layer addresses
```

Second, assign the physical interface to a specific dialer pool.

```
r4(config-if)#dialer pool-member 1 ?
     max-link Maximum number of B channels for pool
     min-link Minimum number of B channels for pool
     priority Priority of interface in pool
     <cr>
```

A physical interface can be associated with multiple dialer pools. A logical "dialer interface" can be associated with only one dialer pool.

Other commonly configured Dialer Profile physical interface configuration commands include:

```
Encapsulation PPP
PPP Authentication CHAP
```

CONFIGURATION OF A LOGICAL DIALER INTERFACE:

Configuration of a Dialer interface includes:

1. Configuring "dialer remote-name"
   - Only one name can be associated with a specific dialer interface. A unique dialer remote-name must be used for every dialer interface created.
2. Associate a dialer pool (a pool of physical interfaces) with the logical dialer interface:
   - Dialer pool 1
   - You can have only one dialer pool per dialer interface.
3. Apply a dialer-group statement to define interesting traffic.
4. Provide a dialer string to call.

This command is needed only if you want the interface to be the "calling" interface. If you want the interface to receive calls only, do not enter a dialer string. Dialer Profiles allow you to have multiple dial strings per dialer interface; however, it is not recommended. If multiple dialer strings are applied to the same logical dialer interface, the same problem of having multiple dialer strings in legacy DDR arises. Listed below are all the dialer parameters (excluding dialer-group) for a Dialer Profile logical interface:

```
r4(config-if)#dialer ?
  callback-secure   Enable callback security
  caller            Specify telephone number to be screened
  enable-timeout    Set length of time an interface stays down be-
                    fore it is available for dialing
  fast-idle         Set idle time before disconnecting line with an
                    unusually high level of contention
  hold-queue        Configure output hold queue
  idle-timeout      Set idle time before disconnecting line
  in-band           Set v.25bis dialing for interface
```

```
  load-threshold     Specify threshold for placing additional calls
  max-call           Specify maximum number of calls
  pool               Specify dialer pool to be used
  remote-name        Configure a remote name
  rotor              Set outbound rotor order
  snapshot           Specify snapshot sequence number for Dialer
                     Profiles
  string             Specify telephone number to be passed to DCE
                     device
wait-for-carrier-    How long the router will wait for carrier
time
```

There are no dialer map statements with dialer profiles. Notice that there is no MAP parameter for the dialer statement under "interface dialer 0":

Notice no next hop parameters like in the dialer map statement.

Notice no broadcast parameter like in the dialer map statement.

A new command, remote-name, exists under logical dialer interfaces that did not exist under physical interface legacy DDR configuration.

Instead of static dialer maps, dynamic dialer maps are automatically generated by dialer profiles:

```
Dynamic dialer map ip 172.16.1.11 name 2001 () on Dialer0
```

OPTIONAL MAP-CLASS CONFIGURATION

With MAP-CLASS statements, you can reduce repetitive configuration of multiple logical dialer interfaces. Instead of typing in commands such as idle-timeout and fast-idle on multiple dialer interfaces, configure a map-class once and apply to as many dialer interfaces as desired.

```
HEADQUARTERS(config-map-clas)#dialer ?
  callback-server         Enable callback return call
  enable-timeout          Set length of time an interface stays down
                          be fore it is available for dialing
  fast-idle               Set idle time before disconnecting line
                          with an unusually high level of contention
  idle-timeout            Set idle time before disconnecting line
  isdn                    ISDN Settings
  voice-call              Dial the configured number as a voice call
  wait-for-carrier-time   How long the router will wait for carrier
HEADQUARTERS(config-map-clas)#dialer isdn ?
  spc                     Semi Permanent Connections
                          speedSet ISDN speed
                          <cr>
```

MINIMAL DIALER PROFILE CONFIGURATION

Displayed below is a minimal dialer profile configuration:

```
interface BRI0
```

```
      no ip address
      encapsulation ppp
      ppp authentication chap
      dialer pool-member 1
!
interface Dialer0
      ip address 172.16.1.3 255.255.255.0
      encapsulation ppp
      dialer remote-name r3
      dialer string 2001
      dialer pool 1
      dialer-group 1
      ppp authentication chap
!
no ip classless
!
dialer-list 1 protocol ip permit
!
```

When a Dialer Profiles based connection is established, messages similar to those listed below appear on the router console:

```
%LINK-3-UPDOWN: Interface BRI0:1, changed state to up
%DIALER-6-BIND: Interface BRI0:1 bound to profile Dialer0
%LINK-3-UPDOWN: Interface BRI0:2, changed state to up
%DIALER-6-BIND: Interface BRI0:2 bound to profile Dialer1
%LINEPROTO-5-UPDOWN: Line protocol on Interface BRI0:1, changed
state to up
%LINEPROTO-5-UPDOWN: Line protocol on Interface BRI0:2, changed
state to up
%ISDN-6-CONNECT: Interface BRI0:1 is now connected to 2002
%ISDN-6-CONNECT: Interface BRI0:2 is now connected to 2003
```

When a connection is established between two DDR interfaces using Dialer Profiles, both the calling and the called interfaces create and maintain dynamic dialer maps. With legacy DDR, if dialer maps are used, the calling side would need to maintain static dialer maps. With Dialer Profiles no interface needs to maintain static dialer maps. With Dialer Profiles, dialer map statements are prohibited.

```
HEADQUARTERS#sh dialer map
Dynamic dialer map ip 140.10.1.20 name SATELLITE-1 on Dialer0
Dynamic dialer map ip 172.16.1.2 name SATELLITE-1 on Dialer1
SATELLITE-1#sh dialer map
Dynamic dialer map ip 140.10.1.1 name backup () on Dialer0
Dynamic dialer map ip 172.16.1.1 name policy-hq () on Dialer1
```

With show dialer, notice the addition of the dialer profile statements at the top of the display:

```
SATELLITE-1#sh dialer

Dialer0 - dialer type = DIALER PROFILE
Idle timer (120 secs), Fast idle timer (20 secs)
Wait for carrier (30 secs), Re-enable (15 secs)
Dialer state is data link layer up

Dial String   Successes   Failures   Last called   Last status

Dialer1 - dialer type = DIALER PROFILE
Idle timer (120 secs), Fast idle timer (20 secs)
Wait for carrier (30 secs), Re-enable (15 secs)
Dialer state is data link layer up

Dial String   Successes   Failures   Last called   Last status

BRI0 - dialer type = ISDN

Dial String   Successes   Failures   Last called   Last status
0 incoming call(s) have been screened.
0 incoming call(s) rejected for callback.

BRI0:1 - dialer type = ISDN
Idle timer (120 secs), Fast idle timer (20 secs)
Wait for carrier (30 secs), Re-enable (15 secs)
Dialer state is data link layer up
Interface bound to profile Dialer1
Time until disconnect 119 secs
Connected to 2019992001 (policy-hq)

BRI0:2 - dialer type = ISDN
Idle timer (120 secs), Fast idle timer (20 secs)
Wait for carrier (30 secs), Re-enable (15 secs)
Dialer state is data link layer up
Interface bound to profile Dialer0
Time until disconnect 39 secs
Connected to 2019992001 (backup)
```

CONFIGURING PPP CHAP AUTHENTICATION WITH DIALER PROFILES

In order to configure PPP CHAP authentication with dialer profiles, enter the "PPP authentication chap" statement at both the physical interface and the logical dialer interface.

At the dialer interface level, make sure that the dialer remote-name of the called party matches the remote peer (calling) router's host name or the remote peer router's manually configured "ppp chap hostname" name.

As with legacy DDR, make sure that each router has a local database entry of either the remote router's host name or ppp chap hostname. These names are case sensitive and the passwords for each remote peer entry must be the same.

The dialer remote-name statement is critical for the called party. It must match the calling parties host name or the name specified in the calling party's ppp chap hostname statement. For the calling party, the PPP name that is critical is the router host name or, if used, the ppp chap host name. Whatever that is for the calling party, that is what is used. The remote-name can be any string for the calling party only. It is not relevant to the authentication process.

Listed below is a sample configuration. It involves a unique configuration: two dialer interfaces configured to call the same remote destination. This configuration can be useful for situations where one dialer interface will be used for dial backup purposes (it will be in standby mode) and the other will be used to route other traffic. The single greatest challenge of the configuration involves the inability to use the same dialer remote-name twice to call the same router. Take note of how this issue is resolved.

```
hostname HEADQUARTERS (The Calling Router)
!
username SATELLITE-1 password cisco
isdn switch-type basic-ni1
!
interface BRI0
      no ip address
      encapsulation ppp
      dialer pool-member 1
      ppp authentication chap
!
interface Dialer0
      ip address 140.10.1.1 255.255.255.0
      encapsulation ppp
      dialer remote-name SATELLITE-1
      dialer string 2002
      dialer pool 1
      dialer-group 1
      no cdp enable
      ppp authentication chap
      ppp chap hostname backup
!
interface Dialer1
      ip address 172.16.1.1 255.255.255.0
      encapsulation ppp
      dialer remote-name policy-1
      dialer string 2002
      dialer pool 1
      dialer-group 1
      no cdp enable
      ppp authentication chap
      ppp chap hostname oregon
!
```

```
dialer-list 1 protocol ip permit
```

Take note of the following settings in the configuration above:

1. Only one username, SATELLITE-1 is listed in router HEADQUARTERS' local database.
2. Even though HEADQUARTERS is calling the same destination, it uses different dialer remote-names. If the same dialer remote-name is entered on two separate dialer interfaces, an error message is generated.
3. Each dialer interface has a different "ppp chap hostname" specified. Under interface dialer 0, the ppp chap hostname is "backup." Under dialer 1, the name is "oregon."

Compare these configuration parameters to those on the called router's configuration script:

```
SATELLITE-1#sh run (The called router.)
hostname SATELLITE-1
!
username HEADQUARTERS password 0 cisco
username backup password 0 cisco
username oregon password 0 cisco
isdn switch-type basic-ni1
!
interface BRI0
      no ip address
      encapsulation ppp
      dialer pool-member 1
      ppp authentication chap
!
interface Dialer0
      ip address 140.10.1.20 255.255.255.0
      encapsulation ppp
      dialer remote-name backup
      dialer pool 1
      dialer-group 1
      ppp authentication chap
!
interface Dialer1
      ip address 172.16.1.2 255.255.255.0
      encapsulation ppp
      dialer remote-name oregon
      dialer pool 1
      dialer-group 1
      ppp authentication chap
!
dialer-list 1 protocol ip permit
```

Take note of the following settings in the configuration above:

1. Three usernames are listed in SATELLITE-1's local database: HEADQUARTERS, backup, and oregon.
2. Even though SATELLITE-1 is calling the same destination, it is using different dialer remote-names. If the same dialer remote-name is entered on two separate dialer interfaces, an error message is generated. Notice how the dialer remote-names match the ppp chap hostnames listed under the dialer interfaces of the HEADQUARTERS router. If they did not match, PPP CHAP authentication will fail.

It is easy to get confused with a configuration like the one displayed above. Make sure that all names and passwords match.

ROUTING TRAFFIC OVER ISDN/DDR

With Frame-Relay, configuration issues are encountered with certain types of routing protocols running over specific types of Frame-Relay topologies. We will see that there is a different set of issues with routing protocols running over ISDN. For example, distance vector routing protocols constantly send out a full routing table on a fixed interval of time (default of 30 seconds for IP RIP; 60 seconds for IPX RIP; 90 seconds for IGRP), such updates would keep the ISDN line up indefinitely.

For link state routing protocols such as OSPF, hello packets are transmitted at fixed intervals to assure that a neighbor is reachable. By default, OSPF multicasts hello packets every 10 seconds in broadcast interfaces and every 30 seconds for nonbroadcast and point-to-multipoint links. Hello packets will keep an ISDN link up indefinitely.

Three configuration methods will be presented for routing over DDR:

1. Static route configuration with use of dialer-lists that filter routing updates
2. SNAPSHOT routing for distance vector routing protocols
3. OSPF Demand Circuit

USING STATIC ROUTES AND RESTRICTIVE DIALER-LIST STATEMENTS

By relying solely on static routes, all dynamic routing processes can be disabled over the DDR link. Static routes are sometimes an undesirable solution because they do not scale well and have limited capabilities to adjust to changes in an internetwork's topology.

However, if you are configuring a static route on a branch office router that uses the ISDN connection as the single path out of the branch office, a static default route is an excellent configuration choice.

If you choose to configure static routes on your ISDN/DDR routers, it is highly likely that you do not need to add the broadcast parameter to your dialer map statements. You can also create restrictive dialer-lists that will further limit any type of router to router update traffic.

SNAPSHOT ROUTING

An alternative to static routes is enabling a distance vector routing protocol, such as RIP and IGRP and enabling snapshot routing. Snapshot routing is designed to provide a remedy for the constant periodic updates generated by distance vector routing protocols. Snapshot routing is not just applied to IP-based distance vector routing protocols. It can be applied to IPX/RIP and AppleTalk RTMP as well.

Snapshot routing operates by defining a routing protocol update "active period" and "quiet period." An active period is defined when distance vector routing processes may exchange routing table updates. After the active period expires, a quiet period is maintained where routing updates are suppressed, but the routes remain in the routing table.

All snapshot routing configuration is performed at the interface configuration mode. Configuration involves defining a snapshot client and snapshot server. Important snapshot routing monitoring and debugging tools are listed below:

1. Show snapshot
2. Clear snapshot
3. Debug snapshot

CONFIGURING SNAPSHOT ROUTING OVER ISDN/DDR

Snapshot routing configuration involves configuring a snapshot client and snapshot server. Typically, the snapshot client is a branch office and the snapshot server is the headquarters or "hub" office. With snapshot routing, the snapshot client is the "calling" party and the snapshot server is the "called" party.

Snapshot routing is useful in a hub and spoke switched topology where spokes need to obtain routing information.

CONFIGURING THE SNAPSHOT CLIENT

Configuring the snapshot client in a legacy DDR environment involves two interface configuration commands:

1. Dialer map snapshot
2. Snapshot client

The dialer-map snapshot interface configuration command specifies a sequence number and a dial string (a telephone number to call to initiate a snapshot "active period").

The snapshot client interface configuration command specifies the snapshot active period and quiet period. Both active and quiet period times are defined in minutes. Two additional parameters can be added to the snapshot client configuration command:

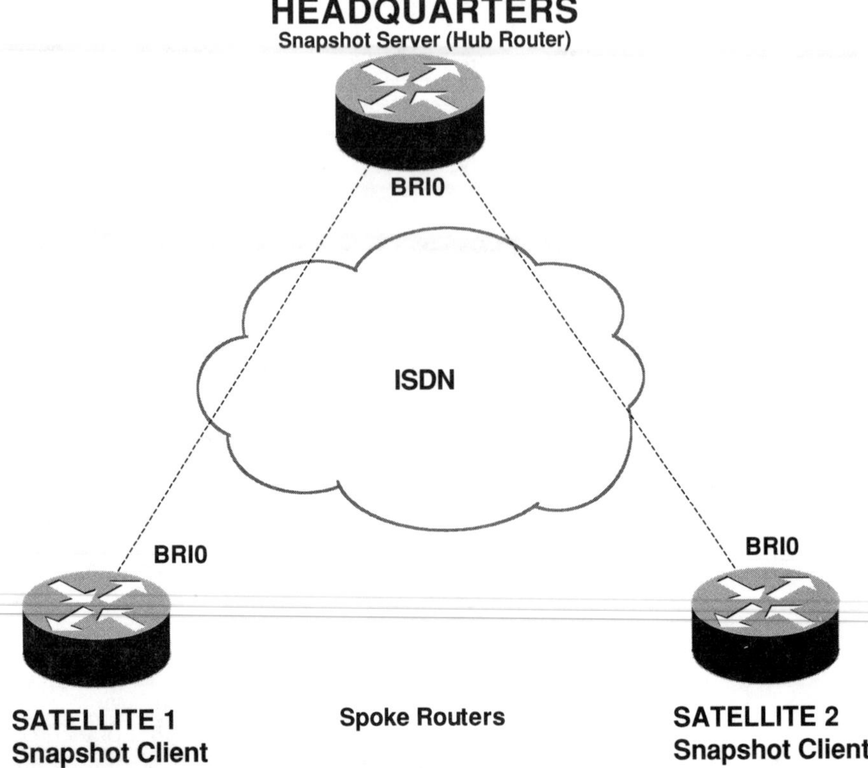

FIGURE 5–3 A snapshot routing configuration

1. Suppress-statechange-updates
2. Dialer

The suppress-statechange-updates parameters prevents routing table updates from being exchanged when other interesting traffic has activated the interface that snapshot routing is configured on.

The dialer parameter enables the snapshot client to initiate a call to start the active period for exchanging routing table updates.

Listed below are sample displays of a snapshot client configuration and output generated by show snapshot, clear snapshot, and debug snapshot.

```
interface BRI0
   ip address 172.16.1.1 255.255.255.0
   encapsulation ppp
   dialer map snapshot 60 2002
   dialer map ip 172.16.1.2 broadcast 2002
   dialer-group 1
   snapshot client 5 1200 supress-statechange-updates dialer
```

In the show snapshot display below, notice that the current snapshot state is "quiet." However, when the clear snapshot command is used, it manually sets the snapshot client into an "active" state.

```
r3#show snapshot
BRI0 is up, line protocol is upSnapshot client
   Options: dialer support
   Length of active period:          5 minutes
   Length of quiet period:           8 minutes
   Length of retry period:           8 minutes
   For dialer address 60
   Current state: quiet, remaining:   7 minutes

r3#clea snapshot quiet-time bri 0

BRI0: snapshot, 2 bytes, interesting (set by snapshot)
BRI0: Dialing cause snapshot
SNAPSHOT: BRI0[60]: Move to active queue (Operator intervention)
SNAPSHOT: BRI0[60]: moving to active queue
```

CONFIGURING THE SNAPSHOT SERVER

The Snapshot server router is the headquarters router. It is the source of all the routing table updates for the spoke routers. The spoke routers act as snapshot clients that call and request routing table updates. When snapshot clients call to request routing table updates, the snapshot server "serves" the updates to the clients.

Configuring a snapshot server requires only one interface configuration command: the snapshot server command. The snapshot server command has two parameters:

1. Active period interval (measured in minutes)
2. Dialer (allowing a DDR call to be made to initiate a snapshot session in the absence of other "interesting" traffic initiating a DDR call)

Listed below are sample displays of a snapshot server configuration and output generated by show snapshot, clear snapshot, and debug snapshot.

```
interface BRI0
   ip address 172.16.1.2 255.255.255.0
   encapsulation ppp
   dialer map ip 172.16.1.1 broadcast 2001
   dialer-group 1
   snapshot server 5 dialer
```

Notice in the show command displayed below that the snapshot server does not list the length of the quiet period. It lists the length of the active period only. The snapshot client defines the quiet period in snapshot routing.

```
r2#sh snapshot
BRI0 is up, line protocol is upSnapshot server
   Options: dialer support
   Length of active period:5 minutes
   For ip address: 172.16.1.1
   Current state: server post active, remaining time: 0 minutes
```

Notice in the following clear snapshot display that the snapshot server cannot initiate a snapshot session. Only the snapshot server can initiate a snapshot session. Remember, only the snapshot client uses the dialer map snapshot statement. Therefore, only the snapshot client is supplied with a dial string (a telephone number) to call.

```
r2#clea snap quiet-time bri0
SNAPSHOT: Interface is not the client side.
```

Notice in the routing table below, that the last entry (150.10.0.0/16) has an age of 10:22. This is well beyond the default hold down and routing entry flush limit of IP RIP. It has been retained in the routing table because it was learned through Snapshot routing.

```
r2#sh ip ro
Codes: C - connected, S - static, I - IGRP, R - RIP, M - mobile,
B - BGP    D - EIGRP, EX - EIGRP external, O - OSPF, IA - OSPF
inter area    N1 - OSPF NSSA external type 1, N2 - OSPF NSSA
external type 2    E1 - OSPF external type 1, E2 - OSPF external
type 2, E - EGP i - IS-IS, L1 - IS-IS level-1, L2 - IS-IS level-
2, * - candidate default U - per-user static route, o - ODR
Gateway of last resort is not set
   172.16.0.0/24 is subnetted, 1 subnets
C     172.16.17.0 is directly connected, Serial0
   177.11.0.0/24 is subnetted, 1 subnets
C     177.11.1.0 is directly connected, BRI0
   149.10.0.0/24 is subnetted, 1 subnets
C     149.10.1.0 is directly connected, Loopback0
R  150.10.0.0/16 [120/1] via 177.11.1.1, 00:10:22, BRI0
```

DEBUGGING SNAPSHOT ROUTING

You can trace snapshot routing operations with the following debugging tools:

1. Debug snapshot
2. Debug dialer packet
3. Debug dialer events

Debug snapshot output always begins with the SNAPSHOT: prompt. It lists the change in state of snapshot operation. Sample debug snapshot output is provided below:

```
SNAPSHOT: BRI0[60]: Move to active queue (Operator intervention)
SNAPSHOT: BRI0[60]: moving to active queue
SNAPSHOT: BRI0[60]: moving to client post active->active queue
```

Debug dialer packet and debug dialer events are also useful for troubleshooting snapshot routing. They illustrate how the snapshot routing process provides an exception to dial-on-demand routing and dialer-lists.

Notice in the debug dialer packet and debug dialer events trace displayed below, that packets that have the destination address of 255.255.255.255 are being defined as "uninteresting" by DDR. Following the word "uninteresting" is "set by snapshot" in parenthesis. This statement means that a dialer-list did not define this packet as uninteresting; the snapshot routing process did. The packet with a 255.255.255.255 is a routing table update being suppressed during the snapshot quiet period.

Debug dialer events displayed the statements "snapshot, 2 bytes, interesting (set by snapshot)" and "Dialing cause snapshot." These statements along with debug snapshot allow an internetwork engineer to trace when a snapshot process is moving from a quiet state to an active state.

BRI0: snapshot, 2 bytes, interesting (set by snapshot)
BRI0: Dialing cause snapshot

```
BRI0: ip (s=172.16.1.2, d=255.255.255.255), 92 bytes,
uninteresting (set by snapshot)
BRI0: ip (s=172.16.1.2, d=255.255.255.255), 32 bytes,
uninteresting (set by snapshot)
BRI0: snapshot, 2 bytes, interesting (set by snapshot)
```

OSPF and DDR

The primary issue with configuring OSPF over an ISDN/DDR link is the OSPF hello traffic will keep the ISDN line up indefinitely. Cisco has a solution to limit OPSF hello traffic over an ISDN link: IP OSPF DEMAND-CIRCUIT (an interface configuration command).

In the show dialer statement below, notice that interface BRI0:1 was activated by a packet with the destination address of 224.0.0.5. This IP address is an OSPF multicast.

```
r2#show dialer
BRI0 - dialer type = ISDN
Dial String  Successes  Failures  Last called   Last status
2001         6          1         00:00:57      successful
0 incoming call(s) have been screened.
0 incoming call(s) rejected for callback.
BRI0:1 - dialer type = ISDN
Idle timer (120 secs), Fast idle timer (20 secs)
Wait for carrier (30 secs), Re-enable (15 secs)
```

```
Dialer state is data link layer up
Dial reason: ip (s=177.11.1.2, d=224.0.0.5)
Time until disconnect 112 secs
Connected to 2001
BRI0:2 - dialer type = ISDN
Idle timer (120 secs), Fast idle timer (20 secs)
Wait for carrier (30 secs), Re-enable (15 secs)
Dialer state is idle
r2#show dialer
```

In the debug dialer packet and debug ip ospf packet output displayed below, you can see that OSPF multicast traffic is constantly going over the BRI0 line:

```
BRI0: ip (s=177.11.1.2, d=224.0.0.5), 68 bytes, interesting (ip
PERMIT)
BRI0: sending broadcast to ip 177.11.1.1
OSPF: rcv. v:2 t:1 l:48 rid:177.11.1.1
   aid:0.0.0.0 chk:B982 aut:0 auk: from BRI0
OSPF: Rcv hello from 177.11.1.1 area 0 from BRI0 177.11.1.1
OSPF: End of hello processing
BRI0: ip (s=177.11.1.2, d=224.0.0.5), 68 bytes, interesting (ip
PERMIT)
BRI0: sending broadcast to ip 177.11.1.1
OSPF: rcv. v:2 t:1 l:48 rid:177.11.1.1
   aid:0.0.0.0 chk:B982 aut:0 auk: from BRI0
OSPF: Rcv hello from 177.11.1.1 area 0 from BRI0 177.11.1.1
OSPF: End of hello processing
BRI0: ip (s=177.11.1.2, d=224.0.0.5), 68 bytes, interesting (ip
PERMIT)
BRI0: sending broadcast to ip 177.11.1.1
```

OSPF OVER ISDN/DDR WITHOUT ON-DEMAND CIRCUIT

In the OSPF show commands displayed below, notice that a timer value is defined in show ip ospf neighbor and no entries are marked DNA (DO NOT AGE) in the link state data base. Therefore, OSPF hello traffic will keep the ISDN link-up indefinitely.

```
r1#show ip ospf neighbor
Neighbor ID    Pri   State    Dead Time   Address      Interface
172.16.201.2   1     FULL/    00:00:37    172.16.1.2   BRI0
r1#show ip ospf database

    OSPF Router with ID (172.16.10.1) (Process ID 100)

       Router Link States (Area 0)
Link ID        ADV Router     Age   Seq#         Checksum  Link  count
172.16.10.1    172.16.10.1    50    0x80000020   0xC655    4
172.16.201.2   172.16.201.2   51    0x80000021   0xF22C    4
```

OSPF OVER ISDN/DDR WITH ON-DEMAND CIRCUIT

By entering the interface configuration command IP OSPF DEMAND-CIRCUIT on one side of a BRI connection, OSPF adjacencies will be formed and on-going OSPF hellos will be suppressed. OSPF hello suppression is manifested in the following show ip OSPF commands. Notice in the show ip ospf interface how it is explicitly listed that this interface is being "Run as demand circuit" and that hellos are suppressed for adjacent neighbor.

```
r2#show ip ospf inte bri0
BRI0 is up, line protocol is up (spoofing)
 Internet Address 177.11.1.2/24, Area 0
 Process ID 100, Router ID 144.10.1.1, Network Type POINT_TO_POINT,
 Cost: 1562
 Configured as demand circuit.
 Run as demand circuit.
 DoNotAge LSA allowed.
 Transmit Delay is 1 sec, State POINT_TO_POINT,
 Timer intervals configured, Hello 10, Dead 40, Wait 40, Retransmit 5
   Hello due in 00:00:03
 Neighbor Count is 1, Adjacent neighbor count is 1
   Adjacent with neighbor 177.11.1.1 (Hello suppressed)
 Suppress hello for 1 neighbor(s)
```

With ip OSPF demand-circuit configured, notice how there is no value for the dead time. Normally, there is an actual value in this column.

```
Neighbor ID     Pri   State    Dead Time   Address       Interface
172.16.201.2    1     FULL/    -           172.16.1.2    BRI0
```

When a packet is received by an OSPF demand-circruit peer at the time of the expiration of the dead timer, the following message debug message was generated:

```
OSPF: Dead event ignored for 177.11.1.1 on demand circuit BRI0
```

With ip OSPF demand-circuit configured, notice how link-state database entries learned over the ISDN interface are marked DNA (Do Not Age)

```
r1#show ip ospf database

        OSPF Router with ID (172.16.10.1) (Process ID 100)

                Router Link States (Area 0)
Link ID         ADV Router      Age        Seq#          Checksum Link count
172.16.10.1     172.16.10.1     216        0x8000001E    0xCA53    4
172.16.201.2    172.16.201.2    6 (DNA)    0x8000001E    0xF829    4
```

Finally, even though the BRI0 interface is down, OSPF retains routes learned via the BRI interface in the routing table.

```
r1#sh ip ro
Codes: C - connected, S - static, I - IGRP, R - RIP, M - mobile
    B - BGP, D - EIGRP, EX - EIGRP external, O - OSPF
    IA - OSPF inter area, N1 - OSPF NSSA external type 1
    N2 - OSPF NSSA external type 2, E1 - OSPF external type 1
    E2 - OSPF external type 2, E - EGP, i - IS-IS
    L1 - IS-IS level-1, L2 - IS-IS level-2
    * - candidate default, U - per-user static route, o - ODR

Gateway of last resort is not set

    172.16.0.0/16 is variably subnetted, 5 subnets, 2 masks
O   172.16.222.0/24 [110/1572] via 172.16.1.2, 00:03:01, BRI0
O   172.16.201.2/32 [110/1563] via 172.16.1.2, 00:03:01, BRI0
C   172.16.10.0/24 is directly connected, Loopback0
C   172.16.1.0/24 is directly connected, BRI0
C   172.16.101.0/24 is directly connected, Ethernet0
```

DIAL BACKUP

Dial Backup allows an ISDN/DDR interface to be set in standby mode so that if a "primary" interface fails or exceeds a pre-established usage threshold, the backup interface will be activated. As discussed in the Dialer Profile section, dial backup can be configured so that either a physical interface is in standby mode (legacy DDR) or a logical dialer interface is placed in standby mode (Dialer Profiles). If the physical interface is placed in standby mode, it cannot be used for anything else. It is recommended to use Dialer Profiles so that only the logical interface is placed in standby mode and the physical interfaces are free to be used for additional DDR traffic.

To configure dial backup for primary link failure, apply the following two interface configuration commands to the primary interface:

```
Backup interface (bri0 or dialer0)
Backup delay XXX YYY
     XXX= amount of time in seconds to wait before activating the
     backup interface
     YYY= amount of time in seconds to wait to place the backup
     interface in standby mode after the primary becomes
     operational again
```

Primary link failure is defined by an interface's "line protocol" attaining a "down" state. Therefore, if anything should cause the line protocol of interface Serial 0 to attain the state of down, dial backup will take interface BRI0 out of standby mode.

Use show ip interface brief to see BRI0 in standby mode. Use show interface XX (XX = interface type and interface number) to view dial backup settings on the primary interface.

```
r2#sh ip inte brie
Interface  IP-Address   OK?  Method Status          Protocol
BRI0       177.11.1.2   YES  manual standby mode    down
Serial0    unassigned   YES  manual up              up

r2#sh interface Serial0
Serial0 is up, line protocol is up
  Hardware is HD64570
  Internet address is 172.16.17.1/24
  Backup interface BRI0, kickin load not set, kickout load not set
    failure delay 20 sec, secondary disable delay 10 sec
MTU 1500 bytes, BW 1544 Kbit, DLY 20000 usec, rely 255/255,
load 1/255
```

You can use dial backup to backup an individual Frame-Relay DLCI by placing that DLCI under a point-to-point subinterface. If the DLCI becomes inactive, the point-to-point subinterface's line protocol attains a state of "down" and the designated backup interface will be come active.

```
r2#sh inte s0.1
Serial0.1 is up, line protocol is up
  Hardware is HD64570
  Backup interface BRI0, failure delay 0 sec, restore delay 0 sec
  MTU 1500 bytes, BW 1544 Kbit, DLY 20000 usec, rely 255/255,
    load 1/255
  Encapsulation FRAME-RELAY
```

To configure dial backup to become active when the primary link exceeds a usage threshold, apply the following two interface configuration commands to the primary interface:

```
Backup interface (bri0 or dialer0)
Backup load XXX YYY
XXX= amount of load to be exceeded to trigger the backup
interface to be activated
YYY= amount of load to be attained to deactivate the backup
interface and place it back into standby mode
```

An alternative to using the dial backup interface configuration command is configuring floating static routes. It is essential that you understand the floating static route alternative to the dial backup statement. Floating static routes provide a greater degree of flexibility than the dial backup command. Floating static routes are covered in Chapter Nine.

TROUBLESHOOTING ISDN

Many technical steps are involved in performing dial-on-demand routing over ISDN. A partial listing of the major steps involved with establishing a DDR connection using ISDN and PPP are listed below along with associated debug and show commands:

1. Is the ISDN DTE device (the router) communicating to the switch?
   Use `show isdn status` and `debug isdn q921`.
2. Is the traffic that is supposed to initiate an ISDN/DDR call properly defined as interesting?
   Use `show run` and `examine dialer-list`.
   If you suspect a problem with your dialer-list command, configure and apply a very broad and permissive dialer-list. If the connection is established with a broad dialer-list, more than likely your problem involves the configuration of the dialer-list.
3. Is the interface that the traffic is supposed to traverse recognizing the traffic as interesting?
   Use `debug ip packet`, `debug dialer packet` and `debug dialer events`?
   Debug ip packet will show you whether the desired packet is being sent out the proper interface.
   Debug dialer packet will show you whether the packet is being defined as interesting.
   Debug dialer events provides other vitally important DDR debugging messages that you do not see with debug dialer alone.
4. Is the router successfully placing the telephone call?
   Use `debug dialer events` and `debug isdn q931`
   Debug isdn will show you the messages exchanged between the calling router and the switch or the called router and the switch. It will supply vitally important information such as "is the number you are calling out of order or in a busy state."
5. If PPP is configured, is PPP negotiation successfully performed?
   Use `debug ppp negotiation` and `show interface briX Y` (X = BRI interface; Y = BRI Channel)
   Once ISDN Q931 has verified that the "calling" party has successfully connected to the "called" party, debug ppp negotiation will supply a step by step trace of the negotiation process between the calling and called parties or PPP peers. Show interface briX Y provides a brief summary of the PPP state status of each BRI channel.
6. If PPP authentication is configured, is the authentication process successfully performed?

Use `debug ppp authentication`.

Possible problems usually involve an incomplete configuration or mistyped user names and passwords. Debug ppp authentication provides excellent messages to pinpoint authentication problems.

Other useful ISDN/DDR troubleshooting tools to are:

- SHOW DIALER
- SHOW DIALER MAP

Show dialer provides a summary of DDR configuration parameters as well as the status of DDR configured interfaces. If a configured DDR interface is currently active, show dialer lists the cause of initiating the call.

Show dialer map provides a brief summary of currently configured and active dialer map statements. Both static and dynamic dialer maps will be listed.

In order to perform any type of troubleshooting effectively, you must be thoroughly familiar with both the normal and abnormal methods of operation of a given technology. This type of familiarity is best developed through hands-on job experience. Another method of obtaining this knowledge basis is to work with the technology in a lab environment. In order to understand ISDN/DDR, get two or more ISDN routers and connect them to an ISDN simulator. Build ISDN/DDR configurations and test them. Record your configuration scripts and debug traces. Keep a personal journal of your experiences. If you do not have access to routers or ISDN switches, a number of companies provide virtual lab access to equipment via the Internet such as the web-site **www.mentorlabs.com.**

Be incremental in your troubleshooting. Make absolutely sure that a given step in the sequence of ISDN/DDR connection setup events has been performed properly before going on to the next step. Do not be sloppy with your analysis. Be precise and rigorous. When you're 99% right in internetwork troubleshooting, more than likely you are 100% wrong!

Remember to troubleshoot both sides of an ISDN/DDR connection. During an ISDN call setup, the calling party performs different operations than the called party. With PPP negotiation and authentication many of the steps performed by two PPP peers are executed in a different sequence depending on which peer is the calling peer and which peer is the called peer.

Pay special attention to whether debug output is all inbound or outbound. If all debug output is outbound, the device you are currently accessing (via TELENT or console port connection) is performing all of the communicating. The remote device is not answering back. If all debug output is inbound, only the remote device is communicating. The local device is not responding.

Summary

This chapter laid a foundation for configuring ISDN BRI interfaces with DDR. It must be stressed that this is a foundational chapter. We are by no means finished with ISDN. We will revisit ISDN in the following chapters:

- Configuring OSPF
- Configuring IPX
- Configuring AppleTalk
- Configuring DECNET
- IP Access-Lists
- IPX Access-Lists
- AppleTalk Access-Lists

Before you begin learning ISDN in these other areas, make sure you know how to set up ISDN with a very broad IP dialer-list. Everything will build upon this. If you can't get such a configuration to work, more than likely, nothing else will work.

ISDN is a topic loaded with issues and pitfalls. You must be systematic and incremental in approaching ISDN configuration and troubleshooting. You must be able to separate the following issues in a layered and incremental fashion:

- ISDN issues (Am I talking to the ISDN switch properly?)
- DIALER-LIST issues (Is the traffic I configured as being interesting actually being found interesting by the router?)

- PPP issues (Are PPP peers negotiating a connection properly?)
- PPP Authentication issues

Once you have mastered the material in this chapter, you will be better prepared to learn ATM (ISDN Q.931 signaling is very similar to ATM Q.2931 signaling), ISDN PRI , and asynchronous modem communication.

Professional Development Checklist

To verify your level of competence in ISDN/DDR configuration and troubleshooting, use the following checklist as a benchmark:

- Basic ISDN configuration with HDLC encapsulation and dialer strings
- Basic ISDN configuration with PPP encapsulation and dialer maps
- Basic ISDN configuration with PPP/One side calling only
- ISDN Configuration for IP
- ISDN Configuration for IPX
- ISDN Configuration for AppleTalk
- ISDN Configuration with CHAP Authentication
- ISDN Configuration with Complex Dialer-List (Using IP, IPX, and AppleTalk Access-List)
- Configure Dialer Profiles
- Snapshot Routing Configuration
- Configure IP OSPF Demand-Circuit
- Configure Dial Backup
- Formulate, Rehearse, and Master ISDN/DDR Troubleshooting Techniques

For Further Study

- Advanced Cisco Router Configuration Course 11.3, Cisco Systems, Inc. This course does an excellent job in covering ISDN topics.
- Cisco IOS WAN Configuration Guide, Cisco Systems, Inc., 1989–1998.
- Cisco IOS WAN Command Reference, Cisco Systems, Inc., 1989–1998.
- Configuring ISDN in Design Guide, Cisco Systems, Inc., 1989–1998.

URLs

- **www.cciecert.com**
- **www.mentorlabs.com**
- **www.cisco.com/univercd/home/home.htm**

Can You Spot the Issues?

1. The BRI interface keeps going up and down. Sample console messages are displayed on page 179. Name possible reasons why the interface keeps going up and down.
2. Your client was using a distance vector routing protocol over an ISDN line. Your local ISDN router had a full internetwork routing table but in order to maintain the table, routing updates keep the connection up indefinitely. You filtered the distance vector routing table updates and now you can't ping or access remote networks on the far-side of the ISDN connection. Why?
3. You enable debug isdn Q931 and you see wrong dial string being dialed. What is the cause of this?
4. You enable debug dialer packet and you see IP packets labeled as "uninteresting." What is the cause of this? How can it be remedied?
5. An ISDN/DDR connection is active and after 120 seconds, the connection drops. Why?
6. You are currently using an ISDN interface for transferring data four times a day to one remote office site. Each of the four connections lasts only five minutes. You also have a frame-relay connection to an information service provider named FINANCE-NET. The link to FINANCENET service provider is critical to your business. FINANCENET informs you that you can configure a hot backup link to the FINANCENET datacenter via ISDN.

You configure the dial backup feature to FINANCENET using your physical ISDN BRI0 interface as the defined dial backup interface. Suddenly your regional office cannot transfer data to your headquarters anymore. What happened? What is the remedy?

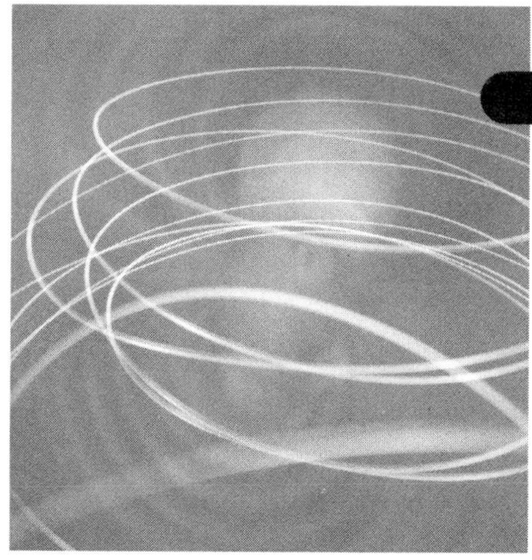

SIX

Configuring the Catalyst 5000 and VLANs

Topics Covered in This Chapter

- Catalyst 5000 Overview
- Introduction to the Catalyst 5000 User Interface
- Basic Catalyst 5000 Configuration
- Configuring virtual local-area networks (VLANs) on a Catalyst 5000
- Routing Between VLANs on a Catalyst 5000
- Trunking on a Catalyst 5000
- Troubleshooting a Catalyst 5000

In its pursuit to provide a cohesive end-to-end solution for an organization's internetworking needs, Cisco has formulated Cisco Fusion. Cisco Fusion combines routing, LAN switching and ATM switching technologies into one scalable and manageable architecture. The primary unifying element of the Cisco Fusion architecture is the Cisco Internetwork Operating System (IOS). Both the Catalyst 5000 and the Catalyst 8500 are the pinnacle of Cisco's efforts to attain the architectural goals of Cisco Fusion. The origins of the Catalyst 5000 are from the LAN switching world and the origins of the Catalyst 8500 are from the routing world. This Chapter focuses on configuring and maintaining the Catalyst 5000. As this Chapter will describe, even though the origins of the Catalyst 5000 come from the LAN switching environment, the Catalyst 5000 has evolved well beyond mere LAN switching. It has evolved into a unique multilayer switching platform. The Catalyst 5000 does not run a single IOS but multiple IOSs. For example, Catalyst route switch modules (RSMs), ATM modules, and Catalyst 8500 switch route modules can be installed inside of a Catalyst 5000. All of these run the standard Cisco IOS; however, the LAN switching modules of the Catalyst 5000 are accessed and managed by an IOS that is different from the standard Cisco IOS. Since the core of this book focuses on the standard Cisco IOS, this Chapter will focus on the nonstandard LAN switching IOS of the Catalyst 5000. When comparing the different IOSs that run on the different modules installed inside of a Catalyst 5000, it is this nonstandard LAN switching IOS that is the primary IOS of the entire Catalyst 5000 platform. When a Catalyst 5000 is booted, it boots into the LAN switching IOS environment. All other modules are accessible through the nonstandard IOS. Therefore, it is essential to master the basic configuration and monitoring commands of the primary LAN switching IOS of the Catalyst 5000. Remember that all versions of the Cisco IOS are constantly evolving. You can be assured that the LAN switching IOS will become more like the standard IOS over time. Before addressing actual LAN switching Catalyst IOS commands, the following sections provide an overview of the entire Cisco Catalyst family as well as fundamental similarities and differences between routing and LAN switching.

Comparing the Catalyst 5000 to the Catalyst 8500

The Catalyst 5000 and the Catalyst 8500 are Cisco's two flagship core multilayer switching platforms. Both platforms blur the traditional boundary lines of conventional LAN switching, ATM switching, and routing.

The Catalyst 5000's origins spring from the LAN switching company formerly known as Crescendo acquired by Cisco in 1994. Since the original Catalyst product-line was developed by a non-Cisco company, its IOS was completely different from the standard Cisco IOS. Over the years, Cisco has taken the former LAN switching Crescendo product and "Cisco-ized" it. From a hardware perspective, the product is no longer merely a LAN switching platform. It is a multilayer switching platform that supports LAN switching, ATM switching, and network layer switching. From an operating system perspective, many of the modules that are installed in the Catalyst 5000 run the standard Cisco IOS, but the core Catalyst IOS is still significantly different from the Cisco standard IOS that operates on the Cisco router product line, LightStream ATM switch product line, and certain Catalyst campus/LAN switches such as the Catalyst 2916, 2924, and 8500. Major differences between the LAN switching IOS and the standard Cisco IOS are:

1. The LAN switching IOS has only two modes of operation: user and enable. The standard IOS has multiple modes of operation such as:

- User
- Privileged
- Global configuration mode
- Interface configuration mode
- Other more specialized configuration modes

2. Instead of having multiple modes of configuration, configuration commands on the Catalyst LAN switching IOS are dominated by SET and CLEAR commands.

A more detailed description of the differences between the standard IOS and the Catalyst LAN switching IOS will be supplied later in this Chapter.

The origins of the Catalyst 8500 product-line are from the routing world. The Catalyst 8500 is high performance layer three switch developed entirely by Cisco Systems. It switches IP and IPX packets over Ethernet, Fast-Ethernet, and Gigabit Ethernet at wire speed. The Catalyst 8500 runs the standard Cisco IOS. Catalyst 8500 modules can be installed into the high-end Catalyst 5000 model: the Catalyst 5500. The functional equivalent of VLANs can be created on a Catalyst 8500 using standard IOS bridging commands. Multiple interfaces on a single Catalyst 8500 can be grouped inside of the same broadcast domain using a standard IOS "bridge-group" command. Interfaces on Catalyst 8500 that are defined within the same broadcast domain with the bridge-group command can be joined to routed interfaces on the same Catalyst 8500 through the standard IOS feature known as Integrated Routing and Bridging. A more detailed description of broadcast domains will be supplied later in this Chapter. Integrated Routing and Bridging is described in Chapter Twenty.

Comparing the Catalyst 5000 Family of Switches to the Constellation of Cisco Catalyst Switches

The Catalyst 5000 is a modular multilayer switch. At the Data-Link Layer, it supports protocols such as Ethernet, Fast-Ethernet, Gigabit Ethernet, Token-Ring, fiber distributed data interface (FDDI), and ATM. At the Network Layer, it can be configured with an RSM, a Supervisor Three Module with a NetFlow Feature Card, or a Catalyst 8500 Switch Route Processor. The most common configuration of a Catalyst 5000 is with Gigabit Ethernet/Fast-Ethernet/Ethernet modules.

The Catalyst 5000 is a single family of switches within a larger constellation of multilayer switch products offered by Cisco. All of Cisco's LAN switching and multilayer products fall under the "Catalyst" product name. Cisco's entry into the multilayer switching market was through the acquisition of three LAN switching pioneer companies: Crescendo, Kalpana, and Grand Junction. Cisco has integrated these acquisitions into their routing and ATM product offerings to provide the high-performance multilayer switching solution known as "Cisco Fusion." The Cisco Catalyst switch product line can be categorized in the three level internetworking hierarchy of "core, distribution, and access." Catalyst model numbers include:

Catalyst Switches Originating from the Grand Junction Acquisition:

- 1800: Fixed configuration LAN switch
- 1900: Menu-driven user interface
- 2820: Menu-driven user interface

From a hardware perspective, these switches are primarily fixed configuration switches with mostly Ethernet 10BASET and some Fast-Ethernet ports. The Model 2820 possesses modular uplink slots for Fast-Ethernet, FDDI, and ATM. These switches are defined as a "workgroup" LAN switch solution for small businesses. When categorized in the three level internetworking hierarchy of "core, distribution, and access," these switches are access-level switches.

From a software "IOS" perspective, these switches' operating systems were originally nothing like the standard Cisco IOS. The IOS was originally possessed a menu driven interface developed by Grand Junction Systems. However, as these products have become "Cisco-ized," their IOS is more Cisco-like. With the latest OS version, it now offers a command line interface that supports a number of show commands.

The Model 1800, 1900, and 2820 switches can be categorized as access-level switches. None of these products have the core-level switching capabilities of the Catalyst 5000 or the Catalyst 8500.

Catalyst Switches Originating from the Kalpana Acquisition:

The Catalyst 3000 switch family has its origins from the Ethernet switching pioneer company Kalpana. In the three level switch hierarchy of core, distribution, and access, the Catalyst 3000 family is categorized as a high performance access-level solution.

From a hardware perspective, Catalyst 3000 switches possess some degree of modularity. Three primary models that make up the Catalyst 3000 family are:

- Catalyst 3000
- Catalyst 3100
- Catalyst 3200

The Catalyst 3000 and 3100 possess limited modularity. The base units of both of these models are comprised of multiple 10BASET switch ports. The Model 3200 possesses a modular chassis with six available slots and one "FlexSlot." All Catalyst 3000 switches can support Fast-Ethernet and ATM for uplink connections. The Model 3100 and 3200 also support a wide-area network (WAN) router module.

A unique hardware feature of the Catalyst 3000 is its "stackable" feature. Up to eight Catalyst 3000 switches can be stacked together providing 3.84

Gbps of aggregate bandwidth. All eight of the switches could be monitored and administered from a single console port.

From a software perspective, the Catalyst 3000 uses an IOS that is completely different from the standard Cisco IOS. It possesses a menu driven user interface.

CATALYST SWITCHES ORIGINATING FROM THE CRESCENDO ACQUISITION:

- 2900: Fixed configuration LAN switch with Catalyst 5000 supervisor engine and LAN modules
- 5000: Modular; multilayer switch with five slots
- 5002: Modular; multilayer switch with two slots
- 5500: Modular; multilayer switch with thirteen slots

Different models of the Catalyst 5000 family can be placed in all three levels of the internetworking hierarchy. For example, a Catalyst 2900, 5002, and 5000 can be placed at the access-level. These platforms are commonly deployed in an organization's wiring closet.

At the distribution level, a Catalyst 5000 with an RSM or Supervisor III Card with a NetFlow feature card can be deployed.

At the core-level, a Catalyst 5500 with the following types of modules:

ATM Switch Processor
Supervisor III Module with a NetFlow Feature Card
Catalyst 8500 Switch Route Processor Module
Gigabit Ethernet Module

Cisco Internally Developed Catalyst Switches:

- Catalyst 2916 and 2924: Modular LAN switch that has a standard Cisco IOS user interface
- Catalyst 8500: A layer three switch router that forwards IP and IPX at wire speed. The Catalyst 8500 runs the standard Cisco IOS.

As reflected above, Cisco offers a wide range of multilayer switching products. Different switch models use different switching technologies. Different switches use different operating systems and user interfaces. The flagship multilayer switch platform of the Cisco product line is the Catalyst 5000 family. Catalyst 5000 switches can be configured as a combination of a LAN switch, ATM switch, router, and high-performance layer three switch. The Catalyst 5000 family is made up of four of the models listed above:

- Catalyst 2900
- Catalyst 5000
- Catalyst 5002
- Catalyst 5500

All of these products use the same core supervisor module and user interface.

In its simplest configuration, a Catalyst 5000 with Ethernet modules is a data-link layer LAN switch that operates much like a multiport transparent bridge. It uses the Spanning Tree Protocol for loop prevention just as a transparent bridge would. By adding additional modules, the Catalyst 5000 can be configured into a high-performance multilayer switch.

As mentioned at the end of Chapter Three, the Catalyst 5000 is a plug and play switch. Out of the box, Ethernet end systems or hubs can plug into a Catalyst port. The Catalyst 5000 will autosense the speed of the connection and pass through the listening and learning states of the spanning tree algorithm. If the spanning tree algorithm places the port in a forwarding state, the port will be able to forward traffic. Once the port is placed in the forwarding state and end systems begin to transfer data through the port, the Catalyst builds a switching table composed of media access control (MAC) addresses, the port number that the MAC address was learned from, and the VLAN number the MAC address is a member of. (A default Catalyst configuration places all ports in VLAN1.) When the table is built, the Catalyst 5000 switches frames based upon this information.

How the Catalyst LAN Switching Process Differs from a Conventional Routing Process

A traditional router running a destination based routing process builds and maintains a routing table of network layer addresses. From this table, packets that enter the router have its data-link layer header removed, and a lookup of each packet's destination network layer address is compared to an entry in a table—a cached switching table derived from the main routing table or the main routing table itself—and a switching decision is made.

A Catalyst switch operating in an exclusively LAN switching mode also builds and maintains a table. However, unlike the router with network layer addresses in its table, the Catalyst LAN switching table consists of MAC layer addresses. The core information in a Catalyst LAN switching table is:

- Destination MAC address
- VLAN membership of destination MAC address
- Port destination MAC address learned from

The Catalyst LAN switching process does not remove the data-link layer header. It adds an extra header onto the data-link frame when the frame is forwarded over an inter-switch connection called a "trunk port." This header is called the VLAN header. For Ethernet switching, two common VLAN headers in a Cisco environment are ISL headers (Cisco specific) and 802.1q headers.

IP routing information can be obtained from a router with the `show ip route` command. Catalyst LAN switching information can be obtained from a Catalyst 5000 with the `show cam` command and its options.

Let's compare the contents of an IP routing table to a Catalyst 5000 CAM table. In the IP routing table below, the two primary units of information for each listing is the destination network address (second column of data) and the local interface to switch packets to get to that destination network (last listing of every line: Serial0, Ethernet0). For example, if an IP packet destined for the subnet of 172.16.200.0/24 is received by the router maintaining the table displayed below, the packet is forwarded out the Serial0 interface. If a packet is received for the destination of 172.16.244.0/24, an address not in the routing table, the packet is dropped and an ICMP "destination unreachable" message is sent to the end system with the source address inside of the dropped packet. This packet is dropped because the "gateway of last resort is not set." If the "gateway of last resort" is set, then the packet destined for the 172.16.244.0 network is forwarded out of the interface designated as the gateway of last resort.

```
R1#sh ip ro
Codes: C - connected, S - static, I - IGRP, R - RIP, M - mobile, B - BGP
    D - EIGRP, EX - EIGRP external, O - OSPF, IA - OSPF inter area
    N1 - OSPF NSSA external type 1, N2 - OSPF NSSA external type 2
    E1 - OSPF external type 1, E2 - OSPF external type 2, E - EGP
    i - IS-IS, L1 - IS-IS level-1, L2 - IS-IS level-2, * - candidate default
    U - per-user static route, o - ODR
```

Gateway of last resort is not set

```
    172.16.0.0/16 is variably subnetted, 3 subnets, 1 mask
O     172.16.200.0/24 [110/74] via 172.16.1.2, 1d13h, Serial0
C     172.16.10.0/24 is directly connected, Ethernet0
C     172.16.1.0/24 is directly connected, Serial0
```

As mentioned earlier, the CAM table contains three units of information for each entry: destination MAC address, VLAN number that the MAC address is a member of, and the port to switch frames out of to get to the destination MAC address. If a frame is received with a MAC address contained in the first listing of the CAM table below (00-80-c7-7a-3d-b8), the frame will get forwarded out module 3 port 3 (3/3) only.

```
cat1 (enable) sh cam dyn
VLAN Dest MAC/Route Des Destination Ports or VCs
---- ------------------ ----------------------------------------
-----------
1    00-80-c7-7a-3d-b8  3/3
1    00-00-86-12-47-68  2/42
1    00-80-c7-38-f0-81  2/45
1    00-80-c7-21-72-d8  2/45
```

```
1     00-60-97-90-b0-96  3/7
1     00-80-c7-5a-a3-bd  3/12
1     00-e0-1e-e4-fe-dd  2/42
1     00-00-86-09-23-ff  3/10
1     00-60-08-23-ca-29  2/42
1     00-60-97-ed-c5-9e  2/45
1     00-60-08-02-fd-0a  3/9
```

If a frame is received with a destination MAC address is not in the Catalyst 5000's CAM table, the frame gets broadcast out all outbound ports of the VLAN. Therefore, the exact opposite is done with unknown frames in a Catalyst LAN switching process compared to what is done with unknown IP packets in a routing process with no "gateway of last resort."

Collision Domains and Broadcast Domains

When comparing switches to routers, the topic of collision and broadcast domains always arises. Take note of the following:

- Repeaters: All repeater ports are in one collision domain and one broadcast domain. A conventional 10BaseT is a multiport repeater. Therefore, all 10BASET hubs are one collision domain and broadcast domain.
- Bridges: Each port of a bridge creates a collision domain but all ports of a bridge are in one broadcast domain.

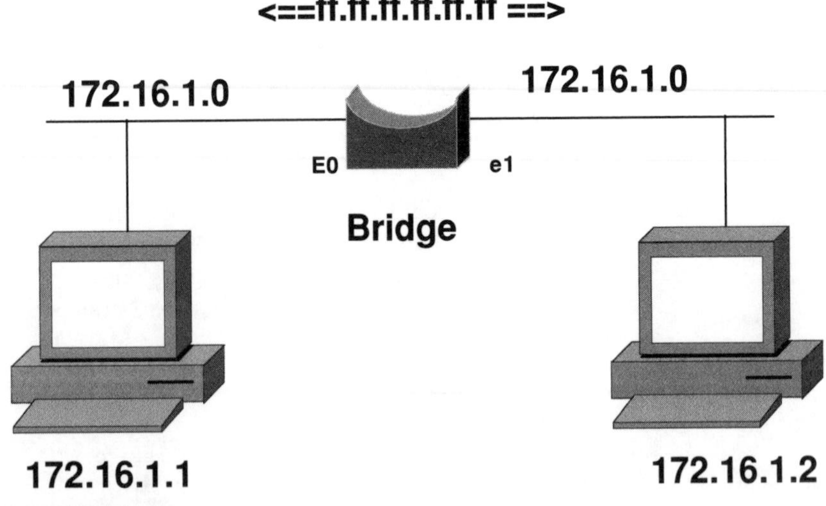

FIGURE 6–1 All bridge ports reside in the same broadcast domain

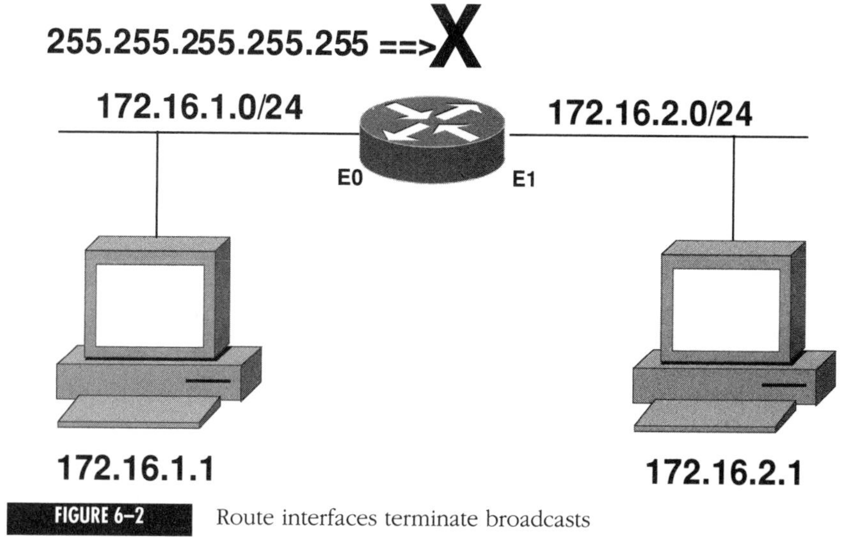

FIGURE 6–2 Route interfaces terminate broadcasts

- Routers: Each interface of a router creates a collision domain and a broadcast domain.
- LAN Switches: Each port of a LAN switch creates a collision domain and each VLAN residing on the switch creates a broadcast domain

The condition of making each port on a switch a separate collision domain is known as "microsegmentation."

By default, all ports on an entire switch are in a single VLAN and thereby in a single broadcast domain. On a switch, broadcast domains are defined by VLANs. One VLAN defines a single broadcast domain. If traffic needs to be forwarded from one VLAN to another, a routing process must be used to route "inter-VLAN" traffic.

In a shared LAN environment, routers perform the operation of creating broadcast domains. In a switched LAN environment, LAN switches create broadcast domains by defining VLANs. Therefore, from the perspective of being the device that defines broadcast domains and collision domains, LAN switches are a direct replacement of routers. However, LAN switches do not have the intelligence to move traffic from one VLAN to another. This is the role of routers in a switched internetwork. Routers are used to switch packets between VLANs.

As an illustration of the role of routers and LAN switches in a campus internetwork consider the two scenarios below.

State of the Art Internetwork Hierarchy of the Early 1990s

The most commonly used components of internetworks installed in the early 1990s was Ethernet 10BASET at the access-level, routers at the distribution level, and FDDI at the core level. A brief description of how each of technologies was deployed is provided below.

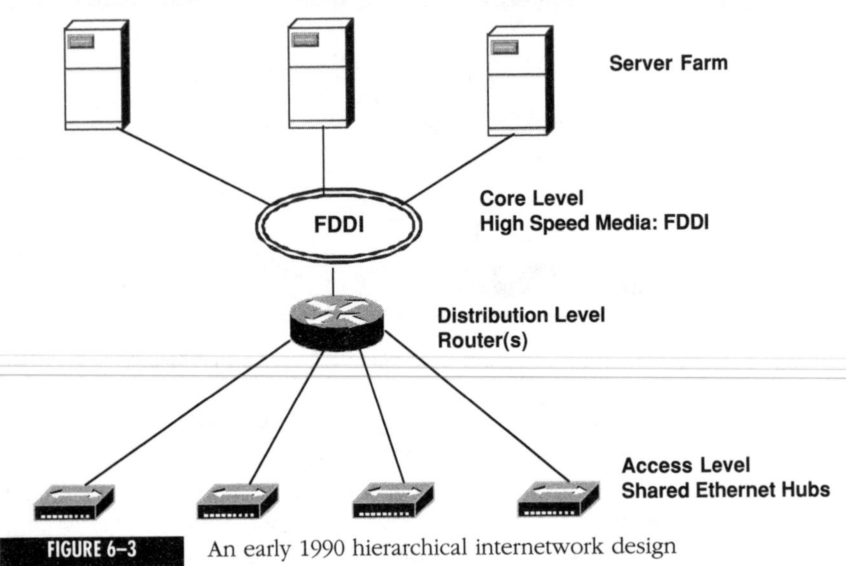

FIGURE 6–3 An early 1990 hierarchical internetwork design

ACCESS-LEVEL: SHARED ETHERNET LANS

Daisy-chained Ethernet hubs formed a single collision domain. Ethernet, especially 10BASET, provided a low cost solution to provide 10 Mbps "shared" bandwidth to desktop users. The dominant suppliers of Ethernet hubs were:

SynOptics
CableTron
Hewlett-Packard
SMC

DISTRIBUTION LEVEL: ROUTERS

Routers defined the boundaries of both broadcast domains and collision domains. Each interface on a router defined a network layer subnet that was a termination point for a given subnet's broadcast and unicast radiation. If too much traffic was on a given Ethernet segment, the number of collisions increased. Routers were used to "divide and conquer" segments suffering from excessive collisions. When segments would reach a point of excessive collisions, the afflicted segment would get divided. Both of the two newly created segments would require a connection to a router interface. The router provided the best of both worlds. It limited and defined the scope of broadcast and unicast radiation. It also provided any to any reachability for all end systems in the internetwork.

Not only did routers define the broadcast domains and collision domains for LAN segments; routers also provided the intelligence of path selection and network layer switching for destinations that were not local to a given segment.

CORE LEVEL: FDDI

The core level provided a high bandwidth backbone that would accommodate the aggregated traffic from the end users. FDDI was the core technology of choice because it supplied a relatively high level of bandwidth (100 Mbps) and sophisticated redundancy features (dual counter rotating rings). Servers were attached directly to the FDDI ring. If the FDDI ring became over utilized, routers would once again provide the "divide and conquer remedy". A single FDDI would be divided into two FDDI rings and routers would provide inter-ring reachability.

State of the Art Internetwork Hierarchy for the Twenty-First Century

Commonly used components of internetworks installed today are switched Ethernet 10BASET and 100BASET at the access-level, a routing process at the distribution level and high speed switching engines using Fast-Ethernet, ATM, or Gigabit Ethernet. A brief description of how each of technologies was deployed is provided below.

ACCESS LEVEL: SWITCHED ETHERNET 10/100 MPBS VLANS

Due to its pre-existing installation base and its low cost and ease of maintenance, Ethernet will continue to be a dominant data-link protocol for desktop connectivity. Instead of connecting Ethernet-based desktop devices to a shared hub, they will be connected to a LAN switch. Each port of the LAN switch will be a separate collision domain. Therefore, from a collision domain perspective, routers are no longer needed to define collision domains. To provide a smooth migration into a switched Ethernet environment, legacy hubs can be connected into a switch port. If devices connected to a hub off of a switch port are generating too much traffic that is resulting in excessive collisions, the "divide and conquer" strategy that was once applied by a router can now be applied by a LAN switch. To reduce collisions, some end systems can remain connected to a legacy hub which is in turn connected to a LAN switch and other end systems will be connected directly to the LAN switch. Even though some end systems are connected to different switch ports than the legacy hub, they all can be configured to remain in the same broadcast domain.

As the prices of LAN switches drop and as the older legacy hubs are retired, all end systems will eventually have a direct connection into a LAN switch. As LAN switches proliferate, a new connectivity issue will arise: the issue of interconnecting switches together. This will be performed by either a routing process or trunking process. A more detailed discussion of the differences between routing and trunking will be supplied in the next section.

As mentioned earlier, each port of a switch defines a collision domain. By possessing this feature, routers are no longer needed to define collision domains in a LAN switched environment. In a legacy environment, routers not only defined collision domains, they also defined broadcast domains. By defining VLANs, LAN switches can now also define broadcast domains. Ports belonging to a given VLAN do not need to reside on the same physical switch. They can be dispersed through out the switched internetwork. The inter-switch "trunking" process will tie all physically separate VLAN ports into a single logical entity.

In a switched environment, LAN switches perform much of the work that routers performed in a legacy "shared LAN" environment. LAN switches now define collision domains on a physical port by port basis and define broadcast domains on a VLAN by VLAN basis. In a campus/LAN environment, a routing process plays the role of providing inter-VLAN communication. Make note that the phrase "routing process" and not "router" was used in the previous sentence. In a campus/LAN environment, routing may not occur on a physically separate device such as 3600 router or a 7500 router. Routing may occur inside of a Catalyst 5000 with the use of the following Cisco technologies:

Route Switch Module
Supervisor III Module with NetFlow feature card
Catalyst 8500 Switch Router Processor Module

By placing the routing process inside of a Catalyst 5000, the Catalyst becomes much more than a LAN switch: it becomes a multilayer switch that will perform both LAN switching and routing.

DISTRIBUTION LEVEL: LAYER THREE SWITCHING PERFORMED BY A ROUTING PROCESS

Just as in the shared LAN architectures of the early 1990s, routing will continue to play a key role at the distribution layer of the switched internetwork hierarchy; however, the routing process will be much more specialized. The routing process will no longer provide the boundary for collision domains and broadcast domains. This will be performed by LAN switches. Routers will

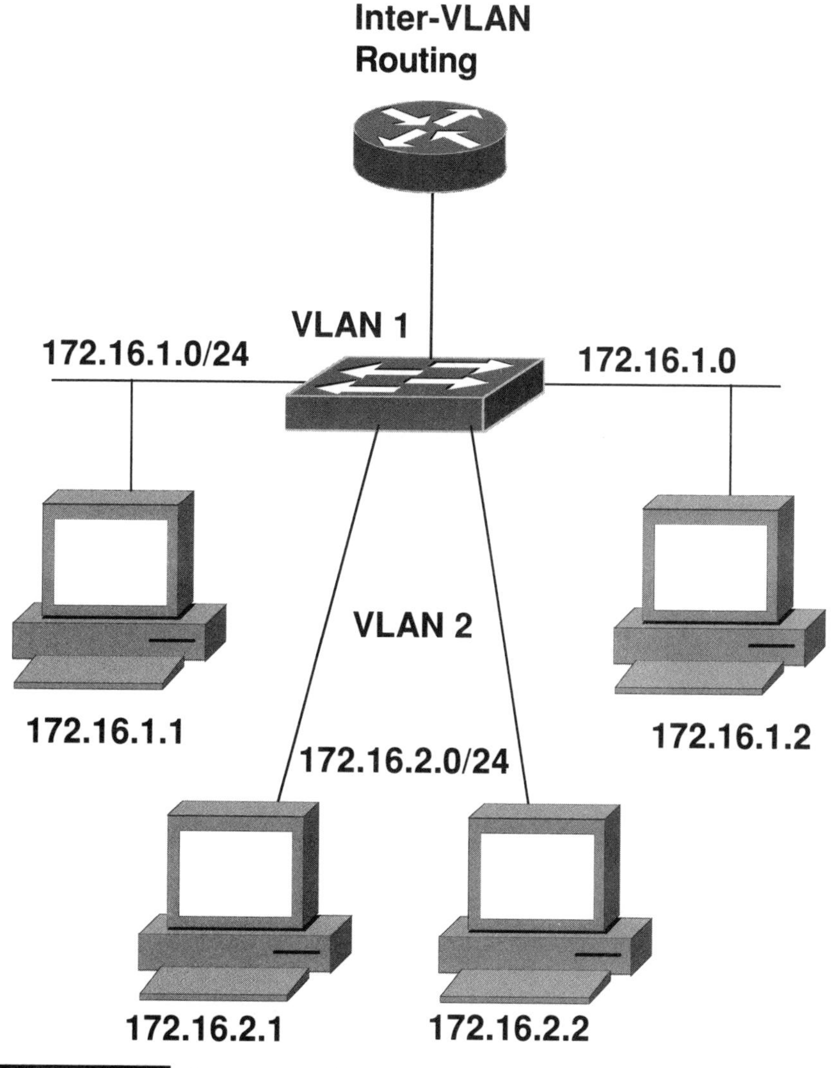

FIGURE 6–4 Routers provide inter-VLAN connectivity

be focused on switching packets between broadcast domains or data-link layer segments. Routers are often derided as the bottleneck in the switching hierarchy. Cisco supplies two techniques to remove the bottleneck created by the routing process:

1. Catalyst 8500 layer three switching at wire speeds
2. Cut through switching using NetFlow and MPOA

By using a Catalyst 8500, conventional routing can be performed. However, it is being performed using the Catalyst 8500's optimized hardware and layer three switching software at wire speed.

By using a cut through switching technique, the first packet is routed in a conventional manner from one VLAN to another by a routing process. After either NetFlow or multiprotocol over ATM (MPOA) learn both the source and destination addresses of a given data flow, they set up a direct connection between the two VLANs. Prior to cut-through switching, the router was involved in the switching process of every single packet. It was the workhorse of inter-VLAN switching. With cut through switching, the router is involved with switching only the first packet of a data flow. Once the first packet is switched, the router is not involved with the switching process of subsequent packets. With cut through switching, the router is no longer the inter-VLAN switching workhorse. This operation is performed by multilayer switches like the Catalyst 5000 (NetFlow) or ATM switches (MPOA). As a result, the routing bottleneck is bypassed altogether.

NetFlow is a Cisco proprietary cut-through switching technology. MPOA is developed by the ATM Forum and is deployed by multiple vendors.

Recommended distribution layer platforms are the Catalyst 5000 and the Catalyst 8500.

CORE LEVEL: HIGH-SPEED SWITCHING

The core level is the aggregating point of all traffic. It should be optimized for packet or cell switching only. High-speed switching platforms should be installed in the core. Platforms include:

- Catalyst 5500 multilayer switches with Gigabit Ethernet or ATM (OC-12 or higher) modules
- Catalyst 8500 layer three switches with Gigabit Ethernet or ATM (OC-12 or higher) modules
- LightStream ATM switches with OC-12 or higher modules

Trunking versus Routing

Routing provides VLAN to VLAN communication or broadcast domain to broadcast domain communication. Trunking provides connectivity for the following types of connections in a multiple VLAN environment:

1. Switch to switch
2. Switch to router
3. Switch to trunk aware interface in an end system

Ports belonging to the same VLAN may reside on different physical switches. Switch-to-switch trunking allows information to be shared by all ports in a given VLAN, even if these ports reside on different physical switches.

Switch-to-router trunking allows a single physical router interface to route inter-VLAN traffic over different subinterfaces. Each subinterface on a trunked router interface is assigned to a specific VLAN. This is known as "one-armed routing," "hairpin routing," or "router on a stick."

Trunking can occur between a switch-to-trunk aware interface in an end system. This allows an end system, like a File Server, to access multiple VLANs over a single physical port.

When traffic transits a trunk link, it is encapsulated inside of a trunking header. Listed below are trunking technologies:

ISL (Inter-Switch Link)
802.1q
Gigabit Ethernet
802.10
ATM LANE

The first three trunking protocols are Fast-Ethernet and Gigabit Ethernet based. ISL is a Cisco proprietary trunking technology developed for Fast-Ethernet. 802.1q is based upon an IEEE specification. When the 802.1q specification matures and is broadly deployed, it will provide a vendor independent solution for inter-switch trunking utilizing Fast-Ethernet technology. Gigabit Ethernet is being developed by organizations like the Gigabit Ethernet Alliance.

The 802.10 trunking technology uses FDDI as its underlying transport. It is popular in environments that already have FDDI backbones installed. Very few organizations are installing new infrastructures with 802.10/FDDI trunks between switches. In most instances, organizations are looking to create new infrastructures with either Gigabit Ethernet or ATM.

ATM LANE was developed by the ATM Forum to provide a method of transporting legacy LAN traffic (Ethernet and Token-Ring) between two or more LAN segments over an ATM network. Two primary benefits of deploying ATM in the core of an organization's internetwork is its ability to be deployed in the LAN, campus as well the WAN and its quality-of-service (QoS) features. By deploying ATM LANE, VLANs can be interconnected by a trunking protocol that spans the WAN.

For example, assume that four switches possess ports that belong to the Engineering VLAN. These switches reside in the geographically dispersed cities of New York, Miami, Los Angeles, and San Jose. By installing ATM LANE to provide inter-switch trunking, all of the ports of VLAN Engineering can reach each other.

ATM is also selected as a strategic technology for an organization's core infrastructure. It provides quality of service parameters that are essential for voice and video traffic. ATM and ATM LANE are covered in greater detail in Chapter Seven.

In a multi-VLAN switching domain, trunking is used to separate data from different VLAN's. Trunking headers allow data sourced from different VLAN's to be distinguished as it transits a single physical "trunk" link. When data has transited trunk links, trunk headers direct the data to the correct destination VLAN.

Trunking can be performed on only specific types of ports. For example, trunking cannot be performed on 10 Mbps Ethernet ports. A minimum of 100 Mbps ports are required for ISL trunking.

If only one VLAN is defined on a group of Catalyst switches, trunking is not necessary. With only one VLAN defined on a group of switches, traffic can be forwarded can be performed on a single Ethernet port with a crossover cable run between two switches.

To summarize the difference between routing and trunking:

1. Routing provides inter-VLAN connectivity.
2. Trunking provides intra-VLAN connectivity between switches that possess ports that belong to the same VLAN.
3. Trunking provides switch-to-router connectivity so that a single router interface can be used to route between multiple VLANs.
4. Trunking provides connectivity between a switch and "trunk aware end system interface" so that an end system, such as a File Server, can communicate with multiple VLAN's over a single physical network interface card.

Both routing and trunking can be bottlenecks in a switched internetwork.

The Catalyst 5000 family of switches possess multi-gigabit per second backplanes; however, many trunk links and router links transfer traffic at rates well below the Gigabit per second level. Listed below is the bandwidth capacity of each trunking technology:

ISL	100 Mbps
802.1q	100 Mbps
Gigabit Ethernet	1 Gbps
802.10/FDDI	100 Mbps
ATM LANE (OC-3)	155 Mbps
ATM LANE (OC-12)	622 Mbps
ATM LANE (OC-48)	2.6 Gbps

The Catalyst 5000 provides a feature of aggregating four ISL trunk links to provide a single 800 Mbps trunk. This feature is known a Fast-EtherChannel. Fast-EtherChannel is promoted as an interim technology for moving towards Gigabit Ethernet.When performing strategic planning for building a high-performance infrastructure, most organizations are focusing their choice on a Fast-Ethernet/Gigabit Ethernet solution or an ATM solution. The Fast-Ethernet/Gigabit Ethernet solution is attractive because it appears to be less expensive and less complex to deploy and maintain. The ATM solution is attractive because it provides robust QoS features for voice and video services, it scales into the wide area network and it scales up to a multi-gigabit per second bandwidth capacity. This is one of the greatest debates in internetwork design: is an organization's primary core technology ATM or Gigabit Ethernet? Arguing the pros and cons of both technologies is beyond the scope of this book. What must be said here is that the Catalyst 5000 family supports both technologies. With its modular hardware design, a Catalyst 5000 can be configured with both Ethernet and ATM ports.

Even if high-performance trunk-links are installed in switched internetworks, a bottleneck may reside in the device that provides inter-VLAN connectivity: the router. Cisco provides many solutions to minimize the router bottleneck including:

Route Switch Module
Supervisor III Module with a NetFlow Feature Card
ATM MPOA
Catalyst 8500

Loop Avoidance in a Multiswitch Network: The Spanning Tree Protocol

When multiple LAN switches are interconnected with multiple connections to all other switches, a looped topology may be formed. A looped topology is often desirable to provide redundancy, but looped traffic is undesirable. LAN switched traffic is especially vulnerable to broadcast loops and the spanning tree protocol (802.1d) was designed to prevent such loops from being formed. The spanning tree protocol was originally developed for bridges. Today, it is also applied to Cisco LAN switch topologies on a per VLAN basis. By applying the spanning tree protocol to a looped LAN switch topology, all VLAN's will be reachable but any points where loops can occur will be blocked on a per VLAN basis.

The Spanning Tree Protocol has four basic phases of operation:

1. Election of a root bridge among a switch group on a per VLAN basis
2. Calculating the shortest path to the root switch by all nonroot switches within a specific VLAN
3. Block highest cost paths to the root switch for loop avoidance if a loop exists
4. Maintaining and recalculating the spanning tree with BPDUs on a per VLAN basis

Once a spanning tree is formed for a given VLAN, all the ports residing in the VLAN know is who the root switch is and what direction the root switch is in. AGAIN, THIS IS PERFORMED ON A PER VLAN BASIS.

Spanning Tree is a Level Five Topic. It will be covered in greater detail in Chapter Twenty.

Scalable Trunking Environments and VTP

The Virtual Trunking Protocol (VTP) is a Cisco proprietary feature that automatically advertises existing VLANs on a given switch within a VTP domain to all other switches in the same domain. It is useful in an environment where there are multiple switches and multiple VLANs. A switch can be in one and only one VTP domain at a given time.

As an example, consider a campus network that is comprised of four Catalyst 5000 switches that are interconnected via trunking. Assume that all of the switches are configured as members of the same VTP domain. Each of the switches has ports that are members of the VLANs listed in the table below:

Switch-1	VLANs 1, 2, and 3
Swich-2	VLANs 1,2, and 4
Switch-3	VLANs 1,3, and 4
Switch-4	VLANs 1,5, and 6

Even though each switch in the table above has its ports configured in three VLANs only, every switch is aware of all six VLANs defined in the VTP domain. If a fourth VLAN out of the six total VLANs in the table above was added to a specific switch, switch wide configuration is minimized due to VTP. For example, in the table above, Switch-1 has all of its ports configured in VLANs 1, 2, and 3. If some of the ports in VLAN 1 and 2 on Switch-1 were added to VLAN 4 on Switch-1, no additional configuration would need to be performed on Switch-2 or Switch-3 (both switches with ports already configured in VLAN 4). Finally, if a fifth switch was added—Switch-5—and its ports were to be assigned to VLANs 1, 3, and 6, all that would need to be done is to add Switch-5 to the VTP domain of the other four switches and assign its specific ports to the respective VLANs. Due to VTP, no additional configuration would need to be performed on the other switches.

Default Catalyst Configuration

In Chapter Two, coverage of the Catalyst boot up process was provided. At the end of Chapter Three, an overview of the default status of Catalyst ports was provided. In these Chapters, show commands were used in a manner similar to show commands used on Cisco platforms that use the standard IOS such as routers and ATM switches.

As mentioned in Chapter Three, the default Catalyst 5000 switch configuration is the following: all ports are members of VLAN1 and no VTP domain has been defined. End systems and hubs can be plugged in with no configu-

ration and be operational. This is why Cisco promotes the Catalyst as being "useable out of the box."

CATALYST 5000 USER INTERFACE

If you are familiar with UNIX, the Catalyst 5000 user interface is similar to a UNIX C Shell interface. The Cisco standard IOS used on Cisco routers, Light-Stream ATM switches, and the Catalyst 8500 possesses a user interface that is similar to a UNIX BASH shell interface.

SIMILARITIES BETWEEN THE CATALYST 5000 USER INTERFACE AND THE ROUTER IOS

Both the Catalyst 5000 IOS and the standard IOS are mode oriented. Both environments have a user and privileged mode. Upon booting up a Catalyst 5000, you are left at the following prompt:

```
catalyst-1> en
Enter password:
```

There is no ">" and "#" prompts with the Catalyst. You know when you are in the "enable" mode when you see the following prompt:

```
catalyst-1> (enable)
```

Both the standard Cisco IOS and the Catalyst IOS allow the user to type command contractions. For example, instead of typing out the full names of the command "show module," you can type the command contraction "sh mod." In order for command contractions to operate properly, you must type enough of the command that makes it a unique string to the IOS. For example, the Catalyst has two commands that begin with the same four characters:

```
Show span
Show spantree
```

"Show spans" lists information on a port listening and diagnostics feature of the Catalyst 5000 known as Switched Port Analyzer (SPAN). "Show spantree" lists information on the spantree configuration for a specific VLAN (VLAN 1 by default). If you type `show span` the Catalyst IOS has not been given enough characters to execute the "show spantree" command. In this particular case, it will default to listing "show span" (switched port analyzer) information. Therefore, if you wanted to view spanning tree information, type `sh spant`.

DIFFERENCES BETWEEN THE CATALYST 5000 INTERFACE AND THE ROUTER IOS

The Catalyst 5000 IOS possesses the following distinguishing features from the standard IOS:

- There is no configuration mode.
- There is no copy run start or write memory command.
- When moving from user to enable mode on a Catalyst 5000, you are prompted for a password even if one does not exist.

Unlike a Cisco router, the arrow up key does not display previous commands. When the arrow up key is pressed, an error message is generated. If you want to execute a previous command, type `!!`. To view a listing of previous commands, type `hist`.

The Catalyst 5000 LAN switching command line interface is markedly different than the standard IOS interface. However, when a route switch module, ATM switch module, ATM LANE module or a Catalyst 8500 switch route module is added to the Catalyst 5000, these modules are configured and managed from the same standard IOS found on Cisco routers and LightStream ATM switches.

GETTING HELP ON A CATALYST 5000

To access a help facility on the Catalyst 5000, type `help` or `?`. When entered, the following main help menu appears in enable mode:

```
Console>                    enable) ?
Commands:
----------------------------------------------------------------------
clear                       Clear, use 'clear help' for more info
configure                   Configure system from terminal/network
disable                     Disable privileged mode
disconnect                  Disconnect user session
download                    Download code to a processor
enable                      Enable privileged mode
help                        Show this message
history                     Show contents of history substitution buffer
ping                        Send echo packets to hosts
quit                        Exit from the Admin session
reconfirm                   Reconfirm VMPS
reset                       Reset system or module
session                     Tunnel to ATM or Router module
set                         Set, use 'set help' for more info
show                        Show, use 'show help' for more info
slip                        Attach/detach Serial Line IP interface
switch                      Switch to standby <clock|supervisor>
telnet                      Telnet to a remote host
test                        Test, use 'test help' for more info
upload                      Upload code from a processor
wait                        Wait for x seconds
write                       Write system configuration to terminal/network
```

A more restricted number of commands will be available in the user mode.

```
Console> ?
Commands:
----------------------------------------------------------------------
enable                   Enable privileged mode
help                     Show this message
history                  Show contents of history substitution buffer
ping                     Send echo packets to hosts
quit                     Exit from the Admin session
session                  Tunnel to ATM or Router module
set                      Set, use 'set help' for more info
show                     Show, use 'show help' for more info
wait                     Wait for x seconds
```

The user mode is limited to show commands, two set commands and no clear commands. Like the router IOS, you cannot see the configuration file from the user mode.

CATALYST SYNTAX

Catalyst 5000 syntax can be categorized into four categories:

1. Show
2. Set
3. Clear
4. Other

The most commonly used show, set and clear commands are reviewed on the following pages:

KEY CATALYST 5000 SHOW COMMANDS

Just as show commands play a critical role in monitoring the operation of a Cisco router, they play a similar role with the Catalyst 5000. Listed below are all the show commands available in enable mode. Some commands such as show port have additional show parameters.

```
Console>                 (enable) show ?
Show commands:
---------------------------------------------------------------------------
show alias               Show aliases for commands
show arp                 Show ARP table
show bridge              Show bridge information
show cam                 Show CAM table
show cdp                 Show Cisco Discovery Protocol Information
show cgmp                Show CGMP info
show config              Show system configuration
show drip                Show DRiP Information
show fddi                Show FDDI module entries
show fddicam             Show FDDI module CAM table
show flash               Show system flash information
```

```
showhelp
how ntp statistics
show port                Show port information
show rif\                Show Routing Information Field (RIF) Table
show rsmautostate        Show RSM derived interface state enabled/disabled
show snmp                Show SNMP information
show span                Show switch port analyzer information
show spantree            Show spantree information
show station             Show Tokenring Station info
show summertime          Show state of summertime information
show system              Show system information
show tacacs              Show TACACS information
show test                Show results of diagnostic tests
show time                Show time of day
show timezone            Show the current timezone offset
show tokenring           Show tokenring information
show trunk               Show trunk ports
show users               Show active Admin sessions
show version             Show version information
show vlan                Show Virtual LAN information
show vmps Show VMPS information
```

Some Catalyst 5000 commands were introduced in Chapters Two and Three. Chapter Two provided an overview of how to initially inspect newly received Catalyst 5000 switches. To examine the hardware components residing in a Catalyst 5000 and the current IOS, the following commands are used:

```
Show version

Show module
```

Chapter Three introduced methods of examining the interface and port status of connections on a Catalyst 5000. Chapter Three provided an overview on the use of the following commands:

```
Show module

Show mac

Show port

Show port status

Show cdp neighbor
```

SHOW CONFIG

Show config is the router IOS equivalent to show running-config and show startup-config combined. Since every command setting gets saved to NVRAM immediately, there is no need for two different show configuration commands or a copy running-config startup-config command. The config file for a Catalyst 5000 is divided into sections. A sample config file is displayed below:

```
Console> (enable) sh config help
Usage: show config [all|system|mod_num]

Console> (enable) sh config

begin
set password $1$FMFQ$HfZR5DUszVHIRhrz4h6V70
set enablepass $1$FMFQ$HfZR5DUszVHIRhrz4h6V70
set prompt Console>
set length 24 default
set logout 20
set banner motd ^C^C
!
#system
set system baud 9600
set system modem disable
set system name
set system location
set system contact
!
#snmp
set snmp community read-only   public
set snmp community read-write   private
set snmp community read-write-all secret
set snmp rmon disable
set snmp trap disable module
set snmp trap disable chassis
set snmp trap disable bridge
set snmp trap disable repeater
set snmp trap disable vtp
set snmp trap disable auth
set snmp trap disable ippermit
set snmp trap disable vmps
!
#ip
set interface sc0 1 0.0.0.0 0.0.0.0 0.0.0.0

set interface sl0 0.0.0.0 0.0.0.0
set arp agingtime 1200
set ip redirect  enable
set ip unreachable  enable
set ip fragmentation enable
set ip alias default     0.0.0.0
!
#Command alias
!
#vmps
set vmps server retry 3
```

```
set vmps server reconfirminterval 60
set vmps tftpserver 0.0.0.0 vmps-config-database.1
set vmps state disable

!
#dns
set ip dns disable
!
#tacacs+
set tacacs attempts 3
set tacacs directedrequest disable
set tacacs timeout 5
set authentication login tacacs disable
set authentication login local enable
set authentication enable tacacs disable
set authentication enable local enable
!
#bridge
set bridge ipx snaptoether  8023raw
set bridge ipx 8022toether  8023
set bridge ipx 8023rawtofddi snap
!
#vtp
set vtp mode server
set vtp v2 disable
set vtp pruning disable
set vtp pruneeligible 2-1000
clear vtp pruneeligible 1001-1005
!
#spantree
#uplinkfast groups
set spantree uplinkfast disable
#vlan 1
set spantree enable   1
set spantree fwddelay 15  1
set spantree hello  2   1
set spantree maxage  20  1
set spantree priority 32768 1

!
#cgmp
set cgmp disable
set cgmp leave disable
!
#syslog
set logging console enable
set logging server disable
set logging level cdp 2 default
set logging level cgmp 2 default
set logging level disl 5 default
set logging level dvlan 2 default
```

```
set logging level earl 2 default
set logging level fddi 2 default
set logging level ip 2 default
set logging level pruning 2 default
set logging level snmp 2 default
set logging level spantree 2 default
set logging level sys 5 default
set logging level tac 2 default
set logging level tcp 2 default
set logging level telnet 2 default
set logging level tftp 2 default
set logging level vtp 2 default
set logging level vmps 2 default
set logging level kernel 2 default
set logging level filesys 2 default
set logging level drip 2 default
set logging level pagp 5 default
!
#ntp
set ntp broadcastclient disable
set ntp broadcastdelay 3000
set ntp client disable
clear timezone
set summertime disable
!
#permit list
set ip permit disable
!
#drip
set tokenring reduction enable
set tokenring distrib-crf disable
!
#module 1 : 2-port 100BaseTX Supervisor
set module name  1
set vlan 1  1/1-2
set port enable   1/1-2
set port level   1/1-2 normal
set port duplex   1/1-2 half
set port trap    1/1-2 disable
set port name    1/1-2
set port security  1/1-2 disable
set port membership 1/1-2 static
set cdp enable  1/1-2
set cdp interval 1/1-2 60
set trunk 1/1 auto 1-1005
set trunk 1/2 auto 1-1005
set spantree portfast  1/1-2 disable
set spantree portcost  1/1-2 19
set spantree portpri   1/1-2 32
set spantree portvlanpri 1/1 0
```

```
set spantree portvlanpri 1/2 0
set spantree portvlancost 1/1 cost 18
set spantree portvlancost 1/2 cost 18
!
!
#module 5 empty
!
#switch port analyzer
set span disable
!
#cam
set cam agingtime 1,1003,1005 300
end
```

Notice that the Catalyst configuration file is divided into sections. The section headings are:

```
Global parameters
#system
#snmp
#ip
#Command alias
# vmps
#dns
#bridge
#vtp
#spantree
#vlan xxxx
#cgmp
#syslog
#ntp
#permit list
#drip
#module xxxx
#switch port analyzer
#cam
```

You can clear the config file without rebooting the Catalyst. Simply type `clear config all` and the switch will reset itself to the default settings.

```
catalyst-1> (enable) clea config all
This command will clear all configuration in NVRAM.
This command will cause ifIndex to be reassigned on the next system startup.
Do you want to continue (y/n) [n]? y
. . . . . .
System configuration cleared.
```

SHOW SYSTEM

The show system command is used to determine the Catalyst 5000's uptime as well as its levels of utilization. A sample `show system` display is provided below:

```
Console> show system

PS1-Status PS2-Status Fan-Status Temp-Alarm Sys-Status Uptime d,h:m:s Logout

---------- ---------- ---------- ---------- ---------- -------------- -----

ok      none    ok      off     ok      0,00:03:53   20 min
PS1-Type  PS2-Type  Modem  Baud Traffic Peak Peak-Time

---------- ---------- ------- ----- ------- ---- -------------------------

WS-C5008A none    disable 9600  0%   0% Sun Jul 12 1998, 23:47:44

System Name        System Location     System Contact

------------------------ ------------------------ --------------------

DC-HQ-2nd-Floor     Washington DC      Bernie Wolzac
```

SHOW VLAN

The `show vlan` command lists the VLANs that are resident on the switch or in the VTP domain if the switch is a member of a VTP domain. Show VLAN also displays which ports are members of which vlan on the local switch. VLANs are identified by a number ranging from 1 to 1024. VLAN numbers 1001 through 1024 are reserved. As an option, a name can also be assigned to a VLAN.

Listed below are the default VLANs listed on a Catalyst 5000 with a Supervisor module in slot one and a twelve port Ethernet module in slot three. VLANs 1002–1005 are default VLANs defined for possible Token-Ring and FDDI modules that can be installed in a Catalyst 5000.

The bottom halves of the displays list summary information for the different types of LAN modules that can be installed in Catalyst 5000: Ethernet/Fast Ethernet, Token-Ring, or FDDI.

```
Console> (enable) sh vlan
VLAN Name                          Status     Mod/Ports,     Vlans
---- -------------------------- ---------- --------------------------------
1    default                       active     1/1-2
                                              3/1-12
1002 fddi-default                  active
1003 token-ring-default            active
1004 fddinet-default               active
1005 trnet-default                 active
```

```
VLAN Type  SAID       MTU   Parent RingNo BrdgNo Stp  BrdgMode Trans1 Trans2
---- ----- ---------- ----- ------ ------ ------ ---- -------- ------ ------
1    enet  100001     1500  -      -      -      -    -        0      0
1002 fddi  101002     1500  -      0x0    -      -    -        0      0
1003 trcrf 101003     1500  0      0x0    -      -    -        0      0
1004 fdnet 101004     1500  -      -      0x0    ieee -        0      0
1005 trbrf 101005     1500  -      -      0x0    ibm  -        0      0

VLAN AREHops STEHops Backup CRF
---- ------- ------- ----------
1003 7       7       off
```

SHOW CAM

The show cam command lists the LAN switch transparent bridging table. It is used to direct the switching of frames through the Catalyst. If a frame enters the Catalyst 5000 and the destination address contained within the frame is in the CAM table, the frame is switched according to the information in the CAM table. If a frame enters the Catalyst 5000 and the destination address contained within the frame is not in the CAM table, the frame is flooded out all out bound ports.

CAM entries can be acquired dynamically or statically. Dynamic CAM entries are acquired by recording the source address of MAC frames that have entered a specific port. Dynamic CAM entries contain the following three elements of information:

MAC address
Port MAC address was learned on
VLAN number of source port

In the example below, a single MAC address is listed after the show cam command:

```
sh cam 00-a0-24-66-81-02

            * = Static Entry. + = Permanent Entry. # = System Entry.

VLAN Dest MAC/Route Des Destination Ports or VCs
---- ------------------ ----------------------------------------------------
3   00-a0-24-66-81-02  3/8
Total Matching CAM Entries Displayed = 1
```

By using the sh cam command with a single MAC address, you can locate a single MAC address out of thousands of entries.

In the example below, show cam dynamic lists all dynamically learned MAC addresses:

```
Console> (enable) sh cam dynamic
VLAN Dest MAC/Route Des Destination Ports or VCs
```

```
---- ----------------- ---------------------------------------------------
2    00-e0-29-0a-07-dc  3/3
3    00-a0-24-66-81-02  3/8
Total Matching CAM Entries Displayed = 2
```

Dynamic CAM entries have a default age of 300 seconds. If a frame containing the MAC address stored in the CAM table is not received on the associated port within the associated VLAN stored in the CAM table within the age expiration time, the entry is flushed.

SHOW PORT

The `show port` command was first introduced in Chapter Three. As the listing below reflects, there are many options to the show port command:

```
Console                    (enable) sh port ?
Usage:                     show port
    show port <mod_num>
    show port <mod_num/port_num>
Show port commands:
---------------------------------------------------------------------------
show port broadcast       Show port broadcast information
show port cdp             Show port CDP information
show port channel         Show port channel information
show port counters        Show port counters
show port fddi            Show port FDDI information
show port filter          Show Token Ring port filtering information
show port help            Show this message
show port mac             Show port MAC counters
show port multicast       Show port multicast information
show port security        Show port security information
show port spantree        Show port spantree information
show port status          Show port status
show port trap            Show port trap information
show port trunk           Show port trunk information
```

Commonly used show port commands are:

```
show port mac             This command provides the same information as show mac
                          x/y (x/y= module/port).
show port status          This command provides a brief summary status of a port
                          or group of ports. Show port status show only the first
                          line of the standard show port command.
show port trunk           This command displays what ports are in a trunking
                          state.
```

Listed below is a sample show port display:

```
Console> (enable) sh port 2/5
Port Name      Status      Vlan    Level    Duplex   Speed   Type
```

```
---- ------------------- ---------- -------- ------ ------ ----- --------
2/5           notconnect 20      normal  auto     auto    10/100BaseTX

Port          Align-Err  FCS-ErrXmit-ErrRcv-Err UnderSize
---- ---------- ---------- ---------- ---------- ----------
2/5           0          0       0         0          0

Port Single-Col Multi-Coll Late-Coll Excess-Col Carri-Sens Runts  Giants
---- ---------- ---------- ---------- ---------- ---------- --------- -----

2/5           0          0       0         0          0       0       0

Last-Time-Cleared
```

```
Thu Oct 9 1997, 11:25:47
```

Show port statistics can be cleared with the `clear` counters command.

SHOW MAC

The `show mac` command was introduced in Chapter Three. The `show mac` command displays the number and type of frames that have been sent and received by a given port. Used in combination with the clear counters command, the `show mac` command can be a useful troubleshooting tool to determine whether frames are being sent and received on a given port. A sample show mac display is provided below:

```
Console> (enable) show mac 3/1
MAC       Rcv-Frms   Xmit-Frms  Rcv-Multi  Xmit-Multi Rcv-Broad  Xmit-Broad
-------- ---------- ---------- ---------- ---------- ---------- ----------
 3/1      28         241        3          227        11         0

MAC       Dely-Exced MTU-Exced  In-Discard Lrn-Discrd In-Lost    Out-Lost
-------- ---------- ---------- ---------- ---------- ---------- ----------
 3/1      0          0          0          0          0          0

Port      Rcv-Unicast          Rcv-Multicast        Rcv-Broadcast
-------- -------------------- -------------------- --------------------
 3/1      14                   3                    11

Port      Xmit-Unicast         Xmit-Multicast       Xmit-Broadcast
-------- -------------------- -------------------- --------------------
 3/1      14                   228                  0

Port      Rcv-Octet            Xmit-Octet
-------- -------------------- --------------------
 3/1      3185                 16780

Last-Time-Cleared
```

```
-------------------------
Sun Jul 5 1998, 12:39:45
```

SHOW PORT SPANTREE

The `show port spantree` command allows you to see the spantree status of a specific port. The different spanning tree states are:

- Learning
- Listening
- Forwarding
- Blocking
- Disabled

```
Console> (enable) show port spantree 3/7
Port     Vlan Port-State    Cost  Priority Fast-Start Group Method
-------- ---- ------------- ----- -------- ---------- ------------
 3/7       1   learning      100   32       disabled
```

It is absolutely essential that you possess a strong understanding of the configuration and operation of the Spanning Tree Protocol. Spanning Tree will be covered in greater detail in Chapter Twenty.

SHOW VTP DOMAIN

The `show vtp domain` command lists the VTP domain that a switch resides in. In the listing below, notice that the VTP domain name "Cisco" has been listed. Remember one switch can only be in one and only VTP domain at any given time. The default configuration is that the switch does not reside in any VTP domain. The listing below reflects a switch's default configuration.

```
Console> (enable) sh vtp domain
Domain Name          Domain Index VTP Version Local Mode Password
-------------------------- ------------ ----------- ----------- ----------
Cisco               1       2      server   -

Vlan-count Max-vlan-storage Config Revision Notifications
---------- ---------------- -------------- -------------
5     1023         0        disabled

Last Updater  V2 Mode Pruning PruneEligible on Vlans
--------------- -------- -------- -------------------------
0.0.0.0     disabled disabled 2-1000
```

SHOW TRUNK

The `show trunk` command provides a summary of the ports in trunking mode on a given switch:

```
Console> (enable) sh trunk ?
```

```
Usage: show trunk
    show trunk [mod_num]
    show trunk [mod_num/port_num]

Console> (enable) sh trunk
Port     Mode       Status
-------- ---------- -----------
 2/1-2   on         trunking
 4/1     on         trunking

Port     Vlans allowed on trunk
-------- ----------------------------------------------------------------------
 2/1-2   1-1005
 4/1     1-1005

Port     Vlans allowed and active in management domain
-------- ----------------------------------------------------------------------
 2/1-2
 4/1

Port     Vlans in spanning tree forwarding state and not pruned
-------- ----------------------------------------------------------------------
 2/1-2
 4/1
```

The `Show trunk` command also displays what VLANs are allowed over a specific trunk link and what VLANs are actually forwarding traffic over a given trunk link.

By default, a trunk port will be assigned for a route switch module and an ATM LANE module if either of these modules are installed.

SH VERSION

The `show version` command was first introduced in Chapter Two. Just as with the standard IOS found on a router or LightStream ATM Switch, show version displays information about IOS used on switch and hardware components:

```
Console> (enable) sh version
WS-C5000 Software, Version McpSW: 3.1(2) NmpSW: 3.1(2a)
Copyright (c) 1995-1998 by Cisco Systems
NMP S/W compiled on Feb 20 1998, 18:56:57
MCP S/W compiled on Feb 20 1998, 19:09:39

System Bootstrap Version: 2.2(2)

Hardware Version: 2.3 Model: WS-C5000 Serial #: 005595417

Module Ports Model      Serial #  Hw     Fw      Fw1     Sw
------ ----- ---------- --------- ------ ------- ------- --------------------
1      2     WS-X5009   005595417 2.3    2.2(2)  2.2(1)  3.1(2a)
2      2     WS-X5156   007514151 2.0    1.3     1.3     3.2(6)
```

```
3    12   WS-X5213A 007403608 2.1   3.1(1)      3.1(2)
4    1    WS-X5302  006806418 4.5   20.1   2.2(4) 11.2(7)P, SHAR

    DRAM            FLASH              NVRAM
Module Total   Used   Free   Total   Used   Free   Total Used Free
------ ------- ------- ------- ------- ------- ------- ----- ----- -----
1     20480K  8206K 12274K  4096K  3584K  512K 256K 100K 156K

Uptime is 0 day, 0 hour, 17 minutes
```

SHOW MODULES

Show modules was featured in both Chapters Two and Three. It provides a summary of the modules and associated software installed in a Catalyst 5000.

```
Console> (enable) show module
Mod Module-Name  Ports Module-Type            Model     Serial-Num Status
--- ------------ ----- ---------------------- --------- ---------- ------
1                2     100BaseTX Supervisor   WS-X5009  005595417  ok
2                2     UTP OC-3 Dual-Phy ATM  WS-X5156  007514151  ok
3                12    10/100BaseTX Ethernet  WS-X5213A 007403608  ok
4                1     Route Switch           WS-X5302  006806418  ok

Mod MAC-Address(es)                Hw    Fw    Sw
--- ---------------------------------------- ------ ------- ----------------
1  00-10-11-3b-88-00 thru 00-10-11-3b-8b-ff 2.3   2.2(2) 3.1(2a)
2  00-e0-1e-e4-fe-dd                  2.0   1.3    3.2(6)
3  00-e0-1e-e7-a7-38 thru 00-e0-1e-e7-a7-43 2.1   3.1(1) 3.1(2)
4  00-e0-1e-91-ce-34 thru 00-e0-1e-91-ce-35 4.5   20.1   11.2(7)P, SHAR
```

SET AND CLEAR COMMANDS

There is no configuration mode on the primary Catalyst 5000 IOS. The functional equivalent to the standard IOS configuration mode are the Catalyst SET and CLEAR commands.

The following set commands can be used in enable mode.

```
Console>                    (enable) set ?
Set commands:
--------------------------------------------------------------------------
set alias                   Set alias for command
set arp                     Set ARP table entry
set authentication          Set TACACS authentication
set banner                  Set message of the day banner
set bridge                  Set bridge, use 'set bridge help' for more info
set cam                     Set CAM table entry
set cdp                     Set cdp, use 'set cdp help' for more info
set cgmp                    Set CGMP (enable/disable)
set enablepass              Set privilege mode password
set fddi                    Set FDDI, use 'set fddi help' for more info
```

```
set help                 Show this message
set interface            Set network interface configuration
set ip                   Set IP, use 'set ip help' for more info
set length               Set number of lines in display (0 to disable 'more')
set logging              Set system logging configuration information
set logout               Set number of minutes before automatic logout
set module               Set module, use 'set module help' for more info
set multicast            Set multicast router port
set ntp                  Set NTP, use 'set ntp help' for more info
set password             Set console password
set port                 Set port, use 'set port help' for more info
set prompt               Set prompt
set rsmautostate         Enable/Disable RSM derived interface state
set snmp                 Set SNMP, use 'set snmp help' for more info
set spa                  Set switch port analyzer
set spantree             Set spantree, use 'set spantree help' for more info
set summertime           Set summertime
set system               Set system, use 'set system help' for more info
set tacacs               Set TACACS information
set time                 Set time
set timezone             Set timezone
set tokenring            Set tokenring information
set trunk                Set trunk ports
set vlan                 Set virtual LAN information
set vmps                 Set VMPS information
set vtp                  Set VLAN Trunk Information
```

The following clear commands can be used in enable mode. Notice that some set commands do not have corresponding clear commands

```
Console>                 enable) clear ?
Clear commands:
---------------------------------------------------------------------------
clear alias              Clear aliases of commands
clear arp                Clear ARP table entries
clear banner             Clear Message Of The Day banner
clear cam                Clear CAM table entries
clear cgmp               Clear CGMP statistics
clear config             Clear configuration and reset system
clear counters           Clear MAC and Port counters
clear drip               Clear DRiP statistics
clear help               Show this message
clear ip                 Clear IP, use 'clear ip help' for more info
clear log                Clear log information
clear logging            Clear system logging information
clear multicast          Clear multicast router port
clear ntp                Clear NTP servers and timezone
clear port               Clear port features
clear snmp               Clear SNMP trap receiver address
clear spantree           Clear spantree parameters
```

```
clear tacacs              Clear TACACS server host/key
clear timezone            Clear timezone
clear trunk               Clear trunk ports
clear vlan                Clear a VLAN
clear vmps                Clear VMPS information
clear vtp                 Clear VTP statistics
```

CONFIGURING THE SC0 INTERFACE

The SC0 interface is a logical interface within each Catalyst 5000. Once it is configured, you can TELNET to the Catalyst to monitor and configure it. If the SC0 interface is not configured, you must use the console connection to access the Catalyst. By default the SC0 interface resides in VLAN 1. Examine the syntax displayed below carefully. The [vlan] option allows you to place the SC0 interface into another VLAN if desired.

```
Console> (enable) set interface
Usage: set interface <sc0|sl0> <up|down>
    set interface sc0 [vlan] [ip_addr [netmask [broadcast]]]
    set interface sl0 <slip_addr> <dest_addr>
```

You can view the SC0 interface configuration with the `show interface` command:

```
Console> (enable) show interface
sl0: flags=51<UP,POINTOPOINT,RUNNING>
    slip 0.0.0.0 dest 0.0.0.0
sc0: flags=63<UP,BROADCAST,RUNNING>
    vlan 2 inet 172.16.32.1 netmask 255.255.255.0 broadcast 172.16.32.255
```

Once the SC0 interface is configured, a default gateway needs to be supplied for it. This is done with the following command syntax:

```
Console> (enable) set ip route
Usage: set ip route <destination> <gateway> [metric]
    (destination and gateway are IP alias or IP address in
    dot notation: a.b.c.d)
```

The set ip route does not create a static route for all traffic transiting the switch. It creates a static route for the SC0 interface. An example of setting the default route for the SC0 interface is displayed below:

```
Console> (enable) set ip route 0.0.0.0 172.16.32.100
Route added.
```

You can view the default route settings for the SC0 interface with the `show ip route` command:

```
Console> (enable) sh ip route
Fragmentation  Redirect  Unreachable
```

```
----------  --------  -----------
enabled     enabled   enabled

Destination            Gateway                Flags  Use        Interface
---------------------- ---------------------- ------ ---------- ---------
default                172.16.32.100          UG                0 sc0
172.16.32.0            172.16.32.1            U                 0 sc0
default                default                UH                0 sl0
```

TESTING AND ACCESSING THE SC0 INTERFACE

From both user and enable mode, you can test SC0 connectivity with PING and TELNET commands.

SET VTP DOMAIN

Configure a VTP domain if you have multiple switches and multiple VLANs. The syntax for configuring a switch to participate in a VTP domain is:

```
Console> (enable) set vtp ?
Usage: set vtp [domain <name>] [mode <mode>] [passwd <passwd>]
         [pruning <enable|disable>] [v2 <enable|disable>
     (mode = client|server|transparent
     Use passwd '0' to clear vtp password)
Usage: set vtp pruneeligible <vlans>
     (vlans = 2..1005
     An example of vlans is 2-10,1005)
```

Switches can be configured to participate in the following three VTP modes:

```
VTP Server
VTP Client
VTP Transparent
```

A VTP server can create and delete VLANs as well as assign ports from one VLAN to another.

A VTP client will receive VLAN advertisements from over VTP participating switches. A VTP client cannot create or delete VLANs. It can assign ports from one pre-existing VLAN to another.

The VTP transparent mode allows a switch to forward VTP traffic but the switch itself will not participate in sending or receiving VLAN information from a given VTP domain.

SET TRUNK

Ports can be placed in a trunking state with the set trunk command. Catalyst 5000s also support dynamic ISL trunking for Fast-Ethernet ports. Certain modules, such as the RSM and the ATM LANE interfaces are automatically defined as trunked connections.

```
Console> (enable) set trunk help
Usage: set trunk <mod_num/port_num> [on|off|desirable|auto|nonegotiate] [vlans]
    (vlans = 1..1005
    An example of vlans is 2-10,1005)
```

As displayed above, the set trunk syntax is straightforward. One point that requires further explanation is the ability to specify which VLANs can be forwarded over a specific trunk port. This is defined by the "vlans" parameter.

To remove a port from trunking mode or to remove specific VLANs from being propagated over a trunk link, use the clear trunk command.

SET VLAN

On a Catalyst 5000, VLANs can be defined either statically or dynamically. Creating static VLANs involves associating a specific port or a discrete collection of ports to a specific VLAN. This can be performed using Catalyst 5000 command `set vlan`. Creating dynamic VLANs involves creating a database with unique end system information such as end system MAC addresses associated to a specific VLAN. On a Catalyst 5000, creating this database involves configuring a Virtual Management Policy Server (VMPS) and enabling specific ports to acquire VLAN membership dynamically. The syntax used on a Catalyst 5000 to enable a port to participate in dynamically joining VLANs is:

set port membership dynamic

Listed below is the set vlan command used for statically assigning Catalyst 5000 ports to a specific VLAN:

```
Console> (enable) set vlan
Usage: set vlan <vlan_num> <mod/ports...>
    (An example of mod/ports is 1/1,2/1-12,3/1-2,4/1-12)
Usage: set vlan <vlan_num> [name <name>] [type <type>] [state <state>]
              [said <said>] [mtu <mtu>] [ring <ring_number>]
              [bridge <bridge_number>] [parent <vlan_num>]
              [mode <bridge_mode>] [stp <stp_type>]
              [translation <vlan_num>] [backupcrf <off|on>]
              [aremaxhop <hopcount>] [stemaxhop <hopcount>]
    (name = 1..32 characters, state = (active, suspend)
    type = (ethernet, fddi, fddinet, trcrf, trbrf)
    said = 1..4294967294, mtu = 576..18190, ring_number = 0x1..0xfff
    bridge_number = 0x1..0xf, parent = 2..1005, mode = (srt, srb)
    stp = (ieee, ibm, auto), translation = 1..1005
    hopcount = 1..13)
```

In the example below, ports five through twelve on module three are being assigned to VLAN 2. As the console messages reflect, these ports are being taken from VLANs 22, 1, and 12:

```
Console> (enable) set vlan 2 3/5-12
VLAN 2 modified.
VLAN 22 modified.
VLAN 1 modified.
VLAN 12 modified.
VLAN Mod/Ports
---- -----------------------
2    3/5-12
```

In its most basic application, the `set vlan` command will assign a single port, a range of ports or a collection of ports to a specific VLAN.

With the `clear vlan` command, notice that you cannot reference individual ports. If you want to clear ports on a VLAN, you must clear the entire VLAN. When the `clear vlan` command is used, the ports formerly belonging to the removed VLAN belong to no VLAN. They attain an "inactive" state. In order to make the ports of a cleared VLAN active again, use the `set vlan` command to assign the ports to an existing VLAN. The syntax of the `clear vlan` command is displayed below:

```
Console> (enable) clear vlan
Usage: clear vlan <vlan_num>
    (vlan_num should be in the range of 2..1000)
```

In the example below, all ports assigned to VLAN 2 are being cleared:

```
Console> (enable) clear vlan 2
```

This command will deactivate all ports on vlan 2

```
in the entire management domain

Do you want to continue(y/n) [n]?y

Vlan 2 deleted
```

Listed below, take note of ports five through twelve on module three. After VLAN 2 has been cleared, all of its ports are in an "inactive" state and they are still listed as being associated with VLAN 2:

```
Console>      (enable)    sh      port    status 3
Port          Name        Status Vlan     Level    Duplex Speed   Type
----- ------------------ ---------- ---------- ------ ------ ----- --------
 3/1          notconnect 1       normal  auto     auto    10/100  BaseTX
 3/2          notconnect 1       normal  auto     auto    10/100  BaseTX
 3/3          notconnect 10      normal  auto     auto    10/100  BaseTX
 3/4          notconnect 10      normal  auto     auto    10/100  BaseTX
 3/5          inactive    2      normal  auto     auto    10/100  BaseTX
 3/6          inactive    2      normal  auto     auto    10/100  BaseTX
 3/7          inactive    2      normal  auto     auto    10/100  BaseTX
 3/8          inactive    2      normal  auto     auto    10/100  BaseTX
 3/9          inactive    2      normal  auto     auto    10/100  BaseTX
 3/10         inactive    2      normal  auto     auto    10/100  BaseTX
 3/11         inactive    2      normal  auto     auto    10/100  BaseTX
 3/12         inactive    2      normal  auto     auto    10/100  BaseTX
```

In order to place them back into an "active" state, assign them to an active VLAN.

REMEMBER: WHEN THE SET VLAN COMMAND IS USED, YOU HAVE CREATED A SECOND BROADCAST DOMAIN. NETWORK LAYER PROTOCOLS LIKE IP AND IPX WILL TREAT THE SECOND VLAN LIKE A SEPARATE NETWORK. IN ORDER TO RETAIN REACHABILITY BETWEEN END SYSTEMS IN TWO OR MORE SEPARATE VLANS, A ROUTING PROCESS MUST BE AVAILABLE FOR EACH AND EVERY VLAN.

SET AND CLEAR SPANNING TREE PROTOCOL PARAMETERS

Catalyst 5000 Ethernet LAN Switch modules operate like a multiport transparent bridge. The Spanning Tree Algorithm eliminates the formation of loops in a transparent bridged environment. The Catalyst 5000 applies the Spanning Tree Algorithm on a per VLAN basis. The Catalyst 5000 supplies a wide range of set and clear commands related to spanning tree configuration:

```
Console> (enable) set spantree ?
Set spantree commands:
----------------------------------------------------------------------------
set spantree disable    Disable spanning tree
set spantree disable    Disable spanning tree
set spantree fwddelay   Set spantree forward delay
set spantree hello      Set spantree hello interval
set spantree help       Show this message
set spantree maxage     Set spantree max aging time
set spantree portcost   Set spantree port cost
set spantree portfast   Set spantree port fast start
set spantree portpri    Set spantree port priority
set spantree portstate  Set spantree logical port state
```

```
set spantree portvlancostSet spantree port cost per vlan
set spantree portvlanpri Set spantree port vlan priority
set spantree priority    Set spantree priority
set spantree root        Set switch as primary or secondary root
set spantree uplinkfast Enable or disable uplinkfast groups
set spantree multicast-addressSet multicast address type for trbrf's

Console> (enable) clea spantr ?
Clear spantree commands:
-----------------------------------------------------------------------------
clear spantree help      Show this message
clear spantree portvlancostClear spantree port vlan cost
clear spantree portvlanpriClear spantree port vlan priority
clear spantree root      Restore STP parameters to default values
clear spantree statisticsClear spantree statistics information
clear spantree uplinkfastClear uplinkfast groups
```

Spanning Tree is an extremely important topic to understand in a LAN switching environment. It is covered in detail in Chapter Twenty.

SET PORT

The `set port` command allows you to custom configure port parameters.

```
Console> (enable) set port ?
Set port commands:
-----------------------------------------------------------------------------
set port broadcast     Set port broadcast traffic limit
set port channel      Set port channel (on/off)
set port disable      Disable a port
set port duplex       Set port transmission type (full/half duplex)
set port enable       Enable a port
set port filter       Set filtering of Token Ring ports
set port help        Show this message
set port level       Set port priority level (normal/high)
set port membership   Set vlan membership assignment to a port
set port multicast    Set port multicast router
set port name        Set port name
set port security     Set port security (enable/disable)
set port speed       Set port transmission speed (4/10/16/100 Mbps)
set port trap        Set port up/down trap (enable/disable)
```

ROUTING BETWEEN VLANS

Cisco offers different ways to perform routing between VLANs including the following high-performance methods:

RSM
Supervisor III Module with a NetFlow Feature Card
Catalyst 8500

Three methods will be reviewed below.

Method One: Assigning a Single Port of a Router to Each VLAN

The simplest inter-VLAN routing solution is to connect a router interface into each VLAN. The router will be configured as if its was connected to a shared Ethernet port. The disadvantage of this method is that as the number of VLANs increase the number of ports needed on a router will increase.

Use of the Cisco 8500 layer three switch is the optimal method for performing this style of routing. The Cisco 8500 switches IP and IPX packets at wire speed. It uses the same Cisco Express Forwarding technology of the Cisco 12000.

Method Two: Performing ISL Trunking between a Switch and a Router Interface

As second method is to perform ISL trunking on a Fast-Ethernet interface of a router. With this configuration, only a single router interface is needed. A single router interface can be divided into multiple ISL subinterfaces. This is known as one-armed routing, hairpin routing, or router on a stick.

Method Three: Using the Route Switch Module (RSM)

RSM is a Catalyst layer three routing module that is inserted directly into the Catalyst. It is the same routing and layer three switching engine found in a Cisco 7500 router. When accessed, its user interface is identical to the Cisco router IOS.

A significant and noticeable difference between a standard Cisco router and the RSM is the absence of physical interfaces. The RSM uses logical interfaces; primarily "vlan interfaces" are defined on the RSM. Therefore, exhausting port density on a router is not an issue with the RSM.

To access the RSM from the Catalyst IOS, type `session #` (# = the module where the RSM resides)

```
Console> (enable) session 4
Trying Router-4...
Connected to Router-4.
Escape character is '^]'.

Router>
```

Once you are at the router prompt, your user interface is identical to what you would expect from a Cisco 2500, 4000, 3600, 7200, or 7500 router.

RUNNING CONFIG ON A ROUTE SWITCH MODULE WITH VLANS CREATED

In the example below, notice that logical "VLAN" interfaces are created. The interface names are titled VLAN1 and VLAN2.

```
Router#sh run
Building conf

Current configuration:
!
version 11.2
no service udp-small-servers
no service tcp-small-servers
!
hostname Router
!
!
!
interface Vlan1
ip address 172.16.1.1 255.255.255.0
!
interface Vlan2
ip address 172.16.2.1 255.255.255.0
!
interface Vlan10
 no ip address
!
no ip classless
!
line con 0
line vty 0 4
 login
!
end
```

Listed below are routing protocols that can be used on the RSM:

```
Router(config)#router ?
 bgp     Border Gateway Protocol (BGP)
```

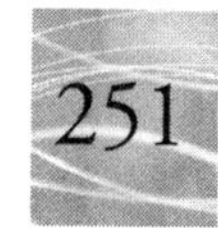

```
egp     Exterior Gateway Protocol (EGP)
eigrp    Enhanced Interior Gateway Routing Protocol (EIGRP)
igrp    Interior Gateway Routing Protocol (IGRP)
isis    ISO IS-IS
iso-igrp IGRP for OSI networks
mobile  Mobile routes
odr     On Demand stub Routes
ospf    Open Shortest Path First (OSPF)
rip     Routing Information Protocol (RIP)
static  Static routes
```

BASIC CATALYST 5000 TROUBLESHOOTING

A recommended method of basic Catalyst 5000 troubleshooting is provided below:

1. Make sure the Catalyst 5000 switch is booting properly. Review the Catalyst 5000 boot up process described in Chapter Two.
2. Make sure that all Catalyst modules are in an "OK" state. Use show module and check the port LEDs.
3. Make sure that all ports that have a connection are in an ACTIVE state. Check the Catalyst LED's and use the show port status command.
4. Make sure that ports are sending and receiving frames. Perform an extended ping on an end system connected on a specific Catalyst port and examine port traffic statistics with the show mac and show port commands. If necessary, use the clear counters command to make the reading of the show mac and show port statistics easier.
5. Check the Catalyst CAM table to make sure that end system MAC addresses are in the CAM table and that the are being associated with the proper port and VLAN. Use the show cam <mac-address> command to locate a single MAC address to examine the CAM table.
6. Use the show system command to view the utilization of a given Catalyst switch.

Summary

LAN switching and multilayer switching is redrawing the contour lines of internetworking. Functions that routers once performed, switches are now performing. All internetworking engineers must know how to design, install, configure, maintain, and troubleshoot LAN switches and multilayer switches. These platforms are at the heart of state-of-the art campus/LAN internetworks.

The Catalyst 5000 is a keystone platform in the entire Cisco product line. It is critical that Cisco internetwork engineers know how to integrate the Catalyst 5000 into a Cisco router environment. This chapter covered only the basics of Catalyst configuration. There is much more to learn about Catalyst configuration and monitoring.

Catalyst configuration issues will be revisited at Level Five, configuring nonroutable technologies (Chapter 20). The key Catalyst related topics covered at Level Five will be transparent bridging, source route bridging, spanning tree configuration, concurrent routing, and bridging as well as integrated routing and bridging.

Important Catalyst 5000 topics not covered in this book include:

- Dynamic VLAN membership configuration
- VLAN security
- Deploying redundancy features in a Catalyst 5000 environment
- VLAN performance tuning

You must pursue these topics independently.

Professional Development Checklist

By reading this chapter, you should be able to perform the following operations:

- Configure SCO interface
- Set the default route of the SCO interface
- Place SCO interface in another VLAN
- Configure VTP Domain Membership
- Configure ISL Trunking
- Configure Multiple VLANs
- Configure inter-VLAN routing by connecting different router interfaces into different VLANs
- Configure inter-VLAN routing with the RSM
- Monitor a Catalyst 5000's port activity and system utilization
- Perform basic Catalyst 5000 troubleshooting

For Further Study

Cisco Certified Training Course: Cisco LAN Switch Configuration (CLSC), Cisco Systems, Inc.

Designing Switched LAN Internetworks

http://www.cisco.com/univercd/data/doc/cintrnet/idg4/idglans.htm

Setting up VLANs Automatically

http://www.cisco.com/warp/customer/732/vlan/vtp_wp.html

URLs

- **http://www.cisco.com/univercd/home/home.htm**
- **www.mentorlabs.com**
- **www.cciecert.com**

Can You Spot the Issues?

1. Three months ago you received a single Catalyst 5000 with three 12 port Ethernet 10/100 port modules. You knew that the Catalyst is a plug and play LAN switch. You plugged 100 end systems into the available Ethernet ports on the Catalyst. Some of the end systems are directly connected to the Catalyst 5000. Others are connected through old 10BASET hubs. Everything was working fine. You did not configure the Catalyst in any way. All of its settings are the default settings. Today, you decided you wanted to optimize your network by dividing your network into two VLANs. You successfully place the ports used to connect 40 of your users into VLAN 2. Suddenly, they cannot ping any of the end systems not in VLAN 2 but they can ping each other. What happened? What is the remedy?
2. You are tired of directly connecting to the Catalyst 5000 console port to access it. You configure the SC0 interface and now you can access the Catalyst from your corporate LAN. The only configuration you performed on the Catalyst was the configuration of the SC0 interface. Everything else on the Catalyst is set to its defaults. You go home and you cannot access it from home. You can access a UNIX system in your office that is connected to the Catalyst but you cannot

establish a TELNET session with the Catalyst switch itself. Why? What is the remedy?

3. Your company purchases a second Catalyst 5000 and you do not feel comfortable about VLANs. You plug 200 end systems into the Catalyst 5000 using a combination of direct connections and hub connections with end systems attached to the hubs. You now have 200 end systems attached off of both Catalysts. This gives you a sum total of 400 end systems attached to two Catalyst switches. Both Catalyst switches are configured with the default configuration only. What is the absolute minimum you need to do to provide inter-switch connectivity with both Catalyst's possessing their default configurations?
4. You want to create three new VLANs on your two Catalysts. Only the SC0 interface will remain in VLAN 1. All three VLANs will have member ports on both switches. The minimal configuration you suggested in Question 3 no longer works. End systems can only ping other end systems in their VLAN on their physical switch. A third Catalyst switch has been delivered and you need to add these three VLAN's to it. What are the issues? What are the remedies?
5. You now have three Catalyst switches with 600 end systems attached. You are just learning about Catalyst switches and you have a lot to learn. You are under the misguided impression that since there are 600 end systems attached to your Catalyst 5000 switch domain, there should be 600 end systems in you CAM table. There are only 240 entries on Switch-1 when you check. This number is constantly changing. The other switches have other MAC addresses and a different total number of MAC addresses in their CAM tables. Why? Is this a cause of concern? Explain.

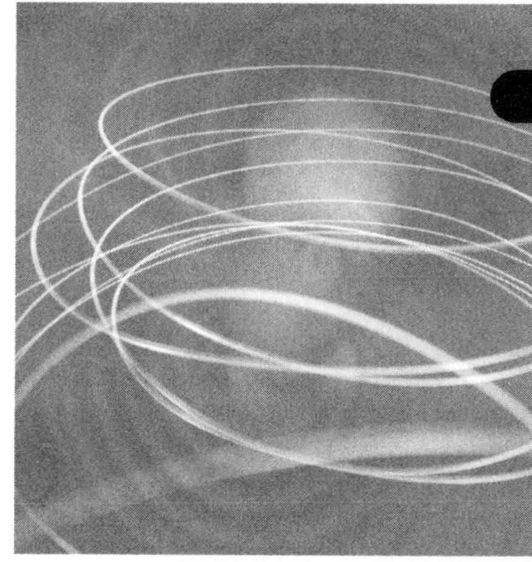

SEVEN

Configuring ATM

Topics Covered in This Chapter

- Configuring ATM PVCs
- Configuring ATM SVCs with MAP-LISTS
- Configuring ATM Classical IP
- Configuring ATM LANE
- ATM Routing Overview
- Troubleshooting ATM

So far we have examined Frame-Relay, ISDN/DDR and Catalyst 5000 configurations. We will now examine ATM, a technology that overlaps and interacts with all that we have seen so far.

Therefore, before beginning this chapter, make sure you have a strong grasp on:

- All Frame-Relay configuration issues. A strong grasp on Frame-Relay PVC configuration and configuring IP routing over Frame-Relay. This will greatly accelerate your learning of ATM PVC configuration and configuring IP routing over ATM. Frame-Relay configuration issues are covered in Chapter 4.
- ISDN/DDR configuration issues. You know how to configure ISDN to talk to an ISDN switch. Review the Q.931 messages displayed for ISDN call set-up and tear down at the beginning of Chapter Five.
- Review the Catalyst 5000 configuration issues. Especially important is the role of trunking, defined in Chapter 6. ATM LANE is identified as one of three primary trunking technologies.

This chapter does not supply an in-depth theoretical description of ATM. It focuses on the configuration of ATM technology with Cisco products. To obtain excellent coverage on ATM theoretical issues, read the following Prentice Hall PTR publications:

ATM (Volume I, II and III) by Uyless Black, ISBN Number: 0-13-784182-5
ATM—The New Paradigm for Internet, Intranet and Residential Broadband Services and Applications, by Timothy Kwok, ISBN Number: 0-13-107224-7

ATM and Frame-Relay Compared

Similarities between ATM and Frame-Relay

Both ATM and Frame-Relay possess the following features:

- Both are virtual circuit based.
- Both are NBMA technologies.
- Both have congestion avoidance techniques.
- Both have burst rate features.
- Both have traffic management features (traffic shaping).
- Frame-Relay FECN is equivalent to ATM EFCI.
- Frame-Relay BECN is equivalent to ATM Relative Rate Marking.

Differences between ATM and Frame-Relay

- ATM is cell based.
- ATM is isochronous. Frame-Relay is not.
- ATM has a LANE deployment. Frame has nothing of the sort.
- Frame-Relay LMI is completely different than ATM ILMI.
- ATM has QOS.

ATM and ISDN Compared

Similarities between ATM and ISDN

- ATM has its origins in B-ISDN.
- ATM switched connections use the same signaling as Narrowband ISDN. ATM SVCs use Q.2931. Q.2931 is a direct descendant of Narrowband ISDN's Q.931. (See Chapter 5 of this book.)
- ATM has one control channel for many data connections.
- ATM and ISDN can support both voice and non-voice traffic.

Differences between ATM and ISDN

- ATM is unchannelized. Narrowband ISDN is channelized.
- Narrowband ISDN is limited by the number of concurrent channels it supports.
- ISDN BRI supports only two B Channels and one D Channel. ISDN PRI supports 23 B Channels and one D Channel.
- ATM is not limited by a predefined number of channels. It is "unchannelized".

ATM Overview

The ATM architectural model can be compared to the OSI Model. Both are layered.

ATM Interface Types

Two types of ATM interfaces are defined:

1. User to Network (UNI)
2. Network to Network (NNI)

The UNI interface is defined as the interface(s) used between an ATM edge device and an ATM switch. Examples of ATM edge devices are workstations with ATM cards and routers.

The NNI is used between two ATM switches and two ATM networks. Also, there is a further classification of ATM UNI and NNI interfaces into either private (private ATM UNI and private ATM NNI) or public interface types (public ATM UNI or public ATM NNI).

ATM Classes of Service

- Class A Supports constant bit rate traffic with stringent timing requirements
- Class B Similar to Class A, but also supports variable bit rate applications
- Class C Supports connection-oriented variable bit rate applications
- Class D Similar to Class C, but supports connectionless services
- Class X "Raw" ATM service

The ATM UNI 3.1 specification supports only classes A, C and X.

ATM Adaptive Layer (AAL) Types

The ATM adaptive layer is divided into two parts:

1. A common part
2. A service specific part

The AAL Common Part is further divided into two sublayers:

1. Convergence sublayer
2. Segmentation and reassembly sublayer

- CBR Constant Bit Rate
- VBR Variable Bit Rate
- ABR Available Bit Rate
- UBR Unspecified Bit Rate

Cisco's Implementation of ATM

Cisco possesses a number of products that support ATM technology. A partial listing of some of the more prominent Cisco ATM products is provided below:

- LightStream 1010 is a full service ATM switch that runs the Cisco IOS
- ATM Interface Processor in 7500 routers
- Out of the box Cisco AIPs support AAL3/4 and AAL5
- In order to support AAL1, you need a CES port adapter
- ATM CES Port Adapter for 7200
- LANE Module in Catalyst 5000

Configuring ATM PVCs with the Cisco IOS

PVC CONFIGURATION ON A CISCO ROUTER OR CATALYST LANE MODULE

Unlike a Frame-Relay connection, where all that needs to be typed is "encap frame", you must manually configure the ATM PVCs with a VPI/VCI pair at the router. Once the ATM PVC is manually configured, INVERSE ARP can be used to map remote network layer addresses with local VPI/VCI pairs. If you don't want to use INVERSE ARP, MAP-LIST statements can be used instead. ATM MAP-LIST statements are the functional equivalent of FRAME-RELAY MAP statements.

Displayed below is a sample configuration of an ATM PVC, along with associated MAP-LIST commands:

```
interface ATM0
ip address 172.10.10.1 255.255.255.0
atm pvc 1 0 40 aal5snap
atm pvc 2 0 50 aal5snap
map-group 1483pvc
map-list 1483pvc
ip 172.10.10.2 atm-vc 1 broadcast
ip 172.10.10.3 atm-vc 2 broadcast
```

A third alternative to using INVERSE ARP and MAP-LIST statements is to use point-to-point subinterfaces. Again, remember to draw parallels between Frame-Relay PVC configuration and ATM PVC configuration.

MANUAL VPI/VCI CONFIGURATION ON THE LIGHTSTREAM ATM SWITCH

Configuration of A LightStream 1010 Switch

Displayed below is a sample PVC configuration on a Light Stream 1010 switch:

```
interface ATM1/1/2
    no keepalive
    atm pvc 1 140 interface ATM1/1/1 0 140
    atm pvc 1 60 interface ATM1/1/1 0 60
```

LS1 #show atm vc int atm 1/1/1

Interface	VPI	VCI	Type	X-Interface	X-VPI	X-VCI	Status
ATM1/1/1	0	5	PVC	ATM2/0/0	0	47	Up
ATM1/1/1	0	16	PVC	ATM2/0/0	0	48	Up
ATM1/1/1	0	18	PVC	ATM2/0/0	0	49	Up
ATM1/1/1	0	140	PVC	ATM1/1/2	1	140	Up
ATM1/1/1	0	60	PVC	ATM1/1/2	1	60	Up

Using show atm Status

You can obtain a summary status of all ATM interfaces with the show atm status command. Listed below is a sample display of show atm status:

ls1010-1#show atm status

NUMBER OF INSTALLED CONNECTIONS: (P2P=Point to Point, P2MP=Point to MultiPoint, MP2P=Multipoint to Point)

Type	PVCs	SoftPVCs	SVCs	TVCs	PVPs	SoftPVPs	SVPs	Total
P2P	5	0	0	0	0	0	0	5
P2MP	0	0	0	0	0	0	0	0
MP2P	0	0	0	0	0	0	0	0

TOTAL INSTALLED CONNECTIONS = 5

PER-INTERFACE STATUS SUMMARY AT 16:54:22 UTC Tue Sep 8 1998:

Interface Name	IF Status	Admin Status	Auto-Cfg Status	ILMIAddr RegState	SSCOP State	Hello State
-------------	--------	------------	--------	------------	---------	--------
ATM0/0/0	UP	up	done	UpAndNormal	Idle	n/a
ATM0/0/1	UP	up	done	UpAndNormal	Idle	n/a
ATM0/0/2	DOWN	down	waiting	n/a	Idle	n/a
ATM0/0/3	DOWN	down	waiting	n/a	Idle	n/a
ATM0/1/0	DOWN	down	waiting	n/a	Idle	n/a
ATM0/1/1	DOWN	down	waiting	n/a	Idle	n/a
ATM0/1/2	DOWN	down	waiting	n/a	Idle	n/a
ATM0/1/3	DOWN	down	waiting	n/a	Idle	n/a
ATM2/0/0	UP	up	n/a	UpAndNormal	Idle	n/a

Using show atm vc

Interface	VCD	VPI	VCI	Type	Encapsulation	AAL/ Kbps	Peak Kbps	Avg. Cells	Burst Status
ATM0	1	0	140	PVC	AAL5-SNAP	155000	155000	94	Active
ATM0	2	0	60	PVC	AAL5-SNAP	155000	155000	94	Active

Configuring PVCs Between Multiple Sites

You must now revisit the same hub and spoke issues encountered with Frame-Relay in Chapter 4. Just as with Frame-Relay, ATM provides three configuration tools for a partially meshed ATM topology:

1. Inverse ARP
2. ATM map statements using the map-list statement
3. Point-to-point subinterfaces

Map-list is equivalent to the Frame-Relay map statement. If you want to forward broadcasts over an ATM PVC, include the broadcast parameter at the end of the map-list statement.

The ATM point-to-point subinterface is comparable to the point-to-point subinterface used in a Frame-Relay environment.

Routing Over ATM PVCs

Many of the same issues related to configuring network layer routing (IP, IPX, AppleTalk, etc.) over Frame-Relay also exist with configuring network layer routing over ATM. For example, when configuring distance-vector routing protocols over a hub and spoke ATM network, be aware of the rule of split horizon.

If different interface types are used with OSPF over an ATM network, be aware of OSPF interface mismatches. As with an OSPF Frame-Relay configuration, use the following OSPF interface configuration command to assure that all OSPF ATM interfaces are of the same type:

```
Ip ospf network
```

Configuring ATM SVCs

As its name suggests, an ATM PVC is permanently active. Conversely, an ATM switched virtual circuit is established only when needed. ATM Switched Virtual Circuit call set up involves three basic steps:

1. Call set up
2. Data transfer
3. Call tear down

In order to accommodate switched virtual circuits, an addressing scheme must be defined to support this on-demand virtual circuit model. This addressing scheme is embodied in the 20-byte NSAP address.

The ATM NSAP Address

An ATM NSAP address is 160 bits (20 bytes) in length. It is made up of the following components:

1. The Initial Domain Part (IDP)

2. The Authority Format Identifier (AFI)
   a. 39 = DCC ATM format
   b. 47 = ICD ATM format
   c. 45 = E.164 format
4. The Initial Domain Identifier (IDI). The IDI is coded as:
   a. A data country code (DCC) in conformance to ISO 3166
   b. An international code designator (ICD)
   c. An E.164 address
4. Domain Specific Part (DSP)
   a. 13 bytes from the switch
   b. 6 bytes from the ES

1 byte: the selector byte The selector byte is not used by the ATM network. The selector byte distinguishes between the LES and the BUS, potentially on the ES or router.

The selector byte is functionally similar to a TCP port number.

Required PVCs for Cisco SVC Connections

Two PVCs must be established for SVC connections to be created on a Cisco router or Catalyst LANE module:

1. QSAAL: Use VPI/VCI pair: 0 5
2. ILMI: Use VPI/VCI pair: 0 16

ATM Addressing and ILMI

The ATM Forum specified Interim Local Management Interface (ILMI) is used primarily for ATM edge device address registration. ILMI information is communicated from an ATM switch to an edge device over the well-known VPI/VCI pair of 0 16.

You can view the dynamically assigned switch prefix with the show atm ilmi command:

r2#show atm ilmi

Interface ATM0 ILMI VCC: (0, 16)
ILMI Keepalive: Disabled
Address Registration: Enabled
ILMI State: UpAndNormal
Peer IP Addr: 172.16.1.11 Peer IF Name: ATM0/0/1
Prefix(s):
47.009181000000001007465F01
Addresses Registered:
Local Table :
47.009181000000001007465F01.0060837BA7B9.01
Remote Table :
47.009181000000001007465F01.0060837BA7B9.00

ILMI activity can also be monitored with the debug atm ilmi command:

```
ILMI Transition : Intf := 1 From  Restarting To  AwaitRestartAck
<ilmi_initiate_addreg>
ILMI: REQ_PROCESSING Reqtype = GETNEXT Reqid = 6 Requester = ILMI, Transid = 1 (ATM0)
%LINEPROTO-5-UPDOWN: Line protocol on Interface ATM0, changed state to up
ILMI: Trap Received (ATM0)
ILMI: REQ_PROCESSING Reqtype = GET Reqid = 7 Requester = ILMI, Transid = 1 (ATM0)
ILMI: REQ_PROCESSING Reqtype = GET Reqid = 8 Requester = ILMI, Transid = 1 (ATM0)
ILMI: REQ_PROCESSING Reqtype = GET Reqid = 9 Requester = ILMI, Transid = 1 (ATM0)
ILMI: VALID_RESP_RCVD Reqtype = GET Reqid = 7 Requester = ILMI, Transid = 1 (ATM0)
ILMI: Peer UNI Version on 1 = 4
ILMI: TERMINATE Reqtype = GET Reqid = 7 Requester = ILMI, Transid = 1 (ATM0)
ILMI: VALID_RESP_RCVD Reqtype = GET Reqid = 8 Requester = ILMI, Transid = 1 (ATM0)
ILMI: TERMINATE Reqtype = GET Reqid = 8 Requester = ILMI, Transid = 1 (ATM0)
ILMI: VALID_RESP_RCVD Reqtype = GET Reqid = 9 Requester = ILMI, Transid = 1 (ATM0)
ILMI: Peer IfName on 1 = ATM0/0/0
ILMI: TERMINATE Reqtype = GET Reqid = 9 Requester = ILMI, Transid = 1 (ATM0)
ILMI: REQ_TIMEOUT Reqtype = GETNEXT Reqid = 6 Requester = ILMI, Transid = 1 (ATM0)
 ILMI Retry count (before decrement) = 3
ILMI: REQ_PROCESSING Reqtype = GETNEXT Reqid = 6 Requester = ILMI, Transid = 1 (ATM0)
ILMI: VALID_RESP_RCVD Reqtype = GETNEXT Reqid = 6 Requester = ILMI, Transid = 1(ATM0)
ILMI Transition :
 Intf := 1 From  AwaitRestartAck To  UpAndNormal  <ilmi_process_response>
ILMI: TERMINATE Reqtype = GETNEXT Reqid = 6 Requester = ILMI, Transid = 1 (ATM0)
ILMI: REQ_PROCESSING Reqtype = GET Reqid = 10 Requester = ILMI, Transid = 1 (ATM0)
ILMI: REQ_PROCESSING Reqtype = GET Reqid = 11 Requester = ILMI, Transid = 1 (ATM0)
ILMI: REQ_PROCESSING Reqtype = GET Reqid = 12 Requester = ILMI, Transid = 1 (ATM0)
ILMI: VALID_RESP_RCVD Reqtype = GET Reqid = 10 Requester = ILMI, Transid = 1 (ATM0)
ILMI: Peer UNI Version on 1 = 4
```

```
ILMI: TERMINATE Reqtype = GET Reqid = 10 Requester = ILMI, Transid = 1 (ATM0)
ILMI: VALID_RESP_RCVD Reqtype = GET Reqid = 11 Requester = ILMI, Transid = 1 (ATM0)
ILMI: TERMINATE Reqtype = GET Reqid = 11 Requester = ILMI, Transid = 1 (ATM0)
ILMI: VALID_RESP_RCVD Reqtype = GET Reqid = 12 Requester = ILMI, Transid = 1 (ATM0)
ILMI: Peer IfName on 1 = ATM0/0/0
ILMI: TERMINATE Reqtype = GET Reqid = 12 Requester = ILMI, Transid = 1 (ATM0)
ILMI: Trap sent. Waiting for Prefix ATM0
ILMI: Notifying Address Addition 47.00918100000001007465F01 (ATM0)
ILMI: Notifying Address Addition 47.00918100000001007465F01 (ATM0)
ILMI: Table is up to date. Sync not done
```

ATM Signaling and ATM SVCs

Calling Party ATM Signaling Messages

```
ATMAPI: SETUP from LANE Client (PC 0x60691768
ATMSIG: index = 227, callref = 227, lic = TRUE
ATMMTP: enter Hash: index = 227, call ref = 227, lic = TRUE
ATMSIG: Called  Party Addr: 47.00918100000001007465F01.0060837BA7B9.01
ATMSIG: Calling Party Addr: 47.00918100000001007465F01.0060837BA729.01
ATMSIG: User Cell Rate IE size = 9
ATMSIG: o Setup msg, Null state, length 116, call ref 227, pad 0
ATMSIG: state changed from Null to Call Initiated
ATMSIG: index = 227, callref = 227, lic = TRUE
ATMSIG: i Rcvd Call Proceeding msg in call Initiated State, length 9, call ref 227
ATMSIG: state changed from Call Initiated to Outgoing Call Proceeding
ATMSIG: index = 11, callref = 11, lic = FALSE
ATMMTP: enter Hash: index = 11, call ref = 11, lic = FALSE
ATMSIG: Rcvd Setup Event in Call Present State
ATMSIG: Called  Party Addr: 47.00918100000001007465F01.0060837BA729.01
ATMSIG: Calling Party Addr: 47.00918100000001007465F01.0060837BA7B9.01
ATMSIG: o Call Proc msg, Call Present state, length 24, call ref 11, pad 2
ATMSIG: notifying Setup event to client
ATMSIG: state changed from Call Present to Incoming Call Proceeding
ATMAPI: RELEASE_COMP from ATMSIG Input (PC 0x60691A84)
ATMSIG: o Rel Complete msg, Incoming Call Proceeding state, length 20, call ref11,
pad 1
ATMSIG: state changed from Incoming Call Proceeding to Null
ATMSIG: removeVC - vcnum = 21, vpi/vci = 0/276
ATMSIG: removeHashEntry: svc remvd from hash table
ATMSIG: index = 227, callref = 227, lic = TRUE
ATMSIG: i Rcvd Connect msg in Out Call Proc State, length 35, call ref 227
ATMSIG: o Connect Ack msg, Outgoing Call Proceeding state, length 16, call ref 227,
pad 3
ATMSIG: state changed from Outgoing Call Proceeding to Active
```

Called Party's ATM Signaling Messages

```
ATMSIG: Rcvd Setup Event in Call Present State
ATMSIG: Called  Party Addr: 47.00918100000001007465F01.0060837BA7B9.01
ATMSIG: Calling Party Addr: 47.00918100000001007465F01.0060837BA729.01
ATMSIG: o Call Proc msg, Call Present state, length 24, call ref 7, pad 2
ATMSIG: notifying Setup event to client
ATMSIG: state changed from Call Present to Incoming Call Proceeding
ATMAPI: CONNECT from ATMSIG Input (PC 0x6069191C)
ATMSIG: o Connect msg, Incoming Call Proceeding state, length 48, call ref 7, pad 0
ATMSIG: state changed from Incoming Call Proceeding to Connect Request
ATMSIG: index = 7, callref = 7, lic = FALSE
ATMSIG: i Rcvd Connect Ack msg in connect Request State, length 0, call ref 7
ATMAPI: notifying Connect Ack event to client
ATMSIG: state changed from Connect Request to Active
```

Using Map-Lists for SVCs

An SVC is established only when needed. Therefore, many of the configuration issues involved with ISDN/DDR are involved. As with ISDN/DDR, you must specify which number to call in order to connect to a desired remote network layer address. With ISDN/DDR, dialer map and dialer string statements are used. With ATM, map-lists can be used. Other, more scalable solutions are Classical IP and ATM LAN Emulation (LANE). Classical IP and LANE will be examined later in this chapter. Listed below is a sample configuration of a switched virtual circuit configuration, using map-list statements:

```
interface ATM0
   ip address 172.16.10.1 255.255.255.0
   atm esi-address 111100000000.00
   atm pvc 10 0 5 qsaal
   atm pvc 20 0 16 ilmi
   map-group CCIE

   map-list CCIE
   ip 172.16.1.2 atm-nsap 47.00918100000006177775444.222200000000.00 broadcast
   ip 172.16.1.3 atm-nsap 47.00918100000006177777777.333300000000.00 broadcast
```

Note the similarities and the differences between the ATM map-lists statements displayed above with the Frame-Relay map and the ISDN/DDR dial map statements.

You can monitor the status of ATM SVC configurations with the show atm interface, show atm map and show atm vc commands.

```
R1#show int atm 0
ATM0 is up, line protocol is up
  Hardware is ATMizer BX-50
  Internet address is 172.16.1.1/24
  MTU 4470 bytes, sub MTU 4470, BW 156250 Kbit, DLY 100 usec, rely 210/255, load 1
  255
  NSAP address: 47.00918100000000617777777.111100000000.00
  Encapsulation ATM, loopback not set, keepalive set (10 sec)
  Encapsulation(s): AAL5 AAL3/4, PVC mode
  1024 maximum active VCs, 1024 VCs per VP, 4 current VCCs
  VC idle disconnect time: 300 seconds
  Signalling vc = 10, vpi = 0, vci = 5
  UNI Version = 3.0, Link Side = user
  Last input 00:00:20, output 00:00:01, output hang never
Last clearing of "show interface" counters never

R1#show atm map
Map list TestSVC : PERMANENT
ip 172.16.1.2 maps to NSAP 47.009181000000006170595555.222220000000.00,  broadcast
ip 172.16.1.3 maps to NSAP 47.009181000000006170595555.333330000000.00,  broadcast,
connection up, VC 105, ATM0
```

R1#show atm vc

Interface	VCD	VPI	VCI	Type	Encapsulation	AAL/ Kbps	Peak Kbps	Avg. Cells	Burst Status
ATM0	1	0	5	PVC	AAL5-SAAL	155000	155000	95	ACT
ATM0	2	0	16	PVC	AAL5-ILMI	155000	155000	95	ACT
ATM0	3	0	100	SVC	AAL5-SNAP	155000	155000	95	ACT

You can view the individual steps involved in ATM SVC set up by enabling debug atm sig-events.

Introduction to ATM Classical IP and ATM LANE

Instead of statically defining network layer addresses with map-list statements, two dynamic methods of mapping network layer addresses with ATM NSAP addresses have been developed:

1. Classical IP (CLIP)
2. LAN Emulation (LANE)

Classical IP is the more limited method of dynamically mapping network layer addresses to ATM NSAP addresses. Classical IP maps only IP addresses to NSAP addresses. If you have IPX running over a classical IP logical IP subnet, it will not map an IPX address to an ATM NSAP address. Only ATM LANE will map multiple network layer protocols to ATM NSAP addresses.

From a configuration perspective, Classical IP is simpler than ATM LANE. Classical IP involves creating an ATMARP server. ATM LANE involves creating three different servers:

1. LAN Emulation Configuration Server
2. LAN Emulation Server
3. Broadcast/Unknown Server

ATM LANE was developed by the ATM Forum, a consortium of ATM manufacturers and users. RFC Classical IP was developed by the IETF and is defined by RFC 1577.

Classical IP Overview

1. Classical IP client registers with the ARP server
2. Classical IP client sends an ATM-ARP request to the ARP server
3. ARP server responds to the ATM-ARP request
4. One Classical IP client directly connects to another Classical IP client

Configuring Classical IP

Enter the following command in Global Configuration Made:

On the ARP server:
Atm arp-server self
On the ARP clients:
Atm arp-server nsap xxx.xxxx....

Show atm map (see dynamic parameter)

Show atm arp
Debug atm arp

ATM LANE Overview

LANE was developed by the ATM Forum to interconnect legacy LANs over an ATM core.

Ethernet and Token-Ring LANE clients have no idea they are connected an ATM backbone. ATM LANE is the ATM community's answer to the VLAN.

At the heart of the ATM LANE process is the operation of the IP protocol Address Resolution Protocol (ARP). To demonstrate the importance of ARP, consider the following scenario:

1. An end system (assume it has an Ethernet interface) generates an ARP broadcast to resolve the remote IP address of another end system on the same LAN with its MAC address.
2. The broadcast is picked up by the LAN Emulation Client (LEC) to which the end system is attached (for example, a Catalyst 5000).

   If the target remote end system is on a segment on the other side of the ATM cloud, the LEC forwards the ARP broadcast to the BUS to which it is attached.
3. The BUS floods the ARP broadcast to all LANE clients.
4. When the remote end system responds to the ARP request, the ARP response can be returned by the BUS or LES. It will be returned by the LES if the remote/target ARP client has an LE-ARP entry for the source MAC address in the ARP request.

The general rules for LANE 1.0 are:

LANE must use AAL5/SNAP
There can be one and only one LECS for every ATM ELAN domain.
There must be one LES/BUS pair for each ELAN.
SSRP is a Cisco solution for the lack of server redunancy in LANE 1.0. Think of SSRP as being like HSRP for routers. LANE 2.0 is supposed to remedy this redundancy problem.

LANE ultimately creates a single LEC-to-LEC connection.

Overview of LANE Components

When configuring ATM LANE, the following components are involved:

LECS (LAN Emulation Configuraton Server)

This manages ELAN membership. The LECS has a "well-known address" defined by the ATM Forum.

Once the LECS has told the LEC about the ELANs to which it belongs, the SVC is torn down. A LECS is optional. It is an administrative tool. You can bypass use of the LECS if you know the NSAP address of each LES you want to use.

LES (LAN Emulation Server)

The LAN Emulation Server performs MAC address-to-NSAP mappings using LAN Emulation (LE-ARP).

BUS (Broadcast Unknown Server)

The Broadcast Unknown Server forwards all broadcast MAC addresses and unknown MAC addresses to all LAN Emulation Clients, until a LAN Emulation Client to LAN Emulation Client can be created.

LEC (LAN Emulation Client)

The LEC has a statement to identify the LECS to which to attach, similar to a preferred server statement in a NetWare NET.CFG file.

The LAN Emulation Client maintains six types of connections in a LANE environment:

- **Configure Direct**. Bi-directional VCC setup initiated by LEC during the LEC-to-LECS connection establishment phase
- **Control Direct**. Bi-directional point-to-point VCC between LEC and LES
- **Control Distribute**. Uni-directional point-to-multipoint VCC between LEC and LES
- **Multicast Send**. Bi-directional point-to-point VCC between LEC and BUS
- **Multicast Forward**. Uni-directional point-to-multipoint VCC between LEC and BUS used to forward multicast/broadcast and unknown traffic to all LECs
- **Data Direct**. Final LEC to LEC connection for end system data transfer

Trunking with ATM LANE

Trunking was introduced in Chapter 6 as a method of providing connectivity for the following devices:

1. One LAN switch to another LAN switch in a multi-VLAN environment
2. One LAN switch to a trunk-aware routing interface in a multi-VLAN environment
3. One LAN switch to a trunk-aware server in a multi-VLAN environment

Trunking technologies include:

1. Fast Ethernet ISL
2. Fast EtherChannel
3. Gigabit Ethernet
4. 802.10 (FDDI)
5. ATM LANE

ATM LANE creates an individual "emulated LAN," or "ELAN," for every VLAN for which it provides trunking services. The design objective of ATM LANE is to provide a transparent backbone/core service for legacy Ethernet and Token-Ring LANs.

With LANE, you can perform trunking over Wide Area Networks.

Configuring ATM LANE in a Cisco Environment

Most of the LANE configuration is performed on the routers or Catalyst switches. Minimal configuration is required on the LightStream ATM switch. Usually, a single command is entered on the ATM switch to identify the location of the LECS. A single Cisco router or Catalyst switch can be a LECS, LES/BUS and a LEC all at one time.

In order to configure ATM, the four previously mentioned LANE components must be configured:

1. LAN Emulation Configuration Server (LECS)
2. LAN Emulation Server (LES)
3. Broadcast/Unknown Server (BUS)
4. LAN Emulation Client (LEC)

Cisco LANE NSAP Addressing Rules

Each LANE service component is identified by a unique NSAP address. As mentioned in the previous section, a single Cisco router or Catalyst switch can be concurrently configured as a LECS, LES/BUS and LEC. Each of these LANE services is differentiated by an NSAP address. To better understand this, closely examine the show lane default display below:

```
ATM>show lane default
interface ATM0:
LANE Client:         47.00918100000000100D328401.0010113B8810.**
LANE Server:         47.00918100000000100D328401.0010113B8811.**
LANE Bus:            47.00918100000000100D328401.0010113B8812.**
LANE Config Server: 47.00918100000000100D328401.0010113B8813.00
```

Notice the entire NSAP address for all four listed addresses, with the exception of the last digit listed (the highlighted digit). This digit increments by a value of one as you move down from row to row. This last digit is numbered in a special manner. The rules for assigning a value to the last digit of an NSAP address is listed below:

1. The last digit of the LEC NSAP address is a given value.
2. The last digit of the LES NSAP address is THE VALUE OF THE LAST DIGIT OF THE LEC + 1.
3. The last digit of the BUS NSAP address is THE VALUE OF THE LAST DIGIT OF THE LEC + 2.
4. The last digit of the LECS NSAP address is THE VALUE OF THE LAST DIGIT OF THE LEC + 3.

Re-examine the show lane default display provided above. Notice how the last digit of the LEC, LES, BUS and LECS NSAP addresses increase by one.

Finally, notice how the selector-byte is represented by two asterisks (**). The selector byte is not explicitly listed, because this value may vary depending upon the number of LANE services configured on a router or Catalyst switch. The actual value of the selector byte will correspond with the sunbinterface number under which LANE services will be configured. For example, if three ELAN LEC clients were configured on a single router, each LEC configuration will reside under a different subinterface. Therefore, the LEC NSAP for each LEC configured on the router will be identical, except for the selector byte. For each LEC configured, the selector byte will be identical to the subinterface under which the LEC was configured. This is an extremely important concept to grasp!

Configuring the LAN Emulation Configuration Server (LECS)

The LECS contains the name of configured LAN Emulation Servers and a respective NSAP address. Even if multiple ELANs are defined, you must configure one and only LAN Emulation Configuration Server. The LECS acts much like a Registrar's Office for a University. Typically, you go to the Registrar's Office only at the beginning of a semester to pay your tuition bill and get your list of classes for the semester. Similarly, the LECS is referenced by a LEC only at the beginning of the LAN emulation process. The LEC must locate the LECS to determine the NSAP address for a specified LES. Once the LEC has located the LES, it no longer needs to communicate with the LECS.

LECS configuration involves at least three steps:

Step 1: Determine the NSAP address of a specified LAN Emulation Server, using the following show command on the router or Catalyst switch that is designated to be the LAN Emulation Server:

```
Router#show lane def inte a0.1
LANE Client:        47.00918100000000 6083C49401.0060837BA711.01
LANE Server:        47.00918100000000 6083C49401.0060837BA712.01
LANE Bus:           47.00918100000000 6083C49401.0060837BA713.01
LANE Config Server: 47.00918100000000 6083C49401.0060837BA714.00
```

Pay particular attention to the ATM selector byte of the NSAP address. The entire address, including the selector byte, must be entered in the LECS database.

Step 2: Create a LANE database with the following global configuration command:

```
lane database name
```

Step 3: Enter the name of LAN Emulation Server with its NSAP address

```
name elan1 server-atm-address  .....
```

Step 4: Activate the LECS database with the following global configuration command:

```
lane config database name
```

Listed below is a sample configuration of a LECS on a Cisco router:

```
ATM#show run
!
lane database cat1
  name elan1 server-atm-address 47.00918100000000006083C49401.00603E115603.01
  name elan2 server-atm-address 47.00918100000000006083C49401.0010113B7011.02
!
interface Loopback0
!
interface ATM0
 mtu 1500
 atm preferred phy A
 atm pvc 1 0 5 qsaal
 atm pvc 2 0 16 ilmi
 lane config auto-config-atm-address
 lane config database cat1

!
interface ATM0.1 multipoint
 lane client ethernet 1 elan1
!
interface ATM0.2 multipoint
 lane server-bus ethernet elan2
 lane client ethernet 2 elan2
```

Configuring the LightStream 1010 to Announce the LECS Address to LECs

When a LAN Emulation Client begins the process of joining a given ELAN, it must first locate the LAN Emulation Server and Broadcast Unknown Server. It finds the information in the LAN Emulation Configuration Server. However, before the LAN Emulation Client locates its LES/BUS pair, it must first locate NSAP of the LAN Configuration Server. The NSAP address for the LECS is supplied by the LEC's directly-connected ATM switch. A well-known LECS address or a specified address can be used. To manually configure a specified LECS address, perform the following steps:

1. Perform a show lane default on the router or Catalyst switch where the LECS resides. Record the last NSAP address listed. Since the NSAP address is a long number, it is strongly advised that you use a cut and paste utility to record the address. This is the NSAP address that identifies the router or Catalyst if it is used as a LECS. Listed below is a sample show lane default display, with the LECS address highlighted:

```
LANE-LEC-1>show lane default
interface ATM0:
LANE Client:         47.00918100000000006083C49401.0010113B7010.**
LANE Server:         47.00918100000000006083C49401.0010113B7011.**
LANE Bus:            47.00918100000000006083C49401.0010113B7012.**
LANE Config Server: 47.00918100000000006083C49401.0010113B7013.00
```

Note: ** is the subinterface number byte in hex. This is what is used for the selector byte.

2. If LANE-LEC-1 is designated as the LECS, the address highlighted above will be typed in on the LS1010 switch as:

Atm LECS-address-default

3. If you use the well-known NSAP LECS address, type "lane config fixed address" (11.2), "lane fixed address" (11.1). If you use a specified address, use "lane auto-config" (11.1) and "lane config auto-config" (11.2). Enter these commands at the physical ATM interface.

On a LightStream 1010, a virtual interface on the LS1010 is 2/0/0. On a Catalyst 5500 with an ATM Switch Processor, the virtual interface is 13/0/0.

LAN Emulation Server (LES)/Broadcast Unknown Server (BUS) Configuration

The LAN Emulation Server (LES) implements the control functions of the emulated LAN. The LES responds to LE-ARP requests with LE-ARP responses. On Cisco routers and Catalyst switches, the LES and BUS are co-located at all times. On other platforms, such as Fore switches, the LES and BUS can be on different devices.

Displayed below is a sample LES/BUS configuration:

```
interface ATM0
 no ip address
 atm pvc 1 0 5 qsaal
 atm pvc 2 0 16 ilmi
 lane config auto-config-atm-address
```

```
!
interface ATM0.1 multipoint
 ip address 172.16.1.2 255.255.255.0
lane server-bus ethernet elan1  (One command for LES/BUS configuration.)
 lane client ethernet elan1
!
interface ATM0.2 multipoint
 ip address 172.16.2.2 255.255.255.0
 ip helper-address 172.16.1.254
 lane client ethernet elan2
```

If you don't use the interface configuration command "lane config auto-config-atm-address," you can manually configure an end system address.

You can validate the operation of a LANE LES and BUS with the following two show commands:

```
r1#show lane server
LE Server ATM0.1  ELAN name: bruce  Admin: up  State: operational
type: ethernet          Max Frame Size: 1516
ATM address: 47.00918100000000006083C49401.0060837BA712.01
LECS used: 47.00918100000000006083C49401.0060837BA714.00 connected, vcd 6
control distribute: vcd 12, 4 members, 346 packets

proxy/ (ST: Init, Conn, Waiting, Adding, Joined, Operational, Reject, Term)
lecid ST vcd  pkts Hardware Addr   ATM Address
  1   O   9   2    0060.837b.a711  47.00918100000000006083C49401.0060837BA711.01
  2   O  18   10   0060.837b.a7ba  47.00918100000000006083C49401.0060837BA7BA.01
  3P  O  21   336  0010.113b.7010  47.00918100000000006083C49401.0010113B7010.01
  4P  O  26   2    0010.113b.8810  47.00918100000000006083C49401.0010113B8810.01

r1#show lane bus
LE BUS ATM0.1  ELAN name: bruce  Admin: up  State: operational
type: ethernet          Max Frame Size: 1516
ATM address: 47.00918100000000006083C49401.0060837BA713.01
data forward: vcd 16, 4 members, 481 packets, 3 unicasts

lecid  vcd     pkts  ATM Address
  1    13       19 47.00918100000000006083C49401.0060837BA711.01
  2    19       18 47.00918100000000006083C49401.0060837BA7BA.01
  3    22      441 47.00918100000000006083C49401.0010113B7010.01
  4    27        3 47.00918100000000006083C49401.0010113B8810.01
```

Notice that the entries for the LES and BUS tables are the same. This is because both addresses are of the LECs of ELAN Bruce.

Configuring the LAN Emulation Client (LEC)

You must create a multipoint subinterface on a router to make it a lane client. Once created, you need to type in only one statement:

LANE client Ethernet ELAN1

Listed below is a sample LAN Emulation Client configuration:

```
interface ATM0
 no ip address
 atm pvc 1 0 5 qsaal
 atm pvc 2 0 16 ilmi
 lane config auto-config-atm-address
!
interface ATM0.1 multipoint
 ip address 172.16.1.2 255.255.255.0
 lane server-bus ethernet elan1   One command for LES/BUS configuration.
 lane client ethernet elan1
!
interface ATM0.2 multipoint
 ip address 172.16.2.2 255.255.255.0
 lane client ethernet elan2
```

If you don't use the auto-config, you can manually configure an end system identifier (ESI) address.

LEC Activation

When the LEC comes up, the first thing it locates is the LECS address via ILMI. The switch will supply the LECS address to the LEC. When the LEC learns its LES/BUS NSAP address, it establishes the following for VCCs with the LES/BUS:

Control Direct. Bi-directional point-to-point VCC between LEC and LES

Control Distribute. Uni-directional point-to-multipoint VCC between LEC and LES

Multicast Send. Bi-directional point-to-point VCC between LEC and BUS

Multicast Forward. Uni-directional point-to-multipoint VCC between LEC and BUS used to forward multicast/broadcast and unknown traffic to all LECs

Once this is performed, the LEC registers its own MAC address with the LES. A summary of the LEC initialization process is supplied below.

When LEC initializes, it looks for the LECS using the following techniques:

1. Via hard coded address (at each LEC subinterface)
2. Via well known PVC 0 17
3. Via ILMI
4. Via well known LECS NSAP address

Once the LEC finds the LECS, it establishes a bi-directional "Configure Direct" VC with the LECS. The LEC tells the LECS which ELAN it wants to join, and the LECS tells the LEC the NSAP address of the LES specified by the LEC. The LEC establishes a bi-directional Control Direct VC with the LES. LEC generates an LE-ARP to register its own address with the LES, and performs an address registration with the LES (MAC to NSAP registration). LES will make the new LEC a leaf on the tree it has with other clients on the LES' point-to-multipoint connection. This leaf connection is a uni-directional connection. LES gives LEC a client ID, and LEC does LE-ARP to LES to find the location of the BUS. The LEC establishes a bi-directional VC with the BUS. BUS will add new LEC as leaf on his point-to multipoint connection. LEC can now establish a "data direct" connection between other LECs.

Remember: When configuring LANE in a Cisco environment, the multipoint subinterface must match the selector byte.

**** Good LANE Monitoring and Configuration Validation PROGRESSION:

On the LANE CLIENT:

1. r2#show lane client

```
LE Client ATM0.1  ELAN name: elan1  Admin: up  State: operational
Client ID: 2                       LEC up for 21 minutes 16 seconds
Join Attempt: 4
HW Address: 0060.837b.a7b9   Type: ethernet          Max Frame Size: 1516

ATM Address: 47.0091810000000001007465F01.0060837BA7B9.01

VCD  rxFrames  txFrames  Type        ATM Address
0    0         0         configure   47.0091810000000001007465F01.0060837BA72C.00
11   1         10        direct      47.0091810000000001007465F01.0060837BA72A.01
12   17        0         distribute  47.0091810000000001007465F01.0060837BA72A.01
13   0         29        send        47.0091810000000001007465F01.0060837BA72B.01
14   57        0         forward     47.0091810000000001007465F01.0060837BA72B.01
```

2. r2#show lane default-atm-addresses

```
interface                ATM0:
LANE Client:             47.0091810000000001007465F01.0060837BA7B9.**
LANE Server:             47.0091810000000001007465F01.0060837BA7BA.**
LANE Bus:                47.0091810000000001007465F01.0060837BA7BB.**
LANE Config Server:      47.0091810000000001007465F01.0060837BA7BC.00
```

note: ** is the subinterface number byte in hex

3. r2#show lane le-arp

```
Max le-arp entries: 4096     Active le-arp entries: 1

Hardware Addr   ATM Address                                    VCD  Interface
0060.837b.a729  47.0091810000000001007465F01.0060837BA729.01   16   ATM0.1
```

4. **r2#show arp**

```
Protocol  Address          Age (min)  Hardware Addr   Type   Interface
Internet  172.16.1.1               7  0060.837b.a729  ARPA   ATM0.1
Internet  172.16.1.2               -  0060.837b.a7b9  ARPA   ATM0.1
```

5. **r2#show atm vc**

```
                                     AAL /          PeakAvg. Burst
Interface  VCD  VPI  VCI  Type  Encapsulation  Kbps     Kbps    Cells  Status
0          1    0    16   PVC   AAL5-ILMI      155000   155000  94     ACTIVE
0          2    0    5    PVC   AAL5-SAAL      155000   155000  94     ACTIVE
0.1        11   0    37   SVC   LANE-LEC       155000   155000  32     ACTIVE
0.1        12   0    38   MSVC  LANE-LEC       155000   155000  32     ACTIVE
0.1        13   0    39   SVC   LANE-LEC       155000   155000  32     ACTIVE
0.1        14   0    40   MSVC  LANE-LEC       155000   155000  32     ACTIVE
0.1        16   0    43   SVC   LANE-DATA      155000   155000  32     ACTIVE
```

6. **r2#show atm vc 16**

```
ATM0.1: VCD: 16, VPI: 0, VCI: 43, etype:0x6, LANE-DATA, Flags: 0x57
PeakRate: 155000, Average Rate: 155000, Burst Cells: 32, VCmode: 0x1
OAM DISABLED, InARP DISABLED
InPkts: 1, OutPkts: 0, InBytes: 66, OutBytes: 0
InPRoc: 1, OutPRoc: 0, Broadcasts: 0
InFast: 0, OutFast: 0, InAS: 0, OutAS: 0
OAM F5 cells sent: 0, OAM cells received: 0
Status: ACTIVE  , TTL: 2
interface =  ATM0.1, call remotely initiated, call reference = 8
vcnum = 16, vpi = 0, vci = 43, state = Active
 aal5lane vc, Unknown, point-to-point call
Retry count: Current = 0, Max = 10
timer currently inactive, timer value = 00:00:00
Remote Atm Nsap address: 47.00918100000001007465F01.0060837BA729.01
```

7. **Debug LAN client**:

```
LEC ATM0.1: action A_REGISTER_ADDR
LEC ATM0.1: predicate PRED_LEC_NSAP FALSE
LEC ATM0.1: state IDLE event LEC_LOCAL_ACTIVATE => IDLE
LEC ATM0.1: action A_REGISTER_ADDR
LEC ATM0.1: predicate PRED_LEC_NSAP FALSE
LEC ATM0.1: state IDLE event LEC_LOCAL_ACTIVATE => IDLE
LANE ATM0: prefix add event for 4700918100000001007465F01 ptr=0x60C41100 len=13
    the current first prefix is now: 4700918100000001007465F01
LEC ATM0.1: atm address changed, recycling
LEC ATM0.1: action A_REGISTER_ADDR
LEC ATM0.1: predicate PRED_LEC_NSAP TRUE
LEC ATM0.1: state IDLE event LEC_LOCAL_PREFIX_SET => REGISTER_ADDR
LEC ATM0.1: action A_POST_LISTEN
LEC ATM0.1: sending LISTEN
LEC ATM0.1:   listen on 47.00918100000001007465F01.0060837BA7B9.01
```

```
LEC ATM0.1: state REGISTER_ADDR event LEC_CTL_ILMI_SET_RSP_POS => POSTING_LISTEN
LEC ATM0.1: received LISTEN
LEC ATM0.1: action A_ACTIVATE_LEC
LEC ATM0.1: predicate PRED_CTL_DIRECT_NSAP FALSE
LEC ATM0.1: predicate PRED_LECS_NSAP FALSE
LEC ATM0.1: state POSTING_LISTEN event LEC_SIG_LISTEN_POS => GET_LECS_ADDR
LEC ATM0.1: action A_ALLOC_LECS_ADDR
LEC ATM0.1: state GET_LECS_ADDR event LEC_CTL_ILMI_SET_RSP_POS => GET_LECS_ADDR
LEC ATM0.1: action A_ALLOC_LECS_ADDR
LEC ATM0.1: state GET_LECS_ADDR event LEC_CTL_ILMI_SET_RSP_POS => GET_LECS_ADDR
LEC ATM0.1: action A_SEND_LECS_SETUP
LEC ATM0.1: sending SETUP
LEC ATM0.1:   callid            0x60C36EF0
LEC ATM0.1:   called party      47.00918100000001007465F01.0060837BA714.00
LEC ATM0.1:   calling_party     47.00918100000001007465F01.0060837BA7B9.01
LEC ATM0.1: state GET_LECS_ADDR event LEC_CTL_ILMI_SET_RSP_NEG => LECS_CONNECT
LEC ATM0.1: received RELEASE
LEC ATM0.1:   callid            0x60C36EF0
LEC ATM0.1:   cause code        3
LEC ATM0.1: action A_SEND_NEXT_LECS_SETUP
LEC ATM0.1: sending RELEASE_COMPLETE
LEC ATM0.1:   callid            0x60C36EF0
LEC ATM0.1:   cause code        31
LEC ATM0.1: sending SETUP
LEC ATM0.1:   callid            0x60C37284
LEC ATM0.1:   called party      47.00918100000001007465F01.0060837BA72C.00
LEC ATM0.1:   calling_party     47.00918100000001007465F01.0060837BA7B9.01
LEC ATM0.1: state LECS_CONNECT event LEC_SIG_RELEASE => LECS_CONNECT
LEC ATM0.1: received CONNECT
LEC ATM0.1:   callid            0x60C37284
LEC ATM0.1:   vcd               17
LEC ATM0.1: action A_SEND_CFG_REQ
LEC ATM0.1: sending LANE_CONFIG_REQ on VCD 17
LEC ATM0.1:   SRC MAC address   0060.837b.a7b9
LEC ATM0.1:   SRC ATM address   47.00918100000001007465F01.0060837BA7B9.01
LEC ATM0.1:   LAN Type  1
LEC ATM0.1:   Frame size        1
LEC ATM0.1:   LAN Name  elan1
LEC ATM0.1:   LAN Name size     5
LEC ATM0.1: state LECS_CONNECT event LEC_SIG_CONNECT => GET_LES_ADDR
LEC ATM0.1: received LANE_CONFIG_RSP on VCD 17
LEC ATM0.1:   SRC MAC address   0060.837b.a7b9
LEC ATM0.1:   SRC ATM address   47.00918100000001007465F01.0060837BA7B9.01
LEC ATM0.1:   LAN Type  1
LEC ATM0.1:   Frame size        1
LEC ATM0.1:   LAN Name  elan1
LEC ATM0.1:   LAN Name size     5
LEC ATM0.1: action A_PROCESS_CFG_RSP
LEC ATM0.1: sending RELEASE
LEC ATM0.1:   callid            0x60C37284
```

```
LEC ATM0.1:   cause code        31
LEC ATM0.1: state GET_LES_ADDR event LEC_CTL_CONFIG_RSP_POS => LECS_RELEASE
LEC ATM0.1: received RELEASE_COMPLETE
LEC ATM0.1:   callid            0x60C37284
LEC ATM0.1:   cause code        16
LEC ATM0.1: action A_SEND_LES_SETUP
LEC ATM0.1: sending SETUP
LEC ATM0.1:   callid            0x60C36EF0
LEC ATM0.1: called party  47.00918100000001007465F01.0060837BA72A.01 (LES Adddress)
LEC ATM0.1:   calling_party     47.00918100000001007465F01.0060837BA7B9.01
LEC ATM0.1: state LECS_RELEASE event LEC_SIG_RELEASE_COMP => CTL_DIRECT_CONN
LEC ATM0.1: received CONNECT
LEC ATM0.1:   callid            0x60C36EF0
LEC ATM0.1:   vcd               18
LEC ATM0.1: action A_SEND_JOIN_REQ
LEC ATM0.1: sending LANE_JOIN_REQ on VCD 18
LEC ATM0.1:   Status            0
LEC ATM0.1:   LECID             0
LEC ATM0.1:   SRC MAC address   0060.837b.a7b9
LEC ATM0.1:   SRC ATM address   47.00918100000001007465F01.0060837BA7B9.01
LEC ATM0.1:   LAN Type  1
LEC ATM0.1:   Frame size        1
LEC ATM0.1:   LAN Name  elan1
LEC ATM0.1:   LAN Name size     5
LEC ATM0.1: state CTL_DIRECT_CONN event LEC_SIG_CONNECT => JOIN_CTL_DIST_CONN
LEC ATM0.1: received SETUP
LEC ATM0.1:   callid            0x60C37170
LEC ATM0.1:   called party      47.00918100000001007465F01.0060837BA7B9.01
LEC ATM0.1:   calling_party     47.00918100000001007465F01.0060837BA72A.01
LEC ATM0.1: action A_PROCESS_CTL_DIST_SETUP
LEC ATM0.1: sending CONNECT
LEC ATM0.1:   callid            0x60C37170
LEC ATM0.1:   vcd               19
LEC ATM0.1: state JOIN_CTL_DIST_CONN event LEC_SIG_SETUP => JOIN
LEC ATM0.1: received CONNECT_ACK
LEC ATM0.1: state JOIN event LEC_SIG_CONNECT_ACK => JOIN
LEC ATM0.1: received LANE_JOIN_RSP on VCD 18
LEC ATM0.1:   Status            0
LEC ATM0.1:   LECID             2
LEC ATM0.1:   SRC MAC address   0060.837b.a7b9
LEC ATM0.1:   SRC ATM address   47.00918100000001007465F01.0060837BA7B9.01
LEC ATM0.1:   LAN Type  1
LEC ATM0.1:   Frame size        1
LEC ATM0.1:   LAN Name  elan1
LEC ATM0.1:   LAN Name size     5
LEC ATM0.1: action A_PROCESS_JOIN_RSP_SEND_REQ
LEC ATM0.1: sending LANE_ARP_REQ on VCD 18
LEC ATM0.1:   SRC MAC address    0060.837b.a7b9
LEC ATM0.1:   SRC ATM address    47.00918100000001007465F01.0060837BA7B9.01
LEC ATM0.1:   TARGET MAC address  ffff.ffff.ffff
```

```
LEC ATM0.1:    TARGET ATM address   00.000000000000000000000000.000000000000.00
LEC ATM0.1: state JOIN event LEC_CTL_JOIN_RSP_POS => GET_BUS_ADDR
LEC ATM0.1: received LANE_ARP_RSP on VCD 19
LEC ATM0.1:    SRC MAC address      0060.837b.a7b9
LEC ATM0.1:    SRC ATM address      47.00918100000001007465F01.0060837BA7B9.01
LEC ATM0.1:    TARGET MAC address   ffff.ffff.ffff
LEC ATM0.1:    TARGET ATM address   47.00918100000001007465F01.0060837BA72B.01
LEC ATM0.1: action A_SEND_BUS_SETUP
LEC ATM0.1: predicate PRED_MCAST_SEND_NSAP FALSE
LEC ATM0.1: sending SETUP
LEC ATM0.1:    callid             0x60C376C8
LEC ATM0.1:    called party       47.00918100000001007465F01.0060837BA72B.01
LEC ATM0.1:    calling_party      47.00918100000001007465F01.0060837BA7B9.01
LEC ATM0.1: state GET_BUS_ADDR event LEC_CTL_ARP_RSP => MCAST_SEND_FORWARD_CONN
LEC ATM0.1: received CONNECT
LEC ATM0.1:    callid             0x60C376C8
LEC ATM0.1:    vcd                20
LEC ATM0.1: action A_PROCESS_BUS_CONNECT
LEC ATM0.1: state MCAST_SEND_FORWARD_CONN event LEC_SIG_CONNECT =>
MCAST_FORWARD_CONN
LEC ATM0.1: received SETUP
LEC ATM0.1:    callid             0x60C379F8
LEC ATM0.1:    called party       47.00918100000001007465F01.0060837BA7B9.01
LEC ATM0.1:    calling_party      47.00918100000001007465F01.0060837BA72B.01
LEC ATM0.1: action A_SEND_BUS_CONNECT
LEC ATM0.1: sending CONNECT
LEC ATM0.1:    callid             0x60C379F8
LEC ATM0.1:    vcd                21
%LANE-5-UPDOWN: ATM0.1 elan elan1: LE Client changed state to up
LEC ATM0.1: state MCAST_FORWARD_CONN event LEC_SIG_SETUP => ACTIVE
LEC ATM0.1: received CONNECT_ACK
LEC ATM0.1: action A_PROCESS_CONNECT_ACK
LEC ATM0.1: state ACTIVE event LEC_SIG_CONNECT_ACK => ACTIVE
```

8. PING Another LANE Client with Debug LANE Client Enabled

```
r2#ping 172.16.1.1
LEC ATM0.1: received LANE_ARP_REQ on VCD 19
LEC ATM0.1:    SRC MAC address      0060.837b.a729
LEC ATM0.1:    SRC ATM address      47.00918100000001007465F01.0060837BA729.01
LEC ATM0.1:    TARGET MAC address   0060.837b.a7b9
LEC ATM0.1:    TARGET ATM address   00.000000000000000000000000.000000000000.00
LEC ATM0.1: action A_SEND_ARP_RSP
LEC ATM0.1: sending LANE_ARP_RSP on VCD 18
LEC ATM0.1:    SRC MAC address      0060.837b.a729
LEC ATM0.1:    SRC ATM address      47.00918100000001007465F01.0060837BA729.01
LEC ATM0.1:    TARGET MAC address   0060.837b.a7b9
LEC ATM0.1:    TARGET ATM address   47.00918100000001007465F01.0060837BA7B9.01
LEC ATM0.1: state ACTIVE event LEC_CTL_ARP_REQ => ACTIVE
LEC ATM0.1: received LANE_ARP_RSP on VCD 19
LEC ATM0.1:    SRC MAC address      0060.837b.a729
```

```
LEC ATM0.1:    SRC ATM address     47.0091810000000001007465F01.0060837BA729.01
LEC ATM0.1:    TARGET MAC address  0060.837b.a7b9
LEC ATM0.1:    TARGET ATM address  47.0091810000000001007465F01.0060837BA7B9.01
LEC ATM0.1: action  A_PROCESS_ARP_RSP
LEC ATM0.1: state ACTIVE event LEC_CTL_ARP_RSP => ACTIVE
LEC ATM0.1: received SETUP
LEC ATM0.1:    callid             0x60C384E8
LEC ATM0.1:    called party       47.0091810000000001007465F01.0060837BA7B9.01
LEC ATM0.1:    calling_party      47.0091810000000001007465F01.0060837BA729.01
LEC ATM0.1: action A_PROCESS_SETUP
LEC ATM0.1: sending CONNECT
LEC ATM0.1:    callid             0x60C384E8
LEC ATM0.1:    vcd                22
LEC ATM0.1: state ACTIVE event LEC_SIG_SETUP => ACTIVE
LEC ATM0.1: received CONNECT_ACK
LEC ATM0.1: action A_PROCESS_CONNECT_ACK
LEC ATM0.1: state ACTIVE event LEC_SIG_CONNECT_ACK => ACTIVE
LEC ATM0.1: received LANE_READY_IND on VCD 22
LEC ATM0.1: action A_PROCESS_READY_IND
LEC ATM0.1: state ACTIVE event LEC_CTL_READY_IND => ACTIVE
LEC ATM0.1: sending LANE_ARP_REQ on VCD 18
LEC ATM0.1:    SRC MAC address     0060.837b.a7b9
LEC ATM0.1:    SRC ATM address     47.0091810000000001007465F01.0060837BA7B9.01
LEC ATM0.1:    TARGET MAC address  0060.837b.a729
LEC ATM0.1:    TARGET ATM address  00.000000000000000000000000.000000000000.00
LEC ATM0.1: received LANE_ARP_REQ on VCD 19
LEC ATM0.1:    SRC MAC address     0060.837b.a7b9
LEC ATM0.1:    SRC ATM address     47.0091810000000001007465F01.0060837BA7B9.01
LEC ATM0.1:    TARGET MAC address  0060.837b.a729
LEC ATM0.1:    TARGET ATM address  00.000000000000000000000000.000000000000.00
LEC ATM0.1: action A_SEND_ARP_RSP
LEC ATM0.1: state ACTIVE event LEC_CTL_ARP_REQ => ACTIVE
LEC ATM0.1: received LANE_ARP_RSP on VCD 19
LEC ATM0.1:    SRC MAC address     0060.837b.a7b9
LEC ATM0.1:    SRC ATM address     47.0091810000000001007465F01.0060837BA7B9.01
LEC ATM0.1:    TARGET MAC address  0060.837b.a729
LEC ATM0.1:    TARGET ATM address  47.0091810000000001007465F01.0060837BA729.01
LEC ATM0.1: action A_PROCESS_ARP_RSP
LEC ATM0.1: state ACTIVE event LEC_CTL_ARP_RSP => ACTIVE
```

Special Issues Involving LANE Configuration on a Catalyst 5000 LANE Module

The Catalyst 5000 LANE module performs the following:

- Implements the assignment of individual VLANs to different emulated ELANs
- Allows the LEC to configure automatically many standard LANE configuration steps such as ILMI and QSAAL PVC configuration.

To see the messages of the ATM LANE mod in the CAT, you must type terminal monitor.

```
interface ATM0
 mtu 1500
 atm preferred phy A
 atm pvc 1 0 5 qsaal
 atm pvc 2 0 16 ilmi
 lane config auto-atm-address
!
interface ATM0.1 multipoint
lane client ethernet 2 elan2
```

You can't supply an IP address on an interface configured on a Catalyst 5000 LANE module.

Using the Dual PHY LANE Modules in a Catalyst 5000

On a two port LANE module in a Catalyst 5500, when the primary part failed, the backup port recreated control VCs in 20 seconds.

Data-direct VCs were built in 55 seconds.

```
ATM0 is up, line protocol is up
  Hardware is Catalyst 5000 ATM
  MTU 1500 bytes, sub MTU 0, BW 156250 Kbit, DLY 80 usec, rely 255/255, load 1/2
55
  Encapsulation ATM, loopback not set, keepalive set (10 sec)
  Encapsulation(s): AAL5, PVC mode
  4096 maximum active VCs, 1024 VCs per VP, 21 current VCCs
  VC idle disconnect time: 300 seconds
  Signalling vc = 1, vpi = 0, vci = 5
  UNI Version = 3.1, Link Side = user
  PHY Type : DUAL PHY; Preferred_phy : PHY_A
  PHY_A: Down; Link Status: DOWN; Errors : Loss of Signal
  PHY_B: Active; Link Status: UP; Errors : None
  Last input 00:00:00, output never, output hang never
  Last clearing of "show interface" counters never
  Queueing strategy: fifo
  Output queue 0/40, 0 drops; input queue 0/75, 0 drops
  5 minute input rate 2000 bits/sec, 1 packets/sec
  5 minute output rate 1000 bits/sec, 1 packets/sec
     2750 packets input, 704256 bytes, 0 no buffer
     Received 0 broadcasts, 0 runts, 0 giants, 0 throttles
     0 input errors, 0 CRC, 0 frame, 0 overrun, 0 ignored, 0 abort
     3074 packets output, 310992 bytes, 0 underruns
     0 output errors, 0 collisions, 11 interface resets
```

More LANE Configuration Information

- UBR has no quality of service parameters
- AAL5SNAP is for all upper-layer protocols
- AAL5MUX is for individual protocols

Troubleshooting ATM

Use many of the same troubleshooting techniques used with Frame-Relay and ISDN/DDR.

Check whether packets are leaving a given ATM interface with debug IP packet and debug atm packet. This method is similar to the methods used with Frame-Relay and Narrowband ISDN.

Is your ATM edge device forwarding cells to its directly-attached ATM switch?

If it is an SVC connection, is the SVC connection being set up properly? Remember to troubleshoot both sides of the connection. Troubleshoot from the calling party's side as well as the called party's side.

Summary

From a technology perspective, ATM is an evolutionary extension of Frame-Relay and Narrowband ISDN. From a learning perspective, studying ATM is a logical progression from Frame-Relay and Narrowband ISDN. ATM provides both PVC and SVC connectivity. With its robust class of service offerings, ATM can support the full spectrum of end-user service requirements, including voice, data and video.

Professional Development Checklist

By using this chapter, you should be able to perform the following operations:

- Configure an ATM PVC on a router
- Configure an ATM PVC on a LightStream Switch
- Configure an ATM SVC using map-lists
- Configure point-to-point subinterfaces with ATM
- Configure ATM Classical IP
- Configure RIP over a partially meshed ATM network
- Configure OSPF over an ATM network
- Configure ATM LANE on a Cisco router
- Configure ATM LANE trunking between two or more Catalyst switches
- Configure PNNI over an ATM network

For Further Study

- Cisco Certified Course: Cisco ATM, Cisco Systems, Inc.
- Cisco Certified Course: Configuring the Catalyst 5000 in a Switching Environment, Cisco Systems, Inc.
- Black, Uyless. *ATM Resource Library*, Prentice Hall, 1998. ISBN: 0-13-083786-5
- Kwok, Timothy. *ATM: The New Paradigm for Internet, Intranet and Residential Broadband Services and Applications*, Prentice Hall, 1998. ISBN: 0-13-107244-7

URLs

- **www.arslimited.com**
- **www.cciecert.com**
- **www.mentorlabs.com**
- **www.cisco.com**

Can You Spot the Issues?

1. What is wrong with the ATM LANE CLIENT configuration below:

```
interface ATM0
 mtu 1500
 atm preferred phy A
 atm pvc 1 0 16 qsaal
 atm pvc 2 0 5 ilmi
 lane config auto-config-atm-address
!
interface ATM0.1 multipoint
 lane client ethernet 2 elan2
```

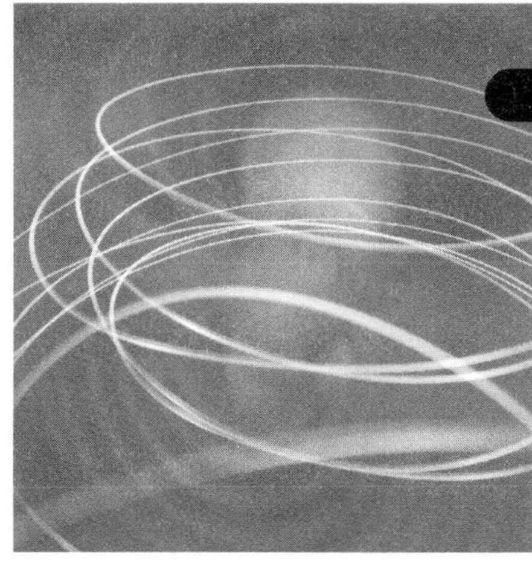

EIGHT

Level One Summary

At this point you should be able to:

- Administratively enable specified interfaces
- Supply specific encapsulation types when requested to do so
- Create any type of virtual interface:

  1. Loopback interfaces
  2. Subinterfaces
  3. Dialer interfaces

     - Configure a Frame-Relay Switch
     - Configure Frame-Relay Interfaces on a Router
     - Configure ISDN/DDR
     - Configure ISDN/DDR Dial Backup
     - Create a VLAN
     - Troubleshoot a Catalyst 5000
     - Create an ATM PVC
     - Create an ATM SVC
     - Configure ATM LANE

You should be able to perform a show ip interface brief and see all interfaces in an up/up state.

You should be able to perform a show cdp neighbor and see the specified routers/switches over the correct interfaces.

You may not be able to see routes in a routing table or even ping neighbors, but all of your interfaces are in an up/up state and you can see all of your neighbors out the proper interfaces with show cdp neighbor.

Your Frame-Relay interfaces should have the appropriate DLCIs assigned to them. If subinterfaces are specified, you should have the appropriate subinterfaces configured. You should know what to expect to see when you type:

```
Show frame pvc
Show frame map
Debug frame packet
```

You have everything configured up to supplying an IP address on your Frame-Relay interfaces. This is a LAYER TWO activity. Stop at this point.

Your ISDN interfaces should be able to talk to the switch. If Dialer Profiles are specified, you have configured them. You should know what to expect to see when you type:

```
Show isdn status
Debug isdn q931
Debug dialer packet
Show dialer
Show dialer map
Debug ppp negotiation
Debug ppp authentication
```

You have everything configured up to supplying an IP address to your ISDN/DDR interfaces. This is a LAYER TWO activity. Stop at this point.

Your Catalyst switch(es) should have the following configurations:

```
SC0 interface configured
Default route for SC0 interface configured
VTP Domain defined if specified
Trunks configured if specified
VLAN's defined if specified
```

Your show commands for verifying proper configuration and operation of the Catalyst 5000 are:

```
Show config
Show interface
Show vtp domain
Show port
Show vlan
```

Your are able to configure ATM switches and routers for:

PVC support
SVC support
ATM LANE Support

You are familiar with using the following ATM show commands:

```
Show atm status (LightStream)
Show atm interface
Show atm vc
Show lane default
Show lane client
Show lane server
Show lane database
Show arp
Show lane le-arp
```

Your mindset for performing all of the tasks above is dominated by the following principles:

Be Incremental in Performing Your Configuration

When you type in a single configuration command, you should be able to predict what will appear as a console message, what will appear when you type the relevant show command or enable the appropriate debug option.

Troubleshoot Both Sides of a Connection

For a synchronous serial connection, troubleshoot both the DCE side and the DTE side. Make sure that encapsulations match on both sides.

For Frame-Relay, make sure the Frame-Relay DTE is communicating properly the Frame-Relay switch.

Make sure that one Frame-Relay DTE is communicating with the other Frame-Relay DTE at the remote side of a PVC. Make sure that packets that are sent by one Frame-Relay DTE are being received by the target Frame-Relay DTE. This can be performed with debug ip packet, debug ip icmp, and debug frame packet.

For ISDN/DDR, make sure the ISDN DTE (the router) is able to communicate with the switch. Make sure that the calling party's ISDN connection setup messages are being received by the called party. This can be performed with debug ISDN Q931.

Measure Your Comfort Level with the Material of Level One

For five to eight routers, configuring the requirements listed above usually takes a CCIE candidate no more than ten to fifteen minutes to perform. *You must know how to perform this configuration step with complete confidence.*

If you have any questions or problems with interface configuration, refer to Volumes I and IV of both the Cisco Router Configuration Guide and Command Reference.

Once, Level One steps are performed, you are now ready to go to Level Two: IP address assignment, IP IGP routing configuration, and IP IGP route redistribution.

It cannot be stressed enough how important successful and rapid level one and two configuration are.

Now, on to Level Two: IP Addressing, IP IGP Routing Protocol Configuration, and Redistribution.

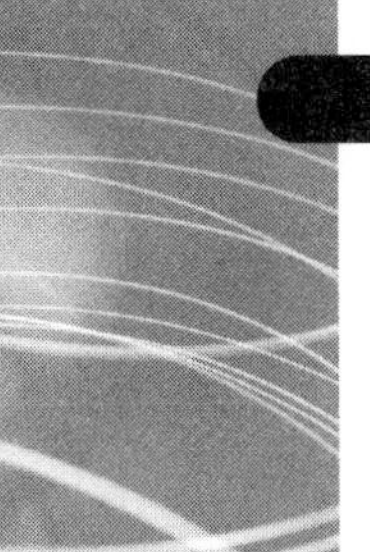

NINE

IP Addressing and the IP Routing Process

Topics Covered in This Chapter

- IP Addressing Overview
- IP Subnetting Overview
- Variable Length Subnet Mask Overview
- Route Summarization Overview
- Dissecting a Cisco Routing Table
- Using Debug IP Packet
- Using Show IP Route
- Configuring Static Routes
- Dynamic Routing Protocol Configuration Basics
- Configuring IP Secondary Addresses
- Configuring Network Address Translation
- Configuring IP Multicast Routing

Level One addressed issues of configuring, monitoring and troubleshooting physical and data-link layer technologies. Mastery of Level One topics assured that all interfaces were in an "Up/Up" state. Proper Level One configuration focused on issues such as whether ISDN, Frame-Relay and ATM interfaces were communicating with the respective switches, and whether Catalyst switch ports were in the correct VLAN and in an active state. However, Level One focused only on getting specific physical and data-link layer technologies operational individually. For example, Frame-Relay configuration was addressed in a manner that was completely separate from ISDN or Catalyst LAN switching. In a real production internetworking environment, all of these technologies are tied together into a single entity with a network layer protocol such as IP. Level One did not address tying together a complex internetwork made up of a combination of physical and data-link layer technologies. Tying together all Level One technologies with IP addressing and IP routing is the sole focus of Level Two.

Level Two builds directly upon Level One. If Level One technologies do not operate properly, Level Two technologies cannot operate and cannot be tied together as a single internetwork. Therefore, both Level One and Level Two provide the foundation of internetworking. Mastery of both topics is an absolute prerequisite for moving any further in CCIE preparation.

Level Two technologies—IP addressing and IP routing protocols—tie all Level One technologies into one administrative entity. Once all Level Two technologies are deployed and associated configuration tasks are completed, you will be able to reach every interface in your internetwork regardless of their physical and data-link layer characteristics.

The four main topics of Level Two are:

1. Possessing a thorough understanding of IP addressing and the IP routing process
2. Designing and deploying an IP addressing plan in a complex internetwork
3. Configuring IP IGP routing (both static routes and dynamic routing protocols)
4. Configuring IP route redistribution

All four topics will be introduced and examined in this chapter. Chapters 10 and 11 will examine individual IP routing protocols in greater detail, and Chapter 12 will examine IP route redistribution. It is absolutely mandatory that CCIE candidates master these topics.

A Brief History of the Evolution of IP Addressing

IP addressing has undergone an evolution over the last twenty years. In the late 1970s and early 1980s, IP addressing was structured in different classes of 32-bit IP addresses (Classes A, B, C, etc.). Categorizing IP addresses into different classes is known as the "classful" model of IP addressing. By the late 1980s, the original classful structure was found to be unable to accommodate the rapid deployment of IP addresses. As a partial remedy, subnetting was introduced to provide a method of address conservation of existing IP address classes. By 1993, the move towards completely abandoning the classful model was underway with the introduction of Classless InterDomain Routing (CIDR). Instead of categorizing networks by an address class, CIDR introduced a model that identified networks by a unique prefix and prefix length. Finally, IP Version 6 is on the horizon to bring even more changes to IP addresses. The following sections review issues associated with classful IP addressing, subnetting, summarization and CIDR.

IP Addressing Overview

One of the most important design decisions of an Internet engineer is how to assign IP addresses—32-bit numbers that identify Internet hosts. These numbers are placed in the IP packet header and are used to route packets to their destination. Several things should be kept in mind about IP address assignment:

Prefix-based addressing. A basic concept of IP addressing is that initial prefixes of the IP address can be used for generalized routing decisions. For example, the first 16 bits of an address might identify Acme Company, the first 20 bits identify Acme's Jonestown office, the first 26 bits identify a particular Ethernet in that office, and the entire 32 bits identify a particular host on that Ethernet. Prefix-based addressing has its origins in IP Address Classes, and has evolved into subnetting and CIDR.

Per-interface assignment. IP addresses are assigned on a per-interface basis. A device might possess several IP addresses if it has several interfaces. For example, a device with both Ethernet and serial interfaces would have an IP address for each. This is an important consequence of prefix-based addressing. An IP address doesn't really refer to a device, but rather to an interface. If a device is known by multiple addresses, then every service on the device can be referred to by multiple names! Addressing this device requires picking one of these. Since the packet is addressed to the interface and not the device itself, path information is introduced into the address. The exact ramifications of this effect depend heavily on network design. In particular, careless design can result in a device becoming reachable by one address but not another. The simplest solution is to select the device's most reliable interface and advertise its IP address as the primary IP address.

IP Address Classes

The original IP addressing design was based on Address Classes. In the original Internet routing scheme developed in the 1970s, sites were assigned addresses from one of three classes: Class A, Class B and Class C. The address classes differ in size and number. Class A addresses are the largest, but there are few of them. Class Cs are the smallest, but they are numerous. Classes D and E are also defined, but are not used in normal operation.

To say that class-based IP addressing is still used would be true only in the loosest sense. Many addressing designs are still class-based, but an increasing number can only be explained using the more general concept of classless interdomain routing (CIDR), which is backwards compatible with address classes.

Suffice it to say that, at one point, you could request an internationally-recognized IP address registration organization, such as the Internet NIC, to assign you a Class A, B or C address. To get the larger Class B addresses, you might have to supply some justification, but only the Class A was really tough to get. In any case, the Internet NIC would set the network bits, or n-bits, to some unique value and inform the local network engineer. It would then be up to the engineer to assign each of his hosts an IP address, starting with the assigned n-bits, followed by host bits, or h-bits, to make the address unique.

Internet routing used to work like this: A router receiving an IP packet extracted its Destination Address, which was classified (literally) by examining its first one to four bits. Once the address' class had been determined, it was broken down into network and host bits. Routers ignored the host bits, and needed only to match the network bits to find a route to the network. Once a packet reached its target network, its host field was examined for final delivery.

Summary of IP Address Classes

Class A - 0nnnnnnn hhhhhhhh hhhhhhhh hhhhhhhh

First bit 0; 7 network bits; 24 host bits
Initial octet: 0 - 127
126 Class As exist (0 and 127 are reserved)
16,777,214 hosts on each Class A

Class B - 10nnnnnn nnnnnnnn hhhhhhhh hhhhhhhh

First two bits 10; 14 network bits; 16 host bits
Initial octet: 128 - 191
16,384 Class Bs exist
65,532 hosts on each Class B

Class C - 110nnnnn nnnnnnnn nnnnnnnn hhhhhhhh

First three bits 110; 21 network bits; 8 host bits
Initial octet: 192 - 223
2,097,152 Class Cs exist
254 hosts on each Class C

Class D - 1110mmmm mmmmmmmm mmmmmmmm mmmmmmmm

First four bits 1110; 28 multicast address bits
Initial byte: 224 - 247
Class Ds are multicast addresses - see RFC 1112

Class E - 1111rrrr rrrrrrrr rrrrrrrr rrrrrrrr

First four bits 1111; 28 reserved address bits
Initial byte: 248 - 255
Reserved for experimental use

Subnetting

Engineers gradually realized that the original class-based addressing design was too inflexible for many applications. In the mid-1980s, subnetting was introduced as an extension to the original scheme.

Subnetting, documented in RFC 950, originally referred to the subdivision of a class-based network into subnetworks, but now it refers more generally to the subdivision of a CIDR block into smaller CIDR blocks. Subnetting allows single routing entries to refer either to the larger block or to its individual constituents. This permits a single, general routing entry to be used through most of the Internet, more specific routes only being required for routers in the subnetted block.

Many lectures and presentations on IP addressing and subnetting teach these topics detached from the subject of routing. This is a flawed method of instruction. It is absolutely essential to understand the relationship between subnetting and specific IP routing protocols. The two topics are inextricably linked. Different routing protocols treat the subnetting process differently. For example, RIP v.1 and IGRP never advertise subnet mask information in their routing table advertisements, whereas EIGRP, OSPF and BGP4 do send subnet mask information, along with the IP prefix, in routing updates.

A subnet mask is a 32-bit number that determines how an IP address is split into network and host portions, on a bitwise basis. The two fundamental rules of subnetting are:

1. If a bit in a subnet mask has a value of one, then the bit in the corresponding IP address is part of the network prefix.
2. If a bit in a subnet mask has a value of zero, then the bit in the corresponding IP address is part of the host suffix.

When applying the two rules of subnetting to classful addresses, the default subnet masks for Class A, Class B and Class C addresses are:

Class A	N.H.H.H	255.0.0.0
Class B	N.N.H.H	255.255.0.0
Class C	N.N.N.H	255.255.255.0

In the table above, 255.255.0.0 is a standard class B subnet mask, since the first two bytes are all ones (network), and the last two bytes are all zeros (host). When a 255.255.0.0 subnet mask is applied to a class B address, no subnetting is performed.

In a subnetted network, the network portion is extended. For example, a subnet mask of 255.255.255.0 would subnet a class B address space using its third byte. Using this scheme, the first two bytes of an IP address would identify the class B network, the next byte would identify the subnet within that network, and the final byte would select an individual host. Since subnet masks are used on a bit-by-bit basis, masks like 255.255.240.0 (four bits of subnet; 12 bits of host) are perfectly normal.

In a traditional subnetted network, several restrictions apply. Many of these restrictions have been lifted by VLSM, CIDR and more flexible routing protocols such as OSPF and EIGRP. However, if older routing protocols (such as RIP Version 1 and IGRP) are used, the two following restrictions must still be observed:

1. All subnet masks must be of a fixed length. Since RIP v.1 and IGRP routing updates do not include subnet mask information, a router must assume that the subnet mask with which it has been configured is valid for all subnets. Therefore, a single mask must be used for all subnets of a given classful network. Different masks can be used for different classful network addresses. This rule is referred to as the Rule of Fixed Length Subnet Masks (FLSM). Later, it will be compared to Variable Length Subnet Masks (VLSM).

   Based on the assumption of FLSM, a router can exchange subnet routes with other routers within the network. Since the subnet masks are identical across the network, the routers will interpret these routes in the same manner. However, routers not attached to the subnetted network cannot interpret these subnet routes, since they lack the subnet mask. Therefore, subnet routes are not relayed to routers on other networks. This leads to our second restriction.

2. A subnetted network cannot be split into isolated portions. All the subnets must be contiguous, since subnet routing information cannot be passed to non-members. Within a network, all subnets must be able to reach all other subnets without passing traffic through other networks.

Variable Length Subnet Masks (VLSM)

A Fixed Length Subnet Mask (FLSM) environment is too inflexible when you need varying types of subnet masks for the same network address. For example, consider a large organization with a single Class B address of 172.16.0.0. Its headquarters site is made up of four IP subnets with 250 end systems on each VLAN. The same organization has ten regional offices, each with a single LAN with less than 60 end systems each. Finally, this organization has 500 field offices. Each field office has a single LAN segment with less than five end systems each. Which of the following subnet masks is best for this organization?

- A 24-bit subnet (255.255.255.0) yielding 254 subnets (each subnet yields 254 valid end system addresses each)

- A 26-bit subnet (255.255.255.192) yielding 1,022 subnets (each subnet yields 62 valid end system addresses each)
- A 29-bit subnet (255.255.255.248) yielding 8,190 subnets (each subnet yields 6 valid end system addresses each)

The answer is either "none of them individually" or "all of them." The 24-bit subnet mask can be deployed at the headquarters site. The 26-bit subnet mask can be deployed at the regional offices. The 29-bit subnet mask can be deployed at the field offices. However, a Fixed Length Subnet Mask environment cannot accommodate deploying all of these different length subnet masks for a single classful network prefix. A Variable Length Subnet Mask environment can.

Routing protocol selection determines whether you are stuck with a FLSM environment or whether you can deploy VLSM. As mentioned earlier, RIP v.1 and IGRP support only FLSM. RIP v.2, OSPF and EIGRP support VLSM. To illustrate this, closely examine the routing updates from debug traces generated by RIP v.1, IGRP, OSPF and EIGRP:

```
IGRP
IGRP: sending update to 255.255.255.255 via Serial0 (172.16.2.1)
subnet 172.16.10.0, metric=8476
subnet 172.16.4.0, metric=1100
network 177.11.0.0, metric=11000
network 177.10.0.0, metric=11000
```

```
RIP
RIP: sending v1 update to 255.255.255.255 via Serial1
(172.16.10.1)
  subnet 172.16.17.0, metric 4
subnet 172.16.4.0, metric 1
subnet 172.16.1.0, metric 4
network 177.10.0.0, metric 1
network 177.11.0.0, metric 1
```

```
OSPF
OSPF: Generate external LSA 179.10.1.0, mask 255.255.255.0, type
5, age 0, metric 20, seq 0x8000000C
OSPF: Generate external LSA 172.16.10.0, mask 255.255.255.0, type
5, age 0, metric 20, seq 0x8000000C
OSPF: Generate external LSA 172.16.1.0, mask 255.255.255.0, type
5, age 0, metric 20, seq 0x8000000C
OSPF: Generate external LSA 172.16.2.0, mask 255.255.255.0, type
5, age 0, metric 20, seq 0x8000000C
```

```
EIGRP
IP-EIGRP: Int 172.16.2.0/24 M 2681856 - 1657856 1024000 SM
2169856 - 1657856 512000
```

```
IP-EIGRP: Ext 10.0.0.0/8 M 2707456 - 1657856 1049600 SM 2195456 -
1657856 537600
```

Notice that no subnet mask length information is contained in the IGRP and RIP routing table advertisements. However, with OSPF and EIGRP, subnet mask length information is included in routing table advertisements. Also, note the distinction between subnet and network routing table updates with IGRP and RIP. At the top of each routing table update for IGRP and RIP, there is a statement that lists the interface on which the update is being generated (Serial 0 or Serial 1) and the IP address of the interface. If the routing table update is advertised on an interface that is a subnet of a classful IP address, that interface will advertise all subnets of its own address; otherwise, it will send out only the classful network prefix. For example, subnets of the 172.16.0.0 network are advertised on both the RIP and IGRP routing update displays because the advertising interface is participating in the subnetting of the 172.16.0.0 network. In the RIP and IGRP routing updates displayed above, the 177.10.0.0 and 177.11.0.0 networks are also being advertised. Since these network addresses are different from the IP address assigned to the interface performing the advertising, they are labeled as "network" advertisements (compared to "subnet" for the 172.16.0.0 updates) and only the classful address is advertised.

To strengthen your understanding of VLSM, let's return to the organization that had a requirement for three different types of subnet masks:

- Four subnets with 24-bit subnet masks for headquarters
- Ten subnets each with a 26-bit subnet mask for each of the ten regional offices
- 500 subnets with a 29-bit subnet mask for each of the 500 field offices

You can allocate the following four subnets 172.16.1.0/24, 172.16.2.0/24, 172.16.3.0/24 and 172.16.4.0/24 for the four headquarters subnets:

You can allocate the following ten subnets for the ten regional offices:

172.16.10.0/26
172.16.10.64/26
172.16.10.128/26
172.16.10.192/26
172.16.11.0/26
172.16.11.64/26
172.16.11.128/26
172.16.11.192/26
172.16.12.0/26
172.16.12.64/26

You can allocate subnets similar to the following sample of 29-bit subnets for the field offices:

172.16.100.0/29
172.16.100.8/29
172.16.100.16/29
172.16.100.24/29
172.16.100.32/29

EIGRP and OSPF will forward all of these subnets because both routing protocols advertise both the network prefix and the subnet mask.

RIP v.1 and IGRP will only advertise the subnets that match the subnet mask of the advertising interface. For example, if a RIP v.1 enabled interface was configured with a 26-bit mask, it will advertise all other 26-bit subnets it knows. It will not advertise any subnets with a mask other than 26 bits.

A critical rule to remember when subnetting in general and variable length subnetting in particular is: DO NOT LET THE ADDRESS SPACE OF ANY SUBNET OVERLAP WITH ANOTHER! In order to assure that this does not happen, remember this basic subnetting technique:

First, determine the largest subnet your organization will require. Remember that the largest subnet will possess the smallest subnet mask. The largest subnet will be assigned the title "baseline subnet." Take one of the baseline subnets and subnet it again using a larger subnet mask. A larger subnet mask will create more subnets, but with fewer hosts per subnet. Keep detailed records of the subnets you assign.

Also, when planning your subnetting, consider your route summarization strategy. Let's return to the hypothetical organization mentioned above. Assume that the organization's network topology is based upon the Cisco hierarchy of core, distribution and access. Assume also that the 500 field offices are connected into ten regional offices in groups of fifty, and that the ten regional offices are connected into the organization's headquarters. Instead of having 500 routing table entries in the headquarters routers, you can have fourteen entries and still maintain full reachability throughout the entire internetwork. This can only be performed with careful and proper subnet address deployment and summarization planning.

When applying the suggested subnets listed above for this hypothetical organization, the subnets selected will fulfill the purpose of avoiding IP address overlapping, but they are an inefficient solution for route summarization purposes. Therefore, when determining an organization's IP addressing requirements, consider the following three factors:

1. Determine the organization's need for subnets of varying lengths.
2. Deploy a subnet strategy that assures that no addresses overlap.
3. Deploy a subnet strategy that facilitates route summarization.

Summarization

Well-planned subnetting yields efficient summarization. Subnetting extends the network prefix with a subnet mask, which extends the network prefix by shifting the prefix from left to right. The more you extend the subnet mask, the more subnets you create, but the fewer hosts you can assign per subnet. But summarization—the reverse process—involves moving the bits of a network prefix in the opposite direction (from right to left, rather than left to right). In this way, summarization builds upon subnetting. In fact, summarization is sometimes often called "supernetting."

Summarization involves a routing process possessing multiple network entries which share a common prefix. Instead of advertising all network entries in the routing table, a router may announce a single network that possesses the common prefix. The router that is the source of the summarized route will advertise a single prefix to its downstream neighbors. When IP traffic is forwarded to the source router, the "summarizing" router will be able to switch packets to the appropriate subnet by applying the longest match rule.

The effectiveness of summarization is limited by poor IP address planning and deployment. For example, if 20 subnets can be summarized by a particular router for the network of 172.16.0.0, a summarization statement should be configured. However, if another ten subnets belonging to the 172.16.0.0 prefix existed in other parts of the internetwork—parts that were not contiguous with the summarized 20 subnets—they would need to be propagated throughout the network in a non-summarized form.

RIP version 1 and IGRP summarize at the classful boundaries only. OSPF and EIGRP pass mask length information in their routing table updates.

OSPF by default does not summarize. You can manually summarize OSPF routing information on a Cisco router with the "area range" and "summary-address" commands. Both of these commands are entered in the routing protocol configuration mode. OSPF summarization will be covered in Chapter 11.

EIGRP by default summarizes by classful network boundaries. You can disable this feature with the interface configuration command "no auto-summary." You can also summarize routing information with EIGRP with the interface configuration command "ip summary-address eigrp." EIGRP summarization will be covered in Chapter 10.

As an example of summarization, assume a university campus made up of several dozen subnetworks. The university has been assigned a single registered address (a Class B address). When the university announces its registered prefix to another non-university router, it does not announce all of the subnets. It announces only one prefix. This prefix is a "summary" of all the university's subnets.

The benefits of summarization are:

- It reduces the size of routing table updates, saving bandwidth.
- It reduces the size of routing tables, saving router memory.
- It limits the scope of failure of network instabilities.

Summarization Tools

Two summarization tools are commonly used. One is graphical. The other is a binary to decimal table.

USING THE ROUTE SUMMARIZATION GRAPH

Take the collection of numbers to be summarized and find their location in Figure 9-1.

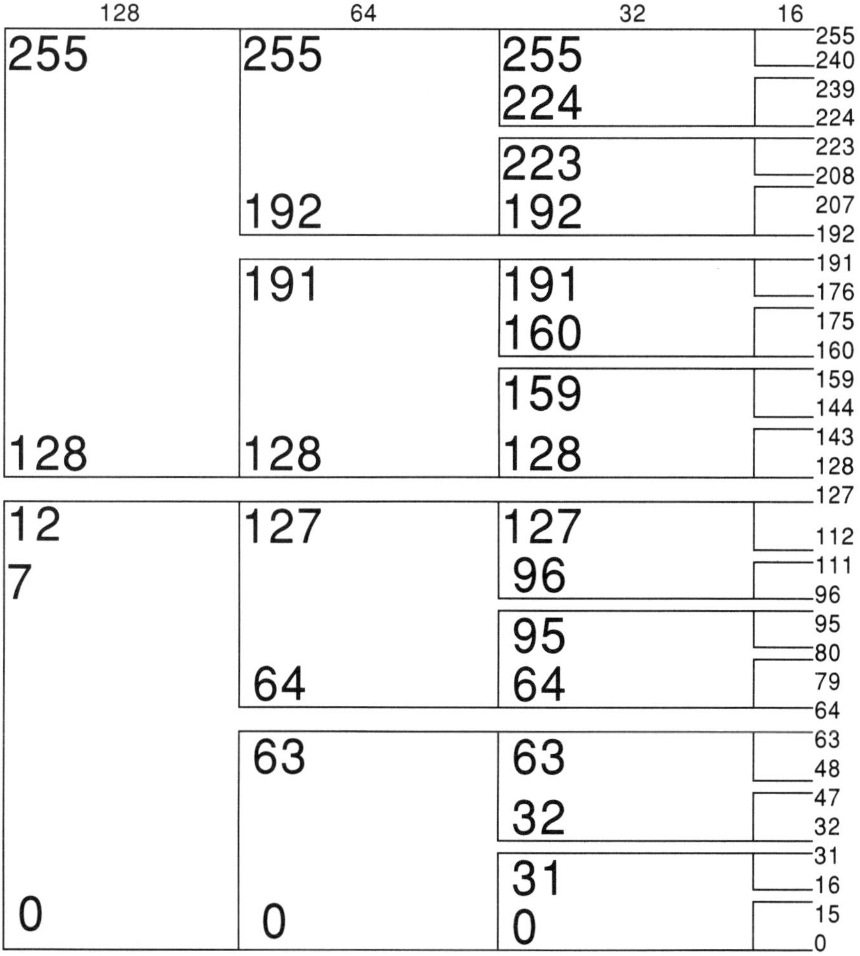

FIGURE 9–1 IP Address Summarization Chart

Select the range that contains all your addresses. This is your summary address. Notice how inefficient your summaries can be, depending on the numbers you select to summarize. Typically, the broader the range of numbers to be summarized, the more inefficient the summarization.

USING A BINARY TO DECIMAL TABLE FOR ROUTE SUMMARIZATION

When using the binary to decimal table for route summarization, perform the following steps:

1. List octets to be summarized in the left-hand column.
2. Convert the octets to a binary format.
3. Locate all the columns with which the octets share common bit values (the shaded area in the tables below).
4. Locate the first column with which the octets *do not* share common bit values.
5. Summarize the block of addresses on the last contiguous bit of common bit values.

Listed below are a few examples.

1. Summarize 172.16.60.0/24, 172.16.61.0/24 and 172.16.62.0/24.

	128	**64**	**32**	**16**	**8**	**4**	**2**	**1**
60	0	0	1	1	1	1	0	0
61	0	0	1	1	1	1	0	1
62	0	0	1	1	1	1	1	0

172.16.60.0 255.255.252.0 summarizes the three addresses above. All three addresses shared the same binary values for their respective first six bits. This is a neat and efficient summarization for the three 24-bit subnets listed above. The summary supports only four address combinations. The 172.16.60.0/22 summary is using three of them. The further apart the addresses to be summarized; the broader the summarization, the more wasteful the summarization.

2. Summarize 172.16.29.0, 172.16.30.0 and 172.16.31.0

	128	**64**	**32**	**16**	**8**	**4**	**2**	**1**
29	0	0	0	1	1	1	0	1
30	0	0	0	1	1	1	1	0
31	0	0	0	1	1	1	1	1

172.16.28.0 255.255.252.0 summarizes the three addresses above. All three addresses shared the same binary values for their respective first six bits.

3. Summarize 172.16.30.0, 172.16.31.0 and 172.16.32.0

	128	**64**	**32**	**16**	**8**	**4**	**2**	**1**
30	0	0	0	1	1	1	1	0
31	0	0	0	1	1	1	1	1
32	0	0	1	0	0	0	0	0

In this example the summary address is 172.16.0.0 255.255.192.0. Only the first two bits are shared by all three addresses. The third address, number 32, crossed a major bit boundary. Even though these three addresses are contiguous, they require the entire block of address space between zero and 63 to be summarized. This is an example of inefficient address summarization.

4. Summarize 172.16.140.0, 172.16.141.0 and 172.16.149.0

	128	**64**	**32**	**16**	**8**	**4**	**2**	**1**
140	1	0	0	0	1	1	0	0
141	1	0	0	0	1	1	0	1
149	1	0	0	1	0	1	0	1

In this example, the summary address is 172.16.128.0 255.255.224.0. Only the first three bits are shared by all three addresses.

5. Summarize 172.16.1.33, 172.16.1.41 and 172.16.1.46

	128	**64**	**32**	**16**	**8**	**4**	**2**	**1**
33	0	0	1	0	0	0	0	1
41	0	0	1	0	1	0	1	0
46	0	0	1	0	1	1	1	1

In this example the summary address is 172.16.1.32 255.255.255.240. Only the first four bits are shared by all three addresses.

6. Summarize 172.16.1.10, 172.16.1.20 and 172.16.1.40

	128	**64**	**32**	**16**	**8**	**4**	**2**	**1**
10	0	0	0	0	1	0	1	0
20	0	0	0	1	0	1	0	0
40	0	0	1	0	1	0	0	0

In this example, the summary address is 172.16.1.0 255.255.255.192. Only the first two bits are shared by all three addresses.

Classless Interdomain Routing (CIDR)

Both subnetting and supernetting are embodied in Classless Interdomain Routing (CIDR), which is the most recent enhancement to Internet addressing. With the advent of CIDR, the original class-based scheme has been almost completely discarded. Instead, subnetting is used to divide "CIDR blocks" of arbitrary size into smaller "CIDR blocks," a process that can be repeated ad infinitum.

Faced with exhaustion of Class B address space and the explosion of routing table growth triggered by a flood of new Class Cs, IETF began implementing CIDR in the early 1990s. CIDR is documented in RFC 1518 and RFC 1519. The primary requirement for CIDR is the use of routing protocols that support it, such as RIP Version 2, OSPF Version 2, or BGP Version 4.

CIDR can be thought of as "subnetting on steroids." The subnetting mask, previously a magic number set in a computer's boot sequence, now becomes an integral part of routing tables and protocols. A route is no longer an IP address, broken down into network and host bits according to its class. A route is now a combination of address and mask. Not only can we break networks into "subnets," but we can also combine networks into "supernets," so long as they have a common network prefix. CIDR defines address assignment and aggregation strategies designed to minimize the size of top-level Internet routing tables. In general, IP-based routing is better served by preface-based addressing over classful network-based addressing. The old classful model (Class A, Class B, Class C) does not scale well.

IP Addressing and the IP Routing Process

In a standard IP network, each network or subnetwork has a unique network prefix. All devices on a given segment have the same network prefix and a unique host suffix (unless IP secondary addresses are used; IP secondary addresses will be covered later in this chapter). Thus, if a given internetwork has ten different subnetworks, ten unique IP subnets must be assigned. Under the most basic circumstances with no route summarization occurring, all routers would possess ten subnet entries in their routing tables. With these entries in their routing tables, routers can forward packets toward any destination in the internetwork. As a result, all end systems will be able to reach each other.

As an example, consider a large college campus with an internetwork made up of 100 subnets. Each of these subnets is identified by a unique subnet prefix, and each subnet is interconnected by a router. When packets leave any end system on campus, the end system must make a decision: Is the destination address in a given IP packet on the directly-attached local network, or is it on some other network? If the destination address is on the local network, the end system generates an ARP request to match the target destination IP address with a remote MAC address. Otherwise, the end system forwards the IP packet to a locally connected router.

If the packet is forwarded to the router, the router examines the destination address of the packet and attempts to match it with the "longest match" in its routing table. If a match is found, the router "switches" the packet out of the local interface associated with the matched destination address. For example, if a router receives a packet containing the destination address of 172.16.1.1 and its routing table contains an entry:

172.16.1.0/24 Serial 0

the router will forward the packet out of its Serial 0 interface. The router's switching decision can be interpreted in plain English as, "To get to 172.16.1.0/24, forward the packet out interface Serial 0." In fact, all switching decisions made by an IGP routing process can be interpreted by the phrase, "To get to x.x.x.x, forward the packet out interface yy (x.x.x.x = any IP prefix; yy = any interface associated with IP prefix x.x.x.x).

At the heart of the routing process is the routing table. If an entry for a destination address is not in the routing table, and there is no default route, packets will be dropped.

IP addressing →	Routing Table	←Routing Protocols
IP packets	Prefix based	RIP, OSPF, IGRP, EIGRP

How are these routing tables created? How are they maintained?

In its most rudimentary form, routing is performed on a packet-by-packet basis, using only the destination address of each IP packet routed. The destination address of each IP packet is matched with the longest match found in a routing table. IT IS ABSOLUTELY CRITICAL THAT YOU UNDERSTAND THE LONGEST MATCH RULE AND HOW IT APPLIES TO SUBNETTED AND SUMMARIZED ROUTING TABLE ENTRIES.

Cisco enhances the conventional packet-by-packet destination address-based IP routing process with several different techniques: fast-cache switching, autonomous switching, NetFlow switching, Tag switching and methods of distributed switching (used on the model 12000 router, the Catalyst 8500 switch router, and Versatile Interface Processor cards in a 7500 router and a Catalyst 5000 multilayer switch). With the Catalyst 8500, IP packets can be forwarded at wire speed! At a minimum, all Cisco routers and routing modules have the IP fast caching performance feature, which is enabled by default.

When IP routing was first introduced, routing tables were made up of three different types of entries:

- Host routes (a complete 32-bit match)
- Network routes (Class A, Class B, Class C)
- A default route (0.0.0.0)

Therefore, when IP routing was first introduced, the destination address in a transiting IP packet could only be matched with the three types of entries listed above.

In the mid-1980s, IP routing tables began to accept subnet entries.

In the early 1990s, routing tables began to exchange variable-length subnets with routing protocols, such as OSPF and EIGRP. Finally, in the early to mid-1990s, classless subnets and supernets were accepted by IP routing tables.

With the enhancements of subnetting, VLSM and CIDR, IP packets transiting a router can perform a more granular match to its destination address. But even with all of these enhancements to the IP routing process, the Longest Match Rule still prevails. IT CANNOT BE STRESSED ENOUGH: KNOW AND THOROUGHLY UNDERSTAND THE LONGEST MATCH RULE!

The core of the standard IP routing process can be divided into the following two processes:

1. Building and maintaining routing tables
2. Switching packets based upon matching the destination address in the IP packet with the longest match in the IP routing table

The following section focuses on building and maintaining interior gateway IP routing tables. Exterior gateway routing will be covered in Chapter 14.

Building Routing Tables

In most cases, IP routers build routing tables with IP address prefixes. Routing tables are constructed with either static IP prefix entries or dynamic entries. Static entries consist of static routes configured by a network administrator. Dynamic entries consist of routing table information exchanged by routing protocols, such as RIP, IGRP or OSPF.

Ideally, all routers in the same routing domain attain a state of "convergence." Convergence is attained when all routers possess a stable, accurate and consistent view of the network topology. It has been said that when routers obtain a state of convergence, they have attained a state of "network nirvana." How routers maintain a state of convergence varies upon their configuration and routing protocols.

Routing protocols are categorized by the underlying technology they use. For example, RIP and IGRP are categorized as Distance-Vector based routing protocols, OSPF is categorized as a Link-State Protocol, and EIGRP is categorized as an enhanced Distance-Vector routing protocol. Common characteristics of Distance-Vector based routing protocols are:

1. A single table (the routing table) consisting of the best paths to all known destination networks is maintained. Link-State protocols maintain three tables, while Distance-Vector protocols maintain only one.
2. A complete copy of the routing table is advertised to its neighbors on a periodic basis. This is performed even if no change has occurred to the network.
3. Several loop-avoidance techniques, such as split-horizon, hold down timers and poison reverse are used. While these techniques prevent routing loops, they also slow down reconvergence time.

Update timers, hold down timers and flush timers can be seen for each distance vector routing protocol with the "show ip protocols" command. The first three lines of the show ip protocols command is displayed below:

```
Routing Protocol is "igrp 100"
       Sending updates every 90 seconds, next due in 72 seconds
       Invalid after 270 seconds, hold down 280, flushed after 630
```

To see the state of holddown for a given routing table entry, type "sh ip route x.x.x.x" (x.x.x.x = a specific network prefix). To bring a single route out of holddown, type "clea ip route x.x.x.x."

In a healthy distance-vector routing environment, routing entries are "forever young." For example, all RIP and IGRP routing entries are never older than the routing protocol's update interval. RIP and IGRP are constantly exchanging routing table updates on every update interval. RIP's default update interval is 30 seconds. IGRP's default update interval is 90 seconds. Therefore, no standard RIP routing table entry should ever be older than 30 seconds, and no IGRP entry should ever be older than 90 seconds.

Common characteristics of a Link-State routing protocols are:

1. All routers participating in Link-State routing maintain an identical map of all the links in the entire internetwork. This map is contained in the link-state or topological database. This topological database is a completely separate table from the main routing table.
2. Each Link-State router locates itself in the link state database and executes a "shortest path first" algorithm to determine the optimal path to all destination networks.
3. The results of executing the shortest path algorithm are posted to the main routing table.
4. Link State routers do not exchange the entire routing table on a fixed periodic basis. Link-State routers exchange locally-sourced Link State Advertisements. Link State Advertisements are exchanged when a change to the network topology occurs.

5. Since all Link-State routers maintain a complete map of the entire internetwork in its topological database, they can rapidly reconverge when a network is declared unreachable. Link-State routing protocols are not subject to the loop avoidance techniques of Distance-Vector routing protocols. They do not use split-horizon or hold down timers.

The mostly commonly used Link-State routing protocol in the IP world is Open Shortest Path First (OSPF). OSPF is covered in detail in Chapter 12.

EIGRP is an enhanced Distance-Vector routing protocol. EIGRP discovers a network like a distance-vector routing protocol, but it adapts to changes in the network in a manner similar to a Link-State protocol. Specifically, it discovers a network like IGRP. Both IGRP and EIGRP use the same metric calculation to determine the best path to a given destination network. Like a Distance-Vector routing protocol, EIGRP applies the Rule of Split Horizon, and like a Link-State protocol, it maintains a topological database to assist it in rapidly reconverging when a change in the network topology occurs. However, the actual contents of the EIGRP topological database is significantly different from a Link-State topological database. EIGRP will be covered in more detail in Chapter 10.

OSPF and EIGRP make changes to their routing tables when there is a change in the network topology. Therefore, if an OSPF or EIGRP network is stable, routing entries should attain an old age.

Maintaining Routing Tables

RIP and IGRP maintain only one table: a routing table. They do this by exchanging the full routing table with neighboring routers on a periodic basis. If a learned RIP or IGRP route is announced as unreachable, RIP and IGRP will mark the route as being in a "possibly down" state and place it in a holddown state. The route is normally placed in a holddown state for a period three times the length of a routing table update interval. If the route has not been re-learned by either the same source, the route is flushed from the routing table. Update timers, hold down timers and flush timers can be viewed with the "show ip protocols" command.

In addition to maintaining a routing table, EIGRP and OSPF also maintain two other tables: a neighbor and a topology table. Each builds upon the other. Both OSPF and EIGRP build and maintain their neighbor tables by exchanging HELLO packets with other OSPF and EIGRP routers. Once HELLO parameters are properly exchanged, both OSPF and EIGRP begin exchanging routing table information with their respective neighbors. This process builds both the OSPF and EIGRP topological database. From the information in its topological database, OSPF executes the shortest path algorithm. OSPF places the results of the shortest path algorithim in the main routing table. However, EIGRP does not execute a shortest path algorithim. It simply places the best learned paths to destination networks in the main routing table. If there is a change in the status of a network's reachability in the main routing table, neither EIGRP nor OSPF will ever place the route in a holddown state. They will both reconverge immediately by using information in their topological databases.

Switching Packets on the Longest Match in the Routing Table

Once the routing table is built, the router switches packets by matching the destination address of an incoming packet with the "longest match" in the routing table. The routing table can be constructed with entries from multiple sources, including:

- Connected routes
- Static routes
- Default routes
- Distance-Vector learned routes (RIP, IGRP)
- Link-State learned routes (OSPF)
- Learned routes from other dynamic routing protocols (IS-IS, EIGRP, BGP4, etc.)

The Anatomy of a Cisco IP Routing Table

Understanding the function of each column in a standard Cisco routing table reveals a great deal about the Cisco IP routing process. It is therefore critical that a CCIE candidate is familiar with every entry and column.

There are seven columns in a Cisco IP routing table:

1. Source of routing information
2. Destination address at issue
3. Administrative distance
4. Metric
5. Next hop of packet/source of routing information
6. Age of the entry
7. Local interface to switch the packet on

Listed below is a sample display of the IOS "show ip route" command.

```
r3#show ip route
Codes: C - connected, S - static, I - IGRP, R - RIP, M - mobile, B - BGP
     D - EIGRP, EX - EIGRP external, O - OSPF, IA - OSPF inter area
     E1 - OSPF external type 1, E2 - OSPF external type 2, E - EGP
     i - IS-IS, L1 - IS-IS level-1, L2 - IS-IS level-2, * - candidate  default
Gateway of last resort is 172.16.3.2 to network 140.10.0.0

1    2            3   4          5                6         7
I*   140.10.0.0 [100/183071] via 172.16.3.2, 00:00:26, Serial1
                [100/183071] via 172.16.4.4, 00:00:45, Serial0
```

```
C    150.10.0.0 is directly connected, Loopback0
     160.10.0.0 255.255.255.0 is subnetted, 1 subnets
S    160.10.1.0 [1/0] via 172.16.3.2
     172.16.0.0 255.255.255.0 is subnetted, 4 subnets
C    172.16.4.0 is directly connected, Serial0
I    172.16.1.0 [100/182571] via 172.16.4.4, 00:00:46, Serial0
I    172.16.2.0 [100/182571] via 172.16.3.2, 00:00:27, Serial1
C    172.16.3.0 is directly connected, Serial1
```

COLUMN ONE: SOURCE OF ROUTING TABLE ENTRY

The single letter on the far left-hand side of the routing table (Column 1) represents the source of the routing table entry. All possible sources of routing table information are listed in the legend directly above the table. Every routing table must have at least one "connected" entry. All entries from sources other than "C" (connected) and "S" (static) are dynamically "learned" routes derived from routing protocols. You can examine groups of routing table entries by typing "show ip route connected," "show ip route static," and "show ip route rip."

COLUMN TWO: DESTINATION IP PREFIX WITH SUBNET MASK INFORMATION

Column Two contains an essential element of the IP routing process: the IP prefix that will be matched with the destination IP address of a packet attempting to be routed. An IP routing table entry can be created without a metric, but not without referencing a destination prefix.

The two core elements of every routing table entry are:

1. Target destination network (the contents of column two of the IP routing table)
2. Local interface to forward packet on to get to destination network (last column of the IP routing table)

Sometimes a routing entry will list a destination network and a next hop address. (See the static routing entry for 160.10.1.0/24 in the sample routnig table above.) If the switching decision is based upon a next hop address rather than a local interface, a second "recursive" look up must be performed to map the next hop address with a local interface. IP switching decisions begin with locating a destination address, using the longest match rule and ending with referencing a local interface to switch the packet on. The IP switching process can be summarized with the phrase, "To get to the destination prefix x.x.x.x, go out interface Y."

Note that some entries in the sample routing table displayed above contain subnet information. By maintaining the subnet information, the routing table can provide a granular application of the Longest Match Rule. If a single classful network address is subnetted with more than one mask, it will be listed as "variably subnetted."

COLUMN THREE: ADMINISTRATIVE DISTANCE

The administrative distance prioritizes routing information derived from different routing table sources. A routing protocol with a lower administrative distance is given preference over one with a higher administrative distance. The default administrative distance settings are listed below:

Connected routes	0
Static routes referencing a local interface	0
Static routes referencing the next hop router	1
External BGP derived routes	20
EIGRP derived routes	90
IGRP derived routes	100
OSPF derived routes	110
RIP derived routes	120
External EIGRP derived routes	170
Internal BGP derived routes	200
Unknown	255

For example, if network 172.16.0.0 is learned from a RIP speaking neighbor and an IGRP-speaking neighbor, the routing information from the IGRP speaker will be given precedence, since IGRP has a lower administrative distance.

Instances when a router would be running more than one routing protocol are:

1. When the router is performing route redistribution
2. When a routing domain is migrating from one routing protocol to another

Administrative distance manipulation is a key component to configuring floating static routes.

Note that a directly connected route does not have an administrative distance associated with it in the routing table display.

COLUMN FOUR: METRIC

While the administrative distance prioritizes routing information derived from different routing table sources, the metric is used to select the best path to a destination network from a single routing source.

When a routing protocol discovers multiple paths to a specific destination, it must select the best path to place in its routing protocol. Metrics are

used to associate a cost for each possible path. Metric values can be comprised of "hop counts" (RIP), cost (OSPF) or composite metric: bandwidth, delay, load, reliability and MTU (IGRP and EIGRP). The path with the lowest metric is selected as the optimal path.

Note that a directly connected route does not have a metric associated with it in the routing table display.

COLUMN FIVE: NEXT HOP OF PACKET/SOURCE OF ROUTING INFORMATION

Column Five specifies the next-hop IP address to forward an IP packet to in order to move the packet closer to its desired destination IP prefix. When the next-hop address is not followed by a local interface listing, a second "recursive" look up must be performed to map the next-hop address with a local interface.

The address listed in Column Five can also correspond to the IP address of the next-hop neighbor that supplied the dynamically-learned routing information. For IP routing table entries learned from dynamic routing protocol neighbors, the address listed in Column Five of a Cisco IP routing table usually corresponds to one of the addresses listed at the bottom of the "show ip protocols" display under the "routing information sources" heading:

```
Routing Protocol is "igrp 100"
      Sending updates every 90 seconds, next due in 72 seconds
      Invalid after 270 seconds, hold down 280, flushed after 630
      Outgoing update filter list for all interfaces is not set
      Incoming update filter list for all interfaces is not set
      Default networks flagged in outgoing updates
      Default networks accepted from incoming updates
      IGRP metric weight K1=1, K2=0, K3=1, K4=0, K5=0
      IGRP maximum hopcount 100
      IGRP maximum metric variance 1
      Redistributing: igrp 100
      Routing for Networks:
        140.10.0.0
        172.16.0.0
      Routing Information Sources:
        Gateway         Distance  Last Update
        172.16.1.4      100       00:00:04
        172.16.2.2      100       00:01:03
      Distance: (default is 100)
```

Note that a directly-connected route does not have a next-hop address associated with it in the routing table display.

COLUMN SIX: AGE OF THE ROUTING TABLE ENTRY

This column lists the age of the routing table entry. Notice that only dynamic routing protocols have this column. Distance-Vector routing protocols keep their entries young; other routing protocols, such as OSPF and EIGRP, allow them to get old.

Compare the age of the entries in the routing table, with the timers listed in "show ip protocol."

```
Routing Protocol is "igrp 100"
      Sending updates every 90 seconds, next due in 72 seconds
      Invalid after 270 seconds, hold down 280, flushed after 630
      Outgoing update filter list for all interfaces is not set
      Incoming update filter list for all interfaces is not set
      Default networks flagged in outgoing updates
      Default networks accepted from incoming updates
      IGRP metric weight K1=1, K2=0, K3=1, K4=0, K5=0
      IGRP maximum hopcount 100
      IGRP maximum metric variance 1
      Redistributing: igrp 100
      Routing for Networks:
        140.10.0.0
        172.16.0.0
      Routing Information Sources:
        Gateway    Distance    Last Update
        172.16.1.4  100          00:00:04
        172.16.2.2  100'         00:01:03
      Distance: (default is 100)
```

Note that a directly-connected route does not have an age of entry timer associated with it in the routing table display.

COLUMN SEVEN: LOCAL INTERFACE TO SWITCH PACKET ON

This is the local interface to switch the packet on to get to the target destination network. If a routing table entry does not end with a local interface listing, the router must perform a "recursive" lookup to match the next-hop routing table entry with a local interface. The IP switching process always ends by selecting a routing table entry that specifies a local interface to switch a packet on.

Understanding each of the columns of a Cisco IP routing table is very useful for monitoring and troubleshooting purposes. Listed below are frequently-asked questions when troubleshooting an IP routing table:

- Are all connected routes listed?
- Is a default route set?
- Is a specific routing table entry in the routing table?
- Is a routing table entry's metric accurate?

- Are packets being switched out the correct interface to get to a specified destination network?
- Are routing table entries aging properly?
- Are any routing table entries in a "possibly down" state? If so, why?

Options of Show IP Route

The following "show ip route" commands allow you to selectively search for a particular network entry, or range of entries, in a routing table. For existing entries in a routing table, type "show ip route x.x.x.x" (where x.x.x.x = existing IP network or subnet). An example of this option is displayed below:

```
r1#sh ip ro 172.16.4.0
Routing entry for 172.16.4.0/24
       Known via "rip", distance 120, metric 1
       Redistributing via rip
       Advertised by rip (self originated)
       Last update from 172.16.1.2 on Serial0, 00:00:15 ago
       Routing Descriptor Blocks:
       * 172.16.1.2, from 172.16.1.2, 00:00:15 ago, via Serial0
       Route metric is 1, traffic share count is 1
```

Notice the additional detail this display provides.

In the two "show ip route" displays shown below, you see the IOS messages generated when a specific entry is not in the routing table:

```
r1#sh ip ro 140.10.0.0
     % Network not in table

r1#sh ip ro 172.16.5.0
% Subnet not in table
```

The error message listed above will only appear if a subnetwork for the specified network exists in the local routing table. This statement will be crucial when troubleshooting subnet reachability issues with RIP and IGRP.

When a remote network is advertised as inaccessible by RIP or IGRP, the routing table places it in a "possibly down" state. Examine the routing table entry 172.16.4.0/24 in the display below:

```
r1#sh ip ro
Codes: C - connected, S - static, I - IGRP, R - RIP, M - mobile, B - BGP
     D - EIGRP, EX - EIGRP external, O - OSPF, IA - OSPF inter area
     N1 - OSPF NSSA external type 1, N2 - OSPF NSSA external type 2
     E1 - OSPF external type 1, E2 - OSPF external type 2, E - EGP
     i - IS-IS, L1 - IS-IS level-1, L2 - IS-IS level-2, * - candidate default
     U - per-user static route, o - ODR
```

```
Gateway of last resort is not set
R    10.0.0.0/8 [120/1] via 172.16.2.3, 00:00:06, Serial1
     172.16.0.0/24 is subnetted, 4 subnets
R    172.16.4.0/24 is possibly down,
     routing via 172.16.1.2, Serial0
C    172.16.1.0 is directly connected, Serial0
C    172.16.2.0 is directly connected, Serial1
R    172.16.3.0 [120/1] via 172.16.2.3, 00:00:07, Serial1
     [120/1] via 172.16.1.2, 00:00:07, Serial0
```

For RIP and IGRP , you can examine the subnets holddown timer with the command "show ip route x.x.x.x":

```
r1#sh ip route 172.16.4.0
Routing entry for 172.16.4.0/24
     Known via "rip", distance 120, metric 4294967295 (inaccessible)
     Redistributing via rip
     Advertised by rip (self originated)
     Last update from 172.16.1.2 on Serial0, 00:00:36 ago
     Hold down timer expires in 159 secs
```

If one or more networks are in holddown, you can automatically reset the entire routing table with a "clear ip route *" command. This command is very useful in a lab environment; however, it can severely impact a live production network. USE "CLEAR IP ROUTE *" ONLY IN EXTREME CIRCUMSTANCES ON A PRODUCTION NETWORK.

The last "show ip route" option is an excellent tool for gaining a grasp on the "longest match rule". By typing "show ip route 172.16.0.0," either the 172.16.0.0 network or all subnets for the 172.16.0.0 network will be displayed. In the example below, all subnets for the 172.16.0.0 network that reside in the routing table are displayed:

```
r1#sh ip ro 172.16.0.0
Routing entry for 172.16.0.0/24, 4 known subnets
     Attached (2 connections)
     Redistributing via rip
R    172.16.4.0 [120/1] via 172.16.1.2, 00:00:07, Serial0
C    172.16.1.0 is directly connected, Serial0
C    172.16.2.0 is directly connected, Serial1
R    172.16.3.0 [120/1] via 172.16.2.3, 00:00:11, Serial1
     [120/1] via 172.16.1.2, 00:00:07, Serial0
```

However, when "show ip route 172.0.0.0" is entered, the following message is generated:

```
r1#sh ip ro 172.0.0.0
% Network not in table
```

When the additional parameters of a network mask (255.0.0.0) and the "longer-prefixes" option are added to the "show ip route command," the following information is displayed:

```
r1#sh ip ro 172.0.0.0 255.0.0.0 longer-prefixes
Codes: C - connected, S - static, I - IGRP, R - RIP, M - mobile, B - BGP
     D - EIGRP, EX - EIGRP external, O - OSPF, IA - OSPF inter area
     N1 - OSPF NSSA external type 1, N2 - OSPF NSSA external type 2
     E1 - OSPF external type 1, E2 - OSPF external type 2, E - EGP
     i - IS-IS, L1 - IS-IS level-1, L2 - IS-IS level-2, * - candidate default
     U - per-user static route, o - ODR

Gateway of last resort is not set
     172.16.0.0/24 is subnetted, 4 subnets
R    172.16.4.0 [120/1] via 172.16.1.2, 00:00:08, Serial0
C    172.16.1.0 is directly connected, Serial0
C    172.16.2.0 is directly connected, Serial1
R    172.16.3.0 [120/1] via 172.16.2.3, 00:00:11, Serial1
     [120/1] via 172.16.1.2, 00:00:08, Serial0
```

Since 172.16.0.0 is a longer match to 172.0.0.0 255.0.0.0, all of its subnets are displayed.

Consider the example below. When "show ip route 160.0.0.0 224.0.0.0 longer-prefixes" is entered, all networks with the range of 160.0.0.0 to 191.0.0.0 will be listed. Since 169.10.0.0, 170.10.0.0 and 172.16.0.0 fall within this range, they are listed.

```
r1#sh ip route 160.0.0.0 224.0.0.0 longer-prefixes
Codes: C - connected, S - static, I - IGRP, R - RIP, M - mobile, B - BGP
     D - EIGRP, EX - EIGRP external, O - OSPF, IA - OSPF inter area
     N1 - OSPF NSSA external type 1, N2 - OSPF NSSA external type 2
     E1 - OSPF external type 1, E2 - OSPF external type 2, E - EGP
     i - IS-IS, L1 - IS-IS level-1, L2 - IS-IS level-2, * - candidate default
     U - per-user static route, o - ODR

Gateway of last resort is not set
R    170.10.0.0/16 [120/1] via 172.16.1.2, 00:00:02, Serial0
R    169.10.0.0/16 [120/1] via 172.16.1.2, 00:00:03, Serial0
     172.16.0.0/24 is subnetted, 4 subnets
R    172.16.4.0 [120/1] via 172.16.1.2, 00:00:03, Serial0
C    172.16.1.0 is directly connected, Serial0
C    172.16.2.0 is directly connected, Serial1
R    172.16.3.0 [120/1] via 172.16.2.3, 00:00:14, Serial1
     [120/1] via 172.16.1.2, 00:00:03, Serial0
```

Using Debug IP Packet

Debug IP packet is an extremely useful tool in a lab and testbed environment. It can be instrumental in helping an internetworking engineer understand the IP routing process. However, it can also be a disastrous tool in a real-world production environment. If debug IP packet is enabled while a moderate-to-high volume of IP packets is being switched through a router, it is certain that the debug process will use all available CPU cycles of the router, and consequently prevent the router from performing its primary function of routing packets. THEREFORE, DO NOT ENABLE DEBUG IP PACKET ON A PRODUCTION ROUTER!

In our first demonstration of "debug ip packet," an existing host address for the 172.16.4.0 subnet is pinged.

The routing table reflects that the 172.16.4.0 subnet is reached through the serial0 interface. When "debug ip packet" traces a successful ping series, you see both packets being sent and received.

```
IP: s=172.16.1.1 (local), d=172.16.4.1  (Serial0), len 100, sending
IP: s=172.16.4.1 (Serial0), d=172.16.1.1 (Serial0), len 100, rcvd 3
IP: s=172.16.1.1 (local), d=172.16.4.1  (Serial0), len 100, sending
IP: s=172.16.4.1 (Serial0), d=172.16.1.1 (Serial0), len 100, rcvd 3
IP: s=172.16.1.1 (local), d=172.16.4.1  (Serial0), len 100, sending
IP: s=172.16.4.1 (Serial0), d=172.16.1.1 (Serial0), len 100, rcvd 3
```

Compare the trace above to the unsuccessful ping displayed below. Here, packets are being sent out, but none are being received. This shows that the router is operating properly, but somewhere beyond this router, the routing process is failing.

```
IP: s=172.16.1.1 (local), d=172.16.4.2 (Serial0), len 100, sending.
IP: s=172.16.1.1 (local), d=172.16.4.2 (Serial0), len 100, sending.
IP: s=172.16.1.1 (local), d=172.16.4.2 (Serial0), len 100, sending.
IP: s=172.16.1.1 (local), d=172.16.4.2 (Serial0), len 100, sending.
IP: s=172.16.1.1 (local), d=172.16.4.2 (Serial0), len 100, sending.
```

When you receive "debug ip packet" output of this type, first check the immediate neighboring router. From there, check all subsequent upstream routers.

An additional troubleshooting tool is "ping 172.16.4.255" combined with "debug ip icmp." The ping 172.16.4.255 will ping all host addresses on the specified subnet. The debug IP icmp will return the valid host addresses for the subnet. Another useful debug tool for a problem of this type is the "traceroute" command.

The following sample debug IP packet trace was seen many times when debugging Frame-Relay, ISDN and ATM:

```
IP: s=172.16.1.3 (local), d=172.16.1.1 (Serial0), len 100, sending
IP: s=172.16.1.3 (local), d=172.16.1.1 (Serial0), len 100, encapsulation
failed.
IP: s=172.16.1.3 (local), d=172.16.1.1 (Serial0), len 100, sending
IP: s=172.16.1.3 (local), d=172.16.1.1 (Serial0), len 100, encapsulation
failed.
```

This debug trace can be interpreted as saying, "The IP routing process is running fine on this router; however, some underlying technology supporting the IP forwarding process is malfunctioning." Since debug IP packet cannot specify which process supporting the IP packet forwarding is malfunctioning, it represents the detected error with the vague message "encapsulation failed." When you see the "encapsulation failed" message in debug IP packet, enable other debug tools for the underlying technologies.

For example, if you see the "encapsulation failed" message when forwarding IP packets over Frame-Relay, enable debug frame packet. If you see the "encapsulation failed" message when forwarding IP packets over ISDN, enable debug dialer packet, debug isdn q931, debug ppp negotiation, or debug ppp authentication. If you see the "encapsulation failed" message when forwarding IP packets over ATM, enable debug atm packet. If you see the "encapsulation failed" message when forwarding IP packets over Ethernet or Token-Ring, enable debug arp.

The following scenario clearly displays a problem with a local routing table. When you see "unroutable" in a debug IP packet trace, check your local router configuration statements or perform a debug trace on the specific routing protocol used on the router generating the "unroutable" messages.

```
IP: s=172.16.1.1 (local), d=192.10.1.1, len 100, unroutable.
IP: s=172.16.1.1 (local), d=192.10.1.1, len 100, unroutable.
IP: s=172.16.1.1 (local), d=192.10.1.1, len 100, unroutable.
IP: s=172.16.1.1 (local), d=192.10.1.1, len 100, unroutable.
IP: s=172.16.1.1 (local), d=192.10.1.1, len 100, unroutable.
```

If you want to see packets being switched by a particular router, disable "ip route-cache" on all interfaces routing ip. You will then be able to see all IP packets transiting the router. Take special caution not to do this on a production router! You are process switching all packets and impacting cpu performance by running debug. This is sure to consume all cpu cycles on a production router.

In a lab environment, perform the debug scenario described above in only limited circumstances. It is useful to gain a strong understanding of the Cisco routing process. Under all circumstances, perform this debug procedure for a very limited period of time.

Displayed below is a debug trace with iproute-cache disabled.

```
IP: s=172.16.2.1 (Serial0), d=172.16.3.3 (Serial1), g=172.16.3.3,
len 104, forward
```

```
IP: s=172.16.2.1 (Serial0), d=172.16.3.3 (Serial1), g=172.16.3.3,
len 104, forward
IP: s=172.16.2.1 (Serial0), d=172.16.3.3 (Serial1), g=172.16.3.3,
len 104, forward
IP: s=172.16.2.1 (Serial0), d=172.16.3.3 (Serial1), g=172.16.3.3,
len 104, forward
```

Debugging the Construction of an IP Routing Table

DEBUG IP ROUTING

"Debug ip routing" is a useful debug tool to trace the events involved with building and maintaining an IP routing table. When the IP routing table is cleared, every entry in the table is re-inserted. Notice in the example below how connected, static, RIP and OSPF are re-inserted in the table.

```
r1#debug ip routing
IP routing debugging is on
r1#clea ip ro *
RT: add 172.16.4.0 255.255.255.0 via 0.0.0.0, connected metric
[0/0]
RT: add 172.16.3.0 255.255.255.0 via 0.0.0.0, connected metric
[0/0]
RT: add 169.10.1.0 255.255.255.0 via 0.0.0.0, static metric [1/0]
RT: add 10.1.1.1 255.255.255.255 via 172.16.3.3, ospf metric
[110/65]
RT: add 172.16.2.0 255.255.255.0 via 172.16.3.3, ospf metric
[110/128]
RT: add 170.10.1.0 255.255.255.0 via 172.16.3.3, static metric
[1/0]
RT: network 10.0.0.0 is now variably masked
RT: add 10.0.0.0 255.0.0.0 via 172.16.3.3, rip metric [120/1]
RT: add 172.16.4.0/24 via 0.0.0.0, connected metric [0/0]
RT: add 172.16.2.0/24 via 0.0.0.0, connected metric [0/0]
RT: add 0.0.0.0/0 via 0.0.0.0, static metric [1/0]
RT: default path is now 0.0.0.0 via 0.0.0.0
RT: new default network 0.0.0.0
RT: add 172.16.17.0/24 via 172.16.2.2, rip metric [120/2]
RT: add 172.16.5.0/24 via 172.16.2.2, rip metric [120/2]
RT: add 172.16.1.0/24 via 172.16.2.2, rip metric [120/1]
RT: add 172.16.117.0/24 via 172.16.2.2, rip metric [120/2]
```

Each IP routing protocol has its own set of debug tools:

- Debug ip rip
- Debug ip igrp events
- Debug ip igrp transactions

- Debug ip ospf adj
- Debug ip eigrp

It is essential that you know how to read the debug traces of all major IP routing protocols, under both normal and abnormal conditions. IP routing debugging tools will be covered in the next two chapters.

Configuring Static Routes

The Cisco IOS provides two types of static route statements. The first references a destination address with a local interface. This type of static route will appear as a "connected" route in the routing table. Since it appears as a connected route, it will be redistributed automatically into routing protocols whose "network" statements are associated with the destination address referenced in the static route.

The second type of static route specifies the next-hop address, instead of a local interface. It will appear in the routing table with an administrative distance of one. It must be manually redistributed into dynamic routing processes.

The syntax of configuring an IP static route in global configuration mode is displayed below:

```
ip route prefix mask {address | interface} [distance] [tag tag]
[permanent]

Syntax Description
    prefix
            IP route prefix for the destination.
    mask
            Prefix mask for the destination.
    address
            IP address of the next hop that can be used to reach
            that network.
    interface
            Network interface to use.
    distance
            (Optional) An administrative distance.
    tag
            (Optional) Tag value that can be used as a "match"
            value for controlling redistribution via route maps.
    permanent
            (Optional) Specifies that the route will not be
            removed, even if the interface shuts down.
```

A static route is appropriate when the Cisco IOS software cannot dynamically build a route to a specified destination prefix. Static routes are also useful when it is undesirable to use dynamic routing protocols. For example, with ISDN/DDR, static routes are often used because they do not generate any traffic like dynamically learned routes. Using static routes on routers with ISDN/DDR interfaces is a common method to avoid the problem of keeping an ISDN/DDR link up and active due to routing protocol traffic.

If you explicitly specify an administrative distance to a static route, you are flagging a static route that can be overridden by "other" information. The source of the "other" routing information can be derived from dynamic routing protocols or other static routes. By adding the administrative distance parameter to a static route, you are creating a "floating static" route. A floating static route only becomes active if the primary routing source is disabled. For example, IGRP-derived routes have a default administrative distance of 100. To have a static route that would be overridden by an IGRP dynamic route, specify an administrative distance greater than 100. Static routes have a default administrative distance of 0 or 1.

In the following example, an administrative distance of 110 is configured at the end of the static route statement. In this case, packets for network 10.0.0.0/8 will be routed through to a router with a next-hop address of 131.108.3.4 if routing information with an administrative distance less than 110 is not available. Since IGRP has an administrative distance of 100, IGRP learned routes will be preferred over the floating static route listed below:

```
ip route 10.0.0.0 255.0.0.0 131.108.3.4 110
```

By default static routes will be removed from a routing table when a directly-connected network that is used to reference the static route disappears. For example, if the interface associated with the next-hop address listed above (131.108.3.4) disappears, the static route will also disappear. However, if a link beyond the directly-connected networks fails, the static route will not adjust to the internal topology change. Therefore, static routes can only adjust to the change of availability of directly-connected networks and interfaces. This is a clear disadvantage of static routes. In contrast, dynamic routing protocols learn about a remote change in a network's topology automatically and consequently adjust to such changes.

Default Routes

When an internetwork is designed hierarchically, default routes are a useful tool to limit the need to propagate routing information. Access-level networks, such as branch offices, typically have only one connection to headquarters. Instead of advertising all of an organization's network prefixes to a branch office, configure a default route. If a destination prefix is not in a branch office's routing table, forward the packet over the default route. The

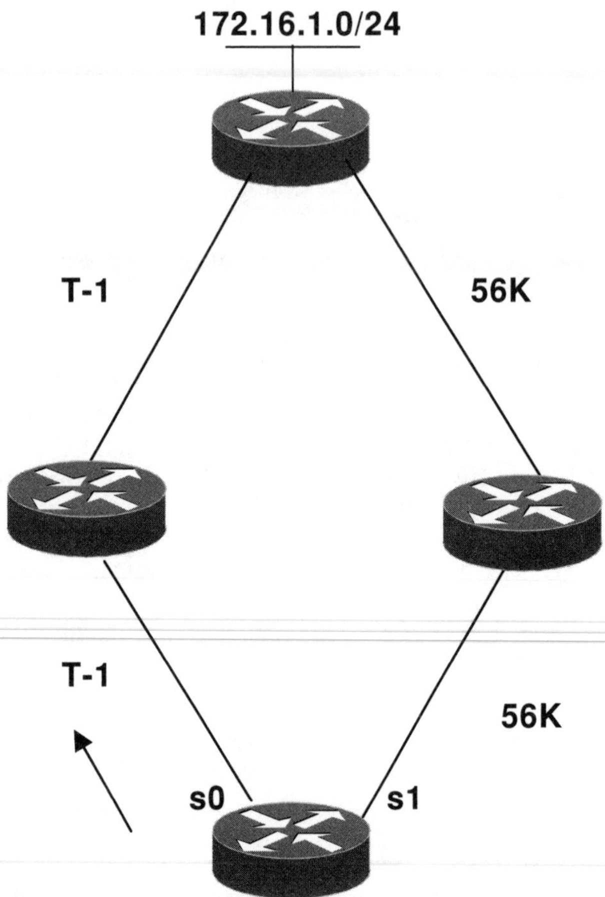

FIGURE 9–2 IP static route: ip route 172.16.1.0255.255.255.0 s0

Cisco IP routing table displays the default route at the top of the routing table as the "Gateway of Last Resort."

The default route is usually configured with the following static route:

IP route 0.0.0.0 0.0.0.0 172.16.1.1

In the language of the Longest Match Rule, no specific routing table entry can have the address 0.0.0.0 0.0.0.0. Therefore, if there is no match in the routing table, use the 0.0.0.0 0.0.0.0 entry.

Once a default route is specified, you must determine how you want downstream routers to receive the default route. How this is performed varies with different routing protocols. For example, RIP automatically redistributes the 0.0.0.0 0.0.0.0 route. On the other hand, IGRP does not recognize the 0.0.0.0 0.0.0.0 route at all. OSPF uses a command called the "default information originate" command to propagate a default route through an OSPF

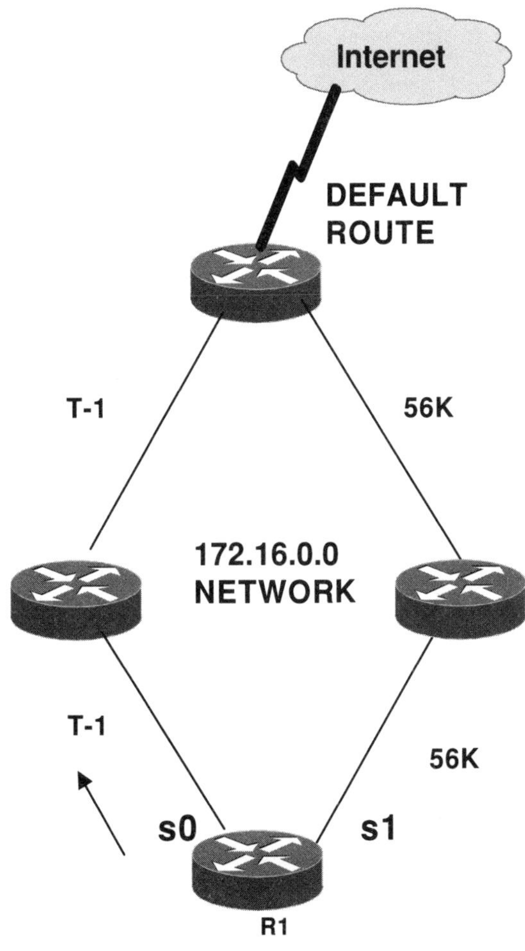

FIGURE 9–3 IP default route: ip route 0.0.0.0. 0.0.0.0. s0

domain. The specifics on how different routing protocols handle the propagation of default routes will be covered in Chapters Ten, Eleven, and Twelve.

Configuring Routing Protocols

By default, no IP dynamic routing protocol is enabled on the Cisco IOS. All IP dynamic routing protocols are enabled by the following global configuration mode command:

```
Router(config)#router ?
   bgp         Border Gateway Protocol (BGP)
```

```
egp           Exterior Gateway Protocol (EGP)
eigrp         Enhanced Interior Gateway Routing Protocol (EIGRP)
igrp          Interior Gateway Routing Protocol (IGRP)
isis          ISO IS-IS
iso-igrp      IGRP for OSI networks
mobile        Mobile routes
odr           On Demand stub Routes
ospf          Open Shortest Path First (OSPF)
rip           Routing Information Protocol (RIP)
static        Static routes
```

When a routing protocol is specified, you access the IP routing protocol configuration mode. This mode is represented by the following prompt:

```
London(config-router)#
```

At the very least, dynamic IGP routing protocols must have at least one "network" statement defined in a given routing protocol mode. This network statement must match the network addresses configured on local interfaces. For RIP, IGRP and EIGRP, network statements will reflect the classful network address used on an interface. For example, if you typed in "network 172.16.33.1" in the RIP, IGRP or EIGRP router configuration mode, only "network 172.16.0.0" will appear in the running configuration script.

When the following statement:

```
London(config-router)#network 172.16.33.1
```

is entered in router configuration mode for RIP, IGRP or EIGRP, the result is the statement below in running-configuration mode:

```
!
router igrp 100
network 172.16.0.0
!
```

Notice that no error message was generated when the "network 172.16.33.1" statement was entered. The address was automatically truncated to its classful boundary. With OSPF, network statement configuration is markedly different.

OSPF also requires at least one "network" statement. However, more specific addresses can be used with OSPF. A sample OSPF network statement is displayed below.

If we enter what we entered for RIP, IGRP and EIGRP with OSPF, we get the "% Incomplete command" error message:

```
London(config-router)#network 172.16.32.0
% Incomplete command.

London(config-router)#network 172.16.0.0
```

```
% Incomplete command.
```

By using the help facility, we see that OSPF is requesting a wildcard mask to follow the network address:

```
London(config-router)#network 172.16.0.0 ?
  A.B.C.D OSPF wild card bits
London(config-router)#network 172.16.0.0 0.0.255.255
% Incomplete command.
```

Even the wildcard mask is not enough. We must supply an "area ID" after the wildcard mask.

```
London(config-router)#network 172.16.0.0 0.0.255.255 ?
  area Set the OSPF area ID
London(config-router)#network 172.16.0.0 0.0.255.255 area ?
  <0-4294967295>OSPF area ID as a decimal value
  A.B.C.DOSPF area ID in IP address format
London(config-router)#network 10.1.1.0 0.0.0.255 area 0
```

Once a network address, wildcard mask and area ID are supplied, OSPF network statement configuration is complete. OSPF network statement configuration is displayed in the following manner in running configuration:

```
!
router ospf 100
  network 172.16.0.0 0.0.255.255 area 0
  network 10.1.1.0 0.0.0.255 area 0
!
```

In summary, no IP dynamic routing protocol is enabled on a Cisco router by default. An IP IGP routing protocol is enabled with a minimum of two commands: one in global configuration mode and one in routing configuration mode. The global configuration command is "router xxx" (xxx = specific routing protocol name).

- To enable RIP, enter "router RIP".
- To enable IGRP, enter "router IGRP #". (# = autonomous system number)
- To enable EIGRP, enter "router EIGRP #". (# = autonomous system number)
- To enable OSPF, enter "router OSPF #". (# = process identification number)

For all IGRP and EIGRP routers in the same IP routing domain, the autonomous system number must be the same. If they are not, they will not automatically exchange routing table information. IGRP and EIGRP routers with different autonomous system numbers can exchange routing table information by manually configuring route redistribution.

The process-ID number for OSPF routers can be the same or different on OSPF routers in the same OSPF domain. The process-ID number is locally significant.

Once the routing process is enabled and routing configuration mode is accessed, enter a minimum of one "network" statement. More detailed discussions of routing protocol configuration will be supplied in the next two chapters.

Configuration Commands Available for Every Dynamic Routing Protocol

When you access a routing protocol configuration mode, type "?" to see all available options. For every dynamic routing protocol, the following commands are available in routing protocol configuration mode:

```
default-metric      Set metric of redistributed routes
distance            Define an administrative distance
distribute-list     Filter networks in routing updates
maximum-paths       Forward packets over multiple paths
network             Enable routing on an IP network
passive-interface   Suppress routing updates on an interface
redistribute        Redistribute information from another
                    routing protocol
timers              Adjust routing timers
```

The default-metric allows you to set the metric for any networks injected into a given routing domain via redistribution.

The distance command allows you to manually reset the administrative distance. This is often used when a router is maintaining both an OSPF and IGRP routing process. IGRP has an administrative distance of 100; OSPF has an administrative distance of 110. If you want OSPF to have lower administrative distance than IGRP, type "distance 95".

Route Redistribution

Route redistribution is the final tool that ties large-scale IP internetworking together. Route redistribution is the process of translating and importing routing table information from one routing source to another. For example, assume a large bank that uses OSPF in its corporate backbone. The bank then acquires another bank that uses RIP throughout is internetwork. In this example, route redistribution is required to pass information between the RIP domain and the OSPF domain.

When route redistribution is performed, information is lost. Information such as metrics cannot be precisely translated when redistributing one type of routing entry into another. The network administrator must manually assign what metrics will be assigned to routes redistributed from another routing source. Route-maps can be used to provide more granularity to route metric translations. Route-maps are covered in Chapter 28.

Two basic types of redistribution exist:

1. One way redistribution
2. Two way redistribution

An example of one-way redistribution is redistributing RIP updates into OSPF, but not redistributing OSPF updates into RIP. An example of two-way redistribution is redistributing RIP updates into OSPF, and redistributing OSPF updates into RIP.

In many cases, redistribution can be avoided by using default routes.

IT CANNOT BE EMPHASIZED ENOUGH HOW IMPORTANT IT IS TO KNOW ALL FORMS OF ROUTE REDISTRIBUTION AND ALL ISSUES ASSOCIATED WITH ROUTE REDISTRIBUTION. Route redistribution will be covered in greater detail in Chapter 12.

Special Tools for IP Address Assignment: IP Secondary Address and Network Address Translation

IP Secondary Address

The IP secondary address interface configuration command is a useful tool when you want to assign more than one IP address to a router interface. Multiple IP addresses may be assigned to a specific segment. In order to provide IP routing services to a segment with more than one IP prefix assigned to it, assign a second IP address to an interface. End the IP address configuration command with a "secondary" parameter. By doing so, you can have more than one IP address assigned to a given router interface.

You may not be able to PING a locally-connected device from an interface with a secondary address. The PING is sent out with the source address of the primary IP address. To avoid this from happening, use the extended PING source address option and specify the secondary IP address.

Network Address Translation (NAT)

Network address translation (NAT) allows you to use an address space within one routing domain, and perform address translation when internal devices attempt to access resources outside of the domain. NAT is a popular solution to the registered IP address shortage. Internally, unregistered IP addresses can be used. However, when a device needs to access a resource outside its internal domain, such as a resource located on the Internet, the packets pass through a device running NAT that maps an unregistered IP address to a registered address.

Bask NAT configuration steps are as follows:

1. Define a NAT address pool.
2. Define a NAT inside address.
3. Define which interfaces are participating in the NAT process.

NAT GLOBAL CONFIGURATION COMMANDS

```
Router(config)#ip nat ?
      inside          Inside address translation
      outside         Outside address translation
      pool            Define pool of addresses
      translation     NAT translation entry configuration
```

NAT INTERFACE CONFIGURATION COMMANDS

Listed below are two IP NAT interface configuration commands.

```
Router(config-if)#ip nat ?
      inside          Inside interface for address translation
      outside         Outside interface for address translation
```

SAMPLE NAT CONFIGURATION

```
ip nat pool ccie 172.16.17.20 172.16.17.30 netmask 255.255.255.0
ip nat inside source list 1 pool ccie
!
!
interface Loopback0
       ip address 172.16.17.1 255.255.255.0
!
!
interface Serial0
       ip address 200.100.10.2 255.255.255.0
       ip nat inside
!
interface Serial1
       ip address 172.16.2.2 255.255.255.0
       ip nat outside
!
!
router rip
       network 172.16.0.0
!
ip classless
access-list 1 permit 200.100.10.0 0.0.0.255
!
```

The first line of the configuration displayed above creates the NAT pool of registered addresses. These addresses are extracted from the address space of the subnet configured on interface loopback 0. The NAT pool must be extracted from a routable address space. Otherwise, destination networks and end systems will not know how to return to the source of the NAT translation. Note that the pool of NAT addresses is extracted from an address other than the address on the interface defined as the "nat outside" interface.

The second line defines the inside addresses that must be matched to be eligible for the NAT process. The syntax in the example above references "list 1" and "pool ccie". "List 1" is a reference to the access-list at the bottom of the configuration script. Whatever is permitted by access-list 1 will be applied to NAT. In the sample configuration above, all IP addresses matching 200.100.10.0 network will be translated into addresses defined in the "ccie" pool: 172.16.17.20 through 172.16.17.30.

NAT SHOW AND DEBUG COMMANDS

NAT operation can be monitored by the following show and debug commands:

```
Show ip nat statistics
Show ip nat translation
Debug ip nat
```

Displayed below are samples of these commands.

```
r2#show ip nat statistics
Total active translations: 1 (0 static, 1 dynamic; 0 extended)
Outside interfaces: Loopback0, Serial1
Inside interfaces: Serial0
Hits: 3180 Misses: 1
Expired translations: 0
Dynamic mappings:
-- Inside Source
access-list 1 pool ccie refcount 1
     pool ccie: netmask 255.255.255.0
        start 172.16.17.20 end 172.16.17.30
        type generic, total addresses 11, allocated 1 (9%), misses 0

r2#show ip nat translations verbose
Pro Inside global   Inside local   Outside local    Outside global
--- 172.16.17.20    200.100.10.1   ---              ---
    create 00:06:09, use 00:00:00, left 23:59:59, flags: none

debug ip nat
NAT: s=200.100.10.1->172.16.17.20, d=172.16.2.3 [2129]
NAT: s=172.16.2.3, d=172.16.17.20->200.100.10.1 [2129]
NAT: s=200.100.10.1->172.16.17.20, d=172.16.2.3 [2130]
NAT: s=172.16.2.3, d=172.16.17.20->200.100.10.1 [2130]
NAT: s=200.100.10.1->172.16.17.20, d=172.16.2.3 [2131]
```

```
debug ip nat detailed
NAT: i: icmp (200.100.10.1, 2262) -> (172.16.2.3, 2262) [2314]
NAT: o: icmp (172.16.2.3, 2262) -> (172.16.17.20, 2262) [2314]
NAT: i: icmp (200.100.10.1, 2263) -> (172.16.2.3, 2263) [2315]
NAT: o: icmp (172.16.2.3, 2263) -> (172.16.17.20, 2263) [2315]
NAT: i: icmp (200.100.10.1, 2264) -> (172.16.2.3, 2264) [2316]
```

Notice the difference between "debug ip nat" and "debug ip nat detailed". The latter provides information about protocols being translated.

You can also clear both NAT statistics and the NAT translation table:

```
r2#clea ip nat ?
  statistics             Clear translation statistics
  translation            Clear dynamic translation
```

IP Multicasting

"Multicast" refers to a network's ability to send a single packet to multiple destinations simultaneously (or nearly so). Obvious applications include newsfeeds with multiple subscribers, routing protocols announcing reachability information, and conference sessions between several sites. Most common LAN technologies, such as Ethernet, support native multicast, while network-layer protocols now provide support for multicasting over wide area links and disparate technologies. IP Class D addresses have been designated for multicast use.

Ethernet supports multicasting by virtue of its operation. Simply by using a special MAC address recognized by multiple NIC cards, a single packet can be received by several machines. In fact, IEEE has designed a special range of MAC addresses for multicast use. RFC 1112, "Host Extensions for IP Multicasting," defines a standard Algorithm to convert IP Class D multicast addresses into Ethernet multicast addresses, allowing IP hosts to reliably multicast over LAN technologies.

Relaying multicast packets across multiple subnets and networks requires routing protocol support, just as unicast packets do. The most important multicast routing protocols at this time are Distance Vector Multicast Routing Protocol (DVMRP - RFC 1075), Multicast OSPF (MOSPF - RFC 1584), and Protocol Independent Multicast (PIM).

When planning your multicast configuration, remember that there is a difference between end systems that can transmit data to a multicast group and end systems that can receive data destined for a multicast group. Any end system can send data to a multicast group. The sending end system does not need to be a member of a multicast group. However, if an end system wants to receive data targeted for a multicast group, it must be a member of that multicast group. End system multicast membership is dynamic. End systems can join and exit multicast groups at will, and can also belong to multiple multicast groups at one time.

Configuring IP Multicast Routing

Configuring IP Multicast Routing on Cisco routers involves two configuration steps:

1. Define which multicast groups to support in your multicast routing process with the interface configuration command "ip igmp join-group x.x.x.x" (x.x.x.x = multicast address).
2. Enable IP multicast routing in global configuration mode and define which multicast routing protocol to enable.

When defining which multicast groups to support for multicast routing, you must have a basic understanding of the Internet Group Management Protocol (IGMP). IGMP is defined in RFC 1112 as follows:

"The Internet Group Management Protocol (IGMP) is used by IP hosts to report their host group memberships to any immediately-neighboring multicast routers. IGMP is an asymmetric protocol and is specified here from the point of view of a host, rather than a multicast router. (IGMP may also be used, symmetrically or asymmetrically, between multicast routers. Such use is not specified here.)"

IGMP end systems generate messages such as "JoinLocalGroup" and "LeaveLocalGroup." Multicast routers generate a "Host Membership Query" message to IGMP end systems. IGMP end systems respond to a Host Membership Query message with a Host Membership Report.

According to RFC 1112, IGMP is used to allow end systems on locally-attached segments to report their membership of specified IGMP multicast groups to a locally-attached multicast router. To allow a Cisco router interface to determine whether there are any members for a specific multicast group on a locally connected LAN segment, enter the following interface configuration command:

```
r1(config-if)#ip igmp join-group 224.10.1.2
```

When entering this command, you must specify which multicast group you want to be listening for. Valid IGMP addresses range from 224.0.0.0 to 239.255.255.255. Specific multicast addresses are reserved. See RFC 1112 for more details. If you type a non-multicast address, you get the following error message:

```
r1(config-if)#ip igmp join-group 172.16.1.1
Not a IP multicast group address
```

You can verify which end systems have joined the multicast group specified in the "ip igmp join-group interface" command by typing "show ip igmp group":

```
r1#show ip igmp group
IGMP Connected Group Membership
Group Address      Interface        Uptime         Expires       Last Reporter
224.0.1.40         Serial0          00:35:02       never         0.0.0.0
224.10.1.2         Ethernet0        00:32:29       neve          172.16.4.1
```

Other IGMP-related show and debug commands are:

- "Show ip igmp interface"
- "Debug ip igmp"

Once you have specified which multicast groups you want to listen for on locally-attached interfaces, you must enable IP multicast routing and specify a multicast routing protocol.

To enable IP multicast routing, enter the following global configuration command:

```
London(config)#ip multicast-routing
```

Once IP multicast routing is enabled, you must select a multicast routing protocol. You can choose among the following:

- Distance Vector Multicast Routing Protocol (DVMRP - RFC 1075)
- Multicast OSPF (MOSPF - RFC 1584)
- Protocol Independent Multicast Sparse Mode (PIM SM)
- Protocol Independent Multicast Dense Mode (PIM DM)

In the example below, PIM Dense Mode is selected. When a router operating in PIM Dense Mode receives a multicast packet, it forwards the packet on all interfaces that have directly-connected IGMP members or remote PIM neighbors. When a PIM-enabled router receives a multicast packet and it does not have any IGMP members or PIM neighbors, it sends a "prune" message back to the source so that no additional packets are forwarded to the router.

Basic PIM Dense Mode configuration is enabled with the following interface configuration mode command:

```
Ip pim dense mode
```

PIM must be enabled on every interface within the internetwork participating in multicast routing. When PIM Dense Mode is enabled on a router interface, IGMP is also enabled on the same interface. When PIM is enabled, a console message like the one displayed below is generated for every PIM participating interface:

```
IGMP: Send v2 Query on Serial0 to 224.0.0.1
IP: s=172.16.1.3 (local), d=224.0.0.1 (Serial0), len 28, sending
broad/multicast
```

You can monitor the status of interfaces participating in the PIM routing process with the "show ip pim interface" command:

```
r3#show ip pim interface
Address         Interface         Mode          Nbr          Query        DR
                                                Count        Intvl
0.0.0.0         Ethernet0         Dense         0            30           0.0.0.0
172.16.1.3      Serial0           Dense         0            30           0.0.0.0
```

You can check for PIM multicast router neighbors with the "show ip pim neighbor" command:

```
r1#sh ip pim neighbor
PIM Neighbor Table
Neighbor Address    Interface     Uptime        Expires     Mode
172.16.2.2          Serial0       00:35:00      00:01:29    Dense
```

To further troubleshoot and verify PIM operation, use debug ip pim.

You can test the reachability of remote multicast devices with the "PING" command:

```
r1#ping 224.10.1.2

Type escape sequence to abort.
Sending 1, 100-byte ICMP Echos to 224.10.1.2, timeout is 2
seconds:

Reply to request 0 from 172.16.1.3, 68 ms
```

When you perform a multicast PING, it operates much like a network broadcast PING. You can also perform a multicast traceroute with the "mtrace" command.

You can examine the IP multicast routing table with the "show ip mroute" command:

```
r2#show ip mroute
IP Multicast Routing Table
Flags: D - Dense, S - Sparse, C - Connected, L - Local, P - Pruned
     R - RP-bit set, F - Register flag, T - SPT-bit set, J - Join SPT
Timers: Uptime/Expires
Interface state: Interface, Next-Hop, State/Mode

(*, 224.0.1.40), 00:07:06/00:00:00, RP 0.0.0.0, flags: DJCL
     Incoming interface: Null, RPF nbr 0.0.0.0
     Outgoing interface list:
     Serial1, Forward/Dense, 00:03:15/00:00:00
     Ethernet0, Forward/Dense, 00:07:06/00:00:00
```

```
(*, 224.1.1.2), 00:07:11/00:00:00, RP 0.0.0.0, flags: DJCL
  Incoming interface: Null, RPF nbr 0.0.0.0
  Outgoing interface list:
    Serial1, Forward/Dense, 00:03:16/00:00:00
    Ethernet0, Forward/Dense, 00:05:02/00:00:00
```

Other show commands to use for monitoring multicast routing are:

- Show ip mroute summ
- Show ip mroute count
- Show ip mroute active

Summary

The topics of this chapter have laid the foundation for the next five chapters. By providing an overview of IP addressing, subnetting, VLSM, summarization, the routing process in general and using tools such as debug ip packet and show ip route, you are now prepared for the next four chapters.

Chapter 10 examines the routing protocols RIP v.1, IGRP and EIGRP.
Chapter 11 examines OSPF.
Chapter 12 examines Route Redistribution.
Chapter 13 is a Level II Summary.
Chapter 14 examines BGP4.

Professional Development Checklist

By using this chapter, you should be able to perform the following operations:

- Plan an IP address scheme for deployment in a complex internetwork.
- Configure variable length subnet masks.
- Configure summarization.
- Configure NAT.
- Set the administrative distance of a routing protocol.
- Configure IP Multicasting.
- Can you subnet on a bit-by-bit basis?
- Can you configure variable length subnets for a given routing protocol?
- Can you summarize on a bit-by-bit basis?
- Do you know the relationship between subnetting techniques and routing protocols?
- Do you know the relationship between summarization techniques and routing protocols?

For Further Study

- Advanced Cisco Router Configuration Course
- *Understanding IP Addressing: Everything You Ever Wanted to Know*; Semeria, Chuck
- Cisco IOS Configuration Guide Volume V
- Cisco IOS Command Reference Volume V

URLs

- **www.cciecert.com**
- **www.mentorlabs.com**
- **www.cisco.com**
- **www.freesoft.org**

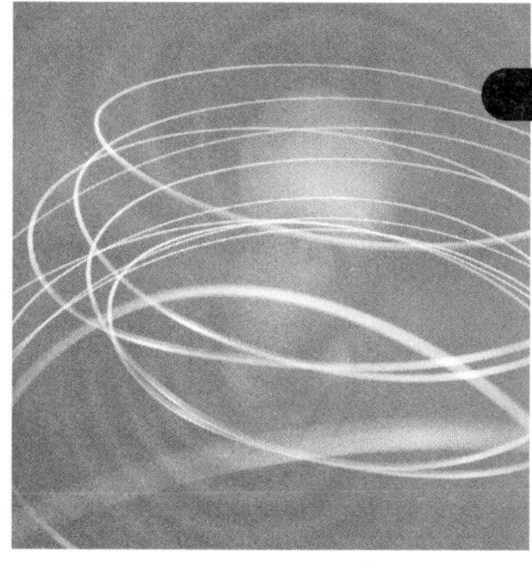

TEN

Configuring RIP, IGRP and EIGRP

Topics Covered in This Chapter

- Configuring RIP
- Configuring IGRP
- Configuring EIGRP
- Performing Route Summarization with EIGRP

This chapter provides a roadmap for learning the configuration basics of RIP, IGRP and EIGRP. They are presented together because they are linked by an evolutionary progression and are configured in a similar manner on a Cisco router.

First, the routing information protocol (RIP) will be examined. RIP is a distance vector routing protocol that uses a "hop count" as a metric. Next we will examine IGRP, a Cisco proprietary distance-vector routing protocol. The primary difference between RIP and IGRP is the metric calculation. While RIP uses a "hop count" as a metric, IGRP uses a composite metric comprised of bandwidth, delay, load, reliability and MTU size. Finally, EIGRP will be examined. EIGRP is an enhanced distance-vector routing protocol. Many Cisco documents categorize EIGRP as a "hybrid" routing protocol that discovers networks like a distance vector routing protocol, but adjusts to changes in network topology similar to a link-state routing protocol. However, EIGRP is not a Link-State routing protocol.

Overview of RIP Operation

RIP v.1 is an open standards based Distance-Vector routing protocol. In the diagram below, RIP will calculate two equal cost paths to network 10.0.0.0 from router R1. Even though the path out of R1's Serial 0 interface uses T-1 connections, and the path out of R1's Serial 1 interface uses 56K connections, both paths appear to RIP as having an equal cost.

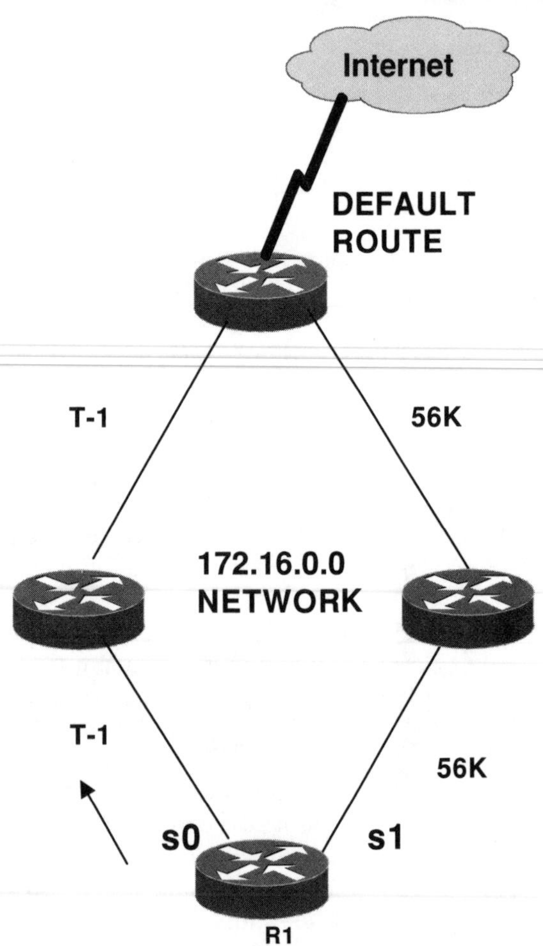

FIGURE 10–1 On router R1, RIP will view the path to the Internet as equal when using interface, S0 and S1.

IGRP Provides a Remedy to RIP

IGRP overcomes the metric calculation limitations of RIP by calculating the shortest path to a destination network with a composite metric. By default, the composite metric is calculated by the smallest bandwidth of outbound interfaces to a given destination network and the sum of delay of all outbound interfaces to a given destination network.

Even though IGRP has a more robust metric calculation than RIP, it still has some of the undesirable characteristics of traditional distance-vector routing protocols—namely, a slow reconvergence time.

EIGRP: The Second Generation IGRP

Finally, Cisco introduced EIGRP, a hybrid routing protocol that discovers that network like a distance vector protocol (namely IGRP) but maintains a "topological database" for rapid reconvergence.

EGRP also possesses the following features:

- It supports variable length subnet masks.
- It supports discontiguous subnets.
- It does not send a complete copy of its routing table to Neighbors on a periodic basis.
- It can be enabled for IPX and AppleTalk, as well as for IP.
- When configured for IP, it automatically redistributes routes with IGRP processes defined in the same autonomous system.
- When configured for IPX, it automatically redistributes routes with IPX/RIP processes.
- When configured for AppleTalk, it automatically redistributes routes with RTMP.

EIGRP performs the same metric accumulation as IGRP. However, when you examine the metric calculation between IGRP and EIGRP, you will see the EIGRP value is much greater. If you divide the EIGRP metric by 256, you get the same IGRP metric value.

Configuring RIP, IGRP and EIGRP

The basic configuration steps of RIP, IGRP and EIGRP are virtually identical. A minimum of two steps are required to enable and configure RIP, IGRP and EIGRP:

1. Enable the routing process.
2. Define locally-connected networks to participate in the routing process.

The global configuration statement for enabling each routing process is displayed below:

- Router rip
- Router igrp XXX
- Router eigrp XXX
- XXX=autonomous system number)

Do not confuse the autonomous system number of IGRP and EIGRP with the BGP autonomous system number. They have nothing to do with each other. If you want all IGRP and EIGRP routers to be in the same routing domain, the same autonomous system number must be supplied to every IGRP and EIGRP process running on every router within a domain.

Once the routing protocol is enabled, at least one "network" statement must be defined within the routing protocol configuration mode. The "network" statement must be entered for a classful address only. Entries of subnets will be truncated to classful boundaries.

Common IOS commands used to verify, monitor and troubleshoot RIP, IGRP and EIGRP operation are:

- Show ip route
- Ping
- Trace
- Specific routing protocol debugging tools (which will be discussed throughout the chapter)

RIP Specific Configuration Issues

Basic configuration of RIP is simple on a Cisco router. As mentioned in the previous section, basic RIP configuration involves a two-step process:

1. Enabling the RIP routing protocol in global configuration mode
2. Identifying the locally connected IP addresses that are intended to participate in the RIP routing process. This is performed by entering one or more "network" statements in routing protocol configuration mode. The address specified with the network statement is a classful network. Subnet entries will be truncated.

The RIP Routing Table

Displayed below is a sample IP routing table with RIP routing entries:

```
r4#show ip route
Codes: C - connected, S - static, I - IGRP, R - RIP, M - mobile, B - BGP
       D - EIGRP, EX - EIGRP external, O - OSPF, IA - OSPF inter area
       N1 - OSPF NSSA external type 1, N2 - OSPF NSSA external type 2
       E1 - OSPF external type 1, E2 - OSPF external type 2, E - EGP
```

```
       i - IS-IS, L1 - IS-IS level-1, L2 - IS-IS level-2, * - candidate default
       U - per-user static route, o - ODR

Gateway of last resort is not set

     172.16.0.0/24 is subnetted, 5 subnets
R       172.16.17.0 [120/1] via 172.16.4.1, 00:00:02, Serial0
C       172.16.4.0 is directly connected, Serial0
R       172.16.1.0 [120/1] via 172.16.4.1, 00:00:02, Serial0
R       172.16.2.0 [120/1] via 172.16.3.3, 00:00:17, Serial1
C       172.16.3.0 is directly connected, Serial1
```

RIP routing table entries are identified by an "R" on the far left side of the routing table. RIP routes have a default administrative distance of 120. RIP metrics are calculated by "hop count." A "hop" is a router that has transited. A "hop count" is the number of routers a RIP update has transited. The metric is the value in the fourth column. In the sample routing table above, subnets 172.16.4.0/24 and 172.16.1.0/24 both possess a metric of 1.

In a stable RIP routing environment, the age of RIP routing entries are never older than the RIP update interval. The default RIP update interval is 30 seconds. In a healthy RIP routing environment, RIP routing entries are "forever young." For the two RIP routing entries in the table above, the age of the entries is listed in the second-to-last column.

You can view more detailed information for a single RIP route with the "show ip route x.x.x.x" command:

```
r4#show ip route 172.16.1.0
Routing entry for 172.16.1.0/24
  Known via "rip", distance 120, metric 1
  Redistributing via rip
  Advertised by rip (self originated)
  Last update from 172.16.4.1 on Serial0, 00:00:14 ago
  Routing Descriptor Blocks:
  * 172.16.4.1, from 172.16.4.1, 00:00:14 ago, via Serial0
      Route metric is 1, traffic share count is 1
```

If a routing entry learned by the RIP routing protocol is declared to be unreachable, it is placed in a hold down state. The hold down period for a RIP learned route is three times the update interval, or 180 seconds. If the unreachable route is still unavailable after the hold down period expires, it is flushed after 240 seconds. RIP timers can be viewed in the top three lines of the show ip protocols display:

```
r4#show ip protocols
Routing Protocol is "rip"
Sending updates every 30 seconds, next due in 8 seconds
Invalid after 180 seconds, hold down 180, flushed after 240
  Sending updates every 30 seconds, next due in 8 seconds
```

```
Invalid after 180 seconds, hold down 180, flushed after 240
Outgoing update filter list for all interfaces is not set
Incoming update filter list for all interfaces is not set
Redistributing: rip
Default version control: send version 1, receive any version
  Interface        Send     Recv      Key-chain
  Serial0           1        1          2
  Serial1           1        1          2
Routing for Networks:
  172.16.0.0
Routing Information Sources:
  Gateway          Distance       Last Update
  172.16.4.1            120       00:00:20
  172.16.3.3            120       00:00:10
Distance: (default is 120)
```

When a RIP learned route is placed in the hold down state, it is listed as "possibly down" in the routing table:

```
r3#show ip route
Codes: C - connected, S - static, I - IGRP, R - RIP, M - mobile, B - BGP
       D - EIGRP, EX - EIGRP external, O - OSPF, IA - OSPF inter area
       N1 - OSPF NSSA external type 1, N2 - OSPF NSSA external type 2
       E1 - OSPF external type 1, E2 - OSPF external type 2, E - EGP
       i - IS-IS, L1 - IS-IS level-1, L2 - IS-IS level-2, * - candidate default
       U - per-user static route, o - ODR

Gateway of last resort is not set

     172.16.0.0/24 is subnetted, 5 subnets
       R       172.16.17.0/24 is possibly down,
               routing via 172.16.3.4, Serial0
       R       172.16.17.0/24 is possibly down,
               routing via 172.16.3.4, Serial0
R       172.16.4.0 [120/1] via 172.16.3.4, 00:00:06, Serial0
R       172.16.1.0 [120/1] via 172.16.2.2, 00:00:06, Serial1
C       172.16.2.0 is directly connected, Serial1
C       172.16.3.0 is directly connected, Serial0
```

You can obtain more detail on the hold down status of a specific route by typing "show ip route x.x.x.x":

```
r3#show ip route 172.16.17.0
Routing entry for 172.16.17.0/24
  Known via "rip", distance 120, metric 4294967295 (inaccessible)
  Redistributing via rip
  Advertised by rip (self originated)
  Last update from 172.16.3.4 on Serial0, 00:01:07 ago
  Hold down timer expires in 127 secs
```

If you enable debug ip rip and debug ip routing, you can view an unreachable network prefix enter into a hold down state and eventually get flushed from the routing table. Listed below are sample debug traces displaying the RIP hold down and flushing messages:

```
RT: no routes to 172.16.17.0, entering holddown
RIP:sending v1 update to 255.255.255.255 via Serial0 (172.16.4.4)
    subnet  172.16.17.0, metric 16

    subnet  172.16.17.0, metric 16
    subnet  172.16.2.0, metric 2
    subnet  172.16.3.0, metric 1
```

When the route is finally flushed from the routing table, debug ip routing generates the following message:

```
RT: garbage collecting entry for 172.16.17.0
```

Like RIP, IGRP also places unavailable routes in a hold down state and flushes them after a fixed period of time. The topic of route hold down states and flush timers will be revisited in the section on IGRP.

Configuring a Default Route for RIP

When the static default route 0.0.0.0 0.0.0.0 is configured on a RIP speaking router, RIP automatically redistributes the 0.0.0.0 entry into the RIP domain. All downstream RIP speaking routers forward the default route. This feature is useful when you have two borders routers to a RIP domain, and you want both borders to be used as default gateways.

For example, assume a company with two Internet connections. The two connections were installed for redundancy; however, since both are active, the company wants to use both connections for load balancing internal Internet access. The two routers maintaining the Internet connection advertise the default route 0.0.0.0 into the company's IGP protocol RIP. Interior corporate routers receive both default routes from the two border routers, and dynamically select the default route with the lowest metric. Therefore, the interior routers closest to one of the border routers selects the most optimal Internet connection. If one of the border routers is disabled, all interior routers dynamically select the single remaining default router.

Another method of advertising a default route with RIP is to use the default information originate statement under the router RIP configuration mode. By entering this statement, a 0.0.0.0 route will be advertised into the RIP domain, even if there is no 0.0.0.0 route on the router that is the source of the default route.

In Chapter 9, RIP v.1 was identified as supporting fixed-length subnet masks. Therefore, only a single subnet mask is supported with a given RIP domain. It was also stated that, in a RIP domain, all subnets must be contiguous. The contiguous subnet requirement can be overcome by using a combination of default routes and the "ip classless" command.

A default route allows a RIP-speaking router to forward all classful "network" prefixes that are not listed in a given router's routing table. However, a default route does not automatically allow a RIP-speaking router to forward all "subnets" that are not listed in a given router's routing table. If a RIP-speaking router is participating in the subnetting of a classful prefix, it assumes that it knows about all subnets due to the contiguous subnet rule. By enabling IP classless, you override the contiguous subnet rule and allow the router to look for the longest match beyond the listed subnets. If a subnet is not listed on a router with IP classless enabled, it will eventually match the 0.0.0.0 entry (the default route). Therefore, the unknown subnet will be forwarded with the default route.

This technique is very useful for routing protocol migrations from RIP to OSPF. It is also useful in environments where RIP many be running at the edges of an internetwork and OSPF is running in the core. In such a scenario, RIP and OSPF may be using the same classful address space. RIP may have a set of fixed-length subnets, and OSPF will have a collection of variable-length subnets. If RIP is running at the edge of the internetwork and OSPF is running at the core, use a combination of default routes and ip classless enabled to assure that all subnets within the entire internetwork can be reached. This topic will be revisited in Chapter 12.

RIP Tuning Parameters

The Cisco IOS allows you to tune RIP with the following routing configuration mode commands:

offset-list. Allows you to adjust metrics for specific routes manually. If a destination network is only three hops away, but you want it to appear to be five hops away, use the "offset-list" command to increase the specific destination network's metric.

Distance Use this command to adjust RIP's administrative distance. Its default administrative distance is 120.

Timers By default, RIP advertises its routing table every 30 seconds. When a remotely learned route is advertised as unreachable, RIP places that route in a hold down state for 180 seconds. Finally, if the route is still unreachable after the hold down period, RIP will flush the route. Update timers, hold down timers and flush timers can all be adjusted with the "timers" command. If you adjust the timers on one router in a RIP domain, adjust the timers on all routers to the exact same settings.

Version You can enable RIP version 2 routing with the version command.

Troubleshooting RIP

The most useful debugging tool for RIP routing is debug ip rip. It allows you to view all routes being advertised from a given RIP speaker, as well as all routes received.

```
Debug ip rip
Clear ip route *
Check the timers with sh ip protocol
```

When examining RIP routing updates, remember the Rule of Split Horizon. If Split-Horizon is enabled, the number and type of routes a router interface receives will directly affect which routes the interface advertises. Beware of split horizon on NBMA networks.

IGRP Specific Configuration Issues

Like RIP, IGRP is a distance vector routing protocol, and its configuration involves the following two steps:

1. Enabling the IGRP routing protocol in global configuration mode with an autonomous system number. The global configuration command is "router igrp xxx" (xxx = autonomous system number). All IGRP routers in the same routing domain must have the same autonomous number.
2. Identifying the locally-connected IP addresses that are intended to participate in the IGRP routing process. This is performed by entering one or more "network" statements in routing protocol configuration mode. The address specified with the network statement is a classful network. Subnet entries will not be accepted.

RIP has a maximum hop count of 15. IGRP has a maximum hop count of 100. RIP uses its hop count as a metric and as a mechanism for loop avoidance. IGRP does not use its hop count as a metric, but for routing loop avoidance only.

The IGRP Routing Table

Displayed below is a sample IP routing table with IGRP routing entries:

```
r3#show ip route
Codes: C - connected, S - static, I - IGRP, R - RIP, M - mobile, B - BGP
 D - EIGRP, EX - EIGRP external, O - OSPF, IA - OSPF inter area
 N1 - OSPF NSSA external type 1, N2 - OSPF NSSA external type 2
 E1 - OSPF external type 1, E2 - OSPF external type 2, E - EGP
 i - IS-IS, L1 - IS-IS level-1, L2 - IS-IS level-2, * - candidate default
 U - per-user static route, o - ODR

              Gateway of last resort is not set

     172.16.0.0/24 is subnetted, 4 subnets
I       172.16.4.0 [100/10476] via 172.16.3.4, 00:00:21, Serial0
I       172.16.1.0 [100/10476] via 172.16.2.2, 00:00:58, Serial1
C       172.16.2.0 is directly connected, Serial1
C       172.16.3.0 is directly connected, Serial0
```

IGRP routing table entries are identified by an “I” on the far left side of the routing table. IGRP routes have a default administrative distance of 100. IGRP metrics are calculated by a composite metric, which is based upon a formula using parameters such as the bandwidth, delay, load and reliability of a given path to a destination network. The metric is the value in the fourth column. In the sample routing table above, subnets 172.16.4.0/24 and 172.16.1.0/24 both have a metric of 10476.

In a stable IGRP routing environment, the age of IGRP routing entries are never older than the standard IGRP update interval of 90 seconds. In a healthy IGRP routing environment, IGRP routing entries are “forever young.” For the two IGRP routing entries in the table above, the age of the entries is listed in the second-to-last column.

You can view more detailed information for a single IGRP route with the “show ip route x.x.x.x” command:

```
r3#sh ip route 172.16.4.0
Routing entry for 172.16.4.0/24
  Known via "igrp 100", distance 100, metric 10476
  Redistributing via igrp 100, eigrp 100
  Advertised by igrp 100 (self originated)
  Last update from 172.16.3.4 on Serial0, 00:00:19 ago
  Routing Descriptor Blocks:
  * 172.16.3.4, from 172.16.3.4, 00:00:19 ago, via Serial0
      Route metric is 10476, traffic share count is 1
      Total delay is 40000 microseconds, minimum bandwidth is 1544 Kbit
```

```
Reliability 255/255, minimum MTU 1500 bytes
Loading 1/255, Hops 0
```

IGRP Metric Calculation

A key benefit of IGRP over RIP is IGRP's metric calculation method. Instead of using a hop count for a metric, IGRP uses a composite metric to determine the best path to a destination network. The composite metric uses the following parameters in the following formula:

```
Metric = (K1*Bandwidth)+(K2*Bandwidth)/(256-load)+(K3* Delay)
```

K1, K2 and K3 are constants. By default, K1=K3=1, K2=0. This yields the default formula:

```
Metric=Bandwidth+Delay
```

Bandwidth is the smallest of all bandwidths on outbound ports in a given path. Delay is the sum of all delays of outbound ports in a path.

Bandwidth and delay are static parameters that can be adjusted with the following interface configuration commands:

```
r3(config-if)#bandwidth ?
  <1-10000000>   Bandwidth in kilobits
r3(config-if)#delay ?
  <1-16777215>   Throughput delay (tens of microseconds)
```

You can view the current settings for the IGRP weight on the fourth line of the "show Interface" command:

```
Serial0 is up, line protocol is up
  Hardware is HD64570
  Internet address is 172.16.3.3/24
  MTU 1500 bytes, BW 1544 Kbit, DLY 20000 usec, rely 255/255, load 1/255
```

You can view IGRP metrics as they are sent and received from a given router with debug ip igrp events and debug ip igrp transactions. Listed below is an outbound "sending" routing table update:

```
IGRP: sending update to 255.255.255.255 via Serial0 (172.16.3.3)
      subnet 172.16.1.0, metric=10476
      subnet 172.16.2.0, metric=8476
```

The following is a "received" routing table update:

```
IGRP: received update from 172.16.2.2 on Serial1
      subnet 172.16.17.0, metric 10576 (neighbor 8576)
      subnet 172.16.4.0, metric 12476 (neighbor 10476)
      subnet 172.16.1.0, metric 10476 (neighbor 8476)
      subnet 172.16.3.0, metric 14476 (neighbor 12476)
```

```
IGRP: Update contains 4 interior, 0 system, and 0 exterior
routes.
IGRP: Total routes in update: 4
```

The IGRP Route Hold Down and Route Flushing Process

In the routing table displayed below, notice that the 172.16.5.0/24 subnet is in a "possibly down" state:

```
r2#show ip route
Codes: C - connected, S - static, I - IGRP, R - RIP, M - mobile, B - BGP
       D - EIGRP, EX - EIGRP external, O - OSPF, IA - OSPF inter area
       E1 - OSPF external type 1, E2 - OSPF external type 2, E - EGP
       i - IS-IS, L1 - IS-IS level-1, L2 - IS-IS level-2, * - candidate default

Gateway of last resort is not set

     172.16.0.0 255.255.255.0 is subnetted, 5 subnets
I    172.16.17.0 [100/8576] via 172.16.1.3, 00:01:12, Serial1
I    172.16.4.0 [100/8576] via 172.16.1.3, 00:01:12, Serial1
I    172.16.5.0 255.255.255.0 is possibly down,
     routing via 172.16.1.3, Serial1
C    172.16.1.0 is directly connected, Serial1
C    172.16.2.0 is directly connected, Serial0
```

When an IGRP learned route is announced as unreachable, it is placed in a hold down state, which is represented by a "possibly down" routing table entry. The IGRP learned route remains in a "possibly down" state for 280 seconds (four minutes and 40 seconds). It stays in this state even if the route once again becomes available. Do not be misled by the "possibly down" listing. The routing table is not stating that the network is definitely down; it is stating that it is "*possibly* down." The routing entry will still be used when it is in a "possibly down" state, and if the path is operational, data will be successfully forwarded. If the path is not operational, traffic will still be forwarded over the "possibly down" path; however, the traffic forwarding will be unsuccessful.

If the hold down timer expires and the routing table entry is still unreachable, it remains in a "possibly down" state for another 350 seconds (for a total of 630 seconds or 10.5 minutes). After 630 seconds, the unusable routing table entry is flushed and an alternate path is learned. Therefore, if you are running IGRP on an IP internetwork with a redundant topology, you can have networks that will be unreachable for 10.5 minutes. Only after 10.5 minutes will IGRP flush the "possibly down" route and learn a new route.

You may ask why IGRP takes so long to flush a "possibly down" route. The answer is that, by doing so, IGRP can prevent the formation of routing loops. If you like, you can adjust the IGRP hold down and flush timers. HOWEVER, IF YOU ADJUST THE IGRP HOLD DOWN AND FLUSH TIMERS FOR

ONE ROUTER, YOU MUST ADJUST THEM FOR ALL ROUTERS IN A GIVEN IGRP ROUTING DOMAIN. You can see which hold down timers are set with the "show ip protocols" command:

```
r2#show ip protocols
Routing Protocol is "igrp 100"
     Sending updates every 90 seconds, next due in 58 seconds
     Invalid after 270 seconds, hold down 280, flushed after 630
     Outgoing update filter list for all interfaces is not set
     Incoming update filter list for all interfaces is not set
     Default networks flagged in outgoing updates
     Default networks accepted from incoming updates
     IGRP metric weight K1=1, K2=0, K3=1, K4=0, K5=0
     IGRP maximum hopcount 100
     IGRP maximum metric variance 1
     Redistributing: igrp 100
     Routing for Networks:
     172.16.0.0
  Routing Information Sources:
     Gateway        Distance        Last Update
     172.16.1.3     100             0:01:20
  Distance: (default is 100)
```

You can watch the timers associated with a given routing entry with show ip route x.x.x.x. In the display below, you see the hold down timer approaching zero.

```
r3#sh ip ro 172.16.17.0
Routing entry for 172.16.17.0/24
  Known via "igrp 100", distance 100, metric 4294967295 (inaccessible)
  Redistributing via igrp 100
  Advertised by igrp 100 (self originated)
  Last update from 172.16.3.4 on Serial0, 00:02:20 ago
  Hold down timer expires in 144 secs
```

You can also track hold down activity with debug ip routing. Listed below are sample messages generated by the IGRP hold down process. The first set of messages generated when the route first went into a hold down state:

```
IGRP: received update from 172.16.3.4 on Serial0
    subnet 172.16.17.0, metric 4294967295 (inaccessible)
RT: delete route to 172.16.17.0 via 172.16.3.4, igrp metric [100/10576]
RT: no routes to 172.16.17.0, entering holddown
```

After the hold down period expires, the following message is generated:

```
RT: 172.16.17.0 came out of holddown
```

If the route is still unreachable after the hold down timer expires, you can track the events and timers leading up to the route being flushed with show ip route and debug ip routing. Note the last update received for the 172.16.17.0/24 network in the show ip route display provided below. It is over ten minutes.

```
r3#show ip route 172.16.17.0
Routing entry for 172.16.17.0/24
  Known via "igrp 100", distance 100,  metric 4294967295 (inaccessible)
  Redistributing via igrp 100
  Advertised by igrp 100 (self originated)
  Last update from 172.16.3.4 on Serial0, 00:10:41 ago
```

When the route is finally flushed, debug ip routing generates the following message:

```
RT: garbage collecting entry for 172.16.17.0
```

Configuring Default Routes for IGRP

IGRP does not advertise the 0.0.0.0 network to downstream IGRP neighbors. RIP and EIGRP do.

With IGRP, you must use the "ip default-network" global configuration command. When using this statement, it is recommended that you assign a classful address. If you use a subnet with "ip default-network", a static route will be created in your running configuration.

Whatever network you reference with the "ip default-network statement" must be in the routing table of the router that is sourcing the default-network.

The selected default-route will appear as an "exterior network" in debug ip igrp events:

```
IGRP: received update from 172.16.2.2 on Serial1
       subnet 172.16.1.0, metric 10476 (neighbor 8476)
       subnet 172.16.2.0, metric 10476 (neighbor 8476)
       exterior network 10.0.0.0, metric 10576 (neighbor 8576)
```

The default network can also be traced with "debug ip routing":

```
RT: default path is now 10.0.0.0 via 172.16.1.1
RT: new default network 10.0.0.0
```

The IGRP default network will be marked as a "candidate default" in the IP routing table, and will appear at the top of the table as a "gateway of last resort":

```
Router#show ip route
Codes: C - connected, S - static, I - IGRP, R - RIP, M - mobile, B - BGP
       D - EIGRP, EX - EIGRP external, O - OSPF, IA - OSPF inter area
       N1 - OSPF NSSA external type 1, N2 - OSPF NSSA external type 2
       E1 - OSPF external type 1, E2 - OSPF external type 2, E - EGP
       i - IS-IS, L1 - IS-IS level-1, L2 - IS-IS level-2, * - candidate  default
       U - per-user static route, o - ODR

Gateway of last resort is 172.16.1.1 to network 10.0.0.0

       172.16.0.0/24 is subnetted, 2 subnets
C         172.16.1.0 is directly connected, Serial1
C         172.16.2.0 is directly connected, Serial0
I*     10.0.0.0/8 [100/8576] via 172.16.1.1, 00:01:10, Serial1
```

IGRP Tuning Parameters

IGRP offers a number of tunable parameters under router igrp xxx configuration mode (xxx= autonomous system). Listed below are some of the most commonly used tunable parameters:

Distance Distance allows you to adjust the administrative distance of IGRP. The default administrative distance for IGRP is 100.

Variance The variance command allows you to perform "unequal-cost load balancing." The variance parameter allows you to specify a factor of a path to use, in comparison to the best metric selected to get to a particular destination network. For example, if variance is set to three, IGRP will load balance over any paths that are no more than three times the amount of the best metric known for a given destination network. IGRP supports up to four unequal-cost load balancing paths at any given time.

Timers You can adjust the update, hold down and flush timers for IGRP with the "timers" command. If you change the timers for one router, change them for all the routers in a single IGRP domain.

Troubleshooting IGRP

Routers should be sending and receiving updates according to the update interval. Go to the source of a given routing update and make sure the router is advertising the update. If the source of a given routing table entry appears to be successfully advertising a given network or collection of networks, go to the direct neighbor of the routing source and make sure the neighbor is receiving the route.

The tools you can use to examine IGRP routing updates are:

- Debug ip igrp transactions
- Debug ip igrp events

A sample debug trace is provided below. Notice the highlighted entry, which is listing an unreachable network.

```
IGRP: sending update to 255.255.255.255 via Serial1 (172.16.2.3)
      subnet 172.16.17.0, metric=4294967295
      subnet 172.16.4.0, metric=10476
      subnet 172.16.3.0, metric=8476
```

EIGRP Specific Configuration Issues

As mentioned earlier, from a configuration perspective, basic EIGRP configuration is identical to IGRP configuration. Basic EIGRP configuration involves a minimum of two steps:

1. Enable the EIGRP routing protocol in global configuration mode with an autonomous system number. All EIGRP routers in the same routing domain must have the same autonomous number. EIGRP routers will automatically exchange routes with IGRP routers in the same autonomous system.
2. Identify the locally connected IP addresses that are intended to participate in the EIGRP routing process. This is performed by entering one or more "network" statements in routing protocol configuration mode. The address specified with the network statement is a classful network. Subnet entries will be truncated.

Once the EIGRP routing protocol is enabled, EIGRP speaking routers create the following three tables:

1. an EIGRP Neighbor Table
2. an EIGRP Topology Table
3. a Main Routing

The EIGRP Neighbor Table

An EIGRP neighbor table is constructed and maintained by EIGRP speaking neighbors exchanging HELLOs. EIGRP HELLOs contain neighbors' IP addresses. HELLOs are advertised every five seconds and use the multicast 224.0.0.10. Once EIGRP speaking routers exchange HELLOs and form a neighbor relationship, they exchange routing update information and build a topology table. A sample EIGRP neighbor table is listed below:

```
Router#sh ip eigrp neighbors
IP-EIGRP neighbors for process 100
```

```
H    Address       Interface  Hold   Uptime     SRTT   RTO   Q     Seq
                              (sec)  (ms)                    Cnt   Num
1    172.16.4.1    Se0        11     00:01:08   60     360   0     86
0    172.16.2.2    Se1        10     00:39:47   38     228   0     70
```

The EIGRP Topology Table

The EIGRP topology table contains destination network reachability information from EIGRP neighbors. EIGRP constructs the topology table by applying the diffused update algorithm (DUAL). DUAL involves the collection of routing table updates from EIGRP neighbors. The topology table consists of at least two entries:

1. The advertised metric to reach a given destination network by a directly connected EIGRP neighbor.
2. The "feasible distance" from a given EIGRP speaker to a given destination network. The feasible distance is the advertised metric of a directly-connected EIGRP neighbor, plus the cost of reaching the directly-connected neighbor. The feasible distance is the metric used by a given router to reach a specific destination network.

   For example, assume router r1 advertises the subnet 172.16.1.0/24 with a metric of 100 to router r2. 100 is the advertised metric of 172.16.1.0/24 from router r1. When r1 advertises the route to r2, it increases the metric to account for accessing the directly-connected link between routers r1 and r2 by 10. Remember, metrics are advertised on outbound interfaces. Router r1 must account for the link between r1 and r2 in its advertisement to r2. Therefore, r1 must increase the metric for 172.16.1.0/24 when it advertises the route to r2. With the increase of 10, r2's metric for reaching the 172.16.1.0/24 subnet via router r1 is 110.

Examine the ip routing table and the EIGRP topology table displayed below. Notice that the metric listed in the routing table is the same as the feasible distance (FD) listed in the topology table. Both are highlighted in the respective tables.

```
r3# show ip route
Codes: C - connected, S - static, I - IGRP, R - RIP, M - mobile, B - BGP
       D - EIGRP, EX - EIGRP external, O - OSPF, IA - OSPF inter area
       N1 - OSPF NSSA external type 1, N2 - OSPF NSSA external type 2
       E1 - OSPF external type 1, E2 - OSPF external type 2, E - EGP
       i - IS-IS, L1 - IS-IS level-1, L2 - IS-IS level-2, * - candidate default
       U - per-user static route, o - ODR

Gateway of last resort is not set

     172.16.0.0/24 is subnetted, 5 subnets
D       172.16.17.0 [90/2707456] via 172.16.3.4, 00:00:07, Serial0
D       172.16.4.0 [90/2681856] via 172.16.3.4, 00:00:13, Serial0
```

```
D       172.16.1.0 [90/2681856] via 172.16.2.2, 02:02:01, Serial1
C       172.16.2.0 is directly connected, Serial1
C       172.16.3.0 is directly connected, Serial0
```

```
r3# show ip eigrp topology
IP-EIGRP Topology Table for process 100
Codes: P - Passive, A - Active, U - Update, Q - Query, R - Reply,
       r - Reply status
P 172.16.17.0/24, 1 successor, FD is 2707456
          via 172.16.3.4   2707456   /2195456 , Serial0
P 172.16.17.0/24, 1 successor, FD is 2707456
via 172.16.3.4 (2707456/2195456), Serial0
P 172.16.4.0/24, 1 successors, FD is 2681856
         via 172.16.3.4 (2681856/2169856), Serial0
P 172.16.1.0/24, 1 successors, FD is 2681856
         via 172.16.2.2 (2681856/2169856), Serial1
P 172.16.2.0/24, 1 successors, FD is 2169856
         via Connected, Serial1
P 172.16.3.0/24, 1 successors, FD is 2169856
         via Connected, Serial0
```

Note the underlined value above 2195456. It is listed as the metric used in the directly connected neighbor's main routing table:

```
r4#sh ip ro
Codes: C - connected, S - static, I - IGRP, R - RIP, M - mobile, B - BGP
       D - EIGRP, EX - EIGRP external, O - OSPF, IA - OSPF inter area
       N1 - OSPF NSSA external type 1, N2 - OSPF NSSA external type 2
       E1 - OSPF external type 1, E2 - OSPF external type 2, E - EGP
       i - IS-IS, L1 - IS-IS level-1, L2 - IS-IS level-2, * - candidate default
       U - per-user static route, o - ODR

Gateway of last resort is not set

     172.16.0.0/24 is subnetted, 5 subnets
D       172.16.17.0 [90/2195456 via 172.16.4.1, 00:08:37, Serial0
C       172.16.4.0 is directly connected, Serial0
D       172.16.1.0 [90/3193856] via 172.16.3.3, 00:08:37, Serial1
D       172.16.2.0 [90/2681856] via 172.16.3.3, 00:08:37, Serial1
C       172.16.3.0 is directly connected, Serial1
```

Therefore, the two values listed in succession in an EIGRP topology table are:

1. The first entry: the feasible distance (local metric) for local router to get to a given destination network
2. The second entry: the metric used by a directly connected EIGRP neighbor to get to the same destination network.

A rule to remember for the second value (the metric used by a directly connected EIGRP neighbor) is: IT MUST BE LESS THAN THE METRIC USED

BY THE LOCAL ROUTER. By assuring that a neighbor's metric to a destination network is less than your own metric to the same destination network, you can avoid creating routing loops. **If a directly connected neighbor's metric to a given destination network is less than your own metric, you cannot create a routing loop by selecting a shorter path to a given destination network.** If a router cannot locate a neighbor with a metric to a given destination network that is less than the current feasible distance, the router must go into an "ACTIVE" state and query its neighbors for routing information. The result of the ACTIVE state query will be to recompute the feasible distance value so that it locates a neighbor with a metric to a given destination network that is less than the feasible distance. If a router maintains its own metrics and routing table selections to destination networks that are greater than its neighbors' metrics to the same destination networks, it can assure that no routing loops will form. Therefore, EIGRP topological database construction and maintenance can be summarized by the following rule: "You cannot form a routing loop by selecting a path with a shorter metric."

Routing loop avoidance is the purpose of maintaining an EIGRP topological database. Since EIGRP maintains this topological database, it does not have to place routes in a hold down state when they become unreachable. It can reference its topological database and locate a neighbor with a metric that is less than its own current feasible distance, and rapidly select an alternate route. It is this technique that allows EIGRP to avoid the slow convergence characteristics of RIP and IGRP. Since EIGRP uses this loop avoidance technique, it does not have any hold down or flush timers. Examine the show IP protocol display for EIGRP. Notice how it does not have the update, hold down or flush timers that RIP and IGRP possess.

```
r4>show ip protocols
Routing Protocol is "eigrp 100"
  Outgoing update filter list for all interfaces is not set
  Incoming update filter list for all interfaces is not set
  Default networks flagged in outgoing updates
  Default networks accepted from incoming updates
  EIGRP metric weight K1=1, K2=0, K3=1, K4=0, K5=0
  EIGRP maximum hopcount 100
  EIGRP maximum metric variance 1
  Redistributing: eigrp 100
  Automatic network summarization is in effect
  Routing for Networks:
    172.16.0.0
  Routing Information Sources:
    Gateway          Distance       Last Update
    172.16.4.1             90       00:44:48
    172.16.3.3             90       00:44:48
  Distance: internal 90 external 170
```

With EIGRP topology table entries, you can obtain detailed information on each by typing "show ip eigrp topology x.x.x.x y.y.y.y" (x.x.x.x = a network prefix, y.y.y.y = a network prefix mask) A sample display is provided below:

```
r4#show ip eigrp topology 172.16.17.0 255.255.255.0
IP-EIGRP topology entry for 172.16.17.0/24
 State is Passive, Query origin flag is 1, 1 Successor(s), FD is 2195456
  Routing Descriptor Blocks:
  172.16.4.1 (Serial0), from 172.16.4.1, Send flag is 0x0
      Composite metric is 2195456  /281600), Route is Internal
      Vector metric:
        Minimum bandwidth is 1544 Kbit
        Total delay is 21000 microseconds
        Reliability is 128/255
        Load is 1/255
        Minimum MTU is 1500
        Hop count is 1
```

Once again, make note of the highlighted entries. These are the metrics used by this router (r4) to get to the network 172.16.17.0/24. On the fifth line of the display (the line beginning with "Composite metric"), the underlined and bolded value is the metric used by the directly connected neighbor to get to the network 172.16.17.0/24. Notice how the metric used by this router (metric 2195456) is greater than the metric used by the neighbor (281600). This complies with the rule, "You cannot form a routing loop by selecting a path with a shorter metric."

The EIGRP Routing Table

EIGRP routing table entries are identified by the letters "D" and "EX". A "D" EIGRP is a route that is internal to a given EIGRP routing domain. An "EX" entry is a route that has been redistributed from another routing protocol or source, such as RIP or OSPF.

EIGRP internal routes ("D" routes) have an administrative distance of 90. "EX" routes have an administrative distance of 170.

Note the massive value in the metric column for EIGRP entries. EIGRP metrics are calculated with the exact same composite metric parameters and formula used by IGRP. The only difference between an IGRP metric and an EIGRP metric is that the EIGRP metric is represented by a value that is larger than IGRP metric by a factor of 256. Therefore, if you take an IGRP metric for a given destination network and multiply it by 256, you will have the EIGRP metric.

Note also the age of the EIGRP routing entries in the table below. In comparison to RIP and IGRP, EIGRP's routing table entries are old. In a stable RIP and IGRP environment, routing table entries are never older than the update interval. Since EIGRP maintains a topological database that is updated only when changes to network topology occur, EIGRP routing will become very old in a stable environment. Constantly young EIGRP routing table entries indicate an unstable network.

```
Router#show ip route
Codes: C - connected, S - static, I - IGRP, R - RIP, M - mobile, B - BGP
     D - EIGRP, EX - EIGRP external, O - OSPF, IA - OSPF inter area
     N1 - OSPF NSSA external type 1, N2 - OSPF NSSA external type 2
     E1 - OSPF external type 1, E2 - OSPF external type 2, E - EGP
     i - IS-IS, L1 - IS-IS level-1, L2 - IS-IS level-2, * - candidate   default
     U - per-user static route, o - ODR

Gateway of last resort is not set

     140.10.0.0/24 is subnetted, 2 subnets
D       140.10.2.0 [90/2809856] via 172.16.2.2, 00:27:08 Serial1
D       140.10.1.0 [90/2809856] via 172.16.2.2  00:27:08 Serial1
     140.11.0.0/24 is subnetted, 1 subnets
D       140.11.2.0 [90/2809856] via 172.16.2.2,00:27:08 Serial1
     172.16.0.0/24 is subnetted, 2 subnets
D       172.16.1.0 [90/2681856] via 172.16.2.2, 00:31:09 Serial1
C       172.16.2.0 is directly connected, Serial1
```

You can obtain detailed information on a single EIGRP routing entry by typing "show ip route x.x.x.x" (x.x.x.x = a specific EIGRP network prefix). A sample display is provided below:

```
r4#show ip route 172.16.17.0
Routing entry for 172.16.17.0/24
  Known via "eigrp 100", distance 90, metric 2195456, type
internal
  Redistributing via eigrp 100
  Last update from 172.16.4.1 on Serial0, 00:12:09 ago
  Routing Descriptor Blocks:
  * 172.16.4.1, from 172.16.4.1, 00:12:09 ago, via Serial0
      Route metric is 2195456, traffic share count is 1
      Total delay is 21000 microseconds, minimum bandwidth is
1544 Kbit
      Reliability 128/255, minimum MTU 1500 bytes
      Loading 1/255, Hops 1
```

EIGRP Routing Table Advertisements

With EIGRP routing table updates, variable length subnetting and supernetting is supported. In the debug ip eigrp output displayed below, notice how the majority of networks are 172.16.0.0/24 entries; however, examine entries seven and nine. Entry seven is using a 27-bit subnet mask, and entry nine is using a 30-bit subnet mask. Also, make note of entry eleven: 161.0.0.0/8.

Under the rules of classful addressing, any address beginning with a first octet of 161 is a Class B network with the first 16 bits allocated to the network prefix. This entry breaks the old classful addressing rules. It is a classless prefix identified by a unique prefix and mask length. Neither variable length subnetting nor classless addresses are supported by RIP v.1 or IGRP.

Even though EIGRP supports variable length subnetting, it automatically summarizes routing table updates at the classful boundaries. In the routing advertisements listed below, notice how all 172.16.0.0 subnets are tagged as "do not advertise." This is because EIGRP automatically summarizes subnetted information at the classful network boundaries. This feature can be disabled, as will be further discussed in the next section.

```
IP-EIGRP: 172.16.3.0/24, - do advertise out Serial1
IP-EIGRP: 172.16.4.0/24, - do advertise out Serial1
IP-EIGRP: Int 172.16.4.0/24 metric 2169856 - 1657856 512000
IP-EIGRP: 172.16.17.0/24, - do advertise out Serial1
IP-EIGRP: Int 172.16.17.0/24 metric 2195456 - 1657856 537600
IP-EIGRP: 172.16.101.64/30, - do advertise out Serial1
IP-EIGRP: Int 172.16.101.64/30 metric 2297856 - 1657856 640000
IP-EIGRP: 172.16.100.32/27, - do advertise out Serial1
IP-EIGRP: Int 172.16.100.32/27 metric 2297856 - 1657856 640000
IP-EIGRP: 161.0.0.0/8, - do advertise out Serial1
IP-EIGRP: Int 161.0.0.0/8 metric 257664000 - 256000000 1664000
```

EIGRP Automatic Network Summarization

By default, EIGRP auto-summarizes subnets at the classful network boundaries. Examine the routing table below. Notice the null0 entries. Each null0 entry is identified as a "summary."

```
r1#show ip route
Codes: C - connected, S - static, I - IGRP, R - RIP, M - mobile, B - BGP
       D - EIGRP, EX - EIGRP external, O - OSPF, IA - OSPF inter area
       N1 - OSPF NSSA external type 1, N2 - OSPF NSSA external type 2
       E1 - OSPF external type 1, E2 - OSPF external type 2, E - EGP
       i - IS-IS, L1 - IS-IS level-1, L2 - IS-IS level-2, * - candidate default
       U - per-user static route, o - ODR

Gateway of last resort is not set

     140.10.0.0/16 is variably subnetted, 3 subnets, 2 masks
C       140.10.2.0/24 is directly connected, Loopback1
D       140.10.0.0/16 is a summary, 00:01:08, Null0
C    140.10.1.0/24 is directly connected, Loopback0
     140.11.0.0/16 is variably subnetted, 2 subnets, 2 masks
C    140.11.2.0/24 is directly connected, Loopback2
```

```
D       140.11.0.0/16 is a summary, 00:01:08, Null0
     172.16.0.0/16 is variably subnetted, 4 subnets, 2 masks
C    172.16.4.0/24 is directly connected, Serial1
D    172.16.1.0/24 [90/3193856] via 172.16.4.3, 00:01:10, Serial1
D    172.16.2.0/24 [90/2681856] via 172.16.4.3, 00:01:10, Serial1
```

A router downstream from the summarizing router will see only the summaries. Downstream routers will see no reference to the null0 interfaces used on the summarizing routers.

```
r1#sh ip ro
Codes: C - connected, S - static, I - IGRP, R - RIP, M - mobile, B - BGP
     D - EIGRP, EX - EIGRP external, O - OSPF, IA - OSPF inter area
     N1 - OSPF NSSA external type 1, N2 - OSPF NSSA external type 2
     E1 - OSPF external type 1, E2 - OSPF external type 2, E - EGP
     i - IS-IS, L1 - IS-IS level-1, L2 - IS-IS level-2, * - candidate default
     U - per-user static route, o - ODR

Gateway of last resort is not set
D     140.10.0.0/16 [90/2809856] via 172.16.2.3, 00:01:53, Serial0
D     140.11.0.0/16 [90/2809856] via 172.16.2.3, 00:01:53, Serial0
     172.16.0.0/24 is subnetted, 2 subnets
D       172.16.4.0 [90/2681856] via 172.16.2.3, 00:05:05, Serial0
C       172.16.2.0 is directly connected, Serial0
```

The summarization process can be traced through debug:

```
IP-EIGRP: 140.10.1.0/24, - don't advertise out Serial0
IP-EIGRP: 140.10.2.0/24, - don't advertise out Serial0
IP-EIGRP: 140.10.0.0/16, - do advertise out Serial0
IP-EIGRP: 140.11.2.0/24, - don't advertise out Serial0
IP-EIGRP: 140.11.0.0/16, - do advertise out Serial0
```

By applying the longest match rule, the downstream routers will forward all destination prefixes using the summary address. Eventually, these routes will be forwarded to the router performing the summarization. The summarizing router will match the destination prefixes with their longer matching subnets. If any of the destination prefixes match the summary address only, the summarizing router will forward these packets to the null interface, and they will be discarded.

If you have discontiguous subnets, you will want to disable the automatic summarization feature of EIGRP. This can be done with the "no auto-summary" command entered in the EIGRP routing protocol configuration mode.

```
r1(config)#router eigrp 100
r1(config-router)#no auto-summary
```

When this command is entered, notice that the summary statements referencing a null0 interface are removed from the routing table:

```
r1#sh ip ro
Codes: C - connected, S - static, I - IGRP, R - RIP, M - mobile, B - BGP
     D - EIGRP, EX - EIGRP external, O - OSPF, IA - OSPF inter area
     N1 - OSPF NSSA external type 1, N2 - OSPF NSSA external type 2
     E1 - OSPF external type 1, E2 - OSPF external type 2, E - EGP
     i - IS-IS, L1 - IS-IS level-1, L2 - IS-IS level-2, * - candidate   default
     U - per-user static route, o - ODR

Gateway of last resort is not set

     140.10.0.0/24 is subnetted, 2 subnets
C       140.10.2.0 is directly connected, Loopback1
C       140.10.1.0 is directly connected, Loopback0
     140.11.0.0/24 is subnetted, 1 subnets
C       140.11.2.0 is directly connected, Loopback2
     172.16.0.0/24 is subnetted, 3 subnets
C       172.16.4.0 is directly connected, Serial1
C       172.16.1.0 is directly connected, Serial0
D       172.16.2.0 [90/2681856] via 172.16.4.3, 00:01:54, Serial1
                    [90/2681856] via 172.16.1.2, 00:01:54, Serial0
```

Manual Network Summarization with EIGRP

The auto-summary feature of EIGRP automatically summarizes at classful network boundaries. You may want to summarize at any subnet or supernet boundary. You can do this manually with the interface configuration command "ip summary-address eigrp":

```
London(config-if)#ip summary-address ?
        eigrp Enhanced Interior Gateway Routing Protocol (EIGRP)
```

When you use this manual summary address command, it inserts a null0 interface entry into the summarizing routing table. A sample routing table display is provided below, in which multiple 140.10.0.0/16 and 140.11.0.0/16 entries are summarized in the 140.0.0.0/8 prefix.

```
r1#sh ip ro
Codes: C - connected, S - static, I - IGRP, R - RIP, M - mobile, B - BGP
     D - EIGRP, EX - EIGRP external, O - OSPF, IA - OSPF inter area
     N1 - OSPF NSSA external type 1, N2 - OSPF NSSA external type 2
     E1 - OSPF external type 1, E2 - OSPF external type 2, E - EGP
     i - IS-IS, L1 - IS-IS level-1, L2 - IS-IS level-2, * - candidate  default
     U - per-user static route, o - ODR
Gateway of last resort is not set

     *    10.0.0.0/24 is subnetted, 1 subnets
C         10.1.1.0 is directly connected, Ethernet0
```

```
     140.10.0.0/16 is variably subnetted, 3 subnets, 2 masks
C       140.10.2.0/24 is directly connected, Loopback1
D       140.10.0.0/16 is a summary, 00:00:59, Null0
C       140.10.1.0/24 is directly connected, Loopback0
     140.11.0.0/24 is subnetted, 1 subnets
C       140.11.2.0 is directly connected, Loopback2
     172.16.0.0/16 is variably subnetted, 4 subnets, 2 masks
C       172.16.4.0/24 is directly connected, Serial1
D       172.16.0.0/16 is a summary, 00:19:24, Null0
D       172.16.1.0/24 [90/3193856] via 172.16.4.3, 00:00:55, Serial1
D       172.16.2.0/24 [90/2681856] via 172.16.4.3, 00:00:56, Serial1
D       140.0.0.0/8 is a summary, 00:00:54, Null0
```

When you examine the debug ip eigrp output below, notice how all 140.10.0.0 and 140.11.0.0 entries are not advertised, but the single 140.0.0.0/8 is.

```
IP-EIGRP: 140.10.1.0/24, - don't advertise out Serial1
IP-EIGRP: 140.10.2.0/24, - don't advertise out Serial1
IP-EIGRP: 140.0.0.0/8, - do advertise out Serial1
IP-EIGRP: 140.10.0.0/16, - don't advertise out Serial1
IP-EIGRP: 140.11.0.0/16, - don't advertise out Serial1
```

RIP, IGRP, and EIGRP over NBMA

All the routing protocols discussed in this chapter—RIP, IGRP and EIGRP—apply the Rule of Split-Horizon: Do not advertise routes out an interface on which you learned the route. Split-Horizon is a useful tool on point-to-point and multi-access segments, but it can cause problems on non-broadcast multi-access segments, such as Frame-Relay and ATM.

Split-horizon is disabled by default for IP on Frame-Relay physical interfaces. However, it is not disabled by default for point-to-point or multipoint subinterfaces. Be aware of these issues when you are configuring RIP, IGRP and EIGRP on NBMA networks. In order for routing information to be propagated through a hub and spoke NBMA network, such as Frame-Relay and ATM, split-horizon must be disabled on the hub router only. Remember that split-horizon is disabled on all physical Frame-Relay interfaces. If the interface is a **spoke** interface in a hub and spoke topology, it is recommended that you manually enable split-horizon. Otherwise, you may get routers advertising routes which they do not actually have. This can wreak havoc on routing tables, especially on routers performing redistribution. This topic will be revisited in Chapter Twelve.

RIP and IGRP over Switched Connections

The Periodic routing table updates of RIP and IGRP will keep a switched connection, such as an ISDN/DDR link, up indefinitely. EIGRP HELLOs will also keep this type of connection up indefinitely. To remedy this problem, consider using static routes or snapshot routing. See Chapter Five for more details on configuring routing protocols over an ISDN/DDR connection.

Troubleshooting EIGRP

When troubleshooting EIGRP, remember the progress of EIGRP operation:

1. EIGRP neighbor relationships must be established.
2. Each EIGRP speaker must build its topological database.
3. The Feasible Distance entries in a given router's topological database must be greater than the directly-connected EIGRP neighbors' advertised metric.
4. The optimal topological database entries will be posted in the main IP routing table.

You can reinitialize this entire process on an EIGRP speaking router by entering the "clear ip eigrp neighbor" command. DO NOT ENTER THIS COMMAND ON A PRODUCTION ROUTER! PERFORM THIS COMMAND IN A LAB OR TESTBED ENVIRONMENT ONLY! When you perform the "clear ip eigrp neighbor" command, use the following commands to observe the EIGRP initialization process:

- Show ip eigrp neighbor
- Show ip eigrp topology
- Show ip route
- Debug ip eigrp

Summary

This chapter introduced you to the basic configuration, monitoring and troubleshooting issues associated with RIP, IGRP and EIGRP. There is a clear progression in learning these routing protocols in sequence. When you begin with RIP, you become aware of the benefits of dynamic routing protocols over static routes. Dynamic routing protocols adjust to changes inside the internetwork, not just to directly-connected interfaces.

You can now enable and maintain RIP, IGRP and EIGRP. We will revisit these topics in Chapter Twelve.

Professional Development Checklist

By using this chapter, you should be able to perform the following operations:

- Enable RIP routing process and define participating local networks.
- Enable IGRP routing process and define participating local networks.
- Enable EIGRP routing process and define participating local networks.

For Further Study

- Advanced Cisco Router Configuration, Cisco Systems, Inc., 1989–1998.
- Cisco IOS Configuration Guide Volume V, Cisco Systems, Inc., 1989–1998.
- Cisco IOS Command Reference Volume V, Cisco Systems, Inc., 1989–1998.
- Huitema, Christian. *Routing in the Internet*, Prentice-Hall, 1995.

URLs

- **www.cciecert.com**
- **www.freesoft.org**
- **www.mentorlabs.com**
- **www.cisco.com**

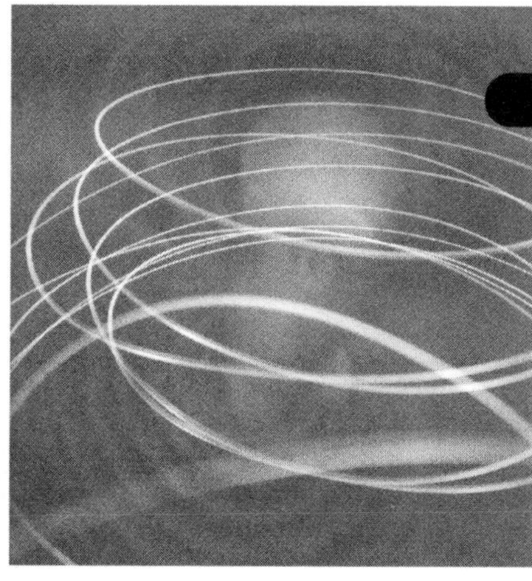

ELEVEN

Configuring OSPF

Topics Covered in This Chapter

- Introduction to OSPF
- Basic OSPF Operation
- OSPF Network Types
- The OSPF Hello Protocol
- Adjacencies
- The Designated Router
- OSPF Areas
- Virtual Links
- Redistribution
- Route Summarization

Distance vector routing algorithms have some important drawbacks, all related to their relatively limited view of the network's topology. Conventional distance vector protocols such as RIP and IGRP implement hold-down timers, which mandate a waiting period before using alternate routes. Often, this waiting period is several minutes in length. The need for a hold-down timer is a direct consequence of distance vector's susceptibility to routing loops, which, in turn, is largely the consequence of inconsistent information exchanged between several routers.

Improvements have been developed, such as EIGRP's DUAL algorithm, but none have achieved the success of OSPF's link state algorithm. This is due partly to the genuinely improved performance offered by link state, and partly to the non-proprietary nature of OSPF and its consequent widespread acceptance as the interior routing protocol of choice.

A link state routing protocol operates by providing each router with enough information to construct a complete map of the network. The elements of this map are contained in the link state router's topological database. The topological database contains a comprehensive and exhaustive listing of all links in a given link state routing domain. For some protocols, such as OSPF, the topological database lists all links in a specific area of a link state routing domain. For every router in a link state routing domain or area, the contents of the topological database are identical. By locating itself in the map constructed from the entries in its own topological database, each router computes a routing table for itself.

Several points should be noted about link state routing. First, its memory requirements are significantly greater than distance vector, since it stores more complete information about the network topology. Its computational requirements are also greater, since it cannot simply compare its neighbors' routing tables against each other. A linkstate router must construct its routing table based on its own network map, typically a more time-consuming process. OSPF allows the engineer to partition the network into areas, which reduces the computational requirements at the cost of added complexity in the configuration. OSPF areas will be discussed in more detail later in this Chapter.

OSPF is certainly not the last word in routing protocols, but it does represent the state of the art in the 1990s. At the time of this writing, OSPF version 2 is in widespread use. Important OSPF-related RFCs include:

- RFC 2178 OSPF Version 2
- RFC 1850 OSPF MIB (for use with SNMP)
- RFC 1793 OSPF Demand Circuits
- RFC 1584 OSPF Multicasting Support
- RFC 1587 OSPF Not-So-Stubby Areas

Basic OSPF Operation

Each OSPF router in a given OSPF area builds an identical topological database, which consists of "link-state advertisements" (LSAs). LSAs use the multicast address of 224.0.0.5. OSPF supports several different types of LSAs, the most important of which are "router" LSAs (one for each router in an area) and "network" LSAs (one for each IP subnet on transiting broadcast and nonbroadcast networks). Each LSA is generated by a single router, then "flooded" throughout the entire OSPF domain or a single OSPF area, so that every other router gets a copy of it. Some LSAs are flooded only to routers residing in a single OSPF area, while others are flooded throughout the entire OSPF domain.

RFC 1247 defines LSAs in the following manner:

LSA Type	Advertisement name	Advertisement description
1	Router links advs.	Originated by all routers. This advertisement describes the collected states of the router's interfaces to an area. Flooded throughout a single area only.

2	Network links advs.	Originated for multi-access networks by the Designated Router. This advertisement contains the list of routers connected to the network. Flooded throughout a single area only.
3,4	Summary link advs.	Originated by area border routers, and flooded throughout their associated areas. Each summary link advertisement describes a route to a destination outside the area, yet still inside the AS (i.e., an inter-area route). Type 3 advertisements describe routes to networks. Type 4 advertisements describe routes to AS boundary routers.
5	AS external link advs.	Originated by AS boundary routers and flooded throughout the AS. Each external advertisement describes a route to a destination in another Autonomous System. Default routes for the AS can also be described by AS external advertisements.

A router will generate at least a single router LSA (LSA Type 1), identifying itself and including (as part of the router LSA) a list of all the networks to which it is attached. For certain types of networks, such as multi-access LANs (Ethernet, Token-Ring, FDDI) and non-broadcast multiaccess networks (Frame-Relay, ATM and X.25), each network possesses a "designated router" responsible for sourcing a network LSA (LSA Type 2) for that network.

For example, consider the following simple network:

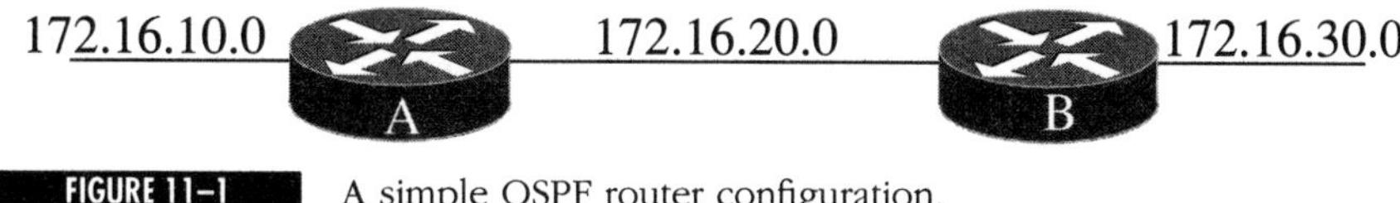

FIGURE 11–1 A simple OSPF router configuration.

Router A will source a router LSA for itself, identifying itself and listing two links to 172.16.10.0 and 172.16.20.0. Likewise, Router B will source a router LSA for itself, listing 172.16.20.0 and 72.16.30.0 as its two links. Additionally, one of the two routers will be elected Designated Router for the 172.16.20.0 network, and will source a network LSA for 172.16.20.0, including the router IDs of two attached routers. Networks 172.16.10.0 and 172.16.30.0 are special. They are considered "stub" networks, since each has only a single router attached, and therefore will not possess network LSAs of their own. Instead, they will be identified as part of the corresponding router LSA.

So our simple network will cause three LSA to be generated and flooded to all the OSPF routers (there are only two of them).

To actually use this information, a routing table must be constructed. OSPF does this with a "shortest path first" algorithm, sometimes called the "Dijkstra algorithm"—a fancy term to describe a trivial procedure for a human, but somewhat more complex for a computer. A router simply finds itself in the network diagram and begins constructing routing table entries for every network it finds, moving outward from the center in a step-by-step process. At each step, the router keeps track of the accumulated cost (the LSAs contain routing metrics) and processes the next LSA with the lowest cost, ensuring that the lowest-cost paths are always selected. If anything changes in the diagram (for example, if new LSAs are received, or existing ones are deleted for some reason), the entire center-out mapping process must be repeated in its entirety.

Already, you can begin to construct some techniques for diagnosing OSPF with the Cisco IOS. The Cisco IOS command "show ip ospf database" will provide you with a one-line summary of every LSA known to the router. A sample show ip ospf database display is provided below:

```
r3#show ip ospf database

       OSPF Router with ID (172.16.101.65) (Process ID 100)

Router Link States (Area 22)   (Type 1 LSA's)

Link ID         ADV Router      Age    Seq#          Checksum    Link count
172.16.2.2      172.16.2.2      618    0x80000004    0x3455      1
172.16.101.65   172.16.101.65   617    0x80000004    0x3510      1

                Net Link States (Area 22) (Type 2 LSA's)

Link ID         ADV Router      Age    Seq#          Checksum
10.1.1.1        172.16.101.65   617    0x80000001    0xD4D0

                Summary Net Link States (Area 22) (Type 3,4 LSA's)

Link ID         ADV Router      Age     Seq#          Checksum
172.16.1.0      172.16.2.2      1173    0x80000001    0xCEAF
172.16.1.0      172.16.101.65   360     0x80000003    0x1EFA
172.16.2.0      172.16.2.2      1173    0x80000001    0x19DB
172.16.2.0      172.16.101.65   360     0x80000003    0x91C6
```

At the very least, a single router LSA (Type 1) should appear for every router in a given OSPF area. Don't be surprised when you see a section labeled "Network Links," but not all of your networks appear! Only the "transit" networks—those with two or more routers attached—will appear. "Stub" networks, serviced by only a single router, will only appear as part of a specific router's router LSA. The "show ip ospf database" command has a number of options which let you view individual LSAs in detail:

```
r1#show ip ospf database ?
  asbr-summary        ASBR summary link states
  database-summary    Summary of database
  external            External link states (LSA Type 5)
  network             Network link states  (LSA Type 2)
  nssa-external       NSSA External link states (LSA Type 7)
  router              Router link states (LSA Type 1)
  summary             Network summary link states (LSA Type 3 & 4)
  <cr>
```

Classification of OSPF Routers

Not only does OSPF define different types of Link State Advertisements, it also defines different types of routers. Different OSPF routers generate different types of LSAs. Also, different types of OSPF routers are defined by their location in the OSPF network. An OSPF network can be divided into areas. Area boundaries are defined by OSPF router interface designations. Conversely, OSPF router types are also defined by interface designation. For example, if router R1 has a single interface in the backbone OSPF area, Area 0, and a second interface in a non-backbone area (Area 2, for example), the router is classified as an "area border router" or "backbone router." If router R2 has all its interfaces in a single area, it is defined as an "internal router" for that area.

Listed below is the summary description of different OSPF router types from RFC 1247:

> **Internal routers.** A router with all directly connected networks belonging to the same area. Routers with only backbone interfaces also belong to this category. These routers run a single copy of the basic routing algorithm.
>
> **Area border routers.** A router that attaches to multiple areas. Area border routers run multiple copies of the basic algorithm, one copy for each attached area and an additional copy for the backbone. Area border routers condense the topological information of their attached areas for distribution to the backbone. The backbone in turn distributes the information to the other areas.
>
> **Backbone routers.** A router that has an interface to the backbone. This includes all routers that interface to more than one area (i.e., area border routers). However, backbone routers do not have to be area border routers. Routers with all interfaces connected to the backbone are considered to be internal routers.
>
> **AS boundary routers.** A router that exchanges routing information with routers belonging to other Autonomous Systems. Such a router has

AS external routes that are advertised throughout the Autonomous System. The path to each AS boundary router is known by every router in the AS. This classification is completely independent of the previous classifications: AS boundary routers may be internal or area border routers, and may or may not participate in the backbone.

IP routes originating from different OSPF router types are represented by unique identifiers in a Cisco IP routing table. Note the highlighted portions of the Cisco IP routing table displayed below:

```
r3>show ip route
Codes: C - connected, S - static, I - IGRP, R - RIP, M - mobile, B - BGP
       D - EIGRP, EX - EIGRP external, O - OSPF, IA - OSPF inter area
       N1 - OSPF NSSA external type 1, N2 - OSPF NSSA external type 2
       E1 - OSPF external type 1, E2 - OSPF external type 2, E - EGP
       i - IS-IS, L1 - IS-IS level-1, L2 - IS-IS level-2, * - candidate default
       U - per-user static route, o - ODR

Gateway of last resort is not set

O E2 200.100.1.0/24 [110/20] via 172.16.3.4, 00:00:43, Serial0
                    [110/20] via 172.16.2.2, 00:00:44, Serial1
     172.16.0.0/16 is variably subnetted, 5 subnets, 2 masks
O       172.16.101.65/32 [110/129] via 172.16.2.2, 00:00:44, Serial1
                         [110/129] via 172.16.3.4, 00:00:44, Serial0
O       172.16.1.0/24 [110/128] via 172.16.2.2, 00:00:44, Serial1
C       172.16.2.0/24 is directly connected, Serial1
C       172.16.3.0/24 is directly connected, Serial0
O       172.16.100.33/32 [110/129] via 172.16.2.2, 00:00:44, Serial1
                         [110/129] via 172.16.3.4, 00:00:45, Serial0
     10.0.0.0/24 is subnetted, 1 subnets
O IA    10.1.1.0 [110/74] via 172.16.2.2, 00:00:45, Serial1
```

Routing table entries represented by the letter "O" only on the far left side of the routing table (column one) represent LSA Type One routes originating from an "internal" area router.

Routing table entries represented by the letters "O IA" on the far left side of the routing table (column one) represent routes originating from an "area border" router or "backbone" router.

Routing table entries represented by the letters "O E2" on the far left side of the routing table (column one) represent routes originating from an "autonomous system border" router.

OSPF Network Types

OSPF can support many different kinds of networks, of which broadcast networks—such as Ethernet, Token Ring, and most other LAN technologies—are just one. Cisco's implementation of OSPF defines five different network types:

- Point-to-point
- Broadcast
- Non-Broadcast
- Point-to-Multipoint
- Loopback

A commonly-used network type used in OSPF networks is the "point-to-point" OSPF interface type. It is used to link two OSPF speaking routers on a connection such as a dedicated leased line. OSPF makes no requirement that a point-to-point link must have IP addresses associated with it (it could be unnumbered), so these links are identified in a router LSA by listing a direct link to the remote router. If, in addition, the link has IP addresses, it is treated as a stub network.

Consider, for example, a Cisco 2501 router with one Ethernet and two serial interfaces. Assume each interface is fully configured with IP addresses and subnet masks, and that a basic OSPF configuration (no areas, tunnels, subinterfaces, etc.) is in use. The router should generate a single router LSA with five links—two for each of the serial interfaces (a point-to-point link to the remote OSPF router, and a stub network for the IP addresses), and one for the Ethernet.

If no other OSPF routers are detected on the Ethernet, its link will be for a stub network. If other OSPF routers are present on the Ethernet, its link will be to a transit network. In this case, the router will also participate in DR election on the Ethernet only (point-to-point links do not have Designated Routers). If elected DR, the router will source a second LSA—a network LSA for the Ethernet.

Be sure to note the difference between the LSAs and the links. The five links are all part of a single LSA—the router LSA.

Another type of network is the non-broadcast multi-access, typified by Frame-Relay or ATM. Neither broadcast nor point-to-point adequately describes an NBMA network. For one thing, the lack of a broadcast facility makes neighbor discovery difficult, and often implies that some routers may not be able to send directly to others, even though they may be on the same network!

The point-to-point network would require too many individual links to be defined in a large NBMA network. OSPF provides two ways of dealing with this situation: "point-to-multipoint" and "nonbroadcast."

A point-to-multipoint network behaves much like a collection of point-to-point networks. Routers advertise individual links to other routers, allowing

OSPF to find a valid path through even the most convoluted collection of Frame-Relay DLCIs or ATM VPI/VCI pairs. Of course, the disadvantage is the increased bandwidth requirements, due both to the router LSAs containing long lists of neighbor links and the lack of a Designated Router to manage the subnet overall.

Another approach is to use OSPF's NBMA mode, which treats the network much more like an Ethernet or other broadcast LAN technology. A Designated Router is elected, which sources a network LSA, and OSPF treats the WAN cloud overall as a transit network. There is one significant drawback, however: every router on the NBMA subnet must be able to communicate with all other routers on the same subnet. This demands either a full mesh configuration or a collection of "frame-relay map" statements on the individual routers. In short, if you have a full mesh or are willing to do some additional configuration work, use NBMA; otherwise, select point-to-multipoint and let OSPF do the hard work for you. Configuring OSPF on an NBMA network can be tricky. It involves addressing arcane NBMA issues, as well as OSPF issues. You must be able to first separate the issues and then make the two technologies (NBMA and OSPF) work together. Cisco offers many combinations for OSPF configuration over NBMA networks. Since NBMA technologies such as Frame-Relay and ATM are commonly used today, it is essential that you understand how to configure OSPF over NBMA networks. A more detailed section on configuring OSPF on NBMA networks is provided later in this Chapter. You should also review Chapter 4 ("Configuring Frame-Relay") and Chapter 7 ("Configuring ATM").

One final point must be emphasized here. No matter what type of network you chose for a subnet, all OSPF routers attached to it must agree on its type. Otherwise, they will refuse to operate at all on that subnet and will instead print warning messages about how other routers do not agree about the network type. While this may seem somewhat extreme, experience has shown that problems related to network type mismatches are easier to solve if the link does not work at all, rather than if it works only under a certain set of conditions.

Use the "show ip ospf interface" command to determine the OSPF interface type defined on a given interface. In the sample show ip ospf interface displays provided below, notice that the first one is an Ethernet interface defined as an OSPF network type "broadcast," and the second is a serial interface defined as an OSPF network type "point-to-point":

```
r2#sh ip ospf interface ethernet 0
Ethernet0 is up, line protocol is up
  Internet Address 172.16.17.2/24, Area 22
  Process ID 100, Router ID 172.16.17.2, Network Type BROADCAST, Cost: 10
  Transmit Delay is 1 sec, State BDR, Priority 1
  Designated Router (ID) 172.16.101.65, Interface address 172.16.17.1
  Backup Designated router (ID) 172.16.17.2, Interface address 172.16.17.2
```

```
  Timer intervals configured, Hello 10, Dead 40, Wait 40, Retransmit 5
    Hello due in 00:00:05
  Neighbor Count is 1, Adjacent neighbor count is 1
    Adjacent with neighbor 172.16.101.65  (Designated Router)
  Suppress hello for 0 neighbor(s)

r2#sh ip ospf interface serial 0
Serial0 is up, line protocol is up
  Internet Address 172.16.2.2/24, Area 0
  Process ID 100, Router ID 172.16.17.2, Network Type POINT_TO_POINT, Cost: 200
  Transmit Delay is 1 sec, State POINT_TO_POINT,
  Timer intervals configured, Hello 10, Dead 40, Wait 40, Retransmit 5
    Hello due in 00:00:04
  Neighbor Count is 1, Adjacent neighbor count is 1
    Adjacent with neighbor 161.11.1.1
  Suppress hello for 0 neighbor(s)
```

In summary, Cisco's implementation of OSPF defines five different network types:

- Point-to-point
- Broadcast
- Non-Broadcast
- Point-to-Multipoint
- Loopback

The "show ip ospf interface command" allows you to determine which network type is defined for a given OSPF participating interface:

```
r2(config-if)#ip ospf network ?
  broadcast             Specify OSPF Type of Network
  non-broadcast         Specify OSPF Type of Network
  point-to-multipoint   Specify OSPF Type of Network
```

OSPF Configuration Basics

Basic OSPF configuration is similar to RIP, IGRP and EIGRP configuration. Basic OSPF configuration involves a minimum of two steps:

1. Enable the OSPF routing protocol in global configuration mode with a process identification number:
   r2(config)#router ospf 100
   r2(config-router)#
   The OSPF process identification number is locally significant to a given router. The same process identification number can be used on the same routers in an OSPF domain, or a different one can be used.
2. Identify the locally-connected IP addresses which are intended to participate in the OSPF routing process. This is performed by entering one or

more "network" statements in OSPF routing protocol configuration mode. OSPF requires at least one "network" statement in router configuration mode. Unlike RIP, IGRP and EIGRP network configuration statements that define networks at the classful address boundaries only, OSPF allows a more specific address in its network statement. You can create an OSPF network statement that defines a particular subnet. You can even create an OSPF network statement that defines a complete 32-bit address match. A sample OSPF network statement is displayed below.

If you enter what is acceptable for a RIP, IGRP and EIGRP configuration with OSPF, you get the "% Incomplete command" error message. First a classful address is entered and rejected:

```
London(config-router)#network 172.16.0.0
% Incomplete command.
```

Second, a subnet address is entered and rejected:

```
London(config-router)#network 172.16.1.0
% Incomplete command.
```

By using the help facility, you see that OSPF is requesting a wildcard mask to follow the network address:

```
London(config-router)#network 172.16.1.0 ?
      A.B.C.D  OSPF wild card bits
```

Cisco's implementation of OSPF uses IP wildcard masks in OSPF network statements. These are the same wildcard masks used by IP access-access lists. Wildcard masks are entered in a decimal format, but are constructed in a binary format. Each wildcard mask is 32 bits in length. If a specific bit equals zero, the corresponding bit in the address must match. If a specific bit equals one, the corresponding bit in the address does not need to match. Using wildcard masks allows you to create a single network statement to define a range of IP addresses assigned to router interfaces that are intended to be included in an OSPF process. To learn more about creating complex wild card masks see Chapters 23 and 24.

In the network statement below, the address 172.16.1.0 is defined with a mask of 0.0.0.255. This can be interpreted as "Include all router interfaces with an IP prefix of 172.16.1.0. Do not care about all of the bits in the fourth octet."

```
London(config-router)#network 172.16.1.0 0.0.0.255
% Incomplete command.
```

However, even the wildcard mask is not enough. You must supply an "area ID" after the wildcard mask.

```
London(config-router)#network 172.16.1.0 0.0.0.255 ?
        area Set the OSPF area ID

London(config-router)#network 172.16.1.0 0.0.0.255 area ?
        <0-4294967295>   OSPF area ID as a decimal value
        A.B.C.D          OSPF area ID in IP address format

London(config-router)#network 172.16.1.0 0.0.0.255 area 0
```

Once a network address, wildcard mask and area ID are supplied, OSPF network statement configuration is complete. OSPF network statement configuration is displayed in the following manner in running configuration;

```
!
router ospf 100
        network 172.16.0.0 0.0.255.255 area 0
        network 10.1.1.0 0.0.0.255 area 0
```

Once you have performed these basic OSPF configuration steps, perform a "show ip OSPF interface" command to verify that OSPF is operational on the desired interfaces. An operational OSPF interface will list information similar to the show ip ospf interface displayed below:

```
r2#sh ip ospf interface ethernet 0
Ethernet0 is up, line protocol is up
  Internet Address 172.16.17.2/24, Area 22
  Process ID 100, Router ID 172.16.17.2, Network Type BROADCAST, Cost: 10
  Transmit Delay is 1 sec, State BDR, Priority 1
  Designated Router (ID) 172.16.101.65, Interface address 172.16.17.1
  Backup Designated router (ID) 172.16.17.2, Interface address 172.16.17.2
  Timer intervals configured, Hello 10, Dead 40, Wait 40, Retransmit 5
    Hello due in 00:00:05
  Neighbor Count is 1, Adjacent neighbor count is 1
    Adjacent with neighbor 172.16.101.65  (Designated Router)
  Suppress hello for 0 neighbor(s)
```

If you perform a "show ip ospf interface" command for a specific interface and you see a listing similar to the one displayed below, YOU MUST GO NO FURTHER IN YOUR OSPF CONFIGURATION!

r4#show ip ospf interface ethernet 0
Ethernet0 is up, line protocol is up
OSPF not enabled on this interface

IF YOU SEE A DISPLAY SIMILAR TO THE ONE ABOVE, YOU MUST RETURN TO YOUR OSPF NETWORK CONFIGURATION STATEMENTS. YOU MUST MAKE SURE THE OSPF NETWORK STATEMENTS INCLUDE THE IP ADDRESS ON THE INTERFACE THAT IS DISPLAYING AN "OSPF not enabled on this interface" STATEMENT. IF A ROUTER'S OSPF ROUTING PROCESS DOES NOT RECOGNIZE THAT OSPF IS RUNNING ON A GIVEN INTERFACE, NO SUBSEQUENT OSPF ACTIVITY WILL BE PERFORMED ON THAT INTERFACE.

Once the OSPF routing protocol is enabled and OSPF is active on the desired interfaces, OSPF speaking routers create the following three tables:

1. an OSPF Neighbor Table
2. an OSPF Link State Database
3. a Main Routing

The OSPF Neighbor Table and OSPF HELLO Packets

OSPF discovers its neighbors by means of a sub-protocol called the Hello protocol. On a pre-defined periodic basis, an OSPF router will transmit a Hello packet on all its configured interfaces. OSPF Hello packets use the multicast address of 224.0.0.5. The interval for sending out a Hello packet varies depending on the OSPF interface type. Below is a table of the default Hello and Dead intervals associated with the different OSPF interface types (the dead interval will be described later in this section):

Interface Type	Hello Interval	Dead Interval
Broadcast	10	40
Point-to-Point	10	40
Non-broadcast	30	120
Point-to-Multipoint	30	120

The Hello packet includes the following information:

1. Router ID(RID)
2. the subnet mask defined on the participating interface
3. a router priority number (discussed in the next section)
4. the timer values ("HelloInterval" and "RouterDeadInterval") associated with the Hello protocol
5. a list of Router IDs from which the router has heard Hellos on this interface

It is critical that you understand the importance of the router ID and how it is selected. The router ID, or "RID", is the 32-bit unique identifier of an OSPF router. EACH OSPF ROUTER MUST HAVE A UNIQUE RID! In a Cisco environment, the RID is selected as the highest IP address on an active interface. If any loopback interfaces exist on a router, the RID is the highest IP address of all active loopback addresses. Loopback interfaces take precedence over physical interfaces in the RID assignment process. Addresses used for OSPF RIDs do not need to be defined by an OSPF network statement. The RID is selected from all active router interfaces, both OSPF-defined interfaces and non-OSPF defined interfaces. IT IS CRITICAL THAT YOU KEEP RID ASSIGNMENTS STABLE AND CONSISTENT IN AN OSPF NETWORK. VIRTUALLY ALL OSPF OPERATIONS INVOLVE REFERENCING THE RID. IF A ROUTER'S RID IS CHANGED IN AN ACTIVE OSPF NETWORK, OTHER ROUTERS WILL BECOME CONFUSED.

Once two OSPF routers see each other and agree on a basic set of parameters, they enter into the "2-way" state. "2-Way" (a technical term defined used in RFC 1247) connectivity is achieved when the router receives a Hello from a neighbor and sees its own RID in the packet's list of RIDs. This indicates that the remote router has seen your Hellos, and of course the local router has just received a Hello from a remote router. The machines have bidirectional communication. At this point the routers are termed "neighbors".

Two OSPF routers will only form a neighbor relationship if the information received in the Hello packets is consistent with local settings. Timer values must also match. The subnet mask must match; otherwise, the routers will not become neighbors and will generate error messages instead. As mentioned before, this behavior is a deliberate decision designed to call attention to potential misconfigurations as early as possible.

You can view the OSPF neighbor formation process with debug ip ospf adj. In the first debug output displayed below, you see the message:

```
OSPF: 2 Way Communication to 172.16.101.65 on Ethernet0, state 2WAY
```

This reflects a successful exchange of Hello packets.

In the debug output below, the Hello packets exchanged do not match with the subnet masks exchanged:

```
OSPF: Mismatched hello parameters from 172.16.17.1
Dead R 40 C 40, Hello R 10 C 10 Mask R 255.255.255.0 C 255.255.255.224
```

If Hello parameters do not match, OSPF neighbors cannot attain a 2-way state. Attaining the 2-way state is a requirement for OSPF neighbors to form an "adjacency." Adjacencies between OSPF neighbors allow OSPF link state databases to be formed.

Adjacencies

Neighbor routers do not necessarily exchange link state updates. They must become "adjacent" for this to occur. Neighbors on point-to-point and point-to-multipoint links always become adjacent. Neighbors with broadcast and non-broadcast OSPF interface types form adjacencies subject to the Designated Router rules, as explained below. Once a router has decided to become adjacent with one of its neighbors, it begins by exchanging a full copy of its link state database, and expects its neighbor to do the same. After proceeding through several phases, the routers will have synchronized their link state databases and become adjacent. (These are the states a pair of OSPF routers will go through: "Down," "Init" (Hello seen, but lacking our RID), "2-Way" (neighbors), "ExStart" (beginning to exchange link state databases), "Exchange," "Loading" (exchange done, retransmitting dropped LSAs), and "Full." NBMA networks also have an "Attempt" phase, roughly between" Down" and "Init.") LSAs will now be generated indicating the presence of the new adjacency to the rest of the network.

Once routers have become neighbors, they continue to exchange Hello packets. If a fixed period of time (the "Dead Interval") passes without a Hello from a neighbor, the neighbor relationship reverts to the "Down" state. If the "Down" neighbor was also adjacent, a link state update is generated, notifying the network that the two devices can no longer communicate. By default, the Dead Interval is four times the Hello interval for a given interface type.

Whenever a router receives a link state update, it immediately forwards the update to all its adjacencies, except the one which sent it. The other routers will also forward it to their adjacencies, and this process continues until all the routers have received copies of the new LSA. LSA updates must be acknowledged, so each router receives a positive confirmation about each update it forwards.

If a router receives an LSA that duplicates one it already has, it basically ignores the duplicate. Thus, a set of routers formed in a loop will simply pass a new LSA around until it reaches a router that has already heard it from another direction.

In a successful OSPF Adjacency formation process, OSPF neighbors will attain the "full" neighbor state. You can examine the status of a router's OSPF neighbor relationships with the "show ip ospf neighbor" command:

```
r2#show ip ospf neighbor

Neighbor ID     Pri   State           Dead Time   Address         Interface
172.16.101.65     1   FULL/DR         00:00:32    172.16.17.1     Ethernet0
161.11.1.1        1   FULL/  -        00:00:32    172.16.2.3      Serial0
172.16.101.65     1   FULL/  -        00:00:32    172.16.1.1      Serial1
```

You can view the results of the adjacency process on an LSA accumulation basis by examining an OSPF router's Link State database. This can be performed on a Cisco router with the "show ip OSPF database" command:

```
r2#show ip ospf database

       OSPF Router with ID (172.16.2.2) (Process ID 100)

            Router Link States (Area 0)
```

```
Link ID         ADV Router      Age    Seq#         Checksum  Link count
161.11.1.1      161.11.1.1      683    0x8000000D   0x6FA4    4
172.16.2.2      172.16.2.2      678    0x80000002   0xCF92    4
172.16.4.4      172.16.4.4      795    0x80000006   0xEA30    5
172.16.101.65   172.16.101.65   683    0x8000000B   0x3190    4

                Summary Net Link States (Area 0)

Link ID         ADV Router      Age    Seq#         Checksum
172.16.17.0     172.16.2.2      609    0x80000001   0xFFA4
172.16.17.0     172.16.101.65   615    0x80000012   0xAA46
```

The table displayed above provides a summary of all the LSAs in a Link State database. If you want more detailed information on a specific LSA, use the show ip ospf database options. Listed below is a sample display of the contents in the first LSA in the Link State database shown above. The LSA is identified by the RID of the router that sourced the LSA. In this case, it is RID 161.11.1.1.

```
r2>show ip ospf database router 161.11.1.1

OSPF Router with ID (172.16.2.2) (Process ID 100)

                Router Link States (Area 0)

  LS age: 939
  Options: (No TOS-capability, DC)
  LS Type: Router Links
  Link State ID: 161.11.1.1
  Advertising Router: 161.11.1.1
  LS Seq Number: 8000000E
  Checksum: 0x6DA5
  Length: 72
   Number of Links: 4

    Link connected to: another Router (point-to-point)
     (Link ID) Neighboring Router ID: 172.16.2.2
     (Link Data) Router Interface address: 172.16.2.3
      Number of TOS metrics: 0
       TOS 0 Metrics: 64

    Link connected to: a Stub Network
     (Link ID) Network/subnet number: 172.16.2.0
     (Link Data) Network Mask: 255.255.255.0
      Number of TOS metrics: 0
       TOS 0 Metrics: 64

    Link connected to: another Router (point-to-point)
     (Link ID) Neighboring Router ID: 172.16.4.4
     (Link Data) Router Interface address: 172.16.3.3
      Number of TOS metrics: 0
```

```
TOS 0 Metrics: 64

Link connected to: a Stub Network
 (Link ID) Network/subnet number: 172.16.3.0
 (Link Data) Network Mask: 255.255.255.0
  Number of TOS metrics: 0
   TOS 0 Metrics: 64
```

You can watch the OSPF adjacency formation process with debug ip ospf adj:

```
OSPF: Build router LSA for area 22, router ID 172.16.1.2
OSPF: 2 Way Communication to 172.16.101.65 on Serial1, state 2WAY
OSPF: Send DBD to 172.16.101.65 on Serial1 seq 0xC54 opt 0x2 flag 0x7 len 32
OSPF: Rcv DBD from 172.16.101.65 on Serial1 seq 0x1F7B opt 0x2 flag 0x7 len 32
state EXSTART
OSPF: NBR Negotiation Done. We are the SLAVE
OSPF: Send DBD to 172.16.101.65 on Serial1 seq 0x1F7B opt 0x2 flag 0x2 len 132
OSPF: Rcv DBD from 172.16.101.65 on Serial1 seq 0x1F7C opt 0x2 flag 0x3 len 152
state EXSTART
OSPF: Send DBD to 172.16.101.65 on Serial1 seq 0x1F7C opt 0x2 flag 0x0 len 32
OSPF: Database request to 172.16.101.65
OSPF: sent LS REQ packet to 172.16.1.1, length 24
OSPF: Rcv DBD from 172.16.101.65 on Serial1 seq 0x1F7D opt 0x2 flag 0x1 len 32
state EXSTART
OSPF: Exchange Done with 172.16.101.65 on Serial1
OSPF: Send DBD to 172.16.101.65 on Serial1 seq 0x1F7D opt 0x2 flag 0x0 len 32
OSPF: Build router LSA for area 0, router ID 172.16.1.2
OSPF: Build router LSA for area 0, router ID 172.16.1.2
OSPF: Retransmitting request to 172.16.101.65 on Serial1
OSPF: Database request to 172.16.101.65
OSPF: sent LS REQ packet to 172.16.1.1, length 12
OSPF: Retransmitting request to 172.16.101.65 on Serial1
OSPF: Database request to 172.16.101.65
OSPF: sent LS REQ packet to 172.16.1.1, length 12
OSPF: Build router LSA for area 0, router ID 172.16.1.2
OSPF: Synchronized with 172.16.101.65 on Serial1, state FULL
```

Notice how the OSPF adjacency process went through a number of states. In the debug output displayed above, the adjacency process moved through the following three states:

1. 2-way
2. exstart
3. full

OSPF Designated Routers

On a broadcast network such as Ethernet, it would be quite inefficient for each OSPF router to form adjacencies with all the others. The duplicate traffic in link state updates would become prohibitive. Furthermore, a network LSA for the Ethernet itself must be generated, and one of the routers must be selected to do this. For these reasons, a Designated Router (DR) is "elected" for each broadcast and NBMA network. A Backup Designed Router (BDR) is also elected to monitor the operation of the DR and step up to fill its role should it fail in some manner. These concepts are applied on a per-subnet basis. Each independent broadcast or NBMA segment will have its own DR and BDR. A single router with multiple Ethernet or Token Ring interfaces might be DR/BDR on all of them, on some but not others, or on none.

Other routers ("DR Other") form adjacencies with the DR and BDR and exchange link state updates with them, preferably through hardware-assisted multicast. Two "DR Other" routers will not become adjacent; instead, they remain in the "2-Way" neighbor state. So DR and BDR routers form full adjacencies with all their neighbors, while "DR Other" routers form only two adjacencies (over a given broadcast segment), regardless of how many neighbors they actually have.

The same rules apply, though with slight modifications, for NBMA networks. DR/BDR election is performed via the Hello Protocol. Every broadcast or NBMA interface can be configured with a "priority" used during the election process. The priorities are announced in the Hello packets, with higher priorities having a greater chance of election. Whenever a new DR or BDR is required, the neighbor with the highest priority is selected. Since all OSPF routers see all Hello packets, agreement between the routers should be implicit. Setting a priority to zero prohibits a router from becoming DR or BDR, even if no other eligible routers exist. If all routers on a subnet have a priority of zero, OSPF will not function.

Once a DR and BDR have been elected, they form adjacencies with all other OSPF speakers on the subnet. The DR will source a network LSA for the subnet and perform all the operations required by the flooding procedure. The BDR will monitor the operation of the DR, ready to become DR if necessary. Since the BDR is already adjacent with the other routers, this should be a fairly rapid process. The BDR will become the new DR upon detecting a failure of the DR, typically by missing its Hello packets. An election process will select a new BDR.

However, every Hello packet also contains the originating router's idea of who the DR and BDR currently are. If a new router joins a network, it learns about the existing DR and BDR from its neighbors and forms adjacencies with them. A new election occurs only when required. In particular, if a new router with a high priority joins a working subnet, it will not supercede out the current DR. The existing DR/BDR will continue to function. If the DR should fail, the BDR will become DR, and the high priority router will then be elected BDR.

There is no way to force a particular router to become DR other than setting all other router priorities to zero.

Use the Cisco IOS "show" commands—in particular, "show ip ospf neighbors" and "show ip ospf interfaces"—to monitor the status of a router's neighbor connections. On point-to-point and point-to-multipoint subnets, a router should form adjacencies with all its neighbors, so the neighbor count and adjacency count should be equal on these network types, and all neighbor entries should show a "Full" status once the network is stable. On broadcast and NBMA networks, the DR and BDR should form adjacencies with all their neighbors, and their output should show all neighbors in the "Full" state. Other routers (not DR or BDR) on these types of networks will only form adjacencies with the DR and BDR, so they should show two adjacencies regardless of how many neighbors they have. The DR and BDR should show "Full" as their state, while other neighbors (DR-OTHER) will show "2-Way."

Manipulating the DR/BDR Election Process on a Cisco Router

You can manipulate the OSPF DR/BDR election process with the following Cisco interface configuration command:

```
r2(config-if)#ip ospf priority ?
  <0-255>  Priority
```

An interface with the highest OSPF priority will become the DR. The second-highest OSPF priority will become the BDR. If an interface has an OSPF priority of zero, it will never become either the DR or BDR.

Areas

A large OSPF configuration can become prohibitively expensive in terms of the memory and computational requirements on the routers. A router connected to a large network via only a 56 Kbps serial link does not need to know about every link failure ten hops away. Nor does it need to recompute its routing table every time such a failure occurs. To address this problem, OSPF's designers introduced the concept of "areas." An area is a group of routers that maintain complete local link state databases, but only export summary advertisements to other areas. However, areas have one major drawback: they must be manually configured, and the configuration can become complex.

Areas are numbered, typically with small integers (although the area number is a 32-bit field). Areas must be contiguous; you cannot split one area up into two disconnected pieces. (Use two different areas in this case.) Area 0 is special; it is called the "backbone" and must have connections to all other areas. All inter-area transit traffic is passed via the backbone. Every valid OSPF configuration must have an area 0, so if you use only a single OSPF area for your entire network, it must be area 0.

In the Cisco IOS configuration language, areas are configured as an extension of the "network" command (network 172.16.0.0 0.0.255.255 area 0), which is used to indicate which interfaces are in which areas. Both interfaces and subnets can only exist in a single area; routers are used to connect areas. A router with interfaces in multiple areas is called an Area Border Router (ABR).

An ABR builds link state databases for each of the areas to which it is connected, using the standard OSPF procedure for each area independently. Network addresses in an area are passed to other areas in the form of Summary LSAs, which include the ABR's computed metric to the destination. A different Summary LSA is generated for every subnet. Thus, routers within an area know about their area's topology, all network addresses in other areas, and the metrics to those inter-area routes at the ABRs. No detailed information about remote topology appears within an area.

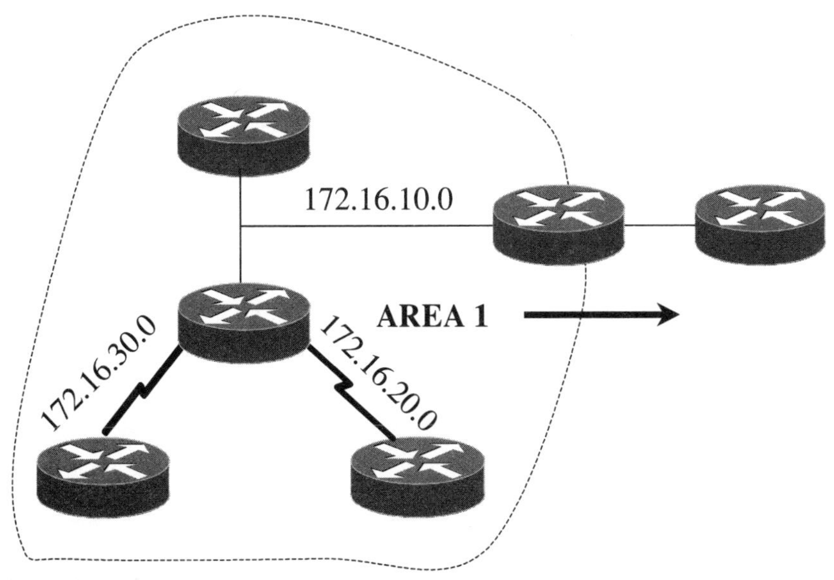

FIGURE 11–2 A third OSPF router is added to the configuration.

Link state updates cause the ABR to recompute its routing table normally. If the new table contains new inter-area routes, new Summary LSAs are generated for them and flooded. If routes have disappeared from the routing table, the corresponding Summary LSAs are retracted. If existing routes have changed metrics, updated Summary LSAs are generated and flooded. Thus, routers within an area receive constant updates as the ABR's view of the network changes. In particular, routers can choose between multiple ABRs based on their advertised metrics.

Virtual Links

Area 0, as has already been mentioned, is special. All other areas must possess a connection to area 0. Normally this is done with a router with interfaces in both area 0 and the other area (an Area Border Router or Backbone Router).

Sometimes, however, an area must be connected to the backbone via a third area. This can be accomplished with a "virtual link." A virtual link connects two ABRs, making both part of area 0.

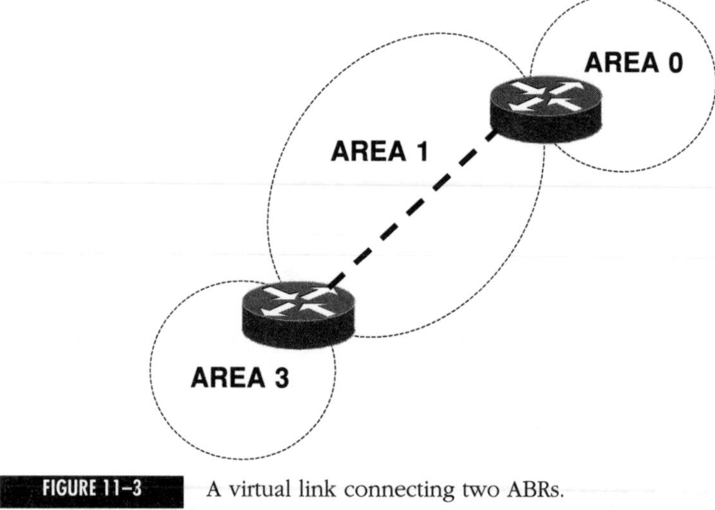

FIGURE 11–3 A virtual link connecting two ABRs.

Virtual links can also be used to connect two discontinuous pieces of area 0. Remember, area 0 cannot simply be split into two different areas.

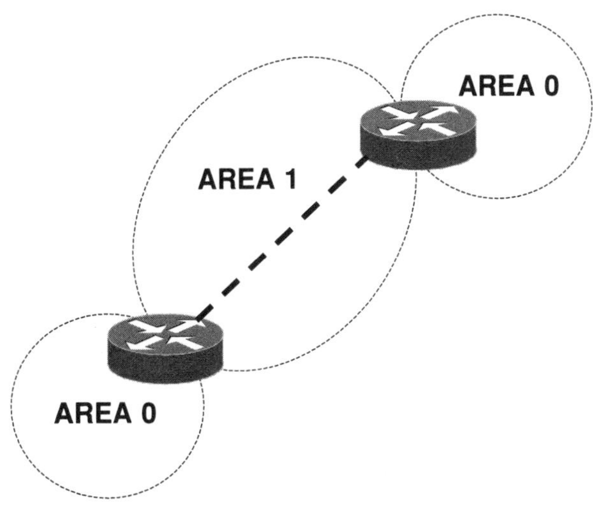

FIGURE 11-4 A virtual link connecting discontiguous Area 0 routers.

Virtual links can also be used to add links to the backbone area to improve its routing behavior.

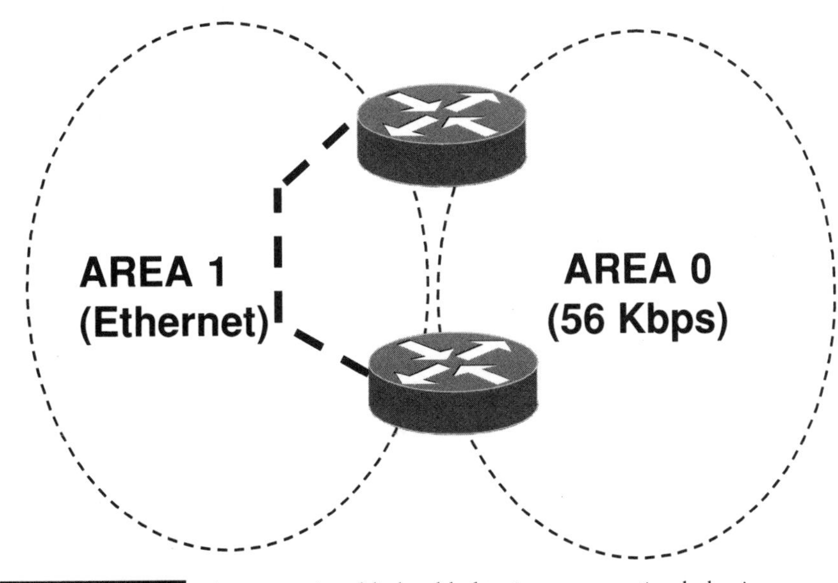

FIGURE 11-5 An extra virtual link added to improve routing behavior.

Configuring Virtual Links

You can configure a virtual link on a Cisco router with the following OSPF routing protocol configuration command:

```
r2(config)#router ospf 100
r2(config-router)#area xxxx virtual-link A.B.C.D
```

xxxx = the area to cross when creating and maintaining the virtual link

A.B.C.D = the remote virtual link's peer RID. The command must be placed on both routers forming the virtual link.

NOTE THAT, IF YOU CHANGE THE RID FOR A ROUTER PARTICIPATING IN A VIRTUAL LINK, YOU MUST RECONFIGURE THE VIRTUAL LINK.

You can view the status of a virtual link with the following "show" command:

```
r2#show ip ospf virtual-links
Virtual Link OSPF_VL0 to router 10.1.1.1 is up
  Run as demand circuit
  DoNotAge LSA allowed.
  Transit area 1234, Cost of using 65535
  Transmit Delay is 1 sec, State UP,
  Timer intervals configured, Hello 10, Dead 40, Wait 40, Retransmit 5
```

OSPF Route Redistribution

OSPF supports redistribution of information from other routing protocols. Such routes are termed "external" and give rise to External LSAs. OSPF routers that generate External LSAs (LSA Type 5) are termed "Autonomous System Boundary Routers" (ASBRs). This term arises because, in a pure OSPF network, external information will only come from BGP or default routes, both of which lead to other autonomous systems. However, any routing source external to OSPF is treated the same way, so a router redistributing RIP into OSPF will become an ASBR.

A default route (0.0.0.0 0.0.0.0) is a special case of an External LSA.

Routes redistributed from non-OSPF sources and a default route are further subclassified as Level One and Level Two exterior routes. A Level One exterior route (identified in a Cisco IP routing table as an "E1" route) increase the metric of the exterior route as it is propagated through the OSPF domain; a Level Two exterior route (identified in a Cisco IP routing table as an "E2" route) does not. For an E2 route, whatever its metric is at the point of route redistribution, it will retain this value as the network is propagated through the OSPF domain.

OSPF route redistribution will be covered in greater detail in Chapter 12.

Stub Areas

OSPF's area structure can be further extended with the concepts of "stub areas", "very stubby areas", and "not-so-stubby areas". Many OSPF areas possess a single connection to the OSPF backbone. These areas can be classified in the Cisco hierarchy of core, distribution and access as "access-level" areas.

A stub area is an area which does not receive or originate any external routes, but instead relies on default routing to reach external destinations. Summary LSAs are propagated normally into stub areas. In other words, routing occurs normally for locations within the OSPF network, but only default routing is used for external locations. A stub area is appropriate for an Internet Provider that imports a large number of external routes via BGP, for example, but does not want to propagate this information beyond the core of the network.

You can configure a stub area on a Cisco router with the following OSPF routing protocol configuration command:

```
r2(config)#router ospf 100
r2(config-router)#area 22 stub
```

This command must be entered on every router in the specified stub area.

A totally stubby area is not part of the OSPF specification. Rather, it is a Cisco extension that is only configured on the ABRs for such an area. Such an ABR will not propagate Summary LSAs, so a very stubby area will depend on default routing, both for external and inter-area routes.

You can configure a totally stubby area on a Cisco router with the following OSPF routing protocol configuration command:

```
r2(config)#router ospf 100
r2(config-router)#area 22 stub
```

Like a stubby area, this command must be entered on every router in the specified stub area.

On the area border router(s) only, enter the following OSPF routing protocol configuration command:

```
r2(config)#router ospf 100
r2(config-router)#area 22 stub no-summary
```

A not-so-stubby area is much like a stub area, except that it is allowed to announce external routes, even though it does not receive external routes. This configuration would be appropriate for a stub area running RIP, for example, where redistribution into OSPF was desired. Since redistributed routes appear as External LSAs, stub areas normally cannot support any kind of redistribution. Not-so-stubby areas use LSA (a Type 7) that allow redistribution to occur within them.

Route Summarization

Surprisingly, OSPF supports route summarization. At first glance, this might seem impossible, since OSPF is based on building a comprehensive, detailed and exhaustive map of a network's topology. Summarization can occur at two points in an OSPF network: (1) at area borders, where ABRs can be configured to announce a single Summary LSA for a range of networks residing within a specific area and (2) on ASBRs at route redistribution points where OSPF routes are being exported to another routing protocol, or non-OSPF routes are being imported into OSPF.

By default, Cisco routers do not summarize OSPF routes. It must be configured manually.

Inter-Area Route Summarization

To configure inter-area route summarization, use the following OSPF routing protocol command on an ABR router:

```
r2(config)#router ospf 100
r2(config-router)#area xxx range A.B.C.D YYY.YYY.YYY.YYY
```

xxx = area to summarize the routes for

A.B.C.D = summary address to announce to other areas

YYY.YYY.YYY.YYY = summary address mask

For example, consider an OSPF area "1234" containing the following subnets:

- 172.16.100.16
- 172.16.100.32
- 172.16.100.48
- 172.16.100.60

	128	**64**	**32**	**16**	**8**	**4**	**2**	**1**
16	0	0	0	1	0	0	0	0
32	0	0	1	0	0	0	0	0
48	0	0	1	1	0	0	0	0
60	0	0	1	1	1	1	0	0

In this example, the summary address is 172.16.100.0 255.255.255.192. Only the first two bits are shared by all four addresses.

You want to summarize these addresses in a single statement and announce them to the other OSPF areas. Enter the following Cisco configuration commands on the ABR router:

```
r2(config)#router ospf 100
r2(config-router)#area 1234 range 172.16.100.0 255.255.255.192
```

Inter-Routing Domain Route Summarization

To configure OSPF route summarization between OSPF and another routing protocol, such as IGRP or RIP, use the following OSPF routing protocol command on an ABR router:

```
r2(config)#router ospf 100

r2(config-router)#summary-address A.B.C.D YYY.YYY.YYY.YYY
```

A.B.C.D = summary address to use during the route redistribution process

YYY.YYY.YYY.YYY = summary address mask

For example, summarize the following routes that are being imported from RIP into OSPF: 172.16.140.0, 172.16.141.0 and 172.16.149.0

	128	**64**	**32**	**16**	**8**	**4**	**2**	**1**
140	1	0	0	0	1	1	0	0
141	1	0	0	0	1	1	0	1
149	1	0	0	1	0	1	0	1

In this example, the summary address is 172.16.128.0 255.255.224.0. Only the first three bits are shared by all three addresses. Configure the summary-address with this address and prefix:

```
r2(config)#router ospf 100
r2(config-router)#summary-address A.B.C.D YYY.YYY.YYY.YYY
```

Configuring OSPF Over Non-Broadcast Multiaccess Networks

When OSPF is configured on the physical interface of a non-broadcast multiaccess technology, such as Frame-Relay or ATM, it assigns the default network type of NON_BROADCAST. When OSPF is configured on point-to-point subinterfaces, OSPF assigns the POINT_TO_POINT OSPF interface type. This causes an acute problem with OSPF. For OSPF to exchange routing information with a neighbor on the same network, the two neighbors must have the same "Hello parameters." When a NBMA network is configured with a combination of physical interfaces and logical interfaces, OSPF network type mismatches are likely to occur. The following debug messages were generated between one Frame-Relay peer, with OSPF configured on a physical interface and a second Frame-Relay peer configured on a point-to-point subinterface:

```
OSPF: Mismatched hello parameters from 172.16.1.1
Dead R 40 C 120, Hello R 10 C 30  Mask R 255.255.255.0 C 255.255.255.0
```

```
OSPF: Mismatched hello parameters from 172.16.1.1
Dead R 40 C 120, Hello R 10 C 30  Mask R 255.255.255.0 C 255.255.255.0
OSPF: Mismatched hello parameters from 172.16.1.1
Dead R 40 C 120, Hello R 10 C 30  Mask R 255.255.255.0 C 255.255.255.0
```

OSPF configured on a physical Frame-Relay interface assumes the default OSPF interface type of non-broadcast. An OSPF non-broadcast interface has settings of 30 seconds for HELLO intervals and 120 seconds for DEAD intervals. A point-to-point subinterface is defined by OSPF as a point-to-point interface type, which has settings of 10 seconds for HELLO intervals and 40 seconds for DEAD intervals. In situations where OSPF is configured on one Frame-Relay physical interface, and OSPF is also configured on another Frame-Relay peer's point-to-point subinterface interface, default OSPF configurations will create "Hello mismatches," the OSPF adjacencies will not form, and OSPF will not work.

A remedy to this problem is to use the Cisco IOS interface configuration command "IP OSPF network" to make sure that OSPF interface types match on a Frame-Relay network. The options of this command are listed below:

```
Satellite-1(config-if)#ip ospf network ?
```

Broadcast	Specify OSPF Type of Network
Non-Broadcast	Specify OSPF Type of Network
Point-to-Multipoint	Specify OSPF Type of Network

By using this command with one of the three options listed above, we can assure that OSPF neighbors on the same Frame-Relay network will have the same network type. A popular selection for OSPF networks is the point-to-multipoint option. By adding this interface configuration statement to every OSPF interface on the Frame-Relay network, the problem of OSPF network type mismatches will be avoided.

When configuring OSPF on an NBMA network, remember the following table:

Interface Type	Hello/Dead Interval	Elects DR/BDR routers
Broadcast	10/40	DR/BDR
Point-to-Point	10/40	no DR/BDR
Non-Broadcast	30/120	DR/BDR
Point-to-Multipoint	30/120	no DR/BDR

Configuring OSPF over ISDN/DDR Links

The primary issue with configuring OSPF over an ISDN/DDR link is that the OSPF Hello traffic will keep the ISDN line up indefinitely. Cisco has a solution to limit OSPF Hello traffic over an ISDN link: IP OSPF demand-circuit (an interface configuration command).

In the show dialer statement below, notice that interface BRI0:1 was activated by a packet with the destination address of 224.0.0.5. This IP address is an OSPF multicast.

```
r2#show dialer

BRI0 - dialer type = ISDN

Dial String    Successes    Failures    Last called    Last status
2001                   6           1    00:00:57       successful
0 incoming call(s) have been screened.
0 incoming call(s) rejected for callback.

BRI0:1 - dialer type = ISDN
Idle timer (120 secs), Fast idle timer (20 secs)
Wait for carrier (30 secs), Re-enable (15 secs)
Dialer state is data link layer up
Dial reason: ip (s=177.11.1.2, d=224.0.0.5)
Time until disconnect 112 secs
Connected to 2001

BRI0:2 - dialer type = ISDN
Idle timer (120 secs), Fast idle timer (20 secs)
Wait for carrier (30 secs), Re-enable (15 secs)
Dialer state is idle
r2#show dialer
```

In the debug dialer packet and debug ip ospf packet output displayed below, you can see that OSPF multicast traffic is constantly going over the BRI0 line:

```
BRI0: ip (s=177.11.1.2, d=224.0.0.5), 68 bytes, interesting (ip PERMIT)
BRI0: sending broadcast to ip 177.11.1.1
OSPF: rcv. v:2 t:1 l:48 rid:177.11.1.1
      aid:0.0.0.0 chk:B982 aut:0 auk: from BRI0
OSPF: Rcv hello from 177.11.1.1 area 0 from BRI0 177.11.1.1
OSPF: End of hello processing
BRI0: ip (s=177.11.1.2, d=224.0.0.5), 68 bytes, interesting (ip PERMIT)
BRI0: sending broadcast to ip 177.11.1.1
OSPF: rcv. v:2 t:1 l:48 rid:177.11.1.1
      aid:0.0.0.0 chk:B982 aut:0 auk: from BRI0
OSPF: Rcv hello from 177.11.1.1 area 0 from BRI0 177.11.1.1
OSPF: End of hello processing
BRI0: ip (s=177.11.1.2, d=224.0.0.5), 68 bytes, interesting (ip PERMIT)
BRI0: sending broadcast to ip 177.11.1.1
```

Configuring OSPF over ISDN/DDR Without ON-DEMAND CIRCUIT

In the OSPF show commands displayed below, notice that a timer value is defined in "show ip ospf neighbor," and no entries are marked DNA (do not age) in the link state database. Therefore, OSPF Hello traffic will keep the ISDN link up indefinitely.

```
r1#show ip ospf neighbor

Neighbor ID     Pri             State    Dead Time     Address       Interface
172.16.201.2    1               FULL/    00:00:37      172.16.1.2    BRI0

r1#show ip ospf database

OSPF Router with ID (172.16.10.1) (Process ID 100)


               Router Link States (Area 0)

Link ID         ADV Router      Age      Seq#          Checksum      Link count
172.16.10.1     172.16.10.1     50       0x80000020    0xC655        4
172.16.201.2    172.16.201.2    51       0x80000021    0xF22C        4
```

Configuring OSPF over ISDN/DDR With ON-DEMAND CIRCUIT

By entering the interface configuration command "IP OSPF demand-circuit" on one side of a BRI connection, OSPF adjacencies will be formed and ongoing OSPF Hellos will be suppressed. OSPF Hello suppression is manifested in the following "show ip OSPF" commands. Notice in the "show ip ospf" interface how this interface is explicitly listed as being "Run as demand circuit," and that Hellos are suppressed for the adjacent neighbor.

```
r2#show ip ospf inte bri0
BRI0 is up, line protocol is up (spoofing)
  Internet Address 177.11.1.2/24, Area 0
  Process ID 100, Router ID 144.10.1.1, Network Type POINT_TO_POINT, Cost: 1562
  Configured as demand circuit.
  Run as demand circuit.
  DoNotAge LSA allowed.
  Transmit Delay is 1 sec, State POINT_TO_POINT,
  Timer intervals configured, Hello 10, Dead 40, Wait 40, Retransmit 5
    Hello due in 00:00:03
  Neighbor Count is 1, Adjacent neighbor count is 1
    Adjacent with neighbor 177.11.1.1  (Hello suppressed)
  Suppress hello for 1 neighbor(s)
```

With IP OSPF demand-circuit configured, notice how there is no value for the dead time. Normally, there is an actual value in this column.

```
Neighbor ID     Pri    State     Dead Time    Address        Interface
172.16.201.2    1      FULL/     -            172.16.1.2     BRI0
```

When a packet is received by an OSPF demand-circuit peer at the time of the expiration of the dead timer, the following message debug message was generated:

```
OSPF: Dead event ignored for 177.11.1.1 on demand circuit BRI0
```

With IP OSPF demand-circuit configured, notice how link-state database entries learned over the ISDN interface are marked DNA (Do Not Age).

```
r1#show ip ospf database

               OSPF Router with ID (172.16.10.1) (Process ID 100)


Router Link States (Area 0)

Link ID         ADV Router      Age       Seq#          Checksum   Link count
172.16.10.1     172.16.10.1     216       0x8000001E    0xCA53     4
172.16.201.2    172.16.201.2    6(DNA)    0x8000001E    0xF829     4
```

Finally, even though the BRI0 interface is down, OSPF retains routes learned via the BRI interface in the routing table.

```
r1#sh ip ro
Codes: C - connected, S - static, I - IGRP, R - RIP, M - mobile, B - BGP
       D - EIGRP, EX - EIGRP external, O - OSPF, IA - OSPF inter area
       N1 - OSPF NSSA external type 1, N2 - OSPF NSSA external type 2
       E1 - OSPF external type 1, E2 - OSPF external type 2, E - EGP
       i - IS-IS, L1 - IS-IS level-1, L2 - IS-IS level-2, * - candidate de fault
       U - per-user static route, o - ODR

Gateway of last resort is not set

       172.16.0.0/16 is variably subnetted, 5 subnets, 2 masks
O      172.16.222.0/24 [110/1572] via 172.16.1.2, 00:03:01, BRI0
O      172.16.201.2/32 [110/1563] via 172.16.1.2, 00:03:01, BRI0
C      172.16.10.0/24 is directly connected, Loopback0
C      172.16.1.0/24 is directly connected, BRI0
C      172.16.101.0/24 is directly connected, Ethernet0
```

Overview of OSPF Operation

As a review, this section will provide a step-by-step method of configuring OSPF and validating the configuration in an incremental manner.

Step One: Enable the OSPF routing process and define specific interfaces with a network configuration command. Remember to configure the network statement with the appropriate wild card mask and area designation.

```
London(config-router)#network 172.16.1.0 0.0.0.255 area 0
```

In the network statement above, all interfaces on the router named "London" with an address of 172.16.1.0/24 will be assigned to the OSPF area 0.

Step Two: Validate your network configuration statement with the show IP OSPF interface command:

```
r1>show ip ospf interface serial 0
Serial0 is up, line protocol is up
Internet Address 172.16.1.1/24, Area 0
Process ID 100, Router ID 172.16.101.65, Network Type POINT_TO_POINT, Cost: 10000
Transmit Delay is 1 sec, State POINT_TO_POINT,
Timer intervals configured, Hello 10, Dead 40, Wait 40, Retransmit 5
Hello due in 00:00:02
Neighbor Count is 1, Adjacent neighbor count is 1
Adjacent with neighbor 172.16.2.2
Suppress hello for 0 neighbor(s)
```

The "show ip ospf interface" command validates that the OSPF process is running on the desired interface. It shows you what IP address is on the interface; what area the interface belongs to; what interface type is defined (point-to-point, broadcast, nonbroadcast, etc.); the RID for the router; the HELLO and DEAD time intervals; and the adjacencies formed.

If you see the following display generated by the show ip ospf interface:

```
London#show ip ospf interface ethernet 0
Ethernet0 is up, line protocol is up
OSPF not enabled on this interface
```

STOP ANY FURTHER CONFIGURATION. INSPECT THE NETWORK CONFIGURATION STATEMENT AND CLOSELY INSPECT THE ADDRESS ASSIGNED AND THE WILD CARD MASK DEFINED. YOU CAN GO NO FURTHER IN SUCCESSFULLY CONFIGURING OSPF UNTIL YOU SEE ALL INTERFACES ACTIVELY DEFINED BY THE OSPF PROCESS.

Step Three: Once you have validated that the desired interfaces have been properly defined by OSPF, check to make sure that OSPF neighbor relationships have been properly formed. You can do this with the "show ip ospf interface" command and the "show ip ospf neighbor" command. At the bottom of the display, show ip ospf interface will provide you with a neighbor count, an adjacency count and a listing of the RIDs of adjacent neighbors. If the interface is participating in a DR/BDR election, "show ip ospf neighbor" will list whether the interface is a DR, BDR or DROTHER.

You can also use the "show ip ospf neighbor" command to gather information on OSPF neighbor relationships:

```
London>sh ip ospf neighbor
Neighbor ID   Pri   State       Dead Time   Address      Interface
172.16.2.2    1     FULL/BDR    00:00:34    10.1.1.2     Ethernet0
172.16.2.2    1     FULL/ -     00:00:34    172.16.1.2   Serial0
172.16.4.4    1     FULL/ -     00:00:35    172.16.4.4   Serial1
```

The "show ip ospf neighbor" command displays a tabular listing of all neighbors by RID (column 1) and by directly-connected IP address (column 5). It also lists the state of the neighbor relationship (INIT, EXSTART, FULL). Under standard operational conditions, the neighbor relationships should be in a FULL state, For networks that participate in DR/BDR elections, it will list the status of the neighbor (whether the neighbor is a DR, BDR or DROTHER). In a stable environment, the Dead Time should never be greater than a single Hello interval.

Step Four: Once you have validated that the OSPF neighbor relationships have been properly formed, inspect the OSPF link state database:

```
r3#show ip ospf database

      OSPF Router with ID (161.11.1.1) (Process ID 100)


                Router Link States (Area 0)

Link ID         ADV Router      Age    Seq#        Checksum  Link
count
161.11.1.1      161.11.1.1      79     0x8000000C  0x71A3    4
172.16.2.2      172.16.2.2      849    0x8000000D  0xB99D    4
172.16.4.4      172.16.4.4      56     0x8000000C  0x83D2    4
172.16.101.65   172.16.101.65   1056   0x8000000F  0xB53E    6

                Summary Net Link States (Area 0)

Link ID         ADV Router      Age    Seq#        Checksum
10.1.1.0        172.16.2.2      839    0x8000000C  0x91C9
10.1.1.0        172.16.101.65   1036   0x8000000C  0x5E5A
```

```
                Summary ASB Link States (Area 0)

Link ID         ADV Router      Age     Seq#        Checksum
172.16.101.65   172.16.2.2      839     0x80000005  0xBD4C

                Type-5 AS External Link States

Link ID         ADV Router      Age     Seq#        Checksum  Tag
200.100.1.0     172.16.101.65   556     0x80000005  0xEFC     0
```

Check to make sure there is an LSA for every router in a given area (LSA Type 1). Make sure each LSA is listing the proper number of links. Remember, for every point-to-point interface type, OSPF will increase the LSA link count by two. Also ensure that the LSAs are aging properly, and that their sequence numbers are incrementing properly. Once you have inspected all Type One LSAs, inspect all of the other categories of LSAs.

Step Five: Inspect the IP routing table:

```
r3#sh ip ro
Codes: C - connected, S - static, I - IGRP, R - RIP, M - mobile, B - BGP
       D - EIGRP, EX - EIGRP external, O - OSPF, IA - OSPF inter area
       N1 - OSPF NSSA external type 1, N2 - OSPF NSSA external type 2
       E1 - OSPF external type 1, E2 - OSPF external type 2, E - EGP
       i - IS-IS, L1 - IS-IS level-1, L2 - IS-IS level-2, * - candidate default
       U - per-user static route, o - ODR

Gateway of last resort is not set

O E2 200.100.1.0/24 [110/20] via 172.16.3.4, 02:16:31, Serial0
                    [110/20] via 172.16.2.2, 02:16:31, Serial1
     172.16.0.0/16 is variably subnetted, 5 subnets, 2 masks
O       172.16.101.65/32 [110/129] via 172.16.2.2, 02:16:31, Serial1
                         [110/129] via 172.16.3.4, 02:16:31, Serial0
O       172.16.1.0/24 [110/128] via 172.16.2.2, 02:16:31, Serial1
C       172.16.2.0/24 is directly connected, Serial1
C       172.16.3.0/24 is directly connected, Serial0
O       172.16.100.33/32 [110/129] via 172.16.2.2, 02:16:31, Serial1
                         [110/129] via 172.16.3.4, 02:16:32, Serial0
     10.0.0.0/24 is subnetted, 1 subnets
O IA    10.1.1.0 [110/74] via 172.16.2.2, 02:16:32, Serial1
```

Make sure that all OSPF entries are listed. Check the listing on a column-by-column basis. Column One displays the proper origin of the routing table entry:

O	Intra area routing table entry
O IA	Inter area routing table entry
O Ex	Exterior routing table entry

Column Two lists specific routing table entries with the appropriate subnet mask. OSPF supports VLSM and supernetting.

Column Three lists the administrative distance of a routing table entry. The default administrative distance for OSPF is 110.

Column Four lists the metric of the routing table entry. Make sure the metrics are accurate.

Column Five lists the next hop for a given destination network.

Column Six lists the age of the OSPF entry. In a stable OSPF network, routing table entries should be very old. Unlike RIP or IGRP, OSPF does not receive periodic updates. It only updates the routing table when the SPF algorithm is executed. In a stable OSPF network, this should be an infrequent occurrence.

Column Seven lists the local interface to forward IP packets out of to get to the destination network. Make sure the appropriate local interface is listed.

Summary

This Chapter introduced you to the basics of OSPF theory and the basics of OSPF configuration on Cisco routers. OSPF is a link state protocol that provides rapid reconvergence. You can create multiple areas with OSPF. To configure OSPF on a Cisco router, you must start by enabling an OSPF process and define which interfaces are going to participate in OSPF routing. Each interface configured for OSPF must be explicitly configured for a specific OSPF area. Additional OSPF commands allow you to summarize OSPF routes and create virtual-links.

Professional Development Checklist

By using this chapter, you should be able to perform the following operations:

- Configure OSPF for a single area.
- Configure OSPF for multiple areas.
- Configure inter area route summarization for OSPF.
- Configure ASBR route summarization for OSPF.
- Configure a virtual link.
- Configure a stub network.
- Configure a totally stubby network.
- Configure a not so stubby network.
- Manipulate the DR/BDR election process.
- Configure OSPF over an NBMA network.
- Configure OSPF over an ISDN/DDR link.

For Further Study

- Cisco Certified Course: Advanced Cisco Router Configuration, Cisco Systems, Inc.
- OSPF Design Guide, Cisco Systems, Inc., 1989–1998.
- Cisco IOS Configuration Guide Volume V, Cisco Systems, Inc., 1989–1998.
- Cisco IOS Command Reference Volume V, Cisco Systems, Inc., 1989–1998.
- RFC 1583, OSPF Version 2 (makes obsolete RFC 1247).

URLs

- **www.cciecert.com**
- **www.freesoft.org**
- **www.mentorlabs.com**
- **www.cisco.com**

Can You Spot the Issues?

1. An OSPF router possesses the following configuration:

```
interface Ethernet0
 ip address 10.1.1.2 255.255.255.0
!
router ospf 100
 network 172.16.0.0 0.0.255.255 area 0
 network 10.0.0.0 0.0.0.255 area 22
```

OSPF has been configured for the classful addresses of 172.16.0.0 and 10.0.0.0.
Its Ethernet interface is in an active state with the ip address 10.1.1.1:

```
r2#show ip interface brie
Interface  IP-Address  OK?  Method  Status  Protocol
Ethernet0  10.1.1.2    YES  manual  up      up
Serial0    172.16.2.2  YES  NVRAM   up      up
Serial1    172.16.1.2  YES  NVRAM   up      up
```

But the OSPF process is not active on the Ethernet interface:

```
r2#show ip ospf interface e0
Ethernet0 is up, line protocol is up
```

OSPF not enabled on this interface
Why? Can you Spot the Issue?

2. Two OSPF neighbors are connected over an ATM network. One neighbor is connected on the physical ATM interface. The second neighbor is configured on an ATM point-to-point subinterface. Both neighbors can ping each other, but they cannot form a neighbor relationship. Why? Can you Spot the Issue?

TWELVE

Redistribution of IP Routes

Topics Covered in This Chapter

- Redistribution Overview
- Redistributing Routes into RIP, IGRP and EIGRP
- Redistributing Routes into OSPF
- Configuring Distribute Lists
- Addressing the VLSM-FLSM Redistribution Problems

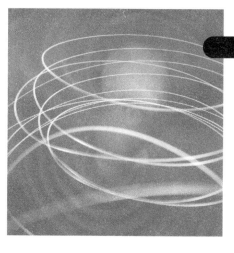

At this point, you are now able to design an IP address plan for your entire internetwork. With this plan, you have taken into consideration when and how to subnet and summarize. You are well aware of the rules of subnetting and summarization for the following IP interior gateway routing protocols: RIP, IGRP, EIGRP and OSPF. You know that RIP and IGRP support fixed length subnet masks only (FLSM); that, by default, RIP and IGRP subnets must be contiguous. You know that Cisco provides a tool (IP classless) which allows you to circumvent the contiguous subnet requirement of RIP and IGRP; and that EIGRP and OSPF support variable length subnetting (VLSM) and classless addressing. At this point, you also know how to enable and configure the routing processes for RIP, IGRP, EIGRP and OSPF. Within a given routing domain for each of these protocols, you are able to see all routes, trace all routes and ping all interfaces.

Now you must tie all these different routing domains together with route redistribution, which is the process of taking routing information from one source and "injecting" it into another source. Route redistribution can be configured as "one-way redistribution" or "two-way (mutual) redistribution." One-way redistribution occurs when only one routing source injects its routes into another routing protocol. Two-way redistribution occurs when two or more routing protocols "mutually" redistribute routes into each other.

Redistribution should be approached with caution. When you perform redistribution, you lose information. Metrics must be arbitrarily reset. For example, if a group of RIP routes with a metric of five hops are redistributed into IGRP, there is no way to translate the five hop RIP metric into the composite metric of IGRP. You must arbitrarily select a metric for the RIP routes as they are redistributed into IGRP. Also, when redistribution is performed at two more points between two dynamic routing protocol domains, routing loops can be formed.

Three Redistribution Scenarios

Listed below are three basic redistribution scenarios. When considering these scenarios, view them from the perspective of the three-tier Cisco internetwork design hierarchy:

- Core
- Distribution
- Access

Access-level routers are typically connected to downstream "stub" routing environments. The access-level router is the single connection point to all other upstream networks in a given internetwork. If a destination network is not among the locally-connected segments, use the default route pointing towards the core of the internetwork. For many organizations with a single Internet connection, the router used for the ISP connection is the stub access point for the vast number of Internet segments.

For stub networking environments, redistribution is relatively simple. If redistribution occurs at all, it will be one-way redistribution. In such environments, configure a default route (IP route 0.0.0.0 0.0.0.0) on the access-level router. Announce this default route to all downstream local routers. Remember, different routing protocols have different methods of propagating default routes.

This scenario is appropriate in an environment with a single stub router connected to a larger upstream internetworking environment.

Route Redistribution Scenario One: Single Border Point Redistribution

In Scenario One, the following parameters exist:

- Default routes are used in stub areas
- Redistribution into a larger upstream routing domain. (Metrics are not important.)

The access-level stub router's directly-connected upstream router may have routes pointing to the access-level router's local networks. If the access-level router has multiple connected subnets, the upstream router's route may be a summary of the downstream subnets. In such a scenario, any redistribution would be "one way" redistribution. The downstream stub router routes will redistribute its routes to the upstream core network. The upstream core networks will not be redistributed to the downstream stub routers. Since the access-level stub router has only a single connection to all other destination networks, configuring a default route is more efficient. Redistributing many upstream routes into a downstream stub routing area with a single connection point is a waste of resources. (If you wanted to redistribute an entire Internet routing table, there could be tens of thousands of routes.)

If route redistribution is performed in such a scenario, metric translation is not an issue, since there is only one exchange point.

Route Redistribution Scenario Two: Multiple Border Point Redistribution (One Way Redistribution)

A single border point creates a single point of failure. If the access-level router or its link to its upstream router is disabled, all non-local connectivity is lost. To avoid such a scenario, a second router with a second upstream connection can be installed. This creates an environment in which two potential redistribution points can exist. One way redistribution can still occur; however, metric translation is important. Thoughtful selection of metric translations will assist the upstream routers in selecting the best path for the downstream networks.

In Scenario Two, the following parameters exist:

- Multiple Border Points (One Way Distribution)
    - Default routes used at the access-level stub routers.
    - Redistribution into larger upstream routing domain. (Metrics are important.)

Route Redistribution Scenario Three: Multiple Border Point Redistribution (Two Way Redistribution)

In this scenario, careful metric selection and use of distribute-lists is highly recommended. A distribute-list is a special filter for routing information in general, and dynamic routing protocol routing table updates in particular. Distribute-lists will be covered later in this chapter.

Routing loops can form if careful metric selection and distribute-lists are not used. BE AWARE OF THIS POSSIBILITY WHENEVER YOU CONFIGURE TWO OR MORE MUTUAL REDISTRIBUTION POINTS BETWEEN TWO ROUTING DOMAINS. It is possible that routes originating from one routing domain will be redistributed into a "target" routing domain and then redistributed back into the original domain as if they were learned from the "target" domain. A detailed scenario of a routing loop will be provided later in this chapter.

In Scenario Three, the following parameters exist:

- Multi-borders: Mutual Redistribution.
- Distribute-lists are important.

Route Redistribution Basics

Route redistribution involves the following steps:

1. Enable routing protocol(s) on border router(s) (the redistributing routers).
2. Specify which networks you want to advertise in each specific routing entry domain.
3. Determine how you want to redistribute:
   Two way (mutual).
   One way.
4. Determine metric for routes redistributed into RIP, IGRP and EIGRP.
5. Apply subnets parameter for subnets redistributed into OSPF.
6. Apply distribute-list (optional).
7. Apply route-maps (optional).
8. Address VLSM/FLSM issues if they exist.

The redistribute command is a routing protocol configuration mode command. As displayed below, it is comprehensive in what it can specify for route redistribution:

```
r1(config-router)#redistribute ?
   bgp          Border Gateway Protocol (BGP)
   connected    Connected
   egp          Exterior Gateway Protocol (EGP)
   eigrp        Enhanced Interior Gateway Routing Protocol (EIGRP)
```

```
igrp          Interior Gateway Routing Protocol (IGRP)
isis          ISO IS-IS
iso-igrp      IGRP for OSI networks
mobile        Mobile routes
odr           On Demand stub Routes
ospf          Open Shortest Path First (OSPF)
rip           Routing Information Protocol (RIP)
static        Static routes
```

The redistribute command is entered in the target routing protocol (the receiver of the redistributed routes). The command will reference the source of the routes to be redistributed. For example, if you wanted to redistribute RIP routes into OSPF, OSPF is the target routing protocol. RIP is the source of the routes to be redistributed. The commands entered to redistribute RIP into OSPF are displayed below:

```
r4(config)#router ospf 100
r4(config-router)#redistribute rip subnets
```

The Metric Requirement for RIP, IGRP and EIGRP

When redistributing routes into a RIP, IGRP and EIGRP domain, providing the "redistribute" command is required, but many times, it is not enough. You must also supply a metric for the routes received. A metric can be defined as an additional parameter of the redistribute command, or a default-metric can be defined with a separate default-metric statement defined in routing protocol configuration mode.

```
r3(config-router)#redistribute rip metric
r3(config-router)#default-metric
```

When a metric is not supplied for routes injected into an IGRP routing domain, the entries will appear with a metric of –1. For IGRP, -1 means the network is unreachable. This problem can be remedied by supplying a metric for redistributed routes.

```
subnet 172.16.17.0, metric=10576
subnet 172.16.10.0, metric=8476
subnet 172.16.1.0, metric=10476
subnet 172.16.2.0, metric=8476
network 177.11.0.0, metric=-1
network 177.11.0.0, metric=-1
```

When a metric is supplied, the routes are injected into IGRP with the manually defined metric:

```
IGRP: sending update to 255.255.255.255 via Serial0 (172.16.2.1)
     subnet 172.16.10.0, metric=8476
```

```
subnet 172.16.4.0, metric=1100
network 177.11.0.0, metric=11000
network 177.10.0.0, metric=11000
```

When a metric is not supplied for routers injected into a RIP routing domain. The entries will appear with a metric of 16. For RIP, 16 means the network is unreachable. Again, this problem can be remedied by supplying a metric for redistributed routes. Displayed below are RIP routing updates of routes that were not supplied a metric during redistribution:

```
RIP: sending v1 update to 255.255.255.255 via Serial1 (172.16.10.1)
     subnet 172.16.17.0, metric 16
     subnet 172.16.4.0, metric 1
     subnet 172.16.1.0, metric 16
     subnet 172.16.2.0, metric 1
```

Displayed below are RIP routing updates of routes that were supplied a metric during redistribution:

```
RIP: sending v1 update to 255.255.255.255 via Serial1 (172.16.10.1)
     subnet  172.16.17.0, metric 4
     subnet  172.16.4.0, metric 1
     subnet  172.16.1.0, metric 4
     subnet  172.16.2.0, metric 1
```

If you want to supply metrics in a granular fashion for routes received via the redistribution process, configure a route-map. Route-maps allow you to specify specific metrics for specific redistributed routes. Route-maps are covered in Chapter 28.

Redistributing Static and Connected Routes

You do not need a metric statement when redistributing static or connected routes into RIP, IGRP, EIGRP and OSPF. You simply need to type the following command in the proper routing configuration mode:

```
Redistribute static
Redistribute connected
```

Redistributing connected routes can be problematic. The "redistribute connected" command indiscriminately redistributes all connected routes into a specified routing domain. If you do not want all connected routes to be redistributed, use a distribute-list out statement to selectively identify which connected routes should be redistributed.

Redistributing Routes Into OSPF

FIGURE 12–1 Redistributing between RIP abd OSPF.

When redistributing routes into OSPF, the "subnets" parameter is required for any subnetted routes. If you omit the subnets parameter, subnetted routes will not be redistributed into OSPF.

Supplying a metric is essential for redistributing routes into RIP, IGRP and EIGRP. It is not required for OSPF. If you redistribute another IGP into OSPF without a default-metric, it will be assigned a metric of 20.

Listed below are two sample redistribution configuration statements for OSPF:

```
r1(config-router)#redistribute igrp 100 subnets

r1(config-router)#redistribute connected  subnet
```

An OSPF router that performs route redistribution is classified as an Autonomous System Border Router (ASBR). OSPF routers that generate External LSAs (LSA Type 5) are termed Autonomous System Boundary Routers (ASBRs). This term arises because in a pure OSPF network, external information will only originate from BGP or default routes, both of which lead to other autonomous systems. However, any routing source external to OSPF is treated the same way, so a router redistributing RIP into OSPF will become an ASBR. A default route (0.0.0.0 0.0.0.0) is a special case of an External LSA.

Routes redistributed from non-OSPF sources and a default route are further subclassified as Level One and Level Two exterior routes. A Level One exterior route (identified in an IP routing table as an "E1" route) increases the metric of the exterior route as it is propagated through the OSPF domain. A Level Two exterior route (identified in an IP routing table as an "E2" route) does not. For an E2 route, whatever its metric is at the point of route redistribution will remain as the network is propagated through the OSPF domain. Note the "E2" routes in the routing table displayed below:

```
r4#show ip route
Codes: C - connected, S - static, I - IGRP, R - RIP, M - mobile, B - BGP
     D - EIGRP, EX - EIGRP external, O - OSPF, IA - OSPF inter area
     N1 - OSPF NSSA external type 1, N2 - OSPF NSSA external type 2
     E1 - OSPF external type 1, E2 - OSPF external type 2, E - EGP
```

```
       i - IS-IS, L1 - IS-IS level-1, L2 - IS-IS level-2, * - candidate default
       U - per-user static route, o - ODR

Gateway of last resort is not set

     179.10.0.0/24 is subnetted, 1 subnets
O E2    179.10.1.0 [110/20] via 172.16.10.1, 00:04:06, Serial0
     177.11.0.0/24 is subnetted, 1 subnets
C       177.11.1.0 is directly connected, Loopback1
     177.10.0.0/24 is subnetted, 1 subnets
C       177.10.1.0 is directly connected, Loopback0
     172.16.0.0/24 is subnetted, 5 subnets
O E2172.16.17.0 [110/100] via 172.16.10.1, 00:13:59, Serial0
C    172.16.10.0 is directly connected, Serial0
O E2    172.16.4.0 [110/100] via 172.16.10.1, 00:08:01, Serial0
O E2    172.16.1.0 [110/20] via 172.16.10.1, 00:04:06, Serial0
O E2    172.16.2.0 [110/20] via 172.16.10.1, 00:04:06, Serial0
     180.10.0.0/24 is subnetted, 1 subnets
O E2    180.10.1.0 [110/20] via 172.16.10.1, 00:04:07, Serial0
```

Note the "Type-5 AS External Link States" in the OSPF Link State database displayed below:

```
r4#sh ip ospf database

     OSPF Router with ID (177.11.1.1) (Process ID 100)
                        Router Link States (Area 0)
 Link ID        ADV Router     Age     Seq#          Checksum     Link       count
 177.11.1.1     177.11.1.1     1047    0x80000005    0xDC55       4
 180.10.1.1     180.10.1.1     991     0x80000008    0xB418       2

                        Type-5 AS External Link States

 Link ID        ADV Router     Age     Seq#          Checksum         Tag
 172.16.1.0     180.10.1.1     930     0x80000002    0x9D83           0
 172.16.2.0     180.10.1.1     930     0x80000002    0x928D           0
 172.16.4.0     180.10.1.1     930     0x80000002    0x9F2E           0
 172.16.10.0    180.10.1.1     930     0x80000002    0x3ADD           0
 172.16.17.0    180.10.1.1     930     0x80000002    0x10B0           0
 179.10.1.0     180.10.1.1     930     0x80000002    0x8A95           0
 180.10.1.0     180.10.1.1     930     0x80000002    0x7DA1           0
```

A debug trace of OSPF redistribution information is displayed below. This debug trace is useful to watch all the redistributed routes get advertised by OSPF Type 5 LSAs.

```
OSPF: Start partial processing Type 5 External LSA 179.10.1.0, mask 255.255.255.0,
adv 180.10.1.1, age 1, seq 0x80000001, metric 20, metric-type 2
  Add better path to LSA ID 179.10.1.0, gateway 172.16.10.1, dist 20
  Add path: next-hop 172.16.10.1, interface Serial0
OSPF: insert route list LS ID 179.10.1.0, type 5, adv rtr 180.10.1.1
OSPF: Start partial processing Type 5 External LSA 172.16.10.0, mask 255.255.255.0,
adv 180.10.1.1, age 1, seq 0x80000001, metric 20, metric-type 2
OSPF: Start partial processing Type 5 External LSA 172.16.1.0, mask 255.255.255.0,
adv 180.10.1.1, age 1, seq 0x80000001, metric 20, metric-type 2
  Add better path to LSA ID 172.16.1.0, gateway 172.16.10.1, dist 20
  Add path: next-hop 172.16.10.1, interface Serial0
  Add External Route to 172.16.1.0. Metric: 20, Next Hop: 172.16.10.1
OSPF: insert route list LS ID 172.16.1.0, type 5, adv rtr 180.10.1.1
```

You can manually initiate an OSPF redistribution process with the following command:

```
r1#clear ip ospf redistribution
```

This command must be performed at the router performing the redistribution only. When it is performed, it generates debug traffic similar to the debug trace displayed below:

```
OSPF: Flushing External Links
OSPF: Start redist-scanning
OSPF: Scan for both redistribution and translation
OSPF: Generate external LSA 179.10.1.0, mask 255.255.255.0, type 5, age 0,
metric 20, seq 0x8000000C
OSPF: Generate external LSA 172.16.10.0, mask 255.255.255.0, type 5, age 0,
metric 20, seq 0x8000000C
OSPF: Generate external LSA 172.16.1.0, mask 255.255.255.0, type 5, age 0,
metric 20, seq 0x8000000C
OSPF: Generate external LSA 172.16.2.0, mask 255.255.255.0, type 5, age 0,
metric 20, seq 0x8000000C
OSPF: Generate external LSA 180.10.1.0, mask 255.255.255.0, type 5, age 0,
metric 20, seq 0x8000000C
```

Redistributing VLSM Subnets into an FLSM Domain

In Chapter 9, we saw how different routing protocols support different subnetting rules. RIP and IGRP are "one size fits all" subnetting environments. When subnetting is performed in a RIP or IGRP environment, all subnet masks for a given classful address must be the same. They are "fixed length subnet mask" (FLSM) environments. Also, for RIP and IGRP, all subnets of a given classful network must be contiguous.

OSPF and EIGRP allow much greater flexibility with subnetting. Both OSPF and EIGRP support variable length subnet masking and classless addresses. Subnets can also be discontiguously located in OSPF and EIGRP.

When OSPF or EIGRP subnets are redistributed into IGRP or RIP, these differences must be taken into account. This is especially the case when both types of routing protocols share the same classful address space.

Consider the following scenario:

Problem: Redistributing Between VLSM and FLSM Environments

FACTS

An OSPF routing domain is using the 172.16.0.0 address space. The OSPF domain contains the following subnets and subnet mask lengths:

```
172.16.1.0/24
172.16.2.0/24
172.16.3.0/24
172.16.4.32/26
172.16.4.64/26
172.16.10.8/29
172.16.10.16/29
172.16.10.24/29
```

An IGRP routing domain is using the 172.16.0.0 address space. The IGRP domain contains the following subnets and subnet mask lengths:

```
172.16.20.0/24
172.16.21.0/24
172.16.22.0/24
```

A router running both OSPF and IGRP must be configured to perform mutual redistribution between OSPF and IGRP, so that all OSPF routers can reach all IGRP networks, and all IGRP routers can reach all OSPF networks.

PROBLEM

Routers in the OSPF domain list all routes redistributed from RIP. Routers in the RIP domain list only those OSPF routes with 24-bit subnet masks. The 24-bit subnet mask matches the RIP subnets own subnet mask. All OSPF routes that do not possess a 24-bit subnet mask are not seen in the RIP domain. All OSPF routes that do not possess a 24-bit subnet mask are not reachable from the RIP domain.

ISSUE

Whether variable subnets (VLSM) of a given classful address space can be redistributed into a fixed length subnet mask environment (FLSM) such as RIP or IGRP.

RULE

Variable length subnets cannot be redistributed into a fixed length subnet mask (FLSM) environment such as a RIP or IGRP environment.

SOLUTION ONE

In order to avoid losing connectivity to variable length subnets during VLSM to FLSM redistribution, summarize the 26-bit and 29-bit OSPF subnets in the scenario described above to a 24-bit summary and redistribute the summaries into IGRP.

SOLUTION TWO

Announce an IP default-network on the redistributing router into the IGRP domain. Enable IP classless on all IGRP routers with the global configuration command "ip classless."

Redistribution and Administrative Distance

When performing two way redistribution in a configuration with two or more redistribution points, be aware of the impact of a routing protocol's administrative distance. The different values of a routing protocol's administrative distance can create an ideal environment for routing loop formation.

As an example, consider the following scenario:

Router RIP-10 announces its own directly connected 172.16.1.0/24 subnet to Border-1 as being one hop away.

Border-1 and Border-2 are RIP speaking routers that are also redistributing RIP routes into OSPF. Therefore, both routers are running both RIP and OSPF.

Border-1 redistributes the 172.16.1.0/24 route into OSPF and advertises the route to Border-2 as being 2 hops away. Border-2 also redistributes the 172.16.1.0/24 subnet into OSPF.

OSPF-11, an internal OSPF speaking router, receives the "E2" route from Border-2 and advertises it back to Border-1. Border-1 receives the route, and since OSPF has a lower administrative distance than RIP, Border-1 replaces the original RIP route with the OSPF route.

A routing loop has been formed! When Border-1 receives a packet destined for the 172.16.1.0/24 subnet, it should send it to RIP-10. However, since it learned the route from OSPF-11, and since OSPF has a lower administrative distance than RIP, Border-1 forwards all packets destined for 172.16.1.0/24 to OSPF-11. OSPF-11 forwards it to Border-2. Border-2 forwards it to Border-1, and Border-1 forwards it back to OSPF-11.

The remedy for this problem is configuring distribute-lists. Create restrictive distribute-lists for both routing protocols so that a given routing protocol

can only announce routes that are native to its domain. Therefore, in the scenario above, deny OSPF border routers from ever injecting the 172.16.1.0/24 subnet into the RIP domain.

EIGRP has an automatic preventive remedy to avoid a scenario like the one described above from ever developing. EIGRP assigns all internally learned EIGRP routes an administrative distance of 90, and marks them as "D" entries in the IP routing table. It assigns an administrative distance of 170 to all routes learned via redistribution and marks them as "EX" (external) routes. The higher administrative distance prevents EIGRP external networks from replacing natively learned networks on routers performing redistribution.

Passive-interface

You can disable the advertising of routing updates on a specific interface with the "passive-interface" command, a router configuration command.

```
r4(config)#router igrp 100
r4(config-router)#passive-interface s1
```

In the example above, no IGRP advertisements will be sent out on interface s1. IGRP advertisements will continued to be received on interface s1, but not advertised.

The passive-interface command is especially useful with RIP, IGRP and EIGRP. Since all three commands define which networks are going to participate in a specific routing process by defining the classful network address only, the passive-interface command is used to silence routing traffic on specific interfaces.

Consider the following example:

The following four subnet addresses are configured on four interfaces of a router:

- 172.16.1.1 255.255.255.0 on e0
- 172.16.2.1 255.255.255.0 on e2
- 172.16.3.1 255.255.255.0 on s0
- 172.16.4.1 255.255.255.0 on s1

The router administrator wants IGRP routing advertisements to be sent out only on interfaces e0 and s0. However, the routing protocol configuration command does not allow subnet specification:

```
r4(config)#router igrp 100
r4(config-router)#network 172.16.0.0
```

When this command is entered, IGRP advertisements will go out on e0, e1, s0 and s1. The passive-interface command can be used to stop IGRP advertisements from going out on e1 and s1.

```
r4(config)#router igrp 100
r4(config-router)#passive-interface e1
r4(config-router)#passive-interface s1
```

Even though routing advertisements will not be advertised out e1 and s1, the subnetwork address configured on e1 and s1 will be advertised by IGRP on e0 and s0. If you want to filter these subnets, you must configure a distribute-list.

Distribute-lists

You can control which routes are advertised or accepted from one routing process to another with distribute-lists. This gives you tremendous management power over the redistribution process. Distribute-lists are essential in situations where there are two or more redistribution points between two routing domains and the possibility of routing loops thereby arises. Distribute-lists are a popular solution for preventing routing loops.

Also, distribute-lists can be used to manually assure that only certain routes are announced from specific routing processes or interfaces.

Distribute-list configuration involve two components:

- Creation of an access-list
- Defining a distribute-list statement

The access-list is used to define which types of routes will be permitted or denied by the distribute-list. The standard rules of access-lists are applied. See Chapters 23 and 24 for a complete description of these rules.

Once the access-list has been created, the distribute-list itself must be defined in routing protocol configuration mode:

```
r4(config-router)#distribute-list ?
<1-199>  IP access list number
```

Notice how the distribute-list requires a reference to an access-list. Once an access-list is referenced, you must select a "distribute-list in" or "distribute-list out":

```
r4(config-router)#distribute-list 1 ?
     in Filter incoming routing updates
     out Filter outgoing routing updates
```

When applying a "distribute-list in" statement, you usually configure the statement under the *same* routing process that is advertising the routes from the remote router.

When applying a "distribute-list out" statement, you usually configure the statement under a *different routing process from the source of the routing table information*. For example, you might apply a "distribute-list out" statement to OSPF for filtering routes coming from RIP.

Distribute-list in

Distribute-list in is more restrictive than Distribute-list out. Distribute-list in can be applied only to interfaces only. Distribute-list out statements can be applied to both interfaces and routing protocols.

```
r3(config-router)#distribute-list 1 in ?
    BRI           ISDN Basic Rate Interface
    Ethernet      IEEE 802.3
    Null          Null interface
    Serial        Serial
    <cr>
```

A DISTRIBUTE-LIST IN SCENARIO

Two RIP routers, R1 and R2, are exchanging routing information. You want to block all routes from 172.16.0.0 and 10.1.1.0 from being advertised from R2 to R1. The following "distribute-list in" statement would provide the desired objective:

```
r2(config)#access-list 1 deny 10.1.1.0 0.0.0.255
r2(config)#access-list 1 deny 172.16.0.0 0.0.255.255
r2(config)#access-list 1 permit any
r2(config)#router rip
r2(config-router)#distribute-list 1 in e0
```

When a distribute-list in statement is placed on the inbound interface of a router speaking RIP, it prevents specific entries from being posted to the router's routing table.

CCIE candidates must know how to configure a granular distribute-list, which will require a strong understanding of IP access-lists. This topic is covered in Chapters 23 and 24.

Distribute-list out

Distributed list-out can be defined for a routing protocol or an interface.

```
r3(config-router)#distribute-list 1 out ?
   BRI          ISDN Basic Rate Interface
   Ethernet     IEEE 802.3
```

```
Null           Null interface
Serial         Serial
bgp            Border Gateway Protocol (BGP)
connected      Connected
egp            Exterior Gateway Protocol (EGP)
eigrp          Enhanced Interior Gateway Routing Protocol (EIGRP)
igrp           Interior Gateway Routing Protocol (IGRP)
isis           ISO IS-IS
iso-igrp       IGRP for OSI networks
ospf           Open Shortest Path First (OSPF)
rip            Routing Information Protocol (RIP)
static         Static routes
<cr>
```

A DISTRIBUTE-LIST OUT SCENARIO

R1 is running both IGRP and OSPF. IGRP is defined on the s0 interface only of R1. OSPF is defined on the E0 interface only of R1. The IGRP routing process lists the following networks on R1:

```
172.16.1.0/24
172.16.2.0/24
10.1.1.0/24
```

The OSPF routing process lists the following networks on R1:

```
172.16.20.0/24
172.16.50.0/24
10.20.30.0/24
```

The following distribute-lists assure that only the above listed networks are redistributed:

```
r2(config)#access-list 1 permit 172.16.1.0
r2(config)#access-list 1 permit 172.16.2.0
r2(config)#access-list 1 permit 10.1.1.0
r2(config)#access-list 2 permit 172.16.20.0
r2(config)#access-list 2 permit 172.16.30.0
r2(config)#access-list 2 permit 10.20.30.0

r2(config)#router ospf 100
r2(config-router)#redistribute igrp 100 subnets
r2(config-router)#distribute-list 1 out igrp 100
r2(config-router)#router igrp 100
r2(config-router)#redistribute ospf 100 metric 10000 1000 255 1 1500
r2(config-router)#distribute-list 2 out ospf 100
```

Summary

With redistribution, you can reach all points of your IP internetwork. Everything that has been covered so far supports the IP redistribution process in a direct or indirect fashion. Getting the physical and data link layer interfaces and ports active, deploying an IP addressing plan that supports well-thought out subnetting and route summarization, configuring routing protocols: all of these tasks allow the route redistribution process to happen. If you cannot comfortably spot the issues and perform the configurations of all Level One and Level Two topics presented so far, you will fail the CCIE lab. Even if you can perform all of these topics, you still can fail the lab.

The issue of IP redistribution will be revisited in Chapter Fourteen, "Configuring BGP4," and Chapter Twenty-Eight, "Configuring Route-Maps." Non-IP route redistribution will be covered in the non-IP routing protocol chapters: Chapters Fifteen–Nineteen.

Professional Development Checklist

By using this chapter, you should be able to perform the following operations:

- Perform two way redistribution between RIP and OSPF.
- Perform two way redistribution between RIP and IGRP.
- Perform two way redistribution between RIP and EIGRP.
- Perform two way redistribution between IGRP and OSPF.
- Perform two way redistribution between IGRP and EIGRP.
- Redistribute static routes into OSPF.
- Redistribute connected routes into OSPF.
- Solve the VLSM to FLSM problem between OSPF and RIP.
- Configure a Distribute-List out.
- Configure a Distribute-List in.

For Further Study

- Advanced Cisco Router Configuration Course, Cisco Systems, Inc.
- Cisco IOS Configuration Guide Volume V, Cisco Systems, Inc., 1989–1998.
- Cisco IOS Command Reference Volume V, Cisco Systems, Inc., 1989–1998.

URLs

- **www.cciecert.com**
- **www.freesoft.org**
- **www.mentorlabs.com**
- **www.cisco.com**

Can You Spot the Issues?

1. Solve the problem below:
   A router is running RIP and OSPF. Both routing protocols are using 172.16.0.0 address space. The router also has two 172.16.0.0 subnets connected. RIP redistribution did not inject the routes into OSPF. Redistribute connected injected them in. Why?
2. Solve the problem below:
   A router is performing mutual route redistribution between EIGRP and OSPF. It has an EIGRP neighbor on an ATM interface, and OSPF routes are successfully redistributed to EIGRP on the redistributing router.
   After a period of time, the redistributing router begins to show entries originating from the OSPF domain as EIGRP routes originating from the EIGRP neighbor on the ATM interface. When this happens, none of the networks are reachable, and when debug IP packet is enabled, pings are sent to the EIGRP neighbor on the ATM connection and not on the correct interfaces.
   What specifically is the problem? How can distribute-lists solve the problem? Is there another solution to the problem?
   Hint: Remember, with ATM physical interfaces, split-horizon is disabled. EIGRP has a lower default administrative distance than OSPF.

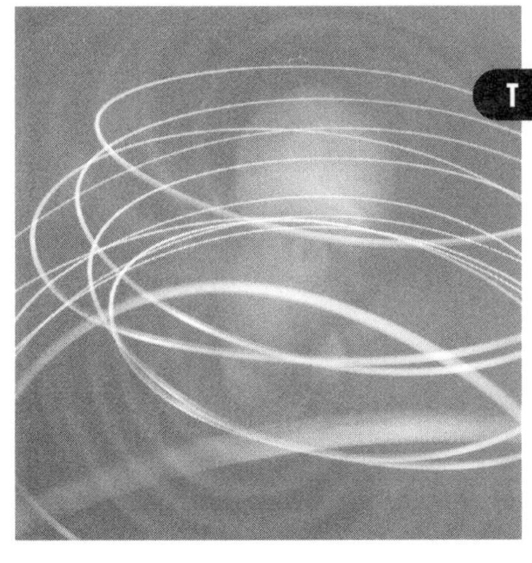

THIRTEEN

Level Two Summary

The Level Two chapters provide you with a set of tools to connect together any type of Level One technology (OSI physical and data link technology). For all Level One technologies —Ethernet, Fast Ethernet, Token-Ring, FDDI, T-1, T-3, Frame-Relay, ATM, ISDN, VLANs, ELANs and others—a Level Two address can be supplied—an IP address. By supplying an IP address to each kind of Level One segment and enabling IP routing on each segment, you can tie an entire collection of dissimilar physical and data-link layer technologies into one administrative entity.

From its very inception, IP addressing and its complementary technology, IP routing, were designed to be "open systems" technologies, which allow any network to connect to any other network. They are designed to provide connectivity to any operating system over any transport media (IP addressing and IP routing are designed to connect anything over everything!). It is this feature of IP addressing and IP routing that has made it the heart of the Internet. Without the open systems technologies of IP addressing and IP routing, we would not have today's Internet.

The Level Two chapters provide you with a starting point of developing a skill set for designing and implementing a well-thought out IP addressing plan, enabling commonly-used IP routing protocols (RIP, IGRP, EIGRP and OSPF) and performing route redistribution between them. When planning an IP internetwork, remember the progression of Level Two:

1. Think through the IP address planning issues first.
2. Take into account an organization's subnetting requirements.
3. Take into account an organization's underlying physical/data-link layer network design.
4. Attempt to plan your IP address deployment on a hierarchical structure (if the organization's underlying physical/data-link layer network design allows you to do so).
5. Take into account the available routing protocols used by the organization. Remember that routing protocol selection will dictate your subnetting techniques (fixed length subnets versus variable length subnets).
6. When developing your subnetting design, consider your route summarization design. The two must complement each other. Remember this general rule: In a hierarchically designed internetwork of core, distribution and access levels—Summarize Up (summarize as you move from the edges to the core, from the access-level to the distribution level to the core level) and Subnet Down (Subnet from the core to the edges; subnet core level summaries at the distribution level; further subnet distribution level subnets at the access-level).
7. When planning your route summarization strategy, remember the Longest Match Rule.
8. Take into account issues of redundancy and load balancing.
9. Select your routing protocols.
10. For stub areas, you may not need any routing protocols. You may use a combination of static routes and default routes.
11. When selecting routing protocols, remember specific routing protocol characteristics like periodic advertisements of the entire routing table (RIP and IGRP) and slow convergence due to hold down timers (RIP and IGRP).
12. You may need to deploy one type of routing protocol at the edges of your network (at the access-level) and another type at the core level. This will require a thorough understanding of IP route redistribution.

The learning strategy applied to this book is:

1. Introduce concepts of IP addressing and IP routing theory. These concepts will be embodied in all routing protocols and route redistribution activities.
2. Introduce how core IP addressing topics and IP routing are performed with the Cisco IOS. Place emphasis on IOS tools, such as show ip route, show ip protocols, debug ip packet and debug ip routing.

3. Introduce commonly-used IP routing protocols, starting with the least complex (RIP) and ending with the most complex (OSPF). Move through the routing protocol progression in the following order: RIP, IGRP, EIGRP and OSPF. Place heavy emphasis on the Cisco IOS tools to configure, monitor and troubleshoot each specific routing protocol. IOS tools are categorized into five basic categories:
   1. Configuration commands
   2. Show commands
   3. Debug commands
   4. Clear commands
   5. Other commands
4. Introduce how to tie all different routing methods (static and dynamic) and routing protocols together into one administrative entity through route redistribution.

This is the road map of Level Two. It is a starting point and not an ending point. You, the CCIE candidate, must build upon the foundation laid in these chapters.

In summary, key Level Two tasks you must perform when faced with an IP routing deployment are:

1. **Plan out your IP addressing.** Be able to perform this task in a systematic and structured manner. Be able to rapidly spot the commonly-overlooked issues of IP address planning, such as planning a subnet strategy for summarization or planning a summarization strategy for route redistribution. Ultimately, all ip routing builds upon ip address deployment.
2. **Enable routing protocols.** Be aware of the characteristics of each routing protocol deployed. Is it bandwidth intensive? Is it CPU intensive? When the network topology changes, how long does it take to re-converge? How well does the routing protocol scale? Be able to spot issues that are specific to a given routing protocol.
3. **Perform route redistribution.** Route redistribution is the tool that ties the different routing protocols together. Be aware of the specific requirements of performing route redistribution for particular routing protocols. For example, RIP, IGRP and EIGRP require an explicit metric defined for all routes received during the route redistribution process. OSPF does not. Know when not to use route redistribution. Know when to use static routes and default routes instead of route redistribution. Know the difference between one way and two way route redistribution.
4. **When performing route redistribution, prevent routing loops with distribute-lists.** When performing route redistribution between two or more border points of two routing domains, be aware of the possibility of routing loop formation. Know how to configure distribute-lists to prevent the formation of routing loops.

Key Level Two IOS Tools to Use

- Show ip route and all of its parameters (know how to read every column of an ip routing table)
- Show ip protocols
- Show cdp neighbors detail
- Ping
- Extended PING (Privileged Mode)
- Traceroute
- Extended Traceroute (Privileged Mode)
- Clear ip route
- Debug ip packet (know the difference between the following types of output: sending/receiving, sending…, encapsulation failed, unroutable)
- Debug ip routing
- Debug ip icmp
- Debug ip rip
- Debug ip igrp transactions
- Debug ip igrp events
- Show ip eigrp neighbors
- Show ip eigrp topology
- Debug ip eigrp
- Clear ip eigrp neighbor
- Show ip ospf interface
- Show ip ospf neighbors
- Show ip ospf database (and its parameters)
- Debug ip ospf packet
- Debug ip ospf events
- Debug ip ospf adj
- Clear ip ospf redistribution

Remember to use all debug and clear commands with extreme caution!

Key Level Two Principles to Remember

1. IP routing decisions are made on a hop-by-hop (router-by-router) basis.
2. IP routing decisions are based upon the Longest Match Rule.
3. IP traffic has two paths: (1) the path to get to a given destination and (2) a return path. Remember to apply Principles 1 and 2 to these two paths. This principle is the functional equivalent of the Level One maxim: "Troubleshoot both sides of the connection."
4. IP routing tables can be built statically or dynamically.
5. All Cisco routing table entries have an administrative distance. When two routing sources exist for a given routing table entry, the routing source with the lower administrative distance will be selected.

Suggested General All-Purpose Level Two Troubleshooting Techniques

1. Can you PING your own interface?
2. Can you PING your locally-attached neighbor's interface?
3. Can you PING your neighboring router's locally-attached neighbor's interface?
4. Can you PING a far side interface on a locally-attached neighboring router?
5. How far are your traceroutes successful? If your traceroutes fail to reach the desired destination, at which router did the traceroute fail?
6. Is the problem detected by the traceroute a problem related to getting to a given destination, or is it a return path problem?
7. How do your routing tables look?
8. Are all routes present in your routing table?
9. Are the routing table entries aging properly?
10. Do the routing table entries possess the correct metrics?
11. When you perform a debug ip packet, do the packets leave the correct interface when you perform a PING?
12. When you perform a debug ip packet, do the packets list the proper sending and receiving messages when you perform a PING? Are all debug messages sending only? Are the debug messages listing the target destination network as unroutable? Are the debug messages displaying an encapsulation failed message?

If you are a CCIE candidate, none of the commands, principles and techniques listed above should be unfamiliar to you. Before you type in any of the commands, you should already know the contents and structure of the show command displays and debug outputs. You should already know the consequences of enabling debug and performing clear commands for every debug and clear command listed above. You should be able to perform Level Two configuration tasks in a structured and incremental manner, and you should feel comfortable and confident in doing so. **If you do not feel comfortable with Level Two topics, tasks and IOS tools, do not go any further in your CCIE preparation. It cannot be stressed enough how important both Level One and Level Two topics are!**

From a learning perspective, many topics in Levels Three through Six will be related to what you have learned in Levels One and Two. The presentations on BGP4 (Level Three) are based upon comparing EGP routing to IGP routing, which is a core topic of Level Two. You will never understand EGP routing if you do not fully understand IGP routing. Level Four presentations will compare IPX, AppleTalk and DECNET operation configuration to IP operation and configuration. If you understand Level Two topics well, you will accelerate your learning of Level Four topics. Level Five compares routing processes to non-routing processes (bridging, DLSw+ and LAN switching). Level Six focuses on traffic management, queuing and route-maps. Many of the Level Six topics relate directly to Level Two topics. Therefore, it is imperative from a learning perspective that you master Level Two topics before addressing Level Three through Six topics.

From an operations and performance perspective, all the topics in Levels Three through Six rely on operational Level One technologies, and many of the topics covered in Levels Three through Six rely on operational Level Two technologies. For example, BGP4, IPX Tunneling, AppleTalk Tunneling and DLSW+ all rely on fully operational Level Two technologies.

A Closing Level Two Comment

For years, many people have been predicting the demise of TCP/IP and IP routing. In the early 1990s, the OSI protocol suite, CLNP and IS-IS, were supposed to surpass TCP/IP by the mid-1990s. Obviously, it did not happen. Since the mid-1990s, many industry pundits have been predicting that end-to-end ATM networks would eventually replace networks based upon IP routing. Many have been predicting the diminution of IP and IP routing in the internetworking world, due to the emergence of a combination of LAN switching and ATM switching. IP critics focus on the premise that IP is an overhead process. For every packet, IP routing requires the removal of the data-link layer header on the ingress interface of an IP router, a routing table lookup and IP switching decision based upon a network layer address, and, finally, the encapsulation of a new data-link layer header on the egress port of an IP router—all of which creates a bottleneck in today's high-speed switched internetworks.

Cisco offers a robust suite of solutions that support traditional IP routing, as well as newer techniques of IP routing, such as ATM's MPOA. For those organizations that want to deploy MPOA, Cisco has a suite of solutions to deploy MPOA. Cisco also has its own set of solutions for high-speed layer three switching. The solutions focus on Cisco's distributed NetFlow architecture and the Cisco Catalyst 8500 layer three switch router. The distributed NetFlow architecture provides a method to perform "cut through" VLAN to VLAN or inter-VLAN switching. The Catalyst 8500 provides the ability to perform IP layer three switching at wire speeds. Whichever solution you desire, Cisco has an IP switching solution. Cisco prides itself on being a "technologically agnostic" company. Whichever IP switching solution you ultimately select, the same IOS discussed in Chapters nine through twelve in this book will be available.

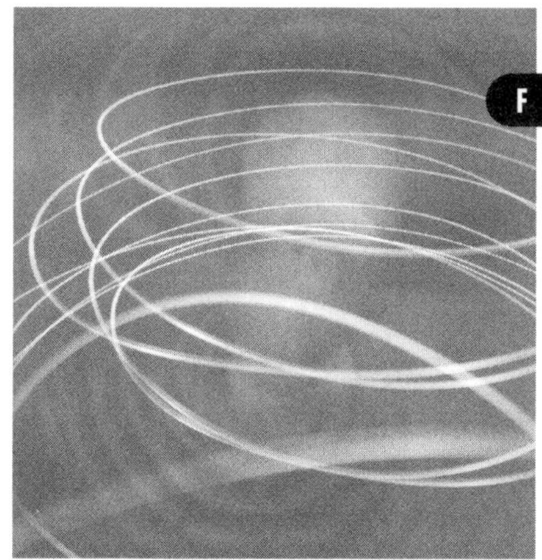

FOURTEEN

Exterior Routing With BGP

Topics Covered in This Chapter

- The BGP-4 Path Selection Process
- Configuring BGP-4 Neighbor Statements
- Advertising Networks Via BGP-4
- Using the NEXT-HOP-SELF Parameter
- Analyzing and Applying the Rule of Synchronization
- Using AS-Path Filters with BGP-4

Throughout this book, references are made to hierarchical internetworking. The standard Cisco hierarchical model for internetworking is made up of three levels: core, distribution and access. This chapter introduces Border Gateway Protocol–4 (BGP4), which is an exterior gateway protocol. Exterior gateway protocols provide inter-autonomous system routing. Inter-autonomous system routing provides a fourth and final level to the three layer hierarchy already described in this book. In order to understand how this is done, the term "autonomous system" must be defined. RFC 1771, the RFC that defines BGP-4, provides the following definition for an autonomous system (AS):

"The classic definition of an Autonomous System is a set of routers under a single technical administration, using an interior gateway protocol and common metrics to route packets within the AS, and using an exterior gateway protocol to route packets to other ASs. Since this classic definition was developed, it has become common for a single AS to use several interior gateway protocols and sometimes several sets of metrics within an AS. The use of the term Autonomous System here stresses the fact that, even when multiple IGPs and metrics are used, the administration of an AS appears to other ASs to have a single coherent interior routing plan and presents a consistent picture of what destinations are reachable through it."

After other terms are defined and a clear comparison is made between "interior gateway protocols" and "exterior gateway protocols," you will see how BGP4 can provide a hierarchy to all of the hierarchical internetworks described in this book. Also, you will see how BGP4, an exterior gateway protocol, ultimately relies on interior gateway protocols for proper operation.

A Brief Review of the IGP Routing Process

Interior Gateway Protocol (IGP) routing is defined as routing performed within an autonomous system. For the purposes of this discussion, IGP routing is not limited to routing with dynamic routing protocols. IGP routing also includes static routes and connected routes.

As mentioned earlier, IGPs provide routing within an autonomous system. Exterior Gateway Protocols, or EGPs, provide routing between autonomous systems. EGPs tell you *what* autonomous systems you need to go through to get to a given IP destination prefix. IGPs tell you *how* to get through a given autonomous system to get to a given IP destination prefix or *how* to get through an autonomous system to get to the next-hop IP address leading to another autonomous system. This may sound confusing at first. The next sections will show how IGPs and EGPs operate in a complementary fashion.

In its most primitive form, any IGP routing table entry can be summarized by the following statement:

To get to the destination IP prefix A.B.C.D/XX, go out local interface Y(Z).

A.B.C.D	=	a given IP prefix
XX	=	a given IP prefix length
Y	=	interface type
Z	=	interface number

Routing decisions are made on a hop-by-hop (router-by-router) basis. As an IP packet destined for a given IP prefix traverses an internetwork, each router makes a decision that can be summarized by the statement above ("To get to destination IP prefix A.B.C.D, go out local interface Y(Z)"). This continues until the packet is delivered to a router with a connected interface that has the target destination IP prefix assigned to it.

An alternative to the statement presented above is a routing entry that specifies a next hop address instead of a local interface:

To get to the destination IP prefix A.B.C.D/XX go to the next-hop N.N.N.N.

A.B.C.D	=	a given IP prefix
XX	=	a given IP prefix length
N.N.N.N	=	the next-hop to forward a packet destined for the prefix A.B.C.D/XX

However, when a next-hop address is used to forward a packet to a destination, the next-hop address itself must be reachable. Also, the packets being forwarded must eventually be forwarded out some interface to get to the next-hop. In order to determine whether the next-hop address is reachable, and to select an interface to forward a packet to the next hop, a second routing table look up must be performed:

1. To get to destination IP prefix A.B.C.D/XX, go to the next-hop N.N.N.N.
2. To get to destination IP prefix N.N.N.N/XX, go out local interface Y(Z).

This second lookup is called a "recursive" lookup. Notice how the next-hop address at the end of statement one is the destination IP prefix to be routed out of a specified interface in statement two.

In Chapter Nine an extensive examination of the IP routing table is provided. Regardless of what type of routing table entry is created—connected routes, static routes, RIP routes, OSPF routes, IGRP routes, EIGRP routes—every one of these routing table entries has one common element: a destination IP prefix. Regardless of what type of routing table entry is created—connected routes, static routes, RIP, routes, OSPF routes, IGRP routes, EIGRP routes—every one of these routing table entries has a second common element that can be one of two types:

1. a corresponding local interface on which to send packets out to get to a given destination IP prefix
2. a corresponding next-hop address on which to send packets to get to a given destination IP prefix

The two available static route configurations confirm this:

```
Ip route 172.16.0.0 255.255.0.0 serial 0
Ip route 172.16.0.0 255.255.0.0 10.1.1.1
```

Routing table entries generated by different dynamic routing protocols may have unique update intervals, hold down timers, methods of calculating metrics, or administrative distances, but they all reference a given destination IP prefix and a corresponding local interface or next-hop address. If a next-hop address is referenced by any routing table entry, a second routing table entry must be performed (a recursive look-up) to determine if the next-hop address is reachable, and to determine which local interface to exit to get to the next-hop.

For a given organization, a well planned internal network applies many of the technologies and techniques mentioned in the Level Two (chapters Nine through Thirteen). A well planned internetwork is hierarchical in design. It deploys a well thought out IP addressing plan that subnets and summarizes efficiently. It has adequate redundancy and load balancing features. It may use static routes and default routes at some of the access-level (stub) networks. It may use a robust dynamic routing protocol (EIGRP or OSPF) at the core-level. In a well planned and maintained private network, end-to-end reachability is possible through routing tables that possess entries providing reachability for every *physical* segment within an autonomous system.

The next section provides an introduction to inter-autonomous system routing or EGP routing. Remember these general rules when comparing intra-autonomous system routing (IGP routing) with inter-autonomous system routing (EGP routing):

1. EGPs provide routing between autonomous systems. EGPs tell you *what* autonomous systems you need to go through to get to a given IP destination prefix.
2. IGPs tell you *how* to get through a given autonomous system to get to a given IP destination prefix, or *how* to get through an autonomous system to get to the next-hop IP address leading to another autonomous system.
3. EGPs view an internetwork as a logical collection of autonomous systems. The underlying network topology of any given autonomous system is unknown to the EGP.
4. IGPs view an internetwork as a physical collection of network segments. They know nothing about the existence of other autonomous systems.
5. EGPs deliver packets to the correct autonomous system, but do not deliver packets to the correct network segment.
6. IGPs deliver packets to the correct network segment.
7. EGPs operate between autonomous systems.
8. IGPs operate inside autonomous systems.

Introduction to Inter-Autonomous System (EGP) Routing

What happens when one organization's internetwork wants to interconnect to another organization's internetwork? Suddenly, you must interconnect to another internetwork that is not under your complete administrative control. For example, how does the MCI IP internetwork interconnect with the AT&T or SPRINT internetwork? This is exactly the issue that BGP-4 is designed to address.

BGP-4 solves this problem by exchanging "BGP table updates" (not routing table updates) containing the following minimum units of information:

- A destination IP prefix
- An origin code (well-known mandatory BGP attribute, Type code 1)
- An autonomous-system path (well-known mandatory BGP attribute, Type code 2)
- A next-hop address (well-known mandatory BGP attribute, Type code 3)

Excluding the destination IP prefix, the other units of information are called "attributes." BGP-4 attributes are a pre-defined collection of "tags" that are associated with a given IP prefix. Attributes are defined in RFC-1771. RFC-2042 lists all attributes that are currently in use. Attributes are used to assist BGP-4 in selecting the best path to a specific destination IP prefix. Using the above listed attributes, a single BGP-4 update provides a minimum of the information listed below:

To get to the destination IP prefix A.B.C.D/XX, go through the AS-PATH X-Y-Z. Your next-hop is N.N.N.N.

A.B.C.D	=	a given IP prefix
XX	=	a given IP prefix length
X-Y-Z	=	a given Autonomous System Path
N.N.N.N	=	the next-hop to forward a packet destined for the prefix A.B.C.D/XX

This information is not posted to an IP routing table, but rather to a BGP table. IP routing tables have no concept of what an AS_PATH or BGP-4 attribute is. Therefore, like EIGRP and OSPF, BGP-4 maintains a separate table from the main IP routing table. As with EIGRP and OSPF topology tables, if the BGP table is not formed properly, the main routing table will not contain the proper BGP routing table entries. Listed below is a sample BGP table.

```
bgp-100#sh ip bgp
BGP table version is 4, local router ID is 172.16.3.1
Status codes: s suppressed, d damped, h history, * valid, > best,
i -internal
Origin codes: i—IGP, e—EGP, ?—incomplete

  Network              Next Hop         Metric LocPrf Weight Path
* 10.1.1.0/24          172.16.1.2       0 200 300 400 i
*>                     172.16.5.5       0 500 400 i
*>192.168.1.0          172.16.1.2       0 200 300 i
*                      172.16.5.5       0 500 400 300 i
```

If a BGP speaker has two or more possible paths to the same destination in its BGP table, it must select the best path. When BGP receives updates for a given destination IP prefix from different ASs, BGP must decide which path to choose in order to reach a specific destination. BGP will select only a single path. The best path is marked by an ">" at the far left hand side of the BGP table. IGP path selection is based upon metrics. BGP-4 does not use metrics (an explanation of why will be provided later in the chapter.) The BGP-4 path selection process is based on evaluating the values of different BGP-4 "attributes," such as next-hop, AS-PATH length administrative weights, local preference, etc. Cisco BGP-4 speaking routers use the following ten-step decision criteria in the sequence presented below to select the best path to a given destination prefix:

1. Discard the BGP path if it references an unreachable next-hop address.
2. Out of all eligible paths, select the one with the largest "weight" attribute. (The weight attribute is a Cisco-specific attribute.)
3. If all "weight" attributes are equal, select the path with the largest local preference attribute.
4. If all local preference attributes are equal, select the path that was originated by BGP running on the local router.
5. If no route was originated on the local router, select the path possessing the shortest AS_PATH attribute.
6. If all AS-PATHs are of equal length, select the path with the lowest origin type attribute (Incomplete>EGP>IGP).
7. If all origin types are equal, select the path with the lowest Multi-Exit Discriminator (MED) attribute.
8. If all paths have the same MED attribute, select the external path over the internal path.
9. If the paths are either all external or all internal, select the path with the nearest IGP neighbor.
10. If all paths have the same nearest neighbor, select the path with the lowest BGP router identifier.

The BGP path selection process will be discussed later in this chapter, as well as in Chapter Twenty Eight. (Route-maps are also covered in Chapter Twenty Eight. Route-maps are a common IOS tool used to adjust and manipulate BGP attributes for path selection purposes.)

Once BGP-4 has selected the best available path in its BGP table, it will insert this path into its own routing table and advertise only the best path to its BGP-4 neighbors in other autonomous systems. The BGP-4 entry in the routing table will have the form:

To get to the destination IP prefix A.B.C.D/XX go to the next-hop N.N.N.N

A.B.C.D = a given IP prefix
XX = a given IP prefix length
N.N.N.N = the next-hop to forward a packet destined for the prefix A.B.C.D/XX.

As mentioned earlier, this type of entry requires a recursive lookup. Listed below is a sample IP routing table with BGP entries:

```
bgp-100#show ip route
Codes: C—connected, S—static, I—IGRP, R—RIP, M—mobile, B—BGP
 D—EIGRP, EX—EIGRP external, O—OSPF, IA—OSPF inter area
 N1—OSPF NSSA external type 1, N2—OSPF NSSA external type 2
 E1—OSPF external type 1, E2—OSPF external type 2, E—EGP
 i-IS-IS, L1—IS-IS level-1, L2 -IS-IS level-2, * -candidate default
 U—per-user static route, o—ODR

Gateway of last resort is not set

     10.0.0.0/24 is subnetted, 1 subnets
B        10.1.1.0 [20/0] via 172.16.5.5, 00:03:16
B     192.168.1.0/24 [20/0] via 172.16.1.2, 00:03:07
     172.16.0.0/24 is subnetted, 3 subnets
C    172.16.5.0 is directly connected, Ethernet0
C    172.16.1.0 is directly connected, Serial0
```

Notice that the BGP entries associate a given destination prefix with a next-hop address. YOU WILL NEVER SEE A BGP ROUTING TABLE ENTRY REFERENCE A LOCAL INTERFACE. In the routing table above, a recursive look-up will be performed to determine the reachability of the next-hop addresses of 172.16.5.5 and 172.16.1.2. BGP provides this information on a hop-by-hop basis.

Hierarchically Designed IGP Internetworks

Until now, IGP routing protocols have been discussed in something of a vacuum. The presented scenarios have shown perhaps half a dozen routers, interconnected by some routing protocol such as OSPF or EIGRP. The most complex configurations have involved two or at most three routing protocols that must "redistribute" routes amongst themselves. The global Internet, when mentioned, was nothing more than a sideshow. While discussing default routes, a serial link has been drawn to a "cloud" near the side of the page, and a vague reference has been made to forwarding traffic to unknown destinations upstream to the "Internet." A general rule observed by many network administrators is: "If a given destination IP prefix is not within an autonomous system's routing domain, the packet is forwarded to the 'net." The alert reader may be wondering what's missing. After all, building the world's largest global data network can't really be that easy.

No, it is not this easy! All the routing protocols presented so far—RIP, OSPF, IGRP and EIGRP,—are all "interior" routing protocols. They function within a single organization ("autonomous system") and operate under a single administrative control. "Exterior" routing protocols, of which BGP is the most important, route between autonomous systems. The entire Internet—every globally unique IP address in the world—is ultimately represented in a single BGP routing entity, which forms the backbone of the Internet. In today's Internet, inter-autonomous system routing conducted by BGP-4 provides a defaultless "top level domain" routing environment.

Routing tables of this kind (and the routers that possess them) are termed "defaultless." Current top level domain BGP-4 routers possess tables with well over 50,000 routes and no default routes! You may wonder how a complete Internet routing table can be constructed with only 50,000-plus routes. You may think that a complete Internet routing table would contain hundreds of thousands, or even millions, of routes. How can the entire Internet be represented by only 50,000-plus routes? The answer is route summarization and classless interdomain routing (CIDR blocking). These topics were introduced in Chapter Nine.

The meaning of the term "defaultless router" is simple. Most routers possess a relatively small routing table and a default route. Often the default route is advertised by a border router that passes packets along a serial link to a service provider. The border router itself has a default route (via the serial line), and often the router on the remote side of the link will have a default route as well. Default routes point to routers with default routes that point to routers with default routes until, eventually, some router has to stop passing the buck. That router is a defaultless router—a machine with no default route, and which therefore must possess routing table entries for every legal address within a given routing domain. When the routing domain is the Internet, a group of routers maintain a complete collection of all prefixes used in the Internet. Many of these prefixes are supernets of CIDR blocked addresses assigned to Internet Service Providers.

So this is the first rule of exterior routing in general, and BGP-4 routing in particular: you don't need to worry about it at all if you can get away with default routes. If your sole connection to the Internet is a single serial line to an Internet provider, you will probably never encounter BGP. Yet just as all roads once led to Rome, with today's Internet, all default routes must eventually lead to BGP—no matter how many hops it takes to get there.

Autonomous Systems

Many—indeed most—Internet users are part of somebody else's autonomous system and don't even know it. The simplest network configuration—a single link to a provider with a default route—does not need to be configured as an independent autonomous system. Since the only way to reach such a network is through its provider, the stub network can be subsumed within the provider's autonomous system, and usually within the provider's IP address space as well. So large Internet providers tend to balloon into gargantuan autonomous systems.

Yet not all autonomous systems are MCI-sized mammoths. Many contain just a few class C addresses. Just as the simplest network configuration (single link with a default route) has no need for autonomous systems information at all, an only slightly more complex one practically requires it. A network with two connections to two independent service providers (where each ISP is defined as its own autonomous system) must run BGP if it wants the world to know that it can be reached via two different autonomous systems, in case either provider experiences an outage.

BGP models the network as a collection of autonomous systems, with arbitrary links interconnecting them. Take the now familiar model of a network of routers, interconnected by links.

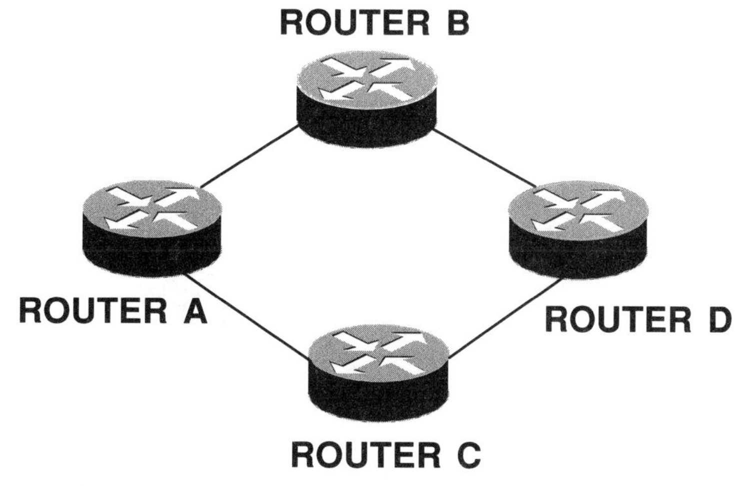

FIGURE 14-1 Intra-autonomous system routing.

Replace the routers with autonomous systems and you get a pretty good representation of how BGP sees its world. Just as an ordinary interior routing protocol assumes that its component routers will have no difficulty forwarding packets from one interface to another, so BGP assumes that a given autonomous system will be capable of forwarding IP traffic between any pair of its (exterior) links. BGP concerns itself little with how routing occurs within an autonomous system. In fact, all but the simplest BGP configurations require an interior routing protocol to run concurrently with BGP. We end up with a layered "hierarchical" routing architecture. BGP takes care of routing between

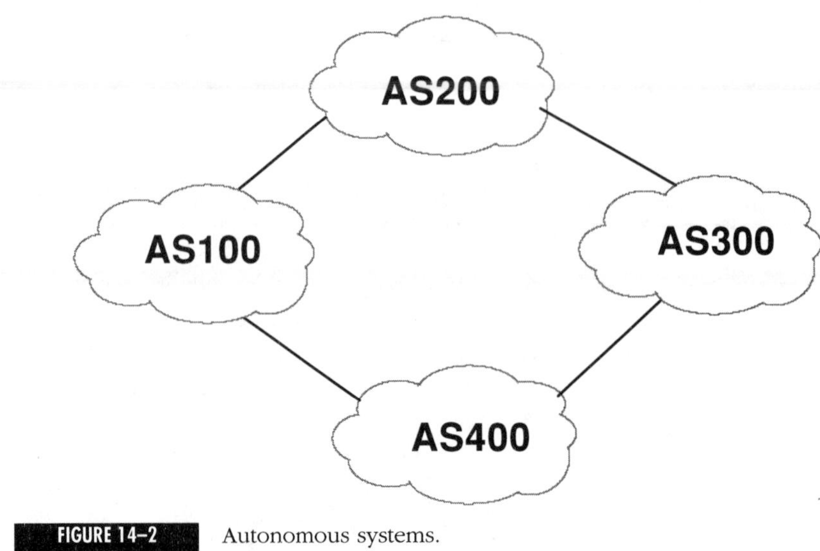

FIGURE 14–2 Autonomous systems.

autonomous systems, and various interior protocols perform routing within each autonomous system.

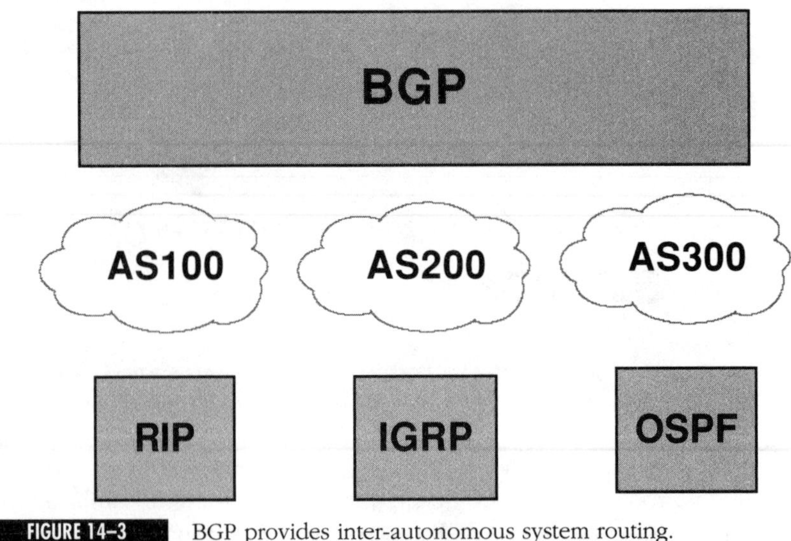

FIGURE 14–3 BGP provides inter-autonomous system routing.

The BGP-4 Protocol (RFC 1771)

As stated in RFC 1771, BGP operates over TCP, using port 179. In this regard, it differs from most other routing protocols, which use either UDP (in the case of RIP) or have their own IP protocol assignments (i.e., OSPF). By using TCP, BGP assures itself of a reliable transport, so the BGP protocol itself lacks any form of error detection or correction. These functions are performed by TCP.

Even more unusual, BGP can operate between peers separated by several intermediate hops, not necessarily running the BGP protocol. Contrast this to more conventional interior routing protocols, in which packets are only exchanged between directly connected routers, and each router in a series must be running the routing protocol to propagate information from one end to the other. Remember that BGP operates over an independent interior routing protocol, so it is not unusual for two routers, connected by a BGP session, to be separated by four or five intermediate routers running only OSPF or RIP.

BGP operates in one of two modes: Internal BGP (IBGP) or External BGP (EBGP). The protocol itself uses the same packet formats and data structures in either case; only the semantics of how the information is processed differs. IBGP is used between BGP speakers within a single autonomous system, while EBGP operates over inter-AS links.

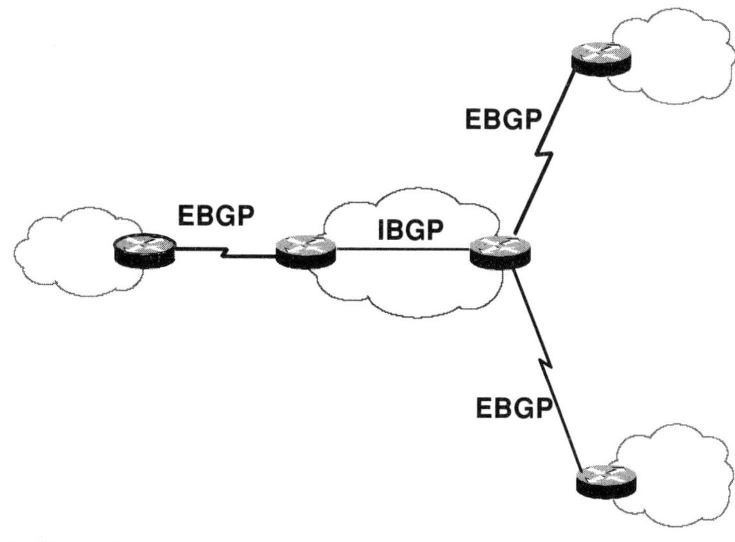

FIGURE 14–4 IBGP operates within an AS; EBGP operates between AS's.

Let's consider EBGP first, since it bears the most resemblance to a conventional interior routing protocol. The link interconnecting two autonomous systems will have an EBGP session running between the two routers on either side of the link. In this case, as in 90 percent of EBGP sessions, the two BGP peers are directly connected by a single shared network connection. Routing updates reflecting changes in the composition of ASs, or in the inter-AS links, are propagated between autonomous systems across EBGP links.

The function of IBGP, on the other hand, is to maintain internal consistency with an autonomous system. For interior routing protocols, this consideration is unimportant—obviously, if a router is advertising information out one of its interfaces, all the other interfaces have access to the same information, all being part of the same router. There is no chance of Ethernet 0 advertising routes via Serial 0, and then Serial 0 suddenly claiming that it doesn't know those routes! In the BGP world, however, many of the interfaces connecting an autonomous system to its neighboring ASs will be on physically different routers. Since BGP regards each AS as an atomic "hop," all the BGP speakers within a single AS must advertise the same information to all bordering EBGP speakers, since IBGP speakers are all part of a single routing entity. Ensuring this consistency is the role of IBGP.

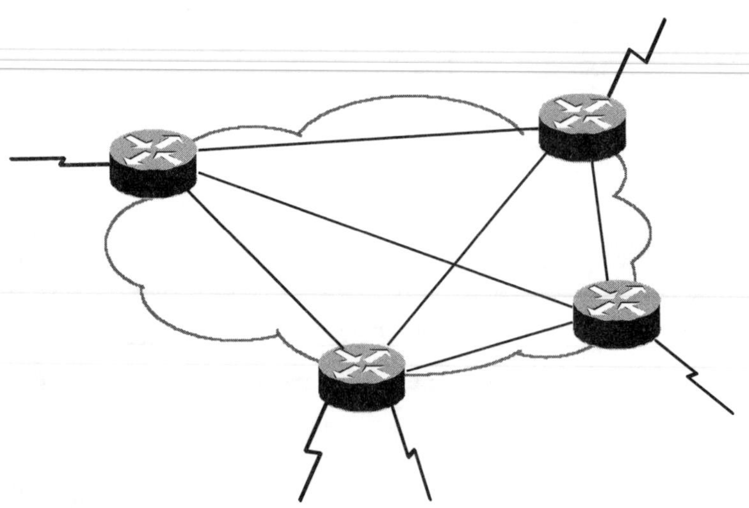

FIGURE 14–5 IBGP speakers are usually fully meshed.

Actually the operation of EBGP and IBGP really isn't as complex as it seems. The rule of thumb is that routing information changes only as it passes over EBGP links. All the routing structures stay the same as they pass over IBGP links. (Cisco IOS provides the ability to edit the routing structures as they pass over any BGP session, but that capability is beyond the scope of this discussion.) Therefore, two BGP speakers within the same autonomous system, interconnected by an IBGP link, should possess identical BGP routing tables. Furthermore, all BGP speakers within an autonomous system must be fully meshed with IBGP sessions (This requirement can be prohibitive for large ASs, and we will see later how it can be relaxed.) Every time a router receives an update over an EBGP link, it processes it and forwards any resulting changes over all its IBGP links, and any other EBGP links. Every time a router receives an update over an IBGP link, it processes it and forwards any changes over only its EBGP links. Routing information never passes from one IBGP link to another, and all BGP routing table changes are immediately announced to all IBGP peers. Thus the autonomous system maintains internal consistency.

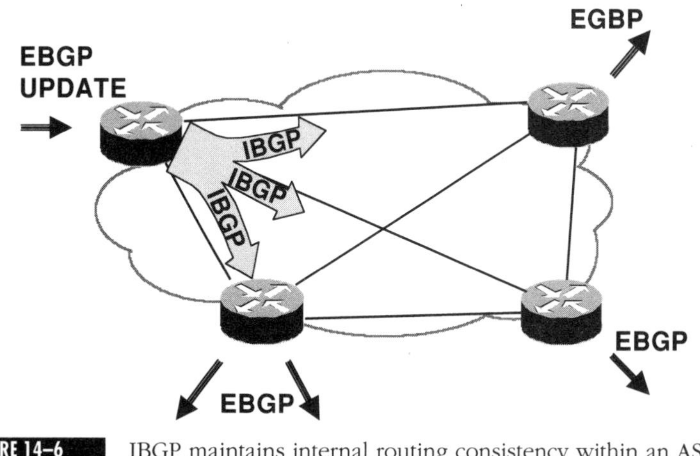

FIGURE 14–6 IBGP maintains internal routing consistency within an AS.

If you think about it for a minute, you'll realize why information cannot be relayed from one IBGP session to another. Since the BGP protocol only communicates inter-AS routing information, all its loop detection mechanisms are based on finding loops among autonomous systems. There is no way BGP could detect a loop among IBGP sessions. Since the information does not change over an IBGP session, relaying information from IBGP session to IBGP session could easily result in an infinite, and undetectable, loop.

BGP-4 Update Messages and BGP Attributes

BGP update messages contain an IP address prefix and associated path attributes. The IP prefix contained in the BGP update message is called the "network layer reachability information" (NLRI). NLRI (IP prefixes) have a collection of "path attributes" associated with them. Regarding BGP-4 path attributes, RFC 1771 states in Section 5:

"Path attributes fall into four separate categories:

1. Well-known mandatory.
2. Well-known discretionary.
3. Optional transitive.
4. Optional non-transitive.

Well-known attributes must be recognized by all BGP implementations. Some of these attributes are mandatory and must be included in every UPDATE message. Others are discretionary and may or may not be sent in a particular UPDATE message."

A path attribute is a "tag," consisting of an attribute type, attribute length, and attribute data. Displayed below is the attribute flag field (bits 0-7) and the attribute type field (bits 9-15) in a BGP-4 update message:

```
 0 1
 0 1 2 3 4 5 6 7 8 9 0 1 2 3 4 5
+-+-+-+-+-+-+-+-+-+-+-+-+-+-+-+-+
|O|T|P|L|       |   Type Code   |
+-+-+-+-+-+-+-+-+-+-+-+-+-+-+-+-+

O = Optional (1) or Well-Known (0)
T = Transitive (1) or Non-transitive (0)
P = Partial (1) or Complete (0)
L = Attribute Length: two bytes (1) or one byte (0)
```

The attribute flag bits allow BGP implementations to process attribute types they do not understand, if the optional bit is set. If the optional bit is clear, the attribute must be understood or the route discarded. The T bit, on an unrecognized optional attribute, specifies whether the attribute should be passed on to other BGP speakers (transitive) or quietly removed from the route (non-transitive). If an unrecognized optional transitive attribute is passed along, its partial bit is set to indicate that at least one BGP speaker handled the route but did not understand the attribute.

The BGP standard, of course, defines a number of well-known attributes that form the core of BGP routing. Listed below are the BGP-4 attributes described in Section 5 of RFC 1771:

5.1 Path Attribute Usage

The usage of each BGP path attributes is described in the following clauses.

5.1.1 ORIGIN (BGP-4 Type Code 1)

ORIGIN is a well-known mandatory attribute. The ORIGIN attribute shall be generated by the autonomous system that originates the associated routing information. It shall be included in the UPDATE messages of all BGP speakers that choose to propagate this information to other BGP speakers.

5.1.2 AS_PATH (BGP-4 Type Code 2)

AS_PATH is a well-known mandatory attribute. This attribute identifies the autonomous systems through which routing information carried in this UPDATE message has passed. The components of this list can be AS_SETs or AS_SEQUENCEs.

When a BGP speaker propagates a route which it has learned from another BGP speaker's UPDATE message, it shall modify the route's AS_PATH attribute based on the location of the BGP speaker to which the route will be sent:

a) When a given BGP speaker advertises the route to another BGP speaker located in its own autonomous system, the advertising speaker shall not modify the AS_PATH attribute associated with the route.

b) When a given BGP speaker advertises the route to a BGP speaker located in a neighboring autonomous system, then the advertising speaker shall update the AS_PATH attribute as follows:

1) If the first path segment of the AS_PATH is of type AS_SEQUENCE, the local system shall prepend its own AS number as the last element of the sequence (put it in the leftmost position).

2) If the first path segment of the AS_PATH is of type AS_SET, the local system shall prepend a new path segment of type AS_SEQUENCE to the AS_PATH, including its own AS number in that segment.

When a BGP speaker originates a route then:

a) The originating speaker shall include its own AS number in the AS_PATH attribute of all UPDATE messages sent to BGP speakers located in neighboring autonomous systems. (In this case, the AS number of the originating speaker's autonomous system will be the only entry in the AS_PATH attribute.)

b) The originating speaker shall include an empty AS_PATH attribute in all UPDATE messages sent to BGP speakers located in its own autonomous system. (An empty AS_PATH attribute is one whose length field contains the value zero.)

5.1.3 NEXT_HOP (BGP-4 Type Code 3)

The NEXT_HOP path attribute defines the IP address of the border router that should be used as the next hop to the destinations listed in the UPDATE message. If a border router belongs to the same AS as its peer, then the peer is an internal border router. Otherwise, it is an external border router. A BGP speaker can advertise any internal border router as the next hop provided that the interface associated with the IP address of this border router (as specified in the NEXT_HOP path attribute) shares a common subnet with both the local and remote BGP speakers. A BGP speaker can advertise any external border router as the next hop, provided that the IP address of this border router was learned from one of the BGP speaker's peers, and the interface associated with the IP address of this border router (as specified in the NEXT_HOP path attribute) shares a common subnet with the local and remote BGP speakers. A BGP speaker needs to be able to support disabling advertisement of external border routers.

A BGP speaker must never advertise an address of a peer to that peer as a NEXT_HOP, for a route that the speaker is originating. A BGP speaker must never install a route with itself as the next hop.

When a BGP speaker advertises the route to a BGP speaker located in its own autonomous system, the advertising speaker shall not modify the NEXT_HOP attribute associated with the route. When a BGP speaker receives the route via an internal link, it may forward packets to the NEXT_HOP address if the address contained in the attribute is on a common subnet with the local and remote BGP speakers.

5.1.4 MULTI_EXIT_DISC (BGP-4 Type Code 4)

The MULTI_EXIT_DISC attribute may be used on external (inter-AS) links to discriminate among multiple exit or entry points to the same neighboring AS. The value of the MULTI_EXIT_DISC attribute is a four octet unsigned number which is called a metric. All other factors being equal, the exit or entry point with lower metric should be preferred. If received over external links, the MULTI_EXIT_DISC attribute may be propagated over internal links to other BGP speakers within the same AS. The MULTI_EXIT_DISC attribute is never propagated to other BGP speakers in neighboring ASs.

5.1.5 LOCAL_PREF (BGP-4 Type Code 5)

LOCAL_PREF is a well-known discretionary attribute that shall be included in all UPDATE messages that a given BGP speaker sends to the other BGP speakers located in its own autonomous system. A BGP speaker shall calculate the degree of preference for each external route and include the degree of preference when advertising a route to its internal peers. The higher degree of preference should be preferred. A BGP speaker shall use the degree of preference learned via LOCAL_PREF in its decision process (see section 9.1.1).

A BGP speaker shall not include this attribute in UPDATE messages that it sends to BGP speakers located in a neighboring autonomous system. If it is contained in an UPDATE message that is received from a BGP speaker which is not located in the same autonomous system as the receiving speaker, then this attribute shall be ignored by the receiving speaker.

5.1.6 ATOMIC_AGGREGATE (BGP-4 Type Code 6)

ATOMIC_AGGREGATE is a well-known discretionary attribute. If a BGP speaker, when presented with a set of overlapping routes from one of its peers (see 9.1.4), selects the less specific route without selecting the more specific one, then the local system shall attach the ATOMIC_AGGREGATE attribute to the route when propagating it to other BGP speakers (if that attribute is not already present in the received less specific route). A BGP speaker that receives a route with the ATOMIC_AGGREGATE attribute shall not remove the attribute from the route when propagating it to other speakers. A BGP speaker that receives a route with the ATOMIC_AGGREGATE attribute shall not make any NLRI of that route more specific (as defined in 9.1.4) when advertising this route to other BGP speakers. A BGP speaker that receives a route with the ATOMIC_AGGREGATE attribute needs to be cognizant of the fact that the actual path to destinations, as specified in the NLRI of the route, while having the loop-free property, may traverse ASs that are not listed in the AS_PATH attribute.

5.1.7 AGGREGATOR (BGP-4 Type Code 7)

AGGREGATOR is an optional transitive attribute which may be included in updates which are formed by aggregation (see Section 9.2.4.2). A BGP speaker which performs route aggregation may add the AGGREGATOR attribute which shall contain its own AS number and IP address."

A highly detailed explanation of the BGP-4 Update message format is provided in section 4.3 of RFC 1771 (A Border Gateway Routing Protocol 4 (BGP 4)). The use of each of the BGP-4 attributes defined in RFC 1771 is covered in section 5 of RFC 1771.

Path Vector Routing

You may be wondering whether BGP-4 can be pigeonholed as either a distance vector or a link state protocol. Unfortunately, neither model really describes the operation of BGP, which has been characterized as a "path vector" protocol. The main difference is the lack of metrics, certainly one of BGP's more unusual features.

All conventional interior routing protocols use metrics in one form or another. RIP uses a hop count; IGRP and EIGRP use a five-element metric based on bandwidth and delay, among other things; OSPF uses a 16-bit metric whose defaults are based on bandwidth. Metrics serve two important purposes. First, they allow the routing protocol to select the best route to a destination when offered a choice between two or more competing alternatives. Second, they eliminate routing loops, since adding extra links which bring data back to a previous location will always result in a larger metric than the original route.

Metrics have one important drawback, however. They require agreement between the routers on how metrics are to be created and interpreted. Obviously, if one router is labeling Ethernet segments with a metric of 10, and another is labeling Ethernet segments with a metric of 100, while yet a third uses 1 for Ethernet metrics, chaos will rule! Normally, this is not much of a problem, since all the routers will be under unified administrative control. The network engineer decides that 10 will be the metric for Ethernet, and configures all the routers accordingly.

This model breaks down for BGP-4, since there is no centralized administrative control to decide on a set of metrics. One autonomous system may use one set of metrics, and a second may use a completely different set of metrics. The BGP-4 solution is not to use metrics at all.

BGP-4 Loop Detection and Loop Avoidance

To BGP-4, loop avoidance is of critical importance. BGP, like any other routing protocol, must have a method of detecting and avoiding loops.

BGP's loop detection algorithm is based on "path vectors." A path vector, included in each BGP update message, is a list of all autonomous systems that have handled the route. Upon receiving a BGP advertisement, a router checks to see if its own AS number is included in the path vector. If so, then the information must be passed around in a loop, so it is simply ignored. If not, then the local AS number is prepended to the path vector before the route is passed along to another autonomous system. The path vector is represented in BGP update messages by the AS_PATH attribute. Every BGP update is tagged with an AS_PATH, which begins as an empty list, and grows as the path propagates through the network.

Thus, the BGP method of loop detection and avoidance is not based on a common set of agreed-upon metrics, but on uniquely assigned autonomous system numbers. These numbers are issued by the Internet Assigned Numbers Authority (**http://www.iana.org/**), the same organization responsible for managing IP address space. Of course, BGP's method of loop detection can only detect loops between autonomous systems, not loops within one system. This only reiterates a point made in the previous section—loops must not be allowed to form via IBGP links, since BGP could not detect them. This is why routing updates are not passed from one IBGP link to another, which leads us directly to the general rule that all BGP speakers within an autonomous system must be fully meshed via BGP/TCP sessions, to insure that all BGP routers receive all BGP updates. (Later in this chapter, we will see that route reflectors and confederations present an exception to this general rule.).

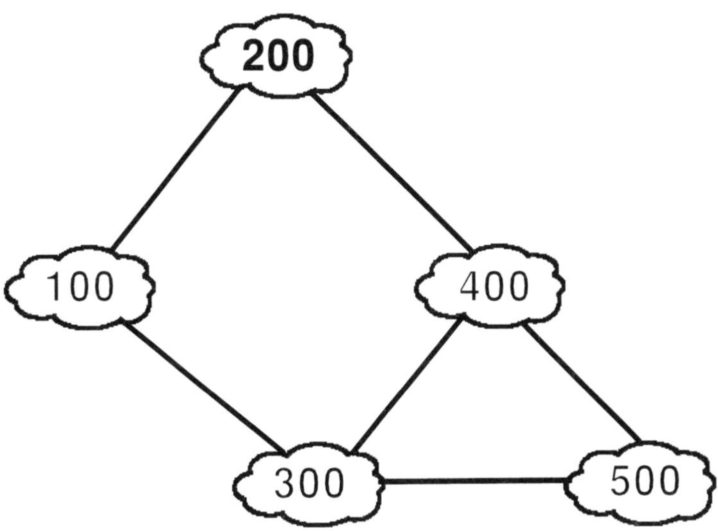

FIGURE 14–7 BGP updates possess an AS_PATH attribute.

BGP-4 Path Selection

Many of the BGP-4 attributes listed in the section on BGP-4 attributes are used in the ten-step BGP-4 path selection process described below. If a BGP speaker possesses two or more possible paths to the same destination IP prefix, it must select the best path. It performs this task by comparing the values in the sequence presented below. For example, if the local preference of one path is greater than another (step 2), the analysis is over. The path with a higher local preference is preferred regardless of what the comparison of values in subsequent steps of the decision process may yield. Also, if all values are the same between two or more possible paths throughout the decision process, the last step is a tie breaker: select the path with the lowest BGP router identifier. Note the highlighted BGP-4 attributes used in the path selection process:

1. Discard the BGP path if it references an unreachable next-hop address **(BGP-4 Type Code 3)**.
2. Out of all eligible paths, select the one with the largest administrative "weight". The administrative weight is a Cisco-specific value. It is locally significant. It is not propagated to any other BGP speaker.
3. If all "weight" attributes are equal, select the path with the largest local preference attribute **(BGP-4 Type Code 5)**.
4. If all local preference attributes are equal, select the path that was originated by BGP running on the local router.

5. If no route was originated on the local router, select the path possessing the shortest AS_PATH attribute **(BGP-4 Type Code 2)**.
6. If all AS-PATHs are of equal length, select the path with the lowest origin type attribute (Incomplete>EGP>IGP) **(BGP-4 Type Code 1)**.
7. If all origin types are equal, select the path with the lowest Multi-Exit Discriminator (MED) attribute **(BGP-4 Type Code 4)**.
8. If all paths have the same MED attribute, select the external path over the internal path.
9. If the paths are either all external or all internal, select the path with the nearest IGP neighbor.
10. If all paths have the same nearest neighbor, select the path with the lowest BGP router identifier.

A common method of manipulating BGP-4 attributes used in the path selection process is configuring route-maps. Configuring route-maps is covered in Chapter Twenty-Eight.

Interaction With IGPS

Once the best path to a given IP prefix is selected, it must be inserted into the BGP speaker's local routing table. Otherwise, it will not be advertised to other EBGP speakers. This restriction supports the following rule stated in RFC 1771:

> "One must focus on the rule that a BGP speaker [will] advertise to its peers (other BGP speakers which it communicates with) in neighboring ASs *only those routes that it itself uses*. This rule reflects the "hop-by-hop" routing paradigm generally used throughout the current Internet…"

BGP-4 interacts with IGPs in a number of ways:

1. The BGP table is populated with information containing the following elements:

To get to the destination IP prefix A.B.C.D/XX, go through the AS-PATH X-Y-Z. Your next-hop is N.N.N.N.

2. After the BGP-4 path selection process is performed, the BGP-4 entry with the best path is inserted in the IP routing table only if the following conditions are met:
   a. The route to be inserted into the IP table already resides in the IGP table. (The Rule of Synchronization.)
   b. The Rule of Synchronization is disabled. (Synchronization will be described later in this section.)

c. The NEXT-HOP attribute listed in the BGP table is reachable by the IGP table.

Listed below is a common language description of the IP routing table entry inserted from the BGP table into the IP routing table:

To get to the destination IP prefix A.B.C.D/XX, go to the next-hop N.N.N.N

A BGP-4 entry will always list a given IP prefix with an associated next-hop address. It will never list an associated local interface. Therefore, a recursive look-up will be performed to determine which local interface to use to get to the next-hop

4. Listed below is a common language description of the recursive look-up for the next-hop address:

To get to destination IP prefix N.N.N.N/XX, go out local interface Y(Z).

The Golden Rule of BGP: Never advertise routes that you don't know how to get to.

Relaying routes between BGP speakers is only part of the story. As discussed earlier, BGP typically resides on top of an interior gateway protocol (IGP). The interaction between the two can take one of three different forms.

1. First, every router in an autonomous system can be running BGP. Since all the routers have BGP routing information, the IGP need only carry routing information for the local AS.
2. If non-BGP speaking routers are present, BGP routing information must be redistributed into the IGP.
3. Default routes can be configured within the autonomous system to allow non-local autonomous system traffic (or inter-autonomous system traffic) to exit out without redistributing all BGP routes into the AS. This technique can be used when an autonomous system is not acting as a transit AS.

The generally recommended procedure is the first approach, primarily because any form of redistribution introduces information loss, but also because it is simpler to understand and administer. Only the first method will be considered here.

The Next-Hop Reachability Requirement

Every time BGP routes pass between autonomous systems—that is, across an EBGP link—the NEXT_HOP attribute is set to the IP address of the sending router. Since BGP attributes are not modified as they traverse IBGP links, every BGP speaker in an autonomous system sees the same NEXT_HOP attribute for each BGP route. That NEXT_HOP is simply the IP address of the first router in the next autonomous system along the BGP path:

NEXT HOP
FOR AS 100

100

200

NEXT HOP
FOR AS 200

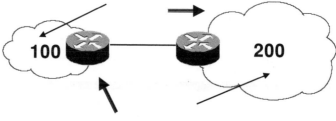

FIGURE 14–8 BGP updates possess a next-hop attribute.

Since we are assuming that all the routers in our autonomous system are BGP speakers, we need only ensure that our IGP possesses routing information for all the NEXT_HOPs, and that all the routers will be able to construct defaultless routing tables. Beginning with the BGP routes, a decision algorithm will be applied to select the best BGP route for each foreign autonomous system. The algorithm's details will be discussed later, but for now, suffice it to say that since all the routers have identical BGP tables (since they are all IBGP peers), and since they all run the same decision algorithm, they will all select the same BGP routes. Next, the routers look up the NEXT_HOP address using the interior gateway protocol (OSPF, EIGRP, etc.), and find an interface and neighbor to which to route the traffic. Finally, all the IP address prefixes in the BGP routing update will be installed into the IP routing table with that interface and neighbor as the next-hop.

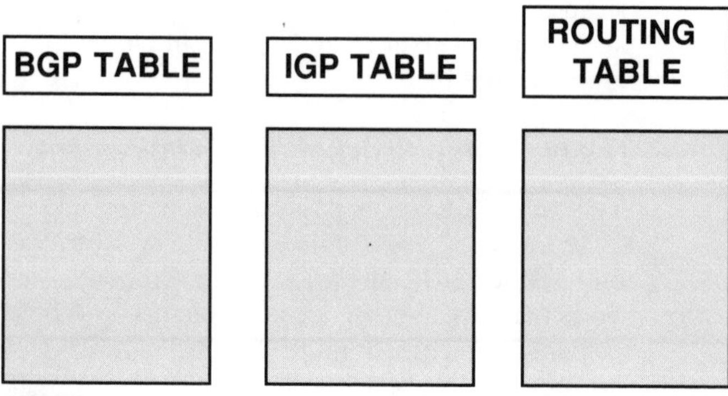

FIGURE 14–9 The tables involved with determining BGP next-hop reachability.

The biggest "gotcha" in the scheme, aside from the memory and processing requirements (which can be substantial), is the issue of NEXT_HOP reachability via the IGP. Let's carefully consider the configuration at the border of two hypothetical autonomous systems, AS 140 and 150. Each of these ASs will have an associated IP address space. Let's assume AS 140 uses the Class B address 140.140.0.0, and AS 150 uses 150.150.0.0. Since routers are wholly owned by their autonomous systems, a router cannot be in two autonomous systems at once. Therefore, one of AS 140's routers must be connected via a shared link to one of AS 150's routers. The shared link must itself be numbered like any other IP link, requiring a subnet number and mask, and this link's address must come out of one ASs address space or the others. Let's assume that it comes from AS 140's address space, and that a 24-bit subnet mask is in use. We will assign 140.140.100.0 to the link.

It must be emphasized that the assumptions used here are completely general. Each router must be in one AS or the other, and the link between them must be numbered out of somebody's address space, so at least one of the autonomous systems will have a local IP address space different from the one used for the link. In this case, that would be AS 150, since the link is numbered out of AS 140's address block.

Now, consider what happens when a BGP routing update proceeds across this link from AS 140 to AS 150. Since this is a EBGP link, the NEXT_HOP attribute will be updated to reflect the address of the sending router—in this case, 140.140.100.140. The BGP route will now be propagated throughout AS 150, with the NEXT_HOP remaining unchanged. So now another router in AS 150, router X for example, attempting to resolve the BGP routes, will need to route to 140.140.100.140—an address that does not appear in any of its IGP routing information, since the IGP only routes for 150.150.0.0.

So what happens? The BGP route will be "ignored" by router X. This must be restated for emphasis, since it is one of the most common configuration problems encountered with BGP: **If the router does not possess an IGP route to the BGP NEXT_HOP, the BGP route will be ignored.** It will appear in the BGP table, but it will not be entered in the IP routing table; nor will it be passed along to other BGP speakers. A BGP speaker will never advertise a route for which it lacks a valid, routable NEXT_HOP, because it could never deliver packets addressed to that route.

What's the solution? In general, the IGP must be extended to cover all links with other autonomous systems, no matter what numbering scheme is in use. Typically, this requires little more than injecting an extra subnet or network route from the border router, usually with a "network" statement. Cisco also provides the ability to change the NEXT_HOP attribute so that it points to a local IP address, using the "next-hop-self" option described in the next section.

Summary of BGP Overview

As RFC 1771 states, the distinguishing features of BGP-4 are as follows:

1. Two BGP-4 neighbors form a TCP connection between each other using TCP port 179. EBGP connections are established between two BGP speakers in different autonomous systems. IBGP connections are established between two BGP speakers in the same autonomous system.
2. Initially, the BGP neighbors exchange their entire routing tables. Once this initial exchange is performed, incremental updates are sent as the routing table changes.
3. BGP-4 supports Classless interdomain routing (CIDR).
4. A BGP speaker advertises to its peers (other BGP speakers with which it has a neighbor relationship) in neighboring ASs only those routes that it itself uses. This rule reflects the hop-by-hop routing paradigm generally used throughout the current Internet.
5. BGP attributes are a set of parameters that describe the characteristics of a prefix. These attributes are part of each BGP update.
6. Within an IGP, you have control over the whole net. Your policy tool is metrics. With EGPs, you do not have control over the whole network. Your policy tool is adjusting path attributes.

For more information on the theoretical operation of BGP-4, see *Routing in the Internet* by Christian Huitema, as well as RFCs 1771 and 1772 (They are very readable RFCs.) For additional references, see the "For Further Study" section at the end of this chapter.

Cisco's BGP Implementation

To enable BGP-4 routing on a Cisco router, a minimum of two statements must be configured:

1. router bgp xxx (xxx = the router's own autonomous system number)
2. neighbor A.B.C.D remote-as xxx (A.B.C.D = remote BGP neighbor's IP address; xxx = remote BGP neighbor's autonomous system number)

Enabling the BGP Routing Process

Like other routing protocols, Cisco's BGP implementation is triggered with a "router bgp" command, with the router's autonomous system number appended. For example, a router in AS 100 would initiate BGP routing with a "router bgp 100" statement.

Establishing a BGP Neighbor Relationship

BGP differs from most other routing protocols in requiring "neighbor" statements. BGP can form neighbor relations with other routers located almost anywhere on the Internet, therefore, for security reasons, Cisco routers will not accept BGP connections from routers not configured as neighbors. Both EBGP and IBGP peers must be configured with the required "remote-as" option indicating the AS number of the neighbor router. IBGP peers will have a "remote-as" number identical to the local "router bgp" number, while EBGP peers will have different "remote-as" numbers.

With BGP-4, you define explicit border-points. With BGP, you do not send out broadcasts for other neighboring BGP speakers to dynamically pick up and process. Unlike OSPF and EIGRP, BGP-4 does not have a dynamic neighbor discovery mechanism. BGP-4 has no equivalent to OSPF's and EIGRP's HELLO protocol. With BGP-4, you must make sure your source IP address matches the IP address that your peer is expecting from you—something like a caller ID service.

Displayed below is a sample configuration of BGP neighbor statements:

```
router bgp 200
 neighbor 10.1.1.1 remote-as 100
 neighbor 172.16.1.2 remote-as 200
 neighbor 172.16.2.3 remote-as 200
```

Once the neighbor statements have been entered on the two routers that are configured to act as BGP neighbors, you can check the status of the BGP neighbor relationship with show ip bgp neighbor and show ip bgp summary. Show ip bgp neighbor provides extensive statistics on each neighbor relationship formed by a given router. Show ip bgp summary gives you a brief summary of each neighbor relationship. Listed below is a sample display of the show ip bgp summary command:

```
r2#show ip bgp summary
BGP table version is 3, main routing table version 3
2 network entries (2/6 paths) using 408 bytes of memory
1 BGP path attribute entries using 92 bytes of memory
0 BGP route-map cache entries using 0 bytes of memory
0 BGP filter-list cache entries using 0 bytes of memory

Neighbor      V  AS   MsgRcvd MsgSent TblVer  InQ Out Q  Up/Down     State/PfxRcd
10.1.1.1      4  100  271     272     3       0   0      01:40:25    0
172.16.1.2    4  200  265     265     3       0   0      01:40:28    0
172.16.2.3    4  200  109     107     3       0   0      01:40:34    2
```

Advertising Networks via BGP-4

The Cisco IOS provides three different methods of announcing networks via BGP-4:

1. Using the "network" statement
2. Redistributing static routes
3. Redistributing dynamic routes

Like other routing protocols, "network" statements are used to declare the local IP network numbers to be advertised via BGP. Since BGP fully supports CIDR, a "mask" option can also be provided to fully specify an IP address prefix. IP addresses configured with the "network" command must be reachable via the IP routing table, either by virtue of being directly connected, or via some interior gateway protocol. BGP will not advertise networks for which it lacks routes.

As a network prefix travels through an inter-autonomous system network, remember these rules:

1. The IP prefix always stays the same.
2. The AS-PATH is prepended as the prefix moves from autonomous system to autonomous system.
3. The next-hop address always changes as it crosses over an EBGP link. Every time you announce a prefix over an EBGP connection the advertising EBGP speaker is the next-hop.
4. By default, the next-hop never changes as it crosses over an IBGP link (remember the Cisco next-hop-self exception).

The BGP-4 Rule of Synchronization

Cisco applies an important and often confusing concept called "synchronization," designed for configurations where BGP is redistributing routing information into an IGP. In this case, the router should not announce BGP routes to other EBGP neighbors until the routes appear in the IGP; nor are the BGP routes posted into the IP routing table. This is designed for cases where not all routers are running BGP in a transit autonomous system. It is important to confirm that routes exist in the interior protocol before announcing them to the outside world. A suggested configuration is to have BGP running on all the routers, with no route redistribution. Therefore, synchronization should be turned off with the "no synchronization" command. As a precaution, synchronization is left on by default, BGP routing updates will not propagate through the network, since they will wait forever for interior routes that will never appear.

A BASIC BGP Configuration

Example One shows four routers in a row, each in a different autonomous system, with EBGP links running between them. No other routing protocols are in use. Since each router forms a complete autonomous system, this is a special case where no IGP is required. The NEXT_HOP addresses change as each link is traversed, so each router can see all its NEXT_HOP addresses because they are directly connected.

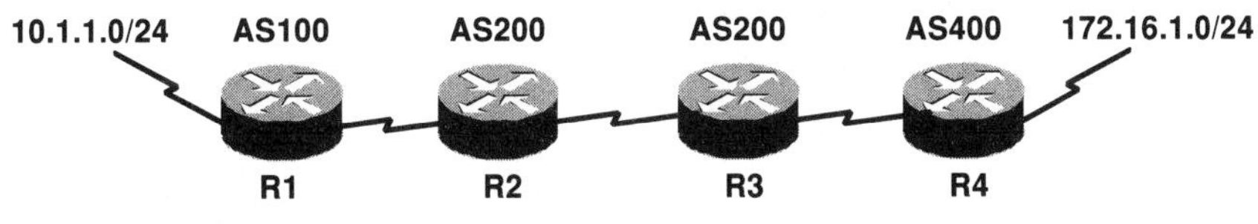

FIGURE 14–10 Example One: Four routers in a row; each in a different AS.

Set up four routers and configure them as shown in Figure 14–10. Remember to verify IP connectivity between adjacent routers—if you cannot ping between two neighbors, BGP will not work either. Use the "show ip bgp neighbor" command to verify correct establishment of the neighbor relationships—correctly configured neighbors will show a timer running under the UP/Down Column heading in slip bgp summary. Make sure you have got the right IP addresses set in the neighbor statements—using a neighbor's IP address other than the one directly connected to you probably will not work. Make sure the neighbor statements are symmetrical—neighbor commands are required on "both" sides of a BGP link.

Congratulations! You have just configured your first BGP network. You might want to make the network more complex by adding a link between the two end routers and forming a loop. Study how BGP deals with loop detection and avoidance, using the "debug ip bgp events" command to watch the routing exchanges.

Now let's move on to a slightly more complex example, where we will reconfigure the two routers in the middle as part of a single autonomous system. We will now have an IBGP link between them, and require the use of either "next-hop-self" or an interior routing protocol. We will just use "next-hop-self," and save the IGP for the example. Notice how the "next-hop-self" statements are associated with the IBGP neighbor relationships.

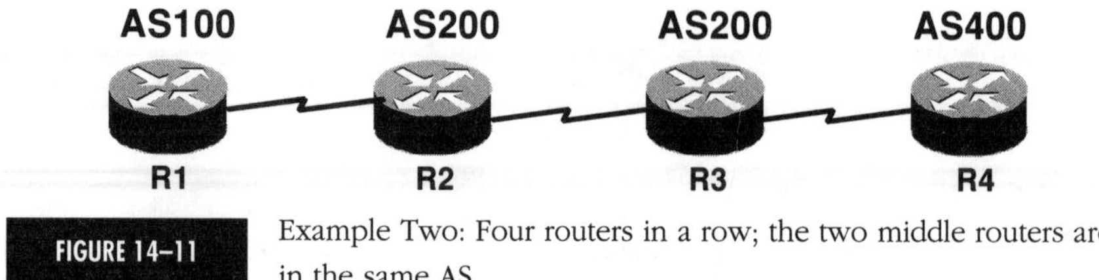

FIGURE 14–11 Example Two: Four routers in a row; the two middle routers are in the same AS.

If we now add a fifth router and remove the "next-hop-self" statements, we can add an interior gateway protocol and start to build a "real" autonomous system. We'll use OSPF in this example. Notice how the network statements are constructed to include the external links. Notice also the full mesh that must be constructed between all the IBGP speakers—each router must have an IBGP session with all other BGP speakers in its autonomous system.

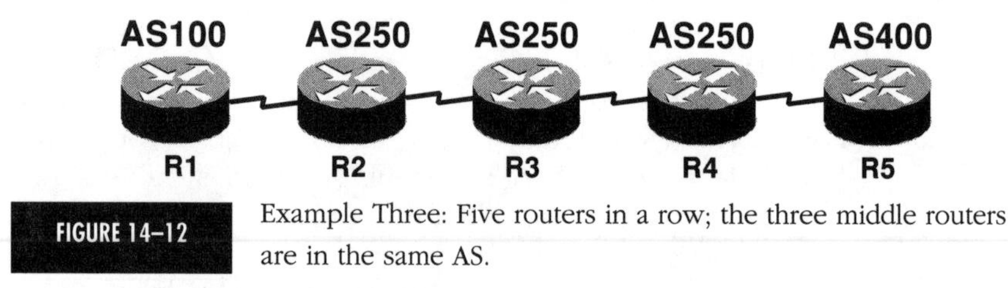

FIGURE 14–12 Example Three: Five routers in a row; the three middle routers are in the same AS.

Route Reflectors and Confederations

The requirement that BGP speakers within an autonomous system must be fully meshed by IBGP links can be troublesome, to say the least. A large AS with 100 BGP speakers would require 4950 IBGP sessions to build a full mesh. (The number of links in a full mesh of N devices is N(N-1)/2].) Perhaps even more troublesome than the amount of network traffic generated by all these links are the configuration requirements. Each of the 100 routers would require 99 neighbor statements! There must be a better way.

Cisco provides two tools for reducing the required number of IBGP links—route reflectors and confederations. Route reflectors are special routers that relay BGP routes from one IBGP session to another. A confederation is like an AS within an AS—BGP uses EBGP rules for inter-confederation links, but all the confederations appear to be a single AS to the outside world. Route reflectors work well for smaller configurations, while confederations are better suited to large networks.

Returning to the previous example, we can make the center router a route reflector, and eliminate the IBGP link between routers R2 and R4. No special configuration should be done on the route reflector clients. The configuration is only on the route reflector server (the router that should relay routes between its IBGP sessions). Place a "route-reflector-client" option on each of the neighbor statements for route reflector clients.

This is the same as Example 3, but the middle router is now a route reflector, and only two IBGP links are used: AS 100, 250, 250, 250, 400.

In general, IBGP links can be classified as either reflecting or non-reflecting. All the non-reflecting IBGP links must form a full mesh among a subset of the routers, which form the core of the BGP routing domain. Any other routers must be connected to the core by one, and only one, reflecting link. The neighbor statement on the core router corresponding to the reflecting link must contain a "route-reflector-client" option. It is most important that route reflector links not be allowed to form a loop, or BGP traffic would cycle indefinitely.

Confederations extend the BGP model by allowing autonomous systems to be broken into subsets which behave like mini-ASs.

Fault Tolerance via Loopbacks

Consider the following scenario. A BGP speaking router has four network connections—two serial links to other autonomous systems running EBGP, an Ethernet within the local AS, and a Token-Ring, also local. Assume that both the Ethernet and Token-Ring have fairly good redundancy within the AS; any other device can be reached via either network. Now we need to configure IBGP sessions. Which IP address should we use to name this router in its peer's "neighbor" statements? If we use the Ethernet's address, and the Ethernet fails, then the IBGP session will fail also, even though the router can still be reached via the Token-Ring. The interior routing protocol will declare the Ethernet's subnet (and all its associated IP addresses) down! Yet if we use the Token-Ring's address, or any of the serial link's addresses, the same problem results if that interface fails.

The solution is to use an IP address associated with an interface that will always be up, because it can never fail—a loopback. The loopback must possess a valid IP address in a subnet all its own, which must be reachable via the IGP. Use using a classless routing protocol such as OSPF, and taking advantage of VLSM to create a number of 30-bit address prefixes. Some can be used for serial links; some for loopbacks. Assign each BGP router a loopback subnet, and configure a loopback interface on each router. Use these IP addresses in all BGP "neighbor" statements. Now your BGP sessions will stay up so long as your IGP can find valid routes through your network.

One issue remains to be addressed. Remember that Cisco's BGP implementation requires that incoming BGP sessions match up with a "neighbor" statement. This creates a chicken-and-egg problem. One router must originate the BGP connection (it's just a TCP session), and it finds the destination address in its "neighbor" statement, but how does it find the source address? Normally, TCP sessions source using the address of whatever interface out of which the packets are routed. In this case, however, we need to insure that the IP source address is the "loopback's" source address, since that is the address from which the remote peer is expecting the connection to come. Any other address would be rejected. Use the "update-source" option on the "neighbor" command to specify which interface's address BGP sessions for that neighbor should be sourced from.

Filtering BGP-4 Updates

In order to enforce the Golden Rule of BGP (never advertise routes that you don't know how to get to), BGP-4 filtering techniques are applied. Two types of BGP-4 filtering methods exist. One is a scalpel-like filtering tool. The second is a sledge hammer-like filtering tool. The distribute-list is a scalpel-like tool since it allows filtering on a prefix by prefix basis. The AS-PATH access-list is a sledge hammer-like tool since it filters all networks associated with a particular autonomous system number.

The distribute-list was first introduced in Chapter Twelve. In Chapter Twelve, distribute-lists were used to filter IP routing updates during the IGP route redistribution process. Whether it is a distribute list or AS-PATH access-list, the basic configuration statements are the same. Since distribute-list configuration was covered in Chapter Twelve, this chapter will focus primarily AS-PATH access-lists.

1. Create a BGP-4 AS-Path access-list.
2. Apply the AS-Path access-list to a BGP-4 neighbor statement.

AS-PATH access-lists are created with regular expressions. Commonly used regular expressions are:

- . Matches any single character
- * Matches 0 or more sequences of a given pattern
- .* Match any pattern
- ^ Beginning of a string
- $ End of string
- _ Beginning of string, end of string or delimter (comma, space, brace, etc.)

Deny all routes transiting AS 300: _300_
Deny all routes originating from AS 300: _300$
Deny all routes sourced from directly connected AS 200 ^200$
Permit all routes transiting directly connected AS 200 ^200_
Deny advertising any routes from my own AS. ^$

To obtain a more detailed description of Regular Expressions, see the Regular Expressions Appendix at the end of Volume III, the Access Service Command Reference.

Troubleshooting BGP

Are Your BGP Neighbor Relationships Established?

- Can you PING your neighbor's address?
- Can you PING your own address?
- Remember to troubleshoot both sides of the connection
- Show ip bgp neighbor
- Show ip bgp summary
- Debug ip bgp events
- Clear ip bgp *

DO NOT USE CLEAR IP BGP * ON A PRODUCTION NETWORK.

Can You See a Given IP Prefix in Your BGP Table?

If a given IP prefix is not in a router's BGP table, check downstream BGP speakers.

If the prefix is not in downstream BGP-4 speakers BGP tables. Check the BGP-4 table of the originator of the route.

Make sure the prefix is in the IGP table of the source of the BGP update.

- Show ip bgp
- Debug ip bgp events
- Debug ip bgp updates
- Clear ip bgp *

DO NOT USE CLEAR IP BGP * ON A PRODUCTION NETWORK.

Is the Route Being Advertised to Other BGP Speakers?

- Is the referenced next-hop address reachable?
- Is the Rule of Synchronization an issue?
- Show ip bgp
- Debug ip bgp events

- Debug ip bgp updates
- Clear ip bgp *

  DO NOT USE CLEAR IP BGP * ON A PRODUCTION NETWORK.

Is the Route Being Inserted in the Local Routing Table?

- Is the referenced next-hop address reachable?
- Is the Rule of Synchronization an issue?
- Show ip bgp
- Show ip route
- Debug ip bgp events
- Debug ip bgp updates
- Clear ip bgp *

  DO NOT USE CLEAR IP BGP * ON A PRODUCTION NETWORK.

Summary

BGP-4 provides inter-autonomous system routing services. The basic BGP-4 configuration steps are summarized below:

1. **Establish neighbor relationships**

   EBGP
   Rule: Direct Connection between EBGP speakers
   Exception: EBGP_Multihop

   IBGP
   Rule: Full Mesh
   Exception: Route Reflectors and Confederations

2. **Announce IP Prefixes**
   - Network (Exact Match Rule)
   - Redistribute static routes
   - Redistribute dynamic routes
3. Sending Network Updates from one EBGP speaker to another:

   Determine whether there is a rule of synchronization issue
   Determine whether there is a next-hop reachability issue
4. Inter-autonomous filtering

   Filtering using distribute-lists
   Filtering using AS-PATH lists

5. Selecting from multiple paths to a given destination network prefix
   - Adiust the administrative weight (keep to yourself)
   - Adjust the local preference (Keep it in the family)

This chapter is only an introduction to BGP4. Topics not covered in this chapter:

- Aggregation
- BGP confederations
- Communities
- Peer-groups
- EBGP_Multihop

Professional Development Checklist

By using this chapter, you should be able to perform the following operations:

- Configure an External BGP neighbor relationship.
- Configure an Internal BGP neighbor relationship.
- Configure the NEXT-HOP-SELF parameter.
- Announce networks with the NETWORK statement.
- Announce network by redistributing static routes.
- Disable synchronization.
- Configure a route reflector.
- Configure an IBGP neighbor relationship using the UPDATE-SOURCE parameter.
- Configure an AS-PATH Access-List.

For Further Study

- RFC 1771, A Border Gateway Protocol 4 (BGP-4).
- RFC 1773, Experience with the BGP-4 Protocol.
  RFCs can be downloaded at **www.freesoft.org**, **www.arslimited.com**.
- Halabi, Bassam. *Internet Routing Architectures*, Cisco Press, 1997.
- Huitema, Christian. *Routing in the Internet*, Prentice Hall, 1995.

URLs

- **www.cciecert.com**
- **www.mentorlabs.com**
- **www.cisco.com**

Can You Spot the Issues?

The two following neighbor statements were configured on BGP speakers R1 and R2. What is wrong with the configuration?

```
Router R1
interface s0
ip address 172.16.10 255.255.255.0
!
router bgp 200
neighbor 172.16.1.2 remote-as 200

ROUTER R2

interface s0
ip address 172.16.1.2 255.255.255.0
!
router bgp 300
neighbor 172.16.1.1 remote-as 200
```

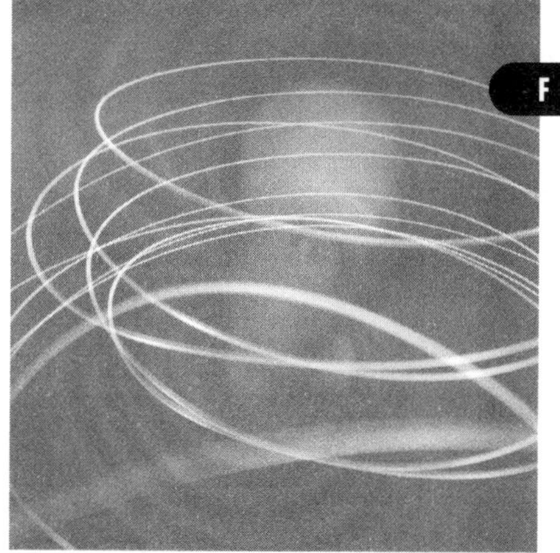

F I F T E E N

Introduction to Configuring non-IP Routing Protocol Suites

Topics Covered In This Chapter

- Review common characteristics that (IP), IPX), AppleTalk, and DECNET share
- Review how EIGRP supports multiple protocols concurrently
- Review the unique characteristics of each protocol suite
- Introduce the "ships in the night" configuration principle
- Introduce the tunneling alternative to "ships in the night" routing
- Learning strategies for IPX, AppleTalk, and DECNET
- Test taking strategies for IPX, AppleTalk, and DECNET
- Comments on ISO CLNS, XNS, VINES, and APOLLO

So far our focus has been IP addressing, routing, and redistribution. Now, we direct our attention to the same topics of addressing, routing, and redistribution using non-IP routing protocols. We are going to use our understanding of IP to accelerate our understanding of non-IP protocols. Let's look at what common characteristics IP routing shares with the non-IP routing protocols: IPX, AppleTalk, and DECNET. Then let's take a look at what is unique about these non-IP protocols.

Common Characteristics of All Protocol Suites that Support Layer Three Routing (IP, IPX, AppleTalk, DECNET)

In Level Two, so far we have seen the following characteristics of IP:

1. IP has an addressing structure consisting of a network prefix and a host suffix.
2. IP routing tables attain a state of equilibrium when they have converged.

3. IP routing tables can be built by using:
   - Static routes
   - Default routes
   - Dynamic routing protocols

4. Dynamic routing protocols can be divided into the following three categories:
   - Distance Vector
   - Link State
   - Hybrid

5. Dynamic routing protocols select the shortest path by using a metric.
6. Dynamic routing protocols will have some "age" value associated with each routing table entry.
7. Distance Vector Routing Protocols advertise their entire routing table on a consistent periodic basis (such as every 30, 60, 90 seconds etc.).
8. The age of networks inserted into a routing table by distance vector routing protocols should be less than the update interval. Distance vector routing entries should stay forever young.
9. Distance vector routing protocols use loop avoidance techniques such as split-horizon and holddown.
10. Link state routing protocols form neighbor relationships with directly connected routers.
11. Once the neighbor relationship is formed, link-state routing protocols form an adjacency and build a topological database.
12. With link state routing protocols, a shortest path selection algorithm is applied to the topological database to select the best paths to insert into the routing table.
13. Link state routing protocols do not advertise their complete routing table on a periodic basis.
14. Link state routing protocols flood link state advertisements when there is a change in link state.
15. In stable networks, the age of networks inserted into a routing table by link state routing protocols should be as old as possible. In stable networks, link state should stay forever old.
16. With link state routing protocols, split horizon and holddown is not used for loop avoidance.
17. Information between two or more routing sources can be exchanged through the process of redistribution.
18. IP routing table update information can be filtered with distribute-lists.

In Level Four, AppleTalk, DECNET, and IPX protocol suites share these same characteristics with IP. A description of these similarities is provided below:

1. IP has an addressing structure consisting of a network prefix and a host suffix. AppleTalk consists of a x-bit network address and a x-bit node address. DECNET addressing consists of a 6-bit area address/10-bit node address. IPX consists of a 32-bit network address and a 48-bit node address.
2. IP routing tables attain a state of equilibrium when they have converged. AppleTalk, DECNET, and IPX routing tables also trend towards convergence.
3. IP routing tables can be built by using:
    - Static routes (Static routes are used by IPX, AppleTalk, and DECNET)
    - Default routes (Default routes are used by AppleTalk, DECNET and IPX)
    - Dynamic routing protocols (Dynamic routing protocols are used by AppleTalk, DECNET, and IPX)
4. Dynamic routing protocols can be divided into the following three categories:
    - Distance Vector IPX RIP, ; AppleTalk RTMP
    - Link State [IPX NetWare Link Services Protocol (NLSP)]
    - Hybrid (DECNET ROUTING, EIGRP for IPX, EIGRP for AppleTalk)
5. Like IP, AppleTalk, DECNET, and IPX dynamic routing protocols, select the shortest path by using a metric.
6. Like IP, AppleTalk, DECNET, and IPX dynamic routing protocols will have some "age" value associated with each routing table entry.
7. Like IP, AppleTalk, DECNET, and IPX distance vector routing protocols advertise their entire routing table on a consistent periodic basis (such as every 30, 60, 90 seconds etc.).
8. For IP as well as AppleTalk, DECNET, and IPX, the age of networks inserted into a routing table by distance vector routing protocols should be less than the update interval. Distance vector routing entries should stay forever young.
9. Like IP, AppleTalk, DECNET, and IPX distance vector routing protocols use loop avoidance techniques such as split-horizon and holddown.
10. Like open shortest path first (OSPF), IPX NLSP Link state routing protocols form neighbor relationships with directly connected routers.
11. Like OSPF, once the neighbor relationship is formed with IPX NLSP, link-state routing protocols form an adjacency and build a topological database.
12. Like OSPF, with IPX NLSP, a shortest path selection algorithm is applied to the topological database to select the best paths to insert into the routing table.
13. Like OSPF, IPX NLSP does not advertise its complete routing table on a periodic basis.

14. Like OSPF, IPX NLSP flood link state advertisements when there is a change in link state.
15. In stable networks, the age of networks inserted into a routing table by link state routing protocols such as OSPF and IPX NSLP should be as old as possible. In stable networks, link state should stay forever old.
16. With OSPF and IPX NLSP, split horizon and holddown is not used for loop avoidance.
17. AppleTalk, DECNET and IPX support redistribution to exchange information between two or more different routing sources.
18. For all protocols (IP, IPX, AppleTalk, DECNET), routing table update information can be filtered with distribute-lists.

The similarities that IPX, AppleTalk, and DECNET possess with IP will accelerate our learning of these protocols. When we cover the Level Four non-IP routing protocols, we will constantly be comparing their operation to what we learned in Level Two about IP routing.

One Level Four topic that deserves special attention is EIGRP for IPX and AppleTalk. This is a Cisco proprietary protocol that offers many advantages in IPX and APPLETALK routing environments.

EIGRP: A Single Routing Protocol that Can Support Multiple Routed Protocols

EIGRP can support IP, IPX, and AppleTalk concurrently. It is an enhanced distance vector routing protocol. It performs a rapid reconvergence when there is a change to the network topology.

Since EIGRP discovers networks like a distance vector routing protocol, the rule of split-horizon is applied to it.

When the EIGRP process is enabled, it creates and maintains the following tables:

- NEIGHBOR TABLE
- TOPOLOGY TABLE
- ROUTING TABLE

It maintains a separate table of each of these for each routed protocol. EIGRP uses the same composite network (bandwidth, delay, load and reliability) for path selection of all routed protocols.

EIGRP automatically redistributes routing table information between itself and IPX/RIP for the IPX routing process and itself and AppleTalk RTMP for the AppleTalk routing process.

Since EIGRP runs only on Cisco routers, it is common to have EIGRP running within the core of an internetwork and the native routing protocols IPX/RIP and AppleTalk RTMP on the edge workgroup (LANs). EIGRP seamlessly handles this configuration with its automatic redistribution feature with IPX/RIP and AppleTalk RTMP. Manual redistribution is required for IPX NLSP and AppleTalk AURP.

For stable networks, the age of routing table entries inserted by the EIGRP routing process should be forever old.

Unique Characteristics of AppleTalk, DECNET, and IPX

In the first part of this chapter, we looked at what IPX, AppleTalk, and DECNET had in common with IP. Now, we want to review what is unique about the protocols.

AppleTalk

AppleTalk is easy on users but tough on network administrators. AppleTalk possesses the following unique characteristics:

- Dynamic network-layer address acquisition
- Dynamic default-gateway selection
- Use of zones to create user "communities of interest" (much like VLANs)
- Dynamic name to address binding through the NBP process

AppleTalk routers must maintain three processes:

1. A routing process
2. A zone process
3. A name binding process

AppletalkTALK Convergence

All routers see all networks (AppleTalk cable-ranges) in the routing table
All routers see all zones in the zone information table

DECNET

DECNET is hostcentric. All routing activity supports connecting to a DEC host.

DECNET possesses the following unique characteristics:

- DECNET addressing identifies the entire router.
- DECNET addressing is not assigned on an interface basis.
- DECNET addressing is area-based

There are two types of routers in DECNET routing: intra-area and inter-area. When DECNET is activated on a LAN interface, it manipulates the MAC address of that interface.

Convergence for DECNET Inter-area Routers

Inter-area routers see entries for all other areas and all other routers within in its respective area.

Convergence for DECNET Intra-area Routers

Intra-area routers see only entries for all other routers within its area.

IPX

IPX is servercentric. All routing activity supports connecting to a Novell server.

IPX possesses the following unique characteristics:

- IPX addresses are in hexadecimal format
- IPX has no ARP process
- Each Novell 3.x and 4.x server possesses a unique internal IPX number
- Routers maintain SAP tables as well as routing tables

Convergence for IPX Routers

All routers see all networks in their respective routing tables. All routers see all SAPs in their respective routing tables.

Non-IP Protocol Configuration Options

There are two fundamental ways of configuring non-IP routing protocols with the Cisco IOS

1. Ships in the Night Configuration
2. Tunnel Configuration

It is critical that you are able to spot the issue of whether you are supposed to perform a ships in the night configuration or a tunneling configuration.

Ships in the Night Configuration on Cisco Routers

Ships in the night configuration entails that protocols other than IP are configured on a given interface. IP packets and non-IP packets are transmitted and received on the same interface concurrently.

Tunnel Configuration on Cisco Routers

An alternative to ships in the night routing, is placing non-IP protocol traffic in IP packets and tunneling the traffic through an IP internetwork. All non-IP traffic can use GRE tunneling. AppleTalk offers alternatives such as AURP and CAYMAN tunneling options. Creating a tunnel involves creating a virtual tunnel interface. The syntax involved with creating a tunnel interface configuration it is displayed below.

The tunnel interface is created by simply typing "interface tunnel x" where x is the interface number of the tunnel.

```
London(config)#interface tunnel 0
```

Once the tunnel is created, you can treat it like any other interface. However, special tunnel parameters must be configured. You must configure the entry point of the tunnel. This can be a local interface or a local IP address. You must then specify the destination endpoint of the tunnel. This must be a remote IP address. The default tunnel mode is GRE. If you want to specify something else, use the tunnel mode command. A listing of the different tunnel options and tunnel modes are listed below:

```
London(config-if)#tunnel ?
  checksum              enable end to end checksumming of packets
  destination           destination of tunnel
  key                   security or selector key
  mode                  tunnel encapsulation method
  sequence-datagrams    drop datagrams arriving out of order
  source                source of tunnel packets

London(config-if)#tunnel mode ?
  aurp     AURP TunnelTalk AppleTalk encapsulation
  cayman   Cayman TunnelTalk AppleTalk encapsulation
  dvmrp    DVMRP multicast tunnel
  eon      EON compatible CLNS tunnel
  gre      generic route encapsulation protocol
  ipip     IP over IP encapsulation
  iptalk   Apple IPTalk encapsulation
  nos      IP over IP encapsulation (KA9Q/NOS compatible)
```

You can check your tunnel configuration with "show interface tunnel."

```
Tunnel0 is up, line protocol is up
  Hardware is Tunnel
  MTU 1500 bytes, BW 9 Kbit, DLY 500000 usec, rely 255/255, load 1/255
  Encapsulation TUNNEL, loopback not set, keepalive set (10 sec)
  Tunnel source 172.16.1.1 (Loopback0), destination 172.16.20.1
  Tunnel protocol/transport GRE/IP, key disabled, sequencing disabled
  Checksumming of packets disabled,  fast tunneling enabled
  Last input never, output never, output hang never
  Last clearing of "show interface" counters never
  Queueing strategy: fifo
  Output queue 0/0, 0 drops; input queue 0/75, 0 drops
  5 minute input rate 0 bits/sec, 0 packets/sec
  5 minute output rate 0 bits/sec, 0 packets/sec
     0 packets input, 0 bytes, 0 no buffer
```

```
Received 0 broadcasts, 0 runts, 0 giants
0 input errors, 0 CRC, 0 frame, 0 overrun, 0 ignored, 0 abort
0 packets output, 0 bytes, 0 underruns
0 output errors, 0 collisions, 0 interface resets
0 output buffer failures, 0 output buffers swapped out
```

Notice that this show command shows you the source and destination address of the tunnel. These addresses determine the entry and exit points of the tunnel. The tunnel mode is listed as GRE/IP. You can troubleshoot the tunneling process with the debug tunnel command.

Common Configuration Steps for non-IP Protocols

For all non-IP routing protocols, at least one global and one interface command must be entered to enable the protocol.

- Global Configuration Command: Enable the non-IP Routing Process

  All protocols expect IP must be enabled manually. The first step for all non-IP routing protocols is to enable the protocol in global configuration mode. Listed below are sample global commands that enable each routing protocol:

  ```
  London(config)#ipx routing
  London(config)#appletalk routing
  London(config)#decnet routing 1.2
  ```

  Details of configuring each of these protocols in global configuration mode will be covered in upcoming chapters.

- Interface Configuration Command: Enable the Protocol in the Desired Interface

  Different non-IP routing protocols require different configuration parameters. IPX requires an eight digit hexadecimal network address. AppleTalk requires a cable-range and a zone. DECNET requires no addressing on an interface. DECENT requires that only a cost be assigned to each DECENT interface.

  The show protocols command will show you what protocols are enabled on the router and what protocols are configured for a particular interface.

  ```
  London#sh protocols
  Global values:
    Internet Protocol routing is enabled
    Appletalk routing is enabled
    DECNET routing is enabled
    IPX routing is enabled
  Ethernet0 is up, line protocol is down
    Internet address is 144.251.100.202/24
    AppleTalk address is 1000.193, zone Backbone
  ```

```
    Decnet cost is 15
    IPX address is 1000.aa00.0400.0204
  Serial0 is down, line protocol is down
    Internet address is 181.8.128.129/25
    AppleTalk address is 1070.217, zone WAN zone 1070
    Decnet cost is 25
    IPX address is 1070.00e0.b05a.9bfb
  Serial1 is administratively down, line protocol is down
```

This gives you a brief snapshot of how both IP and non-IP routing protocols are configured on a given router.

These commands may be entered on physical interfaces only or both physical and logical interfaces such as subinterfaces and tunnel interfaces.

Learning Strategies for IPX, AppleTalk, and DECNET

Compare and relate as much as you possibly can to the operation of each of these protocols —AppleTalk, DECNET, and IPX—to IP. Use the eighteen point comparison as a guideline to compare AppleTalk, DECNET, and IPX to IP.

From a learning perspective, cover the topics in the following order:

1. IPX
2. AppleTalk
3. DECNET

COMMENTS ON APOLLO, ISO CLNS, XNS, AND VINES

Use of the Apollo, XNS and VINES protocol are in decline; however, many installations still use them. If mastery is attained in configuring IP, IPX, AppleTalk,, and DECNET, it will be easier to learn and understand the configuration of these lesser used protocols. For Apollo, XNS and VINES configuration, the following steps must be performed:

1. Enable the protocol in global configuration mode
2. Enable the protocol on specific interfaces

These same steps are also required for IP, IPX, AppleTalk, and DECNET.

IOS support for Apollo, XNS and VINES supports static routes, access-lists, a range of show commands and debug tools.

Finally, ISO CLNS deserves special comment. Although it is not heavily used as an alternative to IP routing, ISO CLNS uses NSAP addresses. NSAP addresses are also used for call routing for ATM switched virtual circuits. Therefore, more attention must be paid to this protocol.

The remainder of the chapter lists all of the following for IPX, AppleTalk and DECNET:

- Show commands
- Debug commands
- Global configuration commands

- Interface configuration commands

Notice that all have show commands that display the following:

- Interface status
- Routing table
- Traffic/protocol statistics

Notice that all protocols have debug commands for the following:

- Packet
- Routing

We have already seen the power of the debug ip packet, debug frame packet and debug dialer packet. Debug ipx, appletalk and decnet will be useful when working with these protocols.

Debug ip rip, debug ip igrp transactions and events are useful in the Level Two environment. We will see that debugging routing activity for the non-IP routing protocols will also be useful.

Notice that all protocols have global configuration commands for the following:

- Routing
- Route (static for AppleTalk)

Notice that all protocols have interface configuration commands for the following:

- Access-group
- Distribute-lists
- Route-cache
- Split-horizon

SHOW IPX

```
r5#sh ipx ?
  accounting     The active IPX accounting database
  cache          IPX fast-switching cache
  compression    IPX compression information
  eigrp          IPX EIGRP show commands
  interface      IPX interface status and configuration
  nasi           Netware Asynchronous Services Interface status
  nhrp           NHRP information
  nlsp           Show NLSP information
  route          IPX routing table
  servers        SAP servers
  spx-protocol   Sequenced Packet Exchange protocol status
  spx-spoof      SPX Spoofing table
  traffic        IPX protocol statistics
```

SHOW APPLETALK

```
r5#sh appletalk ?
  access-lists      AppleTalk access lists
  adjacent-routes   AppleTalk adjacent routes
  arp               AppleTalk arp table
  aurp              AURP information
  cache             AppleTalk fast-switching cache
  domain            AppleTalk Domain(s) information
  eigrp             AppleTalk/EIGRP show commands
  globals           AppleTalk global parameters
  interface         AppleTalk interface status and configuration
  macip-clients     Mac IP clients
  macip-servers     Mac IP servers
  macip-traffic     Mac IP traffic
  name-cache        AppleTalk name cache
  nbp               AppleTalk NBP name table
  neighbors         AppleTalk Neighboring router status
  remap             AppleTalk remap table
  route             AppleTalk routing table
  sockets           AppleTalk protocol processing information
  static            AppleTalk static table
  traffic           AppleTalk protocol statistics
  zone              AppleTalk Zone table information
```

SHOW DECNET

```
r5#sh decnet ?
  <0-3>       Optional ATG network number
  debug       Incomplete network structures for each network
  interface   DECnet interface status and configuration
  map         DECnet Address Translation Gateway table
  neighbors   DECnet adjacent neighbors
  route       DECnet routing table
  static      Display all static routes in static route queue
  traffic     DECnet traffic statistics
  <cr>
```

DEBUG IPX

```
r5#debug ipx ?
  compression      IPX compression
  eigrp            IPX EIGRP packets
  ipxwan           Novell IPXWAN events
  nasi             NASI server functionality
  nlsp             IPX NLSP activity
  packet           IPX activity
  redistribution   IPX route redistribution
  routing          IPX RIP routing information
  sap              IPX Service Advertisement information
```

```
  spoof          IPX and SPX Spoofing activity
  spx            Sequenced Packet Exchange Protocol
```

DEBUG APPLETALK

```
r5#debug apple ?
  arp                      Appletalk address resolution protocol
  aurp-connection          AURP connection
  aurp-packet              AURP packets
  aurp-update              AURP routing updates
  domain                   AppleTalk Domain function
  eigrp-all                All AT/EIGRP functions
  eigrp-external           AT/EIGRP external functions
  eigrp-hello              AT/EIGRP hello functions
  eigrp-packet             AT/EIGRP packet debugging
  eigrp-query              AT/EIGRP query functions
  eigrp-redistribution     AT/EIGRP route redistribution
  eigrp-request            AT/EIGRP external functions
  eigrp-target             Appletalk/EIGRP for targeting address
  eigrp-update             AT/EIGRP update functions
  errors                   Information about errors
  events                   Appletalk special events
  fs                       Appletalk fast-switching
  iptalk                   IPTalk encapsulation and functionality
  macip                    MacIP functions
  nbp                      Name Binding Protocol (NBP) functions
  packet                   Per-packet debugging
  redistribution           Route Redistribution
  remap                    AppleTalk Remap function
  responder                AppleTalk responder debugging
  routing                  (RTMP&EIGRP) functions
  rtmp                     (RTMP) functions
  zip                      Zone Information Protocol functions
```

DEBUG DECNET

```
r5#debug decnet ?
  adjacencies  DECnet adjacency events
  connects     DECnet connect access lists
  events       DECnet major events
  packets      DECnet routing updates and HELLO packets
  routing      DECnet routing table transactions
```

IPX GLOBAL CONFIGURATION COMMANDS

From the listing below, notice that IPX global configuration parameters are dominated by RIP and SAP parameters. (GNS) commands configure a specialized form of SAP request: GET NEAREST SERVER. At the end of the list, a number of "type-20" commands are listed. These are used to propagate NETBIOS traffic over an IPX network.

```
r5(config)#ipx ?
  accounting-list                      Select nets for which IPX accounting
                                       information is kept
  accounting-threshold                 Sets the maximum number of accountin
                                       entries
  accounting-transits                  Sets the maximum number of transit
                                       entries
  backup-server-query-interval         Set minimum interval between successive
                                       backup server table queries
  broadcast-fastswitching              Fastswitch directed broadcast packets
  default-output-rip-delay             Interpacket delay for RIP updates
  default-output-sap-delay             Interpacket delay for SAP updates
  default-route                        Enable default route recognition
  default-triggered-rip-delay          Interpacket delay for triggered RIP
                                       updates
  default-triggered-sap-delay          Interpacket delay for triggered SAP
                                       updates
  eigrp-sap-split-horizon              EIGRP SAP obeys split horizon
  flooding-unthrottled                 NLSP flooding should be unthrottled
  gns-response-delay                   Set msec delay in replying to a GNS
Request
  gns-round-robin                      Round-robin responses to get nearest
                                       server
  internal-network                     Specify internal IPX network for router
  maximum-hops                         Sets the maximum number of hops
  maximum-output-processes             Set maximum number of concurrent output
                                       processes that may run
  maximum-paths                        Forward IPX packets over multiple paths
  nasi-server                          Netware Asynchronous Services Interface
                                       config commands
  netbios-socket-input-checks          Limit input of non-type 20 netbios bc
                                       packets
  per-host-load-share                  Load share per end host (use one path
                                       only)
  ping-default                         Set default to cisco or Novell Standard
                                       Pings
  route                                Set an IPX static routing table entry
  route-cache                          IPX fastswitch cache configuration
  router                               Control IPX routing
  routing                              Enable IPX routing
  sap                                  Set an IPX static SAP table entry
  sap-queue-maximum                    Set maximum SAP processing queue depth
  server-split-horizon-on-server-paths Split horizon SAP on server, not route,
                                       paths
  type-20-helpered                     Forward Type-20 using helper lists,
                                       ignore trace
  type-20-input-checks                 Do additional input checks on type 20
```

```
                                         propagation packets
  type-20-output-checks                  Do additional output checks on type 20
                                         propagation packets
```

IPX INTERFACE CONFIGURATION COMMANDS

Just as with global configuration commands, notice that IPX interface configuration parameters are dominated by RIP and SAP parameters. GNS commands configure a specialized form of SAP request: GET NEAREST SERVER. In the listing below, there are five IPX/RIP related commands, nine IPX SAP related commands and four IPX EIGRP commands and three GNS commands.

```
R5(config-if)#ipx ?
  access-group                   Apply an access list to inbound or outbound
                                 packets
  accounting                     Enable IPX accounting on this interface
  advertise-default-route-only   Only advertise the IPX/RIP default route out
                                 onto this network
  bandwidth-percent              Set EIGRP bandwidth limit
  compression                    Select IPX compression commands
  delay                          Set a Novell delay on the interface, in 'ticks'
  down                           Bring an IPX network administratively down
  encapsulation                  Novell encapsulation
  gns-reply-disable              Disable Get Nearest Server replies on this
                                 interface
  gns-response-delay             Delay in answering GNS on this interface
  hello-interval                 Configures IPX EIGRP hello interval
  helper-address                 Forward broadcasts to a specific address
  helper-list                    Filter helpered IPX packets on input
  hold-time                      Configures IPX EIGRP hold time
  input-network-filter           Filter incoming routing updates
  input-sap-filter               Filter services learned from the Service
                                 Advertising Protocol
  ipxwan                         Configure IPXWAN on this interface
  link-delay                     Set an IPX link delay on the interface, in
                                 microseconds
  netbios                        Setup IPX NetBIOS filters and caching on this
                                 interface
  network                        Assign an IPX network & enable IPX routing
  nhrp                           NHRP interface subcommands
  nlsp                           Select NLSP commands
  output-gns-filter              Filter services reported in response to Get
                                 Nearest Server
  output-network-filter          Filter outgoing routing updates
  output-rip-delay               Interpacket delay for RIP updates
  output-sap-delay               Interpacket delay for SAP updates
  output-sap-filter              Filter services reported via SAP
  pad-process-switched-packets   Pad odd-length packets on output
                                 (process-switched only)
  ppp-client                     Configure interface for PPP client mode
```

```
rip-max-packetsize             Maximum size of RIP packets being sent on
                               interface
rip-multiplier                 Multiple of RIP update interval for aging of
                               RIP routes
route-cache                    Enable fast switching
router-filter                  Filter sources of routing updates
router-sap-filter              Select source router and service type of SAP
                               updates
sap-incremental                Send incremental SAP updates - for IPX EIGRP
                               networks only
sap-interval                   Set SAP update period
sap-max-packetsize             Maximum size of SAP packets being sent on
                               interface
sap-multiplier                 Multiple of SAP update interval for aging of
                               SAP routes
source-network-update          Replace source network with current network if
                               hop count is zero
split-horizon                  Perform split horizon
spx-idle-time                  Set an SPX idle time on the interface, in
                               seconds
spx-spoof                      Spoof SPX keepalives packets
throughput                     Set IPX link throughput in bit per second
triggered-rip-delay            Interpacket delay for triggered RIP updates
                               (override output-rip-delay for triggered
                               updates only)
triggered-sap-delay            Interpacket delay for triggered SAP updates
                               (override output-rip-delay for triggered
                               updates only)
type-20-propagation            Forward IPX type 20 propagation packets
update-time                    Set IPX routing update timer
watchdog-spoof                 Answer Server Watchdog packets for Client
                               machines
```

APPLETALK GLOBAL CONFIGURATION COMMANDS

The most common AppleTalk configuration commands are zone and routing commands. Also, take note of the AppleTalk EIGRP global command.

```
r5(config)#appletalk ?
  alternate-addressing  Use alternate addressing
  arp                   Set Appletalk ARP parameters
  aurp                  Set AURP parameters
  checksum              Enable Appletalk checksumming
  domain                Configure AppleTalk Domain
  eigrp                 AppleTalk EIGRP subcommands
  event-logging         Set appletalk event logging level
  ignore-verify-errors  Allow router to start routing in misconfigured networks
  iptalk-baseport       iptalk-baseport
  local-routing         Allow routing between two local devices on an interface
  lookup-type           Enable cache of service names
```

```
  macip                  Enable MAC-IP
  name-lookup-interval   Set the service polling interval for lookup-type
                         command
  permit-partial-zones   Allow zone routing if part of the zone is visible
  proxy-nbp              Non-extended Appletalk router proxy support
  require-route-zones    Require network/zone associations before advertising
                         routes
  route-redistribution   Leak networks between protocols
  routing                Enable Appletalk routing
  rtmp                   AppleTalk rtmp subcommands
  static                 Configure a static Appletalk route
  strict-rtmp-checking   Enforce maximum checking of routing packets
  timers                 Alter routing timers
  virtual-net            Internal Appletalk Network
  zip-query-interval     Interval between ZIP queries
```

APPLETALK INTERFACE CONFIGURATION COMMANDS

As with AppleTalk global configuration commands, AppleTalk interface commands are dominated by RTMP, EIGRP, and ZONE parameters.

```
r5(config-if)#appletalk ?
  access-group              Appletalk access group
  address                   Set appletalk Phase 1 address
  arp-timeout               arp-timeout
  cable-range               Set appletalk Phase 2 address
  client-mode               Allow PPP client connections.
  discovery                 Reset discovery mode for new cable range discovery
  distribute-list           Filter networks from routing updates
  domain-group              Specify appletalk domain
  eigrp-bandwidth-percent   Set EIGRP bandwidth limit
  eigrp-splithorizon        Enable Split Horizon processing generating AT/EIGRP
                            updates
  eigrp-timers              AT/EIGRP hello and holdtime timers
  free-trade-zone           Enhanced security for one-way shared networks
  getzonelist-filter        Filter zone-list replies
  glean-packets             Glean AARP information from packets
  iptalk                    Encapsulate AT in IP like the CAP and KIP
                            implementations
  protocol                  Select AppleTalk routing protocol
  route-cache               Enable appletalk route cache
  rtmp-splithorizon         Enable Split Horizon processing generating AT/RTMP
                            updates
  rtmp-stub                 Send only RTMP stubs, no routes in updates
  send-rtmps                Send Appletalk routing updates
  zip-reply-filter          Filter ZIP replies
  zone                      Assign an appletalk zone name
```

DECNET GLOBAL CONFIGURATION COMMANDS

DECNET global configuration commands are dominated by area parameters. DECNET can be divided into areas much like OSPF.

```
r5(config)#decnet ?
  <0-3>            ATG network number
  advertise        Advertise a DECnet area imported from OSI
  area-max-cost    Set maximum cost for inter-area routing
  area-max-hops    Set maximum hops for inter-area routing
  attach           Allow an area router to act 'attached'
  conversion       Enable Phase IV/V conversion
  host             Define a name mapping for a DECnet address
  map              Establish an ATG address mapping
  max-address      Set highest node number allowed in current area
  max-area         Set highest area number allowed
  max-cost         Set maximum cost for intra-area routing
  max-hops         Set maximum hops for intra-area routing
  max-paths        Set maximum number of equal cost paths to be kept
  max-visits       Set maximum visits of a packet on this router
  node-type        Specify router node type
  path-split-mode  Specify splitting mode for equal cost paths
  propagate        Allow DECnet static routes to be sent in routing updates
  route            Define a DECnet static route
  routing          Enable DECnet routing
```

DECNET INTERFACE CONFIGURATION COMMANDS

```
r5(config-if)#decnet ?
  <0-3>                 ATG network number
  access-group          Set access control for outgoing packets
  congestion-threshold  Congestion avoidance threshold
  cost                  Set cost value for interface
  hello-timer           Set interval between transmitted HELLO messages
  in-routing-filter     Set up access control for incoming routing information
  multicast-map         DECnet multicast mapping on token ring
  out-routing-filter    Set up access control for outgoing routing information
  route-cache           Enable fast-switching of DECnet datagrams
  router-priority       Set priority for determining default router
  routing-timer         Set interval between transmitted routing messages
  split-horizon         Enable split horizon on interface
```

Summary

When learning, reviewing and mastering the configuration and troubleshooting of non-IP routing protocols, use a comparative learning approach. Compare the configuration and troubleshooting issues associated with non-IP routing protocols with IP routing. Make note of both the similarities and the differences. This Chapter has provided you with a starting point for a comparative learning approach. From an IOS perspective, use the last pages of this Chapter to develop a matrix to locate the common configuration, show and debug commands for all routing protocols.

Also, when studying the non-IP routing protocols, always keep in mind their original design objectives. This will help better understand the unique characteristics of each. For example, since the Novel IPX/SPX protocol suite was originally designed to support a "server-centric" environment, protocols unique to the IPX/SPX environment such as SAP were developed. Since the TCP/IP environment is not server-centric, it does not have a comparable protocol to SAP.

Professional Development Checklist

- List common points between IP and non-IP routing protocols and processes.
- List unique characteristics of non-IP protocols.
- List two configuration methods of non-IP routing protocols (ships in the night or tunneling).
- List what show commands all non-IP routing protocol suites have in common.
- List all debug commands all non-IP routing protocol suites have in common.
- List all configuration commands all non-IP protocol suites have in common.

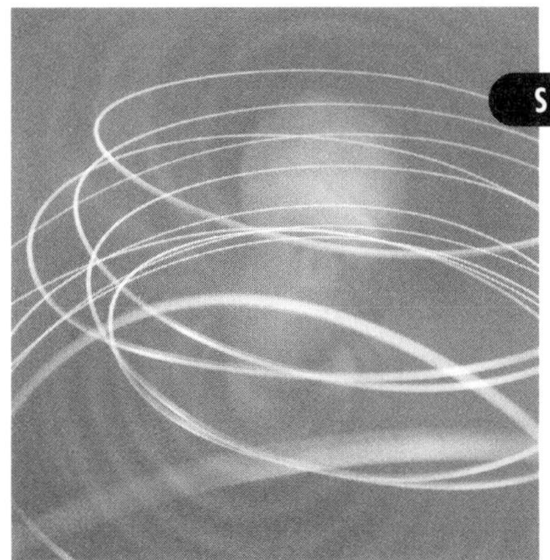

SIXTEEN

IPX Configuration

Topics Covered in This Chapter

- (IPX) Technology Overview
- Review IPX Operating in a Stable Environment with the (IOS)
- Configuring IPX for IPX (RIP)
- Configuring IPX Static Routes
- Configuring IPX Default Routes
- Configuring Static (SAPs)
- Configuring EIGRP for IPX
- Configuring (NLSP)
- Configuring IPX Tunneling
- Configuring IPX over (DDR) Links
- Configuring IPX over (NBMA) Networks
- IPX Idiosyncrasies
- Troubleshooting IPX

IPX Technology Overview

IPX's Design Objective

(IPX) is a derivative of the Xerox XNS protocol. It was adopted by Novell to provide transport services between NetWare clients and NetWare servers.

Novell NetWare's Design Objective

The original design objective of Novell NetWare was to provide shared file and print services to MS-DOS clients. NetWare was a LAN workgroup solution. It was originally **not** designed for wide-area, enterprise networks.

The traditional NetWare operating system is a dedicated file server technology. In a Novell environment, one NetWare client cannot directly communicate with another NetWare client as one can do when utilizing Microsoft Windows 95 or Windows NT. They must communicate through a server. The IPX protocol suite was designed to support this servercentric environment

Also, a user cannot go to the NetWare console and run an application protocol such as Microsoft Word. The NetWare operating system is a *dedicated server technology*. A user must log onto the server to access applications.

MS-DOS clients would connect to a Novell server by loading drivers, most notably the NetWare Core Protocol (NCP)/DOS requester (NETX.COM; X=version of DOS). When NETX.COM was loaded a SAPrequest was generated by the client to attach to the nearest server [GET –NEAREST –SERVER (GNS)]. Once a server is found, the DOS client would receive a prompt stating which server it had attached to. At that time, end users would type a letter such as "F:" and log onto the NetWare file server. End users would treat the NetWare "F:"drive as they would their local "C:" drive.

Key Protocols Used by Novell NetWare: IPX, SPX, IPX/RIP, SAP, NCP

The key protocols of the early releases of NetWare were IPX, (SPX), IPX/RIP, SAP, and NCP. To this day, these protocols are still extremely important to the majority of NetWare installations. In fact, many of these protocols are used by Microsoft networking solutions (Windows 95 and Windows NT).

IPX is at the heart of the original NetWare protocol suite. It performed functions similar to (IP). Like IP, it is a connectionless protocol that supplies a protocol number to identify the protocol that it carried (SPX, SAP, RIP, and NCP). Listed below is a table of protocol numbers used by IP and protocol numbers used by IPX:

IP Upper Layer Protocols	IP Protocol Numbers	IPX Upper Layer Protocols	IPX Protocol Numbers
TCP	6	SPX	5
UDP	17	NCP	17
ICMP	1	SAP	4
IGRP	9	IPX RIP	1
EIGRP	88	NETBIOS	20
OSPF	89		

Like IP, IPX contains a network and node address in each packet. Unlike IP, IPX has an 80-bit network-node address structure that gets translated into hexadecimal format. Unlike IP, IPX uses the MAC address as the node address. Therefore, IPX does not require an ARP-like process. Finally, IPX also contains a source and destination socket address. IP does not contain such information. IP relies on TCP and UDP to provide "socket" or "port" addresses. Since IPX is connectionless and both IP and UDP are connectionless, IPX is oftentimes compared to not just IP but the UDP/IP pair.

SPX is a connection-oriented protocol that is encapsulated within IPX. SPX is used by RCONSOLE and remote printing services.

IPX/RIP provides routing services. Not only does Cisco routers use RIP, but every file server runs a RIP process as well.

SAPs advertise server services. Every Novell file server (NetWare 3.x and less) advertises its services (file servers, print servers, etc.) every sixty seconds. End users needing to login to multiple file servers (NetWare 3.x or less) must do so on a server by server basis.

NCP is the heart of the upper layer protocols for IPX/SPX in NetWare environments. The primary function of NCP was to provide file transfer operations for file and print services. Like network file system (NFS)/remote procedure call (RPC) in the TCP/IP environment, NCP was based upon a request/reply file transfer model. Original implementations of NCP possessed extremely primitive flow control mechanisms.

Cisco Support for IPX

Although Novell file servers have the functionality of a router, the Cisco IOS provides many added features to enhance and scale IPX internetworks.

Primary Cisco IOS features for IPX include:

- EIGRP for IPX
- Full support for NetWare Link Services Protocol (NLSP)
- Robust IPX show commands
- Robust IPX debugging tools
- Sophisticated IPX filtering
- Sophisticated IPX Queuing
- Tools for implementing IPX over DDR links
- Tools for implementing IPX over NBMA links

Cisco IPX solutions can be divided into two broad categories:

1. "Ships in the night" implementations
2. Tunneling implementations

As discussed in the previous chapter, two broad configuration strategies are available for non-IP protocol configuration. The first strategy, the "ships in the night" configuration, involves concurrently configuring IP and IPX on the same interface. Both IP and IPX run concurrently throughout the internetwork.

The second strategy, the tunneling configuration, keeps IPX at the edge of the internetwork. When IPX passes over the core, it is encapsulated in IP packets or "tunneled" in IP packets for transmission across an IP network.

Overview of the IPX Protocol Suite

Just as the TCP/IP protocol suite is made up of a family of protocols, IPX/SPX has its own family members. Just as IP is at the heart of the TCP/IP protocol suite, its Novell counterpart, IPX, is at the heart of the IPX/SPX protocol suite. The next few sections review IPX addressing, other IPX header fields, and other members of the IPX/SPX protocol suite.

IPX Addressing

Listed below are a few points one must remember about IPX addressing:

1. IPX address structure is network:node:socket
   - The network address is 32 bits in length, represented by 8 hexadecimal digits
   - The node address is 48 bits in length, represented by 12 hexadecimal digits
   - The socket address is 16 bits in length, represented in 4 hexadecimal digits
2. Node address uses a MAC address on the router.
3. Wide-area network (WAN) links (serial interfaces) node address is dynamically acquired from the MAC address of the first active LAN interface.
4. With implementations of NetWare 3.x and higher, each NetWare server is assigned a unique internal IPX network number with a node address of 0000.0000.0001.
5. With implementations of NetWare 3.x and higher, multiple addresses can be supported on a single interface when different frame types are needed on that interface.
6. IPX addresses are manually assigned to servers only, clients learn their IPX addresses through the initial server attachment process.

When comparing the IP header to the IPX header, there are many similarities. Both have an address that reflects a network prefix and a host suffix. IPX also has an additional field, the socket address field. IP does not have a socket or port address. It relies on TCP or UDP to supply a port address. Since both IP and IPX are connectionless and since UDP is connectionless, IPX is oftentimes compared to UDP/IP rather than IP alone.

IPX Packet Type

The IPX packet type is called by Cisco the IPX "protocol number." It is similar to the IP protocol type found in an IP header.

```
0     0 or 4 IPX-based communications (RIP, SAP, Serialization)
1     SPX-based communications
17    NCP communications
20    IPX NETBIOS

For Cisco:
1     RIP
2     Cisco IPX PING
3     Error packet
4     IPX
20    IPX NETBIOS
```

IPX Socket Numbers

Socket numbers direct data encapsulation in IPX header to the appropriate upper layer protocols.

```
0x451     NCP
0x452     SAP
0x453     RIP
0x455     NETBIOS
0x456     Diagnostic
0x457     Serialization
0x4001-
0x7FFF    Client socket numbers
0x85BE    IPX EIGRP
0x9001    NLSP
0x9004    IPXWAN
0x9086    IPX PING
```

These sockets will be critical when creating extended IPX access-lists as well as queuing IPX traffic. See Chapter Twenty-Five for IPX access-lists.

IPX/Cisco Frame Types

Novell IPX Name		**Cisco IOS Name**
Ethernet_802.3	←----------→	novell-ether
Ethernet_802.2	←----------→	sap
Ethernet_II	←----------→	arpa
Ethernet_SNAP	←----------→	snap
Token-Ring	←----------→	sap
Token-Ring_SNAP	←----------→	snap
FDDI_SNAP	←----------→	snap
FDDI_802.2	←----------→	sap
FDDI_Raw	←----------→	novell-fddi

Note: The default encapsulation types on Cisco Router interfaces are:

- Ethernet ------------ novell-ether
- Token Ring -------- sap
- FDDI --------------- snap
- Serial --------------- hdlc

IPX RIP (like IP RIP with a twist)

When the IPX routing process is enabled on a Cisco router, IPX RIP is enabled by default. IPX/RIP is very similar to IP RIP. It is a distance vector routing protocol; however, IPX RIP uses ticks and hops as a metric. (Ticks are a measurement of path delay. 1 tick=55 msec. Ticks are added up first and given priority over hops. The hops metric is a tie breaker.) IPX/RIP updates are broadcast every 60 seconds.

Every Novell server will generate an additional routing table entry with its unique internal IPX address. IPX RIP also uses split horizon as a loop avoidance technique.

If IPX/RIP does not receive an update from a neighbor about a particular route, it places that route into holddown. (Three times the udpate; see show ipx interface.)

IPX SAP (Unique to NetWare; NetWare is servercentric)

SAP provides a list to other servers, of services available on the Novell network. Many different server-types generate SAPs: file servers, print servers, HP Jet Direct cards, backup servers. SAP tables are broadcast every 60 seconds.

IPX/RIP routers maintain both a routing table and a SAP table. SAP table entries can be inserted statically or dynamically. Static SAPs have a higher precedence than dynamically learned SAPs. Static SAPs (unlike static IP routes) get propagated without a manual redistribution statement.

By default, there are only seven SAP entries per packet. This can be increased with IOS commands.

If the network that the SAP table entry is referencing is removed from the routing table, the SAP entry also gets removed. **SAP entries are dependent on routing table entries.**

SAPs are identified inside of an IPX packet by socket number 452. This socket number is used in both the source and destination socket number.

SAP TYPES

There are three types of SAPs:

1. SAP Broadcasts
2. SAP Queries
    - General Service Query (Service Type 0x0001)
    - Get Nearest Service Query (Service Type 0x0003)
3. SAP Responses
    - General Service Response (Service Type 0x0002)
    - Nearest Service Response (Service Type 0x0004)

Note the "type 0x2" and the socket number (452) in the IOS debug statement below. Type 0x2 reflects that this is a SAP general service response. Socket number 452 reflects that the IPX packet is carrying a SAP.

```
IPXSAP: Response (in) type 0x2 len 352 src:444.00e0.1e68.31c5
dest:444.ffff.ffff.ffff(452)
```

SAP NUMBERS

Common SAP numbers are listed below. The most common SAP numbers are 0x4 and 0x7. 0x4 identifies a file server. 0x7 identifies a print server.

```
0x4      File Server
0x7      Print Server
0x47     Advertising Print Server
0x112    HP Print Server
0x026B   Time Synchronization
0x278    NDS Server
```

Note: DO NOT filter SAP type 0x4, 0x026B, and 0x278 in a NetWare 4.1 environment.

For a complete listing of the SAP types, go to ftp://ftp.isi.edu/in-notes/iana/assignments/novell-sap-numbers.

SAP HOP COUNT

The SAP Hop Count indicates the number of routers between a server and a client. This value is important when a router searches for the "nearest server," so that when a NetWare client initializes, it can find the nearest server to login to.

All 3.x and 4.x file server SAPs will be at least one hop away from a client on the same network as the file server. This is due to the fact that the NetWare file service (TYPE 4 SAP) is on the internal IPX network. As a result, all file servers must also act as routers.

Get Nearest Server

GNS is a special type of SAP. It is a type 3 SAP request that is generated upon activating the NetWare protocol stack on a client device. A NetWare client is useless unless it can attach to a file server. The GNS SAP request drives this process of attaching to a file server.

The process a workstation goes through when it generates a GNS request is listed below:

- A workstation generates a GNS request (SAP type 3).
- If there is a file server on the workstation's local segment, it sends a GNS response.
- If there is no file server on the workstation's local segment, but there is a Cisco router on the local segment, the router will generate a GNS response from the top of the SAP table.

When a GNS Query is transmitted, the requesting end system will receive a response from each server on the network that provides the service type requested.

The GNS request process can be manipulated with the "preferred server" configuration statement at the workstation. (See Novell NetWare configuration guides for more details.)

When we examine AppleTalk, we will compare and contrast a GNS request to an AppleTalk GETZONELIST request.

SEQUENCED PACKET EXCHANGE (SPX)

SPX is a connection-oriented protocol used for services such as RCONSOLE and remote printer services. It is comparable to TCP in the TCP/IP protocol suite. SPX will continually send acknowledgements between two end systems maintaining a SPX session. This traffic will cause problems over DDR links. As a remedy, the Cisco IOS can spoof SPX traffic over a DDR link.

NETWARE CORE PROTOCOL (NCP)

Once a NetWare client has located a NetWare server to attach to, NCP is used to access bindery information and access files on the file server. For example, NCPs are used to transfer files from the file server disk to the client's RAM. NCPs are based upon a request/reply model. Listed below are some of the more common NCP request and reply numbers:

```
1111     Create a service connection
1112     Service request
3333     Service reply
5555     Destroy service connection
7777     Burst mode transfer
9999     Request being processed
```

The vast majority of Novell traffic is NCP/IPX traffic.

Special IPX Packets

WATCHDOG PACKETS

Watchdog packets are used to clear unused NetWare client connections. If a workstation has been idle for a period of time (default 4 minutes and 56.6 seconds), watchdog packets are transmitted to the workstation.

Workstations can send a Watchdog response packet to a server to reflect that the workstation is still in use. If no response is received from the workstation, the server transmits ten (default) Watchdog query packets at 59.3 (default) second intervals. If the client still does not respond, the server terminates the connection.

Since Watchdog packets are sent continuously, they can keep a DDR link up indefinitely. Just as with SPX, the Cisco IOS provides a command to enable watchdog packet "spoofing" over DDR links.

SERIALIZATION PACKETS

Serialization packets are generated every 66 seconds to protect against NetWare copyright violations. Serialization packets use a destination IPX socket address of 0x457.

CONVERGENCE IPX STYLE

Convergence is the state of internetwork equilibrium. It is when all routers contain the same routing table entries. The entries as an aggregate will be the same. The way they are listed will differ. Each router will list the entries in a manner that reflects its own perspective of the internetwork. Convergence in an IPX internetwork displays:

- All routers see all networks within the internetwork.
- All routers see all SAPs with the internetwork.
- All routes are aging properly.
- All SAP entries are aging properly.
- The metrics of the RIP and SAP entries accurately reflect the relative distance of the networks and servers.

Using the following debug statements, RIP and SAP advertisements should be announced and received consistently with the proper contents:

- Debug ipx routing activity
- Debug ipx routing events
- Debug ipx sap activity
- Debug ipx sap events

Remember: Not all interfaces will announce all networks in an IPX/RIP-SAP environment due to split horizon.

Remember: SAP entries are dependent upon routing table entries.

GENERAL RULES TO REMEMBER ABOUT IPX ROUTING

1. IPX routing is enabled and IPX network addresses are assigned to router interfaces.
2. IPX routers announce locally connected networks to neighboring IPX routers
3. IPX routers accumulate routing information from neighboring routers.
4. Routers create SAP tables through announcements from neighboring IPX routers.
5. SAP entries will only remain in the SAP table if the associated IPX address is in the IPX routing table.
6. SAP entries will be ordered by metric (show ipx server unsorted).

For IPX internetworks, convergence has been achieved when all routers have the same view of all IPX networks *and* all IPX services.

The following IOS show commands display an IPX network operating under stable conditions:

```
r1>sh ipx route
Codes: C - Connected primary network, c - Connected secondary network
     S - Static, F - Floating static, L - Local (internal), W - IPXWAN
     R - RIP, E - EIGRP, N - NLSP, X - External, s - seconds, u - uses

3 Total IPX routes. Up to 1 parallel paths and 16 hops allowed.
No default route known.

C    1A1A (HDLC),           Se0
E    AAA [2297856/0] via    1A1A.0000.0c3b.b5fc, age 0:26:14,
     15u, Se0
E    CCC [2297856/0] via    1A1A.0000.0c3b.b5fc, age 1:12:43,
     4u, Se0

r1>sh ipx servers
Codes: S - Static, P - Periodic, E - EIGRP, N - NLSP, H - Holddown, + = detail
4 Total IPX Servers
```

Table ordering is based on routing and server info.

```
Type  Name     Net       Address      Port       Route          Hops  Itf
E      4 fs1   AAA.1234.1234.1234:0451     2297856/00     2      Se0
E      4 fs2   AAA.1234.1234.1234:0451     2297856/00     2      Se0
E      4 fs3   AAA.1234.1234.1334:0451     2297856/00     2      Se0
E      4 fs5   CCC.1234.1234.4334:0451     2297856/00     2      Se0
```

Configuring IPX

ENABLING THE IPX PROCESS

First, the IPX routing process needs to be enabled on the router—this is performed by entering the following global configuration command:

```
R1(config)#ipx routing
```

Perform the following to verify that the IPX process is running:

```
Show  protocols
sh processes cpu

R1#sh proto
Global values:
Internet Protocol routing is enabled
IPX routing is enabled

R1#sh proc cpu
CPU utilization for five seconds: 3%/3%; one minute: 6%; five minutes: 3%
PID  Runtime(ms)  Invoked  uSecs    5Sec    1Min    5Min      TTY  Process

     1    8        27      296      0.00%    0.00%    0.00%    0    Load Meter
     2    1728     138     12521    0.00%    0.70%    0.39%    0    Exec
```

```
.
.
32    12    3    4000    0.00%    0.01%    0.00%    0    IPX RIP In
33    4     5    800     0.00%    0.00%    0.00%    0    IPX SAP In
34    0     1    0       0.00%    0.00%    0.00%    0    IPX Event Mgr
35    0     1    0       0.00%    0.00%    0.00%    0    IPX RIP Out
36    0     1    0       0.00%    0.00%    0.00%    0    IPX SAP Out
37    4     1    4000    0.00%    0.00%    0.00%    0    IPX Net Mgr
38    0     2    0       0.00%    0.00%    0.00%    0    IPX GNS
39    0     2    0       0.00%    0.00%    0.00%    0    IPX Fowarder
40    0     2    0       0.00%    0.00%    0.00%    0    IPXWAN Input
41    0     2    0       0.00%    0.00%    0.00%    0    IPXWAN Timer
```

When the IPX process is enabled, IPX RIP is enabled by default.

Adding an IPX Network to an Interface

To add an IPX address to an interface, type the following command:

```
R1(config-if)# ipx network 1111
```

This address must match any other IPX interfaces attached to the network. It must be a unique IPX address from others used on other segments. Also, beware of entering overlapping IPX addresses with internal IPX addresses.

Multiple addresses can be assigned to one physical segment with the use of different frame types.

As soon as a new network was added, a flash update was generated immediately by the router. Listed below is a debug trace that reflects what happens immediately after the network statement is added.

```
r1(config-if)#ipx netw 17
r1(config-if)#
IPX: Change state of [itf]:[net] Se1:17 from [unknown] to [up]:[new]
IPX: Change state of [itf]:[net] Se1:17 from [new] to [up]:[up]
IPX: cache flush
IPXRIP: Marking network 17 FFFFFFFF for Flash Update
IPXRIP: General Query src=17.00e0.1eb9.2a05, dst=17.ffff.ffff.ffff, packet sent
IPX: local:17.00e0.1eb9.2a05->17.ffff.ffff.ffff ln= 40 tc=00,
gw=Se1:17.ffff.ffff.ffff
IPX: local:17.00e0.1eb9.2a05->17.ffff.ffff.ffff ln= 34 tc=00,
gw=Se1:17.ffff.ffff.ffff
IPXRIP: positing flash update to 17.ffff.ffff.ffff via Serial1 (broadcast)
IPXRIP: positing full update to 17.ffff.ffff.ffff via Serial1 (broadcast)
IPXRIP: suppressing null update to 17.ffff.ffff.ffff
IPX: Se1:17.0000.0c76.08f9->17.00e0.1eb9.2a05 ln= 56 tc=00, rcvd
IPX: Se1:17.0000.0c76.08f9->17.00e0.1eb9.2a05 ln= 56 tc=00, local
IPXRIP: update from 17.0000.0c76.08f9
IPXRIP: create route to 3AAA FFFFFFFF via 0000.0c76.08f9, delay 7, hops 1
```

```
IPX: cache flush
IPXRIP: Marking network 3AAA FFFFFFFF for Flash Update
     3AAA in 1 hops, delay 7
IPXRIP: create route to 2AAA FFFFFFFF via 0000.0c76.08f9, delay 7, hops 1
IPX: cache flush
IPXRIP: Marking network 2AAA FFFFFFFF for Flash Update
     2AAA in 1 hops, delay 7
IPXRIP: create route to 1AAA FFFFFFFF via 0000.0c76.08f9, delay 7, hops 1
IPX: cache flush
IPXRIP: Marking network 1AAA FFFFFFFF for Flash Update
     1AAA in 1 hops, delay 7
```

The following debug trace displays the debug trace of another router on the same segment:

```
IPXRIP: received request from 17.00e0.1eb9.2a05 for all routes
IPXRIP: positing full update to 17.00e0.1eb9.2a05 via Serial1 (unicast)
IPX: Se1:17.00e0.1eb9.2a05->17.ffff.ffff.ffff ln= 34 tc=00, rcvd
IPX: Se1:17.00e0.1eb9.2a05->17.ffff.ffff.ffff ln= 34 tc=00, local
IPXRIP: src=17.0000.0c76.08f9, dst=17.00e0.1eb9.2a05, packet sent
     network 3AAA, hops 1,  delay 7
     network 2AAA, hops 1,  delay 7
     network 1AAA, hops 1,  delay 7
     network 1AAA, hops 1,  delay 7
```

IPX/RIP: The Default IPX Routing Protocol

As soon as the IPX routing process is enabled and addresses are assigned to interfaces, IPX/RIP begins to advertise networks and build a routing table.

```
r1#sh ipx ro
Codes: C - Connected primary network,    c - Connected secondary network
     S - Static, F - Floating static, L - Local (internal), W - IPXWAN
     R - RIP, E - EIGRP, N - NLSP, X - External, A - Aggregate
     s - seconds, u - uses

4 Total IPX routes. Up to 1 parallel paths and 16 hops allowed.

No default route known.

C    17      (HDLC),         Se1
R    1AAA    [07/01] via     17.0000.0c76.08f9,      1s, Se1
R    2AAA    [07/01] via     17.0000.0c76.08f9,      1s, Se1
R    3AAA    [07/01] via     17.0000.0c76.08f9,      1s, Se1
```

The layout of `show ipx route` is very similar to `show ip route`. On the far left-hand side is the source of the routing information. A "C" reflects a connected route. An "R" reflects a route learned through the RIP process. The [07/01] is not the administrative distance and metric value. Both values are metrics. The first value is the tick count and the second value is the hop count. The remaining values are very similar to an IP routing table. The address preceded by the word "via" is the address of the directly connected IPX/RIP router acting as the next-hop. The "1s" is the age of the entry (one second) and the "Se1" is the local interface to forward the packet out of.

IPX routing activity can be examined more closely with the commands `debug ipx routing activity` and `debug ipx routing events`. Just as "debug ip rip" showed us the entire routing table being periodically announced, these debug commands will do the same. A sample is displayed below:

```
r1#
IPX: Se1:17.0000.0c76.08f9->17.ffff.ffff.ffff ln= 56 tc=00, rcvd
IPX: Se1:17.0000.0c76.08f9->17.ffff.ffff.ffff ln= 56 tc=00, local
IPXRIP: update from 17.0000.0c76.08f9
     3AAA in 1 hops, delay 7
     2AAA in 1 hops, delay 7
     1AAA in 1 hops, delay 7
```

When a route goes down, debug immediately displays it through the IPX flash update process:

```
IPXRIP: update from 17.0000.0c76.08f9
IPX: cache flush
IPXRIP: Marking network 1AAA FFFFFFFF for Flash Update
IPXRIP: Marking network 1AAA FFFFFFFF for Flash Update
     1AAA in 16 hops, delay 7
IPXRIP: positing flash update to 17.ffff.ffff.ffff via Serial1 (broadcast)
IPXRIP: suppressing null update to 17.ffff.ffff.ffff
IPX: Se1:17.0000.0c76.08f9->17.ffff.ffff.ffff ln= 48 tc=00, rcvd
IPX: Se1:17.0000.0c76.08f9->17.ffff.ffff.ffff ln= 48 tc=00, local
IPXRIP: update from 17.0000.0c76.08f9
     3AAA in 1 hops, delay 7
     2AAA in 1 hops, delay 7
```

When a flash update is received about a learned route being down, IPX/RIP places it in a hold down state.

```
r1#sh ipx ro
Codes: C - Connected primary network,    c - Connected secondary network
     S - Static, F - Floating static, L - Local (internal), W - IPXWAN
     R - RIP, E - EIGRP, N - NLSP, X - External, A - Aggregate
     s - seconds, u - uses

4 Total IPX routes. Up to 1 parallel paths and 16 hops allowed.

No default route known.

C    17       (HDLC),          Se1
RH   1AAA     [**/**] via      17.0000.0c76.08f9,      72s, Se1
R    2AAA     [07/01] via      17.0000.0c76.08f9,      12s, Se1
R    3AAA     [07/01] via      17.0000.0c76.08f9,      12s, Se1
```

The hold down state can be removed by clearing the individual entry of the routing table or clearing the entire routing table with `clear ipx route *`.

DO NOT USE CLEAR IPX ROUTE * ON A PRODUCTION NETWORK.

IPX STATIC AND DEFAULT ROUTES

With IP, we can configure static and default routes. We can do the same with IPX. IPX static routes are configured in global configuration mode. The syntax for configuring an IPX static route is:

```
CastlePines(config)#ipx route 1111 ?
  <0-FFFFFFFF>       Network mask
  Loopback           Loopback interface
  N.H.H.H            Address of forwarding host
  Null               Null interface
  Serial             Serial
  Tunnel             Tunnel interface
```

You can complete the static route entry with a next hop address or a local interface. Once either of these is supplied, you can either set the static route as a floating-static route or adjust the routes metrics:

```
CastlePines(config)#ipx route 1111 s0 ?
  <1-65534>          ticks/delay
  floating-static    Permit static route to be overwritten by
                     dynamic in formation
  <cr>
```

You can also configure a default route for IPX. It is used if a destination IPX address is not listed in the IPX routing table. The syntax for configuring an IPX default route is

```
CastlePines(config)#ipx route default ?
  Loopback           Loopback interface
  N.H.H.H            Address of forwarding host
  Null               Null interface
  Serial             Serial
  Tunnel             Tunnel interface
```

Note: Specifying an interface instead of a network.node is intended for use on IPXWAN unnumbered interfaces.

By default, IPX default-route is enabled and uses the network number -2 (0xFFFFFFFE) as the default route. Also, by default, all RIP updates are still advertised out the default interface. If you want to prevent this from happening, enter the following interface configuration command: `ipx advertise-default-route-only network`.

IPX ROUTE REDISTRIBUTION

IPX redistribution is very similar to IP redistribution. You must enter a specific routing protocol's configuration mode and enter the redistribution command. The options for this command are displayed below:

```
r1(config-ipx-router)#redistribute ?
  connected          Connected
  eigrp              Enhanced Interior Gateway Routing Protocol
                     (EIGRP)
  floating-static    Floating static routes
  nlsp               IPX NetWare Link Services Protocol
  rip                Routing Information Protocol (RIP)
  static             Static routes
```

Automatic mutual redistribution occurs between EIGRP and RIP and also between RIP and NLSP. EIGRP must be manually redistributed into NLSP.

Assume R3 has an IPX address AAA assigned to lo0 with an unknown encapsulation. R3 is running IPX RIP. R3 is directly connected to R5, which is running EIGRP. IPX address AAA automatically gets redistributed into R5's EIGRP process.

IPX STATIC SAPS

Not only can you configure IPX static routes, you can also configure IPX static SAPs. The syntax for configuring IPX static SAP configuration is:

r1(config)#**ipx sap** *service-type name network.node socket hop-count*
Ex. R1(config)#ipx sap 4 Fileserv AAA.0000.0c12.1234 451 1

You can display SAP entries with the `show ipx servers` command. Notice the static SAP is identified with an "S" in the far left column:

```
r1#sh ipx servers
Codes: S - Static, P - Periodic, E - EIGRP, N - NLSP, H - Holddown, + = detail
2 Total IPX Servers

Table ordering is based on routing and server info

Type  Name            Net      Address     Port     Route  Hops   Itf
S     4 eng-fs        171.1234.1234.1234:0451       conn   1      Lo0
P     4 accting-fs    1AAA.1234.1234.1234:0451      7/01   2      Se1
```

Static SAPs are automatically advertised. There is no need for redistribution of static SAPs. As soon as a static SAP was entered, this is what was generated by the sourcing router:

```
IPXSAP: positing update to 17.ffff.ffff.ffff via Serial1 (broadcast) (flash)
IPXSAP: positing update to 171.ffff.ffff.ffff via Loopback0 (broadcast) (flash)
IPXSAP: Update type 0x2 len 96 src:17.00e0.1eb9.2a05 dest:17.ffff.ffff.ffff(452)

 type 0x4, "eng-fs", 171.1234.1234.1234(451), 2 hops
```

As soon as a static SAP was entered, this string of messages was received from a neighboring router:

```
IPXSAP: positing update to 17.ffff.ffff.ffff via Serial1 (broadcast) (full)
IPXSAP: Response (in) type 0x2 len 96 src:17.0000.0c76.08f9
dest:17.ffff.ffff.ffff(452)
type 0x4, "accting-fs", 1AAA.1234.1234.1234(451), 2 hops
IPX: SAP queue-hash added for type 4, count 1
IPXSAP: new SAP entry: type 4 server "accting-fs" 2 hops [1/7]
```

With IPX static SAPs, if you place the static SAP on the network that will be propagating the SAPs, it will not get propagated. You get "null updates suppressed" in the DEBUG IPX SAP statements.

In the example above, the SAP needs to be propagated out the s0 interface. If the static SAP is configured on the s0 interface, it will not work. When an attempt to advertise the SAP out the Serial0 interface, the following messages will be generated by the commands `debug ipx sap activity` and `debug ipx sap events`:

```
IPXSAP: positing update to 111.ffff.ffff.ffff via Serial0 (broadcast) (full)
IPXSAP: suppressing null update to 111.ffff.ffff.ffff
```

Notice the "suppressing null update" statement. Therefore, when you create a static SAP, do not associate it with the address of an interface that you want it to go out on or it will get suppressed. This is due to the rule of split horizon, which applies to not only IPX/RIP advertisements but to SAP advertisements as well.

TUNING IPX/RIP AND SAP

SAP update intervals can be adjusted. When the adjustment is made, set it on both sides of a given link. The IPX SAP-INTERVAL command is measured in minutes.

The IPX UPDATE-TIME for RIP allows the update interval for IPX/RIP updates to be calibrated. If this statement is used, configure it on all IPX/RIP routers that communicate with each other. IPX UPDATE-TIME is measured in seconds.

Note: Adjust RIP/SAP update intervals only on serial interfaces.

EIGRP IN AN IPX ENVIRONMENT

The benefits of using EIGRP for IPX include:

- EIGRP does not send out periodic updates of its routing table or SAP table. It propagates SAP information only when something changes or every 120 minutes.
- EIGRP uses a composite metric for shortest path selection.
- EIGRP automatically performs a two-way redistribution with IPX/RIP. To IPX/RIP, the IPX EIGRP cloud appears as a single hop.
- Rapid reconvergence when the network topology changes.
- For IPX, EIGRP is configured in a manner similar for EIGRP for IP.
- The routing process is enabled with the following syntax:
- IPX ROUTER EIGRP *AUTONOMOUS SYSTEM NUMBER*

Like IP EIGRP, the autonomous system number of each IPX EIGRP enabled router must be the same if they are intended to be in the same autonomous system.

After the routing process is enabled, a NETWORK statement must be supplied for each connected network that is to participate in the IPX EIGRP routing process.

If IPX/RIP needs to be disabled for connected network statements, a "NO NETWORK *network number*" statement must be supplied under the IPX ROUTING RIP command.

A sample configuration is supplied below:

```
ipx router eigrp 100
network 1A1A
network AAA
network BBB
network CCC
!
!
ipx router rip
no network 1A1A
no network AAA
no network BBB
no network CCC
!
```

Examine how IPX routing is changed by EIGRP. Cisco usually recommends configuring IPX EIGRP at the WAN core; IPX/RIP at the edges. This greatly reduces the amount of traffic flowing over the WAN core.

- EIGRP neighbor relationships must be established. This can be verified by typing:

```
Sh ipx eigrp neighbor

r2#sh ipx eigrp neighbor
```

```
IPX EIGRP Neighbors for process 100
H  Address              Interface  Hold Uptime  SRTT  RTO   Q  Seq
                        (sec)      (ms)         Cnt   Num
0  1A1A.00e0.b056.1edc  Se0        13 00:05:27  261   1566  0  8
```

The EIGRP IPX topological database must be created. This can be verified by typing:

```
Sh ipx eigrp topology
```

```
r2#sh ipx eigrp top
IPX EIGRP Topology Table for process 100

Codes: P - Passive, A - Active, U - Update, Q - Query, R - Reply,
     r - Reply status

P 1A1A, 1 successors, FD is 2169856
     via Connected, Serial0
P 111, 1 successors, FD is 2297856
     via 1A1A.00e0.b056.1edc (2297856/128256), Serial0
P 222, 1 successors, FD is 2297856
     via 1A1A.00e0.b056.1edc (2297856/128256), Serial0
P 333, 1 successors, FD is 267008000
     via 1A1A.00e0.b056.1edc (267008000/266496000), Serial0
P AAA, 1 successors, FD is 128256
     via Connected, Loopback0
P BBB, 1 successors, FD is 128256
     via Connected, Loopback1
P CCC, 1 successors, FD is 128256
     via Connected, Loopback2
```

- EIGRP selected routes are posted to the IPX routing table. This can be verified by typing:

```
Sh ipx route
```

Displayed below is an IPX routing table with EIGRP routing entries:

```
r1>sh ipx ro
Codes: C - Connected primary network,    c - Connected secondary network
     S - Static, F - Floating static, L - Local (internal), W - IPXWAN
     R - RIP, E - EIGRP, N - NLSP, X - External, s - seconds, u - uses

4 Total IPX routes. Up to 1 parallel paths and 16 hops allowed.

No default route known.

C    1A1A (HDLC),             Se0
E    AAA [2297856/0] via     1A1A.0000.0c3b.b5fc, age 0:39:30, 1u, Se0
E    BBB [2297856/0] via     1A1A.0000.0c3b.b5fc, age 0:35:54, 1u, Se0
E    CCC [2297856/0] via     1A1A.0000.0c3b.b5fc, age 0:35:51, 1u, Se0
```

Notice the age of the routing table entries. Notice they are above 60 seconds.

```
r1#sh ipx server detail
Codes: S - Static, P - Periodic, E - EIGRP, N - NLSP, H - Holddown, + = detail
5 Total IPX Servers

Table ordering is based on routing and server info

Type  Name          Net     Address     Port   Route         Hops   Itf
E     4 fs1         AAA.1234.1234.1234:0451 2297856/00    2      Se0
               -- via Se0:1A1A.0000.0c3b.b5fc, 284s
E     4 fs2         AAA.1234.1234.1234:0451 2297856/00    2      Se0
               -- via Se0:1A1A.0000.0c3b.b5fc, 178s
E     4 fs3         AAA.1234.1234.1334:0451 2297856/00    2      Se0
               -- via Se0:1A1A.0000.0c3b.b5fc, 164s
E     4 fs4         BBB.1234.1234.4334:0451 2297856/00    2      Se0
               -- via Se0:1A1A.0000.0c3b.b5fc, 148s
E     4 fs5         CCC.1234.1234.4334:0451 2297856/00    2      Se0
               -- via Se0:1A1A.0000.0c3b.b5fc,  17s
```

- Notice the age of the SAP entries. With EIGRP, SAP updates on serial interfaces, by default, are sent only when a change occurs.
- When a route is removed from the routing table, associated SAPs will be flushed in 180 seconds.

IPX NLSP CONFIGURATION

Netware Link State Protocols (NLSP) benefits are:

IPX Link state routing
IPX address summarization

IPX NLSP was developed by Novell as a link-state routing protocol for IPX. Like EIGRP, it will greatly reduce the amount of traffic flowing over the WAN core. Like EIGRP, NLSP provides automatic redistribution between itself and IPX/RIP. NLSP also provides IPX route summarization.

Let's examine a basic configuration of NLSP. The basic configuration of NLSP involves a minimum of five commands:

1. Enabling the IPX NLSP routing process.
2. Defining an address summarization range (optional).
3. Defining an internal IPX network number for each router. (Must be unique throughout your network.)
4. Enabling NLSP on desired interfaces.

A sample configuration script with these commands configured is listed below:

```
!
ipx routing 00e0.b05a.9bfb
ipx internal-network 17171
!
interface Ethernet0
 no ip address
ipx network 1AAA
 ipx nlsp enable
!
!
ipx router nlsp
 area-address 0 0
!
```

When using NLSP, remember also to disable RIP/SAP. It is on by default. To disable RIP/SAP on the interfaces, the commands are:

```
IPX NLSP RIP OFF
IPX NLSP SAP OFF
```

Like OSPF, NLSP forms neighbor relationships with neighboring NLSP speaking routers and builds an NLSP link state database by forming adjacencies. These NLSP processes can be monitored with the following show and debug tools:

```
London#sh ipx nlsp ?
     WORD                Routing process tag
     database            NLSP link state database
     neighbors           NLSP neighbor adjacencies
     spf-log             NLSP SPF log

London#debug ipx nlsp ?
     <1-FFFFFFFE>        IPX network
     activity            IPX NLSP activity
     adj-packets         NLSP Adjacency related packets
     checksum-errors     NLSP LSP checksum errors
     events              IPX NLSP events
     local-updates       NLSP local update packets
     protocol-errors     NLSP LSP protocol errors
     snp-packets         NLSP CSNP/PSNP packets
     spf-events          NLSP Shortest Path First Events
     spf-statistics      NLSP SPF Timing and Statistics Data
     spf-triggers        NLSP SPF triggering events
     update-packets      NLSP Update related packets
```

Notice how both the NLSP show and debug tools closely resemble the show and debug tools of OSPF.

NLSP cannot be configured on loopback interfaces or physical Frame-Relay interfaces. Also, it cannot be configured on frame-relay multipoint interfaces; however, it can be configured on frame-relay point-to-point interfaces.

IPXWAN CONFIGURATION

By default, IPX supplies the same number of ticks to all WAN interfaces. Whether the link is a T-1 or a 56K link, to IPX it is the same bandwidth, because by default, six ticks are automatically assigned to a WAN link. This can cause distortions in path selection when multiple WAN connections exist. To remedy this, Novell developed IPXWAN that accurately measures the delay of a WAN link for either IPX/RIP or NLSP. IPXWAN is applied by a single interface configuration command: `ipx ipxwan`.

When IPXWAN is enabled, the interface that it is applied to is momentarily brought down and then back up.

IPXWAN requires:

1. IPX internal address must be supplied for each router.
2. NO IPX network address on an interface that has IPXWAN applied
3. Type IPX IPXWAN on each interface that will have IPXWAN applied. This must be entered on both sides of the WAN connection.

Perform a sh ipx interface s0 to view IPXWAN status.
Perform a sh ipx route to view change of metrics in the routing table.
Use debug ipx ipxwan to view the IPXWAN negotiation process.

IPX OVER NBMA

To configure IPX over an NBMA network such as Frame-Relay, you have some configuration options. For full-mesh configurations, you can rely entirely on inverse ARP.

For hub and spoke NBMA topologies, you can use Frame-Relay map statements on the spoke routers and rely on inverse ARP at the hub. If point-to-point subinterfaces are configured at the spoke routers, then no frame-relay map statements are needed at the spokes.

If you need to supply a frame-relay map statement, use caution when typing in the remote IPX address. You must supply the full network and node address components of the remote-router.

In hub and spoke NBMA networks, split horizon can be an issue with IPX/RIP and EIGRP. Split horizon can never be disabled for IPX/RIP. For EIGRP, disable split-horizon at the hub router only.

Remember how the Frame-Relay map statement disables inverse arp!!! See Chapter Four for more details.

IPX DDR ISSUES

When configuring IPX over DDR links, be aware of the possibility of IPX/RIP and SAP updates keeping the link up indefinitely. A restrictive dialer list can be used to remedy this. However, if a restrictive dialer-list is configured to deny IPX/RIP and SAP updates as interesting traffic, IPX routing and SAP tables will never be properly maintained. This can be remedied with either static IPX routes and static IPX SAPs or with SNAPSHOT routing.

Other parameters you might want to tune for IPX over DDR are:

```
Enable SPX spoofing
Enable watchdog spoofing
Set SPX timeout
```

TUNNELING IPX TRAFFIC

IPX traffic may be tunneled through an IP internetwork with the use of GRE tunneling. In order to do this, create a virtual tunnel interface. Configure the tunnel source and destination. Once this is done, treat the tunnel interface like any other physical IPX interface. Assign an IPX address to it. Enable EIGRP or NLSP on the interface. It is recommended that you use EIGRP or NLSP on the tunnel interface and manually disable IPX/RIP. If you do not, periodic IPX/RIP traffic will be flowing over the tunnel.

GRE tunneling uses IP protocol number 47. Make sure that no access-lists block the passing of IP protocol number 47 traffic.

You can debug IPX tunneled traffic by using standard IPX `show` and `debug` commands as well as `show tunnel` and `debug tunnel`.

TROUBLESHOOTING IPX

Like with IP, make sure that the physical and data-link layer protocols are operating properly. Use the following commands to determine this:

```
Sh ipx interface brie
Sh ipx inte xx
Sh cdp neigh
Sh cdp neighbor detail (Read the IPX address of the far side to verify that it
is correct.)
```

REMEMBER TO BASELINE EVERTHING WITH IP. PERFORM IP PING AND TRACE THROUGHOUT THE INTERNETWORK TO ASSURE THAT EVERYTHING IS OPERATIONAL USING IP.

Once you have determined that everything is operational using IP, use the following IPX specific tools:

```
Ping IPX

DEBUG IPX PACKET
DEBUG IPX ROUTING
DEBUG IPX SAP
CLEA IPX RO *
```

When troubleshooting, remember to troubleshoot both sides of a connection or both directions of a routing path (the destination path and the return path).

THE POWER OF DEBUG IPX PACKET

Like DEBUG IP PACKET, DEBUG IPX PACKET is an extremely valuable troubleshooting tool, primarily in a lab environment. USE DEBUG IPX PACKET ON A PRODUCTION ROUTER WITH EXTREME CAUTION.

Listed below is a sample debug IPX packet trace for an unroutable packet:

```
IPX: Se1:1717.00e0.1eb9.29f9->17.1234.1234.1234 ln=100 tc=00, no route
IPX: Se1:1717.00e0.1eb9.29f9->17.1234.1234.1234 ln=100 tc=00, rcvd
IPX: Se1:1717.00e0.1eb9.29f9->17.1234.1234.1234 ln=100 tc=00, no route
IPX: Se1:1717.00e0.1eb9.29f9->17.1234.1234.1234 ln=100 tc=00, rcvd
IPX: Se1:1717.00e0.1eb9.29f9->17.1234.1234.1234 ln=100 tc=00, no route
```

IPX/SPX IDIOSYNCRASIES AND LANDMINES

- "Novell is Server centric. All internetworking issues ultimately lead up to server connectivity."
- If the network that is associated with an SAP is flushed from the IPX routing table, the SAP will also be flushed.
- Beware of associating a static SAP on an interface you want to advertise the SAP out of. Due to split horizon, the SAP will not get advertised out that interface.
- The node address of a NetWare server is identified by its internal IPX address 0000.0000.0001.
- Beware of split-horizon blocking traffic at the hub of a hub and spoke NBMA network.
- Split horizon can never be disabled for IPX/RIP, but it can be disabled for EIGRP
- Beware of RIP and SAP broadcast traffic from initiating DDR connections.

If RIP and SAP traffic is defined as "uninteresting" for DDR connections, make sure that static routes are used to provide reachability information of remote networks on the opposite side of a DDR link.

If using a tunnel, make sure that all paths through intermediate routers have no access-lists to block the operation of the tunnel.

If IPX is configured on a router and DECNET is configured afterwards, DECNET will alter the MAC address of the LAN interfaces. This will have an impact on WAN map statements.

Summary

IPX/SPX is a protocol suite that highly prevalent on many corporate internetworks. Originally, IPX/SPX was developed to operate solely in Novell NetWare in LAN environments. Today, the protocol suite is also used in Microsoft NT and Lotus Notes environments. With enhancements such as NLSP and NDS, IPX/SPX has also been enhanced to improve its performance in an enterprise environment.

The Cisco IOS provides a wide range of configuration options for IPX/SPX. In a large scale IPX/SPX environment, you can configure IPX/SPX in a hierarchical manner. You can configure either EIGRP or NSLP in the core of your internetwork and use IPX/RIP at the edges. A second alternative to consider is tunneling IPX through an IP core network.

Cisco IPX/SPX router configuration shares many similarities with Cisco IP router configuration. Some of the similarities are:

- The IOS supplies static route support for both IPX and IP routing.
- The IOS supplies default route support for both IPX and IP routing.
- EIGRP supports both IPX and IP

Many of the same issues encountered with configuring IP over Frame-Relay are encountered with configuring IPX over Frame-Relay.

The IOS provides many similar debug tools and show commands for IPX and IP. Some of the similar debugging tools and show commands are:

Debug ip packet	debug ipx packet
Debug ip routing	debug ipx routing activity
Ping ip	ping ipx
Show ip route	show ipx route
Show ip interface brief	show ipx inter

Professional Development Checklist

- Basic IPX configuration using IPX/RIP
- Interface configuration using different LAN encapsulation types
- IPX static route configuration
- IPX default route configuration
- IPX static SAP configuration
- IPX EIGRP configuration
- IPX NLSP configuration
- Enable IPXWAN
- IPX configuration over a DDR link with dialer-maps
- IPX configuration over a DDR link with dialer profiles
- SNAPSHOT routing over a DDR link
- IPX configuration over an NBMA link (full mesh)
- IPX configuration over an NBMA link (hub and spoke)
- IPX tunnel configuration using IPX/RIP (point-to-point)
- IPX tunnel configuration using EIGRP (point-to-point)
- IPX tunnel configuration using EIGRP (hub and spoke)
- Complete review of all pages of the IPX Chapter in the IOS 11.x Configuration Guide
- Complete review of all pages of the IPX Chapter in the IOS 11.x Command Reference

For Further Study

- Ford, Merilee; Lew, Kim; Spanier, Steve; Stevenson, Tim. *Cisco Internetworking Technologies Handbook*, Cisco Press, 1998.
- Naugle, Matthew. *Network Protocols*, McGraw Hill, 1998.

Good Cisco Certified Courses to take for this:

- Introduction to Cisco Router Configuration
- Advanced Cisco Router Configuration
- Cisco Internetwork Troubleshooting

URLs

- **www.cciecert.com**
- **www.mentorlabs.com**
- **www.cisco.com**

Can You Spot the Issues?

1. An IPX configuration is created in a hub and spoke Frame-Relay network, the hub can see all routes but the spokes cannot. Why?
   What would be the course of action to correct the problem?
2. Spoke routers in a Frame-Relay network can see other networks but they cannot PING each other (Spoke routers can PING their hub router but not other spokes.)
   What would be the course of action to correct the problem?
3. A tunnel is configured between R1 and R2. The configuration is correct but the tunnel does not work. Suggest a reason why.
4. Configure IPX networks on the LAN interfaces of a router only, but the routers must be able to reach other IPX networks through the WAN cloud. How can this be done?
5. You have been told that the file server FS1 has been filtered on a router outside of your administrative control. Configure R2 containing FS1in its SAP table.
6. Your IPX network is working fine. You configure DECNET on IPX routers and suddenly IPX is malfunctioning. Why? What is the remedy?
7. Two WAN links (two T-1 lines) are connected between two routers, but only one path is being used. Why? What is the remedy?

8. Two WAN links (one 56-K line and one 1.544-Mbps line) are viewed by IPX routers as equal cost paths. Why? What will allow the IOS to obtain a more accurate view of the difference between the two paths?

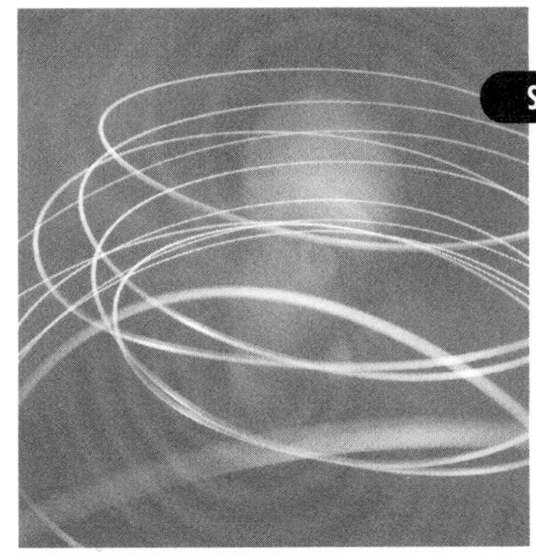

S E V E N T E E N

AppleTalk Configuration

Topics Covered in This Chapter

- AppleTalk Technology Overview
- Configure AppleTalk for RTMP and Only One Zone Per Cable-range
- Configure Static AppleTalk Routes
- Configure EIGRP for AppleTalk
- Configure AppleTalk Tunneling
- Troubleshooting AppleTalk
- AppleTalk Idiosyncrasies
- Troubleshooting AppleTalk

At this point you should have a basic technical understanding of both IP and IPX routing protocol configurations and troubleshooting. This understanding will allow you to more easily acquire the same skill level with the AppleTalk protocol suite. Listed below are some of the similarities that AppleTalk shares with both IP and IPX:

1. Like IP:
   AppleTalk has a network.node addressing scheme (IPX also possesses this address structure).
   AppleTalk provides peer-to-peer connectivity.
2. Like IPX:
   AppleTalk provides mechanisms for end users to seamlessly locate network resources.
   AppleTalk remote file and print sharing is designed so that the user feels that resources being used reside locally.
   AppleTalk was originally designed for local-area networks, not wide-area enterprise internetwork environments.

AppleTalk Design Objectives

The primary design objective of AppleTalk is to make networking transparent and user-friendly. From the end-user perspective, AppleTalk networking is designed to be as "plug and play" as possible. With AppleTalk, the end user can unbox a new Macintosh, plug it into the network, and it would dynamically learn its address, default gateway and default zone. When the end user wants to access a service, he/she accesses the Macintosh Chooser, which is the Microsoft Windows equivalent of Network Neighborhood. From the Chooser, a user selects a service from a graphical menu; services include printing (LaserWriter) and file sharing (AppleShare). Once a service is selected, a zone—the functional equivalent of a VLAN—is selected from a menu of zones. Next, the Chooser performs a search for the specified service in the specified zones. When the search is completed, the AppleTalk Chooser lists all available devices that match the service and zone specified.

For example, if a user wanted to use a LaserWriter printer within the zone "Accounting", he/she would select the service "LaserWriter" and the zone "Accounting" with the easy-to-use, menu-driven "point and click" graphical user interface. The Chooser then lists all the LaserWriter printers within the zone "Accounting". The user can then point and click to the specific desired LaserWriter printer in the zone "Accounting."

Graphical User Interface Networking (The AppleTalk Chooser)

AppleTalk was a pioneer in providing networking services through a graphical user interface. In many ways, the AppleTalk Chooser is like the Microsoft Windows Network Neighborhood. Both are graphical and both allow the user to access remote resources as if they were local. With the Chooser, you click on the type of resource you want. (Resources include file services, print services and mail services.) Once the type of service is selected, you select the services only from a specific zone. (Zones are not limited to physical cable segments, but can span multiple discontiguous cable segments.) When a specific zone is selected, a list of all devices that provide the selected service in the selected zone are listed. You click on the device, and the service is available to you as if it were locally attached.

With the AppleTalk Chooser, everything is name-based. There are no cryptic addresses. All devices are grouped in zones to provide a logical order to device location. Location is not defined by physical or geographic boundaries, but rather by organizational or departmental structure.

Zones

Zones are multicast domains, and are therefore functionally very similar to VLANs. Just as a VLAN allows you to place different devices defined in different VLANs on the same physical switch, zones allow you to place different devices from different zones on the same physical segment.

With AppleTalk, each segment address (called a "cable-range" in AppleTalk) must be unique and cannot overlap with others. Cable-ranges follow the same general rules as IP and IPX segment addressing. However, AppleTalk zones can be assigned to multiple cable-ranges. Multiple zones can also be assigned to a single cable-range.

When configuring AppleTalk routers, all routers connected to a given segment must agree on four things:

1. Cable-range of segment
2. Zones on the segment
3. Which zone is assigned as the default zone
4. Routing protocol (s) active on the segment

AppleTalk From the Perspective of Network Administrators

AppleTalk is "easy on end users, challenging for router administrators."

Easy on Users

To make internetworking easy for users, AppleTalk has the following features:

- Dynamic interface address acquisition (AppleTalk Address Resolution Protocol/ AARP)
- Dynamic default router/gateway selection by end-systems
- Concept of zones to group network resources (much like VLANs)
- Automatic population of end-system zone-table in Chooser
- Network Visible Entities (NVE), a user-friendly naming convention for individual network resources
- An intuitive NVE naming structure: object:type@zone
- Name Binding Protocol (NBP) to process and service NVE activities
- The Apple Chooser, a graphical user interface for accessing network resources

Challenging for Router Administrators

To support dynamic services, zones, and name-to-network address mapping, routers must maintain the following processes and tables:

- Routing process maintained by AppleTalk routing protocols. Routing protocols that can be configured for AppleTalk include the Routing Table Maintenance Protocol (RTMP), EIGRP for AppleTalk, AppleTalk Update Routing Protocol (AURP)
- AppleTalk Routing table
- Zone process maintained by the Zone Information Protocol (ZIP)
- AppleTalk Zone Information Table (ZIT)
- Name binding routing process maintained by the Name Binding Protocol (NBP)

Everything is tied together through the routed protocol DDP, which is at the heart of the AppleTalk protocol suite. DDP is the functional equivalent to IPX in the IPX/SPX protocol suite and IP in the TCP/IP protocol suite. Just as every IP and IPX packet has a source and destination address containing a network prefix and a host suffix, AppleTalk DDP packets functionally contain the same information. When a DDP packet enters an AppleTalk router, the DDP Destination network address is matched with an entry in the AppleTalk routing table. If a match exists, a switching decision is made. Otherwise, the packet is dropped.

Just as SAP tables in the Novell IPX/SPX environment are dependent on information in the IPX routing table, AppleTalk Zone tables are dependent on information in the AppleTalk routing table. Once an AppleTalk router receives a new cable-range, it generates a zone information protocol (ZIP) query targeted to the router that advertised the announced cable-range.

AppleTalk routers spend a lot of time responding to the following types of queries:

- GETZONELIST queries from end systems
- ZIP queries from other routers
- NBP queries from other routers

These queries can generate a tremendous amount of overhead on the network. We will examine them in further detail later in this chapter, as well as in Chapter 25, "Filtering non-IP Routing Traffic."

AppleTalk Technical Overview

AppleTalk Addressing

AppleTalk has two address formats. The original format is known as Phase One Addressing, which supports only a single network number and 127 hosts and 127 servers per segment. In 1988, AppleTalk introduced the Phase Two address format. It supports a range of network numbers and 253 hosts and servers per segment. We will be dealing with Phase Two addresses only.

The AppleTalk address format is 16 bits for the network prefix and 8 bits for the host suffix. The host addresses must range between 1 and 253. The numbers 0, 254 and 255 are reserved for Phase Two networks.

AppleTalk addresses are assigned to a Cisco router interface with the following interface configuration command:

```
r1(config-if)#appletalk cable-range xxx-xxx
```

where xxx-xxx = specified AppleTalk address in cable-range format. The cable-range defines the equivalent of the network prefix in IP, or the network address only in IPX. When configuring an IP address on a Cisco router interface, you must specify both the network prefix and host suffix. When configuring an IPX network address on a Cisco router interface, you specify the network prefix only. The IPX "node address" is acquired by using the MAC address of the interface, or by borrowing a MAC address from a specific source. AppleTalk address assignment is slightly different from both IP and IPX address assignment in that, by default, the assignment of the AppleTalk node address is dynamic. AppleTalk dynamically selects a segment address from the specified cable-range and a node address ranging from 1 to 253. It then verifies that its address is unique by querying other interfaces on the segment. The AppleTalk address acquisition process is managed by the Apple Address Resolution Protocol. This process is discussed in greater detail in the next section.

NOTE: You cannot supply an AppleTalk address cable-range to a loopback interface:

```
Inte lo0
r1(config-if)#appletalk cable-range 1000-1100
% Invalid Appletalk command—interface does not support AppleTalk
```

AppleTalk Address Acquisition: AARP

Once a cable-range is assigned to an interface, AppleTalk dynamically acquires its node address through the AppleTalk Address Resolution Process (AARP). Listed below is a debug trace of the AARP process. This process can be initiated by administratively shutting down the interface and re-enabling the interface.

```
AARP: aarp_ager; starting scan for old AARP entries
AARP: aarp_ager; finished scan; 0 fixed, 0 dynamic examined, 0 deleted
AT: RTMP GC complete (0 PDBs freed, 0 PDBs waiting)
AT: Connected GC complete (1 PDB freed, 0 PDBs waiting)
Serial0: AppleTalk state changed; line down -> restarting
AT: Cache invalidation by atroute_SetPathState
Serial0: AppleTalk state changed; restarting -> probing
%AT-6-ADDRUSED: Serial0: AppleTalk node up; using address 100.153
```

```
%AT-6-ACQUIREMODE: Serial0: AppleTalk interface initializing; acquiring remote peer
Serial0: AppleTalk state changed; probing -> acquiring
Serial0: AppleTalk state changed; acquiring -> checking zones
AARP: aarp_ager; starting scan for old AARP entries
AARP: aarp_ager; finished scan; 0 fixed, 0 dynamic examined, 0 deleted
AT: RTMP GC complete (0 PDBs freed, 0 PDBs waiting)
AT: Connected GC complete (0 PDBs freed, 0 PDBs waiting)
Serial0: AppleTalk state changed; checking zones -> operational
%AT-6-CONFIGOK: Serial0: AppleTalk interface enabled; verified by 100.117
%AT-6-NEIGHBORUP: Serial0: AppleTalk neighbor up; 100.117 has restarted
```

In the debug trace above, notice that the AppleTalk interface randomly selected the address of 100.153. It then searched its segment to determine if this address was being used by any other interface. Finally, the address of 100.153 is verified by interface 100.117. This process takes several seconds to complete.

You can bypass the dynamic address acquisition feature in AppleTalk by manually configuring a node address; however, AppleTalk AARP will still attempt to verify the manually configured address.

AppleTalk Default Router Assignment

Not only can AppleTalk interfaces determine their interface addresses dynamically, but AppleTalk end systems also choose default routers dynamically. Therefore, if there is more than one default router to select on a given segment, any one of them can be selected at system startup. Keep this in mind when planning filtering solutions. For example, place GZL filters on all possible default routers.

Filtering AppleTalk traffic is covered in greater detail in Chapter 25.

AppleTalk Routing Protocols (RTMP, EIGRP and AURP)

Cisco routers support multiple AppleTalk routing protocols, including RTMP, EIGRP and AURP. By default, RTMP is enabled as soon as the AppleTalk routing process is activated on a Cisco router. Both AppleTalk EIGRP and AURP must be manually enabled.

RTMP is a distance vector routing protocol that advertises its full routing table to neighboring RTMP routers every ten seconds. RTMP uses a hop count as a metric. As AppleTalk networks increase in size, RTMP becomes bandwidth-intensive, with its routing tables being advertised every ten seconds. An attractive alternative to RTMP is EIGRP for AppleTalk. It is recommended that you run EIGRP within your AppleTalk network core and RTMP on the edges of your internetwork.

You can examine the contents of an AppleTalk routing table by typing "show apple route".

```
r1#show apple route
Codes: R—RTMP derived, E—EIGRP derived, C—connected, A—AURP
       S—static  P—proxy
4 routes in internet
```

The first zone listed for each entry is its default (primary) zone.

```
C Net 100-100 directly connected, Serial0, zone z1
              Additional zones: 'z111','z11'
R Net 200-200 [1/G] via 100.117, 4 sec, Serial0, zone z2
R Net 300-300 [1/G] via 400.14, 3 sec, Serial1, zone z3
C Net 400-400 directly connected, Serial1, zone z4
```

You can also obtain detailed information on a specific AppleTalk cable-range by typing "show apple route xxx", where xxx is a specific cable-range. An example of this is displayed below:

```
r3#show apple route 300
Codes: R—RTMP derived, E—EIGRP derived, C—connected, A—AURP
       S—static  P—proxy
2 routes in internet

The first zone listed for each entry is its default (primary) zone.

R Net 300-300 [1/G] via 200.119, 5 sec, Serial1, zone z1
     Route installed 00:00:25, updated 5 secs ago
     Next hop: 200.119, 1 hop away
     Zone list provided by 200.119
     Valid zones: "z1"
     There is 1 path for this route
*    RTMP path, to neighbor 200.119, installed 00:00:05 via Serial1
     Composite metric is 256524800, 1 hop
```

AppleTalk Zones

A zone is an arbitrary subset of AppleTalk nodes in an internetwork. Zone configuration is not an issue on a small, single-segment AppleTalk network, which do not require a router. However, zone configuration is a very important issue on multi-segment AppleTalk internetworks. Routers will play a key role in zone management and operation.

One specific AppleTalk node can belong to one (and only one) zone. Nodes choose their zone at system startup from a list of zones assigned and available to a given network segment.

The concept of zones is provided to establish departmental or other user-understandable groupings of entities within an internetwork. As mentioned earlier, think of zones as being functionally equivalent to VLANs.

The AppleTalk cable-range to zone name mapping is performed on routers by the zone information protocol (ZIP). ZIP helps populate the zone information table (ZIT) on the router. An important feature of ZIP is that most of its services are transparent to *nonrouter* nodes. ZIP is implemented primarily by routers. Only routers can tell which cable-ranges are associated with specific zones.

Once the router has built a Zone Information Table, an end system on a local segment can issue a GETZONELIST request. The router will respond by transferring all the zones in its zone table to the end system. A GETZONELIST request is automatically generated by an end system as soon as it opens the AppleTalk Chooser.

Router Interfaces with Multiple Zones

Make sure that a multiple zones per-interface-configuration is identical for all router interfaces on a specific segment. Multiple zone announcements can be monitored with "debug apple zip".

```
AT: 1 query packet sent to neighbor 400.14
AT: Recvd ZIP cmd 2 from 400.14-6
AT: 3 zones in ZIPreply pkt, src 400.14
AT: net 100, zonelen 2, name z1
AT: net 100, zonelen 4, name z111
AT: net 100, zonelen 3, name z11
AT: in CancelZoneRequest, cancelling req on 100-100...succeeded
```

Debug apple zip displays the zip reply for cable range 100-100. Zones z1, z111 and z11 are associated with cable-range 100-100. Once the zones are announced, they are referenced in the AppleTalk routing table and zone table. Listed below, we see Z1 (the default zone) and additional zones z111 and z11 with associated cable-range 100-100.

```
r1#sh apple route
Codes: R—RTMP derived, E—EIGRP derived, C—connected, A—AURP
       S—static  P—proxy
4 routes in internet
```

The first zone listed for each entry is its default (primary) zone.

```
C Net 100-100 directly connected, Serial0, zone z1
              Additional zones: 'z111','z11'
R Net 200-200 [1/G] via 100.117, 4 sec, Serial0, zone z2
R Net 300-300 [1/G] via 400.14, 3 sec, Serial1, zone z3
C Net 400-400 directly connected, Serial1, zone z4
```

AppleTalk Initialization Process

When the AppleTalk routing process is enabled on a router and a cable-range and zone are assigned to an interface, the interface will go through several phases of initialization. The primary phases are summarized below:

- Restart port pending
- Probing for node address
- Acquiring port net information
- Operational

These different phases can be tracked with the "show apple interface" command:

```
r1#sh apple inte s0
Serial0 is administratively down, line protocol is down
  AppleTalk node down, Line protocol is down
  AppleTalk cable range is 100-200
  AppleTalk address is 198.238, Invalid
  AppleTalk zone is "z1"
  AppleTalk address gleaning is not supported by hardware
  AppleTalk route cache is disabled, port down

r1#sh apple inte s0
Serial0 is up, line protocol is up
  AppleTalk node down, Restart port pending
  AppleTalk cable range is 100-200
  AppleTalk address is 198.238, Invalid
  AppleTalk zone is "z1"
  AppleTalk address gleaning is not supported by hardware
  AppleTalk route cache is disabled, port down

r1#sh apple inte s0
Serial0 is up, line protocol is up
  AppleTalk node down, Probing for node address
  AppleTalk cable range is 100-200
  AppleTalk address is 198.238, Invalid
  AppleTalk zone is "z1"
  AppleTalk address gleaning is not supported by hardware
  AppleTalk route cache is disabled, port down

r1#sh apple inte s0
Serial0 is up, line protocol is up
  AppleTalk port disabled, Verifying port zone information
  AppleTalk cable range is 100-200
  AppleTalk address is 198.238, Valid
  AppleTalk zone is "z1"
  AppleTalk port configuration verified by 174.24
  AppleTalk address gleaning is not supported by hardware
  AppleTalk route cache is disabled, port initializing
```

```
r1#sh apple inte s0
Serial0 is up, line protocol is up
  AppleTalk port disabled, Operational
  AppleTalk cable range is 100-200
  AppleTalk address is 198.238, Valid
  AppleTalk zone is "z1"
  AppleTalk port configuration verified by 174.24
  AppleTalk address gleaning is not supported by hardware
  AppleTalk route cache is disabled, port initializing

r1#sh apple inte s0
Serial0 is up, line protocol is up
  AppleTalk cable range is 100-200
  AppleTalk address is 198.238, Valid
  AppleTalk zone is "z1"
  AppleTalk port configuration verified by 174.24
  AppleTalk address gleaning is not supported by hardware
  AppleTalk route cache is enabled
```

The Steps to Attaining AppleTalk Convergence

1. The AppleTalk routing process is enabled and AppleTalk cable-range(s) and zone(s) is (are) assigned to router interfaces.
2. Through AARP, router interfaces dynamically acquire interface addresses and validate that they are unique.
3. AppleTalk routers announce locally-connected networks via a routing protocol to neighbors. The default AppleTalk routing protocol is RTMP.
4. When an AppleTalk router receives a routing update with a new cable-range to add to its routing table, it sends a ZIP query to the source of the new cable-range to acquire at least one zone name for the cable-range.
5. By default, with RTMP, if no zone is supplied for the cable-range, RTMP drops the cable-range from the routing table.
6. For AppleTalk internetworks, convergence has been achieved when all routers have a stable and consistent view of all AppleTalk cable-ranges *and* all AppleTalk zones.

Convergence AppleTalk Style

- All routers see all networks.
- All routers see all zones.
- All routes are aging properly.
- The metrics of RTMP entries accurately reflect the relative cost of network reachability.

The Steps Performed By an End User to Access AppleTalk Services

When an end user (AppleTalk workstation) wants to access AppleTalk services, it performs the following steps:

1. AppleTalk client accesses its Chooser.
2. When the Chooser it accessed, the end-system generates a GZL request to its router to populate its zone list.
3. When the AppleTalk client selects a service (file, print, etc.) and a zone from the Chooser, a list of all services that match the selected service and zone will be displayed on the right side of the Chooser display.

Use the following debug tools to monitor AppleTalk routing and ZIP activity:

- Debug apple routing
- Debug apple zip

Remember: Not all interfaces will announce all networks in an RTMP or EIGRP environment due to split-horizon.

Commonly Used AppleTalk Show Commands

1. **r1#show apple interface serial 1**

```
Serial1 is up, line protocol is up
  AppleTalk port disabled, Acquiring port net information
  AppleTalk cable range is 400-400
  AppleTalk address is 400.159, Valid
  AppleTalk zone is "z4"
  AppleTalk address gleaning is not supported by hardware
```

2. **r2#sh appletalk interface brief**

```
  Interface    Address     Config      Status/Line Protocol    Atalk Protocol
  Ethernet0    4.71        Extended    up                      up
  Ethernet1    unassigned  not config'd  administratively down n/a
  Serial0      1.12        Extended    up                      up
  Serial1      18.17       Extended    up                      up
  TokenRing0   105.60      Extended    up                      up
  TokenRing1   unassigned  not config'd  administratively down n/a
```

3. **r1#show appletalk neighbors**

```
AppleTalk neighbors:
 174.24         Serial0, uptime 00:07:17, 9 secs
      Neighbor has restarted 3 times in 00:34:45.
      Neighbor is reachable as a RTMP peer
 4019.14        Serial1, uptime 00:19:49, 0 secs
      Neighbor has restarted 1 time in 00:20:49.
      Neighbor is reachable as a RTMP peer
```

4. **London#show apple route**

```
Codes: R-RTMP derived, E-EIGRP derived, C-connected, A-AURP
      S-static  P-proxy
8 routes in internet
```

The first zone listed for each entry is its default (primary) zone.

```
E Net 1-1 [1/G] via 18.17, 93838 sec, Serial2, zone frame
E Net 2-2 [2/G] via 18.17, 93789 sec, Serial2, zone r5r4
E Net 4-4 [1/G] via 18.17, 93838 sec, Serial2, zone vlan1
E Net 6-6 [2/G] via 18.17, 93789 sec, Serial2, zone r5ether
E Net 9-9 [3/G] via 18.17, 93765 sec, Serial2, zone r4ether
C Net 18-18 directly connected, Serial2, zone r2r1
C Net 20-20 directly connected, Ethernet0, zone r1ether
E Net 100-110 [1/G] via 18.17, 91394 sec, Serial2, zone test
```

5. **London#show apple zone**

```
Name                Network(s)
r2r1                18-18
r5r4                2-2
r4ether             9-9
r5ether             6-6
Total of 4 zones
```

Basic AppleTalk Configuration

All AppleTalk routers must agree on four things at the interface configuration level:

1. Cable-range applied to a particular interface
2. A common zone-list
3. Default zone
4. Routing protocol used

Global Configuration Commands: Enabling the AppleTalk Process

First, the AppleTalk routing process must be enabled on the router. This is performed by entering the following configuration command:

```
London(config)#appletalk routing
```

Perform the following show commands to verify that the AppleTalk process is properly enabled:

```
London#sh protocols
Global values:
  Internet Protocol routing is enabled
  Appletalk routing is enabled
Ethernet0 is up, line protocol is up
  AppleTalk address is 100.2, zone z1717

London#show processes cpu
CPU utilization for five seconds: 13%/6%; one minute: 9%; five minutes: 10%
PID  Runtime(ms)  Invoked  uSecs  5Sec   1Min   5Min   TTY  Process
1    5344         17596    303    0.00%  0.00%  0.00%  0    Load Meter
2    2432         166      14650  6.79%  1.75%  0.63%  0    Exec
3    152364       1769     86130  0.00%  0.23%  0.14%  0    Check heaps
4    0            1        0      0.00%  0.00%  0.00%  0    Pool Manager
5    8            2        4000   0.00%  0.00%  0.00%  0    Timers
6    0            1470     0      0.00%  0.00%  0.00%  0    ARP Input
7    0            1        0      0.00%  0.00%  0.00%  0    SERIAL A'detect
8    0            1469     0      0.00%  0.00%  0.00%  0    IP Input
9    5708         8799     648    0.00%  0.00%  0.00%  0    CDP Protocol
31   0            135      0      0.00%  0.00%  0.00%  0    AT RTMP
32   4            2        2000   0.00%  0.00%  0.00%  0    LAPB Timer
33   0            1        0      0.00%  0.00%  0.00%  0    AT NBP
34   16           191      83     0.00%  0.01%  0.00%  0    AT Maint
35   4            1        4000   0.00%  0.00%  0.00%  0    AT ZIP
36   4            20       200    0.00%  0.00%  0.00%  0    AT ARP
```

When the AppleTalk process is enabled, the RTMP routing protocol is enabled by default.

Adding an AppleTalk Cable-Range and Zone to an Interface

To add an AppleTalk cable-range to an interface, type the following command in interface configuration mode:

```
appletalk cable-range cable-range [network.node]
```

Syntax Description

1. cable-range

This parameter specifies the start and end of the cable range. Use a hyphen between the specified starting value of the cable range and the ending value. You can use numbers from 0 to 65279. The cable-range specified first (the lower bound cable-range number) must be less than or equal to the second cable-range (the upper bound cable-range number).

2. network.node (optional)
   A manually specified AppleTalk address for the interface. It must be entered in a decimal format conforming to the AppleTalk address structure (16-bit AppleTalk network address and 8-bit node number). The specified network number must be in the range specified in the cable-range parameter.

You can have only one cable-range per interface. The cable-range must not overlap with any other cable—ranges assigned in the AppleTalk internetwork.

Configuring AppleTalk Zones

To add an AppleTalk zone to an interface, type the following command in interface configuration mode:

```
r1(config-if)#appletalk zone xxxx     (xxxx = AppleTalk zone name)
```

Multiple zones can be added to a segment. The same zone name can be assigned to multiple segments. Zone names are case-sensitive and can include spaces. For any given zone, make sure that all zone names are identical in length, case and spaces used (if any). As a general rule, keep zone names as simple as possible.

The order in which you enter zone names for a single interface is critical. The first zone name will be the default zone. Consequently, all router interfaces attached to the same segment must have precisely the same names.

NOTE: You can disable the AppleTalk routing process, which will clear all AppleTalk configuration commands for interfaces running RTMP. This will clear all AppleTalk routing tables, zone tables, active interfaces, etc. You also can re-enable the AppleTalk routing process, and all configuration statements that related to RTMP configuration will reappear.

Tools for Monitoring AppleTalk Configuration

To check your AppleTalk configuration, use the following show commands:

```
Show appletalk route
Show appletalk zone
Show appletalk interface
Show appletalk interface brief
Show cdp neighbor brief
Show appletalk neighbor
```

AppleTalk Static Routes

In previous chapters, you have seen static routes defined for IP and IPX traffic. Static AppleTalk routes can be defined as well. Displayed below are two global configuration mode commands that can be used to configure AppleTalk static routes. The first command configures an AppleTalk static route by cable-range. The second configures a static route by a single network address. Notice that both require that a zone name be associated with the static route.

```
appletalk static cable-range cable-range to network.node [floating] zone zonename
appletalk static network network-number to network.node [floating] zone zonename
```

If the floating parameter is used, the static route will be replaced by a dynamically learned route for the destination network or cable-range referenced. AppleTalk static routes are popular for DDR applications.

Using EIGRP with AppleTalk

Many environments rely exclusively on RTMP for maintaining AppleTalk routing tables. As mentioned earlier, RTMP is a distance vector routing protocol that advertises its entire routing table every 10 seconds.

These features make RTMP unattractive in a large-scale AppleTalk internetwork, especially if AppleTalk traffic is traversing WAN links. Cisco provides a solution to the chattiness of RTMP: EIGRP for AppleTalk. You have already seen EIGRP twice in earlier chapters: EIGRP for IP in Chapter 10 and EIGRP for IPX in Chapter 16.

EIGRP discovers a network like a distance vector protocol, but adjusts to changes in the network topology using the Diffused Update Algorithm (DUAL). By using DUAL, EIGRP can adjust to changes to a network's topology (re-converge) much more rapidly than traditional distance vector routing protocols such as RIP and IGRP. EIGRP for AppleTalk maintains three tables: a neighbor table, a topology table and entries in the AppleTalk routing table.

EIGRP for AppleTalk does not send out periodic updates of its routing table. It sends out updates only when changes to the network topology occur. EIGRP for AppleTalk uses the composite metric to select the shortest path to a given destination AppleTalk network. The composite metric is the same used by IP EIGRP and IPX EIGRP. EIGRP automatically performs a two-way redistribution with RTMP. For many internetwork designs, AppleTalk EIGRP is deployed at the core of the internetwork, and RTMP will remain at the edges. This design is easy to implement, since AppleTalk EIGRP automatically redistributes routes with RTMP.

AppleTalk EIGRP may operate in a similar manner with IP EIGRP and IPX EIGRP. However, the configuration of AppleTalk EIGRP is radically different for AppleTalk than for IP EIGRP and IPX EIGRP.

The AppleTalk EIGRP routing process is enabled with the following syntax:

```
APPLETALK ROUTING EIGRP PROCESS-ID
```

Unlike IP EIGRP and IPX EIGRP, which require a common autonomous-system number, the AppleTalk EIGRP routing process is enabled with a process-ID that is unique to a specific router. When enabling EIGRP for AppleTalk for a group of routers, each router must have a unique process-ID.

After the routing process is enabled in global configuration mode, the following interface configuration statement must be added on every directly-connected interface participating in the AppleTalk EIGRP routing process: "AppleTalk protocol EIGRP". If RTMP needs to be disabled for connected network interfaces, a "No AppleTalk protocol RTMP " statement must be supplied at the interface configuration mode.

A sample configuration is supplied below:

```
London#sh run
!
appletalk routing eigrp 100
appletalk route-redistribution
!
interface Ethernet0
 ip address 172.16.1.1 255.255.255.0
 appletalk cable-range 100-105 100.132
 appletalk zone z1
 appletalk protocol eigrp
 no appletalk protocol rtmp
```

Instead of simply typing "appletalk routing", you now type "appletalk routing eigrp xxx" (xxx = unique AppleTalk EIGRP process ID). Do not forget that the value following the EIGRP parameter must be unique for every AppleTalk router. Also, note the "appletalk route-redistribution" statement following the "appletalk routing eigrp 100" statement. This statement is automatically added when you configure the router for "appletalk routing eigrp".

Examine how AppleTalk routing is changed by EIGRP. Notice the second entry in the routing table, network 3-3. No zone is assigned to the network entry, but the age of the route is over 62,000 seconds. For RTMP routing entries, if no zone is associated with a cable-range, the cable-range will be removed from the routing table by default.

```
r4>sh apple ro
Codes: R-RTMP derived, E-EIGRP derived, C-connected, A-AURP
       S-static  P-proxy
6 routes in internet
```

The first zone listed for each entry is its default (primary) zone.

```
C Net 2-2 directly connected, Ethernet0, zone r4
E Net 3-3 [2/G] via 1005.17, 62305 sec, Tunnel0, no zone set
E Net 4-4 [1/G] via 1005.17, 62305 sec, Tunnel0, zone r5
E Net 1001-1001 [1/G] via 1005.17, 62305 sec, Tunnel0, zone tunnel1
C Net 1002-1002 directly connected, Tunnel1, zone tunnel2
C Net 1005-1005 directly connected, Tunnel0, zone tunnel3
```

You can examine details of a specific EIGRP routing table entry by typing "show apple route XXX" (XXX=network address).

```
r4>sh apple ro 3
Codes: R—RTMP derived, E—EIGRP derived, C—connected, A—AURP S—static  P—proxy
6 routes in internet

The first zone listed for each entry is its default (primary) zone.

E Net 3-3 [2/G] via 1005.17, 62309 sec, Tunnel0, no zone set
  Route installed 17:30:23, updated 62309 secs ago
  Next hop: 1005.17, 2 hops away
  Zone list request retries: 628
  There is 1 path for this route
* EIGRP path, to neighbor 1005.17, installed 17:18:29 via Tunnel0
    Composite metric is 310060544, 2 hops
    Delay is 25616128 microseconds, minimum bandwidth is 284444416 Kbit
    Reliability 255/255, minimum MTU 1476 bytes
    Loading 28/255, 2 EIGRP hops
    Path is derived from CONNECTED from 1
    Path's external metric is 0 hops
```

When we examine the detailed description of AppleTalk cable-range 3-3, we see that no zone is associated with the network, and that 628 zip information protocol requests have been generated. Also, note that both the hop count metric and the composite metric are displayed.

AppleTalk Tunneling

With IPX, the two basic configuration options are: (1) configure IPX on the physical interface, along with other network layer protocols such as IP ("Ships in the Night" configuration) or (2) tunnel IPX traffic through an IP cloud. The same two basic options are available with AppleTalk.

Cisco offers many different methods for tunneling AppleTalk traffic over an IP internetwork. Most common of these methods are GRE tunneling (also known as IPTalk) and AURP tunneling. Even though both methods perform the same general function, the ways in which they operate and are configured are markedly different.

Configuring AURP

The AppleTalk Update Routing Protocol (AURP) is an AppleTalk native protocol that performs both tunneling and routing. Instead of sending out routing table information every 10 seconds like RTMP, AURP sends out routing table information every 30 seconds. A router that runs AURP is called an "exterior" router in the AppleTalk environment.

From a configuration perspective, AURP is unique in that the tunnel interfaces used for AURP do not have AppleTalk cable-ranges or zones assigned to them. The steps for configuring AURP are listed below:

AURP Global Configuration Commands

- AppleTalk route-redistribution

AppleTalk Tunnel Interface Configuration Commands

- Tunnel source
- Tunnel destination
- Tunnel mode aurp
- AppleTalk protocol aurp

A sample configuration is displayed below:

```
London#sh run
!
appletalk routing
appletalk route-redistribution
!
interface Loopback0
ip address 10.1.1.1 255.255.255.0
!
interface Tunnel0
     no ip address
     appletalk protocol aurp
     tunnel source Loopback0
     tunnel destination 172.16.1.2
     tunnel mode aurp
```

Like the AppleTalk EIGRP routing protocol configuration, the "appletalk route-redistribution" statement is added as soon as the "appletalk protocol aurp" statement is added under the tunnel interface configuration mode.

AURP tunnel uses UDP port 387. Be aware of this if you have created IP access-lists.

When you have three or more AURP speakers and you want to provide full connectivity between all of them, you must create a full mesh of AURP tunnels. A hub and spoke configuration will not work with AURP tunnels. A router acting as a hub in an AURP configuration will not forward AppleTalk traffic between two AURP tunnel interfaces.

You cannot ping an AURP tunnel interface since it does not have an AppleTalk cable-range or zone assigned to it.

Cisco provides debugging tools for AURP tunneling:

```
aurp-connection        AURP connection
aurp-packet            AURP packets
aurp-update            AURP routing updates
```

AppleTalk GRE Tunneling

Creating GRE Tunnels differs significantly from creating AURP tunnels. GRE tunnel interfaces require an Apple-Talk cable-range. GRE tunnels can use either EIGRP or RTMP as a routing protocol, and do not need to be configured in a full-mesh. In summary, GRE tunnel interfaces are configured in a manner very similar to AppleTalk physical interface configurations.

Commands used for GRE tunneling using EIGRP include:

```
Appletalk routing eigrp 101
Appletalk route-redistribution
Inte tu0
Tunnel source
Tunnel destination
AppleTalk cable-range
AppleTalk zone
Appletalk protocol EIGRP
No AppleTalk protocol RTMP
```

GRE tunnels use IP protocol number 47. If you have restrictive IP access-lists in the path of a GRE tunnel, make sure you are permitting traffic with the IP protocol number of 47.

GRE and IPTALK

With routers running the Cisco IOS version 11.2 or later, as soon as you enter the AppleTalk zone command on a GRE tunnel, an additional command is added to your tunnel interface configuration: "AppleTalk IPTALK xxxx". This statement was automatically entered at the end of the tunnel interface configuration script displayed below:

```
interface Tunnel0
 no ip address
 appletalk cable-range 700-700 700.244
 appletalk zone zone-tunnel
 appletalk protocol eigrp
 no appletalk protocol rtmp
 tunnel source 172.16.1.1
 tunnel destination 10.1.1.100
 appletalk iptalk 700 zone-tunnel
```

When the iptalk statement is removed with a "no apple iptalk statement", the original AppleTalk cable-range statement is converted to 0-0 with a node address of 65xxx.xx. The configuration script below is the same configuration displayed above after the "no apple iptalk" statement is entered. Notice how the configuration has changed. In particular, examine the changes to line three and the last line:

```
interface Tunnel0
 no ip address
 appletalk cable-range 0-0 65453.244
 appletalk zone zone-tunnel
 appletalk protocol eigrp
 no appletalk protocol rtmp
 tunnel source 172.16.1.1
 tunnel destination 10.1.1.100
 appletalk iptalk 65453 zone-tunnel
```

AppleTalk over DDR

AppleTalk can be configured over both legacy DDR and Dialer profiles. The same configuration steps must be performed for AppleTalk that are performed for IP and IPX:

1. AppleTalk interesting traffic must be specified.
2. For Legacy DDR, AppleTalk dialer maps must be created.
3. For Dialer Profiles, dialer interfaces must be configured with an AppleTalk cable-range.

With debug dialer packet, we can see the AppleTalk traffic being defined as interesting:

```
BRI0: appletalk (s=200.166, d=200.194), 100 bytes, interesting (appletalk PERMIT)
BRI0: appletalk (s=200.166, d=0.255), 29 bytes, interesting (appletalk PERMIT)
BRI0: appletalk (s=200.166, d=200.194), 100 bytes, interesting (appletalk PERMIT)
```

A broad dialer-list statement can be used for AppleTalk:

```
Dialer-list 1 protocol appletalk permit
```

Even with a broad dialer-list, AppleTalk broadcast and multicasts will not be forwarded over the DDR link unless the broadcast parameter is added on to legacy DDR dialer map statements.

If the RTMP routing protocol is used on a DDR link with this dialer-list, routing table updates will be sent over the DDR link every 10 seconds. If AppleTalk EIGRP is used, EIGRP Hellos will be sent over the DDR link every five seconds. Both of these scenarios are untenable. Two alternatives exist:

1. Create restrictive dialer-lists to filter out RTMP updates and/or EIGRP Hellos and use static routes.
2. Configure snapshot routing for RTMP.

AppleTalk Over NBMA Networks

AppleTalk can be configured over NBMA networks, such as Frame-Relay and ATM, using inverse ARP, map statements and subinterfaces. The same configuration steps must be performed for AppleTalk as for IP and IPX.

AppleTalk and Inverse ARP

Inverse ARP supports the AppleTalk protocol in both a Frame-Relay and ATM environment. For example, by simply configuring an interface with the frame-relay encapsulation, the remote AppleTalk address of a directly connected Frame-Relay neighbor will be mapped to a router's local DLCI.

If you accidentally mistype an AppleTalk cable-range, use clear frame-inversearp to have the inverse ARP process occur again. If the clear frame-inversearp does not appear to work properly, reload the router.

AppleTalk and NBMA Map Statements

When using Frame-Relay and ATM (ATM map-list) map statements with AppleTalk, make sure the broadcast parameter is added. This will allow the AppleTalk broadcasts and multicasts to be forwarded over the NBMA network.

If a Frame-Relay map statement for AppleTalk is added to an interface, inverse ARP is disabled for AppleTalk for the DLCI referenced in the Frame-Relay map statement. If you have a combination of inverse ARP and static frame-relay map statements referencing the same DLCI in your frame-relay map table, make sure to replace all dynamic mappings with static mappings. Even though the dynamic and static mappings may co-exist when you first enter a frame-relay map statement, the dynamic map statements will disappear when the router is reloaded.

Displayed below are two statically mapped Frame-Relay map entries. Notice that the broadcast parameter is specified for each.

```
r2#show frame-relay map

Serial0 (up): appletalk 1.17 dlci 201(0xC9,0x3090), static,
     broadcast,
     CISCO, status defined, active
Serial0 (up): appletalk 1.48 dlci 201(0xC9,0x3090), static,
     broadcast,
     CISCO, status defined, active
```

AppleTalk and Subinterfaces

Both point-to-point subinterfaces and multipoint subinterfaces can be used with AppleTalk. If you have multiple DLCIs for a given frame-relay interface, or multiple VCI/VPI pairs for a given ATM interface, and you want to configure an individual point-to-point subinterface for each DLCI, each point-to-point subinterface must have a unique cable-range associated with it.

AppleTalk in a Hub and Spoke NBMA Topology

In an NBMA hub and spoke topology, make sure that split horizon is disabled on the hub router. Do this for both Frame-Relay and ATM. Split horizon can be disabled by entering the following commands at the hub router:

EIGRP

```
London(config-if)#no appletalk eigrp-splithorizon
```

RTMP

```
London(config-if)#no appletalk rtmp-splithorizon
```

AppleTalk Local Routing and NBMA Networks

Also, with multipoint NBMA configurations, use the AppleTalk local routing command to assure that all AppleTalk interfaces on the multipoint subnet can access each other. Enter the following command in global configuration mode:

```
Appletalk local-routing
```

AppleTalk Troubleshooting

Of all of the non-IP routing protocols, configuring AppleTalk requires the greatest care. After practicing AppleTalk configuration many times, you will know what steps must be performed in order to successfully configure AppleTalk in a variety of different ways (Ships in the Night versus tunneling; configuring RTMP versus EIGRP, etc.). Once you have developed confidence in configuring AppleTalk, you may notice that, many times, operations do not perform the way they are supposed to. Certain processes seem to fail or take an extremely long time to perform. If you encounter such scenarios, a good rule of thumb is to reload your routers running the AppleTalk routing process. Reloading is an extreme measure; however, it seems to remedy many AppleTalk configuration problems. This is especially true when AppleTalk tunneling configurations are involved.

"No AppleTalk Routing" Reinitialization Technique

As an alternative to the drastic measure of reloading your router, use the "no appletalk routing" reinitialization technique. When "no appletalk routing" is typed in global configuration mode, all AppleTalk routing configuration statements are removed from the entire running configuration. When "appletalk routing" is re-entered, it re-inserts all commands related to the RTMP routing process only. Any commands not related to RTMP will not be re-inserted (for example, EIGRP and AURP commands). The "no appletalk routing" technique can be useful when the only routing protocol used is RTMP.

Troubleshooting Interface Initialization

Remember that AppleTalk performs a dynamic node address acquisition process. Use the following debug and show commands to monitor and troubleshoot the AppleTalk address acquisition and validation process:

- Debug apple arp
- Show appletalk interface
- Show appletalk neighbors

Troubleshooting Route Zone Table Issues

Use the following debug and show commands to monitor and troubleshoot the AppleTalk zone learning process:

- Show apple zone
- Debug apple zone

Troubleshooting AppleTalk Tunneling Issues

Use the following debug and show commands to monitor and troubleshoot AppleTalk tunneling:

- Debug tunnel
- Debug aurp
- Show AppleTalk Interface

Troubleshooting AppleTalk over a DDR Link

Use the following debug and show commands to monitor and troubleshoot the AppleTalk over ISDN/DDR:

- Debug dialer packet
- Debug ppp negotiation

Troubleshooting AppleTalk over an NBMA Link

Use the following debug and show commands to monitor and troubleshoot the AppleTalk over Frame-Relay:

- Show frame map
- Debug frame packet

Just as for IP and IPX Frame-Relay troubleshooting, debug frame packet helps pinpoint AppleTalk problems over Frame-Relay. When traffic successfully travels through a router Frame-Relay interface, you see frames identified as transporting AppleTalk traffic entering and exiting the interface:

```
Serial0(o): dlci 201(0x3091), pkt type 0x809B(APPLETALK), datagramsize 104
Serial0(i): dlci 201(0x3091), pkt type 0x809B, datagramsize 104
Serial0(o): dlci 201(0x3091), pkt type 0x809B(APPLETALK), datagramsize 104
```

When an AppleTalk interface located within the Frame-Relay cloud is not mapped properly, you see the following messages from debug frame packet:

```
Serial0:Encaps failed--no map entry link 16(APPLETALK)
Serial0:Encaps failed--no map entry link 16(APPLETALK)
```

To configure AppleTalk over ATM, use debug atm packet.

AppleTalk Idiosyncrasies

AppleTalk address acquisition is dynamic. Be patient with the process, and be aware of the specific phases for successful dynamic address acquisition.

When you remove the AppleTalk process with the "no appletalk routing" statement, all AppleTalk configuration statements from both global configuration mode and interface mode are removed. However, when you type "appletalk routing" again, all configuration statements for interfaces configured with RTMP will be re-inserted. For those interfaces that had AppleTalk EIGRP and AURP, the former configuration statements will not be re-inserted. You must manually type in the configuration statements.

When configuring AppleTalk EIGRP, remember that each router must have a unique process ID. For IP EIGRP and IPX EIGRP, the value on the enabling command was an autonomous system number, which needed to be the same for all routers operating within a single EIGRP domain. For AppleTalk, it is the exact opposite.

When adding a AppleTalk zone to a GRE tunnel, an IP Talk statement is inserted. If you remove the IP Talk statement manually, the IOS resets your tunnel interface cable-range number to 0-0 and adds a five digit node address.

If your configuration appears to be correct but it is not working, reload your router!

Summary

AppleTalk requires several steps for configuration. The most basic steps are:

1. Enable the AppleTalk routing process on the router
2. Assign cable-ranges to interfaces
3. Assign a zone(s) to interfaces

When you hear the following AppleTalk terms, associate them with the more commonly-used technologies:

Cable-range	IP address prefix
AARP	RARP, DHCP
Zone	VLAN
Chooser	Microsoft Windows Network Neighborhood

Proceed with caution when configuring AppleTalk. Think through the configuration steps carefully before entering them into the router. If you make a mistake in your configuration, re-initialize the interface or re-initialize the AppleTalk routing process. If this does not remedy the problem, reload the router.

Professional Development Checklist

By using this chapter, you should be able to perform the following operations:

- Configure an AppleTalk interface with one zone.
- Configure an AppleTalk interface with multiple zones.
- Configure AppleTalk static routes.
- Configure AppleTalk default routes.
- Configure AppleTalk with EIGRP.
- Configure AppleTalk over a DDR link with Dialer Maps.
- Configure AppleTalk over a DDR link with Dialer Profiles.
- Configure AppleTalk Tunneling (GRE and EIGRP).
- Configure AppleTalk Tunneling (AURP).

For Further Study

- Sidhu, Gursharan, S; Oppenheimer, Alan, B; Andrews, Richard. *Inside AppleTalk*, Second Edition, Addison Wesley, 1990.
- *Cisco IOS Configuration Guide*, Volume VI, Cisco Systems, Inc., 1989–1998.
- *Cisco IOS Command Reference*, Volume VI, Cisco Systems, Inc., 1989–1998.

URLs

- **www.cciecert.com**
- **www.mentorlabs.com**
- **www.cisco.com**

Can You Spot the Issues?

1. AppleTalk EIGRP is not operating between the two configurations below. Both London and Paris are directly connected on the same point-to-point serial interface:

```
London#show run
!
appletalk routing eigrp 100
appletalk route-redistribution
!
interface Ethernet0
 ip address 172.16.1.1 255.255.255.0
 appletalk cable-range 100-105 100.117
 appletalk zone z1
 appletalk protocol eigrp
 no appletalk protocol rtmp

Paris#show run
!
appletalk routing eigrp 100
appletalk route-redistribution
!
interface Ethernet0
 ip address 172.16.1.2 255.255.255.0
 appletalk cable-range 100-105 100.140
 appletalk zone z1
 appletalk protocol eigrp
 no appletalk protocol rtmp
```

   Can you spot the issue?

2. The router "London" is the hub router in a hub and spoke ATM topology. London has two downstream spoke routers. All of the routers are running EIGRP for AppleTalk. Each spoke router is announcing three cable-ranges to the hub. London sees all six cable-ranges from the two spoke routers; however, the spoke routers cannot see the cable-ranges originating from the other spoke router. Listed below is the configuration script for the hub router London:

```
London#show run
!
appletalk routing eigrp 10
appletalk route-redistribution
!
interface atm 0
 ip address 172.16.10.1 255.255.255.0
 appletalk cable-range 100-105 100.117
 appletalk zone z1
 appletalk protocol eigrp
 no appletalk protocol rtmp
```

Can you spot the issue?

3. You have set up an AURP tunnel over an IP cloud. You have learned the cable-range 100-200 over the AURP tunnel. You want to test the AURP tunnel with an AppleTalk PING command. You try to PING a valid AppleTalk address on the cable-range learned from the remote side of the AURP tunnel, 100.10. You have verified that this is a valid and active address. You cannot PING the address over the AURP tunnel but you can PING it when you telnet to the remote side of the AURP tunnel. Therefore, you can PING 100.10 on the local side of the tunnel but not on the far side; however, the cable-range appears on the far side. Why can you PING the address locally and not remotely, but still see the cable-range remotely?

Configuring DECNET

Topics Covered in This Chapter

- DECNET Technology Overview
- Configure Basic DECNET Environment with One Level Routers
- Configure DECNET for Multiple Levels
- Configure a DECNET Designated Router
- Troubleshooting DECNET
- DECNET Show and Debug Commands

DECNET is the last of the Level Four Non-IP Routable Protocols this book will examine. Just as with IPX and AppleTalk, the learning strategy applied in this Chapter is to compare and contrast DECNET design, operation, and configuration topics with similar IP topics. In particular, when preparing to learn DECNET, review your open shortest path first (OSPF) notes from Chapter Eleven. Review how OSPF configuration involves areas, forming of neighbor relationships and adjacencies. Review how OSPF uses the router identifier (RID) to identify different OSPF routers within an OSPF domain. DECNET possesses all of these features as well. DECNET routers are distinguished by a unique identifier. With DECNET, addresses are not assigned on a per-interface basis. The entire router and all of its interfaces are identified by a unique area.node address combination that is assigned in global configuration mode. Even though DECNET possesses many of the characteristics of OSPF and IS-IS, the version of DECNET covered in this Chapter is not a link-state routing protocol. DECNET also possesses characteristics of distance-vector routing protocols. For example, DECNET uses the rule of split horizon for routing loop avoidance. Therefore, DECNET will be prone to the same issues seen with distance-vector routing protocols (IP RIP, IGRP, IPX/RIP, and RTMP), such as the issues of split-horizon over a partially meshed nonbroadcast multi-access (NBMA) network (Frame-Relay and ATM).

This Chapter focuses on DECNET Phase IV. DECNET Phase IV is a distance-vector routing protocol. DECNET Phase V uses IS-IS as a routing protocol.

DECNET Technical Overview

DECNET is part of the seven layer Digital Network Architecture (DNA) protocol stack.

Throughout the 1980s, Digital Equipment Corporation's slogan was "Digital, the world's second largest computer company." Digital was a giant in the computer industry and a primary competitor of IBM during the 1970s and 1980s. When IBM introduced its proprietary protocol stack SNA in 1974, Digital followed by announcing DNA in 1975. DECNET routing is part of the DNA protocol suite.

DECNET Phase IV routing was first introduced in the early-1980s. Even though OSPF possesses many of the features of DECNET, DECNET possessed many of these features before OSPF existed. For example, DECNET Phase IV routing introduced the concept of areas and adjacencies before OSPF existed.

DECNET Phase IV is a proprietary protocol. In an effort to be open-system compliant, DECNET Phase V uses the open systems interconnection (OSI) protocol suite (FTAM, TP4, IS-IS, etc.). Many DEC installations did not migrate over to DECNET Phase V because it was too radical a change from Phase IV. Therefore, to this day, many DECNET installations are still using DECNET Phase IV.

Four key components of DECNET routing are:

End-nodes: A device in a DECNET network that cannot route. Examples of end-nodes are end systems such as DEC minicomputers with no routing capabilities and personal computers.

Nodes: A routing device in a DECNET network. Examples of nodes are routers and DECNET minicomputers with routing capabilities.

Area: A grouping of end-nodes and nodes.Router-types: DECNET defines two different router types to perform intra-area routing and inter-area routing.

A unique characteristic of DECNET routing is that a DECNET routing table lists all end-nodes and nodes (all end systems and routers) in a given area. This increases the size of a DECNET routing table. By dividing a DECNET routing domain into areas, the routing tables of all routers within a multiple area domain are kept relatively small. DECNET addressing is based upon a 16-bit address divided into two parts: a six-bit area prefix and a ten-bit node suffix. Since the area prefix is limited to six bits, only 63 areas can be assigned to a single DECNET routing domain and only 1023 node addresses can be assigned to a given area.

The DECNET Routing Process

DECNET Phase-IV routing does not neatly fit into the category of any routing protocol technology. Like distance-vector routing protocols, DECNET applies the rule of split-horizon for loop avoidance. DECNET Phase IV is definitely not a link-state routing protocol; however, it possesses characteristics similar to those found in link-state routing protocols such as OSPF and IS-IS. Like OSPF and IS-IS, DECNET possesses the following characteristics:

- DECNET routers are identified by a unique RID.
- DECNET is Area Based.
- DECNET routers send out HELLO packets.
- DECNET routers form adjacencies with directly connected neighbors.
- DECNET routing possess the Designated Router feature.

With OSPF, three commonly used show commands are `show ip ospf`, `show ip ospf interface`, and `show ip ospf neighbor`. Show ip ospf provides a useful summary of an OSPF process running on a router. The Show ip ospf interface displays OSPF interface statistics and configuration settings such as the hello interval, what router is the designated router, and the number of adjacencies formed on the interface Show ip ospf neighbor provides a brief summary of directly connected OSPF neighbors. Three equivalent DECNET commands exist: `show decnet`, `show decnet interface`, and `show decnet neighbor`:

```
r1#show decnet
Global DECnet parameters for network 0:
     Local address is 1.2, node type is area
     Level-2 'Attached' flag is TRUE
     Maximum node is 1023, maximum area is 63, maximum visits is 63
     Maximum paths is 1, path split mode is normal
     Local maximum cost is 1022, maximum hops is 30
     Area maximum cost is 1022, maximum hops is 30
     Static routes *NOT* being sent in routing updates
```

Just as show ip ospf displays the router identifier, show decnet lists the single DECNET routing identifier used by all local interfaces participating in the DECNET routing process. Show DECNET also lists whether the router is a Level One or Level Two router. DECNET Areas and router type assignments (Level One and Level Two) are critical in successfully configuring DECNET. These topics are covered in the next section.

```
r1#show decnet interface s0
Serial0 is up, line protocol is up, encapsulation is HDLC
    Interface cost is 10, priority is 64, DECnet network: 0
    The designated router is 1.1
    Sending HELLOs every 15 seconds, routing updates 40 seconds
    Smallest router blocksize seen is 1498 bytes
    Routing input list is not set, output list is not set
    Access list is not set
    DECnet fast switching is enabled
    Number of L1 router adjacencies is : 1
    Number of non-PhaseIV+ router adjacencies is : 1
    Number of PhaseIV+ router adjacencies is : 0
```

The Show DECNET interface command possesses many similarities with the `show ip ospf interface` command. Both list information on an interface's configured HELLO interval and the number of adjacencies formed.

```
r2#show decnet neighbors
Net        Node      Interface     MAC address      Flags
0          1.1       Ethernet1     aa00.0400.0104   V
```

Like show ip ospf neighbors, show decnet neighbors lists neighbors located on specific interfaces.

DECNET Routing Tables

A DECNET routing table differs from an IP, IPX, and AppleTalk routing table in that it does not list network segment addresses. Instead, it lists every DECNET device (both end systems and routers) that has been assigned a DECNET address. A DECNET address is a 16-bit address composed of two parts: a six-bit area address and ten-bit node address. If a DECNET address is assigned to a router, it can be referred to as a "router-identifier.". One and only one DECNET routing identifier is assigned to a given router. DECNET routes by RID. In DECNET, two neighboring routers may have routing tables that are constructed and displayed in a substantially different manner. This is due to the DECNET design characteristic of categorizing DECNET routers in different levels (Level One and Level Two). By defining different types of routers (Level One and Level Two), DECNET supplies the building blocks needed to group both routers and end systems within a single DECNET domain into discrete areas. By dividing a DECNET routing domain into areas, many of the benefits of areas that an OSPF network enjoys can be realized by a DECNET network.

Routing Levels and Areas

DECENT routers are classified in two categories:

Level One Routers
Level Two Routers

Level One routers only communicate with other Level One routers in the same area. They are the equivalent of intra-area routers in OSPF. Intra-area OSPF routers generate "O" entries in an IP routing table. A DECNET Level One router only lists other routers in its area. Level One routers do not list routers in other areas in its routing table. From a configuration perspective, the Cisco IOS identifies DECNET Level One routers as "routing-iv" DECNET router Level One area designation is assigned with the following global configuration command:

```
r2(config)#decnet node-type routing-iv
```

As mentioned above, DECNET Level One routers only list other routers within their local area. Listed below is a sample show decent route display:

```
r1#show decnet route
Node          Cost     Hops    Next Hop to Node    Expires   Prio
*1.1          0        0       (Local) -> 1.1
*1.2          4        1       Ethernet1 -> 1.2    35        64       V
```

DECNET Level Two routers communicate with other Level One routers in the same local area as well as with other Level 2 routers in other areas. They are the functional equivalent of inter-area routers in OSPF. Inter-area OSPF routers generate "IA" entries in an IP routing table. A DECNET Level Two router lists a single entry for each other area in a DECNET domain as well as all of the other routers in its local area. From a configuration perspective, the Cisco IOS identifies DECNET Level Two routers with the "area" parameter following the decnet node-type global configuration command. DECNET router Level Two area designation is assigned with the following global configuration command syntax:

```
Decnet-border(config)#decnet node-type area
```

As mentioned earlier, DECNET Level Two routers maintain a listing of other areas existing in a DECNET routing domain, as well as all other routers in the router's local area:

```
Decnet-border#show decnet route
Area         Cost    Hops    Next Hop to Node    Expires     Prio
*1           0       0       (Local) -> 1.2
*2           15      1       Serial1 -> 2.1      45          64          A+
```

```
Node         Cost    Hops    Next Hop to Node     Expires     Prio
*(Area)      0       0       (Local) -> 1.2
*1.1         10      1       Serial0 -> 1.1       31          64          V
*1.2         0       0       (Local) -> 1.2
```

Unlike an OSPF inter-area router that belongs to two areas by having one interface configured in area 0 and second interface in an area other than area 0, DECNET Level Two routers belong to one and only one area at all times. The Level Two designation allows the router to exchange routes with a router in a different area. Also, unlike OSPF with its backbone Area 0 requirement, DECNET has no equivalent backbone area requirement.

DECNET Address Manipulation

In order to maintain compatibility with previous versions of DECNET, DECNET does not use a given network interface card's manufacturer assigned mac addresses. When DECNET is applied to a given interface, it multiplies the user-defined DECNET area number by 1024, adds the user-defined node number, swaps the two lower bytes and appends that result to a digital equipment registered mac address prefix of AA00.0400. An example of this address manipulation process is provided below:

```
Area    Node
1       2       1.2     1024 x 1 = 1024 + 2 = 1026 decimal
                        0000.0100.0000.0010 = 1026 binary
                                       0402 = 1026 hexidecimal
                                       0204 = low order byte swap
                             AA00.0400.0204 = decnet mac address
```

In the third line of the partially displayed show interface command listed below, notice how the first Ethernet address listed is different from the burned in address (bia). This is due to the DECNET address manipulation process described above. Notice how the first address listed is identical to the one calculated in the DECNET address manipulation example provided above. The DECNET address applied to the router of the Ethernet interface displayed below is 1.2. The mac address is identical to the one calculated in the address manipulation example.

```
r1#show interface ethernet0
Ethernet0 is up, line protocol is up
  Hardware is Lance, address is aa00.0400.0204 (bia
0000.0c3d.d987)
```

Be advised that this changing of mac address format could cause problems with existing configurations of protocols that use the native mac addresses of a given interface (for example, frame-relay and dialer map statements for IPX). If configuring from the ground up, perform your DECNET configurations first.

Minimum DECNET Configuration

In order to perform a basic DECNET configuration, a minimum of three commands are required (two global configuration commands and one interface command). The commands are:

GLOBAL CONFIGURATION

```
r2(config)#decnet routing area.node
r2(config)#decnet node-type area or decnet node-type routing-iv
```

INTERFACE CONFIGURATION

```
Assign decnet cost
r2(config-if)#decnet cost 4
```

When configuring DECNET, the first command must always be the global configuration command `decnet routing area.node`. This command performs two operations:

1. It enables the DECNET routing process in the Internetwork Operating System (IOS).
2. It assigns a unique area.node (six-bit area address and ten-bit node address) address to the enabled DECNET router.

The requirement of enabling the DECNET routing process first before any other DECNET commands are entered is identical to enabling the IPX and AppleTalk processes first before any subsequent IPX or AppleTalk configuration commands are entered.

The area.node address must be entered so that the area address match the area address of all other routers in a specified area and the node address is unique from the node address of all other routers in a given area. Remember, there are two types of DECNET routers: Level One and Level Two. The DECNET router type definition is based upon whether a router is an "intra-area" router or "inter-area" router. This issue leads directly to the second required DECNET global configuration command: `decnet node-type <area | routing-iv>`. Use the "area" parameter with the `decnet node-type` command if you want the router to be an "inter-area" router. Use the "routing-iv" parameter if you want the router to be an "intra-area" router.

If a DECNET Level One "intra-area" router (the "routing-iv" configuration parameter with the IOS) has a directly connected neighbor that is in another area, the Level One router will ignore the nonlocal router. Therefore, if you want a DECNET router to communicate with neighboring routers in other areas, you must configure the router as a Level Two router.

The final DECNET routing configuration command is the interface configuration command `decnet cost`. Configure every interface that you want to participate in the DECNET routing process with the interface cost command. As mentioned earlier, a distinguishing characteristic of DECNET routing is that it does not assign network addresses to individual interfaces. All interfaces advertise the router's single unique area.node address. The `decnet cost interface configuration` command allows you to adjust the metrics for specific interfaces on a router. Therefore, if you would like to make one interface a more preferred route to a given router over another interface, assign a lower decnet cost to the preferred interface.

BASIC DECNET LEVEL ONE ROUTER CONFIGURATION (INTRA-AREA)

```
r2(config)#decnet routing 1.2
r2(config)#decnet node-type routing-iv
r2(config-if)#decnet cost 4
```

BASIC DECNET LEVEL TWO ROUTER CONFIGURATION (INTER-AREA)

```
r2(config)#decnet routing 1.2
r2(config)#decnet node-type area
r2(config-if)#decnet cost 4
```

DECNET DESIGNATED ROUTER CONFIGURATION

When multiple DECNET devices reside on an Ethernet segment, a single router can become the "designated router" for that segment. The designated router is used by DECNET devices on an Ethernet network (both end systems and other routers) when they do not know where to send a packet. A designated router can be viewed as a dynamically learned default gateway.

The designated router is elected based upon the router with the highest "router-priority" parameter. The IOS interface configuration command to set the designated router priority is displayed below:

```
r2(config)#interface ethernet 0
r2(config-if)#decnet router-priority 75
```

The default router-priority value is 64.

Commonly Used DECNET Show Commands

Once DECNET configuration is completed, use the following show commands to monitor the operation of DECNET:

```
Show decnet
Show decnet interface
Show decnet route
Show decnet traffic
```

Listed below is a complete listing of the DECNET show commands available in IOS 11.2:

```
r1#show decnet ?
  <0-3>              Optional ATG network number
  access-lists       Decnet access lists
  debug              Incomplete network structures for each network
  interface          DECnet interface status and configuration
  map                DECnet Address Translation Gateway table
  neighbors          DECnet adjacent neighbors
  route              DECnet routing table
  static             Display all static routes in static route queue
  traffic            DECnet traffic statistics
  <cr>
```

You can also PING remote DECNET routers with the `ping decnet` command:

```
r3#ping decnet 4.4

Type escape sequence to abort.
Sending 5, 100-byte DECnet Echoes to 4.4, timeout is 5 seconds:
!!!!!
Success rate is 100 percent (5/5), round-trip min/avg/max = 1/2/4
ms
```

DECNET Debugging Tools

The IOS provides the following debugging tools for DECNET:

```
r1#debug decnet ?
  adjacencies        DECnet adjacency events
  connects           DECnet connect access lists
  events             DECnet major events
  packets            DECnet routing updates and HELLO packets
  routing            DECnet routing table transactions
```

DEBUG OUTPUT FROM FORMING A DECNET NEIGHBOR RELATIONSHIP

In the following example, the following debug tools will provide a trace of the steps performed when each basic command is entered during DECNET configuration:

```
r2#show debug
DECNET:
       DECnet packets (errors) debugging is on
```

```
DECnet adjacencies debugging is on
DECnet packet forwarding debugging is on
```

Notice from the debug output that hello packets are being exchanged, adjacencies are being formed and routes are being sent. Closely examine the following step-by-step process of decnet routing being enabled.

First, the DECNET routing process is enabled:

```
r1#configure terminal
Enter configuration commands, one per line. End with CNTL/Z.
r1(config)#decnet routing 1.1
DNET-ADJ: sending hellos
```

Second, the DECNET node-type is defined. It is defined as either area (Level One) or routing-iv (Level Two):

```
r2#configure terminal
Enter configuration commands, one per line. End with CNTL/Z.
r2(config)#decnet routing 1.2
DNET-ADJ: sending hellos
```

Notice in the show decnet neighbors display provided below that no neighbors exist. This is because DECNET has not been configured on any of the interfaces:

```
r1#show decnet neighbors
Net            Node         Interface    MAC address     Flags
```

The third and final basic configuration step is performed with the interface configuration command "decnet cost." When this interface configuration command is applied, DECNET immediately begins generating HELLO packets in an attempt to form an adjacency on that interface. Examine the configuration command entered below as well as the resulting debug output:

```
r1#configure terminal
Enter configuration commands, one per line. End with CNTL/Z.
r1(config)#interface ethernet 1
r1(config-if)#decnet cost 4
DNET-ADJ: sending hellos
DNET: Ethernet1 is up: sending hello and routes
DNET-ADJ: Sending version 2.0 hellos to all PhaseIV routers on
int Ethernet1, blksize 1498
DNET: Sending level 2 routing updates on interface Ethernet1
```

In the debug trace shown above, a DECNET interface was enabled on a segment with no DECNET neighbors. Notice how HELLOs are sent out, but no other DECNET router replies. In the debug trace below, a DECNET interface is enabled on a segment with another DECNET router. Notice in the trace below how the HELLOs get answered and an adjacency is formed.

```
r2#configure terminal
Enter configuration commands, one per line. End with CNTL/Z.
r2(config)#interface ethernet 1
r2(config-if)#decnet cost 4
DNET-ADJ: sending hellos
DNET: Ethernet1 is up: sending hello and routes
DNET-ADJ: Sending version 2.0 hellos to all PhaseIV routers on int Ethernet1,
blksize 1498
DNET: Sending level 2 routing updates on interface Ethernet1
DNET-ADJ: Level 1 hello from 1.2, creating new adjacency
DNET-ADJ: sending triggered hellos
DNET-ADJ: Sending version 2.0 hellos to all PhaseIV routers on int Ethernet1,
blksize 1498
DNET-ADJ: Level 1 hello from 1.1, creating new adjacency
DNET-ADJ: sending triggered hellos
DNET-ADJ: Sending version 2.0 hellos to all PhaseIV routers on int Ethernet1,
blksize 1498
```

Once DECNET is fully configured on two or more routers, show decnet neighbors, show decnet route, and show decnet interface should accurately list the number of DECNET routers configured in your DECNET domain. Examples of each are provided below:

```
r2#show decnet neighbors
Net          Node        Interface    MAC addressFlags
0            1.1         Ethernet1    aa00.0400.0104V

r1#show decnet route
Node         Cost        Hops         Next Hop to Node          Expires    Prio
*1.1         0           0            (Local) -> 1.1
*1.2         4           1            Ethernet1 -> 1.2          35         64V
```

In the two show decnet interface displays listed below, notice that the first display (the r2 display) lists itself as the designated router ("We are the designated router"). Router r2 possesses the DECNET address of 1.2. The second display (the r1 display) also lists r2 as the designated router. (The designated router is 1.2.)

```
r2#show decnet interface ethernet 1
Ethernet1 is up, line protocol is up, encapsulation is ARPA
     Interface cost is 4, priority is 75, DECnet network: 0
     We are the designated router
     Sending HELLOs every 15 seconds, routing updates 40 seconds
     Smallest router blocksize seen is 1498 bytes
     Routing input list is not set, output list is not set
     Access list is not set
     DECnet fast switching is enabled
     Number of L1 router adjacencies is : 1
     Number of non-PhaseIV+ router adjacencies is : 1
     Number of PhaseIV+ router adjacencies is : 0
```

```
r1#show decnet interface ethernet 1
Ethernet1 is up, line protocol is up, encapsulation is ARPA
     Interface cost is 4, priority is 64, DECnet network: 0
     The designated router is 1.2
     Sending HELLOs every 15 seconds, routing updates 40 seconds
     Smallest router blocksize seen is 1498 bytes
     Routing input list is not set, output list is not set
     Access list is not set
     DECnet fast switching is enabled
     Number of L1 router adjacencies is : 1
     Number of non-PhaseIV+ router adjacencies is : 1
     Number of PhaseIV+ router adjacencies is : 0
```

Use ping combined with debug decent packet to get a more detailed look at how a DECNET router is processing a packet. In the example below, a DECNET Level One router (intra-area router) with the source address of 1.3 attempts to ping a node in another area (node 4.4). The debug decnet packet output displays that the packet is forwarded to the Level Two router with a DECNET address of 1.1.

```
r3#ping decnet 4.4

Type escape sequence to abort.
Sending 5, 100-byte DECnet Echoes to 4.4, timeout is 5 seconds:
!!!!!
Success rate is 100 percent (5/5), round-trip min/avg/max = 1/2/4 ms

r3#
DNET-PKT: Packet fwded from 1.3 to 4.4, via 1.1, snpa aa00.0400.0104, Ethernet1
Source address: 4.4
DNET: echo response from 4.4
```

Using DECNET Static Routes

You can configure DECNET static and default routes in the IOS global configuration mode. An example of configuring DECNET static routes along with a default route is displayed below:

```
Router(config)#decnet route 1.4 1.10
Router(config)#decnet route 1.5 1.10
Router(config)#decnet route default 1.100
```

In the examples above, 1.4 and 1.5 are the destination nodes. 1.10 is the next-hop. A DECNET default route is defined with the "decent route default" global configuration command.

Static routes and default routes can be displayed with the `show decnet route` command:

```
Router#show decnet route
  Node        Cost  Hops         Next Hop to Node        Expires  Prio
*1.4           0     0   (STATIC)  forwarding to 1.10
*1.5           0     0   (STATIC)  forwarding to 1.10
*1.10          0     0            (Local) -> 1.10
*DEFAULT* :    0     0    using next hop address of 1.100
```

If you want to forward static routes, use the following global configuration command:

```
r1(config)#decnet propagate static
```

DECNET over ISDN/DDR

If you want to enable DECNET routing over an Integrated Services Digital Network (ISDN)/dial-on-demand routing (DDR) link, you must add the DECNET protocol to your dialer-list. If you want to create a granular dialer-list so that only specific DECNET packets will initiate an ISDN/DDR connection, you must configure a DECNET access-list to be associated with your dialer-list. DECNET access-lists are a Level Six topic. They are covered in Chapter Twenty-Five.

When configuring DECNET over a DDR link, remember that DECNET routers send out HELLO packets every 15 seconds. This will keep an ISDN/DDR link up indefinitely. When configuring DECNET over ISDN/DDR consider using static and default routes.

DECNET over an NBMA Network

If you configure DECNET over a nonbroadcast multi-access (NBMA) network such as Frame-Relay or ATM, you need to decide whether you are going to use physical interfaces or subinterfaces. Review the topics in Chapter Four and Chapter Seven. Determine whether you want to use inverse-arp, map statements or point-to-point subinterfaces. DECNET applies the rule of split-horizon. Be aware of the issues that split-horizon creates in a hub and spoke NBMA network. The hub will see all DECNET nodes, but the spokes will not see nodes announced by other spokes due to split-horizon. DECNET spilt-horizon can only be disabled on a physical interface. It cannot be disabled on a subinterface.

Summary

DECNET Phase IV is a routing protocol that uses a unique router identifier. Other routing protocols that use a unique router identifier are:

- OSPF
- IS-IS
- NetWare Link Services Protocol (NLSP)
- ATM private network node interface (PNNI)

DECNET defines areas. Other routing protocols that define areas are:

- OSPF
- IS-IS
- NLSP
- ATM PNNI
- IGRP
- EIGRP
- BGP4

DECNET routing presents many of the same issues that IP, IPX, and AppleTalk posed: for example, the issue of split-horizon.

Like IPX and AppleTalk, DECNET can be tunneled over an IP backbone.

Even though very few newly installed networks are planning a DECNET routing deployment, many networks around the world are still maintaining large mission-critical DECNET Phase-IV internetworks.

From a learning perspective, mastering DECNET re-enforces an internetworking engineer's understanding of routing theory and the hands-on deployment of any and all routing protocols. If internetworking engineers possess a strong understanding of the routing principles embodied in IP, IPX, AppleTalk, and DECNET routing, they will know what questions to ask and know what to look for when a new routing protocol emerges, or when they encounter a less commonly used routing protocol. With each new routing protocol you learn, the learning process should become easier.

Professional Development Checklist

By using this chapter, you should be able to perform the following operations:

- Enable DECnet Routing
- Assign Decnet Cost to Interfaces
- Configure DECnet on Token Rings
- Configure Level 1 Routers
- Configure Level 2 Routers
- Specify Designated Routers

For Further Study

- Cisco IOS Network Protocols Configuration Guide Part 3, Cisco Systems, Inc., 1989–1998.
- Cisco IOS Network Protocols Command Reference Part 3, Cisco Systems, Inc., 1989–1998.

URLs

- **www.cciecert.com**
- **www.mentorlabs.com**
- **www.cisco.com**

Can You Spot the Issues?

1. DECNET is configured over ISDN/DDR. A restrictive dialer-list has been implemented on DECNET router R1. The dialer-list blocks DECNET traffic from initiating an ISDN/DDR call. A DECNET router R1 is configured with static routes. The remote DECNET router R2 also has a restrictive dialer-list, but no static routes. R1 can set up a call but R2 cannot why?
2. Three DECNET routers R1, R2, and R3 possess three locally discovered end nodes in their routing table. They are interconnected in a hub and spoke NBMA network. R1 is the hub router and R2 and R3 are the spokes. R1 has a complete list of all end-node advertised by R2 and R3; however, R2 does not have the routes from R3 and R3 does not have the routes from R2. Why?
3. How can you configure DECNET so that DECNET traffic can traverse the IP corporate backbone without configuring any of the corporate backbone routers for DECNET?
4. R1 is a Level 1 router in Area 10 and R3 is a Level 1 router in Area 20. They are connected to the same Ethernet segment. Why can't they exchange routing information?

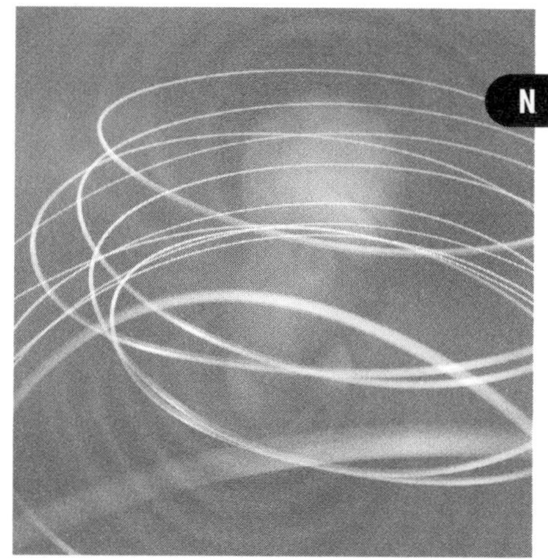

NINETEEN

Level Four Summary Non-IP Routing Summary

In its effort to provide an end-to-end solution, the Cisco Internetwork Operating System (IOS) supports all routing protocols including those used by legacy proprietary protocol suites such as IPX/ SPX, AppleTalk, and DECNET. Cisco categorizes these protocols as "desktop" protocols. At the very least, the Cisco strategy for "desktop" protocols is: Let the native desktop routing protocols reside on the edge of the corporate internetwork (at the access-level) and deploy high-end routing protocols in the core, especially the WAN core.

Cisco offers two fundamental methods of configuring desktop protocols:

1. Concurrently with IP
2. Tunneled inside of IP

Chapters Fifteen–Eighteen provided several examples of how to configure IPX, AppleTalk, and DECNET. While studying these chapters, you encountered many of the same issues you encountered with IP:

- Issues of split-horizon

- Issues of routing table updates keeping Integrated Services Digital Network (ISDN)/dial-on-demand routing (DDR) up
- Issues of route redistribution

Many network designers are attempting to minimize non-IP traffic. Practically every non-IP routing protocol was designed to provide connectivity for a particular end system/operating system:

IPX for Novell Servers
AppleTalk for Apple End Systems
DECNET for DEC Hosts
BANYAN VINES for Banyan Servers
Apollo for Apollo workstations
Systems network architecture (SNA) for IBM end systems

The TCP/IP protocol suite was designed to be operating system independent.

In the late 1980s and early 1990s, the open systems interconnection (OSI) protocol suite (CLNP, TP4, IS-IS, etc.) was heralded as the successor of the TCP/IP protocol suite. Many detailed studies by many highly intelligent internetworking "experts" predicted the demise of IP by the mid-1990s. The U.S Government was ready to bet heavily on the OSI protocol suite. It mandated the adoption of OSI with its Government Open Systems Interconnect Profile (GOSIP) initiative. As history has shown, the OSI protocol suite has not surpassed TCP/IP.

However, there are many advocates for gradually migrating the TCP/IP protocol suite to an asynchronous transfer mode (ATM)-based protocol suite. A glimpse into a possible non-IP future can be gained by reviewing Chapter Seven of this book. Instead of IP, you will have an NSAP address. Instead of TCP, you will have ATM Adaptive Layers. Instead of open shortest path first (OSPF) and routing information protocol (RIP), you will have private network node interface (PNNI).

Absent from the list of proprietary protocol suites is one for Microsoft. Microsoft has never developed its own protocol suite. Originally, Microsoft internetworking protocols relied on IBM developed technologies: namely the nonroutable NETBIOS/NETBEUI. With Windows for Workgroups, Windows NT, and Windows 95, Microsoft began offering three protocols: NETBIOS/NETBEUI, IPX/SPX, and TCP/IP. By supplying, IPX support for its operating system platforms, Microsoft attempted to make the short-term integration efforts of Microsoft and Novell environments easier and the long-term migration from Novell to Microsoft environments easier.

Both Novell and Microsoft developed ODI and NDIS drivers allow their respective clients to maintain multiple protocol stacks over a single network interface card. Today, both Novell and Microsoft aggressively support TCP/IP.

From a theoretical perspective, studying desktop routing protocols re-inforces your understanding of all routing protocols. What you saw with IP RIP and OPSF, you saw with IPX/RIP and NetWare Link Services Protocol (NLSP). From a practical perspective, studying routing protocols re-enforces your understanding of the Cisco IOS. You saw global interface and routing configuration commands used in a manner with the desktop protocols that was similar to those used with IP. You saw `show` and `debug` commands that had IP counterparts.

You should now be able to easily list the similarities between IP routing and non-IP routing processes from both a theoretical and practical IOS perspective.

Key IPX Monitoring and Troubleshooting Tools

```
Show ipx route
Show ipx servers
Show ipx interfaces brief
PING IPX

Debug ipx packet
Debug ipx routing activity
Debug ipx routing events
Debug ipx sap activity
Debug ipx sap events
```

Key AppleTalk Monitoring and Troubleshooting Tools

```
Show appleTalk route
Show appletalk zones
Show appletalk interface
Show appletalk interface brief
Show appletalk neighbors
PING APPLETALK

Debug apple packet
Debug apple routing
Debug apple arp
Debug apple zone
```

Key DECNET Monitoring and Troubleshooting Tools

```
Show decnet route
Show decnet
Show decnet interface
PING DECNET

Debug decnet packet
Debug decnet routing
Debug decnet events
```

Configuration Strategies

Configure DEC first, since it reverses the media access control (MAC) addresses of local-area network (LAN) interfaces. This will have a negative impact on IPX configurations, since IPX uses the MAC address for interface node addresses. Second, configure IPX. Finally, configure AppleTalk last, since its configuration is so prone to potential errors and mishaps.

Remember to thoroughly review the Cisco IOS Configuration Guide and Command Reference Volumes Six and Seven.

Build a checklist for each of the nonrouting protocols. List the particular idiosyncrasies of each protocol. Develop proactive issue-spotting techniques and corresponding configuration strategies for the most common non-IP routing configuration scenarios as well as the most unique. Do not rely solely on this text or any other text for building your Level Four knowledge base and internetworking skills. Get on those routers and practice. Build IPX, AppleTalk, and DECNET internetworks. If you feel motivated, build a BANYAN or Is-Is internetwork! Use the different show commands and debug tools.

If you don't feel comfortable with these topics, do not go to Level Five. It is critical that you possess strong Level Four knowledge before addressing Level Five issues. With Level Five, we move away from routing issues and examine nonroutable protocols in a bridged and switched environment. A key topic covered in Level Five is integrated routing and bridging. You will never grasp this topic if you do not have a strong understanding of routing.

T W E N T Y

Bridging Non-Routable Traffic

Topics Covered in This Chapter

- Bridging Technology Overview
- Configuring Transparent Bridging
- Tuning a Spanning Tree
- Configuring Integrated Routing and Bridging
- Configuring LAT Translation

To Bridge or to Route, That Is the Question

When a frame arrives at a router interface, the router must make a decision: Will the frame be bridged or routed? So far we have examined routing traffic only. At Level Five, we examine bridging and the non-routable traffic that requires bridging. Such non-routable traffic includes SNA, NETBIOS and LAT.

Both SNA and LAT have been implemented for a long time. They carry mission critical traffic between end user terminals and minicomputers and mainframes. SNA was developed by IBM to transport terminal traffic to and from IBM mainframes and minicomputers. LAT was developed by DEC to transport terminal traffic to and from DEC minicomputers.

NETBIOS, a non-routable protocol, was developed by IBM in the mid-80s as part of its LAN implementation strategy. Token-Ring local area network technology was also developed by IBM as part of this strategy. From Token-Ring comes one of two primary bridging technologies: source-route bridging.

DEC played a leading role in developing Ethernet and the second primary bridging technology: transparent bridging. As we will see, these technologies are dramatically different.

During the mid-80s and into the 90s, routing technology was, in most cases, preferred over bridging. A common design slogan was "Route when you can, bridge if you must." However, bridging technology has been reborn with LAN switching. When you examine the operation of a LAN switch such as the Catalyst 5000, you will see bridging technology at the heart of it. With the growing popularity of LAN switching, an often quoted slogan is "Switch when you can, route if must." Cisco adds an alternative to this principle that blurs the boundaries of traditional bridging and routing: Cisco Fusion. With Cisco Fusion, the technologies of routing, LAN switching and ATM switching are combined into a single architecture. The embodiment of Cisco Fusion is the Catalyst 8500 switch router, which performs wire speed layer three forwarding for IP and IPX. A drawback of large-scale LAN switched environments is heavy reliance on the spanning tree algorithm. When redundancy is introduced in a LAN switched environment, at least one path will be blocked by the spanning tree algorithm. By deploying the Catalyst 8500, you can have the best of both worlds: a non-blocking network topology and wire speed forwarding rates.

Cisco routers and the Catalyst 8500 can perform both routing and bridging functions. As stated earlier, for every packet that enters a router's interface, the router makes a decision to either bridge or route the packet. If it cannot bridge or route the packet, the packet will be dropped.

In Level Five, we will first provide a brief definition of both transparent and source route bridging. We will then review hybrids of the two technologies: source-route transparent bridging and source-route translational bridging. We will then list Cisco specific solutions to augment both transparent and source-route bridging. Cisco solutions will include concurrent routing and bridging (CRB), integrated routing and bridging (IRB), remote source-route bridging (RSRB), data-link switching plus DLSw+ and LAT translation.

This chapter will cover the above mentioned definitions, as well as configuring transparent bridging, CRB, IRB and LAT translation. Chapter 22 will cover source-route bridging and DLSw+ in detail.

Transparent Bridging Defined

With routing implementations (IP, IPX, AppleTalk, etc.), routers perform three fundamental functions:

1. Building routing tables comprised of destination addresses.
2. Maintaining the routing table.

3. Switching network layer packets based upon a match of the destination address of a given incoming packet with an entry in the routing table.

Transparent bridges also build and maintain tables and switch frames by matching destination addresses with entries in the transparent bridging table. The major difference between the tables built and maintained by routers and those built and maintained by bridges is that routing tables are based upon network layer addresses, while transparent bridge tables are based upon MAC layer addresses.

The addresses in a routing table can have segment location information contained within them. MAC addresses never contain such information.

Transparent bridging tables are also built differently than routing tables. Routing tables rely on routing protocols to exchange information about different networks which they have learned. With a bridge, each bridge builds its table independently. It learns different MAC addresses by associating the source addresses of transited frames with the port on which the frame arrived into the bridge.

Like routing table information, transparent bridge information has an age associated with it. If the maximum age of a transparent bridge table entry is exceeded, the entry is flushed.

Transparent bridging is named as such because an end system using a transparent bridge is completely unaware of the bridge's existence. The transparent bridge is "transparent" to the end system. The end system does not need any additional software; it does not generate special packets such as "explorer frames," or maintain any types of tables to participate in transparent bridging. For these reasons, we will see how transparent bridging operates in a manner completely different from source-route bridging.

Source Route Bridging Defined

The source route bridging (SRB) algorithm was developed by IBM and proposed to the IEEE 802.5 committee as means to bridge between multiple Token-Ring local-area networks (LANs). The IEEE 802.5 committee subsequently adopted SRB into the IEEE 802.5 Token Ring LAN specification.

SRB has several different combinations, such as:

- SRB – Source route bridging
- SRT – Source route transparent bridging
- SR/TLB – Source route translational bridging

In a source route bridged network, end systems will send what is called an "explorer frame" to the network to find a path from source to destination prior to sending data. The source route bridges will be responsible for adding the path information to these explorer frames and making sure they are passed to and from the appropriate end systems. In addition to passing the explorer frames, they can also store this routing information in a cache. This is called a "RIF cache". Source route bridges will look into a Token-Ring frame and determine whether or not there is any routing information by checking the routing information indicator (RII), and then add to the routing descriptor field (RD) its ring and bridge information.

While transparent bridges build and maintain tables of MAC addresses and associated ports, standard configuration source-route bridges do not. Instead of maintaining an address table, source-route bridges examine the contents of each Token-Ring frame. First, they examine the first bit of a Token-Ring frame's source address to see if it has the value of zero or one. The first bit of the source address in a Token-Ring frame is called the Routing Information Indicator (RII). The value of the RII is set by the source end system of the frame. If the RII is set to zero, no source route information exists in the Token-Ring frame. If the RII is set to one, source route information exists within the frame. Source route information resides in the Routing Information Field (RIF).

Source-Route Transparent Bridging Defined

Source-Route Transparent Bridging (SRT) is a Token-Ring bridge that will either source route bridge or transparent bridge a Token-Ring frame. The decision to source-route bridge or transparent bridge a frame is based upon the RII value. If the RII value is zero, the frame will be transparent bridged. If the RII is one, the frame will be source-route bridged.

See Chapter Twenty-One for more information on the operation and configuration of Source-Route Transparent Bridging.

Source-Route Translational Bridging Defined

Source-Route Translational Bridging (SR/TLB) bridges between Ethernet and Token-Ring segments. SR/TLB is designed to perform several functions:

1. Overcome MTU differences between Ethernet and Token-Ring
2. Token-Ring frames may contain RIFs; Ethernet frames never contain RIFs. SR/TLB reconciles these differences between Ethernet and Token-Ring.
3. Token-Ring addresses are in canonical format; Ethernet addresses are in non-canonical format

SR/TLB bridges assure that all of these differences are resolved when forwarding frames from Token-Ring to Ethernet and Ethernet to Token-Ring.

See Chapter Twenty-One for more information on the operation and configuration of Source-Route Translational Bridging.

Cisco Specific Solutions

Concurrent Routing and Bridging (CRB)

Traditional, intermediate systems would either route or bridge a given network layer protocol out all of its interfaces. When Concurrent Routing and Bridging is configured on a Cisco router, specific protocols can be bridged out specific interfaces and routed out others.

Integrated Routing and Bridging (IRB)

CRB allows bridging and routing of the same protocol to coexist on a single router but never mix the two. Integrated Routing and Bridging (IRB) allows bridged and routed traffic of the same protocol to be interchanged. By creating a logical interface called the Bridge Virtual Interface (BVI), bridged traffic of a given network layer protocol can be forwarded to a routed interface of that same protocol, and vice versa.

Virtual Rings for Multi-Port Source Route Bridges

Standard Token-Ring bridges have only two ports. A Cisco router can be configured as a multi-port source-route bridge by creating a virtual-ring within the router. On a multiport source route bridge, frames from physical interfaces are first forwarded to the virtual-ring, and then to another physical interface.

Remote Source Route Bridging (RSRB)

Remote Source Route Bridging (RSRB) takes the concept of a virtual-ring one step further. Instead of forwarding Token-Ring frames from one physical interface to another through a virtual-ring, RSRB forwards Token-Ring frames from physical Token-Ring interfaces to interfaces connected to an IP cloud through a virtual-ring. This provides a method for performing source route bridging over a WAN.

Data Link Switching Plus (DLSw+)

Data Link Switching Plus (DLSw+) is backwards compatible with RSRB. It performs the same functional tasks as RSRB and much more. Basic configuration of DLSw+ is very similar to RSRB. DLSw+ also supports interconnection of transparent bridging, SRT, SR/TLB, and SDLLCover on IP backbone.

See Chapter 21 for more information on the operation and configuration of DLSw+.

LAT Translation

Finally, with LAT, the IOS takes non-routable terminal traffic and translates it on a router to a protocol, such as TCP. LAT can be translated into TCP/TEL-

NET traffic or translated into TCP traffic as it goes over the IP cloud and back into LAT.

Roadmap of Bridging

In this chapter, we will examine Transparent Bridging, CRB, IRB and LAT translation. In the next chapter, we will examine SRB, SRT, SR/TLB, RSRB and DLSw+.

Configuring Transparent Bridging on Cisco Routers and a Catalyst 8500

The most common transparent bridging configuration involves only Ethernet interfaces. The minimum requirements for Transparent Bridging in an all-Ethernet environment involves the following two steps. One is performed in global configuration mode. The second is performed in interface configuration mode.

Step One: Assign a bridge-group number and select a spanning tree algorithm in global configuration mode.

First, a bridge-group must be assigned and a spanning tree algorithm selected. This is performed by entering the following global configuration command on a Cisco router and Catalyst 8500 switch:

```
r2(config)#bridge 1 protocol ?
  dec    DEC protocol
  ibm    IBM protocol
  ieee   IEEE 802.1 protocol
```

This command is absolutely fundamental to the transparent bridge configuration process. On a Cisco router and Catalyst 8500 switch, it is the starting point of all transparent bridge configurations. The "bridge # protocol xxx" global configuration command is the transparent bridging equivalent to "ipx routing" for IPX configuration or "appletalk routing" for AppleTalk configuration.

Notice there are three spanning tree protocols listed above. Only "dec" and "ieee" can be selected for transparent bridging. The "ibm" selection is for enabling spanning tree for explorer traffic in a source-routing bridging environment.

When configuring transparent bridging, make sure that all bridges within a group are configured with the same bridge group number and spanning tree protocol type.

```
r2(config)#bridge 1 protocol ieee
```

Step Two: Associate the interfaces with the bridge-group that you have created in interface configuration mode.

```
r2(config)#interface ethernet 0
r2(config-if)#bridge-group 1
```

Once these two configuration steps are performed, you must determine which network layer protocols you want to bridge, and which you want to route. By default, all network layer protocols except IP are bridged. If you want to bridge IP traffic in the basic transparent bridge configuration, you must explicitly disable IP routing with the global configuration command "no ip routing." By entering this command, you disable IP routing for the entire router or catalyst 8500 switch! If you want to disable IP routing for selected interfaces, you must configure concurrent bridging and routing or integrated routing and bridging. Configuring concurrent routing and bridging and integrated routing and bridging will be covered later in this chapter.

As a general rule, for all network layer protocols (including IP), do not supply any interface configuration commands for the interfaces that are bridging the designated protocol. For example, if you want to bridge IPX over the Ethernet0 and Ethernet1 interfaces, do not assign an IPX address to these interfaces.

Transparent Bridging for the Catalyst 5000

For Ethernet LAN switch modules on a Catalyst 5000, transparent bridging is enabled by default. When the word "VLAN" is used in the Catalyst 5000 environment, associate it with the word "bridge-group" in the routing environment The two words are functionally synonymous. By default, all LAN switching ports on a Catalyst 5000 are in the same VLAN (VLAN1). Therefore, you can say that all LAN switching ports on a Catalyst 5000 are in the same bridge-group.

The Spanning Tree Protocol

When multiple bridges are interconnected with multiple paths, a looped topology may be formed. A looped topology is often desirable to provide redundancy, but looped traffic is undesirable. Bridged traffic is especially vulnerable to broadcast loops. The spanning tree protocol (802.1d) was designed to prevent such loops from being formed. The spanning tree protocol was originally developed for bridges. Today, it is also applied to LAN switch topologies. By applying the spanning tree protocol to a looped bridged or LAN switch topology, all bridged segments will be reachable, but any points where loops can occur will be blocked.

The spanning tree protocol has four basic phases of operation:

1. Electing a root bridge among a bridge/LAN switch group
2. Calculating the shortest path to the root bridge/LAN switch by all non-root switches
3. Blocking highest cost paths to the root bridge/LAN switch for loop avoidance
4. Maintaining and recalculating the spanning tree with BPDUs

Once a spanning tree is formed, all bridges and LAN switches know who is the root bridge/LAN switch, what direction the root bridge/LAN switch is in, and what is the lowest path cost to the root of the Spanning Tree.

When a bridge port or LAN switch port is first activated, it broadcasts out Bridge Protocol Data Units (BPDUs) with itself as the root of the spanning tree. When a bridge or LAN switch receives BPDUs from other bridges or LAN switches, it conducts a spanning tree election to determine which bridge the root of the spanning tree. Parameters used to determine the spanning tree root is include a spanning tree bridge/LAN switch priority number and a MAC address identifying the bridge or LAN switch. Only one root bridge exists in a single spanning tree at any time.

In its most basic description, a spanning tree topology consists of the following basic components:

1. Bridges/LAN switches
2. Bridge/LAN switch segments

A spanning tree topology consists of the following types of bridges:

1. Root bridge/root LAN switches
2. Designated bridges/LAN switches
3. Non-root bridges/LAN switches
4. Non-designated bridges/LAN switches

At any given time, only one root bridge/LAN switch exists for the entire spanning tree. A root bridge/LAN switch is selected by a spanning tree election process.

A designated bridge/LAN switch is the device closest to the root bridge/LAN switch on a given segment. At any given time, only one designated bridge/LAN switch exists for each bridge segment. A designated bridge/LAN switch is selected by a spanning tree election process. Each bridge segment must have a designated bridge.

The root bridge/LAN switch is the designated bridge for all segments to which it is attached.

A spanning tree topology consists of the following types of ports:

1. One designated port residing on each designated bridge for each bridge/LAN switch segment

2. One root port on every non-root bridge/LAN switch. The root port is the port that provides the most optimal path to the root bridge on a given bridge or LAN switch.

The 802.1d specification defines five spanning tree port states:

1. disabled
2. learning
3. listening
4. forwarding
5. blocking

Root bridge/LAN switch ports and designated ports are never in a blocking state.

The root port on any bridge/LAN switch is never in a blocking state.

When a bridge or LAN switch port is activated, it normally goes through three spanning tree states: learning, listening and forwarding. If the port is the highest cost path to the root bridge in a looped topology, it enters the blocking state. By default, all bridge ports go through the first two states: learning and listening. Based upon the information they obtain during these states, the interface attains a forwarding or blocking state. On a Cisco router and Catalyst 8500, use the "show spanning" and "debug spanning events" commands to watch an interface pass through each of the spanning tree port states.

On a Catalyst 5000, a separate spanning tree is created for each VLAN. Therefore, if a Catalyst 5000 switch has five VLANs defined, five spanning trees will be created and maintained. You can view spanning tree information on a Catalyst 5000 with the "show spantree" command:

```
CAT-5000> (enable) show spantree
VLAN 1
Spanning tree enabled

Designated Root              00-10-7b-38-18-29
Designated Root Priority     100
Designated Root Cost         10
Designated Root Port         3/2
Root Max Age    20 sec    Hello Time 2   sec   Forward Delay 15 sec

Bridge ID MAC ADDR           00-10-79-45-58-00
Bridge ID Priority           32768
Bridge Max Age 20 sec     Hello Time 2   sec   Forward Delay 15 sec

Port      Vlan  Port-State     Cost   Priority  Fast-Start
--------  ----  -------------  -----  --------  ----------
 1/1      1     not-connected    10        32    disabled
 1/2      1     not-connected    10        32    disabled
 3/1      1     forwarding       10        32    disabled
 3/2      1     forwarding       10        32    disabled
```

Configuring the Spanning Tree Protocol on a Cisco Router and the Catalyst 8500 Switch

Cisco router and Catalyst 8500 switch configuration commands for adjusting a Spanning Tree include the statements described in the following sections.

Configuring the Spanning Tree Root Bridge

Selecting the spanning tree root bridge involves comparing a bridge priority value with the bridge priority on each bridge or LAN switch. If the bridge priority value is not manually configured on a Cisco bridge, it assumes a default value of 32768 for IEEE and 128 for DEC. The bridge with the lowest priority value becomes the root bridge. You can manually configure the bridge priority value with the following global configuration command:

```
r3(config)#bridge 1 priority ?
  <0-65535>  Priority (low priority more likely to be root)
```

Upon initial configuration, each bridge assumes that it is the root bridge. If all priority values are the same for all bridges in a bridge-group, the bridge with the lowest MAC address value becomes the root bridge.

Once the root bridge election is complete, all bridges in a bridge group will reflect the same root bridge. All bridge interfaces should be in either the forwarding or blocking mode. This can be verified using the "show spanning tree" command. Listed below are two show spanning tree displays. The first lists the status of the root bridge and its ports. The second lists a downstream neighboring bridge.

When you examine the highlighted portions of the displays, notice the following elements:

1. On the first line of each display it lists the bridge's own identifier.
2. On the fourth line it lists the root bridge. ("We are the spanning tree" or "`Current root has priority 100, address 0010.7b38.1829.`" Notice that the address of the root listed on the non-root bridge is the same address listed on the first line of the root bridge display.
3. Under the port listings, notice that the root bridge is the designated bridge for all segments to which it is connected.
4. For the non-root bridge (r1), notice the listing of "`Current root has priority 100, address 0010.7b38.1829`", the listing of the "root port." Notice how the root port is the port closest to the root bridge.
5. Notice that the Ethernet interface on the non-root bridge (the second display) is in a blocking state.

```
r2#show spanning-tree

Bridge Group 1 is executing the IEEE compatible Spanning Tree protocol
```

```
  Bridge Identifier has priority 100,  address 0010.7b38.1829
  Configured hello time 2, max age 20, forward delay 15
  We are the root of the spanning tree
  Topology change flag set, detected flag set
  Times:  hold 1, topology change 30, notification 30
          hello 2, max age 20, forward delay 15, aging 300
  Timers: hello 2, topology change 12, notification 0

Port 2 (Ethernet0) of bridge group 1 is forwarding
   Port path cost 100, Port priority 128
   Designated root has priority 100, address 0010.7b38.1829
   Designated bridge has priority 100, address 0010.7b38.1829
   Designated port is 2, path cost 0
   Timers: message age 0, forward delay 0, hold 0

Port 5 (Serial1)  of bridge group 1 is forwarding
   Port path cost 647, Port priority 128
   Designated root has priority 100, address 0010.7b38.1829
   Designated bridge has priority 100, address 0010.7b38.1829
   Designated port is 5, path cost 0
   Timers: message age 0, forward delay 0, hold 0

r1#show spanning-tree

Bridge Group 1 is executing the IEEE compatible Spanning Tree protocol
  Bridge Identifier has priority 100, address 00e0.b05a.9bfb
  Configured hello time 2, max age 20, forward delay 15
  Current root has priority 100, address  0010.7b38.1829
  Root port is 4 (Serial0), cost of root path is 100000
   Topology change flag not set, detected flag not set
   Times:  hold 1, topology change 30, notification 30
           hello 2, max age 20, forward delay 15, aging 300
   Timers: hello 0, topology change 0, notification 0

Port 3(Ethernet0) of bridge group 1 is blocking
   Port path cost 100000, Port priority 128
   Designated root has priority 100, address 0010.7b38.1829
   Designated bridge has priority 32768, address 00e0.1eb9.23e7
   Designated port is 2,path cost 747
   Timers: message age 3, forward delay 0, hold 0

Port 4 (Serial0) of bridge group 1 is forwarding
   Port path cost 100000, Port priority 128
   Designated root has priority 100, address 0010.7b38.1829
   Designated bridge has priority 100, address 0010.7b38.1829
   Designated port is 5,path cost 0
   Timers: message age 0, forward delay 0, hold 0
```

Once the root bridge is elected, all non-root bridges elect a designated bridge for each segment and calculate the shortest path to the root bridge. This calculation is performed by accumulating the port costs for each outbound interface. The path with the lowest accumulated port cost is the preferred path.

Use the "debug spanning events command" to watch bridge interfaces move through the different spanning tree ports states on a Cisco router or Catalyst 8500 switch. In the debug spanning events output displayed below, notice how another spanning tree peer is heard with the lower spanning tree priority number and is elected as the root bridge. The highlighted numbers are the spanning tree priority numbers. Notice that the bridge begins declaring itself as the root bridge. As soon as the bridge learns of another bridge with a lower priority (a priority that supersedes its own), it elects that bridge as the new root. Notice the comparison of the priority numbers. The new root has the priority of 100. The old root has a priority of 32768, the default settling.

```
ST: we are the spanning tree root
ST: Serial0 -> listening
ST: Serial0 -> listening
ST: Heard root     100-0000.0c35.f6b0 on Serial0
 Supersedes     32768 -0000.0c06.0ce8
ST: new root is 100, 0000.0c35.f6b0 on port Serial0, cost 100647
ST: sent Topology Change Notice on Serial0
ST: Ethernet0 -> learning
ST: sent Topology Change Notice on Serial0
ST: Serial1 -> forwarding
ST: sent Topology Change Notice on Serial0
ST: Serial0 -> forwarding
```

Manipulating the Spanning Tree Path Cost on a Cisco Router and Catalyst 8500

You can influence the path selected by a non-root bridge to get to the root bridge with the following interface configuration command:

```
r4(config-if)#bridge-group 1 path-cost ?
  <0-65535>  Path cost (higher values are higher costs)
```

By adjusting the path-costs assigned to a given interface, you can influence which path is used to get to the root bridge, and which port will be placed in a blocking state.

For example, consider the scenario below. Bridges br1, br2 and br3 are connected in a mesh topology. A loop exists; therefore, at least one port will be in a blocking state. Bridge br1 is the root bridge. The spanning tree path costs are the values displayed in the diagram below:

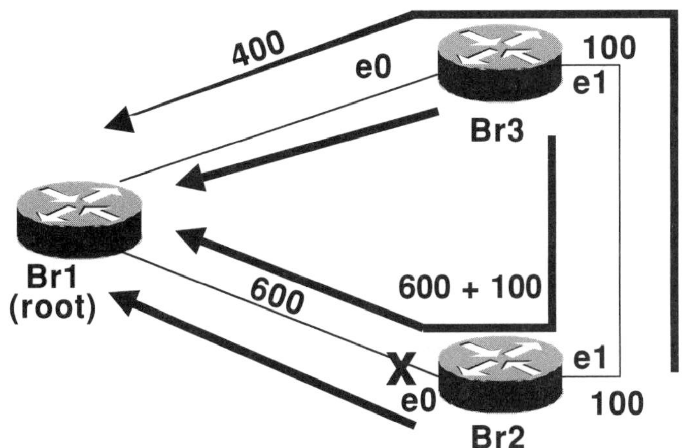

FIGURE 20–1 Spanning tree Scenario One.

Out of all possible paths, the longest path to the root is the Ethernet 0 interface on bridge b2. Therefore, that port enters into a blocking state. Validate the following calculations:

Bridge br3 has two possible paths to the root Bridge br1. One path has a cost of 400. This path is out of Bridge br3's Ethernet 0 interface. The second path has a cost of 100+600=700. This path is out of Bridge br3's Ethernet 1 interface. Given the two possible paths, Bridge br3 selects the path out of Ethernet 0 interface. This path becomes Bridge br3's root port.

Bridge br2 has two possible paths to the root Bridge br1. One path has a cost of 600. This path is out of Bridge br2's Ethernet 0 interface. The second path has a cost of 100+400=500. This path is out of Bridge br2's Ethernet 1 interface. Given the two possible paths, Bridge br2 selects the path out of its Ethernet 1 interface. This path becomes Bridge br2's root port. Since the path that Bridge br2 transits the both the Ethernet 0 and Ethernet 1 ports of Bridge 3, both bridge ports of Bridge br3 must maintain a forwarding state. Therefore, the Ethernet 0 port of Bridge br2 must be placed in the BLOCKING state.

As a second example, assume the path costs are adjusted in the original scenario as displayed below.

The interface Ethernet 1 is now placed in a blocking state. Bridge br3 has two possible paths to the root Bridge br1. One path has a cost of 400. This path is out of Bridge br3's Ethernet 0 interface. The second path has a

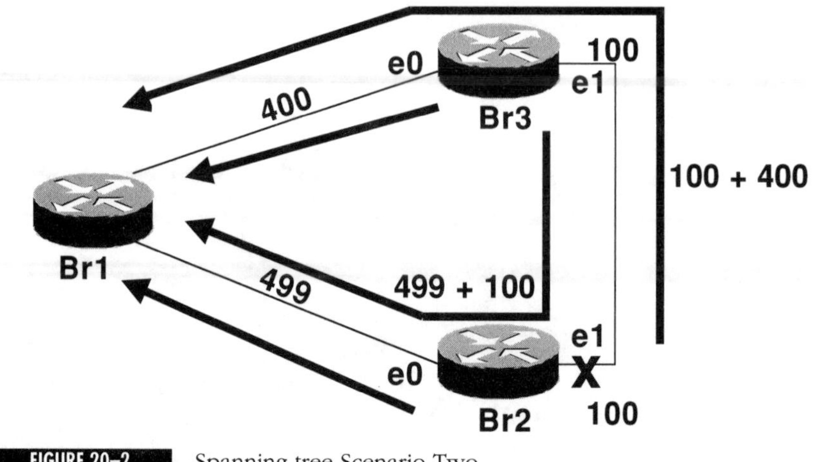

FIGURE 20–2 Spanning tree Scenario Two.

cost of 100+499=599. This path is out of Bridge br3's Ethernet 1 interface. Given the two possible paths, Bridge br3 selects the path out of its Ethernet 0 interface. This path becomes Bridge br3's root port.

Bridge br2 has two possible paths to the root Bridge br1. One path has a cost of 499. This path is out of Bridge br2's Ethernet 0 interface.

The second path has a cost of 100+400=500. This path is out of Bridge br2's Ethernet 1 interface. Given the two possible paths, Bridge br2 selects the path out of its Ethernet 0 interface. This path becomes Bridge br2's root port.

Since the Ethernet 0 ports of both Bridges br2 and br3 are the root ports for the respective bridges, neither can be in a blocking state. Therefore, one of the Ethernet 1 ports of Bridges br2 and br3 will need to be placed in the blocking state.

Adjusting Spanning Tree Parameters on a Catalyst 5000

A key fact to remember when configuring spanning tree parameters on a Catalyst 5000 is that a separate spanning tree instance is maintained for each VLAN.

To manipulate the root bridge election for a specific VLAN, use the following SET command:

```
  CAT-5000> (enable) set spantree priority
  Usage: set spantree priority <bridge_priority> [vlan]
(bridge_priority = 0..65535, vlan = 1..1000)
```

```
CAT-5000> (enable) set spantree priority 500
Spantree 1 bridge priority set to 500.
```

Notice that two parameters are related to the set spantree priority statement: priority number and vlan.

To manipulate the spanning tree path calculation to the root port, enter the following SET command:

```
  CAT-5000> (enable) set spantree portcost
  Usage: set spantree portcost <mod_num/port_num> <cost>
(cost = 1.65535)
```

Catalyst spanning tree BPDUs are exchanged with Cisco routers and Catalyst 8500s with bridging enabled. Listed below is a show spanning tree from a router configured as a root bridge and a directly connected Catalyst 5000. The Catalyst 5000 is connected to the root bridge over port 3/2. Notice that 3/2 is the root port and that the bridge identifier of router r2 (line two of the show spanning tree display below) is the root port for the Catalyst 5000. Notice that the bridge priority of 100 on router r2 (line two of the show spanning tree display below) is also listed in the show spantree display on the Catalyst 5000.

```
r2#show spanning-tree

Bridge Group 1 is executing the IEEE compatible Spanning Tree protocol
  Bridge Identifier has priority 100, address 0010.7b38.1829
  Configured hello time 2, max age 20, forward delay 15
  We are the root of the spanning tree
  Topology change flag set, detected flag set
  Times:  hold 1, topology change 30, notification 30
          hello 2, max age 20, forward delay 15, aging 300
  Timers: hello 2, topology change 12, notification 0

Port 2 (Ethernet0) of bridge group 1 is forwarding

   Port path cost 100, Port priority 1288
   Designated root has priority 100, address 0010.7b38.1829
   Designated bridge has priority 100, address 0010.7b38.1829
   Designated port is 2, path cost 0
   Timers: message age 0, forward delay 0, hold 0

Port 5 (Serial1)   of bridge group 1 is forwarding
   Port path cost 647, Port priority 1288
   Designated root has priority 100, address 0010.7b38.1829
   Designated bridge has priority 100, address 0010.7b38.1829
   Designated port is 5, path cost 0
```

```
Timers: message age 0, forward delay 0, hold 0
```

```
CAT-5000> (enable) show spantree
VLAN 1
Spanning tree enabled

Designated Root                00-10-7b-38-18-29
Designated Root Priority       100
Designated Root Cost           10
Designated Root Port           3/2
Root Max Age    20 sec     Hello Time 2  sec    Forward Delay 15 sec

Bridge ID MAC ADDR             00-10-79-45-58-00
Bridge ID Priority             500
Bridge Max Age 20 sec      Hello Time 2  sec    Forward Delay 15 sec

Port      Vlan  Port-State     Cost   Priority  Fast-Start
--------  ----  -------------  -----  --------  ----------
 1/1      1     not-connected     10        32   disabled
 1/2      1     not-connected     10        32   disabled
 3/1      1     forwarding        10        32   disabled
 3/2      1     forwarding        10        32   disabled
 3/1      1     forwarding        10        32   disabled
 3/2      1     forwarding        10        32   disabled
 3/3      1     not-connected     10        32   disabled
 3/4      1     not-connected     10        32   disabled
 3/5      1     not-connected     10        32   disabled
```

Configuring Transparent Bridging Over WAN Links on a Cisco Router

For point-to-point serial links on a router participating in bridging, configure serial interfaces just as you would an Ethernet interface. Don't be surprised if you see the following message generated when you assign a bridge-group statement to an interface:

```
Note: A random Spanning Tree Bridge Identifier address of
0000.0c52.37dc has been chosen for Bridge Group 1 since there is
no Mac address associated with the selected interface.
```

This appears when an interface without a MAC address (like a serial interface) is assigned the first bridge-group statement.

Configuring Bridging Over Frame-Relay Links

It is important to use the following command when configuring transparent bridging over a Frame-Relay physical interface or multipoint subinterface:

```
Frame-relay map bridge xxxx broadcast
```

Otherwise, bridging traffic will not be forwarded. To validate this, enable debug frame packet in a lab environment and watch the bridged traffic and the BPDUs get forwarded.

Show Commands for Transparent Bridging

On a Cisco router and Catalyst 8500, you can check the contents of the transparent bridging table with the show bridge command:

```
r2#show bridge

Total of 300 station blocks, 297 free
Codes: P—permanent, S—self

Bridge Group 1:

Address           Action     Interface     Age   RX count    TX count
0800.3e1d.1b42    forward    Ethernet0     0     23          10
0800.170c.a417    forward    DLSw Port0    0     10          13
0020.aff2.8344    forward    DLSw Port0    0     79          10
```

For any system that is sending data through the bridge, you should be able to locate its MAC address in the bridging table.

When the spanning tree changes due to a new root bridge election or a link going down, the bridge tables are not flushed automatically. Therefore, it is possible that traffic will continue to be forwarded to a blocked path. This will continue until either the bridge entries age out or the bridge table is cleared with the "clear bridge" command.

The Catalyst 5000 equivalent to the router and Catalyst 8500 "show bridge" command is "show cam dynamic:"

```
cat1 (enable) sh cam dynamic
VLAN  Dest MAC/Route Des  Destination Ports or VCs
----  ------------------  ------------------------
1     00-80-c7-7a-3d-b8   3/3
1     00-00-86-12-47-68   2/42
1     00-80-c7-38-f0-81   2/45
1     00-80-c7-21-72-d8   2/45
1     00-60-97-90-b0-96   3/7
1     00-80-c7-5a-a3-bd   3/12
```

```
1       00-e0-1e-e4-fe-dd    2/42
1       00-00-86-09-23-ff    3/10
1       00-60-08-23-ca-29    2/42
1       00-60-97-ed-c5-9e    2/45
1       00-60-08-02-fd-0a    3/9
```

Additional Transparent Bridging Commands on a Cisco Router and Catalyst 8500 Switch

Global Configuration

Displayed below are all the optional transparent bridging parameters that can be set in global configuration mode on a Cisco router and a Catalyst 8500 switch:

```
r2(config)#bridge 1 ?
  acquire                  Dynamically learn new, unconfigured stations
  address                  Block or forward a particular Ethernet address
  aging-time               Set forwarding entry aging time
  bridge                   Specify a protocol to be bridged in this bridge group
  circuit-group            Circuit-group
  domain                   Establish multiple bridging domains
  forward-time             Set forwarding delay time
  hello-time               Set interval between HELLOs
  lat-service-filtering    Perform LAT service filtering
  max-age                  Maximum allowed message age of received Hello BPDUs
  multicast-source         Forward datagrams with multicast source addresses
  priority                 Set bridge priority
  protocol                 Specify spanning tree protocol
  route                    Specify a protocol to be routed in this bridge group
```

The only option required from all of the parameters above is the protocol option. This option defines which spanning tree protocol to use for a given bridge group. Another option worth noting is aging time, which sets the age interval of an entire bridge table. If a frame with a source address listed in the bridge table is not received within the age-interval, the bridge will flush the entry.

The bridge and route parameters will be covered in detail in the concurrent routing and bridging and integrated routing and bridging section.

The forward-time, hello-time, max-age and priority parameters are all spanning tree tuning parameters. With the exception of the priority parameter, changes to any of these parameters should be reflected on all bridges and switches in a given bridge-group.

Additional Interface Configuration Commands on a Cisco Router and Catalyst 8500 Switch

When you type the "bridge-group" interface command, only one parameter exits: a bridge group number.

This command is the only transparent bridging interface command:

```
r4(config-if)#bridge-group ?
  <1-63>  Assign an interface to a Bridge Group.
```

However, when you type "bridge-group # ?" (# = bridge-group number), an extensive list of parameters is displayed:

```
r4(config-if)#bridge-group 1 ?
  <cr>
  circuit-group              Associate serial interface with a circuit group
  input-address-list         Filter packets by source address
  input-lat-service-deny     Deny input LAT service advertisements matching a
                             group list
  input-lat-service-permit   Permit input LAT service advertisements matching
                             a group list
  input-lsap-list            Filter incoming IEEE 802.3 encapsulated packets
  input-pattern-list         Filter input with a pattern list
  input-type-list            Filter incoming Ethernet packets by type code
  lat-compression            Enable LAT compression over serial inter faces
  output-address-list        Filter packets by destination address
  output-lat-service-deny    Deny output LAT service advertisements matching a
                             group list
  output-lat-service-permit  Permit output LAT service advertisements matching
                             a group list
  output-lsap-list           Filter outgoing IEEE 802.3 encapsulated packets
  output-pattern-list        Filter output with a pattern list
  output-type-list           Filter outgoing Ethernet packets by type code
  path-cost                  Set interface path cost
  priority                   Set interface priority
  spanning-disabled          Disable spanning tree on a bridge group
```

These parameters are dominated by filtering and spanning tree options. The more commonly used filtering options will be covered in Chapter Twenty-Six.

Concurrent Routing and Bridging

When bridging IP, one configuration method is to disable the routing process entirely on the router. This is an extreme scenario. In this extreme scenario, you are not able to route IP over any interfaces. When using this configuration method, you can bridge only or route only but not both.

The remedies for this undesirable scenario are concurrent routing and bridging and integrated routing and bridging. Concurrent routing and bridging

(CRB) allows you to route and bridge a network layer protocol at the same time on a single router. When CRB is enabled, you can bridge and route the same protocol on a router, but the bridged traffic of a given network layer protocol will never be forwarded to a routed interface of the same network layer protocol. This issue is remedied by integrated routing and bridging (IRB).

Configuring CRB

To enable CRB, you must first configure transparent bridging, as described in the previous sections. In global configuration, enable a bridge group and an associated spanning tree protocol. In interface configuration mode, enable each interface that will belong to a bridge-group.

Once this is done, type the following global configuration command:

```
r1(config)#bridge crb
```

When you enable CRB, all network layer protocols are assumed to be bridged for every interface belonging to a bridge group. However, if you have network layer protocol configurations on interfaces that have also been assigned to a bridge group, you will see console messages like those listed below when you enable CRB:

```
r4(config)#bridge crb
CRB: generating 'bridge 1 route ip' configuration command
CRB: generating 'bridge 1 route novell' configuration command
```

In the example above, an IP and IPX address had been assigned to an Ethernet interface that was also defined to be in a bridge group:

```
interface Ethernet0
  ip address 140.10.1.4 255.255.255.0
  ipx network 17A
  bridge-group 1
```

You can view which network layer protocols are bridged and which are routed over a given interface with the "show interface crb" command:

```
r1#sh inte crb

Ethernet0

   Bridged protocols on Ethernet0:
   appletalk    clns       decnet     ip
   vines        apollo     ipx        xns

Software MAC address filter on Ethernet0
Hash        Len      Address             Matches    Act      Type
0x00:       0        ffff.ffff.ffff      3078       RCV      Physical broadcast
0x24:       0        0900.2b00.000f      0          RCV      LAT multicast
```

```
0x2A:      0      0900.2b01.0001    0         RCV     DEC spanning tree
0x2F:      0      0900.2b02.0104    0         RCV     LAT multicast
0xC0:      0      0100.0ccc.cccc    386       RCV     CDP
0xC2:      0      0180.c200.0000    3527      RCV     IEEE spanning tree
0xDA:      0      00e0.1e68.31c4    0         RCV     Interface MAC address

       Serial0

         Not bridging this sub-interface.

       Serial0.1

         Routed protocols on Serial0.1:
         ip

         Not bridging this sub-interface.

       Serial0.2

         Bridged protocols on Serial0.2:
         appletalk    clns     decnet     ip
         vines        apollo   ipx        xns

Software MAC address filter on Serial0.2
Hash       Len    Address           Matches   Act     Type
0x00:      0      ffff.ffff.ffff    24        RCV     Physical broadcast
0x2A:      0      0900.2b01.0001    0         RCV     DEC spanning tree
0xC0:      0      0100.0ccc.cccc    65        RCV     CDP
0xC2:      0      0180.c200.0000    0         RCV     IEEE spanning tree
0xDA:      0      00e0.1e68.31c4    0         RCV     Interface MAC address
```

When CRB is enabled, all network layer protocols are bridged by default. You can selectively bridge some protocols and route others on a bridged interface. This is performed with the following global configuration command:

```
bridge xxx route protocol
no bridge xxx route protocol
```

Syntax Description

bridge-group

Bridge-group number. It must be the same number specified in the bridge protocol command.

Protocol

One of the following protocols: apollo, appletalk, clns, decnet, ip, ipx, vines, xns.

The default is to bridge all of these protocols.

Interpret these commands in the following manner:

The first bridge bridge-group parameter defines the particular bridge group.

The second parameter, either bridge or route, is always followed by a network layer protocol:

```
r4(config)#bridge 1 bridge ?
  apollo       Apollo Domain
  appletalk    AppleTalk
  clns         ISO CLNS
  decnet       DECnet
  ip           IP
  ipx          Novell IPX
  vines        Banyan VINES
  xns          Xerox Network Services

r4(config)#bridge 1 route ?
  apollo       Apollo Domain
  appletalk    AppleTalk
  clns         ISO CLNS
  decnet       DECnet
  ip           IP
  ipx          Novell IPX
  vines        Banyan VINES
  xns          Xerox Network Services
```

When the two components of the second parameter are taken together ("bridge ip" or "route ip"), you are configuring CRB to manually bridge or route a given protocol for a particular bridge group.

For example, when CRB is enabled, all network layer protocols are bridged by default. This is reflected in the following "show interface crb" display:

```
r4#sh interface crb

Ethernet0

  Bridged protocols on Ethernet0:
  appletalk   clns      decnet    ip
  vines       apollo    ipx       xns
```

The following global configuration command is entered:

```
r4(config)#bridge 1 route ipx
```

When this command is entered, view "show interface crb" again. Notice how IPX has moved from being a bridged protocol to a routed protocol.

```
r4#sh interface crb

       Routed protocols on Ethernet0:
```

```
    ipx

Bridged protocols on Ethernet0:
appletalk     clns      decnet    ip
vines         apollo    xns
```

Integrated Routing and Bridging

CRB allows a router to both bridge and route traffic for a given network layer protocol at the same time. However, CRB does not allow bridged traffic of a network layer protocol to be forwarded over to a routed interface and vice-versa. Integrated routing and bridging (IRB) overcomes this limitation. IRB makes it possible to take packets from a routed interface and bridge them across another interface in the same router, and take packets from a bridged interface and route them across another interface within the same router.

This can be a useful feature on the Catalyst 8500. For example, if you want to directly connect a number of servers into the Catalyst 8500 and define this server group as one subnet or VLAN, use the bridging commands already presented in this chapter to place all the servers in the same subnet. After the bridge group is defined, use IRB to route between this bridge-group and the other routed interfaces on the Catalyst 8500. Using IRB on the Catalyst 8500 gives you the best of both worlds:

1. Wire speed layer three forwarding of IP and IPX traffic
2. The functionality of VLANs

You can configure the Cisco IOS software to route a specific protocol between routed interfaces and bridge groups, or to route a specific protocol between bridge groups.

Using integrated routing and bridging, you can:

- Switch packets from a bridged interface to a routed interface
- Switch packets from a routed interface to a bridged interface
- Switch packets within the same bridge group

This functionality of integrated routing and bridging is made possible through the use of a Bridge Group Virtual Interface (BVI). The BVI is a logical routed interface that does not support bridging. You will never configure any bridging parameters on the BVI. The BVI will borrow a MAC address from one of the bridged interfaces in the bridge group associated with the BVI, and you will assign any necessary routed protocol addressing for routing across the BVI. The BVI is associated with a bridge group by configuring the BVI interface with the same number that corresponds to the configured bridge group. For example, if you define the bridge group with the statement "Bridge 1 protocol ieee," you have created a bridge group 1. Therefore, the BVI for bridge-group 1 must also be identified by the number 1.

Once the BVI is configured, any packets that must be routed from the bridge group will be sent to the BVI. The BVI will then forward the packets to the appropriate outbound routed interface. This can be witnessed with debug tools such as debug ip packet or debug ipx packet.

```
IPX:  BV1:17A.00e0.1eb9.29fa  ->17A.ffff.ffff.ffff ln= 40 tc=00 pt=01 ds=0453
ss=04 53, rcvd
IPX:  BV1:1717.0000.0c34.794b ->1717.0000.0c46.ebd0 ln= 48 tc=00 pt=01 ds=0453
ss=0453, rcvd
```

Configuring IRB

Integrated routing and bridging is an extension of transparent bridging. Therefore, to configure IRB, you must also perform a basic transparent bridging configuration. The minimum configuration steps for integrated routing and bridging are:

1. Assign a bridge group number and define the spanning tree protocol (standard transparent bridging).

- Configure interfaces (standard transparent bridging).
- Enable integrated routing and bridging.
- Configure the bridge-group virtual interface
- Configure protocols for routing or bridging with the bridge x route yy, no bridge x route yy, etc. (x = bridge-group number; yy= specific protocol).

Sample commands to configure IRB:

```
r2(config)#bridge 1 protocol ieee
r2(config)#int e0
r2(config-if)#bridge-group 1
r2(config)#bridge irb
r2(config)#interface BVI1
r2(config)#bridge 1 bridge ipx
```

By default, IRB bridges all protocols. Therefore, "bridge # route protocol" must be used to assure that bridged protocols are routed through the BVI to other routed interfaces.

If you are doing nothing but bridging for a given protocol, do not configure the BVI interface for the protocol. If you are performing routing for a given protocol and want to route packets over interfaces defined to be part of a bridge-group, use the "no bridge # bridge protocol" statement.

Listed below are IRB configuration options. They are used to specify what protocols will be bridged and what protocols will be routed on interfaces configured in a given bridge group.

```
r1(config)#bridge 1 bridge ?
```

```
  apollo              Apollo Domain
  appletalk           AppleTalk
  clns                ISO CLNS
  decnet              DECnet
  ip                  IP
  ipx                 Novell IPX
  vines               Banyan VINES
  xns                 Xerox Network Services

r1(config)#bridge 1 route ?
  apollo              Apollo Domain
  appletalk           AppleTalk
  clns                ISO CLNS
  decnet              DECnet
  ip                  IP
  ipx                 Novell IPX
  vines               Banyan VINES
  xns                 Xerox Network Services
```

You should be familiar with the four configuration combinations displayed below (xxx = bridge-group number):

```
Bridge XXX route protocol
No bridge XXX route protocol
Bridge XXX bridge protocol
No bridge XXX bridge protocol
```

Integrated Routing and Bridging Show Commands

You can view the status of the BVI interface with following show command:

```
r2#show interfaces bvi 1
BVI1 is up, line protocol is up
  Hardware is BVI, address is 0000.0c3d.d988 (bia 0000.0000.0000)
  Internet address is 172.16.3.2/24
  MTU 1500 bytes, BW 10000 Kbit, DLY 5000 usec, rely 255/255, load 1/255
  Encapsulation ARPA, loopback not set, keepalive set (10 sec)
  ARP type: ARPA, ARP Timeout 04:00:00
```

Compare the MAC address used by the BVI interface above with the MAC address of the Ethernet interface displayed below:

```
Ethernet0 is up, line protocol is up
  Hardware is Lance, address is 0000.0c3d.d988 (bia 0000.0c3d.d988)
  Hardware is Lance, address is 0000.0c3d.d988 (bia 0000.0c3d.d988)
  MTU 1500 bytes, BW 10000 Kbit, DLY 1000 usec, rely 255/255, load 1/255
  Encapsulation ARPA, loopback not set, keepalive set (10 sec)
  ARP type: ARPA, ARP Timeout 04:00:00
```

Note: BVI uses the MAC address of one of the bridged interfaces in the bridge group.

You can view what protocols will be bridged and what protocols will be routed on a per interface basis with the following show command:

```
r2#show interfaces irb

BVI1

 Routed protocols on BVI1:
 ip                 ipx

Ethernet0

Routed protocols on Ethernet0:
ip

   Bridged protocols on Ethernet0:
   appletalk    clns       decnet      ip
   vines      apollo       ipx        xns

Software MAC address filter on Ethernet0
Hash     Len  Address           Matches   Act      Type
0x00:    0    ffff.ffff.ffff    49        RCV      Physical broadcast
0x2A:    0    0900.2b01.0001    0         RCV      DEC spanning tree
0x84:    0    0000.0c3d.d988    138       RCV      Interface MAC address
0x84:    1    0000.0c3d.d988    0         RCV      Bridge-group Virtual Interface
0xC2:    0    0180.c200.0000    1869      RCV      IEEE spanning tree

Serial0

  Routed protocols on Serial0:
Ip
```

Notice how ip appears under both routed protocols for Ethernet 0 and bridged protocols for the same interface Ethernet 0. For concurrent bridging, a given protocol will appear under one listing (routed protocols or bridged protocols), but not both.

If a network layer protocol is configured on an interface that is defined in a bridge-group, a console message will be generated as soon as the global configuration command "bridge irb" is entered.

A Word About LAT

A Cisco solution for transporting LAT over an internetwork is not limited to bridging alone. With LAT, a Cisco router will translate LAT traffic into TCP/IP terminal traffic: TELNET. In order to translate LAT traffic, perform the following steps:

Translating LAT into TCP

Enter the following interface configuration command:

```
LAT enable (With IOS version 11.2, LAT is enabled by default.)
```

Enter the following commands in global configuration mode:

```
Translate lat XXX tcp A.B.C.D
XXX = the target LAT host name
A.B.C.D = the target IP address to begin a TELNET session at or
to perform a translation from TCP back to LAT.
```

If all you want to do is support an end system that initiates a LAT session that needs to be translated into a TELNET session, you need only to configure the two commands listed above. If you are running 11.2 and higher, you need only to configure the translate command. The options for the translate command are displayed below:

```
r5(config)#translate ?
  A.B.C.D   IP address
  lat       DEC LAT protocol
  tcp       TCP/IP Telnet
  x25       X.25
```

Once these commands are entered, all the LAT speaking end user will need to do is type "LAT XXX" and a TELNET session will transparently open for him/her the specified device with the IP address listed in the translate statement.

You can monitor your LAT to TCP translation activity with the "show translate" command. You can debug your LAT to TCP translation activity with the "debug translate" command. Listed below is a sample show translate display:

```
r5#sh translate

Translate From: TCP 150.100.4.5 Port 23
          To:   LAT ALR
          0/0 users active, 1 peak, 3 total, 0 failures

Translate From: LAT R1
          To:   TCP 150.100.1.1 Port 23
          1/0 users active, 1 peak, 3 total, 0 failures
```

Summary

You now have an overview of non-routable protocols and solutions. You know how to configure transparent bridging, CRB, IRB and LAT. With transparent bridging, you can configure a Cisco router, a Catalyst 8500 and a Catalyst 5000. You can also tune spanning tree parameters on these platforms.

Professional Development Checklist

After reading this chapter, you should be able to perform the following operations:

- Perform transparent bridging.
- Assign a bridge group number and define the spanning-tree protocol.
- Assign each network interface to a bridge group.
- Configure spanning tree parameters.
- Concurrent routing and bridging.
- Integrated routing and bridging.
- Assign a bridge group number and define the spanning-tree protocol.
- Configure interfaces.
- Enable integrated routing and bridging.
- Configure the bridge-group virtual interface.
- Configure protocols for routing or bridging.

For Further Study

- Perlman, Radia. *Interconnections: Bridges and Routers*, Addison Wesley, 1992. ISBN: 0201563320.

URLs

- **www.cciecert.com**
- **www.cisco.com/univercd/home/home.htm**
- **www.mentorlabs.com**

Can You Spot the Issues?

Based on the following configurations can you spot the issues?

Bridge R2:

```
hostname r2

!
enable password cisco
!
ipx routing 0000.0c3d.d988
!
interface Ethernet0
  no ip address
  bridge-group 11
!
interface Serial0
  ip address 172.16.1.2 255.255.255.0
!
interface Serial1
  no ip address
  shutdown
!
interface BVI1
   ip address 172.16.3.2 255.255.255.0
   ipx network 22
   bridge-group 1
!
router igrp 100
   network 172.16.0.0
```

```
!
no ip classless
!
bridge irb
bridge 1 protocol ieee
   bridge 1 route ipx
!
line con 0
line aux 0
line vty 0 4
   password cisco
   login
!
end
```

Bridge R1:

```
hostname r1
!
enable password cisco
!
ipx routing 0000.0c3d.d988
!
interface Ethernet0
    no ip address
    bridge-group 1
!
interface Serial0
    ip address 172.16.1.1 255.255.255.0
!
interface Serial1
    no ip address
    shutdown
!
interface BVI1
    ip address 172.16.3.1 255.255.255.0
    ipx network 22
!
router igrp 100
    network 172.16.0.0
!
no ip classless
!
bridge irb
bridge 1 protocol dec
  bridge 1 route ip
  bridge 1 route ipx
!
line con 0
line aux 0
```

```
line vty 0 4
  password cisco
  login
!
end
```

TWENTY ONE

Configuring Source-Route Bridging and DLSw+

Topics Covered in This Chapter

- DLSw Technology Overview
- Configure Source-Route Bridging
- Configure DLSw+ for a Token-Ring to Token-Ring Connection Using TCP
- Configure DLSw+ for a Token-Ring to Token-Ring Connection
- Configure DLSw+ for a Token-Ring to Ethernet Connection Using TCP
- Configure DLSw+ for an Ethernet-to-Ethernet Connection Using TCP
- Configure DLSw+ Using Border Peers with Peer-on-Demand Defaults
- DLSw+ Checklist

This chapter addresses technical issues involved with configuring, maintaining and troubleshooting source route bridging and Data Link Switching Plus (DLSw+). Although the two topics are closely related and are often configured together, DLSw+ encompasses much more than only an extension to source-route bridging. Cisco's DLSw+ is an enhancement to open standards-based Data Link Switching (DLSw). As stated in RFC 1795, the primary design objective of DLSw is to provide a TCP/IP tunnel for SNA and NetBIOS traffic transported in Logical Link Control Two (LLC2) packets ("To make the corporate network appear as one big LLC2 LAN.") With SNA, much of this traffic originates and terminates at the host in Token-Ring frames. Therefore, DLSw is used to take SNA branch office traffic, transport it over a company's IP backbone, and deliver it to the Token-Ring based mainframe Data Center. By providing this solution, DLSw allows companies to abandon dedicated SNA networks and ultimately reduce the number of WAN circuits they need to order for branch-to-data center connectivity.

A common misconception about DLSw concerns its relationship with source-route bridging. Even though DLSw is commonly used to link two source-route bridged networks over an IP backbone, it is not a pure extension of source-route bridging. In fact, a DLSw session terminates both source-route bridge RIFs and LLC2 sessions at both ends of the DLSw connection. A DLSw peer will also terminate LLC2 traffic that traverses directly connected Ethernet, FDDI, X.25 and SDLC networks. Therefore, to state that DLSw is merely an extension to source-route bridging is incorrect.

To learn more about DLSw, read RFC 1795 (**www.fressoft.org**) cover to cover. It is an easy to read RFC. It provides a deep insight into the internals of DLSw.

Cisco's DLSw+ provides all the functionality of DLSw and more. Enhancements that DLSw+ possesses beyond DLSw are:

1. **Multiple Encapsulation Types.** DLSw specifies a single encapsulation type: TCP/IP. DLSw+ offers four encapsulation types: TCP/IP; FST/IP; Direct encapsulation for point-to-point connections; and straight LLC2 encapsulation for Frame-Relay connections (DLSw+ Lite). Non-TCP encapsulation types can be used for greater DLSw+ connection performance.
2. **Reachability Caching.** Although the DLSw specification mentions the use of reachability caching, it does not stress that it is required. A Cisco DLSw+ peer maintains both a local and remote reachability cache. By maintaining these caches, DLSw+ peers can respond to explorer traffic locally and reduce the amount of explorer traffic on the IP backbone.
3. **Border-Peer Groups and On-Demand Peers.** If all DLSw peers need to communicate with each other, DLSw requires a direct connection between all peers. Therefore, in order to maintain any-to-any connectivity, multiple DLSw peers must be fully meshed. This requirement causes problems with scaling DLSw networks. Cisco's DLSw+ border peer and on-demand peer features provide a solution to this limitation of DLSw. A DLSw+ border peer maintains a peering relationship with multiple downstream clients, creating a hub and spoke relationship with border peer clients. When a border peer client needs to establish a connection with another client, it forwards explorer traffic to the border peer. The border peer processes the explorer request. Once the border-peer client has the destination address of the other client, it can establish a direct "on-demand" connection. By doing so, the need to maintain a full mesh for any-to-any connectivity is eliminated.
4. **Backwards Compatibility with Remote Source Route Bridging.** DLSw+ is backwards compatible with RSRB. This feature provides a clear migration path from RSRB to DLSw+.

Other DLSw+ features include enhanced redundancy and load-balancing. More in-depth coverage of these features will be supplied later in the chapter.

DLSw+ combines many older Cisco IOS "tunneling SNA over IP" services. For example, both RSRB and SDLLC (older IOS "tunneling SNA over IP" solutions) are now performed by DLSw+ alone. DLSw+ is a key technology in Cisco's end-to-end SNA-based Data Center solution. Before getting into the technical configuration and implementation issues of DLSw+ , a review of Cisco's SNA/Data Center solutions will be provided, along with a brief overview of common technical developments that have occurred in many Data Centers that make DLSw+ so attractive .

Technical coverage of SNA-based Data Center issues is a vast topic. This Chapter will only provide a brief sketch of SNA connectivity issues. Essentially, the goal of DLSw+ is to do away with a separate corporate SNA network. DLSw+ takes SNA traffic and tunnels it through the IP corporate internetwork into the SNA Data Center. Once the data is delivered to the Data Center, the SNA network specialists assure that the traffic gets delivered to the correct mainframe.

Although transporting SNA traffic over Token-Ring networks and DLSw+ connections will be the primary topic of this Chapter, coverage of transporting NetBIOS over the same types of connections will also be provided. DLSw+ connectivity is useful for transporting pure NetBIOS traffic because NetBIOS is a non-routable protocol. NetBIOS was an important technology to OS/2 and IBM LAN Server in the late 80s and early 90s. Today, NetBIOS is still important to these platforms, but it is also important to Windows 95, 98 and NT.

The Cisco End-to-End Data Center Solution

Cisco provides traditional SNA customers with an end-to-end mainframe solution that includes options such as placing a version on the IOS on the mainframe itself, all the way down to providing Web access to the mainframe. Code named "CiscoBlue", Cisco's SNA (or "Data Center") solutions are based on two themes:

1. Combining SNA networks with corporate multiprotocol internetworks
2. Providing end-to-end TCP/IP access to mainframe resources

Four key components of Cisco's end-to-end SNA solution are:

- Cisco IOS for S/390
- Cisco Channel Interface Processor
- Cisco APPN/HPR support
- Tunneling SNA traffic over IP internetworks (STUN, RSRB and DLSw+)

1. Cisco IOS for S/390

The Cisco IOS for S/390 places a TCP/IP stack and TCP/IP services directly on the mainframe. With Cisco IOS for S/390 on the mainframe, end users can connect to the mainframe via a 3270 telnet session without using SNA at all! Forget SNA integration with a multiprotocol corporate internetwork. Place Cisco IOS for S/390 on the mainframe and dispose of SNA altogether. Cisco IOS for S/390 was jointly developed with Interlink Computer Sciences, (**www.interlink.com**) and is compatible with IBM's MVS and OS/390 UNIX System Services (formerly OpenEdition). Both MVS and OS/390 are strategic IBM mainframe operating system environments, which assure that the mainframe can become integrated into large-scale Internet and intranet environments. To learn more about the TCP/IP features and Internet support features of OS/390 and MVS, visit the IBM Web site (**www.ibm.com**).

2. Cisco Channel Interface Processor Family (CIP)

By placing a Cisco Channel Interface Processor into a Cisco 7500 router or a Channel Port Adapter (CPA) in a Cisco 7200 router, Cisco has a direct "channel attached" connection to an IBM mainframe. With a Channel Interface Processor, a 7500 router can become a Front End Processor Replacement. It must be stressed that a Cisco router with a CIP card installed is not an SNA Physical Unit Type 4, but rather a Front End Processor replacement. It is beyond the scope of this book to explain the difference between the two, but it is an important distinction. Instead of terminating TN3270 sessions on the mainframe, sessions can be terminated on a CIP or CPA.

A whole career can be made configuring, maintaining and troubleshooting a Channel Interface Processor. The Cisco Web site (**www.cisco.com**)has extensive documentation on the Channel Interface Processor. To learn more about mainframe channel attached technologies, access the IBM web site.

3. Cisco APPN/HPR Support

Advanced peer-to-peer networking (APPN) and high performance routing (HPR) were developed by IBM to provide dynamic and distributed routing in an SNA environment. In a traditional SNA environment, all traffic flowed to a limited number of SNA host devices in one or two data centers. With APPN and HPR, dynamic routing of SNA traffic can be performed between widely dispersed hosts known as "network nodes" in APPN/HPR terminology. To accommodate delay-sensitive SNA traffic, APPN and HPR use Class of Service for path determination. The Cisco IOS fully supports APPN and HPR. To learn more about APPN and HPR, see the IBM and Cisco Web sites.

4. Tunneling SNA Traffic Over IP Internetworks (STUN, RSRB and DLSw+)

While IBM developed APPN and HPR to provide dynamic and distributed routing in an SNA environment, it also developed Data Link Switching (DLSw) as a method of transportating SNA/LLC2-based traffic over an IP backbone.

Both DLSw and LLC2 are strategic technologies. LLC2 provides connection-oriented services for both SNA and NetBIOS traffic, and can be transported by Token-Ring and Frame-Relay. Like SNA, LLC2 is sensitive to delay and is vulnerable to timing out over temporarily-congested WAN links. DLSw was developed to locally terminate LLC2 sessions at the DLSw peer (usually a router). Data Link Switching is defined in RFC 1795 as being the technology that allows an organization's enterprise network to appear as "one big LLC2 LAN." Therefore, both LLC2 and DLSw work hand-in-hand. LLC2 provides a mechanism to transport SNA traffic over a Token-Ring LAN. DLSw provides a highly scalable mechanism to transport LLC2 traffic over an enterprise IP backbone.

Cisco announced Data Link Switching Plus (DLSw+) as a fully compliant superset to the RFC-based DLSw. Prior to DLSw+, Cisco offered other technologies that encapsulated SNA traffic into IP. Cisco's Serial Tunneling (STUN) transported SDLC traffic over an IP cloud, and Remote Source Route Bridging (RSRB) transported SNA traffic in Token-Ring frames over an IP cloud.

This concludes the overview of Cisco's end-to-end IBM Data Center solutions strategy. The remainder of this chapter is dedicated to taking a closer look at source-route bridging and DLSw+. We will see why DLSw+ is a strategic component of the Cisco Data Center end-to-end solution. To find out more about Cisco IOS/390, CIP card configuration and Cisco support for APPN/HPR, access the Cisco Web site. In order to set the stage for DLSw+, the following section provides a technical background for implementing DLSw+.

Recent Technical Developments that Make DLSw+ Attractive

SNA Is Everywhere

Since the invention of the computer, IBM has been the dominant mainframe systems supplier. For the past several years, many computer pundits have been predicting the decline of mainframe use. But the mainframe is alive and well, and will be for a long time to come. When communicating with a mainframe, the traditional protocol suite used is SNA. To this day, SNA is all around us. It transports traffic from bank ATM machines, point of sale terminals, credit card processing devices, airport reservation terminals and supermarket cash registers to data centers containing clusters of IBM mainframes.

When examining large SNA networks, the majority of the network is WAN based. Traditionally, SNA connections originate from a 56K Line Interface Coupler (LIC) inside a Front End Processor. From the LIC, SNA connections travel over dedicated WAN circuits, which are distributed by multidrop technology. Finally, the SNA connection is terminated at an SNA cluster controller at a branch office or to a modem attached to an ATM machine. At the heart of the SNA network is a WAN cloud. If the WAN connection between a branch office and the data center goes down, all SNA terminals at the branch are "temporarily out of service." Prior to technologies such as X.25 and Frame-Relay, large SNA networks required a number of dedicated circuits. Even though X.25 and Frame-Relay have reduced the number of physical dedicated circuits used by SNA networks, the SNA network is still a completely separate network from the LAN-based multiprotocol corporate internetwork.

IP, the Internet and Intranets Are Everywhere

The Internet has become ubiquitous. It is no longer used to merely browse Web sites. People are purchasing items, checking their bank accounts and paying student loans on the Internet. Much of this information resides on an IBM mainframe computer. While pure SNA is the traditional method of accessing the mainframe, IP access to the mainframe is an alternative that is growing in popularity. Traditional IBM mainframe customers once had a single SNA data connection between each branch office and the corporate Data Center. Since Internet connectivity is so important, many of these branch offices now have a second IP connection to the Internet. With two connections to branch offices, many MIS directors are evaluating whether the two connections can be combined into a single connection. Even though a single combined connection would reduce direct costs, MIS directors are concerned about the compromise in SNA security and the ability to maintain consistent SNA performance when combining the two connections.

WINTEL Is Everywhere

Since the mid-80s, PCs and PC networking has been exploding. No corporation can operate without its private LANs and Internet access. The same large corporations that use mainframes also have extensive LAN internetworks. The dominant client platform in the corporate LAN environment is a Microsoft Operating System (Windows 95, Windows 98 and NT) with an Intel processor. From a server perspective, the dominant platforms are NT, UNIX and NetWare. In the past, mainframe networks and data networks were separate. Merging the two networks would have a greater impact on mainframe traffic than on LAN traffic. Also, mainframe traffic normally supports mission critical services and is delay sensitive. Mainframe traffic is primarily terminal-based. An end user at a terminal enters approximately 100 bytes of keyboard input and receives a screen full of characters consisting of approximately 2000 bytes. The majority of LAN traffic is file transfer-based. Applications and user files are downloaded from a file server (NT, UNIX, NetWare) to the memory of a client workstation. Such traffic creates "packet trains" that can starve out delay-sensitive mainframe terminal sessions for bandwidth. Eventually, mixing mainframe and LAN traffic became problematic, especially since mainframe traffic is mission critical to the entire organization.

The Token-Ring Solution

Token-Ring was, and still is, a strategic technological LAN solution for IBM. Unlike Ethernet, Token-Ring is a deterministic LAN protocol with configuration and management features that allow a LAN to better support delay-sensitive mainframe services and file transfer-oriented LAN services concurrently. IBM provided Token-Ring solutions from the mainframe Front End Processor all the way to the desktop. Mid-range computers like the AS-400 can be directly attached to a Token-Ring LAN. Many large IBM mainframe customers implemented the IBM Token-Ring end-to-end solution. Token-Ring Interface Couplers (TICs) were installed in IBM Front End Processors (FEP). A TIC card supplied 16 million bits of bandwidth—a staggering increase of bandwidth in comparison to the TIC's predecessor, the Line Interface Coupler (LIC), which has a maximum bandwidth of 56Kbps per port. For many large IBM mainframe customers, Token-Ring was installed throughout the corporate network: in the data center and in the corporate LANs.

As large deployments of Token-Ring were being planned and performed, Source-Route Bridging became an extremely important topic. Large Source-Route Bridged networks needed to be deployed that provided both redundancy and a high level of performance.

Another major issue was interconnecting Token-Ring networks over the WAN. Since the early 90s, a popular solution has been interconnecting Token-Ring networks over Frame-Relay networks using LLC2 encapsulation end-to-end.

From a technical perspective, Token-Ring seemed to have a bright future; however, it never gained the broad popularity of 10BASET Ethernet. Since Ethernet was less expensive and easier to install and maintain, it surged ahead of Token-Ring in deployment. Today, Ethernet switching has made Ethernet more popular. However, Token-Ring is still broadly deployed in large IBM mainframe sites, especially in the data centers.

The Cisco End-to-End SNA/Data Center Solution

Cisco is the industry leader in merging SNA networks with LAN-based multiprotocol internetworks. Virtually every office with SNA traffic also has requirements for corporate LAN interconnectivity and Internet connectivity. Instead of maintaining two separate networks—one for SNA traffic and another for all other data traffic—Cisco developed a number of solutions to combine the two. At the heart of all the Cisco solutions is the "tunneling SNA traffic over and IP backbone" technique. A few of the most prominent Cisco "tunneling SNA traffic over an IP backbone" solutions are:

SERIAL TUNNELING (STUN)

STUN transports SDLC traffic over an IP cloud. If the FEP has Line Interface Couplers, and the cluster controllers in the branch offices accept SDLC traffic,

STUN will connect the data center to the regional offices. This will be performed over the same WAN connection providing corporate inter-LAN and Internet connectivity. If the traffic is purely SDLC traffic end-to-end, STUN is a viable solution.

REMOTE SOURCE ROUTE BRIDGING (RSRB)

RSRB transports LLC2/Token-Ring traffic over an IP cloud. If the FEP has a Token-Ring Interface Coupler (TIC), and Token-Ring devices in the branch offices, RSRB will connect the data center to the regional offices over an IP WAN backbone. Again, this will be performed over the same WAN connection providing corporate inter-LAN and Internet connectivity. Essentially, RSRB provides a form of encapsulated bridging over an IP backbone. When source-route bridged frames are transmitted over an RSRB IP tunnel, the original RIF remains.

When RSRB was announced, IBM had nothing comparable to it. IBM's WAN solution to RSRB was a device known as a "half-bridge" that performed data link layer encapsulated bridging.

DATA LINK SWITCHING PLUS (DLSW+)

IBM's response to Cisco's RSRB was the development of Data Link Switching (DLSw). Data Link Switching is RFC-based (RFC 1795) and contains enhancements that go beyond RSRB. Cisco's latest innovation in providing SNA connectivity over an IP backbone is DLSw+ (first introduced in IOS version 10.3(2)). DLSw+ is a superset of both RSRB and DLSw. It is fully backward compatible with both. Before Cisco's DLSW+ is examined, a strong foundational understanding of DLSw must be attained, as well as an understanding of the following bridging technologies:

- source-route bridging
- transparent bridging
- source-route transparent bridging
- source-route translational bridging

This chapter focuses on interconnecting the following types of data-link segments with each other over an IP cloud using DLSw+:

- Token-Ring to Token-Ring
- Token-Ring to Ethernet
- Ethernet to Ethernet
- Token-Ring to SDLC

Queuing

When tunneling SNA traffic over an IP backbone, bandwidth is always an issue for SNA traffic. SNA does not need a lot of bandwidth, but what it does need must always be there. Cisco provides a range of queuing technologies to assure that, if congestion occurs on a WAN link, specified traffic (such as SNA traffic) will have priority. Queuing is covered in Chapter Twenty-Eight.

In the following sections, source-route bridging topics will be covered first, followed by a technical overview of DLSw and DLSw+. Coverage of transparent bridging is supplied in Chapter Twenty. Coverage of transparent bridging in this Chapter will be limited to how it relates to DLSw+. The next section provides a configuration overview of source-route bridging.

Source-Route Bridging

Source-route bridging applies the same deterministic principles to inter-ring bridging as Token-Ring applies to LAN access. Unlike transparent bridging, which is applied to both Ethernet and Token-Ring LANs, source-route bridging is applied exclusively to Token-Ring networks. An end system participating in a source-route bridged network must learn the complete path to its destination before sending any data. Therefore, an end system participating in the source-route bridge process is a primary participant in the bridging process. In comparison, an end system connected to a transparent bridged network has no idea that its data is forwarded by a transparent bridge. The entire bridging process is "transparent" to the end system.

Another significant difference between source-route bridging and transparent bridging is that the transparent bridge builds and maintains a bridge table and switches frames based upon the contents of the bridge table. If a broadcast or unknown frame address is encountered by the transparent bridge, it floods it out all ports except the port through which the frame originally entered the bridge. With a baseline implementation of source-route bridging, no bridge table is built. The source-route-bridge examines the first byte of the Token-Ring source address. If the value is zero, the bridge does not attempt to forward the frame. If the value is one, the bridge examines the routing information field of the Token-Ring frame. It locates the token-ring number on which the frame entered into the bridge, as well as the bridge's own bridge number. Once these two elements of information are located, the bridge locates the next ring upon which the frame should be forwarded, and forwards the frame accordingly. Therefore, the source-route bridge does not make a switching decision based upon information it has accumulated in its own bridge table. Rather, the decision is based upon the contents of each data packet's routing information (RIF) field.

A benefit of source-route bridging over transparent bridging is that it is inherently loop-free. There is no need for a spanning tree algorithm to assure that suboptimal looped paths are in a blocking state. Source-route bridging can use the spanning tree algorithm to limit the amount of explorer traffic.

The RIF is constructed by the end system that generates explorer frames. With source-route bridging, the source end system knows what destination it wants to reach; it just does not know how to get there. It uses explorer frames to locate the destination end system. Three types of explorer frames exist:

- Local explorer
- All routes explorer
- Spanning tree explorer

When a source-route bridge receives an all routes explorer, it appends its source-route information in the RIF and floods the explorer out all outbound ports. Without spanning tree enabled for explorer traffic, replicas of the original explore frame will traverse all rings in the source-route bridge network. Most of the explorer frames will expire, since they will never locate the target end system. Those that do will be returned to the source end system.

Once explorer frames return to the source end system, the RIF offering the best path to the destination is used in every data packet sent to the specific destination. The IBM Token-Ring implementation specifies a maximum of eight rings and seven bridges within a single RIF. The IEEE 802.1d implementation specifies a maximum of 14 rings and 13 bridges in a single RIF. Therefore, if the IBM implementation of source-route bridging is used, the source-route bridge network can have a maximum diameter of eight rings. If the IEEE 802.1d implementation is used, the network diameter is 14 rings.

Configuring Source-Route Bridging on a Two-Port Bridge

Originally, standard source-route bridges had only two ports. To make a Cisco router a two-port source-route bridge, enter the following commands in interface configuration mode:

```
interface TokenRing0
 no ip address
 ring-speed 16
 source-bridge 10 1 20
!
interface TokenRing1
 no ip address
 ring-speed 16
 source-bridge 20 1 10
```

When you add the source-route bridge interface configuration command, it reinitializes the Token-Ring interface. While the interface is being reinitialized, the router console is frozen for a few seconds. All bridge ports connected to the same ring must use the same ring number, and all ring numbers within a source-route bridged network must be unique. After you have configured source-route bridging, use the show source and show interface token X (X = interface number) to monitor source-route bridging performance. A sample show source and show interface token command is displayed below:

```
r1#show source

Local Interfaces:                                receive      transmit
             srn bn  trn r p s n  max hops        cnt           cnt          drops
To0           10  1   20    * b    7  7  7         11            0             0
To1           20  1   10    * b    7  7  7          0            0             0

Remote Source Route Bridging not enabled.

Explorers: ------- input -------             ------- output -------
         spanning  all-rings     total       spanning  all-rings      total
To0             0          0         0              0          0          0
To1             0          0         0              0          0          0

  Local: fastswitched 0        flushed 0          max Bps 38400

         rings       inputs          bursts          throttles     output drops
           To0            0               0                  0                0
           To1            0               0                  0                0

r1#show interfaces TO0
TokenRing0 is up, line protocol is up
  Hardware is TMS380, address is 0006.c1de.e548 (bia 0006.c1de.e548)
  MTU 4464 bytes, BW 16000 Kbit, DLY 630 usec, rely 255/255, load 1/255
  Encapsulation SNAP, loopback not set, keepalive set (10 sec)
  ARP type: SNAP, ARP Timeout 04:00:00
  Ring speed: 16 Mbps
  Single ring node, Source Route Transparent Bridge capable
  Source bridging enabled, srn 10 bn 1 trn 20
    proxy explorers disabled, spanning explorer disabled, NetBIOS cache disabled
  Group Address: 0x00000000, Functional Address: 0x0800011A
  Ethernet Transit OUI: 0x000000
  Last input 00:00:00, output 00:00:01, output hang never
  Last clearing of "show interface" counters never
  Queueing strategy: fifo
  Output queue 0/40, 0 drops; input queue 0/75, 0 drops
  5 minute input rate 0 bits/sec, 0 packets/sec
  5 minute output rate 0 bits/sec, 0 packets/sec
     559 packets input, 19785 bytes, 0 no buffer
     Received 448 broadcasts, 0 runts, 0 giants, 0 throttles
     0 input errors, 0 CRC, 0 frame, 0 overrun, 0 ignored, 0 abort
```

```
135 packets output, 10068 bytes, 0 underruns
0 output errors, 0 collisions, 1 interface resets
0 output buffer failures, 0 output buffers swapped out
3 transitions
```

Configuring Source-Route Bridging on a Multiport Bridge

To configure a multiport source-route bridge (a source-route bridge with more than the standard two ports), a virtual ring must be created. All locally-connected Token-Ring interfaces will forward non-local traffic to the virtual ring, which will then forward the traffic to the correct outbound ring. Assume a source-route bridge with three Token-Ring interfaces attached to rings 100, 200 and 300.

If traffic from ring 100 must be forwarded to ring 200, the traffic is forwarded to virtual-ring 1000 first and then to ring 200. Notice how this forwarding sequence is reflected in a multiport bridge configuration script:

```
source-bridge ring-group 1000
!
interface TokenRing0
 no ip address
 ring-speed 16
 source-bridge 100 1 1000
!
interface TokenRing1
 no ip address
 ring-speed 16
 source-bridge 200 1 1000
           !
interface TokenRing1
 no ip address
 ring-speed 16
 source-bridge 300 1 1000
```

When a virtual ring is added, notice how the show source and show interface token displays change. Show interface token now has a "ring group" listing on its source-route bridging configuration line:

```
r1#show interfaces to0
TokenRing0 is up, line protocol is up
  Hardware is TMS380, address is 0006.c1de.e548 (bia 0006.c1de.e548)
  MTU 4464 bytes, BW 16000 Kbit, DLY 630 usec, rely 255/255, load 1/255
  Encapsulation SNAP, loopback not set, keepalive set (10 sec)
  ARP type: SNAP, ARP Timeout 04:00:00
  Ring speed: 16 Mbps
  Single ring node, Source Route Transparent Bridge capable
    Source bridging enabled, srn 10 bn 1 trn 1000 (ring group)
```

Show source now has a section dedicated to virtual ring statistics:

```
r1#show source

Local Interfaces:                                 receive     transmit
             srn bn  trn r p s n  max hops         cnt          cnt          drops
             srn bn  trn r p s n  max hops         cnt          cnt          drops
To1           20  1 1000 * * b    7  7  7           0            0            0

Global RSRB Parameters:
 TCP Queue Length maximum: 100

Ring Group 1000:
  No TCP peername set, TCP transport disabled
   Maximum output TCP queue length, per peer: 100
  Rings:
   bn: 1  rn: 10   local  ma: 4006.c1de.e548 TokenRing0                fwd: 0
   bn: 1  rn: 20   local  ma: 4006.c1de.e5a8 TokenRing1                fwd: 0

Explorers: ------- input -------              ------- output -------
         spanning  all-rings      total      spanning  all-rings      total
To0             0          0          0             0          0          0
To1             0          0          0             0          0          0

  Local: fastswitched 0          flushed 0          max Bps 38400

         rings       inputs          bursts          throttles      output drops
           To0            0               0                  0                 0
           To1            0               0                  0                 0
```

The virtual ring plays a critical role in RSRB and DLSw+ configuration. For RSRB, a virtual ring is created to make the IP backbone appear as another ring to all RSRB neighbors. RSRB performs RIF passthrough. The virtual ring and its underlying IP backbone appear as another hop in the source-route bridge network. All RSRB peers must use the same virtual ring address.

For DLSw+, a virtual ring must be created for any DLSw+ peer that is bridging traffic from a Token-Ring interface. Since RIFs are terminated locally for TCP encapsulated DLSw+ connections, the virtual ring number does not need to be the same for a peers. More information on this topic will be supplied when DLSw+ configuration is covered later in this chapter.

Source-Route Transparent Bridging

Source-Route Transparent Bridging allows a bridge to perform both source-route bridging and transparent bridging for Token-Ring networks.

One of the greatest challenges of maintaining a source-route bridged network is assuring that all end systems have operational source-route bridging software installed. An alternative to maintaining source-route bridge software on end systems is to perform source-route transparent bridging (SRT).

With SRT, no configuration needs to be performed on end systems that participate in Token-Ring transparent bridging. SRT configuration and operation involves the same configuration command used for configuring transparent bridging for Ethernet, as discussed in Chapter Twenty.

SRT is transparent bridging for all Token-Ring networks. Do not confuse SRT with source-route translational bridging (SR/TLB). SR/TLB involves bridging between Token-Ring and Ethernet segments, and is covered in the next section.

A sample configuration SRT configuration script is displayed below:

```
interface TokenRing0
 no ip address
 ring-speed 16
 bridge-group 1
 source-bridge 100 1 200
!
interface TokenRing1
 no ip address
 ring-speed 16
 bridge-group 1
 source-bridge 200 1 100
!
bridge 1 protocol ieee
```

SRT is performed by using the same RII used by source-route bridging to determine if the traffic is destined for a local end system or a non-local end system. If a frame's RII has a value of 1, it is accepted by the SRT bridge for SRB forwarding. If the frame contains a RIF (RII=1), the frame is source-route bridged. If the frame does not possess a RIF (RII=0), it is transparent bridged.

Show commands used to monitor the transparent bridging process in a Token-Ring environment are:

- Show interface to0
- Show bridge
- Show span

Source-Route Translational Bridging

Source-Route Translational Bridging (SR/TLB) is used to bridge traffic between Ethernet and Token-Ring networks. The SR/TLB process involves several challenges in converting an Ethernet frame into a Token-Ring frame and vice-versa. A partial listing of Ethernet to Token-Ring frame translation issues is displayed below:

1. Ethernet addresses are in a cannonical format. Token-Ring addresses are in a non-cannonical format.
2. Ethernet and Token-Ring have different MTUs.
3. A Token-Ring source-route bridged frame has a RIF; Ethernet has nothing comparable.

SR/TLB automatically converts Ethernet cannonical addresses into Token-Ring non-cannonical formats and vice-versa. The conversion is performed on an octet-by-octet basis. To illustrate the issue, consider the scenario below. An Ethernet interface of a Cisco router has the following MAC address:

```
Router#show interfaces ethernet 0
Ethernet0 is up, line protocol is up
Hardware is Lance, address is 0060.837b.a711 (bia 0060.837b.a711)
```

SR/TLB will convert the Ethernet address into the following non-cannonical address so that it can be properly interpreted by Token-Ring:

```
0006.c1de.e588
```

Again, the cannonical to non-cannonical conversion is performed on an octet-by-octet basis. MAC addresses are in a hexadecimal format. A pair of digits in a hexadecimal address represents a single octet (eight bits), or "byte." Each individual digit represents four bits, or a "nibble". Therefore, the cannonical to non-cannonical conversion is performed on one pair of hexadecimal digits at a time. For example, the Ethernet Mac address listed above is: 0060.837b.a711. An Ethernet MAC address is made up of 48 bits. These 48 bits can be divided by eight bits to yield six bytes. However, when a 48 bit MAC address is represented in hexadecimal form, it yields a 12-digit hexadecimal string, such as 0060.837b.a711. It is can be divided from left to right into the following six hexadecimal address pairs:

1	00
2	60
3	83
4	7b
5	a7
6	11

These address pairs are converted from a cannonical to non-cannonical format in the table below:

	Cannonical Address	**Non-cannonical Address**
1	00	00
2	60	06
3	83	c1
4	7b	de
5	a7	e5
6	11	88

Use the following chart to verify the conversion performed above:

First Nibble of cannonical address (below)	**Second nibble of cannonical address (across)**															
	0	1	2	3	4	5	6	7	8	9	A	B	C	D	E	F
0	00	80	40	C0	20	A0	60	E0	10	90	50	D0	30	B0	70	F0
1	08	88	48	C8	28	A8	68	E8	18	98	58	D8	38	B8	78	F8
2	04	84	44	C4	24	A4	64	E4	14	94	54	D4	34	B4	74	F4
3	0C	8C	4C	CC	2C	AC	6C	EC	1C	9C	5C	DC	3C	BC	7C	FC
4	02	82	42	C2	22	A2	62	E2	12	92	52	D2	32	B2	72	F2
5	0A	8A	4A	CA	2A	AA	6A	EA	1A	9A	5A	DA	3A	BA	7A	FA
6	06	86	46	C6	26	A6	66	E6	16	96	56	D6	36	B6	76	F6
7	0E	8E	4E	CE	2E	AE	6E	EE	1E	9E	5E	DE	3E	BE	7E	FE
8	01	81	41	C1	21	A1	61	E1	11	91	51	D1	31	B1	71	F1
9	09	89	49	C9	29	A9	69	E9	19	99	59	D9	39	B9	79	F9
A	05	85	45	C5	25	A5	65	E5	15	95	55	D5	35	B5	75	F5
B	0D	8D	4D	CD	2D	AD	6D	ED	1D	9D	5D	DD	3D	BD	7D	FD
C	03	83	43	C3	23	A3	63	E3	13	93	53	D3	33	B3	73	F3
D	0B	8B	4B	CB	2B	AB	6B	E8	1B	9B	5B	DB	3B	BB	7B	FB
E	07	87	47	C7	27	A7	67	E7	17	97	57	D7	37	B7	77	F7
F	0F	8F	4F	CF	2F	AF	6F	EF	1F	9F	5F	DF	3F	BF	7F	FF

The shaded entries are palandromic addresses. Palandromic addresses remain the same during the cannonical to non-cannonical bit-translation.

The topic of address conversion is also very important for DLSw+ configurations that involve Token-Ring and Ethernet segments.

Configuring SR/TLB involves four steps:

1. Configure source-route bridging on the Token-Ring interfaces to be bridged using a virtual ring.
2. Configure transparent bridging on Ethernet interfaces to be bridged.
3. Select a "pseudo-ring" number to make all of your Ethernet segments appear to the IOS as a second virtual token-ring.
4. Configure the global configuration command: source-bridge transparent <virtual ring-group> <pseudo-ring> <source-route bridge number> <transparent bridge-group>.

Listed below is a sample SR/TLB configuration:

```
source-bridge ring-group 200
source-bridge transparent 200 70 1 10
```

```
!
interface Ethernet0
 no ip address
 bridge-group 10
!
interface TokenRing0
 no ip address
 ring-speed 16
 source-bridge 100 1 200
!
interface TokenRing1
 no ip address
 ring-speed 16
 source-bridge 300 1 200
!
no ip classless
!
bridge 10 protocol ieee
```

In the configuration above, the Token-Ring interfaces are configured for source-route bridging using a virtual ring. The Ethernet interface is configured for transparent bridging. The only new command is the global configuration command "source-route transparent". Four parameters follow the source-route transparent command. Each is described below:

200	This is the virtual-ring number created.
70	This is the pseudo-ring created to make the Ethernet transparent bridged segment appear as a single ring to the source-route bridged segments.
1	This is the source-route bridge number used under interfaces tokenring 0 and tokenring 1. This bridge number is being mapped to the transparent bridge number 10.
10	This is the transparent bridge-group number for the Ethernet segment.

Notice that in the show source below, three rings are defined under the virtual ring (Ring Group 200). The third ring, 70, is the pseudo-ring. If you can interpret each parameter in the third line, you have developed a solid foundational understanding of SR/TLB. Notice that the MAC address listed in the third line is interface Ethernet 0's address in a non-cannonical format. Use the bit conversion chart displayed earlier to validate the address conversion. (Note: The first byte of the address in the show source display below—"40"—does not translate into the original first byte of the Ethernet address—"00").

```
r1#show source

Local Interfaces:                                 receive      transmit
             srn bn   trn r p s n   max hops        cnt          cnt          drops
To0          100  1   200 * * b     7  7  7          12            0            0
To1          300  1   200 * * b     7  7  7           0            0            0
```

```
Global RSRB Parameters:
 TCP Queue Length maximum: 100

Ring Group 200:
  No TCP peername set, TCP transport disabled
   Maximum output TCP queue length, per peer: 100
  Rings:
   bn: 1  rn: 100  local  ma: 4006.c1de.e548 TokenRing0          fwd: 0
   bn: 1  rn: 300  local  ma: 4006.c1de.e5a8 TokenRing1          fwd: 0
   bn: 1  rn: 70   locvrt ma: 4006.c1de.e588 Bridge-group 10     fwd: 0

Explorers: ------- input -------              ------- output -------
         spanning  all-rings     total      spanning  all-rings     total
To0             0          0         0             0          0         0
To1             0          0         0             0          0         0

  Local: fastswitched 0         flushed 0         max Bps 38400
         rings      inputs         bursts          throttles     output drops
           To0           0              0                  0                0
           To1           0              0                  0                0
```

From the SR/TLB transparent bridging perspective, examine the show spanning display below. Notice that a bridge port 21 has been created for "Ring Group 200," and that the Ethernet addresses listed under port 21 are in a non-cannonical format.

```
Bridge Group 10 is executing the IEEE compatible Spanning Tree protocol
  Bridge Identifier has priority 32768, address 0060.837b.a711
  Configured hello time 2, max age 20, forward delay 15
  We are the root of the spanning tree
  Topology change flag not set, detected flag not set
  Times:  hold 1, topology change 30, notification 30
          hello 2, max age 20, forward delay 15, aging 300
  Timers: hello 2, topology change 0, notification 0

Port 6 (Ethernet0) of bridge group 10 is forwarding
   Port path cost 100, Port priority 128
   Designated root has priority 32768, address 0060.837b.a711
   Designated bridge has priority 32768, address 0060.837b.a711
   Designated port is 6, path cost 0
   Timers: message age 0, forward delay 0, hold 0

Port 21 (RingGroup200) of bridge group 10 is forwarding
   Port path cost 10, Port priority 0
   Designated root has priority 32768, address 0060.837b.a711
   Designated bridge has priority 32768, address 0060.837b.a711
   Designated port is 21, path cost 0
          Timers: message age 0, forward delay 0, hold 0
```

Configuring Source-Route Bridging Over an IP Backbone

So far, all the configuration scenarios of this chapter have involved configuring source-route bridging and its variations using LAN interfaces only (Token-Ring and Ethernet interfaces only). Now, WAN interfaces will be introduced to configuring source-route bridging and its variations.

Cisco's first solution for configuring source-route bridging over the WAN was Remote Source-Route Bridging (RSRB). Introduced in 1991, RSRB encapsulated source-route bridged traffic into TCP/IP, FST/IP or HDLC tunnels and transported it over an IP backbone. The original RIF was maintained while the source-route bridged traffic traversed the IP backbone.

In the mid-90s, Cisco introduced Data Link Switching Plus (DLSw+). DLSw+ provides full backwards compatibility with RSRB; however it also does much more than RSRB. RSRB links only remotely attached Token-Ring source-route bridged networks. DLSw+ interconnects non-routable traffic using dissimilar data-link protocols such as Ethernet, Token-Ring, SDLC, FDDI and X.25. To appreciate the flexibility of DLSw+, consider the following scenario:

The Wolzac Media Corporation has a mainframe with Token-Ring Interface Couplers ("TIC cards") in its Front End Processor. The mainframe is used for classified advertisement billing for several of Wolzac's newspapers printed throughout the country. The Wolzac mainframe supports 45 billing offices around the United States and Canada. The Western United States region is comprised of 15 offices with PCs connected to Token-Ring LANs. The Eastern Region of the United States is comprised of fifteen offices. Each Eastern Region office has 3270 terminals communicating with a cluster controller via SDLC. The Canadian Region is comprised of 15 offices. Each Canadian office has workstations connected to a Catalyst 5000 with Ethernet modules.

Eastern Region U.S. offices are using SDLC terminals to communicate with a Token-Ring interface residing in the Wolzac mainframe's Front End Processor, located in Washington D.C. Western Region U.S. offices are using Token-Ring connected workstations to communicate with a Token-Ring interface residing in the Wolzac mainframe's Front End Processor located in Washington D.C.; Canadian offices are using Ethernet connected workstations to communicate with a Token-Ring interface residing in the Wolzac mainframe's Front End Processor.

Each of the billing offices can install a Cisco router and configure DLSw+ to provide branch office SNA connectivity over an IP backbone. DLSw+ is recommended over RSRB for the following reasons:

Both DLSw+ and RSRB can connect two remotely-connected Token-Ring networks; however, the scenario above also involves Ethernet and SDLC networks. DLSw+ can provide Ethernet to Token-Ring connectivity. In fact, DLSw+ performs source route translational bridging automatically for Ethernet and Token-Ring segments connected together via DLSw+. RSRB does not perform automatic source-route translational bridging. DLSw+ can also connect

SDLC based networks to Token-Ring/LLC2 networks; RSRB cannot. Another Cisco solution—SDLLC—was required.

Since DLSw+ is backward compatible with RSRB and offers more robust features than RSRB, the remainder of the Chapter will focus on DLSw+.

DLSw+ Technical Overview

DLSw+ builds upon both RSRB and DLSw. In fact, it can be said that DLSw+ provides the best of both RSRB and DLSw. DLSw+ is reverse compatible with both RSRB and DLSw, and many of the Cisco IOS commands used to configure RSRB have similar counterparts in DLSw+. The protocols and intelligence specified in RFC 1795 that defined DLSw are also used in Cisco's DLSw+.

Even though DLSw+ builds on RSRB and DLSw, it offers much more than both. RSRB provided source-route bridging services over an IP backbone. The RIF was retained while the frame was transported over the IP backbone. DLSw+ operates in a different manner. It terminates the RIF and uses a RFC 1795-defined collection of switch-to-switch protocol (SSP) messages to set up a DLSw+ circuit over the WAN for two remotely-connected end systems. RSRB was limited to connecting two Token-Ring segments over the WAN. DLSw+ can connect the following types of segments over the WAN:

- Token-Ring to Token-Ring
- Token-Ring to Ethernet
- Ethernet to Ethernet
- Token-Ring to SDLC
- Token-Ring to QLLC
- Ethernet to QLLC

Standard DLSw is defined by RFC 1795. That specification defined the core elements of DLSw; however, it did not specify how to implement many of the enhancements, such as caching reachability information of both locally and remotely connected end systems. Cisco's DLSw+ fully conforms to the core elements of DLSw. At the same time, it adds many enhancements, such as:

Multiple Encapsulation Types. DLSw specifies a single encapsualtion type: TCP/IP. DLSw+ offers four encapsulation types: TCP/IP; FST/IP; direct encapsualtion for point to point connections and straight LLC2 encapsulation for Frame-Relay connections (DLSw+ Lite). Non-TCP encapsulation types can be used for greater DLSw+ connection performance.

Reachability Caching. Although the DLSw specification mentions the use of reachability caching, it does not stress that it is required. A Cisco DLSw+ peer maintains both a local and remote reachability cache. By maintaining these caches, DLSw+ peers can respond to explorer traffic locally and reduce the amount of explorer traffic on the IP backone.

Border-Peer Groups and On-Demand Peers. If all DLSw peers need to communicate with each other, DLSw requires a direct connection between all peers. Therefore, in order to maintain any-to-any connectivity, multiple DLSw peers must be fully meshed. This requirement causes problems with scaling DLSw networks. Cisco's DLSw+ border peer and on-demand peer features provide a solution to this limitation of DLSw. A DLSw+ border peer maintains a peering relationship with multiple downstream clients, creating a hub and spoke relationship with border peer clients. When a border peer client needs to establish a connection with another client, it forwards explorer traffic to the border peer. The border peer processes the explorer request. Once the border-peer client has the destination address of the other client, it can establish a direct "on-demand" connection. By doing so, the need to maintain a full mesh for any-to-any connectivity is eliminated.

DLSW+ also offers several back-up, security, and load balancing features that are not defined in the DLSw standard. Even though DLSw+ offers many enhancements over DLSw, DLSw is still at the very core of DLSw+.

The best way to gain an understanding of the core operation of DLSw+ is to read RFC 1795. The following pages provide excerpts from RFC 1795 as well as interpretations.

In Section Two of RFC 1795, the Overview Section, the design objective of DLSw is clearly stated:

"Data Link Switching was developed to provide support for SNA and NetBIOS in multi-protocol routers. Since SNA and NetBIOS are basically connection oriented protocols, the Data Link Control procedure that they use on the LAN is IEEE 802.2 Logical Link Control (LLC) Type 2. Data Link Switching also accommodates SNA protocols over WAN (Wide Area Network) links via the SDLC protocol.

IEEE 802.2 LLC Type 2 was designed with the assumption that the network transit delay would be predictable (i.e., a local LAN). Therefore the LLC Type 2 elements of procedure use a fixed timer for detecting lost frames. When remote bridging is used over wide area lines (especially at lower speeds), the network delay is larger and it can vary greatly based upon congestion. When the delay exceeds the time-out value LLC Type 2 attempts to retransmit. If the frame is not actually lost, only delayed, it is possible for the LLC Type 2 procedures to become confused. And as a result, the link may be eventually taken down if the delay exceeds the T1 timer times N2 retry count.

Given the use of LLC Type 2 services, Data Link Switching addresses the following bridging problems:

- DLC Time-outs
- DLC Acknowledgments over the WAN

- Flow and Congestion Control
- Broadcast Control of Search Packets
- Source-Route Bridging Hop Count Limits

NetBIOS also makes extensive use of datagram services that use connectionless LLC Type 1 service. In this case, Data Link Switching addresses the last two problems in the above list."

After defining the primary design objective of DLSw, RFC 1795 provides an insightful comparison between Data Link Switching (DLSw) and bridging:

"The principal difference between Data Link Switching and bridging is that for connection-oriented data DLSw terminates the Data Link Control whereas bridging does not. The following figure illustrates this difference based upon two end systems operating with LLC Type 2 services.

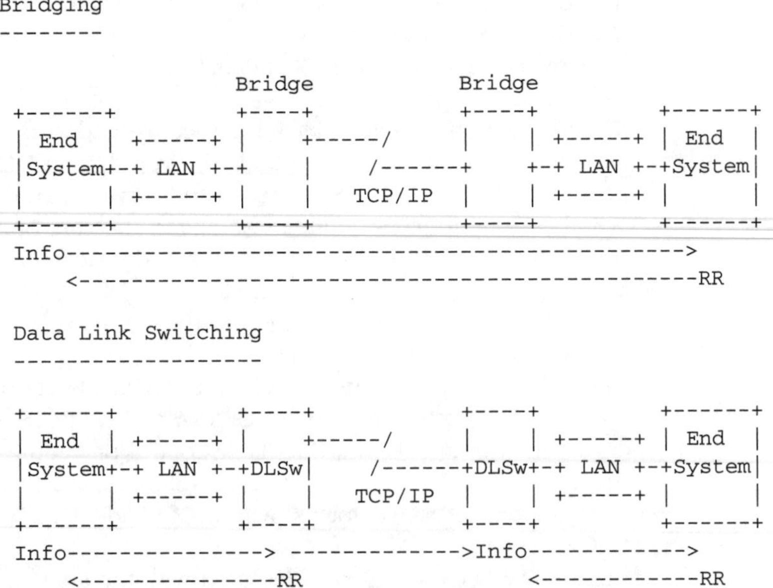

```
Bridging
--------

                     Bridge             Bridge
 +------+           +-----+            +-----+           +------+
 | End  | +-----+ |     +-----/     |     | +-----+ | End  |
 |System+-+ LAN +-+     |    /------+     +-+ LAN +-+System|
 |      | +-----+ |     |   TCP/IP  |     | +-----+ |      |
 +------+           +-----+            +-----+           +------+
 Info----------------------------------------------------->
     <-------------------------------------------------RR

 Data Link Switching
 -------------------

 +------+           +-----+            +-----+           +------+
 | End  | +-----+ |     +-----/     |     | +-----+ | End  |
 |System+-+ LAN +-+DLSw|    /------+DLSw+-+ LAN +-+System|
 |      | +-----+ |     |   TCP/IP  |     | +-----+ |      |
 +------+           +-----+            +-----+           +------+
 Info--------------> ------------->Info------------>
     <---------------RR              <-------------RR
```

In traditional bridging, the Data Link Control is end-to-end. Data Link Switching terminates the LLC Type 2 connection at the switch. This means that the LLC Type 2 connections do not cross the wide area network. The DLSw multiplexes LLC connections onto a TCP connection to another DLSw. Therefore, the LLC connections at each end are totally independent of each other. It is the responsibility of the Data Link Switch to deliver frames that it has received from a LLC connection to the other end. TCP is used between the Data Link Switches to guarantee delivery of frames.

As a result of this design, LLC time-outs are limited to the local LAN (i.e., they do not traverse the wide area). Also, the LLC Type 2 acknowledgments (RRs) do not traverse the WAN, thereby reducing traffic across the wide area links. For SDLC links, polling and poll response occurs locally, not over the WAN. Broadcast of search frames is controlled by the Data Link Switches once the location of a target system is discovered. Finally, the switches can now apply back pressure to the end systems to provide flow and congestion control."

DLSw was designed to accommodate the characteristics of three protocols:

- SNA
- NetBIOS
- LLC2

Later in the specification, RFC 1795 states that the design objective of DLSw+ is to make "the corporate internetwork appear as one big LLC2 LAN." Each DLSw+ peer terminates LLC2 traffic and source-route bridge RIFs. When you examine the RFC 1795 DLSw diagrams displayed above, you notice that a given end system-to-end system DLSw "circuit" involves a total of three connections:

1. A connection from the originating end system to the originating DLSw peer
2. A connection between the originating DLSw peer and the target DLSw peer
3. A connection from the target DLSw peer to the target end system

In the bridging diagram displayed above, a single end system-to-end system connection is required. When Cisco IOS DLSw+ debug traces are generated, you will see two different sets of debug output:

1. Messages generated between an end system and a DLSw+ peer
2. Messages generated between two DLSw+ peers

In order to understand DLSw, a basic understanding of LLC1, LLC2 and the DLSw Switch-to-Switch Protocol (SSP) is required.

Logical Link Control Overview

IEEE data link specifications divide the data link layer into two sublayers: the media access control layer and the logical link control layer. The media access control sublayer lies directly above the physical layer, and the logical link control sublayer lies directly above the media access control layer. Commonly-used IEEE specified media access control protocols are 802.3 (Ethernet) and 802.5 (Token-Ring).

Commonly-used logical link control protocols include LLC1 and LLC2. LLC1 is a connectionless protocol. A widely-used LLC1 implementation is LLC1/SNAP. LLC2 is a connection-oriented protocol. It is used heavily in IBM SNA environments. It provides a reliable connection between the mainframe and end user devices. LLC2 traffic, like mainframe traffic, is delay sensitive.

LLC2 is the IEEE specification for an ITU-T specification: HDLC/Asynchronous Balanced Mode (ABM). HDLC itself is a descendant of the original IBM SNA data link protocol SDLC. Using LLC2 over a deterministic MAC protocol like Token-Ring can provide robust SDLC-like functionality with more flexibility.

Since LLC1 is connectionless and LLC2 is connection-oriented, the latter is much more complex in its operation. Displayed below are the three different LLC2 frame types and their associated commands and responses. (LLC1 does not possess multiple frame types.)

- Unnumbered frame (U-frame)
- Supervisory frame (S-frame)
- Information frame (I-frame)

LLC2 operates on a command and response model. Each of the frame types listed above generate a specific collection of commands and responses:

LLC2 Frame Type	Command	Response
Unnumbered	SABME	UA
	DISC	UA
		DM
		FRMR
Supervisory	RR	RR
	RNR	RNR
	REJ	REJ
Information	I	I

Unnumbered frames are used for connection setup and disconnect. The LLC2 peer initiating a connection will send a Set Asynchronous Balance Mode Extended (SABME) to the target LLC2 peer. The target peer will respond with an unnumbered acknowledgment (UA). An LLC2 session is terminated with the "disconnect" (DISC) unnumbered frame. A DISC is also answered with an unnumbered acknowledgment (UA). Unnumbered commands and responses do not carry end user data. In summary, LLC2 unnumbered frames are used to setup and tear down a connection.

Once the unnumbered frames have set up the connection, supervisory frames are used to maintain the connection. Supervisory frames include the following three command/response pairs:

- Receive Ready (RR)
- Receive Not Ready (RNR)
- Reject (REJ)

Supervisory frames perform functions such as sequencing packets and polling connections. SNA implementations that use LLC2 rely on Supervisory RR commands to poll the availability of a downstream device. It is precisely these RR polls that DLSw+ terminates. By terminating RR polls and responses,

DLSw+ prevents this traffic from traversing the WAN. Like Unnumbered frames, Supervisory frames do not carry data.

Finally, LLC2 information frames transport actual end user data.

Since LLC1 is a connectionless protocol, it does not require the connection setup and maintenance features of LLC2. With LLC1, no SABME U-frames or RR S-frames are used. LLC1 operates in a single mode: the information transfer mode. LLC1 uses three types of frames:

- Unsequenced information (UI)
- Exchange identification (XID)
- Test (TEST)

The UI frame is used to transfer data between two end systems in a connectionless manner (i.e., no unackowledgments are used).

The XID frame is used for services such as locating a remote end system and testing for duplicate addresses.

The Test frame is used for connection testing purposes, such as loop-back testing. The LLC1 specification does not require an LLC1 device to generate a TEST frame, but it does require an LLC1 device to respond to a TEST frame.

Logical Link Control Addressing

Both LLC1 and LLC2 use the same address format, which consists of a 16-bit address field divided into an eight-bit destination address and an eight-bit source address. LLC addresses are called "service access points" (SAP). The destination address is known as a DSAP, and the source address is known as an SSAP. They are ordered in the LLC header in the following manner: DSAP first, SSAP second. Both addresses are represented in a hexadecimal format. Since they are eight bits in length, they are represented by two hexadecimal digits ("nibbles"). DSAP and SSAP addresses are registered with the IEEE. RFC 1795 lists the following SAP addresses as being important to know for DLSw+ implementation:

- 0x04 SNA
- 0x08 SNA
- 0x0C SNA
- 0xF0 NetBIOS
- 0x00 Null SAP

This concludes the brief introduction of LLC1 and LLC2. It is beyond the scope of this book to examine LLC1 and LLC2 to a high level of detail. Since DLSw+ is designed to manage LLC2 connections, it is essential that you have a strong understanding of LLC2. Also remember that LLC2 is derived from HDLC/ABM, which is, in turn, a more flexible and robust variant of the original SDLC. You have already encountered variations of LLC in this book. In the ISDN/DDR chapter (Chapter Five), both Q.921 and PPP are variations of

HDLC. In the ATM chapter (Chapter Seven), SSCOP is based upon HDLC and RFC 1483 ATM encapsulation uses LLC1/SNAP. Therefore, it is recommended that you supplement your reading of LLC1, LLC2, HDLC and SDLC with some of the resources listed at the end of this chapter.

DLSw+ Addressing

Two basic types of connections exist in DLSw+:

1. A DLSw+ to DLSw+ peer connection
2. An end system to end system circuit traversing a DLSw+ peer-to-peer connection

When a DLSw+ to DLSw+ connection is made, the two peers have attained the DLSw+ peer "connected" state. DLSw+ peer-to-peer connections can be monitored with the "show dlsw peers" command:

```
r2#show dlsw peers
Peers:            state     pkts_rx    pkts_tx   type  drops ckts TCP   uptime
TCP 172.16.40.4   CONNECT   117        223       conf  0     0    0     00:52:32
```

End system-to-end system connections that traverse DLSW+ peer-to-peer connections are called DLSw+ "circuits." DLSw+ end system-to-end system circuits can be monitored with the "show dlsw circuits" command:

```
Router# show dlsw circuits

Index    local addr(lsap)     remote addr(dsap)    state
75-00    1000.5acc.5acc(F0)   1000.5acc.800d(F0)   CONNECTED
119-00   1000.5acc.88ea(04)   1000.5acc.800d(08)   CONNECTED
121-00   4006.315b.568e(F0)   0006.311d.eea1(F0)   CONNECTED
```

As the "show dlsw" commands reflect, these two types of DLSw+ connections use different address formats.

A DLSw+ peer-to-DLSw+ peer connection must be established before an end system-to-end system DLSw+ circuit can be established. DLSw+-to-DLSw+ peer connections can be established using different encapsulation methods, such as TCP/IP and FST/IP. These connections are identified by a TCP port and an IP address when the TCP/IP encapsulation method is used, and by an IP protocol number (91) and an IP address when FST/IP is used.

End system-to-end system circuits that traverse DLSw+ connections use a collection of different address and identifiers, including:

- Data Link Identifier (14 bytes)
- Origin Circuit Identifier (8 bytes)
- Target Circuit Identifier (8 bytes)

The Data Link identifier is used during end system-to-end system circuit establishment. It is not used when actual information is flowing between end systems. The Data Link Identifier is composed of the following four elements:

	Number of Bytes	Number of Bits
MAC address of one end system	6	48
MAC address of second end system	6	48
SAP address of one end system	1	8
SAP address of second end system	1	8
Total:	14	112

Origin and Target Circuit Identifiers are used during circuit set up as well as during end system-to end-system information exchange. Once the end system-to-end system circuit is established, the origin circuit identifier will be the same number as the target circuit identifier.

In DLSw+, all MAC addresses are represented in non-cannonical (Token-Ring) format. Therefore, all participating Ethernet end systems will have their address converted into a non-cannonical format.

Switch to Switch Protocol Overview

At the heart of the DLSw+ process is the Switch-to-Switch Protocol (SSP), which is involved in virtually every DLSw+ operation. The SSP operates by exchanging different types of messages between DLSw+ peers:

```
Command           Description                           Type     flags/notes
-------           --------                              ------   -----------
CANUREACH_ex      Can U Reach Station-explorer          0x03     SSPex
CANUREACH_cs      Can U Reach Station-circuit start     0x03
ICANREACH_ex      I Can Reach Station-explorer          0x04     SSPex
ICANREACH_cs      I Can Reach Station-circuit start     0x04
REACH_ACK         Reach Acknowledgment                  0x05
DGRMFRAME         Datagram Frame                        0x06     (note 1)
XIDFRAME          XID Frame                             0x07
CONTACT           Contact Remote Station                0x08
CONTACTED         Remote Station Contacted              0x09
RESTART_DL        Restart Data Link                     0x10
DL_RESTARTED      Data Link Restarted                   0x11
ENTER_BUSY        Enter Busy                            0x0C     (note 2)
EXIT_BUSY         Exit Busy                             0x0D     (note 2)
INFOFRAME         Information (I) Frame                 0x0A
HALT_DL           Halt Data Link                        0x0E
DL_HALTED         Data Link Halted                      0x0F
NetBIOS_NQ_ex     NetBIOS Name Query-explorer           0x12     SSPex
NetBIOS_NQ_cs     NetBIOS Name Query-circuit setup      0x12     (note 3)
NetBIOS_NR_ex     NetBIOS Name Recognized-explorer      0x13     SSPex
```

```
NetBIOS_NR_cs     NetBIOS Name Recog-circuit setup    0x13    (note 3)
DATAFRAME         Data Frame                          0x14    (note 1)
HALT_DL_NOACK     Halt Data Link with no Ack          0x19
NetBIOS_ANQ       NetBIOS Add Name Query              0x1A
NetBIOS_ANR       NetBIOS Add Name Response           0x1B
KEEPALIVE         Transport Keepalive Message         0x1D    (note 4)
CAP_EXCHANGE      Capabilities Exchange               0x20
```

Each of these messages is defined in RFC 1795. SSP messages are used during DLSw+ peer-to-DLSw peer connection set up, as well as during end system-to-end system circuit establishment.

When a DLSw+ peer needs to locate a remotely located device, it sends the following SSP explorer messages to other DLSw+ peers searching for a specific destination MAC address or NetBIOS name:

CANUREACH_ex	(Can You Reach Explorer)
ICANREACH_ex	(I Can Reach Explorer)
NetBIOS_NQ_ex	(NetBIOS Name Query Explorer)
NetBIOS_NR_ex	(NetBIOS Name Response Explorer)

Once the DLSw+ peer has located the desired remotely-located device, it begins to exchange a sequence of SSP messages with the target remote DLSw+ peer. Listed below is a step-by-step flow diagram of a DLSw+ circuit setup. Note the SSP messages used and the DLSw+ identifiers used (Data Link identifiers, Origin Circuit identifiers, Target Circuit identifiers).

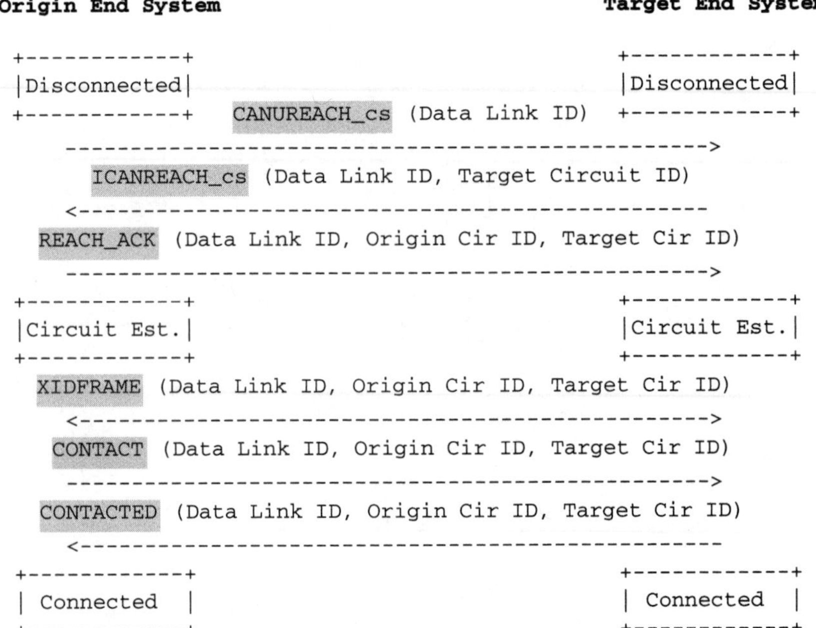

```
  INFOFRAME  (Remote Circuit ID = Target Circuit ID)
-------------------------------------------------->
  INFOFRAME  (Remote Circuit ID = Origin Circuit ID)
<--------------------------------------------------
```

This flow diagram is extracted directly from page 12 in RFC 1795. It provides an excellent summary of the use of different DLSw+ addresses and SSP messages. For more details on DLSw+ addressing and SSP message types, see RFC 1795.

The Four Basic Stages of DLSw+ Operation on a Cisco Router

On a Cisco router, the four basic stages of DLSw+ operations are:

1. DLSw+ connection setup between two DLSw+ peers
2. DLSw+ capabilities exchange between DLSw+ peers
3. DLSw+ peer searching for a destination MAC address or NetBIOS name
4. DLSw+ peer circuit setup for two remotely-connected end systems

DLSw+ Connection Setup Between Two DLSw+ Peers

The DLSw+ peer-to-DLSw+ peer connection setup is always the starting point for any DLSw+ session. No other DLSw+ process can occur between two DLSw+ peers before a connection is established. Four different DLSw+ encapsulation types can be used to establish a DLSw+ peer to peer connection:

- TCP
- FST
- Direct Encapsulation
- DLSw+ Lite LLC2 over Frame-Relay

Once a DLSw+ connection is established, use the "show dlsw peers" command to obtain status and statistics on a given DLSw+ peer connection:

```
r2#show dlsw peers
Peers:            state    pkts_rx    pkts_tx   type  drops ckts TCP   uptime
TCP 172.16.40.4   CONNECT  117        223       conf  0     0    0     00:52:32
```

DLSw+ Peer States are:

- CONNECT (Connected)
- DISCONN (Disconnected)
- CAP_EXG (Capabilities Exchange)
- WAIT_RD
- WAN_BUSY

Configuration types are designated by the "type" heading in the show dlsw peer display. Three different configuration types exist:

- Conf manual configuration
- prom promiscuous
- pod peer on demand

Each of these connection types will be described in the configuring DLSw+ section later in this Chapter.

You can observe a debug trace of the DLSw+ peer connection process with debug dlsw peers. A sample debug trace is displayed below:

```
r2#debug dlsw peers
DLSw peer debugging is on
DLSw: action_b(): opening write pipe for peer 172.16.40.4(2065)
DLSw: peer 172.16.40.4(2065), old state DISCONN, new state CAP_EXG
DLSw: CapExId Msg sent to peer 172.16.40.4(2065)
DLSw: Recv CapExId Msg from peer 172.16.40.4(2065)
DLSw: Pos CapExResp sent to peer 172.16.40.4(2065)
DLSw: action_e(): for peer 172.16.40.4(2065)
DLSw: Recv CapExPosRsp Msg from peer 172.16.40.4(2065)
DLSw: action_e(): for peer 172.16.40.4(2065)
DLSw: peer 172.16.40.4(2065), old state CAP_EXG, new state CONNECT
DLSw: peer_act_on_capabilities() for peer 172.16.40.4(2065)
DLSw: dlsw_tcpd_fini() for peer 172.16.40.4(2065)1
DLSw: dlsw_tcpd_fini() closing write pipe for peer 172.16.40.4
DLSw: action_g(): for peer 172.16.40.4(2065)
DLSw: closing write pipe tcp connection for peer 172.16.40.4(2065)
DLSw-CORE : Sending enable port
 DISP Sent : CLSI Msg : ENABLE.Req   dlen: 56
 DLSW Received-ctlQ : CLSI Msg : ENABLE.Cfm CLS_OK dlen: 56
Core: CLS_TBRIDGE mtu 1500, setting to 1500
DLSw-CORE : Sending activate ring to DLSw Port0
 DISP Sent : CLSI Msg : ACTIVATE_RING.Req   dlen: 64
 DLSW Received-ctlQ : CLSI Msg : ACTIVATE_RING.Cfm CLS_OK dlen: 64
DLSw Received ActRingcnf from DLSw Port0^Z
DLSw: Keepalive Request sent to peer 172.16.40.4(2065))
DLSw: Keepalive Response from peer 172.16.40.4(2065)
```

Notice how the DLSw+ peer moved from the DISCONN state to the CAP_EXG state and finally to the CONNECTED state. Also, make note of the "CLSI" messages at the bottom of the debug trace. CLSI messages are between the DLSw+ peer and locally-connected or configured devices. Finally, make note of the keepalive messages exchanged between the two DLSw+ peers. The TCP encapsulation type was used in the debug trace above. This can be verified by the list of "2065" on many of the debug output lines. 2065 is one of the ports used by TCP-based DLSw+ connections.

DLSw+ Capabilities Exchange

Once two DLSw+ peers attain a CONNECTED state, they perform a mutual capabilities exchange. During this process, two DLSw+ peers share information such as what version of software a peer is using, as well as other capabilities parameters. You can review a remote DLSw+ peer's listed capabilities by using the "show dlsw capabilities" command:

```
Router#show dlsw capabilities
DLSw: Capabilities for peer 172.16.1.1(2065)
  vendor id (OUI)          : '00C' (cisco)
  version number           : 1
  release number           : 0
  init pacing window       : 20
  unsupported saps         : none
  num of tcp sessions      : 1
  loop prevent support     : no
  icanreach mac-exclusive  : no
  icanreach netbios-excl.  : no
  reachable mac addresses  : 1234.1234.1234 <mask ffff.ffff.ffff>
  reachable netbios names  : none
  cisco version number     : 1
  peer group number        : 0
  border peer capable      : no
  peer cost                : 3
  biu-segment configured   : no
  local-ack configured     : yes
  priority configured      : no
  peer type                : prom
  version string           :
Cisco Internetwork Operating System Software
IOS (tm) 4500 Software (C4500-JS-M), Version 11.2(11), RELEASE
SOFTWARE (fc1)
Copyright (c) 1986-1997 by cisco Systems, Inc.
Compiled Mon 29-Dec-97 20:50 by ckralik
```

In the capabilities listing above, DLSw+ peer 172.16.1.1 can reach the MAC address of 1234.1234.1234, and it is a promiscuous peer type. Virtually all capabilities exchange parameters are defined by global configuration commands.

During capabilities exchange, you can list which SAP services are not reachable with DLSw+ peer. Conversely, you can list which MAC addresses and NetBIOS names are reachable by a peer. For example, if a DLSw+ peer resides in a Data Center, and the MAC address of Token-Ring interface in a FEP is reachable through the peer, configure the capabilities exchange to exclude all NetBIOS searches and any searches for other MAC addresses. By configuring your capabilities exchange parameters in this manner, you can greatly reduce DLSw+ explorer activity on IP internetwork.

DLSw+ Search for a Destination MAC Address or NetBIOS Name

When a locally-connected end system is searching for a remote end system with which to communicate, its local DLSw+ peer must locate it. First the DLSw+ peer examines its reachability cache. If it cannot find the target end system in its reachability cache, the local DLSw+ peer begins to exchange the following DLSw+ SSP explorer messages with remote DLSw+ peers:

- CANUREACH_ex (Can You Reach Explorer)
- ICANREACH_ex (I Can Reach Explorer)
- NetBIOS_NQ_ex (NetBIOS Name Query Explorer)
- NetBIOS_NR_ex (NetBIOS Name Response Explorer)

Once the target address or NetBIOS name is located, the local DLSW+ peer begins the circuit setup procedure. Listed below is a sample DLSw+ reachability cache display:

```
r2#show dlsw reachability
DLSw MAC address reachability cache list
Mac Addr            status     Loc.       peer/port               rif
0004.f54f.c122      FOUND      REMOTE     172.16.32.3(2065)
1000.7cb8.d842      FOUND      LOCAL      TBridge-001          --no rif--
1000.e830.25e8      FOUND      REMOTE     172.16.18.5(2065)

DLSw NetBIOS Name reachability cache list
NetBIOS Name        status     Loc.       peer/port               rif
95WKSTN             FOUND      REMOTE     172.16.32.3(2065)
JEC                 FOUND      REMOTE     172.16.18.5(2065)
RDC                 FOUND      LOCAL      TBridge-001          --no rif–
```

The DLSw+ reachability cache states are:

- FOUND
- NOT_ FOUND
- SEARCHING
- UNCONFIRMED
- VERIFY
- FRESH (substate)
- STALE (substate)

A connection becomes stale if no circuit is established after 15 minutes. Entries can also be time-stamped according to when added to cache and when last used.

A RIF will be listed if the cache entry is local. If the address was acquired from a local segment using a media other than Token-Ring (Ethernet or SDLC), DLSw+ lists a "—no rif—" prompt for the listing.

The DLSw+ reachability cache can be statically configured with the following global configuration commands:

- Dlsw mac-addr
- Dlsw netbios-name

These statements are the functional equivalent of a static route.

When traffic begins to flow through DLSw+ peers, DLSw+ peers begin caching both remotely-learned and locally-learned MAC and NetBIOS addresses:

```
R1#show dlsw reachability
DLSw Remote MAC address reachability cache list
Mac Addr        status     Loc.    port                 rif
0000.83f0.7f08  FOUND      LOCAL   TokenRing0

DLSw Local MAC address reachability cache list
Mac Addr        status     Loc.    peer
0000.6148.2efc  FOUND      REMOTE  172.16.1.1(2065)
0001.e327.8469  FOUND      REMOTE  172.16.1.1(2065)

DLSw Local NetBIOS Name reachability cache list
NetBIOS Name    status     Loc.    port                 rif
365XDTK         SEARCHING  LOCAL
LOURDES         FOUND      LOCAL   TokenRing0

DLSw Remote NetBIOS Name reachability cache list
NetBIOS Name    status     Loc.    peer
BROOKLYN        FOUND      REMOTE  172.16.1.1(2065)
```

Instead of constantly generating explorer traffic, DLSw+ can make switching decisions based upon entries in the reachability cache. Applying a common language interpretation to the reachability cache displayed above, you can say, "To get to the NetBIOS workstation named "LOURDES" go to DLSw+ remote peer 172.16.1.1." If the target destination MAC address or NetBIOS name is not in the reachability cache, then generate explorer traffic.

Remember: with DLSw+, everything is MAC address or NetBIOS name-based. Every DLSw client has a MAC address. All MAC addresses are converted to a non-cannonical format.

DLSw+ reachability exchanges can be viewed with debug dlsw reachability. When viewing debug traces, the DLSw prompts are:

- CSM Circuit Setup Message (between DLSw+ peers)
- CLSI Common Layer Services Interface (messages sent between locally configured devices and the local DLSw+ peer)

With CLSI messages, a string appended with ".Ind" is sourced from an end system residing on a locally-connected LAN. A string appended with a ".Rsp" is sourced from the DLSw+ peer targeting an end system on a locally connected LAN.

When viewing debug statements, look for change in DLSw+ state and DLSw+ SSP messages exchanged.

```
r2#debug dlsw reachability
DLSw:
  DLSw Peer debugging is on
DLSw reachability debugging is on at event level for all protocol traffic
  DLSw basic debugging for peer 172.16.40.4(2065) is on
DLSw: Keepalive Request sent to peer 172.16.40.4(2065))
DLSw: Keepalive Response from peer 172.16.40.4(2065)
CSM: Received CLSI Msg : UDATA_STN.Ind   dlen: 228 from DLSw Port0
CSM:   smac 1000.7cb8.d842, dmac ffff.ffff.ffff, ssap E0, dsap E0
DLSw: sending bcast to BP peer 172.16.40.4(2065)
CSM:   smac 1000.7cb8.d842, dmac c000.0000.0080, ssap F0, dsap F0
CSM: Received frame type NetBIOS NAME_QUERY from 1000.7cb8.d842, DL0
DLSw: sending bcast to BP peer 172.16.40.4(2065)
CSM: Received CLSI Msg : UDATA_STN.Ind   dlen: 79 from DLSw Port0
CSM:   smac 1000.7cb8.d842, dmac c000.0000.0080, ssap F0, dsap F0
CSM: Received frame type NetBIOS NAME_QUERY from 1000.7cb8.d842, DL0
CSM: Received CLSI Msg : UDATA_STN.Ind   dlen: 133 from DLSw Port0
CSM:   smac 1000.7cb8.d842, dmac c000.0000.0080, ssap F0, dsap F0
CSM: Received frame type NetBIOS NAME_QUERY from 1000.7cb8.d842, DL0
DLSw: Pak from peer 172.16.40.4(2065) with op DLX_RELAY_RSP
DLSW: creating a peer-on-demand for 172.16.18.5
DLSw: passing pak to core originally from 172.16.18.5 in group 40
CSM: Received CLSI Msg : CONECT_STN.Ind   dlen: 43 from DLSw Port0
CSM:   smac 1000.7cb8.d842, dmac 1000.e830.25e8, ssap F0, dsap F0
CSM: Received CLSI Msg : UDATA_STN.Ind   dlen: 133 from DLSw Port0
CSM:   smac 1000.7cb8.d842, dmac ffff.ffff.ffff, ssap E0, dsap E0
DLSw: sending bcast to BP peer 172.16.40.4(2065)
```

DLSw+ Circuit Setup

Finally, when the desired DLSw+ remote address or NetBIOS name is located, an end system-to-end system circuit is established. You can view a listing of currently active DLSw+ circuits with the "show dlsw circuits" command:

```
Router# show dlsw circuits

Index    local addr(lsap)    remote addr(dsap)    state
75-00    1000.5acc.5acc(F0)  1000.5acc.800d(F0)   CONNECTED
119-00   1000.5acc.88ea(04)  1000.5acc.800d(08)   CONNECTED
121-00   4006.315b.568e(F0)  0006.311d.eea1(F0)   CONNECTED
```

The following is sample output from the "show dlsw circuits" command with the detail argument:

```
Router# show dlsw circuits detail

Index    local addr(lsap)    remote addr(dsap)    state
```

```
194-00  0800.5a9b.b3b2(F0)  0800.5ac1.302d(F0)  CONNECTED
        PCEP: 995AA4        UCEP: A52274
        Port: To0/0         peer 172.18.15.166(2065)
        Flow-Control-Tx CW:20, Permitted:28; Rx CW:22, Granted:25
        RIF = 0680.0011.0640
```

Configuring DLSW+

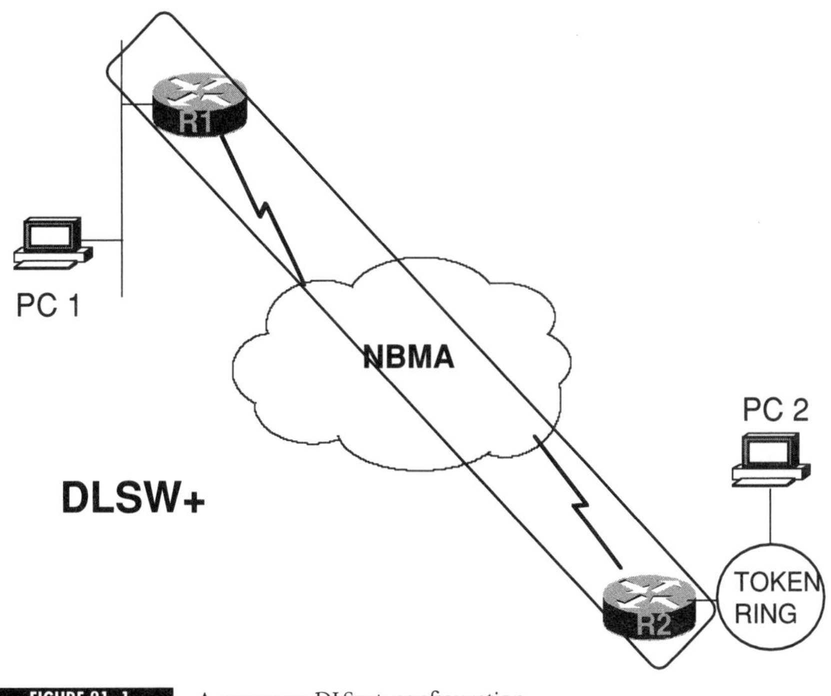

FIGURE 21–1 A common DLSw+ configuration.

When configuring DLSw+, you can divide your configuration tasks into two groups:

1. DLSw+ configuration
2. Local interface/local bridging configuration

The purpose of DLSw+ is to provide backbone connectivity to remotely-connected non-routable traffic. If the traffic originated on an Ethernet segment and terminated on a Token-Ring segment, the DLSw+ configuration will involve transparent bridge configuration on the Ethernet segment and SRB or SRT configuration on the Token-Ring segment.

All DLSw+ commands are global configuration commands. A listing of the DLSw+ global configuration commands is displayed below:

```
r2(config)#dlsw ?
bgroup-list             Configure a transparent bridge group list
bridge-group            DLSw interconnection to transparent bridging
disable                 Disable DLSw without altering the configuration
duplicate-path-bias     Configure how duplicate paths will be handled
explorerQ-depth         Configure depth of DLSw explorer queue
icannotreach            Config a resrce not locally reachable by this router
icanreach               Configure resources locally reachable by this router
local-peer              Configure local peer
mac-addr                Configure a static MAC address - location or path
netbios-name            Configure a static NetBios name - location or path
peer-on-demand-defaults Change peer-on-demand defaults
port-list               Configure a port list
prom-peer-defaults      Change prom-peer-defaults
remote-peer             Configure a remote peer
ring-list               Configure a ring list
timer                   Configure DLSw timers
touch-timer             Configure DLSw touch timers
```

Most of the global dlsw configuration commands are used for capabilities exchange purposes (icanreach, icannnotreach), static DLSw reachability configuration (mac-addr, netbios-name), default settings (prom-peer-defaults, timer, peer-on-demand-defaults, explorerQ-depth), and DLSw+ access-lists (port-list and ring-list).

The two most commonly used DLSw global configuration commands are:

- Dlsw local-peer
- Dlsw remote-peer

At a minimum, all DLSw+ peers must have a local peer statement. Otherwise, they must be configured in the “promiscuous” mode. A listing of the DLSw local peer statement parameters is displayed below:

```
r2(config)#dlsw local-peer ?
  biu-segment          XID3 max receivable i-field spoofing and BIU segmenting
  border               Capable of operating as a border peer
  cost                 Set peer cost advertised to remote peers
  group                Set the peer group number for this router
  init-pacing-window   Initial Pacing Window Size for this local peer
  keepalive            Set the default remote peer keepalive interval
  lf                   Local peer largest frame size
  max-pacing-window    Maximum Pacing Window Size for this local peer
  passive              This router will not initiate remote peer connections
  peer-id              local-peer IP addr; required for TCP/FST & peer groups
  promiscuous          Accept connections from non-configured remote peers
  <cr>
```

If you configure a DLSw+ peer with no remote peer statements, it can never initiate a DLSw+ connection. However, if the DLSw+ peer has no remote peer statements but its local peer statement is configured with the promiscuous parameter, the DLSw+ peer can accept remotely initiated connections.

When configuring a DLSw remote-peer connection, you must first determine what type of encapsulation method to use:

```
r2(config)#dlsw remote-peer 0 ?
  frame-relay  Use Frame Relay for remote peer transport
  fst          Use fast sequence transport (FST) for remote peer
               transport
  interface    Use a direct interface for remote peer transport
  tcp          Use TCP for remote peer transport
```

TCP provides the highest level of reliability and resiliency. If your TCP connection is temporarily interrupted due to an underlying internetwork problem, TCP will adjust to the disturbance with its windowing and retransmission features. The other encapsulation methods operate with less overhead than TCP. If you feel your DLSw+ connections are reliable, you may consider using an encapsulation method other than TCP. For example, if you have a fixed point-to-point link between two sites and no routing is going on between the two sites, you may consider using the "interface" direct encapsulation method. Also, the FST and DIRECT encapsulation types do not support local acknowledgment of frames. Finally, certain types of encapsulation types can only be used in limited configurations. For example, FST can only be used for DLSw+ peers that are both supporting locally attached Token-Ring segments. FST encapsulation does not support Token-Ring to Ethernet DLSw+ configurations.

Listed below are the parameters for the TCP and FST encapsulation types:

TCP Encapsulation

```
r2(config)#dlsw remote-peer 0 tcp 172.16.40.4 ?
backup-peer         Configure as a backup to an existing TCP/FST peer
bytes-netbios-out   Configure netbios bytes output filtering for this peer
cost                Cost to Reach this Remote Peer
dest-mac            Exclusive destination mac-addr for remote peer
dmac-output-list    Filter output destination mac addresses
dynamic             Enable dynamic connection for this remote peer
host-netbios-out    Configure netbios host output filtering for this peer
inactivity          Dynamic peer inactivity
keepalive           Set keepalive interval for this remote peer
lf                  Largest Frame Size for this Remote Peer
linger              Backup peer linger
lsap-output-list    Filter output IEEE 802.5 encapsulated packets
```

```
no-llc              dynamic peer no LLC
pass-thru           Remote peer is capable of locally acknowledging DLC sessions
priority            Enable prioritization features for this remote peer tcp only
tcp-queue-max       Maximum output TCP queue size for this remote peer
timeout             Set retransmission timeout value for this remote peer
  <cr>
```

FST Encapsulation

```
r2(config)#dlsw remote-peer 0 fst 172.16.40.4 ?
  backup-peer          Configure as a backup to an existing TCP/FST peer
  bytes-netbios-out    Configure netbios bytes output filtering for this peer
  cost                 Cost to Reach this Remote Peer
  dest-mac             Exclusive destination mac-addr for remote peer
  dmac-output-list     Filter output destination mac addresses
  dynamic              Enable dynamic connection for this remote peer
  host-netbios-out     Configure netbios host output filtering for this peer
  inactivity           Dynamic peer inactivity
  keepalive            Set keepalive interval for this remote peer
  lf                   Largest Frame Size for this Remote  Peer
  linger               Backup peer linger
  lsap-output-list     Filter output IEEE 802.5 encapsulated packets
  no-llc               dynamic peer no LLC  pass-thru Remote peer is capable of
                       locally acknowledging DLC sessions
  timeout              Set retransmission timeout value for this remote peer
  <cr>
```

DLSw+ Preconfiguration Checklist

It is now time to tie all the topics together from Chapters Twenty-One and Twenty-Two:

- Transparent bridging
- Source-route bridging
- Source-route transparent bridging
- Source-route translational bridging
- DLSw+ local peer statements
- DLSw+ local peer statements with the promiscuous parameter
- DLSw+ remote peer statements with TCP encapsulation
- DLSw+ remote peer statements with FST encapsulation

When planning your DLSw+ configuration, you must ask the following questions:

1. Which type of edge networks are being interconnected via DLSw+:
   - Ethernet
   - Token-Ring
   - SDLC
   - If Ethernet, then transparent bridging must be configured with DLSw+ (beware of the cannonical to non-cannonical addressing issue). With transparent bridging, the DLSw+ peer appears as a bridge port in show spanning display.
   - If Token-Ring, the SRB with a virtual ring statement must be configured or SRT must be configured.
   - If both Ethernet and Token-Ring on the same DLSw+ peer router, then both Transparent Bridging, SRB and SR/TLB must be configured on the edge LAN segments.
   - If SDLC is involved in a DLSw+ configuration, then a Virtual MAC address must be supplied.
2. Select the IP addresses you want to use in your DLSw peer statements. Test reachability of the selected remote DLSw+ peer IP address with a PING command.
3. Are there any access-lists or firewalls that will restrict transiting DLSw+ traffic?
4. What common MAC addresses should be announced during the capabilities exchange? What type of traffic should be filtered during the capabilities exchange? Remember DLSw+ circuits are formed with end system MAC LSAP address combinations.

For NetBIOS, you might want to filter the default names PUBLIC and WORKGROUP during the capabilities exchange.

Basic DLSw+ Configurations

Ethernet to Ethernet (Transparent Bridging)

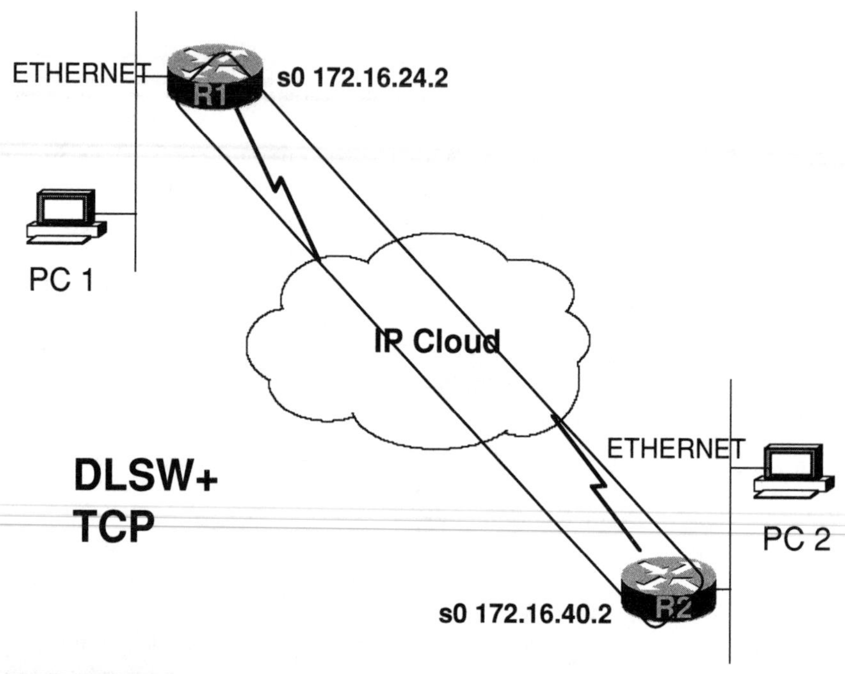

FIGURE 21–2 A DLSw+ configuration using TCP encapsulation between two Ethernet segments.

- Global configuration (Router RI):
  - dlsw local-peer peer-id 172.16.24.2
  - dlsw remote-peer 0 tcp 172.16.40.4
  - dlsw bridge-group 1
  - Bridge I protocol icee
- Interface configuration for ethernet interface:
  - bridge-group 1 (configuration will be the opposite on the other router)

Token-Ring to Token-Ring Using FST (Source-Route Bridging)

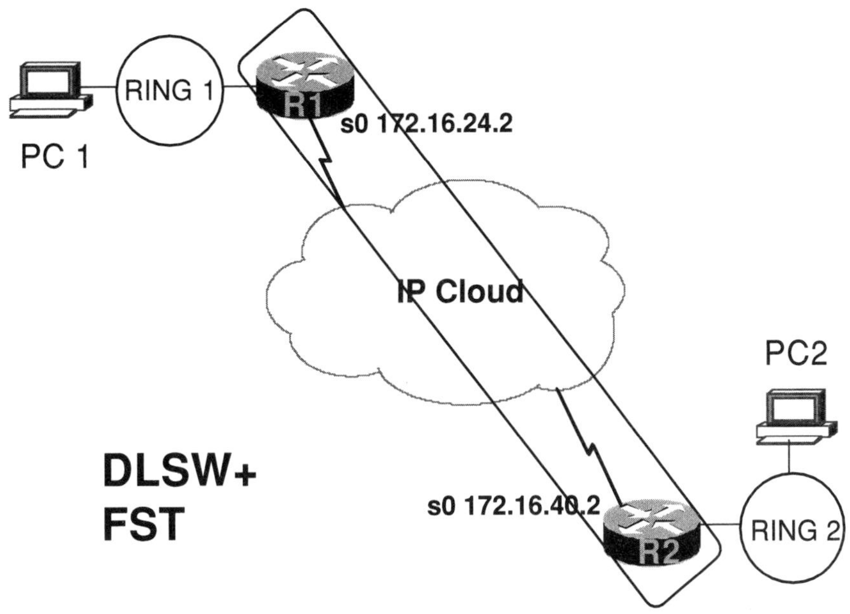

FIGURE 21-3 A DLSw+ configuration using FST encapsulation.

- Global configuration (Router RI):
  - dlsw local-peer peer-id 172.16.24.2
  - dlsw remote-peer 0 for 172.16.40.4
  - source-bridge ring-group 200
- Interface configuration:
  - source-bridge 20 1 200
  - source-bridge spanning (configuration will be the opposite on the other router)

DLSw+ Configurations Using the Promiscuous Parameter

Configuring for promiscuous connections: the DLSw+ local peer promiscuous parameter will allow router 1 to accept connections from other routers. With the promiscuous parameter, router 1 does not require a remote peer statement.

ETHERNET TO ETHERNET (TRANSPARENT BRIDGING)

- Global configuration: router 1
  - dlsw local-peer peer-id 172.16.24.2 promiscuous
  - dlsw bridge-group 1
- Interface configuration:
  - bridge-group 1
- Global configuration: router 2
  - dlsw local-peer peer-id 172.16.40.4
  - dlsw remote-peer 0 tcp 172.16.24.2
  - dlsw bridge-group 1
- Interface configuration:
  - bridge-group 1

TOKEN-RING TO TOKEN-RING (SOURCE-ROUTE BRIDGING)

- Global configuration: router 1
  - dlsw local-peer peer-id 172.16.24.2 promiscuous
  - source-bridge ring-group 200
- Interface configuration:
  - source-bridge 20 1 200
  - source-bridge spanning
- Global configuration: router 2
  - dlsw local-peer peer-id 172.16.40.4
  - dlsw remote-peer 0 tcp 172.16.24.2
  - source-bridge ring-group 200
- Interface configuration:
  - source-bridge 20 1 200
  - source-bridge spanning

Configuring DLSw+ Border Peer Groups

With the above configurations, any-to-any connections will require full mesh connectivity. In order to achieve any-to-any connections without a full mesh, use border peer configurations.

When an end system wants to establish a connection with another end system using DLSw+, one system will send a test frame or name query to its local DLSw+ peer. The local DLSw+ peer will check its cache for the specified destination address, and if the address exists in the local router reachability cache, it will send a Circuit setup request to the listed remote DLSw+ peer. If the target destination address is not in its reachability cache, the local DLSw+ will forward a CANUREACH explorer frame to all its remote peers looking for the destination. When the destination is found, the connection will be established, and the end systems can pass information. Just think of the amount of traffic that could be generated in an any-to-any full mesh environment! The border peer configuration can help reduce the amount of traffic dispersed throughout the network while providing any-to-any connectivity.

DLSW BORDER PEER CONFIGURATION

Global configuration: router 1 border peer for group 40

- dlsw local-peer peer-id 172.16.24.2 group 40 border promiscuous
- dlsw remote-peer 0 tcp 172.16.34.2
- source-bridge ring-group 100

Interface configuration:

- source-bridge 10 1 100
- source-bridge spanning

Global configuration: router 2 (spoke DLSw+ peer)

- dlsw local-peer peer-id 172.16.18.5 group 40 promiscuous
- dlsw remote-peer 0 tcp 172.16.24.2
- source-bridge ring-group 200

Interface configuration:

- source-bridge 20 1 200
- source-bridge spanning

Global configuration: router 3 (spoke DLSw+ peer)

- dlsw local-peer peer-id 172.16.40.4 group 40 promiscuous
- dlsw remote-peer 0 tcp 172.16.24.2
- source-bridge ring-group 300

Interface configuration:

- source-bridge 30 1 300
- source-bridge spanning

Global configuration: router 1 border peer for group 50

- dlsw local-peer peer-id 172.16.34.2 group 50 border promiscuous
- dlsw remote-peer 0 tcp 172.16.24.2
- source-bridge ring-group 100

Interface configuration:

- source-bridge 10 1 100
- source-bridge spanning

Global configuration: router 2 (spoke DLSw+ peer)

- dlsw local-peer peer-id 172.16.28.5 group 50 promiscuous
- dlsw remote-peer 0 tcp 172.16.34.2
- source-bridge ring-group 200

Interface configuration:

- source-bridge 20 1 200
- source-bridge spanning

Global configuration: router 3 (spoke DLSw+ peer)

- dlsw local-peer peer-id 172.16.30.4 group 50 promiscuous
- dlsw remote-peer 0 tcp 172.16.34.2
- source-bridge ring-group 300

Interface configuration:

- source-bridge 30 1 300
- source-bridge spanning

The above configurations for groups 40 and 50 will allow any-to-any communications without a configured full mesh. When an end system sends an explorer frame, the border peer will take care of finding the destination address and let the sender know where to go. When the local router gets the response, it will set up a "dlsw on-demand-peer" with the destination router and a circuit will be established and traffic can pass. The command "dlsw peer-on-demand-defaults tcp" is the default. (This command will not show up in your configuration.) You can make adjustments to this parameter by using the "dlsw peer-on-demand-defaults" command with optional parameters:

```
r2(config)#dlsw peer-on-demand-defaults ?
bytes-netbios-out  Configure netbios bytes output filtering for p-o-d peers
cost               Configure cost to reach p-o-d peers (default is 3)
dest-mac           Exclusive destination mac-addr for pod peer
dmac-output-list   Filter output destination mac addresses
fst                Configure FST for p-o-d transport (default is TCP)
host-netbios-out   Configure netbios host output filtering for p-o-d peers
inactivity         Configure inactivity interval to disconnect p-o-d peers
keepalive          Configure p-o-d keepalive interval (default is 30 secs)
lf                 Configure largest frame size for p-o-d peers
lsap-output-list   Configure LSAP output filtering for p-o-d peers
port-list          Configure a port-list for p-o-d peers
priority           Configure prioritization for p-o-d peers (default is off)
tcp-queue-max      Maximum output TCP queue size for p-o-d peers
```

The two show dlsw peer displays reflect the establishment of a "peer on demand" (POD) connection created through the configuration of border peer groups. Router R2 (172.16.28.5) in border peer group 50 establishes a peer on demand session with R2 in border peer group 40 (172.16.18.5). This is reflected by the last line in the second show dlsw peer display provided below:

```
R2#show dlsw peers (before explorer is sent)
Peers:          state   pkts_rx   pkts_tx  type  drops  ckts  TCP   uptime
TCP 172.16.40.4 CONNECT 117       223      conf  0      0     0     00:52:32
```

```
R2#show dlsw peers (after explorer is sent)
Peers:           state    pkts_rx   pkts_tx  type  drops  ckts  TCP   uptime
TCP 172.16.40.4 CONNECT  117       223      conf  0      0     0     00:52:32
TCP 172.16.18.5 CONNECT  20        14       pod   0      0     0     00:00:1
```

BASIC DLSW+ SHOW COMMANDS

You can monitor DLSw+ operation with the following "show" commands:

```
r2#show dlsw ?
  capabilities    Display DLSw capabilities information
  circuits        Display DLSw circuit information
  fastcache       Display DLSw fast cache for FST and Direct
  local-circuit   Display DLSw local circuits
  peers           Display DLSw peer information
  reachability    Display DLSw reachability information
```

BASIC DLSW+ DEBUG COMMANDS

You can debug DLSw+ processes with the following debugging tools:

```
r2#debug dlsw ?
  core            Debug DLSw core
  local-circuit   Debug DLSw local circuit events
  peers           Debug DLSw peer events
  reachability    Debug DLSw reachability (explorer traffic)
  <cr>
```

Building a DLSw+ Testbed

Not every network has a mainframe with a TIC installed inside its FEP. Even if a network has extensive SNA equipment, it is not advisable to attempt to learn about DLSw+ on a production environment.

With a handful of 1600, 2500, 3600 and/or 4000 routers, you can build your own DLSw+ experimental lab. A minimal DLSw+ test lab consists of two 2501 routers, or two 1600 routers and two Windows 95 workstations with Token-Ring cards or Ethernet cards. Configure the routers for transparent bridging if DLSw+ will involve Ethernet interfaces. Configure the routers for source-route bridging if the work stations support source-routing bridging.

Configure the routers for source-route transparent bridging if the DLSw+ session will involve Token-Ring interfaces but the Windows 95 workstations do not have source-route bridging support for the Token-Ring interfaces.

On the Windows 95 workstation, perform the following two configuration steps:

1. Make sure that NetBIOS is configured. Check this under the Network icon in the Control Panel.
2. Configure one workstation to share a directory.

When you want to test your DLSw+ connection, perform the following steps on a Windows 95 workstation:

- Press the Start button.
- Select "Find" from the Windows 95 main menu.
- Select "Computer" from the Windows 95 Find submenu.

Enter a specific NetBIOS workstation name in the dialog box. Press Enter. If DLSw+ is properly configured, the Windows 95 workstation will find the other Windows 95 workstation located on the far side of your DLSw+ connection.

With this minimal testbed, you can perform the following:

1. Practice establishing DLSw+ peers
2. Watch the reachability caches become populated
3. Create border peer groups
4. Filter DLSw+ connections
5. Generate DLSw+ debug traces
6. Watch DLSw+ circuits form when a Windows 95 end system begins accessing files from a remotely located shared directory

Summary

Cisco's DLSw+ provides connectivity for non-routable traffic over an IP backbone. DLSw+ is compatible with DLSw and RSRB. However, DLSw+ offers features that neither DLSw nor RSRB possess. Unique DLSw+ features include special encapsulation types like FST and border peer configurations. In order to configure DLSw+, you must understand both DLSw+ commands and bridging commands.

Professional Development Checklist

By using this chapter, you should be able to perform the following operations:

- Define a DLSw+ local peer for the router.
- Define DLSw+ remote peers.
- Define a source-bridge ring group for DLSw+ supported Token-Ring edge segment.
- Define a DLSw+ ring list or port list.
- Define a DLSw+ bridge group list.
- Enable DLSw+ on an Ethernet interface.
- Assign Token-Rings to virtual ring groups.
- Tune the DLSw+ configuration.

For Further Study

- RFC 1795, Data Link Switching.
- Cisco IOS Configuration Guide Bridging and IBM Networking Command Reference Configuration Guide, Cisco Systems, Inc., 1989–1998.
- Cisco IOS Configuration Guide Bridging and IBM Networking Command Reference, Cisco Systems, Inc., 1989–1998.
- Cisco Certified Course SNA for Multi-Protocol Networks (SNAM), Cisco Systems, Inc.

URLs

- **www.cciecert.com**
- **www.mentorlabs.com**

Can You Spot the Issues?

There are several problems with the border peer configuration scripts below. Can you spot the issues?

Configuration for r1:

- dlsw local-peer peer-id 172.16.24.2 group 40 border promiscuous
- source-bridge ring-group 100

Interface configuration:

- source-bridge 10 1 10
- source-bridge spanning

Configuration for r2

- dlsw local-peer peer-id 172.16.18.5 group 40 promiscuous
- dlsw remote-peer 0 fst 172.16.24.2
- dlsw bridge-group 1

Interface configuration:

- bridge-group 1

Global configuration: *router 3*

- dlsw local-peer peer-id 172.16.40.4 group 40 promiscuous
- dlsw remote-peer 0 tcp 172.16.18.5
- source-bridge ring-group 300

Interface configuration:

- source-bridge 30 1 300
- source-bridge spanning

T W E N T Y T W O

Level Five Summary

This summary will first provide an overview of transparent bridging configuration, followed by a summary of the integration source route bridging and other non-routing technologies with DLSw+.

The Rebirth of Transparent Bridging

The first topic, the rebirth of transparent bridging and the spanning tree algorithm, is due primarily to the ascendancy and proliferation of LAN switching technology in general, and the Cisco Catalyst family of LAN switches and multilayer switches in particular. As the role of LAN switching grows in importance, Level Five issues also grow in importance. In the late 80s and early 90s, the general rule was "Route when you can, bridge when you must". An often-quoted maxim of the late 90s is "Switch when you can, route when you must." Recall the hierarchical internetwork model presented in Chapter Two:

Core Distribution Access

Today, the cores of many organizations' internetworks are predominantly switched VLAN environments. In many organizations, LAN switches are interconnected with trunk connections, not routers. Routers play the role of routing traffic between VLANs. If desired, Cisco can provide such a solution. However, with Cisco Fusion and Cisco's multilayer switching platforms, like the Catalyst 5000 and Catalyst 8500, Cisco can also provide a robust wire speed Layer III switching solution.

Whether you are a proponent of Layer II switching, Layer III switching, or multilayer switching, you must be able to argue the pros and cons of all configurations and architectures. To do this you must have a strong understanding of the following technologies:

1. LAN switching architectures
2. Transparent bridging
3. The spanning tree algorithm
4. Trunking technologies (ISL, Fast EtherChannel, 802.1q, Gigabit Ethernet, 802.10 and ATM LANE)
5. Layer III switch routing (Catalyst 8500)
6. Integrated routing and bridging

Chapter Twenty, the first Level Five chapter, focused on the IOS specific topics listed above: configuring, monitoring and troubleshooting transparent bridging, the spanning tree algorithm and integrated routing and bridging on Cisco routers and Catalyst switches. This summary provides a review of these topics. Reference the Cisco Web site at www.cisco.com for more information on LAN switching architectures, trunking technologies and Layer III switch routing.

A recommended order of configuring transparent bridging and directly related topics is displayed below:

Design and Planning Tasks

1. Determine what type of traffic is going to bridged (IP, IPX, AppleTalk, NetBIOS, DECNET, DEC LAT, SNA, etc.).
2. Identify which router interfaces and switch ports are going to participate in the transparent bridging process. Determine whether the topology is looped. Identify which router or switch you want to make the root of the spanning tree. If a looped topology exists, determine which port or ports you want to set in a "blocking" state.

Configuration Tasks

1. Perform the basic transparent bridging configuration on all Cisco router interfaces and Catalyst switch ports.
2. Perform spanning tree configuration (if any) and verify proper spanning tree operation on Cisco routers and Catalyst switches.

3. Monitor transparent bridging tables on Cisco routers and Catalyst switches.
4. Configure integrated routing and bridging on Cisco routers and Catalyst 8500 switch routers if necessary.

For Cisco routers and the Catalyst 8500 switch router, transparent bridging configuration monitoring and troubleshooting is identical from the IOS perspective. Transparent bridging is enabled by default on Catalyst 5000 LAN switch modules. The Catalyst 5000 uses a different set of configuration commands than the Cisco routers and Catalyst 8500 switch router. See Chapters 2, 3 and 6 for an overview of the basic Catalyst 5000 IOS commands.

Overview of Configuration Tasks

Basic Transparent Bridging Configuration

The following two commands are the basic Cisco router and Catalyst 8500 transparent bridging configuration commands:

GLOBAL CONFIGURATION

Whichever spanning tree algorithm you select, use the same one on all routers and Catalyst 8500s belonging to the same bridge-group:

```
Bridge # protocol [ieee | dec]  (# = bridge-group number)
```

INTERFACE CONFIGURATION

Place the following command on all router interfaces and Catalyst 8500 ports that you want to participate in a specific bridge group:

```
Bridge-group # (# = bridge-group number)
```

For a Catalyst 5000 LAN switching module, transparent bridging is enabled by default. Therefore, no commands need to be entered on a Catalyst 5000 to enable transparent bridging on its LAN switching modules. They are "plug and play" modules.

Checking the Basic Transparent Bridging Configuration

Once the basic configuration commands are entered on a Cisco router or Catalyst 8500 performing transparent bridging, use the following command to verify that basic transparent bridging is operational:

```
r2#show spanning-tree

Bridge Group 1 is executing the IEEE compatible Spanning Tree protocol
     Bridge Identifier has priority 32768, address 0060.837b.a729
     Configured hello time 2, max age 20, forward delay 15
     We are the root of the spanning tree
     Topology change flag not set, detected flag not set
     Times:  hold 1, topology change 30, notification 30
     hello 2, max age 20, forward delay 15, aging 300
     Timers: hello 2, topology change 0, notification 0

Port 4 (Ethernet0) of bridge group 1 is forwarding
     Port path cost 100, Port priority 128
     Designated root has priority 32768, address 0060.837b.a729
     Designated bridge has priority 32768, address 0060.837b.a729
     Designated port is 4, path cost 0
     Timers: message age 0, forward delay 0, hold 0
```

All participating routers and Catalyst 8500 switch routers must elect the same root bridge. If one of the routers or 8500 switches continues to elect itself as the root bridge while all other devices have elected a different root bridge, more than likely the device electing itself is misconfigured.

For Catalyst 5000 LAN switch modules, a separate spanning tree is created for each VLAN. For each switch trunked with another switch and that is participating in the same VLAN, perform a show spantree xx (xx= vlan number). Make sure that all switches agree on who is the root switch for the specific VLAN.

Adjust the Spanning Tree Parameters (Optional)

Use the following two commands on a Cisco router and Catalyst 8500 switch router to adjust the spanning tree configuration.

The following global configuration command influences the spanning tree root bridge election process:

```
r3(config)#bridge 1 priority
 <0-65535>  Priority (low priority more likely to be root)
```

The following interface configuration command influences the path used by non-root bridges to get to the root bridge:

```
r1(config-if)#bridge-group 1 path-cost
  <0-65535>  Path cost (higher values are higher costs)
```

The results of these configuration commands can be monitored with the following commands:

```
Show span
Debug span events
```

On a Catalyst 5000, use the following two commands to influence the spanning tree root bridge election process and the cost of paths used by the non-root bridges to get to the root bridge:

```
Set spantree
Set spantree
```

Verify and monitor the adjustments made to the spanning tree on the Catalyst 5000 with the following command:

```
Show spantree xxx
```

Monitor Transparent Bridging Tables

To monitor bridging tables on Cisco routers and Catalyst 8500 switch routers, use the following command:

```
Show bridge
```

Look for the specific MAC address that should be bridging traffic. Make sure frames are being transmitted and received properly. If necessary, you can clear the bridge table with a "clear bridge" command.

To monitor bridging tables on a Catalyst 5000 switch, use the following commands:

```
Show cam dynamic
```

(This command will list all MAC addresses learned by the Catalyst 5000. It will also list the port which the MAC address is learned and its associated VLAN.)

```
Show mac
```

(This command lists the number of frames transmitted and received on a given port. Unlike the "show bridge" command on the Cisco routers and Catalyst 8500 switch router, show mac does not associate a MAC address to the number of frames transmitted and received on a given port.)

If necessary, you can clear the CAM table with the "clear cam" command and clear the mac statistics with the "clear counters" command.

Configure Integrated Routing and Bridging on Cisco Routers and Catalyst 8500 Switch Routers (Optional)

If you want to route packets of a given protocol on a specific interface and bridge the same type of protocol on another set of interfaces, you must configure either concurrent routing and bridging (CRB) or integrated routing and bridging (IRB) on a Cisco router or Catalyst 8500 switch router. This feature cannot be configured on a Catalyst 5000 LAN switching module. If you want to exchange packets of the same protocol between bridged interfaces and routed interfaces, you must configure integrated routing and bridging (IRB) only.

IRB configuration and show commands include:

- Bridge irb
- Bridge x route yy
- Bridge x bridge yy
- No bridge x route yy
- No bridge x bridge yy
- Interface bvi x
- Show interface irb
- Show interface bvi x
- x = bridge-group number
- yy = protocols (ip, ipx, appletalk, decnet, etc.)

By default, both Cisco routers and the Catalyst 8500 switch router will attempt to route IP and bridge all other protocols. Use the bridge/no bridge commands listed above to assure that the appropriate protocols are bridged and routed on the proper interface.

If you are a CCIE candidate, none of the transparent bridging commands, principles and techniques described above should be unfamiliar to you. Before you type in any of the commands, you should already know the contents and structure of the show command displays and debug outputs. You should be able to perform the transparent bridging commands described above in a structured and incremental manner, and you should feel comfortable and confident in doing so. If you do not feel comfortable with the transparent bridging topics described above, do not go any further in your CCIE preparation. It cannot be stressed enough how important transparent bridging topics are in today's internetworking environment. Transparent bridging is at the heart of today's Ethernet LAN switching technologies.

Configuring Source Route Bridging and DLSw+

As mentioned at the beginning of this chapter, the Level Five topics covered in this book are dominated by two topics:

1. The rebirth of transparent bridging and the spanning tree algorithm through LAN switching
2. The integration of source route bridging, transparent bridging, source route transparent bridging, source route translational bridging and LLC2-based SNA traffic over an IP backbone using DLSw+

This section will provide an overview of the second topic: integrating source route bridging and other bridging technologies over an IP backbone using DLSw+.

Source route bridging is a bridging technology deployed on Token-Ring networks. Both source-route bridging and Token-Ring are commonly found in data centers housing IBM mainframes and minicomputers. It is not uncommon to encounter organizations with Token-Ring in data centers supporting IBM mainframes and Ethernet based LANs in downstream branch offices. In fact, many organizations have a combination of Token-Ring, Ethernet and SDLC controllers in their branch offices. How do these organizations tie all of these different data-link layer technologies together? A Cisco solution is to deploy DLSw+.

DLSw+ will tie all of the above listed data-link layer technologies (and more) over an IP backbone. If you are going to configure DLSw+, you must know DLSw+ configuration commands as well as bridging commands. Common DLSw+ configurations involve connecting transparent bridged segments to source route bridged segments. In fact, DLSw+ automatically performs source route translational bridging. Since transparent bridging has already been reviewed, the following review will focus only on source route bridging and DLSw+ configuration and monitoring.

Important source route bridging commands to know are:

- source-bridge xx y zz (xx = local ring y = bridge number zz = target ring)
- Source-bridge ring-group xx (xx = virtual ring number)
- Show source

Important DLSw+ commands to know are:

- Dlsw local-peer (the single required command of DLSw+)
- Dlsw remote peer (you do not need this command if your local-peer statement is defined as promiscuous)
- Dlsw bridge xx (allows a transparent bridge group to participate in a DLSw+ session)
- Show dlsw peer
- Show dlsw reachability
- Show dlsw circuit
- Debug dlsw peer
- Debug dlsw reachability
- Debug dlsw core

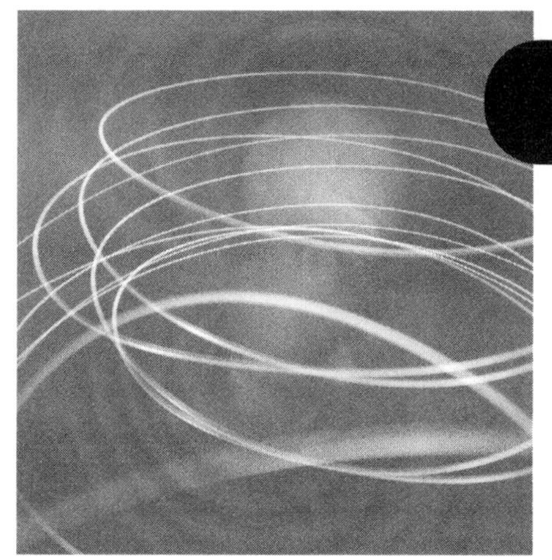

TWENTY THREE

Managing Traffic

Topics Coverted in This Chapter

- Overview of Using Access-lists, Queue-lists, and Route-Maps
- General Guidelines that Apply to All Access-List Configurations
- Points of Caution When Applying Access-Lists
- A Suggested Approach to Constructing Access-Lists for a Range of IP and DECNET Addresses

We have reached the final level: Level Six!

All Level One Tasks Have Been Performed

All of your router interfaces and switch ports are operational. Your Frame-Relay based router interfaces are communicating properly with the Frame-Relay switch. Your ISDN-based router interfaces are communicating properly with the ISDN switch. Your ATM interfaces on both routers and Catalyst switches are communicating properly with the ATM switch. All Catalyst trunk ports between switches are operating properly.

All Level Two Tasks Have Been Performed

An IP addressing numbering plan has been designed and deployed. All of your IP IGP routing protocols have been configured and redistribution is occurring between them. All routers' IP routing tables have converged and all IP addresses can be pinged.

All Level Three Tasks Have Been Performed

All EBGP and IBGP neighbor relationships have been formed and IP inter-autonomous system traffic is being transferred. All BGP tables contain the desired information.

All Level Four Tasks Have Been Performed

The non-IP routing protocol suites—IPX, AppleTalk, and DECNET—have been configured to operate concurrently with IP ("ships in the night") or tunneled through IP. All IPX routing and SAP tables have converged. All AppleTalk routing and zone tables have converged. All DECNET Level One and Level Two routing tables have converged. All IPX, AppleTalk, and DECNET addresses can be successfully pinged.

All Level Five Topics Have Been Performed

Where required, transparent bridging and source route bridging have been configured. Also, integrated routing and bridging (IRB) and DLSw+ have been configured as well. Frames forwarded by transparent bridging are reaching their destinations properly. DLSw+ peer connections are being established. DLSw+ end system to end system circuits are being established as well.

Now you must filter, prioritize, and manipulate traffic in each of the above listed levels (Level Two through Level Five). You must filter specified routing table updates. You must queue specified types of traffic. You must manipulate the metrics of routing table updates at redistribution points. You must manipulate BGP attributes. Different tools will be used for different protocols, but almost all of the tools can be categorized into the following three general categories:

1. Access-lists
2. Queue-lists
3. Route-maps

Now that baseline connectivity has been established for all protocols over all methods of transport, you can begin to tune your network for performance, efficiency, and security. Access-lists, queue-lists, and route-maps provide tools to help you tune your network.

For example, your client might ask you to:

Block access to specific Internet sites
Reduce the amount of overhead traffic (routing table updates) throughout the internetwork
Restrict what users have in bound access to a given network
Assure that terminal traffic (TELNET and SNA traffic) always receive a minimum amount of available bandwidth
Make sure that only specified types of traffic initiate an ISDN/DDR call
For traffic destined to network x.x.x.x, use autonomous system XX instead of autonomous system YY

All of the above listed customer requests are handled through access-list, queue-list, and route-map configuration.

When a network is designed in the Cisco recommended three level hierarchy of core, distribution, and access, you want to closely examine the amount and type of traffic originating from access-level workgroup networks. As access-level traffic is forwarded to distribution level routers and ultimately core-level routers, it gets aggregated. You want to divide traffic types into the general categories of user traffic and overhead traffic. You want to keep overhead traffic to a minimum. Types of overhead are:

Routing table updates
DHCP traffic
DNS traffic
IPX SAP traffic
AppleTalk Zone and NBP queries
LLC2 S-Frames
Spanning Tree BPDUs

In the best of all possible worlds, you want to keep overhead traffic to a minimum, especially in the internetwork core. As an example, consider the following scenario: An organization has 100 branch offices throughout the United States. Each branch office has a 100 node Novell LAN consisting of two IPX segments. Each branch office possesses the following types of servers:

two file servers
four print servers
one backup server
one fax server
one SNA gateway server

Therefore, each branch office maintains a routing table of four local IPX addresses (two for each of the physical segments and two for the internal IPX numbers of the file servers) and a SAP table of only nine local SAPs. Currently, each of these Novell-based branch offices is an "island unto itself." There is no office to office Novell connectivity. The organization plans to provide complete office to office connectivity. When all of the organization's branch offices are interconnected with no IPX filtering applied, all branch office routers and servers maintain a routing table of 400 IPX routes and 900 SAPs. By default, all of the organization's internetwork segments from each workgroup LAN segment to the corporate backbone will be impacted by an IPX routing update consisting of 400 routes and an IPX SAP update consisting of 900 listed services *every sixty seconds!* If the organization has a hub and spoke Frame-Relay topology, the Frame-Relay hub routers will need to replicate these broadcasts for each PVC every sixty seconds!

Also, as a result of this unrestricted propagation of RIP and SAP updates, users at all 100 branch offices will receive a listing of unneeded Novell resources from other offices. For example, users in New York will see listings of print servers and backup servers in San Diego. Users in New York will never use the print servers and backup servers in San Diego!

Two solutions exists to remedy this problem:

1. Implement a routing protocol such as EIGRP or NLSP that do not advertise periodic routing table updates in the internetwork core.
2. Filter routing and SAP updates at the access-level.

Both of these solutions are not mutually exclusive. They can be deployed to complement each other. Unlike IPX RIP and SAP, both EIGRP and NLSP do not send out the periodic updates. When the IPX network is stable, both of these routing protocols require minimum network resources to operate. IPX access-lists can be deployed with any routing protocol. Like all access-lists, IPX access-lists should be deployed at the edge of an organization's internetwork (ideally at the access-level router).

A brief and partial listing of access-list, queue-list, and route-map uses is provided below.

Level Two

Filter IP traffic by specified protocol characteristics such as well known port numbers (access-lists)
Filter specified traffic based upon IP source and destination address (access-lists)
Filter routing table updates with distribute-lists (access-lists)
Define IP interesting traffic with dialer-lists in a granular manner (dialer-lists combined with access-lists)
Define addresses to applied to a NAT process (access-lists)

Assure that delay sensitive traffic (TELNET) always receives a percentage of available bandwidth (queue-lists)

Assure that delay sensitive traffic (TELNET) from specified addresses always receives a percentage of available bandwidth (queue-lists combined with access-lists)

Level Three

Filter BGP4 updates by network prefix (distribute-lists combined with access-lists)
Filter BGP4 updates by autonomous system path (AS-Path Access-Lists)
Define BGP4 updates for route-map manipulation (route-maps combined with access-lists)

Level Four

Filter IPX traffic by specified protocol characteristics such as pre-defined socket numbers (access-lists)
Filter specified traffic based upon IPX source and destination address (access-lists)
Filter IPX routing table updates (access-lists)
Filter IPX SAP updates (access-lists)
Filter IPX GNS requests (access-lists)
Define IPX interesting traffic with dialer-lists in a granular manner (dialer-lists combined with access-lists)
Assure that delay sensitive traffic always receives a percentage of available bandwidth (queue-lists)
Assure that delay sensitive traffic from specified addresses always receives a percentage of available bandwidth (queue-lists combined with access-lists)
Filter AppleTalk traffic based upon AppleTalk source and destination address (access-list)
Filter AppleTalk GET-ZONE-LIST queries (access-list)
Filter AppleTalk Zone Rely queries (access-list)
Filter AppleTalk Name Binding Protocol queries (access-list)
Filter AppleTalk routing table updates (access-list)
Filter DECNET traffic based upon source and destination address (access-list)
Filter DECNET routing table updates (access-list)

Level Five

Filter transparent and source-route bridged traffic by MAC address (access-list)
Filter transparent and source-route bridged traffic by LSAP type (access-list)
Filter NETBIOS traffic by name and byte-count (access-list)
Assure that delay sensitive traffic (DLSw+/LLC2) always receives a percentage of available bandwidth (queue-lists)
Assure that delay sensitive traffic (DLSw+/LLC2) from specified addresses always receives a percentage of available bandwidth (queue-lists combined with access-lists)

Access-List configuration, in its most basic configuration, is the most common method of controlling traffic. With access-lists, you either permit or deny the processing of a packet based upon a list of conditions. For packets processed by access-lists, it is a life and death situation. If a packet meets the permit conditions of an access-list, it gets processed. If it does not, it gets discarded.

If you meet one of the defined conditions, you are either explicitly permitted or denied. If you meet none of the defined conditions, you are implicitly denied.

It is absolutely critical to remember that access-lists are not used solely for filtering traffic. Access-lists are also used by queue-lists and route-maps. Queue-lists use access-lists to provide a highly granular method of identifying what types of traffic get assigned to specific queues. Route-maps use access-lists to identify specific addresses or address ranges for adjustment and manipulation.

Queue-lists are not as extreme as access-lists. With queue-lists, all data gets through. However, some types of traffic may get through an interface before other types do.

If you meet one of the defined conditions, you are assigned to the explicitly assigned queue. If you do not meet the defined conditions, you are assigned to the default queue.

Route-maps provide an alternative to the type of routing we have done so far. All routing performed so far has been destination based routing. Route-maps allow routing decisions to by made on criteria other than the destination address of the routed packet. Other criteria can by source address of packet or source autonomous-system. Route-maps are also used to manipulate routing table update information. Route-maps can be used to manipulate IGP metrics during the route redistribution process. Route-maps can also be used to manipulate BGP-4 updates.

With route-maps, if you meet a defined "match" criteria, you are manipulated by the specified "set" command.

Roadmap of Level Six Coverage

Since access-lists are involved in both queuing and route-map configuration, access-lists will be covered first. Three separate access-list chapters are provided:

Chapter Twenty-Four:	IP Access-Lists
Chapter Twenty-Five:	Non-IP Routing Access-Lists
Chapter Twenty-Six:	Non-Routable Traffic Access-Lists

Just as with Level Four and Level Five topics, your access-list learning process will be baselined by IP. Once you master all of the subtleties of IP access-lists, move onto the non-IP Routing Access-Lists (IPX, AppleTalk, and DECNET) and the nonroutable access-lists. When you are learning IPX, AppleTalk, and DECNET access-lists compare the issues to what you have already learned with IP access-lists.

Once access-lists have been covered, queuing will be covered second; followed by route-map configuration.

General Rules to Apply to All Access-List Configurations

When configuring access-lists, remember the following six general rules of access-lists:

1. Design/define access-lists statements from most specific to most general match criteria.
2. When configuring access-lists, you must possess strong understanding of the protocol stack involved.
3. Access-list configuration and application involve two components:
   - The configuration of the access-list itself in global configuration mode
   - The application of the access-list in interface-configuration mode
4. Access-lists have direction. Access-lists can effect inbound or outbound traffic. Some access-lists can be explicitly applied to inbound or outbound traffic.
5. You can have one access-list per protocol per interface per direction.
6. When adding access-list statement they are appended to the bottom of the list.

In sum, think of access-lists from the following three perspectives:

1. Top to bottom
2. Specific to general
3. Applications Layer to Physical Layer

Points of Caution When Applying Access-Lists

When configuring access-lists, remember the following six points of caution:

1. When configuring access-lists, you are playing with fire.
   When you configure access-lists, you run the risk of accidentally blocking the flow of unforeseen traffic. For example, you set up an IP access-list to allow only EIGRP routing table updates, all outbound TCP traffic and specified UDP traffic (DNS and DHCP traffic). Several months after you have configured these IP access-lists, you attempt to configure AURP tunneling. It does not work because AURP uses UDP port 387. The IP access-lists must be adjusted to accommodate AURP tunneling. Therefore, when configuring access-lists, it is imperative that you understand protocol characteristics to a high level of detail. For example, you must know the well-known port numbers used by TCP and UDP. You must know when these well-known port addresses are designated as the source port as well as the destination port.
2. When configuring access-lists, assume deny: Remember the implicit deny rule.
3. Be sensitive to access-lists direction.
4. Think through wildcard masks.
5. Think through access-lists position in network.
6. When adding access-list statements, new statements go to the bottom of the list.

Binary to Decimal/Decimal to Binary Address Conversion and Binary to Hexadecimal/ Hexadecimal to Binary Address Conversion

It is important to have a mastery of binary to decimal address conversion and hexadecimal to binary address conversion. Binary to decimal address conversion is important for:

Standard subnetting
Variable length subnetting
Route Summarization for OSPF and EIGRP
Route Aggregation for BGP4
Wildcard mask configuration for OSPF
Wildcard mask configuration for IP Access-Lists
Wildcard mask configuration for DECNET Access-Lists

Binary to hexadecimal address conversion is important for:

IPX addressing
IPX address summarization
Wildcard masks for IPX access-lists
Wildcard masks for LSAP access-lists
Wildcard masks for MAC address access-lists
Manipulating the IOS Configuration-Register

A Suggested Approach to Constructing Access-Lists That Manipulate a Range of IP and DECNET Addresses

The following access-list construction technique is useful for IP and DECNET access-list configuration. In the example below, the technique is applied to an IP access-list. The same technique can be applied to a DECNET access-list.

Often, a network engineer desires to match a range of addresses using a Cisco access list. For example, a network's security policy may demand that hosts with an IP fourth octet address of 40 through 49 be permitted network access, while all others be blocked. A naive attempt to construct such an access list might result in something like this:

```
access-list 10 permit 10.10.10.40 0.0.0.10
```

This, of course, won't work. The 10 in the mask will be interpreted in binary as 00001010, the 40 in the address is 00101000, so the resulting pattern will be 0010x0x0, matching the set 32 34 40 42. This is not what we wanted. What's needed, of course, is something like the following:

```
access-list 10 permit 10.10.10.40 0.0.0.7
access-list 10 permit 10.10.10.48 0.0.0.1
```

It's all well and good to present such a list of access-list commands, and the reader should verify for himself that this list works. But how is the access-list generated?

That task can be performed using the following algorithm, a method of converting any address range into a set of access-list statements that exactly match the range.

Access List Algorithm

Let `$(min, max)$` be a range of a numbers between 0 and 255 inclusive. This algorithm generates a list of binary number/mask pairs that exactly match the range.

```
Step 1.       Find the first number on the following chart that lies
              within the range $(min, max)$.  Call this number $chart$.
                                        128
                                      64 192
                                  32 96 160 224
                          16 48 80 112 144 176 208 240
                8 24 40 56 72 88 104 120 136 152 168 184 200 216 232 248
                   4 12 20 28 36 44 52 60 68 76 84 92 100 108 116 124
             132 140 148 156 164 172 180 188 196 204 212 220 228 236 244 252
                      2 6 10 14 18 22 26 30 34 38 42 46 50 54 58 62
                 66 70 74 78 82 86 90 94 98 102 106 110 114 118 122 126
             130 134 138 142 146 150 154 158 162 166 170 174 178 182 186 190
             194 198 202 206 210 214 218 222 226 230 234 238 242 246 250 254
Step 2.       Iterate over the following procedure, starting with$low = chart$
              and $high = max$.
Step 2A.      Subtract $low$ from $high$ and find the largest of the
              following numbers less than or equal to $high-low$.  Call this
              number $mask$:  0 1 3 7 15 31 63 127
Step 2B.      Add a new address/mask pair to the access list:
              $low$ and $mask$
Step 2C.      Compute a new $low$ by adding $mask+1$ to $low$.
Step 2D.      If $low > high$, then continue to Step 3.
              Otherwise, return to Step 2A.
Step 3.       Iterate over the following procedure, starting with
              $low = min$ and $high = chart-1$.
Step 3A.      If $low > high$, then done.  Otherwise, continue to Step 3B.

Step 3B.      Subtract $low$ from $high$ and find the largest of the following
              numbers less than or equal to $high-low$.  Call this number
              $mask$:  0 1 3 7 15 31 63 127
Step 3C.      Add a new address/mask pair to the access list:
              $high-mask$ and $mask$
Step 3D.      Compute a new $high$ by subtracting $mask-1$ from $high$.
Step 3E.      Return to Step 3A.
```

Example

Construct an access list that matches the range 40 to 49.

```
Step 1.       48, on the fourth line of the chart, is the first number on the
              chart between 40 and 49, so $chart = 48$.
Step 2.       Start with $low = 48$ and $high = 49$.
Step 2A.      $high-low$ is 1.  The largest number in the list less
              than or equal to 1 is 1.  $mask = 1$
Step 2B.      Add a new address/mask pair using $low = 48$ and $mask = 1$:
              access-list 10 permit 10.10.10.48 0.0.0.1
Step 2C.      Compute a new $low = low+mask+1 = 48+1+1 = 50$.
Step 2D.      $low=50$ is greater than $high=49$, so continue to Step 3.
Step 3.       Start with $low = 40$ and $high = 47$.
Step 3A.      $low=40$ is less than $high=47$, so continue.
Step 3B.      $high-low$ is 7.  The largest number is the list less than
```

```
              or equal to 7 is 7.  $mask = 7$
Step 3C.      Add a new address/mask pair using $high-mask = 40$ and $mask = 7$:
              access-list 10 permit 10.10.10.40 0.0.0.7
Step 3D.      Compute a new $high = high-mask-1 = 47-7-1 = 39$
Step 3E.      Return to Step 3A. Step 3A:  $low=40$ is greater than $high=39$,
              so we're done.
The resulting access list is:
access-list 10 permit 10.10.10.48 0.0.0.1
access-list 10 permit 10.10.10.40 0.0.0.7
```

Summary

Access-lists, queue-lists, and route-maps are useful for manipulating traffic and routing table updates. Do not configure access-lists until all of your basic connectivity requirements have been fulfilled (your Level Two through Level Five requirements). Configuring access-lists when your basic connectivity requirements are not fulfilled compounds the complications involved with connectivity troubleshooting.

Access-Lists are at the heart of the Cisco IOS traffic management took kit. Not only are access-lists used to permit or deny traffic on a given interface, they are also used to make queue-lists and route-maps more granular. Before moving onto queue-lists and route-maps, master access-list configuration first.

When configuring access-lists, you are playing with fire! Make sure that you understand the protocol suite for which you configure the access-list.

Can You Spot the Issues?

1. Your DLSw+ TCP peer connections are never becoming active. You can PING the remote DLSw+ peer connection from the local DLSw+ peer. Three months ago you placed an access-list on your local DLSw+ peer allowing only routing table updates, WWW, SMTP, DNS and ICMP echoes. Why is your DLSw+ peer connection getting established?
2. IP hosts 172.16.1.30 -172.16.1.63 are permitted with the following access-list statements:

   Access-list 101 permit ip any 172.16.1.30 0.0.0.1
   Access-list 101 permit ip any 172.16.1.32.0.0.0.31

   You only wanted to block hosts with the last octet of 30 to 47. What happened?

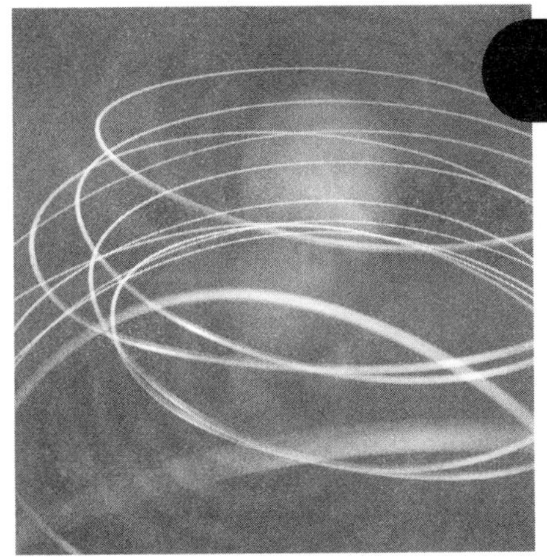

T W E N T Y F O U R

Configuring IP Access-Lists

Topics Covered in This Chapter

- Configuring Internet Protocol (IP) Standard Access-Lists
- Configuring IP Extended Access-Lists
- Configuring a Range of IP Access-Lists
- Configure an IP Access-List with the Established Parameter
- Configure Dynamic Access-Lists

Standard and Extended Access-Lists

The first Internet Protocol (IP) access-list topic covered is standard (access-lists 0-99) and extended (access-lists 100-199) IP access-lists. These types of access lists can be considered "Legacy" and will be used as a baseline for the newer type of access-lists Cisco has developed.

Standard and extended access-lists are used in a variety of applications:

- Security
- Defining interesting traffic on dialer interfaces
- Network Address Translation
- Queuing
- Filtering Routing Updates with Distribute-Lists

Standard Access-Lists

Standard access-lists are used when the source address alone needs to be used as the matching criteria. The basic format is:

```
Access-list number [permit|deny] [ip address] [mask]
```

Each access-list is given a unique number. This number tells the router which type of access-list you are defining. Standard IP access-lists are defined with the numbers within the range of 1-99. With 11.2 named access-list were introduced which allows you to define names for your access-list.

Lets look at an example of the use of a standard access-list.

Senario 1: Standard Access-List to Allow a Specific Host

Figure 24-1 shows a typical scenario of two sites connected to the Internet. Router I connects a network of Windows 95 machines to the internet. Router L connects a UNIX workstation operating as a Web, FTP, and Gopher Server to the Internet. We would like to allow the PC 192.168.87.20 access to the UNIX machine and the services available on the machine.

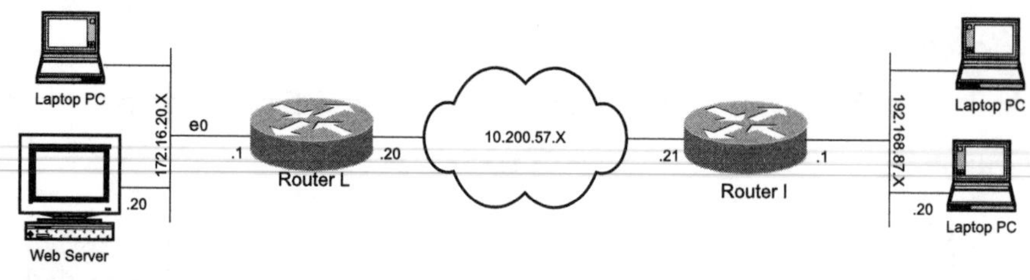

FIGURE 24–1 A standard access-list scenario

The problem specifies that the laptop 192.168.87.20 is required to communicate with the Web Server 172.16.20.20. This may be accomplished by installing a standard access-list on the Ethernet interface of Router L. The configuration will look as follows:

```
hostname RouterL
!
interface Ethernet0
     ip address 172.16.20.1 255.255.255.0
     ip access-group 1
!
access-list 1 permit 192.168.87.20
```

The configuration in Scenario 1 allows ONLY the IP address of 192.168.87.20 through the Ethernet interface. This computer will have full access to all IP servers on the Ethernet network 172.16.20.X. No other computer outside the Ethernet network will have access to the Ethernet network.

Also, notice there are no deny statements. By default, there is an implied *deny all* statement at the end of the list. Anything that is not explicitly permitted is denied. Therefore, EVERY ACCESS-LIST MUST HAVE AT LEAST ONE PERMIT STATEMENT TO BE USEFULL. Without the permit statement all traffic will be denied!

Note: Access-lists do not effect the router that the access-list resides. A user that Telnets to Router L will still have full connectivity to network 172.16.20.x, even though the access-list only allows access from the machine 192.168.87.20. To prevent access from the router, an access-class statement must be used.

Scenario 2: Deny a Specific Host

Deny the host 192.168.87.20 from accessing IP services from the network 172.16.20.x. Allow all other machines access.

Because there is an explicit *deny all* associated with every access-list, we must explicitly permit all hosts except 192.168.87.20. The configuration is as follows:

```
hostname RouterL
!
interface Ethernet0
     ip address 172.16.20.1 255.255.255.0
     ip access-group 1
!
access-list 1 deny 192.168.87.20
access-list 1 permit any
```

The order of the statements in Scenario 2 is critical to the operation of the access-list. The router does NOT find the best match in the list. It uses the first match. If the statements were ordered as follows:

```
access-list 1 permit any
access-list 1 deny 192.168.87.20
```

All machines, including the host 192.168.87.20 will be allowed access.

EXTENDED ACCESS-LISTS

Standard access-lists work well if you only want to filter based upon a source address. Extended access-lists allow filtering on not only the source address, but the destination address, protocol, and port number. The basic format is as follows:

```
access-list access-list-number {deny | permit} protocol source source-wildcard
destination destination-wildcard [operator]
```

Extended access-lists have a range of 100-199 or with IOS version11.2 named access-list may be used.

The protocols that may be specified are:

```
eigrp        Cisco's EIGRP routing protocol
gre          Cisco's GRE tunneling
icmp         Internet Control Message Protocol
igmp         Internet Gateway Message Protocol
igrp         Cisco's IGRP routing protocol
ip           Any Internet Protocol
ipinip       IP in IP tunneling
nos          KA9Q NOS compatible IP over IP tunneling
ospf         OSPF routing protocol
tcp          Transmission Control Protocol
udp          User Datagram Protocol
```

If the protocol is not listed, you may enter the protocol number (between 1-255).

Protocols commonly used but not possessing an IP protocol number key word are:

```
FST (DLSW+ and RSRB) 71
```

Scenario 3: Using the Router RI as a Firewall

The management that operates Router I has decided to allow only Web, Telnet, and FTP access from the Internet. Set Router I to prevent all other services.

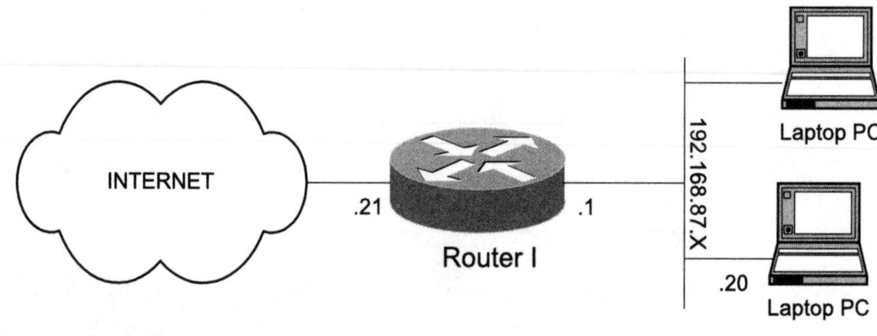

FIGURE 24–2 Limit the outbound access for network 192.168.87.0

We can use an extended access-list to prevent all traffic besides Web, Telnet, and FTP from leaving the router.

```
hostname RI
!
interface Serial0
```

```
  ip address 10.200.57.21 255.255.255.0
  ip access-group 100 out

!
no ip classless
access-list 100 permit tcp any any eq www log
access-list 100 permit tcp any any eq telnet log
access-list 100 permit tcp any any eq ftp log
```

While not explicitly stated, this configuration acts as a "poor man's" firewall. The configuration will allow the laptops on the 192.168.87.x network to access Web, Telnet, and FTP services while preventing outsiders from accessing services that are available on the 192.168.87.x network.

Let us review how a tcp connection is established. The originating machine picks a source and destination port number to be used in the connection. The destination port number is usually a well known number defined in the /etc/services file (or in Windows 95/NT the \windows\services file). In our example, the following port numbers were used:

```
TELNET      23
WWW         80
FTP         21
```

Because these numbers are commonly employed, Cisco has defined the above keywords to represent the port numbers. Therefore, in our configuration we may specify www or 80 as the port number. Earlier releases of the IOS require the numeric representation. As of version 11.3, the following TCP port numbers have keywords:

```
bgp                 Border Gateway Protocol (179)
chargen             Character generator (19)
cmd                 Remote commands (rcmd, 514)
daytime             Daytime (13)
discard             Discard (9)
domain              Domain Name Service (53)
echo                Echo (7)
exec                Exec (rsh, 512)
finger              Finger (79)
ftp                 File Transfer Protocol (21)
ftp-data            FTP data connections (used infrequently, 20)
gopher              Gopher (70)
hostname            NIC hostname server (101)
ident               Ident Protocol (113)
irc                 Internet Relay Chat (194)
klogin              Kerberos login (543)
kshell              Kerberos shell (544)
login               Login (rlogin, 513)
lpd                 Printer service (515)
```

```
nntp                  Network News Transport Protocol (119)
pop2                  Post Office Protocol v2 (109)
pop3                  Post Office Protocol v3 (110)
smtp                  Simple Mail Transport Protocol (25)
sunrpc                Sun Remote Procedure Call (111)
syslog                Syslog (514)
tacacs                TAC Access Control System (49)
talk                  Talk (517)
telnet                Telnet (23)
time                  Time (37)
uucp                  Unix-to-Unix Copy Program (540)
whois                 Nicname (43)
www                   World Wide Web (HTTP, 80)
```

Commonly used TCP port number without keywords are:

```
DLSW+ TCP (read)     2065
DLSW+ TCP (write)    2067
```

UDP keywords are:

```
<0-65535>        Port number
biff             Biff (mail notification, comsat, 512)
bootpc           Bootstrap Protocol (BOOTP) client (68)
bootps           Bootstrap Protocol (BOOTP) server (67)
discard          Discard (9)
dnsix            DNSIX security protocol auditing (195)
domain           Domain Name Service (DNS, 53)
echo             Echo (7)
mobile-ip        Mobile IP registration (434)
nameserver       IEN116 name service (obsolete, 42)
netbios-dgm      NetBios datagram service (138)
netbios-ns       NetBios name service (137)
ntp              Network Time Protocol (123)
rip              Routing Information Protocol (router, in.routed, 520)
snmp             Simple Network Management Protocol (161)
snmptrap         SNMP Traps (162)
sunrpc           Sun Remote Procedure Call (111)
syslog           System Logger (514)
tacacs           TAC Access Control System (49)
talk             Talk (517)
tftp             Trivial File Transfer Protocol (69)
time             Time (37)
who              Who service (rwho, 513)
xdmcp            X Display Manager Control Protocol (177)
```

Commonly used UDP port numbers without IOS keywords are:

```
AURP   387
```

After the destination number is chosen a source port is selected. The source port is usually a number above 1023 that is not currently in use.

On the receiving side, the source and destination numbers are swapped. For example, suppose Host A initiates a Web connection to Host B. Host A will choose the destination port number of 80 and an unused port number greater then 1023. Host B will respond with the source of 80 and the destination of the chosen number above 1023:

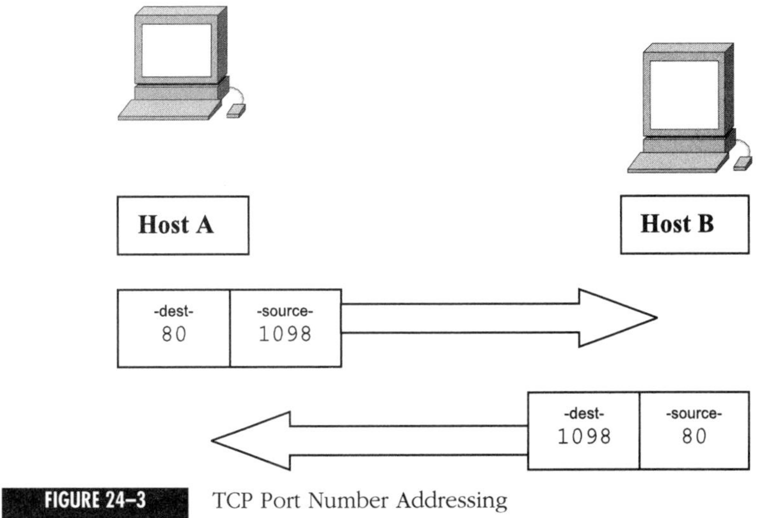

FIGURE 24–3 TCP Port Number Addressing

The configuration specified in Scenario 3 allows only TCP packets with the destination ports of 80, 21, and 23 through the Serial0 interface. All responses to a service request will be denied, since the response will contain a destination port number that is not 80, 21, or 23.

SCENARIO 3A: NAMED ACCESS-LISTS

Configure the access-list to increase readability and management.

With Cisco's IOS Release 11.2, named access-list became available to increase readability and manageability of the access-list statements. Instead of applying a number to the access-list, a name is given. Named access-lists also allow the removal of individual access-list statements. See the Cisco Documentation "Network Protocols Configuration Guide Part 1" for more details. The configuration of Router I is as follows:

```
hostname RI
!
interface Ethernet0
```

```
     ip address 192.168.87.1 255.255.255.0
!
interface Serial0
     ip address 10.200.57.21 255.255.255.0
     ip access-group webpolicy out

!
ip access-list extended webpolicy
     permit tcp any any eq www log
     permit tcp any any eq telnet log
     permit tcp any any eq ftp log
```

Note: Named access-lists are not backward compatible with previous versions of the IOS. If an earlier version is run, the access-list will be deleted.

Scenario 4: Allow Access to the Web Server on Router L

Allow access to the Web server from any machine on the network. Do not allow access to any other device or service on the 172.16.20.x network. Allow all machines on the 172.16.20.x network to have full access to all TCP-based Internet services.

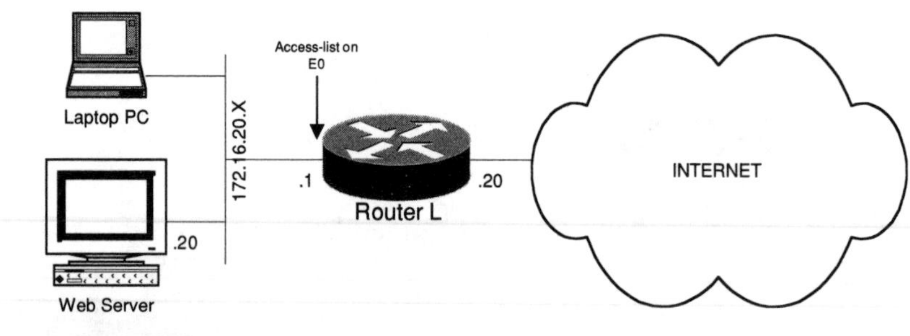

FIGURE 24-4 Using the ESTABLISED parameter

This problem may be split into two issues. The first is to allow access to the Web server from any machine on the network, but deny access to all other services. The second issue is to allow all machines from the 172.16.20.x network full access to ALL TCP services from anywhere on the network. In order to satisfy both issues, we need to use extended access-list with the key work established. The established command matches if the TCP segment has it's ACK bit set.

The configuration on Router L is displayed below:

```
hostname RLocal
!
```

```
interface Ethernet0
     ip address 172.16.20.1 255.255.255.0
     ip access-group 100 out
!
access-list 100 permit tcp any host 172.16.20.20 eq www
access-list 100 permit tcp any any gt 1023 established
```

The line `access-list 100 permit tcp any any gt 1023 established` matches only if the arriving packet is a response to a request from the network 172.16.20.x.

The `establish` command works by taking clues from the arriving packet. If the packet has the correct bits set to represent a response (the ACK bit is set), it is allowed through the router. The router does not remember if a connection was requested. Because the router does not keep track of the state of the connection, it is not considered "stateful" and may be subjected to spoofing attempts. For true stateful functionality, look at the Cisco PIX firewall. With IOS version 11.3 (3) Cisco implemented a security feature set on the 2500 and 1600 series routers to allow true stateful capability.

Scenarion 5: Place access-list on inbound interface

Place an access-list on Router L's Serial0 to allow access to the Web server from any machine on the network. Do not allow access to any other device or service on the 172.16.20.x network. Allow all machines on the 172.16.20.x network to have full access to all TCP-based Internet services.

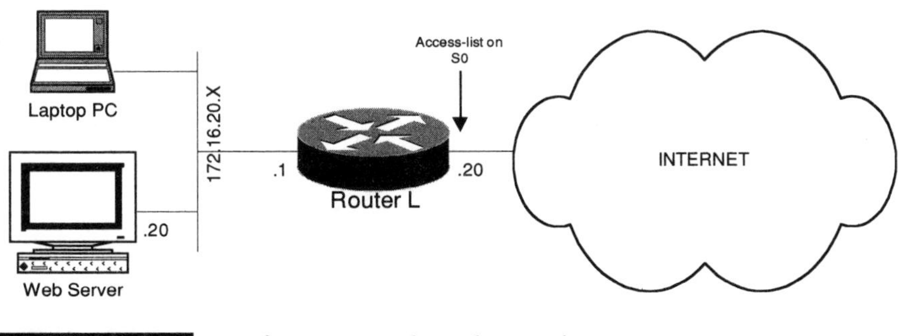

FIGURE 24-5 Configuring an in-bound access-list

This is the same problem as Scenario 4 with the exception that it specifies placement of the access-list on the Router's Serial0. Up to now, we have been using outbound access-list that filter packets as they leave the router. With this problem, we will use an inbound access-list to filter packets as they arrive at the router. Because the packets are being filtered before "entry" in the router, special care must be used to allow for routing updates.

```
hostname RLocal
!
interface Ethernet0
 ip address 172.16.20.1 255.255.255.0
!
interface Serial0
     ip address 10.200.57.20 255.255.255.0
     ip access-group 100 in
!
!
router rip
     network 10.0.0.0
     network 172.16.0.0
!
access-list 100 permit tcp any host 172.16.20.20 eq www
access-list 100 permit tcp any any gt 1024 established
access-list 100 permit udp any any eq rip
```

Inbound access-lists are denoted with the keyword `in` on the `IP access-group` statement. If `in` is not specified, the default value is outbound. In general, inbound access-list offer a special problem since packets are filtered before "entry" in the router. Therefore, special care must be used to insure routing updates are not filtered. Here are a few examples of allowing selected routing protocols.

```
access-list 100 permit udp any any eq rip
access-list 100 permit igrp any any
access-list 100 permit eigrp any any
access-list 100 permit ospf any any
```

Notice that RIP uses UDP while the other routing protocols define their own transport segment.

Scenario 6: Allowing a Range of IP Addresses

Multiple Web servers have been installed on 172.16.20.x. The Web servers are all within the range of 172.16.20.16-23. Allow access to the Web servers only from machines that are located at 192.168.87.16-31. Allow all machines that are located on the 172.16.20.x network to have full TCP access and allow them the capability to ping anywhere in the network for troubleshooting purposes.

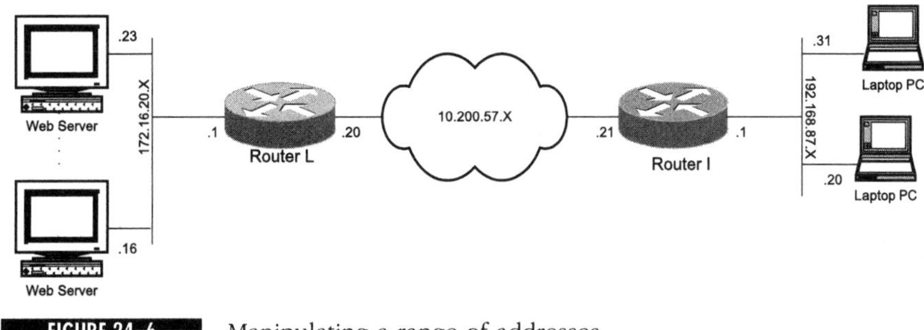

FIGURE 24–6 Manipulating a range of addresses

This problem requires a total of four statements with selective use of network masks. We will place the access-list on the inbound Serial port on Router L.

```
hostname RLocal
!
interface Ethernet0
  ip address 172.16.20.1 255.255.255.0
!
interface Serial0
  ip address 10.200.57.20 255.255.255.0
  ip access-group 100 in
!
router rip
  network 10.0.0.0
  network 172.16.0.0
!
access-list 100 permit tcp 192.168.87.16 0.0.0.15 172.16.20.16
  0.0.0.7 eq www
access-list 100 permit tcp any any gt 1023 established
access-list 100 permit icmp any any echo-reply
access-list 100 permit udp any any eq rip
```

Through the use of masking, we can specify the Web access as a single statement.

Let us review how network masks are created. With an access-list mask, a given bit can possess a value of:

0 = MUST MATCH

1 = MUST NOT MATCH

With the above example, the value 15 is binary equivalent to 0000 1111. This mask stands for "check first four bits and ignore the last four bits." With the IP addresses fourth octet of 16 the access-list will match on:

0001 0000 = 16

0000 1111 = 15

0001 xxxx = 16 to 31

A similar case may be made for the second part of the access-list matching between 16 and 23.

Here are some examples of access-list masks and their effect:

TABLE 24.1

Decimal	Binary Equiv.	Action
0	0000 0000	Check all bits
1	0000 0001	Ignore the last bit
7	0000 0111	Ignore the last three bits
63	0011 1111	Check the first two bits
195	1100 0011	Check the middle four bits
254	1111 1110	Check the last bit
255	1111 1111	Ignore all bits

Access-list masks allow for a wide range of options to match upon. See the end of Chapter Twenty-Three, for additional techniques to calculate a range of IP addresses.

Scenario 7: Filter Out Selective Access-List

Create an access-list to match on the following addresses:

```
172.16.200.x
172.16.216.x
172.16.232.x
172.16.248.x
```

This may be done using a single statement:

```
access-list 1 permit 172.16.200.0 0.0.48.255
```

Scenario 8: Filter Range of Addresses

Create an access-list to permit only ip addresses within the range of 172.16.20.x where x is a value divisible by four.

This again may be done using a single statement that checks the third bit.

```
Access-list 1 permit 172.16.20.4 0.0.0.252
```

Scenario 9: Dynamic Access-Lists (Lock and Key Access-Lists)

Create an access-list on Router L that authenticates a user based upon an assigned Username and Password before granting access to the Web server. Make sure only the machine in which the authentication took place is allowed through the router. Allow machines on the 172.16.20.x network full access to all TCP-based Internet services. Assume the router is using RIP as the routing protocol.

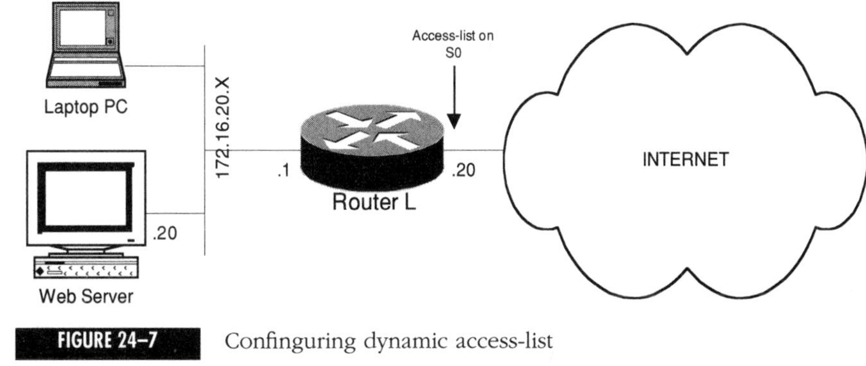

FIGURE 24–7 Confinguring dynamic access-list

This problem requires a dynamic access-list configuration, a new feature of 11.2. With dynamic access-lists, a user Telnets to a router for authentication. After a successful authentication, the user is granted access based upon the defined access-list. In this example, if we place the access-list on the Serial0 interface, we must be careful to allow Telnet access to the router.

```
hostname RLocal
!
username paul password cisco
!
interface Ethernet0
  ip address 172.16.20.1 255.255.255.0
!
interface Serial0
  ip address 10.200.57.20 255.255.255.0
  ip access-group 100 in
!
router rip
```

```
  network 10.0.0.0
  network 172.16.0.0
!
access-list 100 permit udp any any eq rip
access-list 100 permit tcp any host 10.200.57.20 eq telnet
access-list 100 permit tcp any any gt 1023 established
access-list 100 dynamic firewall timeout 60 permit tcp any host
  172.16.20.20 eq www
!
line vty 0 4
 login local
 autocommand access-enable host
```

To verify a dynamic access-list is working, use the following command:

```
show access-list
```

In our example, this command gave the following output:

```
Extended IP access list 100
  permit udp any any eq rip (10 matches)
  permit tcp any host 10.200.57.20 eq telnet (39 matches)
  permit tcp any any gt 1023 established
  Dynamic firewall Max. 60 mins. permit tcp host 0.0.0.0 host 172.16.20.20 eq
www timeout 60 min.
  permit tcp host 192.168.87.20 host 172.16.20.20 eq www (8 matches)
  permit tcp host 10.200.57.21 host 172.16.20.20 eq www
```

Summary

When configuring and applying access-lists, be aware of the unforeseen impact on other traffic. For example, IPX and AppleTalk tunnels as well as DLSw+ connections rely on IP connectivity. If you create a restrictive IP access-list, you might preclude the ability to create tunnels and DLSw+ connections.

Restrictive inbound access-lists can also filter routing protocol information as well.

Professional Development Checklist

By using this chapter, you should be able to perform the following operations:

- Configure IP Standard Access-Lists
- Configure IP Extended Access-Lists
- Configure IP Access-Lists blocking a range of addresses
- Configure an IP Access-List with the Established Parameter
- Configure a Dynamic IP Access-List

For Further Study

- Cisco Certified Course: Advanced Cisco Router Configuration, Cisco Systems, Inc.

URLs

- **www.cciecert.com**
- **www.mentorlabs.com**
- **www.arslimited.com**

Can You Spot the Issues?

1. An inbound access-list has been defined to allow only TCP traffic. Suddenly none of your traffic is leaving your routers. You did not have a default route on your router. You relied on a dynamic routing protocol to build and maintain a routing table. When you view your routing table, there is nothing in the routing table. What happened?
2. You attempt to limit in-bound traffic into a router with the following access-list and it does not work:

```
interface Serial0
       ip address 10.200.57.20 255.255.255.0
       ip access-group 100
!
!
access-list 100 permit udp any any eq rip
access-list 100 permit tcp any host 10.200.57.20
eq telnet
access-list 100 permit tcp any any gt 1023
established
```

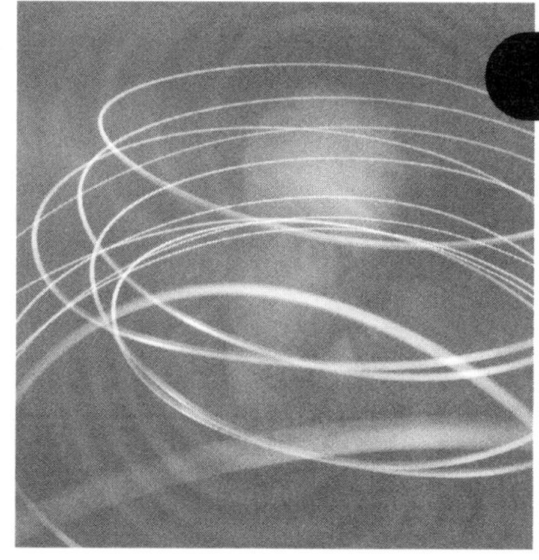

TWENTY FIVE

Configuring Non-IP Routing Access-Lists

Topics Covered in This Chapter

- Configuring standard IPX access-lists
- Configuring extended IPX access-lists
- Configuring SAP filters
- Configuring AppleTalk access-Lists
- Configuring AppleTalk GZL Filters
- Configuring AppleTalk ZIP Reply Filters
- Using the AppleTalk Permit Partial Zones Command
- Configuring DECNET access-lists

This chapter provides an overview of IPX, AppleTalk, and DECNET access-list configuration. First IPX will be examined, followed by AppleTalk and ending with DECNET.

Configuring IPX Access-Lists

Like IP access-lists, IPX has a standard and extended access-list. With the IP standard access-list (access-lists 1-99), only the source IP address can be specified. With standard IPX access-lists (access-lists 800-899), both the source and destination IPX address can be specified. Standard IPX access-lists provide no reference to IPX protocol numbers and socket addresses.

Like IP extended access-lists, IPX extended access-lists (access-lists 900-999) provide granular control over selecting what criteria to use to match IPX traffic. IPX extended access-lists use the IPX protocol number and IPX socket numbers as well as the IPX network and node addresses.

In addition to IPX standard and extended access-lists, two other IPX access-lists are available. Access-lists 1000-1099 provide SAP table filtering and access-lists 1200-1299 provide IPX route summarization.

Configuring IPX Standard Access-Lists

IPX standard access-lists (800-899) allow a match based upon IPX source and destination network and node address only. Notice the simplicity of the standard IPX access-list syntax:

```
access-list access-list-number {deny | permit} source-network[.source-node
[source-node-mask]] [destination-network[.destination-node [destination-node-
mask]]]
```

When configuring IPX access-lists, the value "–1" represents any networks. The options are listed below:

```
r2(config)#access-list 800 permit ?
     -1              Any IPX net
     <0-FFFFFFFF>    Source net
     N.H.H.H         Source net.host address
     <cr>
```

The following IPX access-list statement permits any IPX network with any protocol number and any socket address:

- Access-list 800 permit -1
  When IPX access-lists are viewed by the `show ipx access-lists` command, the "-1" is represented by eight Fs (FFFFFFFF).

```
r2#sh ipx access-lists
IPX access list 800
     deny AAA FFFFFFFF
     permit FFFFFFFF
```

Configuring IPX Extended Access-Lists

Standard IPX access-lists allowed us to filter by source and destination IPX network and node address only. Extended IPX access-lists (access-lists 900-999) can filter on these criteria as well as IPX protocol numbers and IPX socket numbers. When only "access-list 900 permit ?" is typed, the following listing is displayed:

```
r2(config)#access-list 900 permit ?
     <0-255>         Protocol type number (DECIMAL)
     any             Any IPX protocol type
     ncp             NetWare Core Protocol
```

```
netbios        IPX NetBIOS
rip            IPX Routing Information Protocol
sap            Service Advertising Protocol
spx            Sequenced Packet Exchange
```

Where the standard IPX access-list displayed source address parameters and "-1," extended IPX access-lists display different IPX protocols that can be transported inside of an IPX packet. Notice that "-1" is not an option. When "-1" is used with extended IPX access-lists, it must be followed by the enter key. If you try to access help after entering a "-1" in an extended IPX access-list, an error will be generated:

```
r2(config)#access-list 902 permit -1 ?
% Unrecognized command
```

"-1" can be used with IPX extended access-lists; however, it is recommended you use the "any" parameter in its place. With the "any" parameter, the help facility feature is retained.

Displayed below is the syntax for an extended IPX network statement:

```
access-list access-list-number {deny | permit} protocol [source-
network][[[.source-node] source-node-mask]
| [.source-node source-network-mask.source-node-mask]]
[source-socket] [destination.network][[[.destination-node] destination-node-
mask] | [.destination-node destination-network-mask.destination-nodemask]]
[destination-socket]
[log]
```

The first parameter after "deny | permit" specifies IPX protocol numbers. It is represented by the key word "protocol" in the IPX extended access-list. Commonly referenced IPX protocol numbers include:

0	Any/Unknown
1	RIP
4	SAP
5	SPX
17	NCP
20	NETBIOS

If a value of zero is used, it means to disregard the protocol parameter and reference the values for the IPX socket numbers.

IPX masks can also be applied to IPX access-list. Place ones in the bit positions to be masked. For example, if you wanted to permit IPX networks 700 through 7FF, configure the following IPX access-list statement:

```
Access-list 900 permit -1 700.0000.0000.0000 FF.FFFF.FFFF.FFFF
```

The network address is eight hexadecimal characters in length. If you configure a network address such as 700, you do not need to include the five leading zeros (00000700). Notice that the mask above contains only two FFs for the network portion. This indicates that the first five hexadecimal digits are zeros in the masks.

Notice when IPX masks are entered, mask values for the IPX network address will always be in uppercase and masks for IPX node addresses will be in lowercase, when displayed with show commands such as "show run" and "show ipx access-lists." For example, the following statements contain one access-list with a mask of FF.FFFF.FFFF.FFFF and another with ff.ffff.ffff.ffff:

```
r2(config)#access-list 902 deny -1 800.0000.0000.0000 FF.FFFF.FFFF.FFFF
r2(config)#access-list 902 deny -1 800.0000.0000.0000 ff.ffff.ffff.ffff
r2(config)#access-list 902 permit -1
```

When these statements are displayed by show commands, they are modified:

```
r2#show run
Building configuration...

access-list 902 deny any 800.0000.0000.0000 FF.ffff.ffff.ffff
access-list 902 deny any 800.0000.0000.0000 FF.ffff.ffff.ffff
access-list 902 permit any

IPX access list 902
     permit any 800.0000.0000.0000 FF.ffff.ffff.ffff
     deny any 800.0000.0000.0000 FF.ffff.ffff.ffff
     permit any
```

Remember, IPX address masking is in hexadecimal.

Applying IPX Access-Lists

To apply an IPX access-list to an interface, use the following two commands:

```
r3(config-if)#ipx access-group 900 ?
     in             inbound packets
     out            outbound packets
```

To apply an IPX access-list to filter routing table updates for IPX/RIP, use the following two interface configuration commands:

```
ipx output-network-filter
ipx input-network-filter
```

To apply an IPX access-list to filter routing table updates for IPX EIGRP, use the following command under the IPX EIGRP routing protocol mode:

```
r2(config)#ipx router eigrp 100
r2(config-ipx-router)#distribute-list 800 ?
   in            Filter incoming routing updates
   out           Filter outgoing routing updates
```

The default is to apply the access-list on outbound interface traffic. IPX access-lists can also be applied to dialer-lists and queue-lists.

IPX SAP Filters

You can filter individual SAP updates with SAP filters. SAPs can be filtered by address, SAP service type and server name. The syntax of a SAP filter is:

```
access-list access list number {deny | permit} network[.node] [network-
mask.node-mask] [service-type [server-name]]
```

The most basic SAP access-list filter is by network address only.

```
R1(config)#Access-list 1000 deny AA
R1(config)#Access-list 1000 permit -1
```

As with other IPX access-lists, "-1" represents all networks.

SAPs can also be filtered by SAP type. A value of 0 means all services.

4	File server
5	Job server
9	Archive server
21	Network Application Support Systems Network Architecture (NAS SNA) gateway

Note: DO NOT filter SAP type 0x4, 0x026B, and 0x278 in a NetWare 4.1 environment.

For a complete listing of the SAP types, goto **ftp://ftp.isi.edu/in-notes/iana/assignments/novell-sap-numbers**

Finally, SAPs can be filtered by server name. You can use the "*" wildcard at the end of a string to filter groups of SAPs. For example, if you want to filter all SAPs beginning with "texas"

```
Access-list 1000 deny -1 0 texas*
Access-list 1000 permit -1
```

To apply an IPX SAP filter on an interface, use the following commands:

```
ipx input-sap-filter
ipx output-gns-filter
ipx output-sap-filter
ipx router-sap-filter
```

IPX Dialer-Lists

IPX RIP/SAP updates can keep a dial-on-demand routing (DDR) link up indefinitely. Use the following access-list statements to filter IPX routing information protocol (RIP) and IPX SAP.

```
R1(config)#access-list 901 deny -1 ffffffff 0 ffffffff rip
R1(config)#access-list 901 deny -1 ffffffff 0 ffffffff sap
```

Apply it to a dialer-list with the following command:

```
R1(config)#dialer-list 1 protocol ipx permit list 901
```

This will prevent IPX RIP and SAP traffic from initiating a DDR connection.

Configuring AppleTalk Access-Lists

Adhering to its easy–to–use orientation, AppleTalk access-lists (access-lists 600-699) are configured with easy–to–understand language-based commands. There are no tables of well-known port numbers and well-known socket numbers to use with AppleTalk. There are no standard and extended access-lists for AppleTalk. AppleTalk access-lists can be configured to filter the following types of traffic:

```
AppleTalk traffic
GetZoneList(GZL) replies
Zone Information Protocol (ZIP) Replies
routing table updates
Name Binding Protocol (NBP) replies
```

General AppleTalk Access-List Issues

Listed below are the basic options displayed for AppleTalk access-list configuration:

```
r1(config)#access-list 600 permit ?
   <1-65279>           Appletalk network number
   additional-zones    Default filter action for unspecified zones
   cable-range         Filter on cable range
   includes            Filter on cable range inclusively
   nbp                 Specify nbp filter
   network             Filter an appletalk network
   other-access        Default filter action
   other-nbps          Default filter action for nbp
   within              Filter on cable range exclusively
   zone                Filter on appletalk zone
```

```
"access-list includes" command is used to define an access-list that overlaps,
either partially or completely, any part of a network or cable-range.

   Ex. R1(config)#access-list 600 permit includes 100-105
       R1(config)#access-list 600 permit other-access

"access-list within" command is used to define a network or cable-range that
is included within a specified cable-range.

   Ex. R1(config)#access-list 600 permit within 100-105
       R1(config)#access-list 600 permit other-access
```

A basic AppleTalk access-list denying cable-range 100–200 is displayed below:

```
Ex. R1(config)#access-list 600 deny cable-range 100-200
Ex. R1(config)#access-list 600 permit other-access

r1(config)#inte s0.2
r1(config-subif)#appletalk access-group 600 ?
```

You can verify what access-lists are on which interfaces with the commands `show appletalk interface` and `show appletalk access-list`:

```
r1#sh appletalk access-lists
AppleTalk access list 600:
    deny cable-range 400-400
    permit other-access
r1#sh apple inte s0.2
Serial0.2 is up, line protocol is up
    AppleTalk cable range is 33-33
    AppleTalk address is 33.33, Valid
    AppleTalk zone is "33_wan"
    Routing protocols enabled: EIGRP
    AppleTalk port configuration verified by 33.4
    AppleTalk discarded 7 packets due to output errors
    AppleTalk address gleaning is not supported by hardware
    AppleTalk route cache is enabled
    AppleTalk outgoing access list is 600
```

AppleTalk Routing Update Filters

When you filter a cable-range with a zone that is associated with multiple cable-ranges, that zone will also be filtered even if the other cable-ranges are advertised. This can be remedied with the following global configuration command:

```
Appletalk permit-partial-zones
```

AppleTalk GETZONELIST Reply Filters

When an end-system opens its Chooser (a functional equivalent to the Windows 95 network neighborhood), it generates a GETZONELIST Request to its default router. By default, the router responds by providing a complete list of all zones in its zone information table. Specific zone names can be filtered from end systems with a GETZONELIST reply filter. Therefore, use GETZONELIST reply filters only to filter zone list requests from an end system to a router. If you want to filter router to router zone updates, use the ZIP reply filter.

AppleTalk ZIP Reply Filters

When a Cisco router running an AppleTalk routing process receives a newly learned cable-range, it generates a ZIP request to match a zone with the cable-range. For routes advertised by routing table maintenance protocol (RTMP), every cable-range must have at least one zone associated with it by default. This is not a requirement for EIGRP.

In the previous section, GETZONELIST reply access-list statements filtered zone updates between an end system and a router. ZIP reply filters zone update information between two routers.

Placement of ZIP Reply Filters

If you want to filter zone information from a certain router, you do not place the ZIP reply filter on that router. ZIP reply filters are placed on all neighboring routers that can announce the particular zone to the target router.

TRACING THE EFFECTS OF A ZIP REPLY FILTER

In the example below, zone "z250" is filtered by a ZIP reply filter. When applying a ZIP reply filter, the first thing that is impacted is entries in the AppleTalk routing table referencing the filtered zone. In the routing table below, cable-range 250-250 is associated with zone "z250."

```
r1#sh apple ro
Codes: R - RTMP derived, E - EIGRP derived, C - connected, A -
AURP
     S - static  P - proxy
4 routes in internet
```

The first zone listed for each entry is its default (primary) zone.

```
C Net 150-155 directly connected, Serial1, zone z150
R Net 250-255 [31/B] via 154.157, 80 sec, zone z250
```

```
R Net 350-355 [2/G] via 154.157, 0 sec, Serial1, zone z350
R Net 650-655 [2/G] via 154.157, 0 sec, Serial1, zone z650
```

Since zone "z250" is filtered and since cable-range 250-250 has only one zone associated with it (the filtered zone), cable range 250-250 is flushed from the routing table.

```
AT: Time to notify neighbor for route 250-255
AT: RTMP from 154.157 (new 0,old 2,bad 0,ign 0, dwn 0)
AT: src=Serial1:152.180, dst=150-155, size=16, 1 rte, RTMP pkt sent
AT: Route ager starting on Main AT RoutingTable (4 active nodes)
AT: in CancelZoneRequest, cancelling req on 250-255...failed; not on list
%AT-6-DELROUTE: AppleTalk network deleted; 250-255 removed from routing table
```

Even though the route is gone, the route and its associated zone remain in the zone information table (ZIT).

```
r1#show apple zone
Name                Network(s)
z150                150-155
z250                250-255
z350                350-355
z650                650-655

r1#show apple zone z250
AppleTalk Zone Information for z250:
   Valid for nets: 250-255
   Not associated with any interface.
   Not associated with any access list.
```

Eventually, the route associated with the zone is dropped from the ZIT. Notice in the show statement below, how the reference to cable-range 250-250 is gone.

```
r1#show apple zone z250
AppleTalk Zone Information for z250:
   Not associated with any routes in the current internet.
   Not associated with any interface.
   Not associated with any access list.
r1#show apple zone
Name                Network(s)
z150                150-155
z250
z350                350-355
z650                650-655
```

After a few minutes, the filtered zone is flushed from the zone information table.

```
AT: atzip_GC() called
AT: freeing zip entry for z250, 0x13EEB4
AT: freeing zip entry for z250, 0x13EEB4
```

You can accelerate this process by reinitializing the AppleTalk routing process. This is performed by typing the following two global configuration commands in immediate succession:

NO APPLETALK ROUTING

APPLETALK ROUTING

By performing a `no appletalk routing` command, it removes `all appletalk` statements. By adding it back, it restores all RTMP information, but not EIGRP information. Therefore, if you use NO APPLETALK ROUTING and RTMP is turned off on an interface and when APPLETALK ROUTING is restored, all appletalk information will be restored on the interfaces still running RTMP and not on those running EIGRP.

Configuring DECNET Access-Lists

DECNET access-lists (access-lists 300-399) are constructed in a manner similar to IP access-lists. Both DECNET and IP use the same decimal format and wildcard masks. Unlike IP's four octet, 32-bit address structure, DECNET has a six-bit area and ten-bit node address format. For example, the wildcard mask for IP that permits all traffic is 255.255.255.255 (all binary ones). The DECNET wildcard mask that permits all traffic is 63.1023 (all binary ones).

DECNET uses access-list 300.

DECNET access-lists can be constructed with the following parameters:

1. Source address only
2. Source and destination address
3. Source address plus DECNET specific parameter matches
4. Source and destination address plus DECNET specific parameter matches

Scenario:

```
Filter DECNET routers 30-63 in area 10

R1(config)#access-list 300 deny 10.30 0.1
R1(config)#access-list 300 deny 10.32 0.31
R1(config)#access-list 300 permit 0.0 63.1023

R1(config-if)#decnet access-group 300
```

Summary

Non-IP routing protocol access-lists are useful for localizing traffic in large-scale enterprise networks. A general internetwork design principle is to limit the amount of overhead traffic that traverse the internetwork core. For example, IPX SAP filters can limit the amount of SAP traffic broadcasted throughout an internetwork. AppleTalk ZIP reply filters can limit the amount of ZIP update traffic propogated. If an internetwork is designed in a hierarchical manner, non-IP overhead traffic can be managed in an efficient manner through a combination of well thought out name and address assignment, routing protocol selection and well designed access-lists.

Professional Development Checklist

By using this chapter, you should be able to perform the following operations:

- Configure IPX Standard Access-Lists
- Configure IPX Extended Access-Lists
- Configure IPX routing table update filters for IPX/RIP and EIGRP
- Configure IPX SAP filter
- Configure GNS reply filter
- Configure an AppleTalk access-list that applies to all AppleTalk traffic
- Configure AppleTalk GZL filter
- Configure Apple Talk ZIP-Reply filter
- Configure AppleTalk routing table update filters for RTMP and EIGRP
- Configure a DECNET access-list that applies to all DECNET traffic

For Further Study

- Cisco Certified Course: Advanced Cisco Router Configuration, Cisco Systems, Inc.
- Cisco IOS Network Protocols II Configuration Guide (Volume VI), Cisco Systems, Inc., 1989–1998.
- Cisco IOS Network Protocols II Command Reference (Volume VI), Cisco Systems, Inc., 1989–1998.
- Cisco IOS Network Protocols III Configuration Guide (Volume VII), Cisco Systems, Inc., 1989–1998.
- Cisco IOS Network Protocols III Command Reference (Volume VII), Cisco Systems, Inc., 1989–1998.

URLs

- **www.cciecert.com**
- **www.mentorlabs.com**
- **www.arslimited.com**

Can You Spot the Issues?

1. You are trying to deny SAP updates with the following command. Why is it not blocking SAP traffic?
   R1(config)#access-list 901 deny -1 ffffffff 0 ffffffff 457
2. You are trying to block the advertisement of three Print Server SAPs: PS1, PS2, and PS3. You use the following access-list:
   R1(config)#access-list 901 deny -1 ffffffff 0 ffffffff 452
   Now no SAPs are in your SAP table. What happened?
3. You want to block the AppleTalk zone "acctg-zone" from appearing in R1's routing table. R1 learns acctg-zone from only R2 through R1's Serial0 interface. You configure R1 in the following manner:
   r1(config)#access-list 600 deny zone acctg
   r1(config)#access-list 600 permit additional-zones
   r1(config)#inte s0
   r1(config-if)#appletalk getzonelist-filter 600
   For some reason, it does not work. Why not?
4. You place the GZL statement on R2's directly connected interface to R1. What is the problem now?
5. You create an AppleTalk distribute list to block cable-range 700-800. Cable –range 700-800 has zone "publishing" assigned to it. The "publishing" zone is also assigned to cable-ranges 1000-1100, 1200-1400. When

the distribute-list blocking 700-800 was applied, cable-ranges 1000-1100 and 1200-1400 were also blocked. Why? What is the remedy?

6. You want to block the range of DECNET nodes 30 to 63 from area 1. You plan to use the following decnet access-list but the IOS does not take the last line. Why?

```
R1(config)#access-list 300 deny 10.30 0.1
R1(config)#access-list 300 deny 10.32 0.31
R1(config)#access-list 300 permit 0.0 255.255
```

T W E N T Y S I X

Access-Lists for Nonroutable Traffic

Topics Covered in This Chapter

- Configuring MAC address based access-lists
- Configuring LSAP based access-lists
- Configuring NETBIOS host access-lists
- Configuring Access-Expressions

In the previous two chapters, we examined access-lists for routable traffic. We now turn our attention to access-lists for nonroutable traffic.

- Filter by LSAP address (access-list 200)
- Filter by MAC address (access-list 700)
- Filter by NETBIOS name

Finally, these access-lists can be combined through access-expressions. Make note that LSAP and MAC addresses and their corresponding masks are configured in hexadecimal format.

MAC Address Access-Lists (Access-Lists 700 and 1100)

MAC address access-lists (access-lists 700 and 1100) provide filtering for inbound and outbound bridged traffic only. Access-list 700 filters on a single MAC address statement. Addresses specified by access-list 700 can be specified as the source or destination address by the statements that apply the access-list.

Access-lists 1100-1199 are extended MAC address filters. Access-lists 1100-1199 filter both source and destination MAC addresses. Access-lists 1100-1199 are applied at the end of a bridge-group interface statement with the "input-pattern-list" and "output-pattern-list" parameters.

Remember that MAC addresses on Ethernet are bit swapped when compared to MAC Token-Ring addresses. (See the cannonical to non-cannonical bit conversion chart in Chapter Twenty-One) Access-lists on Ethernet use a cannonical address format. Token-Ring and FDDI use a non-cannonical address format. Keep these points in mind. An access-control list designed for Ethernet may not work for Token-Ring or FDDI.

When filtering Token-Ring MAC addresses, use the mask 8000.0000.0000 for the source address of any traffic that requires an exact match and needs to be source-route bridged. The high-order bit is set to one to provide for the different values of the routing information indicator.

MAC address access-lists are applied to the end of both transparent bridging and source-route bridging statements:

```
Bridge-group # input-address-list (# = bridge-group number)
Bridge-group # output-address-list (# = bridge-group number)
Source-bridge output-address-list
Source-bridge output-address-list
```

For DLSW+, the MAC access-lists can be placed on remote-peer statements:

```
Dmac-output-list
```

You can view your MAC address access-lists with the `show access-lists` statement:

```
r4#sh access-lists

Extended Bridging access list 1100
            permit 1111.2222.3333 0000.0000.0000 1111.2222.3333
0000.0000.0000

r4#sh access-lists
Bridge address access list 700
deny 00a0.2466.81020000.0000.0000
permit      0000.0000.0000        ffff.ffff.ffff
```

LSAP Access-Lists

LSAP access-lists (access-list 200) allow you to filter by logical-link control layer or equivalent addresses. LSAP addresses are eight bit addresses displayed in a two digit hexadecimal format. Many of these addresses are registered with the IEEE. Commonly used IEEE LSAP addresses are displayed below:

```
00   Null LSAP
AA   SNAP
04   SNA Path Control (individual)
05   SNA Path Control (group)
F0   IBM NETBIOS
0C   SNA
0D   SNA
```

The addresses are paired in a source and destination format. For example, 0xF0F0 represents a source and destination LSAP pair for NETBIOS in hexadecimal format.

LSAP access-lists only filter bridged traffic. It is not possible to use such access-lists to filter routed traffic.

For Token-Ring interfaces, LSAP filters are placed at the end of source-bridge statements:

```
Source-bridge input-lsap-list
Source-bridge-output-lsap-list
```

For DLSW+, the LSAP access-lists can be placed on remote-peer statements:

```
Lsap-output-list
```

Applying an LSAP Access-List to an Ethernet Interface

For Ethernet interfaces, LSAP access-list statements are applied at the end of a bridge-group statement. You must specify which frame type is being used by the filtered Ethernet traffic. Two options are available for filtering LSAP traffic on a bridged Ethernet interface:

```
input-lsap-list  Filter incoming IEEE 802.3 encapsulated packets
input-type-list  Filter incoming Ethernet packets by type code
```

For example, IP traffic is transported in an Ethernet II frame format. If you wanted to filter IP traffic transported by Ethernet II frames, use the "input-type-list." If the wrong list type is used, the access-list will not be applied.

NETBIOS Access-Lists

NETBIOS traffic can be filtered by NETBIOS name and byte-count. Only NETBIOS name filtering will be covered in this section. A NETBIOS name filter does not have an access-list number associated with it. However, like other access-lists, NETBIOS access-lists have two components: an access-list defined in global configuration mode and statements to apply the access-list to a token-ring interface and a DLSW+ remote peer connection.

The syntax of a NETBIOS host-name access-list is displayed below:

```
netbios access-list host name {permit | deny} pattern
```

The most confusing aspect of configuring NETBIOS host-name access-lists is a prompt encountered when you are constructing the access-list in global configuration mode. When you are supposed to supply the name of the NETBIOS access-list, you are prompted with the ambiguous help message "WORD NETBIOS station name." Many users are confused by this statement. Many interpret this prompt to mean enter the NETBIOS name to be permitted or denied. This prompt references the name to be used for the NETBIOS host-name access-list. Remember, NETBIOS access-lists do not have a number associated with them. You must supply a name for the access-list and the access-list name immediately follows the "host" parameter:

```
r4(config)#netbios access-list host ?
     WORD NETBIOS station name
```

Once the NETBIOS access-list name is supplied, then a pattern matching the NETBIOS end system names to be permitted or denied must be supplied. An exact match can be supplied. Note that NETBIOS names are case sensitive. If a partial match is desirable, use the following MS-DOS like wildcard symbols:

```
* Used at the end of a string to match any character or string of characters.
? Matches any single character. When using this wildcard enter CTRL+V first. If
you don't, the it is possible the IOS will interpret the "?" as a request for help.
```

If you are creating a NETBIOS host-name access-list to deny on specific host-names, remember to end the access-list with a permit all statement. A NETBIOS host-name access-list permit all statement is displayed below:

```
r4(config)#netbios access-list host acctg permit  *
```

NETBIOS Host-Name Access-List Scenario

```
Deny all NETBIOS names beginning with FLA
Deny all three letter NETBIOS names beginning with C
Permit all other NETBIOS names

r4(config)#netbios access-list host abc deny FLA*
r4(config)#netbios access-list host abc deny C??
r4(config)#netbios access-list host abc permit *
```

Applying NETBIOS Access-Lists

NetBIOS access-lists can be used with the following:

1. dlsw remote-peer statements notice all filters are outbound only
   - dlsw remote-peer 0 tcp 172.16.24.2 host-netbios-out mylist
   - dlsw remote-peer 0 tcp 172.16.24.2 bytes-netbios-out mylist
2. Token-Ring interfaces only
   - netbios output-access-filter host mylist
   - netbios output-access-filter bytes mylist
   - netbios input-access-filter host mylist
   - netbios input-access-filter bytes mylist

Note: If applying a NETBIOS access-list to an interface, you can use Token-Ring interfaces only.

Access-Expressions

Access-Expressions combine the filtering services of Access-List 200, Access-List 700, NETBIOS name, and NETBIOS byte-count with the Boolean operators: "and," "or," and "not." Access-Expressions can be constructed to provide a single statement to test filtering criteria such as: Permit all NETBIOS end systems with name beginning with FLA and with the MAC address of 1234.4567.8901.

Access-Expressions must be used in replacement of access-lists 200, 700 NETBIOS name, and NETBIOS byte-count. Access-expressions will not work on an interface that already has access-lists 200, 700, or NETBIOS filters.

To understand access-expressions, an understanding of truth tables is essential. Displayed below are two truth tables; one for the "and" operator and one for the "or" operator.

A truth table for an "AND" Boolean operator:

TRUE	AND	TRUE	=	TRUE
TRUE	AND	FALSE	=	FALSE
FALSE	AND	TRUE	=	FALSE
FALSE	AND	FALSE	=	FALSE

A truth table for an "OR" Boolean operator:

TRUE	OR	TRUE	=	TRUE
TRUE	OR	FALSE	=	TRUE
FALSE	OR	TRUE	=	TRUE
FALSE	OR	FALSE	=	FALSE

By applying truth table logic to the statement: "Permit all NETBIOS traffic from the MAC address of 1234.4567.8901," the statement will be reformulated as: "Permit NETBIOS traffic" and "Permit traffic whose source MAC address is 1234.5678.8901." This will be formulated in the following access-expression:

```
Access-expression in (lsap (200) & smac (700))
```

Configuring Access-Expressions

Access-expressions are configured using the following Boolean operators:

~ not
& and
| or

Access-expressions use the Boolean operators displayed above to combine the following keywords that reference the associated access-lists:

```
Lsap(2xx)
Type(2xx)
Smac(7xx)
Dmac(7xx)
Netbios-host(netbios access-list name)
Netbios-bytes(netbios access-list name)
```

NETBIOS-HOST and NETBIOS-BYTES access-expression terms will always return FALSE for frames that are not NETBIOS frames.

The steps involved in creating an access-expression are:

1. Create access-lists (Access-list 200, Access-list 700 and NETBIOS access-lists).
2. Combine the access-lists with an access-expression on paper.
3. Apply the access-expression on an interface.

Access-lists are created in global configuration mode and then applied with a separate statement in interface configuration mode. Access-expressions have no global configuration mode component. Access-expressions are configured entirely at the interface mode. Access-expressions reference access-lists created in global configuration mode.

The following example applies these configuration steps:

Permit NETBIOS frames *or* SNA frames with a destination address of 1234.1212.1111

1. Create access-list (200) permitting SNA traffic
2. Create access-list (201) permitting NETBIOS frames
3. Create access-list (701) permitting MAC address
4. Create the access-expression on paper.
5. Apply the access-expression to an interface

Global configuration mode:

```
Access-list 200 permit 0x0404 0x0001 (Permits SNA command or
response)
Access-list 200 permit 0x0004 0x0001 (Permits SNA explorers with
NULL DSAP)
```

```
Access-list 201 permit 0xfofo 0x0001 (Pass NETBIOS frames;
command or response)
Access-list 701 permit 1234.1212.1111
```

Interface configuration mode:

```
Access-expression in lsap(201) | (lsap(200) & dmac(701))
```

When creating an access-expression, make sure there are no spaces between the key words (lsap, dmac, etc.) and the access-list numbers (200, 700, etc.). Spaces will generate an error message.

Applying Access-Expressions

Access-expressions are applied to interfaces only. They are not applied to DLSW+ remote peer statements.

To apply an access-expression, type the following interface configuration command:

```
Access-expression {in|out} expression
```

Monitoring and Troubleshooting Access-Expressions

The IOS provides access-expression show and debug commands. Listed below is a sample show access-expression command:

```
R1#show access-expression
Interface Ethernet0:
        Input: ((dmac(700) & lsap(201)) | lsap(200))
```

Access-expression debugging has fifteen different levels:

```
r4#debug access-expression ?
        <0-15>  Debugging level (0=No Debugging)
        <cr>

r4#debug access-expression 1
        Boolean access expression debugging is on: expression-tree
r4#debug access-expression 2
        Boolean access expression debugging is on: operator-stack
r4#debug access-expression 3
        Boolean access expression debugging is on: expression-tree
        operator-stack
r4#debug access-expression 4
        Boolean access expression debugging is on: return-code
r4#debug access-expression 5
        Boolean access expression debugging is on: expression-tree
        return-code
r4#debug access-expression 6
```

```
        Boolean access expression debugging is on: operator-stack
        return-code
r4#debug access-expression 7
        Boolean access expression debugging is on: expression-tree
        operator-stack return-code
r4#debug access-expression 8
        Boolean access expression debugging is on: system-calls
r4#debug access-expression 9
        Boolean access expression debugging is on: expression-tree
        system-calls
r4#debug access-expression 10
        Boolean access expression debugging is on: operator-stack
        system-calls
r4#debug access-expression 11
        Boolean access expression debugging is on: expression-tree
        operator-stack system-calls
r4#debug access-expression 12
        Boolean access expression debugging is on: return-code
        system-calls
r4#debug access-expression 13
        Boolean access expression debugging is on: expression-tree
        return-code system-calls
r4#debug access-expression 14
        Boolean access expression debugging is on: operator-stack
        return-code system-calls
r4#debug access-expression 15
        Boolean access expression debugging is on: expression-tree
        operator-stack return-code system-calls
```

A sample debug trace of an access-expression is displayed below:

```
EXPR: (011) Dump of the ExpressionTree:
Address     Lchild      Ld  Rchild      Rd  Flags     Value
0x001EA694  0x00000000  0   0x00000000  0   Dmac      700
0x001EA640  0x00000000  0   0x00000000  0   Lsap      201
0x001EAD78  0x001EA694  1   0x001EA640  1   Operator  &
```

Summary

The nonroutable protocol access-lists provide filtering capabilities for bridged traffic and DLSw+ traffic. Each of the nonroutable access-lists is relatively simple; however, they can be combined to create access-expressions.

Professional Development Checklist

By using this chapter, you should be able to perform the following operations:

- Configure MAC access-lists for Ethernet frames
- Configure MAC access-lists for Token-Ring frames
- Configure LSAP access-lists
- Configure NETBIOS host name access-lists
- Configure an access-expression

For Further Study

- Cisco IOS Configuration Guide Volume VIII (Bridging and IBM Networking), Cisco Systems, Inc., 1989–1998.
- Cisco IOS Command Reference Volume VIII (Bridging and IBM Networking), Cisco Systems, Inc., 1989–1998.

URLs

- **www.cciecert.com**
- **www.mentorlabs.com**
- **www.arslimited.com**

Can You Spot the Issues?

1. You have created an access-expression, but it does not work. The access-expression is supposed to deny all NETBIOS end systems beginning with FLA and permit a single NETBIOS end system with a name beginning with ACCTG1 and the MAC address of 1234.1234.1234. You have created the following access-expression and it does not work:

```
Access-expression in netbios-host ((fla-filter) |
netbios-host (acctg)) & dmac(700)
```

2. The following NETBIOS host-name access-list is supposed to block only NETBIOS names beginning with FLA. Instead it is blocking everything. Why?

```
r4(config)#netbios access-list host abc deny FLA*
r4(config)#netbios access-list host abc permit .*
```

TWENTY SEVEN

Prioritizing Traffic

Topics Covered in This Chapter

- Overview of IOS Queuing Methods
- Configuring Priority Queuing
- Monitoring and Troubleshooting Priority Queuing
- Configuring Custom Queuing
- Monitoring and Troubleshooting Custom Queuing

Cisco queuing features allow a router to prioritize traffic during periods of temporary congestion. Queuing is activated only when network congestion occurs. Network congestion is defined when an interface queue possesses a depth >=1. Therefore, when the queue depth = 0, packets are forwarded on a first in first out basis.

There are four possible queuing algorithms used:

1. First-in-first-out (FIFO)
2. Weighted fair queuing
3. Priority queuing
4. Custom queuing

With IOS 11.2, serial interfaces at E1 (2.048 Mbps) and below use weighted fair queuing by default. When no other queuing strategies are configured, all other interfaces use FIFO by default.

The Cisco IOS can be configured to support the following types of queuing methods for prioritizing internetwork traffic:

- Weighted fair queuing
- Priority queuing
- Custom queuing

You can configure weighted fair queuing, priority queuing or custom queuing, but you can assign only one type to an interface at any given time. Therefore, different queuing methods are mutually exclusive.

A brief description of each of the configurable queuing methods is provided below.

Weighted Fair Queuing

Weighted fair queuing dynamically categories traffic by protocol type. Protocols that are bandwidth intensive such as FTP and WWW are interleaved so that lower volume traffic such as TELNET does not get crowded out. Of the three configurable queuing methods provided by Cisco, weighted fair queues possesses the least configuration options.

Custom Queuing

Custom queuing allows up to sixteen configurable queues to be created. Each queue can have different protocols or traffic from specific interfaces associated with it. Each queue will also have a "byte-count" associated with it. The "byte-count" determines how many bytes can be forwarded from a specific queue at one time. For example, if four custom queues are configured and each has a byte count of 1500 bytes, queue one will forward 1500 bytes, followed by queue two forwarding 1500 bytes. Queues three and four would be serviced in the same round-robin fashion. If you want to assure that each queue has an fixed percentage of bandwidth, custom queuing is the queuing method to use.

Priority Queuing

Priority queuing is the most extreme type of queuing. Priority queuing is composed of four queues: high, medium, normal, and low. All traffic in the high queue takes precedence over all other queues. Only when the high queue is empty will other queues be serviced. The order of priority of priority queues is:

1. High queue
2. Medium queue
3. Normal queue
4. Low queue

If the high priority queue constantly has packets in it, the lower queues will experience prolonged periods of no access to bandwidth.

You can determine what queuing techniques are currently being used on a given interface with the show interface command and the show queuing command:

```
r4#show interfaces s0
Serial0 is up, line protocol is up
  Hardware is HD64570
  Internet address is 172.16.33.4/24
  MTU 1500 bytes, BW 1544 Kbit, DLY 20000 usec, rely 255/255, load 1/255
  Encapsulation FRAME-RELAY, loopback not set, keepalive set (10 sec)
  LMI enq sent  108, LMI stat recvd 103, LMI upd recvd 0, DTE LMI up
  LMI enq recvd 0, LMI stat sent  0, LMI upd sent  0
  LMI DLCI 0  LMI type is ANSI Annex D  frame relay DTE
  FR SVC disabled, LAPF state down
  Broadcast queue 0/64, broadcasts sent/dropped 941/0, interface broadcasts 904
  Last input 00:00:06, output 00:00:01, output hang never
  Last clearing of "show interface" counters never
  Input queue: 0/75/0 (size/max/drops); Total output drops: 0
  Queueing strategy: weighted fair
  Output queue: 0/64/0 (size/threshold/drops)
  Conversations  0/1 (active/max active)
  Reserved Conversations 0/0 (allocated/max allocated)
  5 minute input rate 0 bits/sec, 0 packets/sec
  5 minute output rate 0 bits/sec, 0 packets/sec
  434 packets input, 21994 bytes, 0 no buffer
  Received 73 broadcasts, 0 runts, 0 giants, 0 throttles
  0 input errors, 0 CRC, 0 frame, 0 overrun, 0 ignored, 0 abort
  1071 packets output, 54894 bytes, 0 underruns
  0 output errors, 0 collisions, 7 interface resets
  0 output buffer failures, 0 output buffers swapped out
  8 carrier transitions
  DCD=up DSR=up DTR=up RTS=up CTS=up

r4#show queueing
Current fair queue configuration:

Interface      Discard    DynamicReserved
               threshold  queue countqueue count
Serial0        64         2560
Serial1        64         2560

Current priority queue configuration:
Current custom queue configuration:
Current RED queue configuration:
```

Configuring Priority Queuing

Configuring priority queuing involves creating a priority queue-list made up of four pre-defined queues: high, medium, normal, and low. If specific protocols or traffic from specific interfaces need a specific priority, they must be explicitly configured. Otherwise, all unspecified traffic will be placed in the default queue. The default queue itself can be explicitly configured as being the high, medium, normal, or low queue.

If the high priority queue constantly has packets in it, the lower queues will experience prolonged periods of no access to bandwidth. If you want to assure that all traffic types are guaranteed some bandwidth on a periodic basis, use custom queuing or weighted fair queuing.

The two required steps for defining and applying priority queuing are similar to the required steps of access-list configuration. First a priority queue must be defined in global configuration mode. Second, the priority queue must be applied to an interface with the interface configuration command "priority-group."

Priority-lists can be defined for a given protocol or for an interface that is the source of traffic to be prioritized.

To establish priority queuing based upon the protocol type, use the following syntax:

```
priority-list list-number protocol protocol-name {high | medium | normal | low}
queue-keyword
keyword-value
```

Keywords and keyword-values include access-list numbers and tcp and udp port numbers.

To establish priority queuing based upon source interface, use the following syntax:

```
priority-list list-number interface interface-type  {high | medium | normal | low}
```

Assigning a Default Priority Queue

Assign a priority queue for those packets that do not match any other rule in the priority list.

```
priority-list list-number default {high | medium | normal | low}
```

Priority Queuing Scenario

- Place all DLSW+ and TELNET traffic in the high priority queue
- Place all IPX/NCP traffic in the medium priority queue
- Place all other traffic in the default queue: normal

```
r4(config)#priority-list 1 protocol dlsw high
r4(config)#priority-list 1 protocol ip high tcp 23
r4(config)#priority-list 1 protocol ipx medium list 900
r4(config)#priority-list 1 default normal
r4(config)#access-list 900 permit ncp any 451 any 451
```

```
r4(config)#inte s0
r4(config-if)#priority-group 1
```

Priority queuing status and operation can be monitored by show interface, show queuing and debug priority.

```
r4#sh queuing
Current fair queue configuration:

 Interface        Discard        Dynamic          Reserved
                  threshold      queue count      queue count
 Serial1          64             256              0

Current priority queue configuration:

List          Queue        Args
1             high         protocol dlsw
1             high         protocol ip         tcp port telnet
1             medium       protocol ipx        list 900

Current custom queue configuration:
Current RED queue configuration:
```

In the "debug priority" trace below, notice how all unspecified traffic goes to the default queue "normal." However, TELNET traffic is placed in the high queue.

```
PQ: Serial0: bridge (defaulting) -> normal
PQ: Serial0: cdp (defaulting) -> normal
PQ: Serial0: bridge (defaulting) -> normal
PQ: Serial0: bridge (defaulting) -> normal
PQ: Serial0: ip (defaulting) -> normal
PQ: Serial0: ip (defaulting) -> normal
PQ: Serial0: ip (tcp 23) -> high
PQ: Serial0: ip (tcp 23) -> high
PQ: Serial0: ip (tcp 23) -> high
```

Custom Queuing

Custom queuing is more democratic than priority queuing. Custom queuing services all of its defined queues in a sequential "round-robin" fashion. Each queue will have an opportunity to forward a specified number of packets defined by a byte count. Once the specified byte count is attained, the next custom queue is serviced. Even the default queue is guaranteed a consistent service interval. To give greater queuing resources to a specific traffic type, the "byte-count" servicing limit can be increased over other queues.

Therefore, if a given scenario, requires you to allocate a percentage of bandwidth for a certain traffic type, use custom queuing.

Configuring Custom Queuing

Configuring custom queuing involves creating a custom queue-list (called a "queue-list") made up of a maximum of sixteen queues plus one system queue. If specific protocols or traffic from specific interfaces need to be placed in a specific queue, they must be explicitly configured. Otherwise, all unspecified traffic will be placed in the default queue. The default queue itself can be explicitly configured.

The two required steps for defining and applying custom queuing are similar to the required steps of access-list configuration. First a custom queue-list must be defined in global configuration mode. Second, the custom queue-list must be applied to an interface with the interface configuration command "custom-queue-list."

Custom-queue-lists can be defined for a given protocol or for an interface that is the source of traffic to be prioritized.

To configure a custom queue-list based upon the protocol type, use the following syntax:

```
queue-list list-number protocol protocol-name queue-number queue-keyword
keyword-value
```

Keywords and keyword-values include access-list numbers and tcp and udp port numbers.

To configure a custom queue-list based upon source interface, use the following syntax:

```
queue-list list-number interface interface-type interface-number queue-number
```

Assigning a Default Priority Queue

Assign a specific queue for those packets that do not match any other rule in the queue-list.

```
queue-list list-number default queue-number
```

Adjust the Byte-Count Value for a Specific Queue

Adjusting the byte count is a critical parameter with Custom-Queuing. The byte-count defines how many bytes will be serviced for a given queue for one polling session. For example, if a queue has 4500 bytes waiting to be forwarded and its byte-count is set to 1500, only 1500 bytes will be forwarded at any given time. After 1500 bytes are forwarded, the custom-queuing algorithm services the next queue. The remaining 3000 bytes will require two more forwarding sessions with the custom-queuing algorithm (1500 bytes per session).

The default byte-count for each queue is 1500 bytes. This can be manually adjusted with the following command:

```
Queue-list list-number queue queue-number byte-count byte-count-number
```

If you want to assure that a certain protocol receives a fixed percentage of bandwidth, increase the byte-count for the queue that services that protocol. The following formula can help to determine a byte-count that will reflect a reservation 50% of access to the bandwidth of a given interface by a specific queue:

(n*c)-c

n=number of custom queues

c=byte count constant

For example, if four queues were defined and you wanted one queue to reserve 50% of available bandwidth, (n*c)-c yields (4*1500)-1500 = 4500. Configure the queue that needs to reserve 50% of available bandwidth with a byte-count of 4500 bytes. This formula is extremely limited by two premises. One is that all queue byte-count sizes are initially the same size. After the formula is executed, all non-50% queues will still remain with the original byte-count size. The second limitation of the formula is that it performs a calculation for a single queue to reserve 50% of available bandwidth. If another percentage is desired, another formula must be created.

A hidden issue with custom-queuing and the byte-count parameter is that custom queuing will not fragment packets. If the custom queuing byte-count is set at 1500 bytes and only frames of 3000 bytes are in a custom-queue, the 3000 byte frames will get forwarded. Therefore, if the frame sizes are different for each queue and frame sizes do not match byte-count settings, the desired percentages of bandwidth allocation for each queue will not be attained.

Custom Queuing Scenario

- Place all DLSW+ and TELNET traffic in a queue that receives 50% of the bandwidth of interface s1
- Place all IPX/NCP traffic in a queue that receives 25% of the bandwidth of interface s1
- Place all other traffic in the default queue

```
r4(config)#queue-list 2 protocol dlsw 1
r4(config)#queue-list 2 protocol ip 1 tcp 23
r4(config)#queue-list 2 protocol ipx 3 list 900
r4(config)#queue-list 2 queue 1 byte-count 3000
r4(config)#queue-list 2 default 4
r4(config)#access-list 900 permit NCP any 451 any 451
```

```
r4(config)#inte s1
r4(config-if)#custom-queue-list 2
```

Custom queuing status and operation can be monitored by show interface, show queuing, and debug custom-queue.

```
r4#show interfaces s1
Serial1 is up, line protocol is up
        Hardware is HD64570
        Internet address is 172.16.34.4/24
        MTU 1500 bytes, BW 1544 Kbit, DLY 20000 usec, rely 255/255, load 1/255
        Encapsulation HDLC, loopback not set, keepalive set (10 sec)
        Last input 00:00:02, output 00:00:03, output hang never
        Last clearing of "show interface" counters never
        Input queue: 0/75/0 (size/max/drops); Total output drops: 0
        Queuing strategy: custom-list 2
        Output queues: (queue #: size/max/drops)
            0: 0/20/0 1: 0/20/0 2: 0/20/0 3: 0/20/0 4: 0/20/0
            5: 0/20/0 6: 0/20/0 7: 0/20/0 8: 0/20/0 9: 0/20/0
            10: 0/20/0 11: 0/20/0 12: 0/20/0 13: 0/20/0 14: 0/20/0
            15: 0/20/0 16: 0/20/0
        5 minute input rate 0 bits/sec, 0 packets/sec
        5 minute output rate 0 bits/sec, 0 packets/sec
        768 packets input, 59742 bytes, 0 no buffer
        Received 153 broadcasts, 0 runts, 0 giants, 0 throttles
        0 input errors, 0 CRC, 0 frame, 0 overrun, 0 ignored, 0 abort
            768 packets output, 59574 bytes, 0 underruns
            0 output errors, 0 collisions, 1 interface resets
            0 output buffer failures, 0 output buffers swapped out
            4 carrier transitions
  DCD=up DSR=up DTR=up RTS=up CTS=up
```

```
r4#show queuing
Current fair queue configuration:

Interface  DiscardDynamicReserved
           thresholdqueue countqueue count
Serial0    64  2560

Current priority queue configuration:
Current custom queue configuration:

List    Queue    Args
2       4        default
2       1        protocol dlsw
2       1        protocol ip        tcp port telnet
2       3        protocol ipx       list 900
2       1        byte-count 3000
  Current RED queue configuration:
```

DEBUG CUSTOM-QUEUE

You can debug custom queuing with the debug custom-queue command. Sample debug output is displayed below:

```
PQ: (Pk size: 104) Q # was 4 now 4
PQ: (Pk size: 104) Q # was 4 now 4
PQ: (Pk size: 98) Q # was 4 now 4
PQ: (Pk size: 47) Q # was 1 now 1
PQ: (Pk size: 47) Q # was 1 now 1
PQ: (Pk size: 53) Q # was 1 now 1
PQ: (Pk size: 44) Q # was 1 now 1
```

Summary

When there is a temporary shortage of bandwidth, a decision must be made to allocate bandwidth to different types of traffic. This is especially important for delay sensitive traffic such as TELNET, SNA/LLC2, voice, and video. Queuing methods can be used to allocate bandwidth to different types of queuing. Cisco offers three types of adjustable queuing methods:

Weighted Fair-Queuing
Priority Queuing
Custom Queuing

Weighted Fair-Queuing allows only minimal adjustments from a router administrator. It has only one adjustable parameter.

Priority queuing is the most extreme type of queuing. It consists of four queues: high, medium, normal and low. Whatever traffic is in the higher queues always gets serviced first. Priority-queues can be configured in a granular manner with access-lists.

Custom queuing is a more democratic form of queuing. Queues are serviced in a round-robin manner. On a given service interval, each queue is serviced according to its byte count. If you want to reserve more available bandwidth for one queue over another, increase its byte-count.

Custom-queues can be made more granular with access-lists. If you ever encounter a requirement specifying a certain percentage of bandwidth to be allocated for a type of traffic, apply custom queuing.

Professional Development Checklist

By using this chapter, you should be able to perform the following operations.

- Construct a standard priority-queuing configuration.
- Construct a granular priority queuing configuration with an access-list.
- Construct a standard custom-queuing configuration.
- Construct a granular custom queue with an access-list.
- Adjust the custom-queue byte-count.

For Further Study

- Cisco Certified Course: Advanced Cisco Router Configuration, Cisco Systems, Inc.

URLs

- **www.cciecert.com**
- **www.mentorlabs.com**
- **www.arslimited.com**

Can You Spot the Issues?

1. You implemented priority queuing on interface serial0. You placed all TCP traffic in the high queue. Now all TCP traffic is being placed in the high queue. You only wanted TELNET traffic placed in the high queue. How do you remedy the problem?
2. You want to further define your priority queuing scheme. You do not want all TELNET traffic in the high queue. You only want TELNET traffic with a source address from the 172.16.1.0 /24 subnet.
3. You want to allocate 50% of available bandwidth to TELNET and DLSw+ traffic. What type of queuing method do you use and how do you configure it?

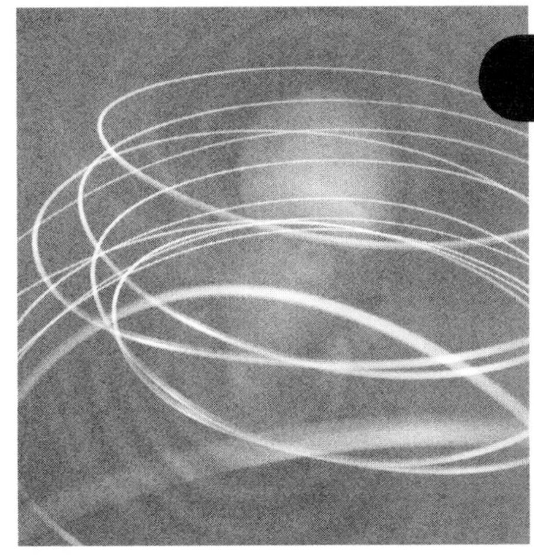

TWENTY EIGHT

Configuring Route-Maps

Topics Covered in This Chapter

- Configuring Route-Maps as a Substitute for Static Routing
- Configuring Route-Maps to Manipulate IGP Metrics
- Configuring Route-Maps to Manipulate BGP4 Attributes

Route-maps provide a mechanism for a network administrator to manipulate routing decisions and manually adjust routing updates on specified routers, especially BGP4 speaking routers. The mechanism is an "if/then" device whereby, if a certain condition is matched (IP address, source interface, autonomous system number, etc.), then a certain routing variable is adjusted (local interface to switch packet on, metric, BGP weight, etc.). Route-maps are applied to IP traffic.

Route-maps rely on access-lists to identify or "match" the packets to be manipulated. Therefore, a full understanding of IP access-lists is a prerequisite for configuring route-maps.

In this chapter, route-maps will be examined at three levels:

1. The first level provides an examination of route-maps acting as a substitute for static routes.
2. The second level provides an examination of route-maps supplementing the IGP route redistribution process.

3. The third level provides an examination of route-maps manipulating the BGP update process.

Route-Maps as a Substitute for Static Routes

Thus far, all IP routing decisions have been made by examining the destination address of inbound IP packets. A packet arrives at a router interface; the destination address of the IP packet is matched with the longest match in the IP routing table; if there is no match, you use the default route; if there is no match and no default route, discard the packet and send an ICMP message to the source of the packet.

Route-maps offer an alternative to this method of "destination address-based routing." Consider the following scenario:

A packet with a source address of 172.16.117.0/24 arrives at a router interface. The router interface has a route-map applied to it, specifying, "All packets arriving on this interface with a source address of 172.16.117.0/24 will be forwarded out of interface Ethernet 0." Because of the route-map, the packet will be forwarded out the Ethernet 0 interface regardless of what destination address it had and regardless of any information contained in the routing table.

Like access-lists and queue-lists, route-maps used as a substitute for static routes have two components: (1) a list of route-map statements, and (2) a statement to apply the route-map to a specific interface. Unlike access-lists and queue-lists, creating a route-map is not performed in global configuration mode. A route-map is created in the "route-map" configuration mode. Provided below is a listing of route-map configuration mode commands:

```
r4(config)#route-map acctg

r4(config-route-map)#?
Route Map           configuration commands:
   default          Set a command to its defaults
   exit             Exit from route-map configuration mode
   help             Description of the interactive help system
   match            Match values from routing table
   no               Negate a command or set its defaults
   set              Set values in destination routing protocol
```

The two primary route-map commands are "match" and "set". Match commands set the conditions which packets must match if the specified route-map action will be performed. The set commands specify the action to be performed when the match criteria is met.

The syntax for accessing route-map configuration mode is:

```
Route-map [map-tag] [[permit|deny] [sequence-number]]
```

When beginning the route-map configuration process, you have the option to define the route-map with a "permit" or "deny" statement. A sequence number can be added to every route-map statement to assure an order of execution of route-map statements. If you do not specify a "permit" or "deny" parameter, or a sequence-number, a "permit" parameter and a sequence number of 10 will be added to the statement.

For example, if the following statement is entered with no permit/deny statement or sequence number:

```
r4(config)#route-map cisco
```

the IOS will add a permit statement and a sequence number of 10.

```
!
route-map cisco permit 10
!
```

If any additional route-map statements are added without permit/deny parameters and a sequence number, the contents of the additional route-maps will be added to the route-map with a sequence number of 10. Therefore, it is highly recommended that all route-map statements are manually configured with permit/deny statements and unique sequence numbers that reflect the route-map statements' desired order of execution.

Route-Map Match Options

Displayed below are route-map match options:

```
r4(config-route-map)#match ?
   as-path          Match BGP AS path list
   clns             CLNS information
   community        Match BGP community list
   interface        Match first hop interface of route
   ip               IP specific information
   length           Packet length
   metric           Match metric of route
   route-type       Match route-type of route
   tag              Match tag of route
```

Notice that two of the match options are explicitly BGP-related. To use a route-map as an alternative to a static route, use the "match ip" option:

```
r4(config-route-map)#match ip ?
   address          Match address of route or match packet
   next-hop         Match next-hop address of route
   route-source     Match advertising source address of route
```

All the "match ip" options require an access-list to specify an IP "address," "next-hop" and "route-source."

```
r4(config-route-map)#match ip address ?
  <1-199> IP access-list number
  WORD    IP access-list name
```

Use the "match ip address x" command (x = access-list number) to define the source address of a packet to be policy routed.

Route-Map Set Options

Displayed below are route-map set options:

```
r4(config-route-map)#set ?
   as-path                    Prepend string for a BGP AS-path attribute
   automatic-tag              Automatically compute TAG value
   clns                       OSI summary address
   community                  BGP community attribute
   dampening                  Set BGP route flap dampening parameters
   default                    Set default information
   destination-preference     BGP destination preference path attribute
   interface                  Output interface
   ip                         IP specific information
   level                      Where to import route
   local-preference           BGP local preference path attribute
   metric                     Metric value for destination routing protocol
   metric-type                Type of metric for destination routing protocol
   origin                     BGP origin code
   tag                        Tag value for destination routing protocol
   weight                     BGP weight for routing table
```

Notice that seven of the set options are explicitly related to BGP. To configure a route-map as an alternative to static routing, use the "set interface" and "set ip next-hop" parameters.

Configuring a Route-Map as a Substitute for a Static Route

The configuration steps are as follows:

1. Designate a route-map name with a permit/deny parameter and sequence number.
2. Specify "match" criteria (in most cases, this involves defining an access-list).
3. Use the statement "match ip address 1."
4. Specify "set" parameters for packets that meet the "match" criteria.

5. Use the recommended statement "set ip interface xx" (xx = local interface to switch matched packets on).
6. Repeat steps 2-3, using a higher sequence number for additional match/set statements.
7. Apply route-map to an interface with the "ip policy xxxx" statement (xxxx = route-map name).

Consider the following scenario:

All packets arriving on interface serial 1 with a source address of 172.16.117.0/24 will be forwarded out of interface Ethernet 0:

```
interface Serial1
     ip address 172.16.34.4 255.255.255.0
     ip policy route-map acctg
!
access-list 1 permit 172.16.117.0 0.0.0.255
!
route-map acctg permit 10
     match ip address 1
     set interface Ethernet0
!
```

Notice that five statements are involved in the configuration:

1. Route-map acctg permit 10
2. Match ip address 1 (1 references standard access-list 1)
3. Set interface Ethernet 0 (this is the interface to forward packets that match the source address specified by access-list 1)
4. Access-list 1 defining the source IP address as 172.16.117.0 0.0.0.255
5. Apply the route-map to interface serial 1 with the "ip policy" statement

Route-map configuration information can be viewed with the "show ip policy" and "show route-map" statements:

```
r4#show ip policy
     Interface     Route map
     Serial1       acctg

r4#show route-map
route-map acctg, permit, sequence 10
     Match clauses:
     ip address (access-lists): 1
  Set clauses:
     interface Ethernet0
  Policy routing matches: 1911 packets, 197278 bytes
```

Debug traces of route-map performance by using "debug ip policy" and "debug ip packet".

In the debug trace below, notice that packets entering interface serial 1 do not meet the "match" criteria of route-map acctg. If the route-map match criteria are not met, the packets are forwarded in their normal manner: matching each packet's destination address with the longest match in the routing table.

```
IP: s=172.16.34.6 (Serial1), d=172.16.33.1 (Serial0), len 100, policy rejected
-- normal forwarding
IP: s=172.16.34.6 (Serial1), d=172.16.33.1 (Serial0), g=172.16.33.1, len 100,
forward
IP: s=172.16.34.6 (Serial1), d=172.16.33.1 (Serial0), len 100, policy rejected
-- normal forwarding
IP: s=172.16.34.6 (Serial1), d=172.16.33.1 (Serial0), g=172.16.33.1, len 100,
forward
IP: s=172.16.34.6 (Serial1), d=224.0.0.10, len 60, policy rejected -- normal
forwarding
IP: s=172.16.34.6 (Serial1), d=172.16.34.4 (Serial1), len 94, policy rejected -
- normal forwarding
IP: s=172.16.34.6 (Serial1), d=172.16.33.1 (Serialal0), len 100, policy
rejected -- normal forwarding
IP: s=172.16.34.6 (Serial1), d=172.16.33.1 (Serial0), g=172.16.33.1, len 100,
forward
```

In the trace below, packets are meeting the match criteria. Notice how "debug ip policy" identifies each packet that meets the "match" criteria specified in the route-map. It then displays a statement reflecting that the operation specified in the "set" statement has been performed. Still, other packets that do not meet the route-map "match" criteria are forwarded in a "normal" (destination based routing) process.

```
IP: s=172.16.117.1 (Serial1), d=172.16.33.1, len 100, policy match
IP: route map acctg, item 10, permit
IP: s=172.16.117.1 (Serial1), d=172.16.33.1 (Ethernet0), len 100, policy routed
IP: Serial1 to Ethernet0 172.16.33.1
IP: s=172.16.117.1 (Serial1), d=172.16.33.1 (Ethernet0), g=172.16.33.1, len
100, forward
IP: s=172.16.34.6 (Serial1), d=224.0.0.10, len 60, policy rejected -- normal
forwarding
IP: s=172.16.34.6 (Serial1), d=224.0.0.10, len 60, rcvd 2
IP: s=172.16.34.6 (Serial1), d=172.16.34.4 (Serial1), len 94, policy rejected
-- normal forwarding
IP: s=172.16.117.1 (Serial1), d=172.16.33.1, len 100, policy match
IP: route map acctg, item 10, permit
IP: s=172.16.117.1 (Serial1), d=172.16.33.1 (Ethernet0), len 100, policy routed
IP: Serial1 to Ethernet0 172.16.33.1
IP: s=172.16.117.1 (Serial1), d=172.16.33.1 (Ethernet0), g=172.16.33.1, len
100, forward
IP: s=172.16.117.1 (Serial1), d=172.16.33.1 (Ethernet0), len 100, policy routed
IP: Serial1 to Ethernet0 172.16.33.1
```

With policy routing, if the interface is down and the policy is to switch the packet over that interface, policy routes will fail if the interface is not available. An alternative to using the "set interface" command is to use the "set next-hop" command. Set Next-hop allows the routing process to make a recursive routing decision. Using the physical address does not let the routing process make a recursive routing decision.

Route-Maps and IGP Redistribution

Route-maps can also be used to manipulate routing update parameters, such as metrics during IGP redistribution. In the example below, EIGRP routes are being redistributed into OSPF. Any EIGRP routes with the first two octets of 169.10.0.0 will be assigned a metric of 257; all EIGRP routes will be assigned a metric of 500 when redistributed into OSPF.

```
router ospf 100
redistribute eigrp 100 metric 110 subnets route-map redist
     network 172.16.33.0 0.0.0.255 area 0
!
access-list 1 permit 169.10.0.0 0.0.255.255
!
route-map redist permit 10
     match ip address 1
     set metric 257
!
route-map redist permit 20
     set metric 500
```

The configuration of the route-map can be viewed with "show route-map":

```
r4#sh route-map
route-map redist, permit, sequence 10
     Match clauses:
       ip address (access-lists): 1
     Set clauses:
       metric 257
     Policy routing matches: 0 packets, 0 bytes
route-map redist, permit, sequence 20
     Match clauses:
     Set clauses:
       metric 500
     Policy routing matches: 0 packets, 0 bytes
```

The results of the route-map can be viewed in the routing table of a directly connected OSPF neighbor:

```
r1>sh ip ro
Codes: C - connected, S - static, I - IGRP, R - RIP, M - mobile, B - BGP
       D - EIGRP, EX - EIGRP external, O - OSPF, IA - OSPF inter area
       N1 - OSPF NSSA external type 1, N2 - OSPF NSSA external type 2
       E1 - OSPF external type 1, E2 - OSPF external type 2, E - EGP
       i - IS-IS, L1 - IS-IS level-1, L2 - IS-IS level-2, * - candidate default
       U - per-user static route, o - ODR

Gateway of last resort is not set

       169.10.0.0/24 is subnetted, 3 subnets
O E2   169.10.3.0 [110/257] via 172.16.33.4, 00:00:34, Serial0.2
O E2   169.10.2.0 [110/257] via 172.16.33.4, 00:00:34, Serial0.2
O E2   169.10.1.0 [110/257] via 172.16.33.4, 00:00:34, Serial0.2
       140.10.0.0/24 is subnetted, 3 subnets
O E2   140.10.3.0 [110/500] via 172.16.33.4, 00:00:34, Serial0.2
O E2   140.10.2.0 [110/500] via 172.16.33.4, 00:00:34, Serial0.2
O E2   140.10.1.0 [110/500] via 172.16.33.4, 00:00:35, Serial0.2
```

Notice how the 169.10.0.0 routes have a metric of 257, and the 140.10.0.0 routes have a metric of 500.

If the second route-map statement is omitted, all routes that do not match the first route-map's "match" statement will not be redistributed. Therefore, an implicit deny is applied to route-maps during redistribution. If you want all routes to be redistributed, even those that do not match any of the "match" statements—add a line similar to the one displayed below at your "permit any" equivalent for route-maps performing redistribution:

```
r4(config)#route-map redist-to-ospf  permit  20
```

Route-Maps and BGP Updates

One of the major features of BGP4 is its ability to be routed based upon policy decisions. Policy decisions are defined as routing decisions determined by a network administrator, rather than a dynamic routing protocol. BGP4 updates have a number of "attributes" which allow them to be manipulated based upon several "policy-oriented" criteria.

Route-maps can be applied to BGP4 updates to manipulate BGP4 attributes. As mentioned earlier, a route-map creates an "if/then" mechanism to directly manipulate the actual router switching decisions or update parameters. For example, when an autonomous system has two or more paths to a destination prefix, it must decide which path to select. IGP routing protocols such as RIP, IGRP, OSPF and EIGRP use a metric to select the shortest path to a destination prefix. BGP4 uses different attribute values for path selection.

Route-maps can be surgically used to manipulate specific attributes to influence the BGP4 path selection process.

Before you examine the route-map syntax used to manipulate BGP4 attributes, it is essential to know which attributes take precedence in the BGP4 path selection process. BGP4 uses the following ten-step decision criteria to select the best path to a given destination prefix:

1. Discard the BGP update if its path references an unreachable next-hop address. (See next-hop reachability requirement in Chapter 14.)
2. Out of all eligible updates, select the update that has the path with the largest "weight" attribute. (The weight attribute is a Cisco specific attribute.)
3. If all "weight" attributes are equal, select the path with the largest local preference attribute.
4. If all local preference attributes are equal, select the path that was originated by BGP running on the local router.
5. If no route was originated on the local router, select the path with the shortest AS_PATH attribute.
6. If all AS-PATHs are of equal length, select the path with the lowest origin type attribute (Incomplete>EGP>IGP).
7. If all origin types are equal, select the path with the lowest Multi-Exit Discriminator (MED) attribute.
8. If all paths have the same MED attribute, select the external path over the internal path.
9. If all paths are either all external or all internal, select the path with the nearest IGP neighbor.
10. If all paths have the same nearest neighbor, select the path with the lowest BGP router identifier.

With these criteria, network administrators can manipulate BGP4 routing decisions using route-maps to manipulate the different attributes that influence the path selection process. This chapter will focus only on the manipulation of the weight and local preference attributes (listed in steps two and three of the ten step decision criteria described above). For additional information on manipulating other BGP4 attributes, see the "For Further Study" section at the end of this chapter.

In most cases, BGP4 updates received have equal values for the weight and local preference attributes. If no attribute manipulation is performed, most BGP4 paths would be selected based upon the shortest AS-PATH attribute. Therefore, most BGP4 path selection processes stop at step five of the ten-step decision criteria.

Manipulating the weight attribute (listed under step two) has very powerful consequences. If you manipulate a BGP4 update's weight to be greater than the weights of all other possible paths, the BGP4 path selection process is over! The update with the highest weight wins, and there is no need to examine any other BGP4 attribute.

The weight attribute is a very special attribute because it does not propagate to any other BGP4 speaker (neither EBGP nor IBGP speakers). You use the weight attribute when you want to influence the path selection process of only one BGP speaker.

If you want to influence the path selection process of all IBGP speakers in a given autonomous system, manipulate the Local Preference attribute. When the Local Preference attribute is manipulated, its value is forwarded to all other IBGP speakers. Therefore, if a BGP4 speaker XX is receiving BGP4 updates from the EBGP4 neighbor YY, and is increasing the Local Preference as the routes are received, the BGP4 speaker's path to YY will be the guaranteed "preferred" path for all routes received from YY. BGP4 speaker XX's preference can only be overridden by two factors:

1. Other IBGP speakers possessing a higher local preference for the routes YY advertised to XX
2. Other IBGP speakers possessing a higher weight for the routes YY advertised to XX. Remember, the weight attribute is never propagated to other BGP speakers (EBGP or IBGP), but a higher weight attribute takes precedence over the local preference attribute.

For example, consider the following scenario:

Company A has a full T-3 connection to the Internet through the Internet Service Provider AAA-101.NET. Company A acquires Company B, which has a T-1 connection to the Internet through the Internet Service Provider BBB-202.NET. Company A wants to keep both Internet connections, but route all its traffic through the T-3 connection, with the exception of packets originating from the AS of BBB-202.NET (BBB-202.NET's AS is 202). All traffic originating from AS 202 will use the T-1 Internet connection.

To perform this task, you must understand route-maps, BGP attributes and access-lists (both IP prefix access-lists—access-list 0-199—and AS path access-lists). From a BGP4 attributes perspective, a local preference can be used to direct all Internet traffic not originating from AS 202 to the T-3 connection. On the former Company B router, the following route-map, AS-Path access-list and local preference increase will be configured:

```
router bgp 1000
 neighbor 10.1.1.1 remote-as 1000
 neighbor 172.16.1.100 remote-as 202
 neighbor 172.16.1.100 route-map AS-200-IN in
!
no ip classless
ip as-path access-list 1 permit _300$
!
route-map AS-200-IN permit 10
```

```
 match as-path 1
 set local-preference 200
!
route-map AS-200-IN permit 20
!
```

1. router bgp 1000
2. neighbor 10.1.1.2 remote-as 1000
3. neighbor 172.16.100.1 remote-as 101
4. bgp default local preference 150

Summary

Route-maps provide a tool to manipulate the IP routing process. Three different uses of route maps are:

- Route-maps used as an alternative to static routes.
- Route-maps used to manipulate the metrics of ICP routes during the route redistribution process.
- Route-maps used to manipulate BGP-4 attributes.

Professional Development Checklist

By using this chapter, you should be able to perform the following operations:

- Configure a route-map to act as a substitute to a static route.
- Configure a route-map to manipulate an IGP redistribution process.
- Configure a route-map to manipulate a BGP update process.

For Further Study

- *Using the Border Gateway Protocol for Interdomain Routing*
- Halabi, Bassam, *Internet Routing Architectures*

URLs

- **www.cciecert.com**
- **www.mentorlabs.com**
- **www.cisco.com**

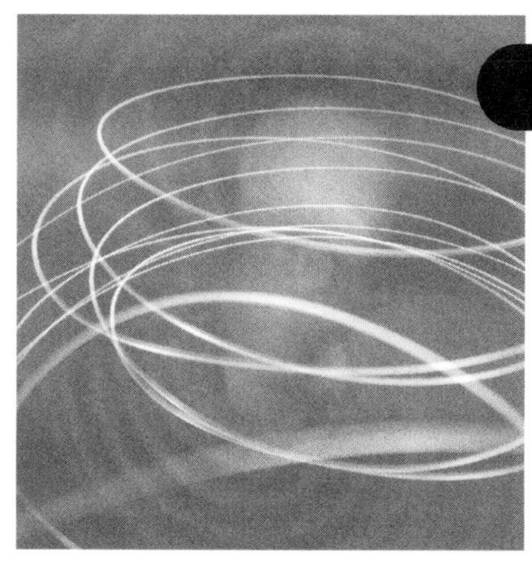

TWENTY NINE

Level Six Summary

You have reached the configuration summit now! You have completed a basic introduction to access-list, queue-list, and route-map configuration. These topics, especially access-lists, span all of the material covered in Level Two through Level Five. Access-lists, queue-lists, and route-maps are the Internetwork Operating System (IOS) equivalent to the high-level programming language "If..then" construct. This module has shown you how you can control traffic and manipulate routing table updates with the Cisco IOS. As a review, some of the tasks that can be performed by access-lists, queue-lists, and route-maps are:

You can filter network layer traffic on a per protocol and per direction basis.
You can filter BGP updates on a per Autonomous System basis.
You can filter data-link layer and nonroutable traffic
You can prioritize traffic when congestion occurs.
You can use route-maps to direct traffic via policy routing.

You can use route-maps to manipulate metrics during route redistribution.
You can use route-maps to manipulate BGP4 attributes.

Access-lists have many uses. In addition to filtering traffic, access-lists can also be used for:

Filtering routing updates with Distribute-Lists
Defining "interesting traffic" with Dialer-Lists
Defining what addresses need to be translated by Network Address Translation (NAT)

Access-lists must be designed and implemented with caution. Remember how IP access-lists can cause problems for other traffic like DLSW+ and GRE tunnels.

Access-lists not discussed in this book are:

XNS
Novell NETBIOS access-lists
Novell Route Summarization access-lists

As a summary, listed below is a display of all of the explicit "permit any" parameters for the different access-lists:

IP	any
IPX	–1
APPLETALK	OTHER-ACCESS
	ADDITIONAL ZONES
DECNET	0.0 63.1023
NETBIOS Names	*
IP AS-PATH	.*
LSAP	0_x00000_xFFFFF

Access-lists, queue-lists and route-maps should be deployed only when it has been verified that stable and consistent baseline connectivity for a given protocol has been attained.

Chapters Twenty-Three to Twenty-Eight provided a mere introduction to the topic of internetwork traffic control. Listed below is a minimal professional development checklist to help you get started with developing your access-list configuration skills:

- Configure IP Standard Access-Lists
- Configure IP Extended Access-Lists
- Configure IP Access-Lists blocking a range of addresses
- Configure an IP Access-List with the Established Parameter
- Configure a Dynamic IP Access-List
- Configure IPX Standard Access-Lists

- Configure IPX Extended Access-Lists
- Configure IPX routing table update filters for IPX/RIP and EIGRP
- Configure IPX SAP filter
- Configure GNS reply filter
- Configure an AppleTalk access-list that applies to all AppleTalk traffic
- Configure an AppleTalk GZL filter
- Configure an Apple Talk ZIP-Reply filter
- Configure an AppleTalk routing table update filters for RTMP and EIGRP
- Configure a DECNET access-list that applies to all DECNET traffic
- Configure MAC access-lists for Ethernet frames
- Configure MAC access-lists for Token-Ring frames
- Configure LSAP access-lists
- Configure NETBIOS host name access-lists
- Configure an access-expression
- Construct a standard priority-queuing configuration
- Construct a granular priority queuing configuration with an access-list
- Construct a standard custom-queuing configuration
- Construct a granular custom queue with an access-list
- Adjust the custom-queue byte-count
- Configure a route-map to act as a substitute to a static route
- Configure a route-map to manipulate an IGP redistribution process
- Configure a route-map to manipulate a BGP update process

This completes Level Six. Access-lists are a critical tool in assuring optimum performance in a Cisco three hierarchical network. When routers are deployed at the access-level, make every attempt to configure access-lists here. In a campus/LAN environment, LAN switches are deployed at the access-level. In a campus/LAN environment, routers are deployed at the distribution level. Therefore, in a campus/LAN environment, configure access-lists at the distribution level.

T H I R T Y

Troubleshooting Routers and Switches

Topics Covered in This Chapter

- General Rules of Troubleshooting
- Catastrophic Troubleshooting
- Reviewing Router and Switch Boot Up Processes
- Upgrading the IOS
- Recovering a Lost Password

In order to perform troubleshooting optimally, you must understand characteristics of protocols and internetworking technology. For example, if you need to troubleshoot Frame-Relay, you must understand the operational characteristics of Frame-Relay. You need to know how Frame-Relay operates under normal conditions. If you know how the technology is supposed to work, you can spot the issues that are causing it not to work.

This chapter provides methods of performing catastrophic troubleshooting as well as brief checklists and associated IOS tools for troubleshooting the technologies covered in this book.

Some General Rules of Troubleshooting

1. Record the symptoms of the problem.
2. Has anything changed since the problem began?
3. Before changing anything during your troubleshooting efforts, record all settings and back up all configurations.

4. Attempt to define the issues related to how the technology is supposed to operate. Use your issue spotting skills!
5. Be incremental. Change one variable at a time and check the results of the change.
6. Be systematic:
   Check physical layer issues first.
   Check data-link layer issues second.
   Check data-link layer issues on a segment by segment basis. Understand an internetwork failure from an exclusively Data-Link Layer basis. Be able to clearly separate Data-Link Layer issues from Network Layer issues.
   Check routed protocol issues third.
   Check routing protocol issues fourth.
   Be able understand an internetwork failure from an exclusively Network Layer basis. Be able to clearly separate Network Layer issues from Data-Link Layer or Transport Layer issues.
7. Attempt to isolate the problem(s).
8. Know what to look for. Know how the protocols operate under normal conditions.
9. Three things you never want to run out of on a router or switch:
   Bandwidth
   CPU cycles
   Memory
10. Examine the running-configuration script.
11. Troubleshoot both sides of the connection, distinguishing between what the "calling" party is doing and what the "called" party is doing.
12. Troubleshoot both paths of the routing traffic (the path from source to destination, as well the path from destination to source (the "return path")).

Catastrophic Troubleshooting

One of the most extreme troubleshooting situations is when the router or switch will not boot up. When this occurs, remove all non-essential components and attempt to boot the router or switch up. For example, if a Cisco 4500 router fails to boot up properly, remove all non-essential components and attempt to boot it. If a Catalyst 5000 fails to boot up properly, remove all modules except the supervisor module and see if it boots up properly. Once you have gotten the router or switch to boot up with a minimal hardware configuration, begin re-installing the non-essential components one by one and see if the device continues to boot up properly.

If the router or switch still does not boot up with all non-essential components removed, check the hardware LEDs on router or switch. For example, on a Cisco 2500 router, the LED next to the AUX port on the back of the router should always be solid green. If it is flashing, it indicates a hardware problem on the 2500. For Cisco 7500 routers, LightStream 1010 ATM switches, Catalyst 5000 switches and Catalyst 8500 switch routers, check the LEDs on the route switch processor (Cisco 7500 routers), ATM switch processor (LightStream 1010), Supervisor module (Catalyst 5000) and switch route processor (Catalyst 8500).

Make sure the router or switch is installed in an environment with:

1. Proper climatic settings; make sure the room is not too hot or humid.
2. Proper ventilation; make sure the router's or switches' internal air flow is unobstructed. A router or switch with blocked ventilation will overheat and malfunction.
3. Proper and consistent power sources. Power spikes can destroy routers and switches; brown outs can cause erratic performance.

Router and Switch Boot Up Sequence

It is very important to assure that the router or switch is booting up properly. Therefore, it is extremely important to know the proper boot up sequence of Cisco routers and switches. Review the boot up sequence by power cycling a switch or router several times in a lab environment. After watching the boot up sequence several times, you should know every step of the process. For example, within seconds of applying power to the router, you should see the following three lines while plugged into the router's console port:

The first three lines seen during the boot up process of a Cisco 2500 router:

```
System Bootstrap, Version 5.2(8a), RELEASE SOFTWARE
Copyright (c) 1986-1995 by cisco Systems
2500 processor with 6144 Kbytes of main memory
```

The first three lines seen during the boot up process of a Cisco 4000 router:

```
System Bootstrap, Version 5.3(10) [tamb 10], RELEASE SOFTWARE (fc1)
Copyright (c) 1994 by cisco Systems, Inc.
C4500 processor with 16384 Kbytes of main memory
```

The first three lines seen during the boot up of a Cisco 7500 router:

```
System Bootstrap, Version 5.3.2(3.2) [kmac 3.2], RELEASE SOFTWARE
Copyright (c) 1994 by cisco Systems, Inc.
RSP processor with 32768 Kbytes of main memory
```

The first three lines seen during the boot up of the LightStream 1010 ATM Switch:

```
System Bootstrap, Version 201(1025), SOFTWARE
Copyright (c) 1986-1996 by cisco Systems
ASP processor with 16384 Kbytes of main memory
```

Notice that line three displays the router or switch processor, as well as the amount of memory in each router and switch. Check to make sure that the amount of memory displayed matches how much you physically installed in the router or switch.

If you do not see something similar to the three lines displayed above during the first few seconds of the router or LightStream switch boot up process, check that you have a good console cable and that your terminal session is configured properly in your workstation (for example, HyperTerminal on Windows 95). If both of these prove to be working properly, you must perform hardware troubleshooting on your Cisco router. As mentioned earlier, remove all non-essential components and attempt to boot the router or switch. If you still do not see something resembling the first three lines listed above, replace the memory modules and try to reboot again. On a 7500 router or Catalyst 5000 RSM, make sure your memory modules are placed in the correct SIMMS sockets. When you replace memory modules for any Cisco router or switch, consult the platform's hardware configuration guide. Make sure you install only Cisco-approved memory modules in all Cisco products.

If the router or ATM switch has no configuration, it will end the boot up process at "setup" mode. You are about to access "setup" mode when you are prompted with the following message:

```
Notice: NVRAM invalid, possibly due to write erase.
        --- System Configuration Dialog ---

At any point you may enter a question mark '?' for help.
Use ctrl-c to abort configuration dialog at any prompt.
Default settings are in square brackets '[]'.
Would you like to enter the initial configuration dialog? [yes]:
```

If you decline to enter the initial configuration dialog, you will end up at the following prompt:

```
Router>
```

From this point, you can begin configuring your router or ATM switch.

If you encounter the following three prompts, your router is not fully operational:

```
>
rommon 1 >
Router(boot)>
```

The first two prompts, ">" and "rommon1>", indicate that your router has booted but has not loaded an IOS. You are in the "ROM Monitor" mode. By pressing the question mark key, a list of microprocessor specific commands will be listed to assist you in getting your router properly booted. When you are in this mode, consider your router as being in a coma. It is alive, but in a vegetative state.

Different commands are available depending upon the type of main processor the router or switch possesses.

If you boot your router and end up with the "Router(boot)>" prompt, your router is still not operational. You have loaded an emergency backup copy of the IOS that allows you to perform IOS commands, but it does not allow the router to route. For example, if you go into configuration mode and you type the command "router ?", you should receive a listing of the routing protocols you can enable; however, when a router is in (boot) mode, no routing process can be enabled:

```
r4(boot)#configuration terminal
Enter configuration commands, one per line.  End with CNTL/Z.
r4(boot)(config)#router ?
% Unrecognized command
```

If this happens, check your configuration register to see from which source your router is set to boot. This can be determined by examining the last hexadecimal digit of the configuration register. The configuration register can be viewed in the last line of the show version display.

If the last digit of the configuration register has the following values, it will attempt to boot from the corresponding sources:

- 0 Your router or switch will boot into ROM MONITOR (COMA MODE)
- 1 Your router or switch will boot into BOOT ROM (LIFEBOAT MODE)
- 2–F Your router or switch will first scan its start configuration script and look for any boot system commands. Then it will attempt to boot from flash. If it cannot boot from flash, it will attempt to boot from a TFTP server. If this is unsuccessful, it will attempt to boot from BOOT ROM.

Catalyst 5000 Boot Up Process

The Catalyst 5000 multilayer switch boot up process takes much longer than a router boot-up process. Common prompts seen during the initial phase of a Catalyst 5000 switch boot up process with a Supervisor I module are:

```
ROM Power Up Diagnostics of Mar 26 1997

Init NVRAM Log
LED Test .................... done
ROM Checksum ............... passed
Dual Port RAM r/w Test ..... passed
ID PROM .................... passed
System DRAM Size(mb) ....... 20
DRAM Data Bus Test ......... passed
DRAM Address Test .......... passed
DRAM Byte/Word Access Test .. passed
EARL Test .................. passed


BOOTROM Version 2.2(2), Dated Mar 26 1997 16:29:34
BOOT date: 06/23/98 BOOT time: 22:56:43
SIMM RAM address test
SIMM Ram r/w 55aa
SIMM Ram r/w aa55
Uncompressing NMP image.  This will take a minute...
```

After approximately four to five minutes of testing the different modules and loading the Catalyst IOS, a successful Catalyst boot up process will terminate with the following console prompt and messages:

```
Cisco Systems Console


Enter password:
7/4/1998,20:27:00:SYS-5:Module 1 is online

Console>
7/4/1998,20:27:22:SYS-5:Module 3 is online
7/4/1998,20:27:25:SYS-5:Module 2 is online
7/4/1998,20:27:33:SYS-5:Module 4 is online
```

For each module installed on a Catalyst 5000, a console message should display that the specific module is now "online." Also, under healthy operational conditions, the system status LED for all modules on a Catalyst should be green.

It is important to be aware of the different stages of the Catalyst 5000 boot up process. When watching the Catalyst bootup process, you will notice different LEDs changing colors (green, orange and red). You will also notice the console generating different messages at different times. If you watch the Catalyst 5000 boot up process closely, you will notice that LED color changes occur in synchronization with the display of many of the console messages. A general chronology of the Catalyst 5000 of the console messages displayed and the associated LED color changes is provided below:

- Upon boot up, all module status LEDs are red.
- Within seconds of bootup, the supervisor module status LED turns orange. All other modules status LEDs are red.
- During testing of the EARL the supervisor status LED turns back to red. All other modules status LEDs are red.
- Once the Catalyst 5000 boot ROM is loaded, the supervisor status LED turns green. All other modules status LEDs are red.
- During a RAM test, the supervisor module status LED turns RED again. All other modules status LEDs are red.
- As the NMP image is uncompressed, the supervisor LED turns orange. All other modules status LEDs are red.
- Once the NMP image is loaded, the supervisor status LED turns green. All other modules status LEDs turn orange.
- Supervisor ports go through a self-test. They will flash between the combinations of orange and green. Finally, all active LEDs in the supervisor module turn green.

A console message similar to the one listed below will then appear for the supervisor module:

```
7/4/1998,20:27:00:SYS-5:Module 1 is online
```

All ports on other modules go through self-tests. After several seconds of self-testing, the status LEDs of the non-supervisor modules turn green and a console message is displayed that they are now "on-line."

Below is a sample display of the Catalyst 5000 bootup process. To the right of each line is a description of the supervisor module LED status light color, and the approximate time elapsed from the moment the bootup process began to reach the specified stage:

```
ROM Power Up Diagnostics of Mar 26 1997

Init NVRAM Log
LED Test .................. done   (red/one second)
ROM Checksum ............... passed (orange/less than five seconds)
Dual Port RAM r/w Test ..... passed (orange/less than five seconds)
ID PROM .................... passed (orange/less than five seconds)
System DRAM Size(mb) ....... 20     (orange/less than five seconds)
DRAM Data Bus Test ......... passed (orange/less than five seconds)
DRAM Address Test .......... passed (orange/less than five seconds)
DRAM Byte/Word Access Test .. passed (orange/less than five seconds)
EARL Test .................. passed (red/six seconds)


BOOTROM Version 2.2(2), Dated Mar 26 1997 16:29:34 (green/26 seconds)
BOOT date: 06/23/98 BOOT time: 22:56:43
SIMM RAM address test (red/ begin at 55 seconds)
SIMM Ram r/w 55aa (red)
```

```
SIMM Ram r/w aa55 (red)
Uncompressing NMP image.  This will take a minute... (orange)
```

Loading a New IOS on a Router

Many router or switch crashes are caused by bugs in the IOS (especially with new features). Cisco is very good about posting IOS bugs on its Web site, so check the Cisco Web site to stay current with the Cisco bug reports. If you need to load a new IOS image onto a router or switch, perform the following steps:

1. Determine how much flash the new image requires. Make sure your router or switch has enough memory to hold the new image.
2. Determine how much RAM the new image requires. Make sure your router or switch has enough RAM to accommodate the new image.
3. **IF YOU NEED TO DELETE THE OLD IMAGE TO MAKE ROOM FOR THE NEW ONE, BACK UP THE OLD IMAGE!** You do not want to be in a situation where your new IOS will not load due to a lack of flash or memory, and you no longer have the old IOS. This can result in a router and switch being down for several hours.
4. If you are going to upgrade the IOS on a "run from flash" router, such as a Cisco 2500, you must reload the router into ROM boot mode. This can be performed by changing the configuration register to 0x1. You can avoid manually changing the configuration register on a 2500 router by simply typing "copy tftp flash". The 2500 router will then prompt you through the IOS upgrade process. However, if you want more control over the process, change the configuration register.
5. Copy the new IOS to a device that will act as a TFTP server. The device can be a UNIX system, an NT system or even a Cisco router. To make a Cisco router act as a TFTP server, type the following global configuration mode command:
   r1(config)#tftp-server flash xxxx-xxxx-xxxx-xxxx
   Warning: xxxx-xxxx-xxxx-xxxx not in Flash for TFTP serving
   (xxxx-xxxx-xxxx-xxxx = the IOS image name in flash memory.)
   Note of the warning directly below the command. The file name entered in the router tftp-server command must be identical to the file name of the IOS image to be served in flash memory.
6. If necessary, delete the old IOS image (REMEMBER TO BACK UP THE OLD IOS IMAGE FIRST IF YOU NEED TO DELETE IT!). To erase flash, enter the following privileged mode command:
   r1#erase flash

   System flash directory:

File Length Name/status
1 7738060 c2500-j-l.112-5
[7738124 bytes used, 650484 available, 8388608 total]

Erase flash device? [confirm]
With release 12.0 of the IOS (and even some 11.3 IOS images), new file system functionality will be added. You can use both DOS-like and UNIX-like delete and copy commands to erase and copy files. However, the old commands, like erase flash, will also remain.

7. Copy the new file to flash with the "copy tftp flash" command.

The Cisco Web site is extremely useful in providing online assistance for IOS upgrades. The site has IOS planners that list how much memory and flash you need to install a given IOS. For those that have the proper maintenance agreement, you can download IOS images for practically all Cisco router and switch platforms directly from the Cisco Web site.

Cisco offers several graphical tools that make this process easier, such as CiscoWorks and Cisco Resource Manager. These tools can further simplify the IOS upgrade process.

Recovering from a Lost or Unknown Password on a Router

Sometimes a router password is forgotten. You must be able to break into the router without knowing the password. The key is to manipulate the configuration register. The default configuration register setting for most Cisco routers is 0x2102. Bit number 6 of the configuration register is used to bypass the startup configuration during system boot up. If you can change the configuration register from 0x2102 to 0x2142, you can bypass the start up configuration script. Since all router passwords are in the startup configuration script, bypassing this script at bootup allows you to bypass any password restrictions. To perform this procedure, perform the following steps on the following Cisco routers 1600, 2500,2600, 3600,4000,7200,7500, AS-5200, AS-5300, MC-3810:

1. Attach a console cable directly to the router console port and activate a terminal session with a product like Windows HyperTerminal.
2. Power the router down and power it back on.
3. Enter a break sequence during the first seconds of the router boot up process.
4. When the break sequence is entered, you will be in the router ROM monitor. You will see one of two prompts:
   >

rommon 2 >

If you are at the ">" prompt, you are in the ROM monitor mode of a 2500 router or a router with Motorola processor. Perform the following steps to complete the password recovery process on a 2500 router or a router with a Motorola processor.

Press the letter "o" at the ">" and get a list of the current configuration register setting:

```
>o
Configuration register = 0x2102 at last boot
Bit#    Configuration register option settings:
15      Diagnostic mode disabled
14      IP broadcasts do not have network numbers
13      Boot default ROM software if network boot fails
12-11   Console speed is 9600 baud
10      IP broadcasts with ones
08      Break disabled
07      OEM disabled
06      Ignore configuration disabled
03-00   Boot file is cisco2-2500 (or 'boot system' command)
```

Notice that bit 6 is listed as "Ignore configuration disabled." You want to change the setting to "Ignore configuration enabled." You will do this by setting the sixth bit of the configuration register to one. Notice that the sixth bit is currently set to zero. (The sixth bit is located in the third digit in the configuration register.) Since this value is currently zero (see the first line of the display above), bits 4, 5, 6 and 7 are set to zero. At the very least you want to make the third digit a four. Therefore, you want to change the configuration register from 0x2102 to 0x2142.

You can also type "e/s 2000002" to get a listing of the current configuration setting. If you use "e/s 2000002", remember to press "q" for quit to get back to the ">" prompt. If you press enter, it continues to show you values located in memory registers:

1. >e/s 2000002
   2000002: 2102
2. q

Change the configuration register from 0x2102 to 0x2142 by entering the following command:

```
>o/r 0x2124
```

Reload the router from ROM MONITOR mode by entering the letter "i "

```
>i
```

When the router reboots, it will act as if it has no start-up configuration scripts. You will encounter the following prompt when the router completes its boot up process:

```
Notice: NVRAM invalid, possibly due to write erase.
         --- System Configuration Dialog ---

At any point you may enter a question mark '?' for help.
Use ctrl-c to abort configuration dialog at any prompt.
Default settings are in square brackets '[]'.
Would you like to enter the initial configuration dialog? [yes]:
```

Answer "no" to entering the configuration dialog and get to a standard router prompt. Enter privileged mode and inspect the running configuration. You will notice that only the default configuration is there. Now inspect the startup configuration. You will see your saved startup configuration still intact. It has just been bypassed! If your old password is encrypted, you must type in a new one.

Do not celebrate too much because you still can make a disastrous move. Do not type in a new password and save it to nvram! If you do this, you will save your new password and the default router configuration to nvram. Your old startup configuration will be lost forever.

Instead of performing the disastrous move described above, perform the following steps:

1. Perform a "copy start run." (yes, copy start run!) This will copy the start up configuration script to running configuration. It does not overwrite the entire running configuration. It merges the startup configuration script with the running configuration script. Therefore, you must manually remove any administrative shutdown statements if you want to activate your interfaces.
2. Enter a new enable password and/or VTY password.
3. Perform a copy run start or wr mem.

Recovering a Password on a RISC-Based Router (4500, 4700, 36xx, 72xx, 75xx)

The procedure for recovering from a forgotten password on a router with a RISC processor is almost the same as recovering from a lost password on a router with a Motorola processor. The only differences are the commands entered in ROM monitor mode. Instead of typing "o" to obtain a current listing of configuration register settings, and "o/r" to change the configuration register, you type a single command that allows you to both view and change the configuration register at the same time. The command is "confreg." Listed below is a sample display of "confreg":

```
rommon 2 > confreg

Configuration Summary
enabled are:
load rom after netboot fails
ignore system config info
console baud: 9600
boot: image specified by the boot system commands
      or default to: cisco2-C4500

do you wish to change the configuration? y/n  [n]:  y
enable  "diagnostic mode"? y/n  [n]:
enable  "use net in IP bcast address"? y/n  [n]:
disable "load rom after netboot fails"? y/n  [n]:
enable  "use all zero broadcast"? y/n  [n]:
enable  "break/abort has effect"? y/n  [n]:
disable "ignore system config info"? y/n  [n]:  y
change console baud rate? y/n  [n]:
change the boot characteristics? y/n  [n]:

    Configuration Summary
enabled are:
load rom after netboot fails
console baud: 9600
boot: image specified by the boot system commands
      or default to: cisco2-C4500

do you wish to change the configuration? y/n  [n]:  n
```

With confreg, you go through a series of prompts, beginning with:

```
do you wish to change the configuration? y/n  [n]:  n
```

When you see this prompt for the first time, enter "y" for yes. Select the defaults (press the enter key) for all of the prompts until you get to the following prompt:

```
"ignore system config info"? y/n  [n]:
```

Answer this prompt with a yes. Once you have done this, select the defaults for all remaining prompts (press the enter key) until you come to the very first prompt you encountered:

```
do you wish to change the configuration? y/n  [n]:
```

This time answer this prompt with a "n." Once this is performed you type "reset" to reload the router:

```
rommon 3 > reset
```

After you reload the router, you will end up at setup configuration mode, just as the routers with the Motorola processors did (the Cisco 2500s). At the setup mode, perform the same steps described in the previous section.

Building a Detailed Troubleshooting Checklist

The following checklists provide a brief reference for the technologies and protocols covered in this book. You, the CCIE candidate, must elaborate and expand these lists:

Level One Troubleshooting

- Are the interfaces in an "Up/Up" State?
- Show ip interface brief
- Show atm interface status
- Show ports (CAT 5000)
- Show MAC (CAT 5000)
- General interface troubleshooting: show controllers
- Which end of the connection is the DTE and which end is the DCE?
- Show cdp neighbor

TROUBLESHOOTING FRAME-RELAY

- Is the router properly communicating to the frame-relay switch?
- Does the show frame pvc display the DLCIs as active?
- Are your packets leaving the router? (debug frame packet/Show frame pvc (packets in/packets out))
- Are your frame relay map statements correct? (Show frame map)
- Favorite Frame-Relay Troubleshooting Tool in a lab enviroument: debug frame packet

TROUBLESHOOTING ISDN/DDR

ISDN

- Is the router properly communicating to the ISDN switch?
    - Show isdn status
    - Debug isdn q921
    - Debug isdn q931
    - Favorite ISDN Troubleshooting Tool: debug isdn q931

DDR

- Is outbound traffic being interesting?
    - Sh dialer
    - Sh dialer map
    - Debug dialer packet
    - Debug dialer events
    - Remember—when in doubt, keep dialer-list configurations very simple.
- Is the ISDN call being set up properly?
    - Debug isdn q931
- What are the q931 messages being generated by the calling party?
- What are the q931 messages being generated by the called party? Favorite DDR Troubleshooting Tool: debug dialer packet
- Is PPP Authentication occurring properly?
    - Debug ppp authentication

TROUBLESHOOTING THE CATALYST 5000

- Is the port active?
    - Show port
- Is the port passing frames
    - Clear counters
    - Sh mac module/port
- Is a specific MAC address in the CAM table?
- show port
- show mac
- show cam dynamic
- show vlan
- show trunk
- show spantree

TROUBLESHOOTING ATM

- Show atm interface status
- Show atm ilmi
- Sh atm vc

TROUBLESHOOTING ATM LANE

- Is the LANE device building all its management and control VCs properly?
    - Show lane default
    - Sh lane client
    - Sh lane server
    - Sh lane database

- Sh lane le-arp
- Debug lane client all

Level Two Troubleshooting

IP ADDRESSING

- What are all of the IP addresses assigned to the interfaces on a particular router?
  - Show ip interface brief
- What are all of the IP addresses of the interfaces of my directly connected neighbors?
  - Show cdp neighbor detail
- Can you ping your own interface?

IP PACKET FORWARDING FROM A SPECIFIC ROUTER

- Are IP packets leaving the router in the desired manner?
  - Ping (standard ping/extended ping)
  - Debug ip packet
- Is the packet leaving the router through the correct interface?
- If debug ip packet displays "unroutable" messages, check the routing table. (show ip route)
- If debug ip packet displays "encap failed" messages, check processes that support the forwarding of IP packets out of a particular interface.
- If the "encap failed" message appears on a multiaccess interface, such as Ethernet or Token-Ring, enable debug arp to make sure the ARP process is working properly.
- If the "encap failed" message appears on a non-broadcast multiaccess interface, such as Frame-Relay or ATM, enable debug frame packet or debug atm packet to make sure the packet has a mapping to the destination address.
- If the "encap failed" message appears on a switched connection, such as an ISDN/DDR link, enable debug isdn q931 to make sure the call is being set up properly; debug dialer packet to make sure the traffic is being defined as interesting; or debug ppp authentication to make sure ppp authentication is occurring properly.
- If debug ip packet displays only "sending" messages, all IP forwarding processes are operating properly on this router. Check all intermediate routers or the return path of the routing traffic.

IP ROUTING

- Are IP routing updates sending the correct prefixes out the correct interfaces?

- Are you receiving the correct routing updates on the correct interfaces?
    - Debug ip rip
    - Debug ip igrp transactions
    - Debug ip igrp events
    - Debug ip eigrp

TRACING A PACKETS PATH THROUGH AN INTERNETWORK

- Traceroute (standard traceroute/extended traceroute)

OSPF

- Is OSPF enabled on each interface that is supposed to be participating in the OSPF process?
    - Show ip ospf interface
- Are OSPF neighbor relationships correctly formed?
    - Show ip ospf neighbors
- Are OSPF adjacencies being formed properly?
    - Shut/no shut
    - Debug ip ospf adjacencies

OSPF OVER NBMA NETWORKS (FRAME-RELAY AND ATM)

- If different combinations of interfaces are being used (physical, point-to-point subinterface and multipoint subinterface), is there an interface mismatch?

OSPF OVER DDR

- Are OSPF Hello packets keeping the interface up indefinitely?

IP ROUTE REDISTRIBUTION

- Enable the appropriate routing protocol debugging tools to verify that the routes are getting passed through the redistribution process.
- Is there an FLSM/VLSM conflict in the route redistribution process?
    - Sh ip protocols
    - Clear ip ospf redistribution

Level Three Troubleshooting

- Is your BGP neighbor relationship formed?
    - Sh ip bgp summary
- Are your BGP networks being advertised?

- Are the networks to be advertised in the BGP speaker's IGP table?
  - Show ip route
- Can your IBGP speakers ping the advertised next-hop address?
  - If not, consider using next-hop-self.
- Is your BGP table being formed properly?
  - Clear ip bgp *
  - Debug ip bgp events
  - Debug ip bgp updates
- Should synchronization be turned off?
  - Show ip bgp
  - Show ip route

Level Four Troubleshooting

IPX

- Is the IPX process running on a specific router?
  - Show protocols
  - Show ipx interface brief
  - Show cdp neighbor brief
- Is IPX traffic exiting a specific router properly?
  - Ping ipx
  - Debug ipx packet
- Are you sending and receiving the correct IPX routing updates on the correct interfaces:
  - Debug ipx routing activity
- Are your IPX routing tables converging properly?
  - Clear ipx route *
  - Show ipx route
- Are your SAP tables converging properly?
  - Clear ipx route *
  - Show ipx servers
- If using IPX EIGRP, are EIGRP neighbor relationships being formed properly?
- Are the contents of the EIGRP topological database correct and complete?
- Are EIGRP metric calculations reflecting the correct cost of the shortest path?
- If tunneling IPX traffic, is the tunnel operating properly?
  - Show tunnel/Debug tunnel

- Remember—IPX tunneling relies on IP connectivity between the tunnel endpoints.
- To assure that one tunnel endpoint is reachable from another, ping the tunnel endpoints.
- If the pings are successful and the tunnel still does not work, check for access-lists on all intermediate routers. Access-lists could be blocking the tunneling traffic.

APPLETALK

- Is the AppleTalk process running on a specific router?
  - Sh protocols
  - Sh AppleTalk interface brief
  - Show AppleTalk interface
  - Sh cdp neighbor brief
  - Sh apple neighbor
- Is AppleTalk traffic exiting a specific router properly?
  - Ping AppleTalk
  - Debug AppleTalk packet
- Are you sending and receiving the correct routing updates on the correct interfaces:
  - Debug AppleTalk routing activity
- Are your AppleTalk routing tables converging properly?
  - No AppleTalk routing/AppleTalk routing (RTMP only)
  - Show AppleTalk route
- Are your Zone tables converging properly?
  - No AppleTalk routing (RTMP only)
  - Show AppleTalk zones
  - Debug AppleTalk zone
- If using APPLETALK EIGRP, are EIGRP neighbor relationships being formed properly?
  - Are the contents of the EIGRP topological database correct and complete?
  - Are EIGRP metric calculations reflecting the correct cost of the shortest path?
- If tunneling AppleTalk traffic, is the tunnel operating properly?
  - Show tunnel/Debug tunnel
  - Remember—AppleTalk tunneling relies on IP connectivity between the tunnel endpoints.
  - To assure that one tunnel endpoint is reachable from another, ping the tunnel endpoints.

- If the pings are successful and the tunnel still does not work, check for access-lists on all intermediate routers. Access-lists could be blocking the tunneling traffic.

DECNET

- Is the DECNET process running on a specific router?
  - Sh protocols
  - Show DECNET
  - Show decnet interface
  - Sh cdp neighbor brief
- Is DECNET traffic exiting a specific router?
  - Ping decnet
  - Debug decnet packet
- Are you sending and receiving the correct routing updates on the correct interfaces:
  - Debug decnet routing activity
- Are your decnet routing tables converging properly?
  - Show decnet route

Level Five Troubleshooting

TRANSPARENT BRIDGING

- Are all bridge-group members listing the same root bridge?
  - Show span
- Is your spanning tree being formed properly?
  - What ports in the bridge-group (if any) are in a blocking state?
  - Debug span events
  - Show spantree
  - Debug arp

CRB AND IRB

- Are the proper protocols being bridged over the correct interface? Are the proper protocols being routed over the correct interface?
  - Show interface crb
  - Show interface irb
  - Show interface bvi

LAT

- Debug translate
- Sh translate

SOURCE-ROUTE BRIDGING

- Show source

DLSW+

- Troubleshoot both sides of the DLSw+connection.
- Can you ping your DLSw+ peer?
    - Dlsw disable
    - Show dlsw peer
    - Show dlsw reachability
    - Debug dlsw peer
    - Debug dlsw reachability
    - Debug dlsw core
    - Show span
    - Show source

Level Six Troubleshooting

ACCESS-LISTS

- Remember implicit deny
- Remember that access-lists have direction
- Sh access-lists
- Show access-expressions
- Debug access-expressions

QUEUING

- Sh queue
- Debug custom
- Debug priority

POLICY ROUTING AND ROUTE MAPS

- Sh ip policy
- Debug ip policy

Summary

A skilled troubleshooter must have a strong understanding of the technology he/she is examining. Common troubleshooting tools are CiscoWorks and the Network Associates SNIFFER. This chapter is a starting point for your troubleshooting skills development.

Professional Development Checklist

- Thoroughly learn the router boot up sequence.
- Thoroughly learn the Catalyst 5000 boot up sequence.
- Perform password recovery on a 2500 router.
- Perform password recovery on a router with a RISC processor.

For Further Study

- Cisco Certified Course: Cisco Internetwork Trouble-shooting, Cisco Systems, Inc.

URLs

- **www.cciecert.com**
- **www.nai.com/services/education/nai/nai_edu_list.asp**
- **www.mentorlabs.com**

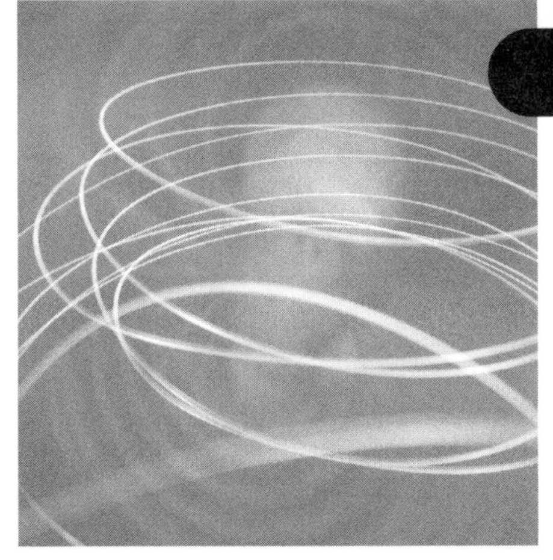

THIRTY ONE

Test Preparation Checklist and Test-Taking Techniques

Topics Covered in This Chapter

- General Test Taking Techniques
- Final CCIE Test Preparation Checklist
- CCIE Issue Spotting Checklist
- CCIE Landmine Checklist

All things are ready if our minds be so....
Henry V, William Shakespeare

We have now covered the core of the features available in the Cisco Internetwork Operating System (IOS). At a minimum, a CCIE candidate should possess a strong understanding of the core topics of the Cisco IOS. What has been covered in this book should be perceived as a beginning rather than an end. You, the CCIE candidate, must now construct a CCIE outline and checklist. You must systematically go through topics listed in your outline and checklist. You must list what key issues and landmines are associated with each topic. Finally, you must time yourself and evaluate your issue spotting, configuration, and troubleshooting skills on the merits of quality and speed. For example, if you cannot configure open shortest path first (OSPF) over a Frame-Relay network for nine routers in a testbed in less than thirty minutes, you must re-evaluate your Frame-Relay issue spotting, configuration, and troubleshooting skills.

Your most precious resource during CCIE testing will be time.

If you approach final CCIE test preparation in a disciplined and systematic fashion, you will greatly increase your chances of success. When you take the actual test, you should have already performed multiple practice scenarios. You should also possess an extensive checklist to guide your approach to IOS configuration and troubleshooting issues. Your checklist should include issue spotting techniques, an inventory of configuration commands for a given topics, and an incremental sequence of show and debug commands to use when testing and verifying a given configuration. All of these checklists should be engrained in your mind.

Also, you must possess a detailed approach as to how you are going to take the test itself.

You should have a pre-planned strategy of diagrams and tables you are going to create during the test itself. Recommended diagrams and tables to draw are listed as follows. Draw a master diagram of the internetwork you configure. On the diagram, keep track of:

Interfaces used.
Addresses assigned to interfaces. (IP, IPX, AppleTalk, DECNET, VINES)
Routing protocols enabled on which router and which interface
Protocols enabled on which router and on which interface
Where access-lists have been defined and applied
Which routers and which interfaces are using virtual interfaces

Create an IP address listing for planning and address allocation purposes.

Create an IP address matrix to keep track of all IP addresses on every router in a clean and easy to read matrix. This will dramatically reduce the amount of time you spend in testing IP reachability of all addresses in your examination internetwork.

Review what common issues can arise for different scenarios.

Create a list of common problems associated with particular implementations.

Preparing for the Actual CCIE Lab Day

The following test-taking strategies are extrapolated from general test techniques and are applied to any type of hands-on test involving the configuration of internetworking equipment. These test-taking techniques apply to hands-on tests on Cisco, Bay Networks, or Fore Systems equipment. Therefore, they can be applied to taking the hands-on portion of the CCIE lab.

Step One

As with any test, read the CCIE test instructions carefully. Prioritize which topics you feel comfortable with and those with which you don't.

Step Two

Physically inspect your rack(s) of routers and switches. Make note of what types of router and switch models have been supplied. Make note of the number and type of interfaces for each router and switch.

If the examination supplies a diagram or a set of diagrams of how the routers and switches have been cabled, verify that it is accurate through physical inspection.

Step Three

Proactively search out and spot configuration issues in the examination instructions. Quickly mark what topics you feel comfortable with and what topics you feel weak with.

Step Four

Attach to each console port and run show version to see what IOS each of the routers and switches are running. Also check to make sure that the number and type of interfaces you made note of in Step Two match what is listed at the bottom of the show version display.

Step Five

Manage your actual test taking performance with a structured approach like the one outlined in this book.

You should not need to write down a checklist to guide you. By the time you take the actual CCIE lab, all of your checklists, configuration strategies, and testing and verification strategies should be engrained in your mind. For example, just as the structure of this book suggests, perform access-list configuration problems only after basic internetwork connectivity is successfully achieved. If the examination questions allow you to answer questions in any order you want, place your access-list configuration problems at the end of all other configuration problems.

Step Six

Keep track of your time. When possible, perform the tasks you feel most comfortable with. After you have thoroughly tested these topics, attack the topics you feel less comfortable with. Do not spend a lot of time on a topic you feel weak with before you have performed all of the topics you feel strong with. TIME WILL FLY IN THE CCIE LAB!!! MANAGE YOUR TIME WELL!!!

Summary CCIE Preparation Checklist

Listed below are suggested activities and scenarios you should review before you take any CCIE examination. It is a suggested and partial list. Expand and modify this list to accommodate your preparation strategy.

As you expand and modify this list, mark what you feel strong with and what you feel weak with. Make note of what you have extensive hands on experience with.

Getting Started Checklist

Know the router boot up process
Know the LightStream boot up process
Know the Catalyst 5000 boot up process
Know how to check hardware components and IOS version via the IOS
If no DNS is supplied, disable DNS lookup on router.
Configure SNMP agent support
Configure a terminal server
Break out of SETUP mode
Review IOS shortcut keystrokes

LEVEL ONE BASIC INTERFACE CONFIGURATION

Configure Ethernet and Fast Ethernet interfaces
Configure a Token-Ring interface
Configure an ATM interface
Configure a Back-to-Back Serial Connection
List and describe the use of virtual interfaces

CONFIGURING FRAME-RELAY

Configure a simple point-to-point physical Frame-Relay interface with inverse ARP
Describe the limitations of inverse ARP
Describe how a Frame-Relay map statement operates
Describe what is the broadcast parameter used for on a Frame-Relay map statement
Describe the effect of Frame-Relay map to inverse ARP

Configure IP on a hub and spoke Frame-Relay topology with physical interfaces only
Configure IP on a hub and spoke Frame-Relay topology with a physical interface at the hub and logical point-to-point subinterfaces at the spokes
Configure IP on a hub and spoke Frame-Relay topology with a multipoint interface at the hub and logical point-to-point subinterfaces at the spokes
Configure IP on a hub and spoke Frame-Relay topology with a multipoint interface at the hub and subinterfaces at the spokes
Configure a Frame-Relay switch to provide a full mesh topology
Configure a Frame-Relay switch to provide a hub and spoke topology
Describe network layer routing issues for distance vector routing protocols over a hub and spoke Frame-Relay topology
Describe OSPF issues in a Frame-Relay network where a combination of interfaces are used (physical at the hub; logical at the spokes, etc.)
Describe OSPF configuration issues over Frame-Relay using nonbroadcast OSPF interface types
Describe OSPF configuration issues over Frame-Relay using broadcast OSPF interface types
Describe OSPF configuration issues over Frame-Relay using point-to-multipoint interface types

CONFIGURING ISDN/DDR

Configure router to communicate with ISDN switch
Configure basic dialer-list/dialer-group statements for IP only
Configure basic dialer map statements
Configure PPP encapsulation with CHAP authentication using dialer map statements
Configure a basic dialer profile
Configure a dialer profile with PPP CHAP
Configure dial backup with dialer profiles
Configure snapshot routing
Configure ip OSPF demand circuit
Configure ppp multilink

CONFIGURE THE CATALYST 5000

Configure the SC0 interface
Configure a default route for the SCO interface
Place the SCO interface in another VLAN
Place a switch into a VTP domain
Configure multiple port based VLANs

Configure ISL trunking between two switches
Configure Fast EtherChannel on a switch
Configure ATM LANE on a Catalyst switch

Level Two

IP ADDRESS PLANNING AND CONFIGURATION

Fill out an IP address planning form
Know the relationship of IP addressing to routing protocols
Configure VLSM subnets
Know the relationship between subnet planning and route summarization planning
Plan and implement IP addresses that allow routing protocols to summarize routes
Configure the IP default network statements
Configure IP classless
Configure NAT
Configure Multicasting

CONFIGURING RIP, IGRP, AND EIGRP

Enable RIP, IGRP and EIGRP and assign locally connected IP addresses to each routing process with the NETWORK command
Use IP default network with IGRP and RIP
Use IP classless with IGRP and RIP
Perform address summarization with EIGRP
Use NO AUTO SUMMARY with EIGRP

CONFIGURING OSPF

Configure OSPF area 0
Configure OSPF nonarea 0
Create a VLSM network in OSPF
Summarize inter-area routes with OSPF using the AREA RANGE statement
Create a virtual link
Create a stub area
Create a totally stubby area
Configure OSPF over a Frame-Relay network using non-broadcast interfaces

Configure OSPF over a Frame-Relay network using broadcast interface
Configure OSPF over a Frame-Relay network using point-to-multipoint interfaces
Configure OSPF over ISDN using IP OSPF demand circuit
Configure default originate information always
Manipulate the Designated Router election on a multia-ccess network
Manipulate the Designated Router election on an NBMA network

REDISTRIBUTING IP ROUTING TABLES

Perform Mutual of Redistribution of RIP and IGRP
Perform Mutual of Redistribution of RIP and OSPF (don't forget the subnets option)
Perform Mutual of Redistribution of IGRP and OSPF
Perform Mutual of Redistribution of EIGRP and OSPF
Redistribute static routes into OSPF
Redistribute connected routes into OSPF
Control redistribution with distribute-list in
Control redistribution with distribute-list out

Level Three

CONFIGURING BGP4

Establishing an EBGP neighbor relationship
Establishing an IBGP neighbor relationship
Announcing networks into BGP with the NETWORK command
Announcing networks into BGP with redistribution of static routes
Describe the use of NO AUTO-SUMMARY when redistributing subnetted static routes
Announcing network into BGP with redistribution of dynamic routes
Describe the rule of synchronization
Configure no synchronization
Describe the next hop rule
Configure NEXT-HOP-SELF
Filtering BGP routes with AS-PATH
Filtering BGP routes with distribute-lists
Load balance IBGP traffic
Using the UPDATE-SOURCE parameter
Using EBGP_Multihop
Configuring ROUTE-REFLECTORS

Level Four

CONFIGURING IPX

Basic configuration of IPX throughout your lab entire internetwork
Configuring EIGRP for AppleTalk in the WAN core
Tunneling IPX over IP
Configuring NLSP
Using IPXWAN
Mutual Redistribution between EIGRP and NLSP
Configuring IPX over a Frame-Relay full mesh topology
Configuring IPX over a Frame-Relay hub and spoke topology
Configuring IPX over ISDN/DDR
Configuring static SAPs
Configuring TYPE 20 propagation

CONFIGURING APPLETALK

Basic configuration of AppleTalk throughout your lab entire internetwork
Configuring EIGRP for AppleTalk in the WAN core
Tunneling AppleTalk over IP with GRE
Tunneling AppleTalk over IP with AURP
Creating a hub and spoke/full meshed AURP tunnel configuration
Configuring AppleTalk over a Frame-Relay full mesh topology
Configuring AppleTalk over a Frame-Relay hub and spoke topology (Don't forget AppleTalk LOCAL ROUTING)
Configuring AppleTalk over ISDN/DDR

CONFIGURING DECNET

Basic configuration of DECNET throughout your lab entire internetwork using a single area
Basic configuration of DECNET throughout your lab entire internetwork using multiple areas
Configuring DECNET over a Frame-Relay full mesh topology
Configuring DECNET over a Frame-Relay hub and spoke topology
Configuring DECNET over ISDN/DDR
Forcing a DECNET router to be the designated router in an area

Level Five

CONFIGURING NONROUTABLE PROTOCOLS TRANSPARENT BRIDGING/CRB/IRB

Configuring Transparent Bridging over Ethernet
Configuring Transparent Bridging over a serial link
Configuring Transparent Bridging over a Frame-Relay full-mesh topology
Configuring Transparent Bridging over a Frame-Relay hub and spoke topology
Forcing a router/bridge to become Spanning Tree Root
Forcing a bridge interface to be in forwarding mode
Forcing a bridge interface to be in blocking mode
Configuring Concurrent Bridging and Routing over Ethernet
Configuring CRB over a Frame-Relay full-mesh topology
Configuring CRB over a Frame-Relay hub and spoke topology
Configuring IRB over Ethernet
Configuring IRB over a Frame-Relay full-mesh topology
Configuring IRB over a Frame-Relay hub and spoke topology

SOURCE ROUTE BRIDGING

Configuring a two port SRB
Configuring a multi-port SRB with a virtual-ring statement
Configuring SRT
Configuring SR/TLB

Configuring DLSw+

Configure DLSw+ between two token-ring LANs with TCP
Configure DLSw+ between two token-ring LANs with FST
Configure DLSw+ between one Ethernet and one Token-Ring LAN
Configure DLSw+ between two Ethernets
Configure a DLSw+ local-peer with the promiscuous parameter
Configure DSLw+ in a hub and spoke topology with border groups and peer groups
Adjust LLC2 timers

CONFIGURING LAT AND PROTOCOL TRANSLATION

Enable LAT on an interface
Configure Translation on a LAT to TCP translating router
Enable the LAT server option

Level Six

CONTROLLING TRAFFIC IP FILTERS

Configure IP standard access-lists
Configure IP extended access-lists for outbound traffic
Configure IP extended access-lists for inbound traffic
Configure IP extended access-lists with the ESTABLISHED parameter
Configure IP Dialer-Lists
Configure IP access-lists to permit or deny a range of addresses (Baccala's Algorithm)

IPX FILTERS

Configure IPX access-lists to block RIP and SAP updates (Access-List 800 and 900)
Configure a SAP filtering access-list (Access-List 1000)
Configure GNS-Reply Filters
Configure IPX Dialer-Lists

APPLETALK FILTERS

Configure standard AppleTalk access-lists (Access-List 600)
Configure AppleTalk GZL filters
Configure AppleTalk ZIP Reply filters
Filter Zones with the PERMIT PARTIAL ZONES command
Configure NBP filters
Configure AppleTalk Dialer-Lists

DECNET FILTERS

Configure standard DECNET access-lists (Access-List 300)
Configure DECNET access-lists to permit or deny a range of addresses (Baccala's Algorithm)

LSAP FILTERS (ACCESS-LIST 200)

STANDARD MAC ADDRESS FILTERS (ACCESS-LIST 700)

NETBIOS NAME FILTERS

Apply NETBIOS Name filter to DLSw+ remote peer statement Apply NETBIOS Name filter to Token-Ring interface

ACCESS-EXPRESSIONS

Create Access-Expression combining LSAP and SMAC
Create Access-Expression combining LSAP and DMAC
Create Access-Expression combining NETBIOS NAME and SMAC
Create Access-Expression combining NETBIOS NAME and DMAC
Create Access-Expression combining LSAP or SMAC
Create Access-Expression combining LSAP or DMAC
Create Access-Expression combining NETBIOS NAME or SMAC
Create Access-Expression combining NETBIOS NAME or DMAC

QUEUING

Configuring Priority Queuing
Configuring Custom Queuing
Configure Custom Queuing byte-count parameter to assure percentage of bandwidth for a given queue

POLICY ROUTING AND ROUTE MAPS

Configure route-maps for policy routing
Configure route-maps to manipulate IGP route redistribution
Configure route-maps to manipulate BGP attributes

TROUBLESHOOTING AND SYSTEM MAINTENANCE

Configuring a router as a TFTP server
Loading the IOS onto a router with no IOS
Bypassing startup configuration on a router

Remember to review the topics listed above in the Cisco IOS Configuration Guides and Command References. These will be available in the CCIE lab. Remember to review the topics listed above on the Cisco IOS CD-ROM set. These will be available in the CCIE lab. Do not forget to review the materials included in the Cisco Design Guide and Case Studies. They have valuable configuration examples.

Create an Issue Spotting Checklist

A key factor in successful configuration and troubleshooting is being able to spot both obvious issues and hidden issues. Listed below is a suggested partial listing of issues to be on the look out for when configuring and troubleshooting internetworking technologies. They are categorized in the Levels used in this book.

Level One

NBMA (Frame-Relay, ATM, SMDS and X.25)
Does the configuration requirement require point-to-point or multipoint subinterfaces?
Do I need a map statement for an NBMA neighbor?
For ISDN, is this a Legacy DDR scenario or a Dialer Profile scenario?

Level Two

Are there any FLSM to VLSM redistribution issues with any of the routing protocols that redistribution is being performed on?
Do my interface types match between OSPF neighbors?
Are there any split-horizon issues?
If only certain routing updates need to be permitted or denied, use a distribute-list.

Level Three

Is the BGP next-hop reachable via my IBGP speakers?
Is the route I am advertising in my IGP?
Do I need to disable synchronization?
If one BGP speaker cannot form a neighbor relationship with another BGP speaker, use a route reflector.

Level Four

Do I configure my IPX, AppleTalk and DECNET concurrently with my IP traffic (ships in the night) or do I tunnel it?

If AppleTalk traffic is tunneled, I must use the GRE encapsulation method if EIGRP is used over the tunnels.

Level Five

TRANSPARENT BRIDGING

Who needs to be the root in the spanning tree?
What interface should be in blocking in spanning tree?
Does the configuration scenario require IRB?

DLSW+

What type of encapsulation type do I use on my remote peer statements?
Who needs to be in promiscuous mode?

Who needs a peer group statement?
Who needs a border peer statement?

Level Six

If ZIP replies need to be filtered between routers, use a ZIP reply filter. If traffic must be permitted or denied by LSAP address and NETBIOS name, consider using access-expressions.

If a percentage of bandwidth is required to allocate by a queuing strategy, use custom queuing.

Create a Landmine Checklist

A key factor in successful configuration and troubleshooting is being able to spot landmine issues that can create complications in internetwork configuration and troubleshooting. Listed below is a suggested partial listing of landmines to be on the lookout for when configuring and troubleshooting internetworking technologies. They are categorized in the Levels used in this book.

Level One

Enabling a Frame-Relay physical interface disables split-horizon. This can cause routes learned on an interface to be advertised back out the same interface.

Level Two

Beware of IP address assignment overlaps. Beware of redistributing connected routes.

Level Three

Beware of redistributing with dynamic routing protocols. This can cause route flapping.

Level Four

DECNET address manipulation of MAC address and its impact on IPX addresses.

Level Five

Beware of which interface goes into blocking mode in a transparent bridge group. Remember that Catalyst switches participate in the spanning tree process.

Level Six

Beware of IP access-lists. They can block many other types of traffic such as IPX tunnels, AppleTalk tunnels and DLSw+ connections.

Beware of inbound IP access-lists. They can block routing table update traffic as well.

Use the 8000.0000.0000 mask for Token-Ring MAC address filters to allow for changes in the RII.

Summary

Are you prepared to take the CCIE lab? Good indicators of whether you are ready to take the lab are:

How large is your personal outline?
How detailed is your personal outline?
How much hands-on experience do you have?
How many hands-on scenarios have you performed in a testbed environment?
How many combined scenarios have you performed (scenarios that will take a full day or at least one-half day to perform)?
Do you have an issue spotting checklist?
Do you have a timebomb/land mine checklist?

The Cisco recommended strategy for preparing for CCIE certification includes the following three elements:

Formal training
Self-study
Hands-on experience

How much of each of these elements have you satisfied? Have you structured and organized your experiences in a manner described in this book. If you have not, the likelihood of attaining CCIE certification is greatly reduced.

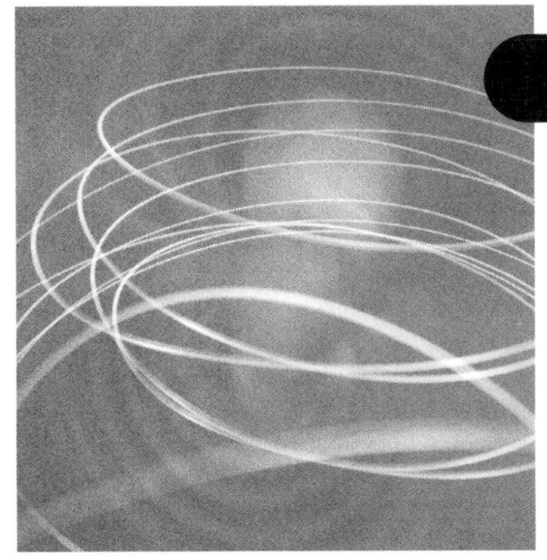

THIRTY TWO

Sample Scenarios

Topics Covered in This Chapter

- Spot specific issues in each scenario supplied
- Take inventory of the configuration tools used for each scenario
- Determine which show and debug commands do you have to use to validate and troubleshoot for your configuration?

"Practice does not make perfect. Perfect practice makes perfect."

An excellent method to prepare for any test is to take as many practice tests as possible. This chapter provides nine Cisco internetworking scenarios to help refine your test-taking skills. With each scenario, you must answer the following questions:

1. What issues are involved with this scenario?
2. What are the available configuration tools that be applied to this scenario?
3. What configuration steps are required for all SMDS configurations, and which are optional?
4. What is the sequence of configuration steps in this scenario?
5. How can you validate your configuration? Which show and debug commands can you use?

Some of the scenarios below involve topics not covered in this book. You, the CCIE candidate, must use external Cisco resources to solve the scenarios. You must use external resources, such as the Cisco Web site and the Cisco Documentation set (the Documentation set is also available on the Cisco Web site.)

Scenario One: SMDS Configuration

In the diagram below is a partial mesh "hub and spoke" SMDS topology. You must supply spoke to spoke connectivity. Approach this problem in a manner similar to partially meshed Frame-Relay and ATM topologies. You must take two other issues into consideration:

1. Unique SMDS addressing characteristics
2. SMDS DXI mode configuration

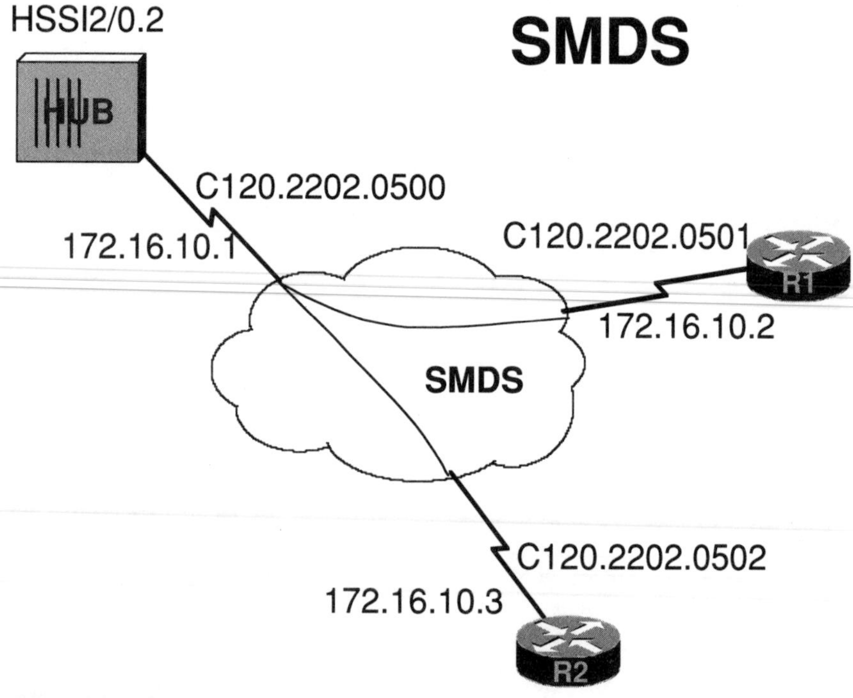

FIGURE 32–1 An SMDS configuration scenario.

1. What issues are involved with this scenario?
2. What are the available configuration tools that can be applied to this scenario?
3. What configuration steps are required for all SMDS configurations, and which are optional?
4. What is the sequence of configuration steps in this scenario?
5. How can you validate your configuration? Which show and debug commands can you use?

Scenario Two: HSRP Configuration

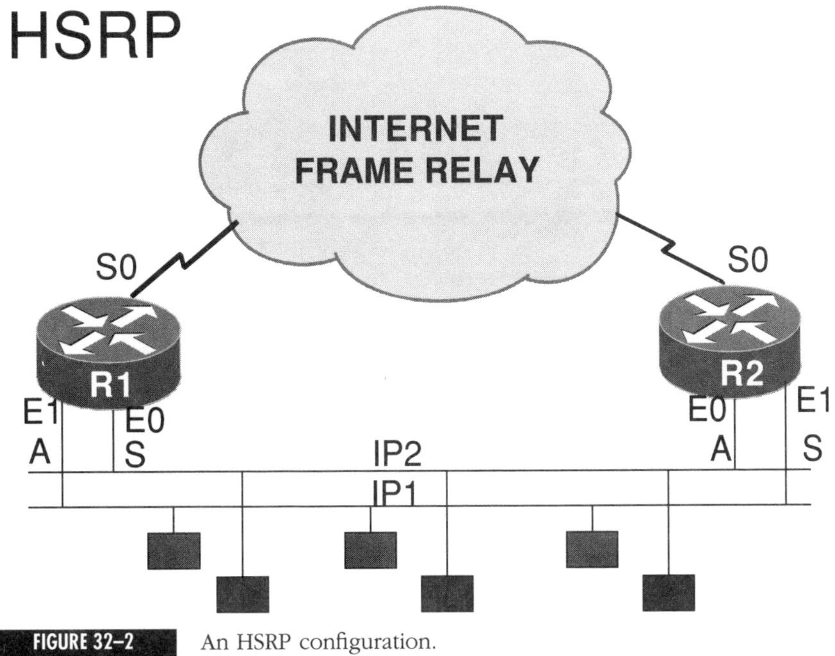

FIGURE 32–2 An HSRP configuration.

Configure router R1 as the active HSRP router for subnet one. Configure router R2 as the active router for subnet two. If either serial link fails on either router, make sure the active HSRP interface shifts to the opposite router.

1. What issues are involved with this scenario?
2. What are the available configuration tools that can be applied to this scenario?
3. Which configuration steps are required for all HSRP configurations, and which are optional?
4. What is the sequence of configuration steps in this scenario?
5. How can you validate your configuration? Which show and debug commands can you use?

Scenario Three: An OSPF Authentication

Enable OSPF MD5 authentication for Area 0.

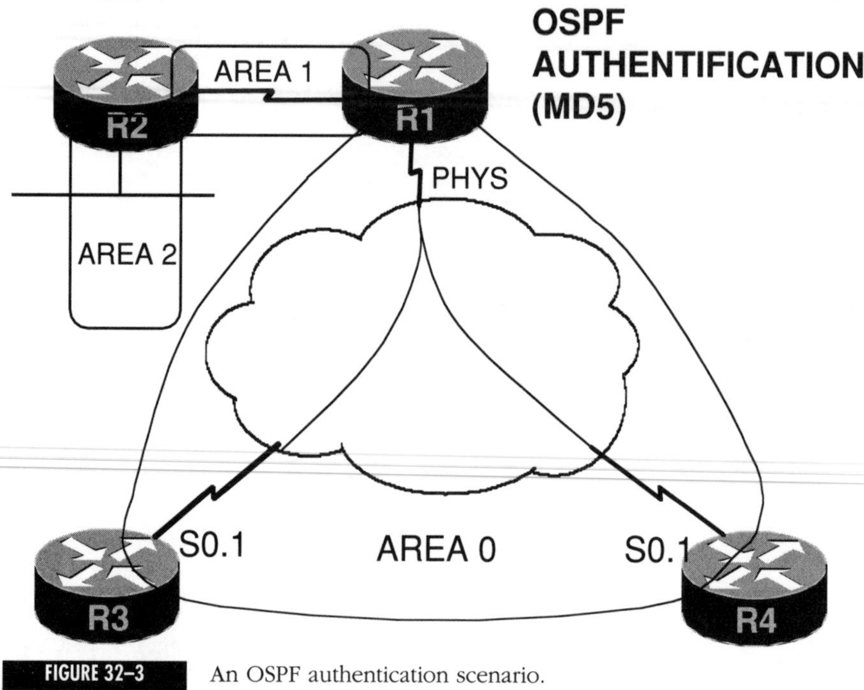

FIGURE 32–3 An OSPF authentication scenario.

1. What issues are involved with this scenario?
   HINT 1: All Area 0 interfaces must participate in authentication if authentication is applied to area.
   HINT 2: Make note of router R2. It has an interface in area 2. Area 2 is not adjacent to area 0.
2. What are the available configuration tools that can be applied to this scenario?
3. Which configuration steps are required for all OSPF configurations, and which are optional?
4. What is the sequence of configuration steps in this scenario?
5. How can you validate your configuration? Which show and debug commands can you use?

Scenario Four: Redistribution of Connected Routes Into OSPF

Redistribute the connected Ethernet route on router R2 into OSPF. Make sure you do not accidentally redistribute the R2 interface serial 0 into the OSPF area.

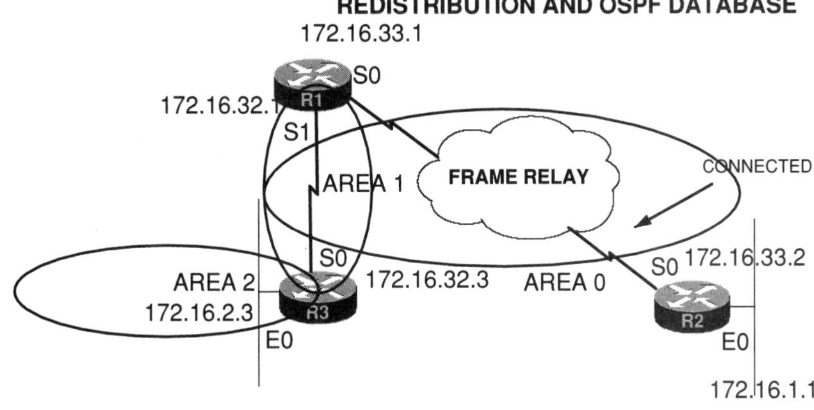

FIGURE 32–4 Redistributing connected routes into OSPF.

1. What issues are involved with this scenario?
2. What are the available configuration tools that can be applied to this scenario?
3. Which configuration steps are required for all route redistribution configurations, and which are optional?
4. What is the sequence of configuration steps in this scenario?
5. How can you validate your configuration? Which show and debug commands can you use?

Scenario Five: IGRP and OSPF Redistribution

Redistribute IGRP into OSPF on router R3. Make sure that the redistributed routes do not activate the BRI0 interface.

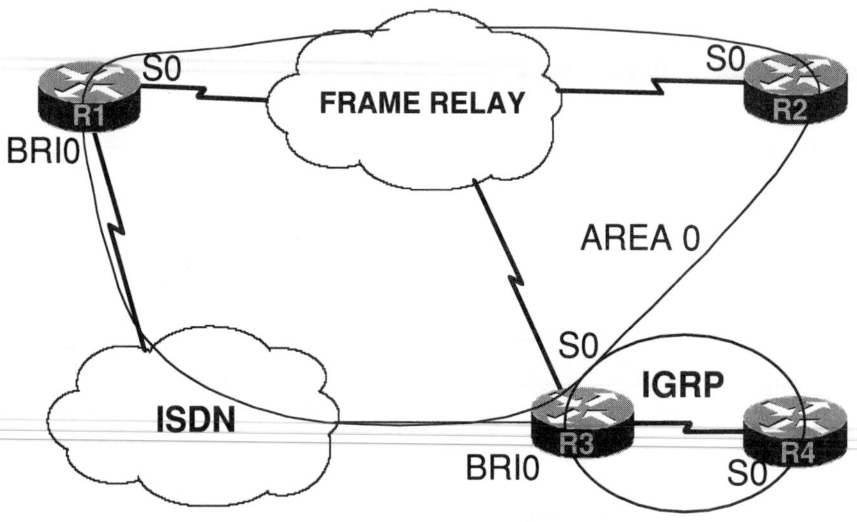

FIGURE 32–5 An OSPF and IGRP redistribution scenario.

1. What issues are involved with this scenario?
2. What are the available configuration tools that can be applied to this scenario?
3. Which configuration steps are required for all route redistribution configurations, and which are optional?
4. What is the sequence of configuration steps in this scenario? (Be incremental!)
5. How can you validate your configuration? Which show and debug commands can you use?

Scenario Six: A Basic Transparent Bridging Scenario

Configure transparent bridging on the bridges in the following diagram. Make R1 the root bridge and place the E0 of R2 into a blocking state:

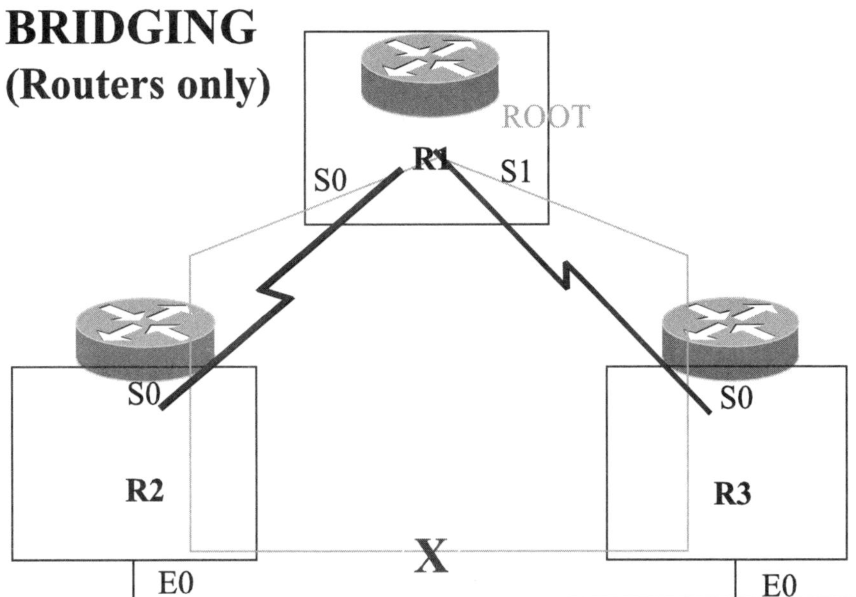

FIGURE 32–6 Configuring transparent bridging with routers only.

1. What issues are involved with this scenario?
2. What are the available configuration tools that can be applied to this scenario?
3. Which configuration steps are required for all bridging configurations, and which are optional?
4. What is the sequence of configuration steps in this scenario?
5. How can you validate your configuration? Which show and debug commands can you use?

Scenario Seven: Transparent Bridging Involving Cisco Routers and Catalyst Switches

This scenario is similar to the previous scenario, except that bridges B2 and B3 are interconnected via a VLAN on a Catalyst switch. Make the Catalyst switch the root bridge. Place the S0 interface of R1 into a blocking state. Create a BVI interface on R1. Be able to ping the BVI interface on R1 from the SC0 interface on the Catalyst switch.

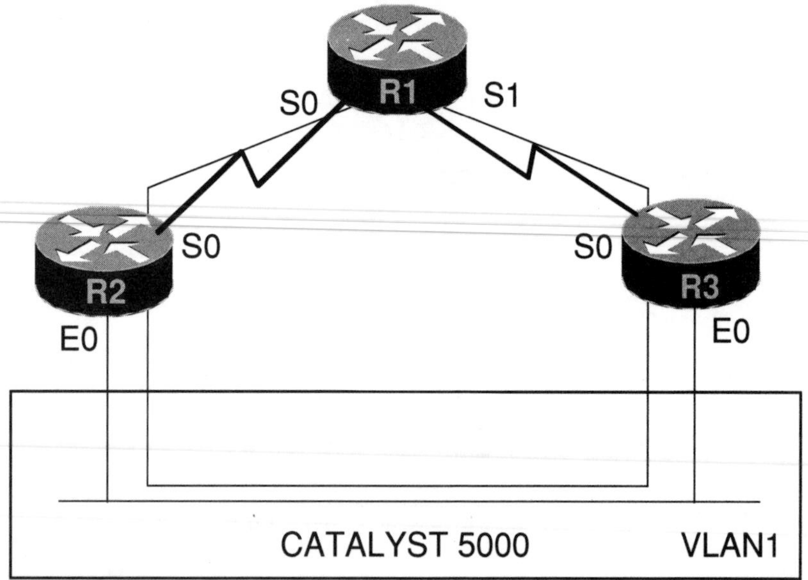

FIGURE 32–7 Configuring transparent bridging with routers and catalyst switches.

1. What issues are involved with this scenario?
2. What are the available configuration tools that can be applied to this scenario?
3. Which configuration steps are required for all bridging configurations, and which are optional?
4. What is the sequence of configuration steps in this scenario?
5. How can you validate your configuration? Which show and debug commands can you use?

Scenario Eight: DLSw+ Promiscuous Mode Configuration

In the diagram below, you have a hub and spoke DLSw+ configuration. The spokes (routers R1 and R3) have a DLSw+ remote peer configuration statement to the hub, but they do not have a manually configured remote peer statement to each other. Make sure end system PC1 can access PC3.

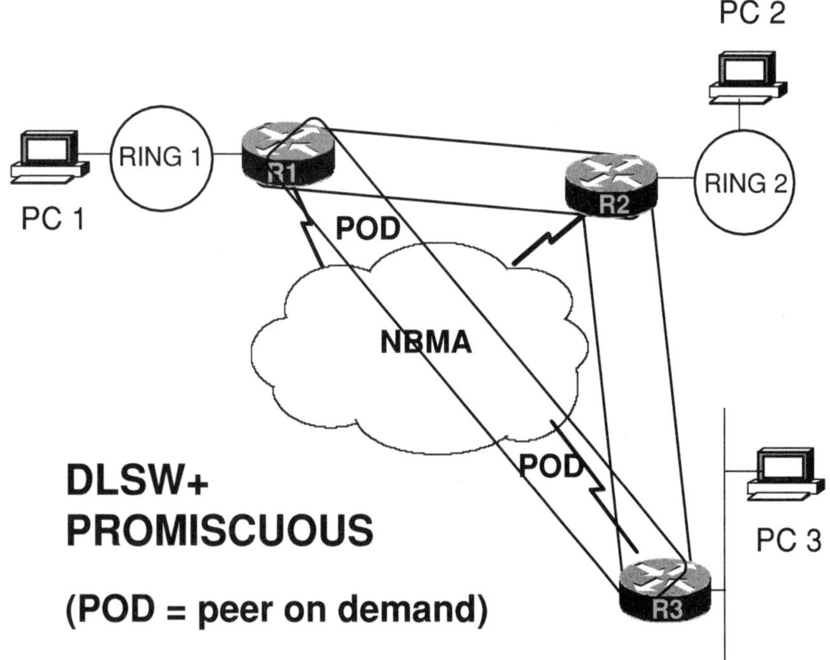

FIGURE 32–8 A DLSw+ configuration using the promiscuous parameter.

1. What issues are involved with this scenario?
2. What are the available configuration tools that can be applied to this scenario?
3. Which configuration steps are required for all DLSw+ configurations, and which are optional?
4. What is the sequence of configuration steps in this scenario?
5. How can you validate your configuration? Which show and debug commands can you use?

Scenario Nine: NAT and Policy Routing

This scenario combines NAT and policy routing issues. Make sure that all 172.16.0.0 internal routes get routed using a routing protocol using subinterface S0.2. For all traffic destined for non-172.16.0.0 networks, forward the packets using a default route on R1 to the "NAT" router. Translate the 172.16.0.0 addresses to 10.0.0.0 addresses. Policy route the NAT'ed packets received by R1 to subinterface s0.1.

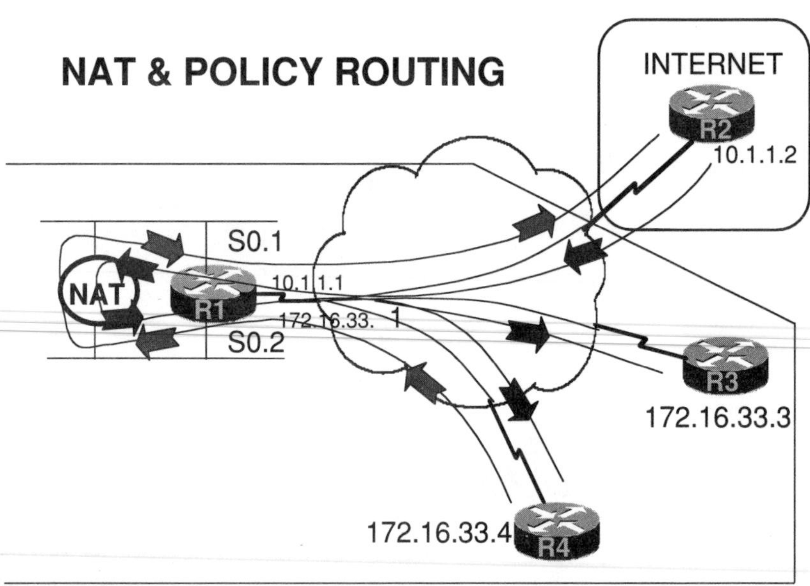

FIGURE 32–9 A NAT and policy routing scenario.

1. What issues are involved with this scenario?
2. What are the available configuration tools that can be applied to this scenario?
3. Which configuration steps are required for all NAT and policy routing configurations, and which are optional?
4. What is the sequence of configuration steps in this scenario?
5. How can you validate your configuration? Which show and debug commands can you use?

Summary

If you are a strong CCIE candidate, no internetwork scenario is too complex for you. You will attack the problem in a structured, systematic and incremental manner.

As a CCIE candidate, you must be prepared for anything and everything. To prepare for the CCIE certification lab, perform as many scenarios as possible; even better, obtain as much hands-on experience as possible.

See for more details on the scenarios listed above and additional scenarios **www.cciecert.com** and for additional scenarios go to **www.mentorlabs.com**.

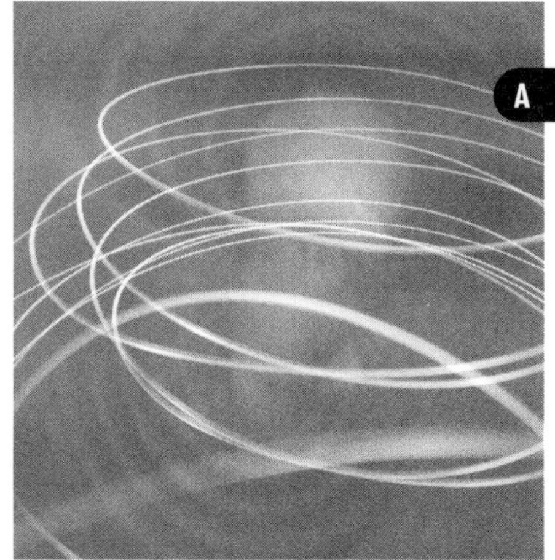

Navigating the Cisco IOS

For Cisco routers, LightStream 1010 ATM switch, AS-5200, AS-5300 and UBR7200 Cable router.

IOS Operation Mode Prompts

Router Prompt	**Mode Name**	**How to Access Mode**
Router>	User Mode	
Router#	Privileged Mode	Router>en
Router(config)#	Global Configuration Mode	Router#conf t
Router(config-if)#	Interface Mode	Router(config)#inte s0 (or equivalent)
Router(config-subif)#	Subinterface Mode	Router(config)#inte s0.1 (or equivalent)
Router(config-router)#	Routing Protocol Mode	Router(config)#router *xxx*
Router(config-line)#	Line Mode	Router(config)#line xxx

The IOS has other configuration modes. The ones listed above are the most commonly used.

IOS Help Facility

When in doubt, type:

```
HELP
```

Help will explain the use of the "?" command.

Using the "?"

?	Shows all commands in a particular mode
c?	Shows all commands that begin with the letter "c"
con?	Shows all commands that begin with the letters "con"

If only one command begins with "conf" in a particular mode, this is all that needs to be typed to complete the command. However, be aware that the command might require additional parameters. To check this, type:

```
Router#conf  ?
```

Notice the single space between the letter "f" and the question mark. Typing this will list any additional parameters (if any) for the string "conf."

Remember, typing the "?" in different IOS modes will yield different results *because different modes have different commands associated with them.*

IOS Command Line Shortcuts

Command contractions	Type the "least unique character string" (i.e., conf t)
TAB	Completes a command entry
CONTROL+A	Takes cursor to the beginning of a line
CONTROL+E	Takes cursor to the end of the line
CONTROL+R	Redisplays a line
ARROW UP or CONTROL+P	Displays previous line
ARROW DOWN or CONTROL+N	Displays the next line
Show history	Provides a list of previous commands typed
Pasting commands to the terminal	Use your terminal to cut and paste entries at the command line

Cisco Command Reference Summary

Moving Between Different Router Modes

ENABLE	Accesses privileged mode
DISABLE	Returns user from privileged mode to user mode
CONFIGURE TERMINAL	Accesses Global Configuration Mode. Must be in privileged mode to access this mode.
INTERFACE E0	
INTERFACE S0, S1	Accesses a particular interface. Must be in Global Configuration mode to access this mode.
ROUTER RIP	
ROUTER IGRP auto-sys-#	Accesses a particular router mode. Must be in Global Configuration mode to access this mode.
EXIT	Moves up one level in the configuration mode. For example, if you are in the interface mode and you type "EXIT," it will place you in Global Configuration Mode. Typing "EXIT" in privileged mode or in user mode will exit out of the router.
CONTROL+Z	Exits a user completely out of all configuration modes.

Configuration Commands

GLOBAL CONFIGURATION COMMANDS (PERFORMED AT THE "CONFIG" PROMPT)

HOST name	Changes the router's internal host name
NO IP DOMAIN-LOOKUP	Disables DNS look ups by router

INTERFACE CONFIGURATION COMMANDS (PERFORMED AT THE "CONFIG-IF" PROMPT)

CLOCK RATE xxxxx	Provides clocking for an interface that is acting as a DCE. Used for synchronous serial interfaces only. An example of using this would be CLOCK RATE 56000 for a link with the speed of 56000.
IP ADDRESS x.x.x.x subnt-mask	Assigns an IP address to a specific interface. It must include a subnet mask as well.
SHUT	Administratively shuts down an interface
NO SHUT	Administratively activates an interface

ROUTER CONFIGURATION COMMANDS (PERFORMED AT THE "CONFIG-ROUTER" PROMPT)

NETWORK x.x.x.x	Enters a directly connected segment into the router's routing table
NO NETWORK x.x.x.x	Removes a directly connected segment from a router's routing table

Show Status Commands

SHOW INTERFACE	Shows status of all interfaces
SHOW INTERFACE e0	
SHOW INTERFACE s0, s1	Shows the status of a specific interface
SHOW CONTROLLER s0, s1, sx	Shows whether a given serial connection is the DCE or DTE
SHOW IP INTERFACE BRIEF	Shows a summary of all interfaces and their IP addresses
SHOW VERSION	Shows information about a specific version of the Cisco IOS
SHOW FLASH	Shows the contents of flash memory
SHOW IP ROUTE	Shows the contents of the IP routing table
SHOW PROTOCOLS	Shows which protocols have been enabled on the router
SHOW RUNNING-CONFIG	Shows the running-configuration in the RAM of the router
SHOW STARTUP-CONFIG	Shows the startup-config stored in NVRAM

Troubleshooting Commands

PING x.x.x.x or name	Issues an ICMP echo request to test a connection at the network layer
TRACE x.x.x.x or name	Issues a series of ICMPs to trace the path to a given destination
TELNET x.x.x.x or name	Allows access to another router
SHOW INTERFACE	
SHOW INTERFACE e0, s0, sx	Shows the status of particular interfaces. Includes information such as whether the link is up or down and whether any packets are being sent and received from specific interfaces.
SHOW RUNNING-CONFIG	Shows the active configuration file stored in memory
SHOW IP ROUTE	Shows the contents of the IP routing table
SHOW IP PROTOCOL	Shows the status of IP protocols in use (in particular, information about routing protocols)
SHOW CDP NEIGHBOR DETAIL	Shows information about directly connected neighbors through data link packet exchanges

DEBUG options	Advanced troubleshooting tool that allows all information exchanged about specific protocols
U AL	Stops all debugging processes (undebug all)

General Maintenance Commands

SHOW RUNNING-CONFIG	Shows the contents of the active configuration file
SHOW STARTUP-CONFIG	Shows the contents of the startup configuration file stored in NVRAM
COPY RUN START	Copies the contents of running-config to startup-config
COPY START TFTP	Copies the contents of startup-config to a TFTP server
COPY TFTP START	Copies the contents of a file on a TFTP server to startup-config
WR	Shortcut to copy contents of running-config to NVRAM

Basic Cisco Router Configuration Step-By-Step

Step One: Physical Layer Installation and Configuration

Action:	Connect blue synchronous serial cable(s) to router.
Verification:	Type sh controllers s 0 (sh cont s 0)
	Router will display cable type: v.35, RS-232, etc.
	Router will display whether connection is DTE or DCE.
	If router displays "no cable", check cable connection.

Step Two: Data-Link Layer Configuration

Action:	Administratively enable interface
	If connection is DCE (see step one), supply clocking on that interface
IOS Configuration:	en
	conf t
	host r*n* (optional step: supply router a name)
	inte s0
	clock rate 56000 (if connection is DCE)
	CONTROL+Z
	wr
Verification:	Show interface s0 (sh inte s0)
	The first line of the display should read:
	Serial0 is up, line protocol is up
	Show cdp neigh (sh cdp nei)

Router will display the router name of the directly connected neighbor.

Step Three: Network Layer/Routed Protocol Configuration

Action: Supply "routed" protocol (IP or IPX) addresses to respective interfaces.

IOS Configuration:
en
conf t
inte s0
ip address 172.16.1.1 255.255.255.0
CONTROL+Z
Wr

Verification:
Show cdp neighbor detail (sh cdp nei d)
Router will display name and IP address of directly-connected neighboring router.
Show IP interface brief (sh ip inte brie)
Router lists summary of IP addresses for each interface as well as the data link and physical layer status of the interface.
PING x.x.x.x (neighbor's IP address)
A series of !!!!! reflects the successful transmission and reply of echo packets between one router and a neighboring router.
Show IP route (sh ip ro)

The contents of the routing table should contain entries for the routers directly-connected networks only. Note how the contents of the routing table changes after step four is performed.

Step Four: Network Layer/Routing Protocol Configuration

Action: Enable dynamic routing process. Configure routing protocol.

IOS Configuration:
En
Conf t
Router igrp 100
Network x.x.x.x
CONTROL+Z
Wr

Verification:	Show ip route (sh ip ro) The contents of the routing table should contain entries for *all* the networks within a given internetwork. PING x.x.x.x and TRACE x.x.x.x IP addresses on routers beyond the interfaces of directly connected neighbors should be able to be pinged. TRACE x.x.x.x will list the path of routers traversed to access the specified IP address. Notice how slow TRACE operates. See step five to remedy this problem.

Step Five: General Maintenance Configuration

Action:	Supply "privileged mode" or "enable" password. Supply "vty" or "TELNET" password. Disable router DNS lookups if no DNS server is not accessible by router.
IOS Configuration:	En Conf t Enable password san-fran No ip domain-lookup Line vty 0 4 Login Password cisco CONTROL+Z Wr
Verification:	Sh running-configuration (sh run) This command provides complete listing of current active or "running" configuration. TELNET x.x.x.x This command provides terminal access to another router. Type "exit" at remote host to terminate TELNET session. TRACE x.x.x.x Notice how the speed of TRACEs has improved. This is due to the "no ip domain-lookup" placed in global configuration.

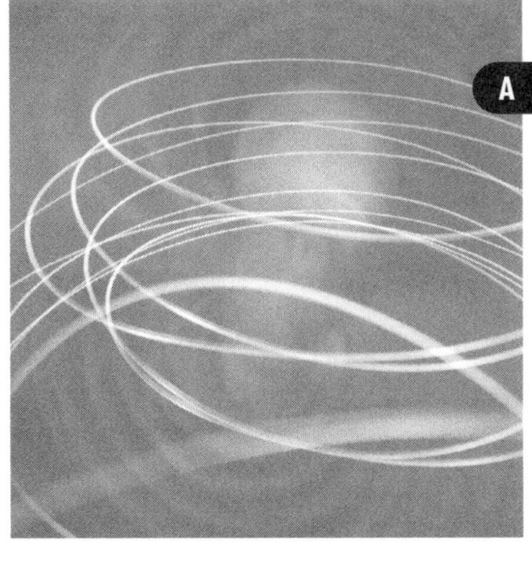

APPENDIX B

Can You Spot the Issues Answer Key

Chapter 1

Paragraph 1 • You cannot perform Fast EtherChannel on a Supervisor I module. You must use Supervisor II modules, as well as other specified modules to configure FastEther Channel. See the Cisco Web site for more details on Fast EtherChannel.

Paragraph 2 • Spanning Tree is extremely important for Catalyst switches. It is essential that anyone configuring Ethernet LAN switching in a multi-switch environment have a strong understanding of Spanning Tree. The Spanning Tree algorithim involves a root bridge as well as designated bridges on a per segment basis. See Chapter Twenty for more details on Spanning Tree. For a more detailed explanation of LANE, see Chapter Seven. To make the Catalyst switch Sw1 the root bridge for a given VLAN, assign it the lowest spanning tree priority number for the specified VLAN. Assign the second lowest spanning tree priority number to Sw2 to make it the backup switch. Remember, catalyst switches maintain a separate spanning tree instance for each VLAN configured.

Paragraph 3 • To learn more about dynamic VLANs, access the Cisco Web site. The administrative port on a Catalyst switch is the SC0 interface. It can be configured with the "set interface" command. The SC0 interface can be configured with the "set interface" command, and the SC0 interface can be placed in a specific VLAN with this command as well. To make sure that the SC0 interface can be accessed anywhere within the WMC internetwork, you must configure the "set ip route" command. See Chapter Six for more details.

Paragraph 4 • Configure HSRP for VLAN4.

Paragraph 5 • The first issue in paragraph 5 is a VLSM problem. See Chapter Nine for more details on VLSM. The second issue in paragraph 5 is an inter-VLAN routing issue. Yes, inter-VLAN routing can be performed on a single interface; however, it cannot be performed on an Ethernet interface. It can be performed on a Fast-Ethernet interface. See Chapter Six for more details.

Paragraph 6 • See Chapters Six, Ten, and Eleven for details.

Paragraph 7 • Yes, loopbacks can be used to simulate networks to be advertised. Subnets of different mask lengths for a given classful IP address cannot be used with RIP version 1 and IGRP. Subnets of different mask lengths can be used with RIP version 2, EIGRP and OSPF.

Paragraph 8 • This is a classic FLSM environment/VLSM environment redistribution problem. Read Chapter Twelve for more details.

Paragraph 9 • Two issues are included in paragraph 9. The first issue involves Frame-Relay configuration. In order for R6 and R7 to PING each other without Frame-Relay map statements, use point-to-point subinterfaces. See Chapter Four for more details. The second issue involves summarizing the OSPF routes from router R6 using the OSPF "area range" command. See Chapter Eleven for more details.

Paragraph 10 • This paragraph involves two additional subnetting issues. One involves a 21-bit subnet; the other involves a set of 30-bit subnets. See Chapters Nine and Eleven for more details.

Paragraph 11 • This will require the OSPF "ip summary configuration" command. See Chapter Eleven.

Paragraph 12 • You can create a single point-to-point subinterface on R2. Assign the DLCI point to the remote IGRP speaker to the point-to-point subinterface. Allow the other DLCIs (the DLCIs pointing to the remote OSPF speakers) to the physical interface. See Chapter Four.

Paragraph 13 • By default, split-horizon is disabled on physical Frame-Relay interfaces. R7 is advertising routes back to R2. Since IGRP has a lower administrative distance than OSPF, the routes are being inserted into the R2 routing table. The remedy is to enable split-horizon on router R7.

Paragraph 14 • Since R7 has a 172.16.0.0 network assigned to one of its interfaces and is running IGRP, it assumes that it knows all 172.16.0.0 subnets. R7 does not have the other WMC 172.16.0.0 subnets listed in its routing table. The remedy is to create a default route on R7 and enable "ip classless." See Chapter Nine.

Paragraph 15 • Configure Dial Backup. See Chapter Five.

Paragraph 16 • Configure Dial Backup using Dialer Profiles. Place a logical dialer interface in standby mode. To assure that only specific types of traffic activate a dialer interface, create a granular dialer interface. See Chapter Five.

Paragraph 17 • This requires an EIGRP route summarization configuration. See Chapter Ten. To get the 10.0.0.0 network into the WMC network, use redistribute connected.

Paragraph 18 • Configure NAT. See Chapter Nine.

Paragraph 19 • Configure X.25 on R11.

Paragraph 20 • R10 and R11 require Frame-Relay map statements. See Chapter Four. Split-horizon must be disabled on R3. See Chapter Ten.

Paragraph 21 • You must configure multicast routing. See Chapter Nine.

Paragraph 22 • Configure an IP access-list with the "established" parameter. See Chapter Twenty-Four.

Paragraph 23 • You must configure BGP4. See Chapter Fourteen.

Paragraph 24 • Configure NAT. See Chapter Nine.

Paragraph 25 • To reference BGP4 configuration basics, see Chapter Fourteen.

Paragraph 26 • To break into a router with an unknown password and make a router a TFTP server, see Chapter Thirty.

Paragraph 27 • WMC will need to configure IPX and filter SAP traffic. See Chapters Sixteen and Twenty-Five.

Paragraph 28 • This requirement involve IPX Type 20 propogation.

Paragraph 29 • Configure IPX/RIP and EIGRP over the WAN links. See Chapter Sixteen.

Paragraph 30 • Configure IPX over an IP tunnel. See Chapter Sixteen. Configure IPX/EIGRP over Frame-Relay. Remember to disable split-horizon at the hub. See Chapter Sixteen.

Paragraph 31 • You must create a static SAP and SAP filter. See Chapter Sixteen and Chapter Twenty-Five.

Paragraph 32 • Configure the "portfast" parameter. See Chapter Six.

Paragraph 33 • Configure an IPX dialer-list. See Chapters Five and Twenty-Five.

Paragraph 34 • Configure IPX Type 20 Propogation.

Paragraph 35 • Configure Integrated Routing and Bridging. See Chapter Twenty.

Paragraph 36 • Configure AppleTalk RTMP and AppleTalk EIGRP. See Chapter Seventeen.

Paragraph 37 • Configure LAT to TCP translation. See Chapter Twenty.

Paragraph 38 • RSRB is a form of encapsulated bridging. DLSw+ is more than just encapsulated bridging; however, it is reverse compatible with RSRB. See Chapter Twenty-One for more details.

Paragraph 39 • You need to know a lot about all forms of bridging. See Chapters Twenty and Twenty-One.

Paragraph 40 • To configure a partial-mesh of DLSw+ peers, use the border-peer configuration. See Chapter Twenty-One.

Paragraph 41 • Check to make sure an IP access-list is not preventing a DLSw+ connection from being formed.

Paragraph 43 • You must configure source-route translational bridging. See Chapter Twenty-One.

Paragraph 44 • Configure custom queuing. See Chapter Twenty-Eight.

Paragraph 45 • Configure a terminal server. See Chapter Two.

Chapter 2

1. The IP host table is referencing an undefined IP address: 11.1.1.1. It should be using the 1.1.1.1 address defined on interface loopback 0. Also, the "transport input all" statement is not defined under the "line" configuration.
2. Enter the "no ip domain-lookup" global configuration command.
3. Review Chapter 2 and draft a summary listing the key configuration details for each router and switch access method.

Chapter 3

1. Check to make sure that both sides of the back-to-back encapsulations match, and that the end with the DCE connection is supplying clock rate.

2. R1 and R2 serial interface encapsulations must match. R1 is configured for the default HDLC, and R2 is defined with the PPP encapsulation type. This mismatch will prevent the interfaces from attaining the "Up/Up" state. Also, R2 must supply clock rate in this back-to-back configuration.

Chapter 4

1. If WMC wants all satellite offices to communicate with each other without a full mesh Frame-Relay topology, inverse-ARP will not be sufficient. Inverse-ARP is used only for directly connected Frame-Relay connections.
2. Using Frame-Relay map statements will disable inverse-ARP for the protocol referenced in the Frame-Relay map statement, as well as the DLCI associated in the Frame-Relay map statement.

Chapter 5

1. PPP authentication problems.
2. The routing updates also were filtered. Therefore, no entries in the routing table existed.
3. The wrong dial string (phone number) is entered in a dialer map statement or dial string statement.
4. The protocol listed as "uninteresting" by debug dialer packet must be defined as interesting by dialer-list commands.
5. The dial idle timer expired. No interesting traffic traversed for a period of 120 seconds.
6. When dial backup was configured on the BRI physical interface, the interface goes into "STANDBY" mode. No traffic can be used on an interface when it is in "STANDBY" mode. The remedy is to configure Dialer profiles and place a logical Dialer interface in "STANDBY" mode.

Chapter 6

1. When you divide a given VLAN into two or more VLANs, you must adjust the IP addressing of the new VLAN to be unique. You must also provide a routing service between the two VLANs.
2. You must supply the SC0 interface with a default interface.
3. If a single VLAN resides on all Catalysts to be connected, only a single crossover cable is needed.
4. Trunking must be configured on the switches if multiple switches and multiple VLANs are involved. Some form of trunking must be configured between the switches.

5. CAM table entries are not like routing table entries. Review the section in Chapter 6 comparing the routing to the LAN switching process.

Chapter 11

1. The address on Ethernet 0 is 10.1.1.2, and the OSPF network statement is 10.0.0.0. Octets two and three configured for the Ethernet interface and the OSPF network statement do not match. The OSPF network statement's wild card mask specified that octets two and three must match (0.0.0.255). The remedy is to change the OSPF network statement to the following:
   Network 10.1.1.10 0.0.0.255 area 22
2. One OSPF neighbor is configured with an OSPF interface type of "point-to-point" and the other is configured as "nonbroadcast." The interface mismatch type will prevent the OSPF routers from forming a neighbor relationship.

Chapter 12

1. Even though two of the directly-connected subnets are defined as RIP subnets, they are listed as connected subnets on the router. Therefore, redistribute connected must be used to redistribute the routes into OSPF.
2. By default, split horizon is disabled on physical ATM interfaces. Since split horizon is disabled on the EIGRP interface, the EIGRP routes learned from the OSPF process are advertised back to the EIGRP/OSPF router. Since EIGRP has a lower administrative distance than OSPF, the routes are inserted into the routing table. A distribute-list can prevent this from occurring. Enabling split horizon on the EIGRP router will also prevent this from occurring.

Chapter 16

1. This is the issue of split horizon. Configure EIGRP on the Frame-Relay network and disable split-horizon.
2. Spoke to spoke frame-relay map statements.
3. Restrictive IP access-list is blocking tunnel traffic.
4. Configure IPX tunnels.
5. Configure a static SAP.
6. DECNET configuration manipulates MAC address formats (see Chapter 18). Configure IPX using manually assigned MAC addresses.
7. You must enable load balancing over the WAN links.
8. Configure IPXWAN on both links.

Chapter 17

1. Both EIGRP processes have the same process-id. All EIGRP routers must have a unique process-id.
2. Split-horizon must be disabled on the hub router only.
3. AURP does not have a cable-range. There is no AppleTalk source address defined for the PING initiated on the AURP interface.

Chapter 18

1. Since R1 is configured with static routes, it will not advertise routes to R2 over the ISDN link. Therefore, R2 has no routes and does not know how to get to any destinations on the far side of the ISDN link.
2. Split-horizon is preventing the routes from being forwarded from spoke to spoke over the NBMA network.
3. Through tunneling DECNET over an IP cloud.
4. Both routers must be DECNET Level Two routers.

Chapter 20

1. The incorrect bridge-group is defined under the Ethernet 0 interface of R2. An illegal bridge-group statement is listed under the BVI interface of R2.

Chapter 21

1. The virtual ring number defined on router R1 does not match the target ring number on the source-bridge interface configuration command. The incorrect IP address is used in the dlsw remote peer statement, defined on router R3.

Chapter 23

1. The restrictive IP access-list is blocking DLSw+ connections. Check the access-list configuration and make sure it is not blocking DLSw+ traffic.
2. The second access-list statement is too broad. To block IP addresses 172.16.1.30 to 172.16.1.47, remove the second access-list and enter the following access-list:
   Access-list 101 permit ip any 172.16.1.32 0.0.0.15

Chapter 24

1. The inbound access-list also filtered out routing table update traffic.
2. By default, ip access-group statements are applied to outbound traffic. If you want to apply an access-list to inbound traffic, you must explicitly configure an "ip access-group in" statement.

Chapter 25

1. You are specifying the wrong IPX socket number. Socket 457 defines IPX serialization packets. If you want to specify IPX SAP traffic, specify the IPX socket number 452.
2. The listed access-list blocks all SAP traffic, not just specific SAP types.
3. The configuration should not be placed on R1. It should be placed on R2.
4. A GZL statement filters end system GZL requests, not router-to-router ZIP requests. A ZIP reply statement should be configured on router R2.
5. When the same zone is configured on multiple cable-ranges and one of the cable-ranges is filtered, the zone is also filtered. This can be overridden with the AppleTalk permit partial zones global configuration command.
6. 255.255 does not work because DECNET uses the following address format: six-bit area address and ten-bit node address. The "permit any" mask of DECNET is 63.1023.

Chapter 26

1. The first bracket grouping "fla-filter" and "acctg" is misplaced. It should group the NetBIOS access-list "acctg" with access-list 700.
2. The permit any statement is invalid. The statement should end with "*", not " .*".

Chapter 27

1. In addition to specifying TCP traffic, you must also specify port 23 for TELNET.
2. You must configure an access-list specifying the 172.16.1.0/24 subnet and attach it to the appropriate priority queuing statement.
3. Custom queuing.

Index

Symbols and Numbers

A

D

K

L

M

P

Q

R

S

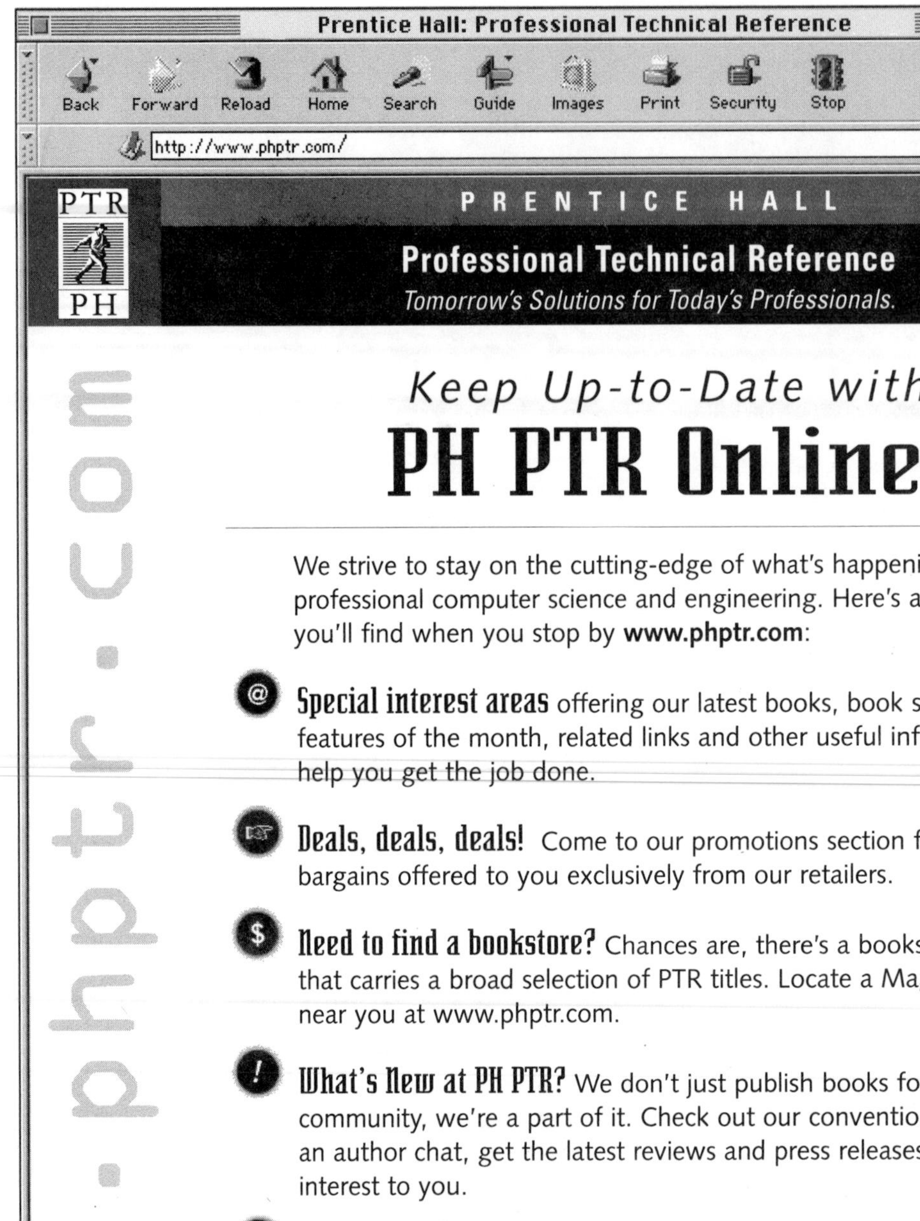

Prentice Hall: Professional Technical Reference
Back Forward Reload Home Search Guide Images Print Security Stop
http://www.phptr.com/
PTR PH
PRENTICE HALL
Professional Technical Reference
Tomorrow's Solutions for Today's Professionals.
www.phptr.com
Keep Up-to-Date with
PH PTR Online!
We strive to stay on the cutting-edge of what's happening in professional computer science and engineering. Here's a bit of what you'll find when you stop by www.phptr.com:
Special interest areas offering our latest books, book series, software, features of the month, related links and other useful information to help you get the job done.
Deals, deals, deals! Come to our promotions section for the latest bargains offered to you exclusively from our retailers.
Need to find a bookstore? Chances are, there's a bookseller near you that carries a broad selection of PTR titles. Locate a Magnet bookstore near you at www.phptr.com.
What's New at PH PTR? We don't just publish books for the professional community, we're a part of it. Check out our convention schedule, join an author chat, get the latest reviews and press releases on topics of interest to you.
Subscribe Today! Join PH PTR's monthly email newsletter!
Want to be kept up-to-date on your area of interest? Choose a targeted category on our website, and we'll keep you informed of the latest PH PTR products, author events, reviews and conferences in your interest area.
Visit our mailroom to subscribe today! http://www.phptr.com/mail_lists